History in the Humanities and Social Sciences

This interdisciplinary volume explores the relationship between history and a range of disciplines in the humanities and social sciences: economics, political science, political theory, international relations, sociology, philosophy, law, literature and anthropology. The relevance of historical approaches within these disciplines has shifted over the centuries. Many of them, like law and economics, originally depended on self-consciously historical procedures. These included the marshalling of evidence from past experience, philological techniques and source criticism. Between the late nineteenth and the middle of the twentieth centuries, the influence of new methods of research, many indebted to models favoured by the natural sciences, such as statistical, analytical or empirical approaches, secured an expanding intellectual authority while the hegemony of historical methods declined in relative terms. In the aftermath of this change, the essays collected in *History in the Humanities and Social Sciences* reflect from a variety of angles on the relevance of historical concerns to representative disciplines as they are configured today.

Richard Bourke is Professor of the History of Political Thought and a Fellow of King's College at the University of Cambridge. He has published widely in the History of Political Ideas and Intellectual History, including *Empire and Revolution: The Political Life of Edmund Burke* (2015) and, as co-editor, *The Political Thought of the Irish Revolution* (Cambridge, 2022).

Quentin Skinner is Emeritus Professor of Humanities at Queen Mary University of London. He was at the Institute for Advanced Study at Princeton between 1974 and 1979, and was Regius Professor of History at the University of Cambridge 1996–2008. He is the author of numerous books on Renaissance and Modern Intellectual History, most recently *From Humanism to Hobbes: Studies in Rhetoric and Politics* (Cambridge, 2018).

T0364226

History in the Humanities and Social Sciences

Edited by

Richard Bourke
University of Cambridge

Quentin Skinner
Queen Mary University of London

CAMBRIDGE
UNIVERSITY PRESS

Shaftesbury Road, Cambridge CB2 8EA, United Kingdom

One Liberty Plaza, 20th Floor, New York, NY 10006, USA

477 Williamstown Road, Port Melbourne, VIC 3207, Australia

314–321, 3rd Floor, Plot 3, Splendor Forum, Jasola District Centre, New Delhi – 110025, India

103 Penang Road, #05–06/07, Visioncrest Commercial, Singapore 238467

Cambridge University Press is part of Cambridge University Press & Assessment, a department of the University of Cambridge.

We share the University's mission to contribute to society through the pursuit of education, learning and research at the highest international levels of excellence.

www.cambridge.org
Information on this title: www.cambridge.org/9781009231046

DOI: 10.1017/9781009231053

First published 2023

A catalogue record for this publication is available from the British Library.

Library of Congress Cataloging-in-Publication Data
Names: Bourke, Richard, author, editor. | Skinner, Quentin, author, editor.
Title: History in the humanities and social sciences / edited by Richard Bourke, University of Cambridge, Quentin Skinner, Queen Mary University of London.
Description: Cambridge ; New York : Cambridge University Press, 2023. | Includes bibliographical references and index.
Identifiers: LCCN 2022024928 | ISBN 9781009231046 (hardback) | ISBN 9781009231053 (ebook)
Subjects: LCSH: History – Philosophy. | History – Study and teaching. | Humanities – Study and teaching. | Social sciences – Study and teaching. | Social sciences and history. | BISAC: POLITICAL SCIENCE / History & Theory
Classification: LCC D16.9 .H567 2023 | DDC 901–dc23/eng/20220720
LC record available at https://lccn.loc.gov/2022024928

ISBN 978-1-009-23104-6 Hardback
ISBN 978-1-009-23100-8 Paperback

Contents

Figures

Contributors

RICHARD BOURKE, University of Cambridge
PAMELA CLEMIT, Queen Mary University of London
HANNAH DAWSON, King's College London
DANIEL FEDOROWYCZ, University of Oxford
JOEL ISAAC, University of Chicago
SUSAN JAMES, Birkbeck College, University of London
STATHIS N. KALYVAS, University of Oxford
HAZEM KANDIL, University of Cambridge
IRA KATZNELSON, Columbia University
MICHAEL LOBBAN, University of Oxford
SAMUEL MOYN, Yale University
SHEILAGH OGILVIE, University of Oxford
JENNIFER PITTS, University of Chicago
CATHY SHRANK, University of Sheffield
MIRA SIEGELBERG, University of Cambridge
QUENTIN SKINNER, Queen Mary University of London
ADAM TOOZE, Columbia University

Acknowledgements

This volume began life as a collaborative enterprise designed to investigate the role of historical consciousness in the humanities and social sciences. The editors would like to thank the United Kingdom's Arts and Humanities Research Council for the funding that enabled a series of workshops in which the contributors to this volume participated. We are naturally also indebted to the contributors for their work, and their involvement in the intellectual exchanges which helped refine the project.

We would like to thank Emma Yates at Queen Mary University of London and Allison Ksiazkiewicz at the University of Cambridge for assistance in administering the award. We are also grateful to Jesus College, King's College, and Corpus Christi College for hosting events. In addition, we would like to record our very particular thanks to Vanessa Lim for her extensive work helping to organise each of our workshops and for designing the website that advertised our activities. Thanks also to Charlotte Johann for her input in relation to the Introduction. The editors would like to express their further gratitude to Elizabeth Friend-Smith who commissioned this book on behalf of Cambridge University Press for her confidence in the venture. We are also indebted to two anonymous reviewers of the penultimate version of the typescript for their constructive comments, to Natasha Whelan for taking care of the production process, to Mary Starkey for managing the copy-editing process, and to Balaji Devadoss for overseeing the proofs.

Introduction

This book addresses the role of history in the humanities and social sciences. Its purpose, however, is not narrowly conceived as a study of relationships between discrete subjects understood in terms of the contemporary division of academic labour. The volume does not ask how history as a discipline within a faculty ought to relate to other forms of inquiry in the human sciences. Its concern is less with the university subject than with historical consciousness more generally. The chapters in the book variously explore the role of historical knowledge in the fields of economics, anthropology, political science, political theory, international relations, sociology, philosophy, law and literature. Many of these disciplines had their roots in historical study, only later to develop into purely analytical or positivistic modes of investigation. Three examples will serve to illustrate the point: legal scholarship in the sixteenth century was regarded as dependent on historical information; politics in the eighteenth century was seen all round as involving historical judgement; and sociology, even at the end of the nineteenth century, was cultivated by many as a branch of historical science. It would be easy to multiply such cases. Each of these activities was distinct from history as a discipline, yet they were all nonetheless historical in character.

This pervasive historicism declined in the course of the twentieth century. The decline began with a perceived crisis. Ernst Troeltsch explicitly broached the problem in his 1922 essay 'Die Krisis des Historismus', which argued that the nineteenth-century ambition to reconstruct the world in terms of the developmental specificity of its components had an inevitably relativising impact on the judgement of values. The historicist vision, he noted, located all reality 'in the flow of becoming', emphasising particularity over universality, and subjecting truth to historical determination.[1] The only solution, Troeltsch argued, was to regard the cumulative fate of the West as offering a historical benchmark. He had

---

[1] Troeltsch 1922, p. 573. See also Troeltsch 2008 [1922].

1

already arrived at this conclusion twenty years earlier, when he recognised that the historical study of Christianity from Spinoza to David Strauss had progressively undermined its claim to universality.[2] But it was during and after the 1920s that more widespread debate ensued, eliciting arguments from all sides, including from Mannheim, Hintze, Heidegger, Heussi, Arendt and Leo Strauss.[3] In the aftermath of the crisis, the central importance of historical sensibility within the humanities and social sciences was steadily challenged. The shift coincided with the rise of American power to pre-eminence after the Second World War, the newfound prestige of US research universities, and the gravitational pull of statistical, analytical and scientistic methods on a substantial proportion of the professoriate. Viewed within a long-term perspective, this amounted to a sudden reversal of an established trend.

This book explores what is lost by misusing or disregarding historical understanding in the pursuit of knowledge about society, politics and culture. Such a rendering of accounts must begin by asking what it means to examine a subject historically. This Introduction lays the groundwork for that enterprise by outlining the emergence of historical mindedness in the aftermath of the scientific revolution, between the Enlightenment and the early twentieth century. In his great work of 1748, *The Spirit of the Laws*, Montesquieu declared that 'laws should be so appropriate to the people for whom they are made that it is very unlikely that the laws of one nation can suit another'.[4] This amounted to claiming, as Montesquieu went on to make plain, that for laws to be effective they had to conform to the nature of the government under which they operated and the animating principle that gave a regime its momentum. This meant that in the case of a monarchy, for example, legal provisions should be compatible with the type of administration and with the principle of 'honour' that Montesquieu believed made it function in the way it did. More than this, a system of laws should be attuned to a people's economic way of life, their political values, their physical environment, their manners and their forms of worship. A state, in other words, was a product of its historical conditions. It followed that the science of politics, at least in part, depended on historical understanding and judgement.

It is true that politics for Montesquieu was not exclusively a matter of adjusting laws and legislation to prevailing attitudes and institutions. There was also the issue of the fundamental values against which

---

[2] Troeltsch 1902.
[3] Mannheim 1968 [1924]; Hintze 1927; Heussi 1932. For Heidegger see Bambach 1995; for Arendt and Strauss see Keedus 2015.
[4] Montesquieu 1989 [1748], p. 8.

contingent arrangements had to be estimated. From Montesquieu's perspective this meant that law ought to be evaluated by reason in accordance with transcendent norms of justice: 'relations of fairness' (*rapports d'équité*) were necessarily prior to 'the positive law that establishes them'. Even the Creator's decrees had to accord with 'invariable' rules.[5] Montesquieu's historicism, therefore, did not entail an endorsement of relativism. To that extent his aims were continuous with mainstream Christian thought. Nonetheless, *The Spirit of the Laws* did mark an epochal shift in political understanding. Montesquieu dedicated just one brief chapter in the first book of his *magnum opus* to an examination of the laws of nature. The remaining thirty books were concerned with civil laws and their manifold relations situated in comparative and historical contexts.

A glance at the great natural law texts of the seventeenth century underscores the major shift in approach. Hobbes, whose humanist training inspired him to translate Thucydides early in his career, largely excluded empirical analysis from *Leviathan*. He conceded that prudence, which formed part of politics, was grounded on the experience of the past. However, true wisdom, which begins with definitions, involved pure rational appraisal, or the 'summing up of the consequences of one saying to another'.[6] In the preceding generation Grotius had confined his use of historical data to illustrating the laws of nations recorded by ancient authorities. His primary goal was to examine fundamental rights as 'Mathematicians consider figures abstracted from Bodies'. In pursuit of that objective, he generally endeavoured to withdraw his mind 'from all particular facts'.[7]

Set alongside these exercises in mathematical reasoning, the eighteenth century signalled a clear break with earlier traditions of political philosophy. Even so, one has to be careful not to overdraw the contrast. For instance, the ancient historians regarded their works as offering instruction in practical principles. Over a millennium and a half later, but in much the same spirit, Machiavelli commended the study of the past as a guide to the present, complaining in the preface to his *Discourses* that the example of the Romans was 'sooner admired than imitated'.[8] Again in this vein, Bodin insisted that history presented the surest method of acquiring 'reliable maxims'.[9] However, during the Enlightenment a change of emphasis becomes apparent. By mid-century the utility of

---

[5] Montesquieu 1989 [1748], p. 4.
[6] Hobbes 2012 [1651], I, p. 58.
[7] Grotius 2005 [1625], I, p. 132.
[8] Machiavelli 1989 [1521], I, p. 190.
[9] Bodin 1945 [1566], p. 9.

history no longer consisted in a record of achievements to be imitated. Instead, inspecting the past aided the discovery of regularities that could assist judgement. For that reason, history did not merely yield exemplary episodes; rather, it uncovered the conditions that structured possibilities. In Hume relations between property, government, law, the sciences, commerce, mores and opinion constituted an object of systematic study. Writing just six years before Montesquieu, he made clear that social science relied on general principles. That implied uncovering the underlying causes of phenomena. While chance for Hume played a definite role in human affairs, many outcomes in social life came about for ascertainable reasons: patterns could be seen to emerge 'from certain and stable causes'.[10] Society and politics were historically relative.

In much the same way that Hume examined the systematic interconnections that determined relations between society and government, Adam Smith analysed the factors that conditioned the growth of opulence in the *Wealth of Nations*. This involved explaining fluctuations in national riches, which depended in turn on the extent of the division of labour, the proportion of the population engaged in work, and the quantity of capital available to sustain employment. These interdependent variables relied in turn on the accumulation of stock. How they operated was then shaped by the way in which industry was applied either in cultivating the agriculture of the countryside or the manufactures of the towns as policy and circumstances have varied across time, although Smith concentrated on the particular transition from the Roman Empire to the states of modern Europe.[11] Only on the basis of comprehensive analysis of this kind could the causes of the wealth of nations be determined. There was yet another consideration that Smith included in his account: the role of theory in formulating policy. His example of a scheme of false assumptions that had guided the approach of sovereigns was the 'mercantile system', which he explicated in Book IV of the *Wealth of Nations*. The 'sophistical' precepts of balance-of-trade theory had governed the management of European empires since the discovery of the New World.[12]

From the perspective advanced by Smith, history was not simply a product of human needs. Rather, any arrangement concerned with the supply of necessities and the creation of luxuries was governed by the conception of how the system ought to operate. On this reckoning, a

[10] Hume 1985 [1742], p. 111.
[11] Smith 1976 [1776]. These various factors are analysed respectively in Books I, II and III.
[12] Smith 1976 [1776], I, p. 433.

crude assessment of the relative impact of thought and material circumstances on the historical process was intrinsically simplifying and would inevitably lead to facile conclusions. The crucial factor in Smith's analysis of economic improvement was the role played by the division of labour. This emphasis had three important consequences. First, it revealed Smith's awareness of the pivotal significance of the peculiar human aptitude for barter in driving change: an animal, by contrast, can plead but not bargain. Second, since the practice of exchange gave rise to coordinated action it was amenable to causal analysis. Smith contrasted causal relations with 'accidental' concurrences which he illustrated with the example of two greyhounds pursuing their prey down a racetrack: their behaviour was symmetrical although they did not directly collaborate. Finally, the scale of change brought about by the division of labour was wholly unintended: the benefits it generated were 'not originally the effect of any human wisdom, which foresees and intends the general opulence to which it gives occasion'.[13] This insight involved a philosophical thesis that transformed the nature of historical explanation. From Vico to Hegel, the doctrine of unintended consequences exercised a powerful influence on how social processes were understood.[14] It provided the basis for the notion of a 'spirit of the age' which linked intentions with predictable outcomes in the absence of design. If not properly understood, the idea is liable to be mistaken for a piece of empty metaphysics, as it often is in commentaries on Hegel.

Truth, Hegel argued in the preface to the *Phenomenology*, is only the process of its own becoming. Knowledge, he thought, was not a matter of specifying an object in order to grasp its abstract identity but rather the progressive recognition of its meaning through its development.[15] The role of philosophy in bringing about this outcome was likewise viewed by Hegel as historical in nature. It was constructed out of the materials of its age and so could not be regarded as feeding on a timeless constant. Yet while philosophical effort was relative to its epoch, it also pressed forward into the future. In addition, the stages in its forward movement should be grasped on their own terms rather than as a series of dispensable preparations: as Hegel noted in his 1801 study of Fichte and Schelling, philosophy was no more an overture for what was to come than Sophocles was a prelude to Shakespeare.[16] Reason, we might say, unfolded out of the past, carrying what it accumulated as it advanced by its own labour. There is

---

[13] Smith 1976 [1776], I, pp. 25–6.
[14] Hirschman 1977, pp. 17 ff.
[15] Hegel 2018 [1807], p. 18.
[16] Hegel 1977 [1801], p. 89.

a sense in which this historical vision of philosophy amounted to a thoroughgoing critique of Kant. When, in the final chapter of the *Critique of Pure Reason*, Kant surveyed the history of metaphysical thinking, he claimed to see nothing but 'ruins' as he looked backwards.[17] The implication was that philosophy must always begin anew rather than reflecting constructively on its course. However, at the same time, Kant presented his thought as a period-specific response to a crisis of reason that drove philosophy to seek 'satisfaction'.[18] As some scholars have noted, a basic impulse of Hegel's project was to make good on Kant's demand for reason to be gratified.[19] It follows that, at least in some sense, even Kant was not exempt from a historical conception of his own practice.

By the end of the eighteenth century most subjects had become eligible for historical investigation. For example, Germaine de Staël related national literatures to prevailing social and political conditions whilst also examining their reciprocal influence on manners. She contrasted the experience of France with that of England. Because English liberty favoured commerce, the national culture was utilitarian in character. Correspondingly, the world of letters – including philosophy and works of imagination – was geared towards practical application. French thought, by comparison, was divorced from public power. Its function was consequently to refine attitudes rather than serve government. Its chief achievement, de Staël went on, had been to alleviate the burden of social distinctions without challenging their existence: literary elegance 'obscures all differences without destroying any'.[20] Three aspects of de Staël's reasoning deserve to be singled out. First, it was focused on explaining a particular occurrence – the role of literature in England by comparison with France. Second, the form of analysis employed involved accounting for the object investigated by situating it within a nexus of relations. Finally, both the object and its nexus were viewed dynamically. As with Montesquieu and Hegel, understanding was inferential, holistic and developmental. Moreover, describing change included reference to the operation of reciprocal influences: in Montesquieu, for instance, manners impacted on laws, which shaped manners in turn.

Collingwood took this approach to be characteristic of historical thinking as such which he believed had become the distinguishing feature of Western civilisation since the eighteenth century.[21] He contrasted history with mathematics and physical science as forms of knowledge whose era

---

[17] Kant 1998 [1781], A852/B880.
[18] Kant 1998 [1781], A855/B883.
[19] Pippin 1989.
[20] De Staël 1800, II, p. 8.
[21] Collingwood 1993 [1946], p. 208.

of dominance had passed. Historical reasoning, he claimed, occupied a position in his own time analogous to the role played by physics in Locke's day or mathematics in the age of Plato. He illustrated this change by differentiating how Greek thought in the fourth century BCE conceived of the polis from how city-states came to be understood during the Enlightenment and beyond: 'The political philosophy of Plato and Aristotle teaches in effect that city-states come and go, but the idea of the city-state remains for ever as the one social and political form towards whose realization human intellect, so far as it is really intelligent, strives.'[22] Among the moderns, on the other hand, the form of the city-state was itself a temporally specific phenomenon. It was a relative rather than a universal ideal whose conditions of existence had now passed. This fact shows that particulars are not simply examples of ideas; ideas themselves could take different historical forms. This conclusion applied to all human artefacts – to every product of labour, in the language of Hegel and Marx – ensuring that the science of human nature must be historical. This did not rule out discovering patterns of behaviour or recurrent habits and dispositions. A social type, such as a feudal baron, exhibited predictable features. Nonetheless, those features were conditioned by the environment that produced the type: 'In order that behaviour-patterns may be constant, there must be in existence a social order which recurrently produces situations of a certain kind.'[23] What historical awareness foregrounds, however, is that social orders are perpetually modified.

In developing the doctrine of historicity, Collingwood drew explicitly upon an idealist heritage that encompassed Bradley and Oakeshott in England, Dilthey, Windelband and Rickert in Germany, and Croce in Italy. The key precursor of this tradition was of course Hegel, whose own roots were traceable to an Enlightenment historicism developed between Montesquieu and Rousseau. The rise of this species of sensibility amounted, Friedrich Meinecke argued, 'to one of the greatest intellectual revolutions that has ever taken place in Western thought'.[24] What is striking in this verdict is that for Meinecke as much as Collingwood the transformation under review was a consummation: the historical approach represented a culmination that they believed would endure. It is also notable that for both of them historicism was a single package, although in actual fact the term includes a diversity of meanings.[25] Historical sensibility did not assume a specific shape.

---

22 Collingwood 1993 [1946], pp. 210–11.
23 Collingwood 1993 [1946], p. 223.
24 Meinecke 1972 [1936], p. liv. See also Toews 2004.
25 Iggers 1968, rev. ed. 1983; Beiser 2011.

Meinecke's conclusion was based on an argument ultimately drawn from Savigny. In his 1814 contribution to debate about legal codification in Germany, *Of the Vocation of the Age for Legislation and Jurisprudence*, Savigny declared that a 'historical spirit has been everywhere awakened'.[26] He cited Justus Möser and Gustav Hugo as predecessors in creating the relevant climate in which this sensibility could prosper.[27] But what exactly did he think the historical approach involved? In considering relations between history and the human sciences, there is a danger of treating historical study as if the purpose of the enterprise were self-evident. However, the very subject matter of history has been variously understood since the eighteenth century. For many, like Ranke, it is concerned with the life of the state; for others, like Buckle, it charts the course of civilisation; and for still others, like Lamprecht, its focus is on society. In each case it was far from certain what the object under examination was. Equally, the rationale of history has been disputed. While Ranke, again, believed that the historian could serve statecraft without confusing that role with the vocation of the politician, he also thought that the study of historical particulars revealed individual instances of the divine will: 'In power itself a spiritual essence manifests itself.'[28] The nature of historical causation has likewise proved contentious, as illustrated by Burkhardt's critique of mono-causal explanation in favour of the idea of 'reciprocal influence' operating between culture, religion and the state.[29]

These debates are not confined to professional historians, but are relevant to the study of society more generally. The problem of delimiting the subject matter of a discipline and isolating the objects of analysis within it is shared across the humanities and social sciences. So too is the question of how to determine relations of causation, how controversial issues can be treated impartially, and how empirical description can inform our choice of values. Prominent figures in the late nineteenth century such as Comte and Spencer opted to circumnavigate the most difficult aspects of these problems by investigating society on the model of the natural sciences, thus bucking the trend that Meinecke and Collingwood thought they had identified. From this perspective, events were best explained 'nomothetically', in Windelband's phrase – by abstracting from particulars with a view to subordinating individual cases under general causal laws.[30] Many others, however, persisted with the historical approach,

---

[26] Savigny 1831 [1814], p. 22.
[27] Savigny 1831 [1814], p. 31.
[28] Ranke 2011, p. 6.
[29] Burkhardt 1979 [1905].
[30] Windelband 1894.

endeavouring to develop a science of discrete entities – establishing what an item was and how it came about – without invoking law-like causal regularities. To many the individualising method still seemed salutary since the components that made up the human sciences – objects such as torts, prices, rights, tribes, money, constitutions and genres – were in essential respects unlike the bodies of classical mechanics or the particles of modern physics. With rapid progress in the biological sciences through the nineteenth century, analogising across the natural and the human worlds looked promising. The idea of a social organism began to thrive, as did the concept of political evolution. But still, to most observers, humanity seemed crucially different from the rest of the plant and animal kingdom since freedom, morality and reflexivity were regarded as distinctive features of human life.

Questions surrounding freedom, morality and reflexivity raised their own peculiar difficulties. But there were two more immediate dilemmas thrown up by the historical method. First, there was what looked like the simple empirical question of how one could identify relevant particulars: in seeking to account for wealth creation by observing the indeterminate mass of economic reality, where was one to begin? The sheer scale and complexity of the whole world of experience was too vast to form the subject matter of coherent empirical analysis. Second, there was the historical question proper: how does one construe the process of change to which empirical data is subject? If nomological explanation was not applicable in the cultural realm, the manner in which social events conditioned one another still had to be analysed. These quandaries became prominent during the so-called *Methodenstreit* waged between the German historical school of economics and Austrian economic theorists at the end of the nineteenth century. The leading document in that dispute is Carl Menger's *Investigation into the Method of the Social Sciences with Special Reference to Economics*. Menger accepted that the accumulation of statistical information, which he associated with German historical economists from Roscher to Schmoller, yielded relevant forms of explanation in economics, usually based on inductive inference. Yet Menger also wished to defend the utility of what Schmoller, in responding to Menger, had branded the hypothetico-deductive method.[31] Scholler's characterisation did not capture Menger's actual procedure. In his own words, what Menger wished to justify was the role of abstraction in reflecting scientifically on economic behaviour. He believed that social scientists did not merely collect data. They also focused on empirical 'forms' or

---

[31] Schmoller 1888 [1883].

'types' – such as exchange, price, supply and rent.[32] Economists were interested, that is, not solely in concrete particulars, but also in general phenomena which could be analysed and even explicated in mathematical languages.

It might seem as if this amounted to a plea on Menger's part for theory in place of history. This, however, is only a partial reading. Menger, as a working economist, was certainly concerned with economic theory, but he was also interested in economic change. He was preoccupied, therefore, not only with formal abstractions but with the appropriate relations between them: with, for example, 'the effect on prices of the increasing or decreasing of supply and demand, the effect of population increase on ground rent', and so on.[33] Underlying this focus was a theoretical reliance on 'atomism' in economic analysis, by which Menger meant a commitment to methodological individualism.[34] This formed the basis of his view that numerous social institutions – such as language, money and the state – were not products of deliberate design but emerged as unintended consequences of self-interested pursuit.[35] Here, in short, was a theory of historical change. In advocating it, Menger identified his project with Burke, and still more boldly with Hugo and Savigny – thus employing the founding figures of historical jurisprudence for his own purposes, and reclaiming them in the process from their customary association with German historicists such as Schmoller.[36]

From the point of view of this discussion the achievement of Menger was twofold. First, while advocating a pluralistic approach to economic research, he defended the aspiration to pursue the 'exact' analysis of economic behaviour by the use of ideal abstractions. But second, he also retained the ambition to account for change within an economy. What interested him most, of course, were theoretical adjustments – how demand, for example, affected supply *in principle* – rather than individual, concrete change. What he lacked, therefore, was a theory of historical causation, which remained a problem in the field of technical economics, and naturally in the social sciences more broadly. Although Max Weber's academic formation was within the German historical school, his debt to the Austrians is obvious. Writing to Lujo Brentano on 30 October 1908, he argued that Menger had largely been right in his

---

[32] Menger 2009 [1883], p. 35.
[33] Menger 2009 [1883], p. 42.
[34] Menger 2009 [1883], pp. 90 ff.
[35] Menger 2009 [1883], pp. 131 ff.
[36] Menger 2009 [1883], pp. 172 ff.

'quarrel' with Schmoller.[37] What he admired was his recognition of the role of idealisations or 'types' in social scientific explanation. Yet Weber also believed that both sides in the dispute had failed to reconcile theory with history in economic science. A systematic accommodation required not just an appreciation of the role of concepts, but also an understanding of causation in the human sciences.

Already at the start of the twentieth century, Weber believed, unlike Collingwood and Meinecke later on, that the tremendous success of the natural sciences had corrupted the self-conception of the historical sciences. By increasingly associating rigorous knowledge with generalising abstractions, explanation as such became increasingly identified with the discovery of 'law-like regularities' under which empirical particulars could be subsumed.[38] Schmoller's as much as Menger's views had been distorted by this pervasive prejudice. Weber sought to rethink what occurred in successful research in the cultural sciences where the focus of study was invariably on objects of value rather than physical occurrences. This programme included elucidating how impartial analysis was possible, how the construction of concepts assisted empirical investigation, and how causal accounts could be developed without reduction to generally valid laws. The resulting procedures, he thought, could illuminate policy choices, and generally clarify the consequences of alternative courses of action, but they could not determine the actual preferences to be followed. Historical inquiry could impartially weigh up options, but it could not resolve the plurality of values.[39]

This was a notable lapse from the claim to normative authority originally promised by the progenitors of the historical school of jurisprudence. For Savigny and Hugo, historical custom by its very existence served to legitimise the validity of laws. Marx, as a student of Eduard Gans, had joined the battle against the German historical jurists for this reason: legitimisation by historical precedent was merely 'positive' and thus 'uncritical'.[40] This was the substance of Hegel's own complaint against Hugo in the *Elements of the Philosophy of Right*. In his 1790 textbook on Roman law, Hugo had cited jurists against philosophers as the best guides to the meaning of laws.[41] But, Hegel replied, since the methods employed by legal scholars could only account for the circumstances of specific provisions, they could never offer insight into the rightfulness

---

[37] Weber 1984–, II/5, pp. 688–9.
[38] Weber 2012 [1904], p. 122.
[39] Weber 1984–, I/7, pp. 98–9.
[40] Marx 1975–2004 [1842], II, p. 203.
[41] Hugo 1818 [1790], § 53.

of legislation. Faced with the oppressiveness of Roman family law, or the licensing of debt bondage under the Twelve Tables, this deficiency was highly significant in Hegel's view. Empirical scholarship could explain the rationale behind the arrangement, but it could not actually justify the relevant ordinances. Accordingly, Hegel concluded, the science of right was not simply charged with the collection of data from the past in a mechanically historical fashion. Instead, the study of right ought properly to be philosophical-historical after the manner of Montesquieu, for whom particular determinations only made sense within the context of a 'totality'.[42] Justification was not just a matter of recounting narrow legal reasons. These had to be set in a wider framework of interdependent 'moments' and ultimately judged according to world historical standards.

Taken together with the arguments and insights assembled so far in this Introduction, the Hegelian attempt to unite historical and philosophical judgement into a combined method for analysing socio-political phenomena is an index of the variety and complexity of the issues thrown up by attempts to think historically about culture. These issues have included those of historical relativity, social and political causation, concept formation, and the interpretation of meaning. They have also provoked subsidiary debate about objectivity in the analysis of human behaviour as well as about the evaluation of moral norms. Carl Schorske has written that down to around 1945 'history as a mode of understanding suffused the world of learning'.[43] Yet during the Cold War, in the United States in particular, approaches rose to prominence within the humanities and social sciences that strove to transcend the strictures of historical reasoning. In general, these approaches – for instance functionalism, structuralism, logical positivism, formalist criticism, behaviourism and economic formalism – had their roots in European intellectual life. However, positivist methods gained a decisive authority after their translation into the United States. The preceding survey of the intellectual landscape before these developments took place is not intended as an argument against the emergence of post-war methods. But it is an invitation to reflect on how the study of society, politics and mind can hope to succeed if, as a matter of principle, it excludes examination of the issues raised by the historical sciences in the past.[44]

It seems clear that human beings do not passively react to their environment, like iron rusting. They self-consciously form preferences in

---

[42] Hegel 1991 [1821], § 3.
[43] Schorske 1997, p. 292.
[44] The conjunction 'society, politics and mind' is taken from Isaac 2012, p. 8.

response to empirical input. In fact, over time they reappraise the values they have chosen, thereby helping to motivate social change. Making sense of such variation is not a matter of reducing conduct to predictable regularities but of accounting for the meaning of behaviour. Despite this, there still exists a marked tendency in some parts of our academic culture to present physical science as a standard for all social explanation. Quine famously contended that 'philosophy of science is philosophy enough'.[45] From Paul Lazarsfeld to B. F. Skinner, the naturalistic ambitions of sociology and psychology were similarly trailed. Experimental knowledge has certainly contributed to advances in these subjects, but it is hard to claim that it convincingly exhausts them. While the blunt application of a hermeneutics of suspicion to all domains of inquiry is surely inappropriate, rampant claims of scientism are also overblown. Today a positivistic spirit persists within influential strands of the social sciences. One consequence has been that the value of historical understanding has been increasingly misunderstood and ignored. The aim of this volume is not to promote anything like an anti-scientific agenda, but it is certainly to redress the balance by illustrating how the cultivation of historical understanding can enrich and improve a range of social-scientific as well as humanistic disciplines.

This is not to suggest that the study of history can be held up to other disciplines as a beacon of enlightenment. As several contributors observe, it might be argued that contemporary historians have not always shown themselves effective practitioners of their own trade. Pamela Clemit maintains in Chapter 13 that some purportedly historical approaches to the study of literature – notably New Historicism – are so unhistorical that they amount to little more than discourse analysis. Samuel Moyn offers a broader and strongly worded criticism in Chapter 2, complaining that many contemporary historians hold a disastrously mistaken view of their discipline. They are far too ready to privilege the ideational over the material world, and far too prone to emphasise contingency over causal determination. He makes a plea for legal as well as historical studies to enrich themselves by reconnecting with central traditions of social thought, thereby engaging once again with the basic question of what holds together our social world.

A majority of contributors argue no less strongly that the pursuit of historical understanding has much more to contribute to the social sciences than is currently believed. Some concentrate on what they take to be current misuses of history in the humanities as well as the social sciences.

[45] Quine 1953, p. 446.

Jennifer Pitts in Chapter 3 criticises the study of international law for its reliance on merely schematic narratives centred on the rise of the modern system of nation-states. Too often these states are still treated as the sole agents in the international political arena. One resulting weakness, which remains to be remedied, has been that international relations theorists have largely failed to comprehend or even address questions about the origins and extent of global domination. Michael Lobban issues a similar rebuke in Chapter 1 to legal historians who turn to the history of law only with the aim of clarifying current legal concepts and judgments. He insists on the need for a rigorously historical approach, showing that anachronistic conclusions can hardly be avoided if we fail to recapture the unfamiliar moral as well as legal assumptions that may have underpinned the cases being discussed. Speaking more synoptically in Chapter 5, Stathis N. Kalyvas and Daniel Fedorowycz survey the misuses of history in a range of the social disciplines, especially economics, sociology and political science, all of which they indict for being excessively inclined to treat a knowledge of the past simply as a means of arriving at allegedly nomothetic forms of explanation.

A further group of contributors focus less on the misuses of history than on a prevailing disregard for historical knowledge and understanding. For some what is missing is a sense of historical and practical possibility. Richard Bourke in Chapter 7 considers John Rawls's *A Theory of Justice* from this point of view. While Rawls acknowledges that his ideal of justice as fairness is a utopian vision, he insists that his utopia is a realistic one. When he lays out his theory, however, he confines himself for the most part to normative construction, with little of real consequence to offer about the historical conditions that would need to be met before his ideal could become a practical possibility. If Rawls had been more historically minded he might have been forced to recognise that his theory was more utopian and less viable than he liked to assume.

For other contributors what is missing is an adequate degree of historical knowledge and awareness. Hazem Kandil argues in Chapter 6 that historical sociology is currently limited by its fixation on a single type of narrative in which different forms of power are treated as the causes of social change. Kandil pleads for more attention to be paid to narratives as re-enactments of events, in which the aim is less to try to explain why a particular outcome happened than to give an account of how events unfolded. More emphasis should be placed on the role of interacting social agents, thereby doing more justice to the open-ended nature of the historical process itself.

Cathy Shrank analogously considers how a lack of historical awareness can radically impoverish our appreciation of literary texts. She opens her discussion in Chapter 12 with a detailed analysis of a poem by Thomas Wyatt. There is no possibility, she argues, of comprehending Wyatt's text if we follow the anti-historical techniques of practical criticism. To decode his allusions we need a knowledge of the Old Testament; to evaluate his moral stance we need an acquaintance with classical Stoicism; to explain his tone of anxiety we need to be aware of his position at court. If we aspire to uncover such layers of meaning there is no alternative to a historical approach.

A similar sense of the impoverishment that can result from a failure to think historically underlies Quentin Skinner's discussion of political philosophy in Chapter 8 as well as Michael Lobban's examination of legal theories in Chapter 1. Both show that some pivotal terms in legal and political discourse have undergone a change of definition over time. Lobban considers our current view of criminal responsibility, in which the concept of *mens rea* plays a central role. This emphasis has led to an abandonment of the earlier belief that judges should be more concerned with evaluating character than attempting to uncover a guilty mind. Skinner similarly examines our current understanding of civil liberty, which is generally defined in terms of non-interference. He illustrates how this definition replaced the earlier belief that the antonym of freedom is subjection to the will of others. Lobban and Skinner both show how one pathway of analysis was closed off in favour of another and strongly contrasting one. But was this a gain or a loss? A study of the history of legal and political concepts may serve to uncover abandoned ways of thinking that in some cases may be of greater value than prevailing orthodoxies.

Several other contributors offer a closely related but stronger criticism: that in some disciplines the refusal to think historically produces results that are not merely partial but misconceived. In Chapter 9 Susan James pursues this objection by way of scrutinising what she describes as the classical conception of philosophy. According to this view, philosophy is a form of enquiry endowed with a unique capacity to illuminate universal truths. This belief has the effect of categorically distinguishing philosophy from history, which is taken to be limited to the uncovering of particular truths. James counters by arguing that what needs to be given up is the belief that philosophy is a discipline capable of supplying us with a transcendent form of knowledge. Only at that point will it be possible for a more fruitful relationship between philosophy and its history to be explored.

Hannah Dawson arrives at a similar conclusion in Chapter 10 from the direction of feminist studies. She begins by observing that a fantasy about the nature of reasoning still holds sway in much contemporary philosophy. We are presented with an image of the human mind that is not only outside time, but is also devoid of gender, race and class. Dawson argues that, from as early as the eighteenth century, feminist writers saw through this fantasy. They were well placed to recognise that a range of concepts to which male philosophers attributed fixity were largely a product of culture and power. The moral she draws is that we need to acknowledge the extent to which, as the early feminists were among the first to insist, our concepts are not the outcome of transcendental reasoning but are more appropriately regarded as tools forged to suit our immediate purposes.

The belief that some current attitudes in the social sciences stand in need of reconsideration likewise underpins Adam Tooze and Ira Katznelson's chapters on economics and political science. In Chapter 11 Katznelson traces the emancipation of political science from history, especially in the United States in the early twentieth century. The historians became more isolated as political scientists increasingly valued causal explanation at the expense of a narrative approach, and the gulf subsequently widened as political scientists became increasingly preoccupied with contemporary experience. Katznelson argues that the resulting separation of the disciplines is now acting to the detriment of political science, which would benefit from an infusion of what he describes (following Richard Hofstadter) as analytical history. Katznelson ends by calling for more emphasis on chronology and the contextualising of events, more willingness to ask about the meaning of statistical data, and above all (echoing earlier chapters) a greater awareness of the role of contingency in the explanation of social change.

Adam Tooze in Chapter 15 uncovers an analogous weakness in the discipline of economics. Many economists are prone to repudiate the outlook of historians, seeing them as too much interested in things that happened and too little in why they happened. This impatience has in recent times led to some ruinous consequences. Here Tooze follows Paul Krugman's intellectual odyssey, and especially his awakening to the value of studying historical precedents. Like Krugman, Tooze argues that the failure of capitalist economies to cope with the economic crisis of 2008 can be attributed at least in part to a wholesale ignorance of what was done to overcome the Great Depression in the 1930s. If economics is to be a practical science, Tooze concludes, a greater willingness to study and learn from the past will be indispensable.

It would be misleading, however, to give the impression that the contributors to this volume are mainly preoccupied with critique. Some place much greater emphasis on celebrating the value of adopting a historical approach across the humanities as well as the social sciences. In Chapter 13 Pamela Clemit reaffirms, from a distinctive angle, the value of a historical approach to literary texts. She takes the case of textual editing, showing how it can provide a means of re-establishing contact with writers who may have become unjustly neglected. As she illustrates, by recovering lost sources we can hope to enlarge our sympathies, thereby helping to prevent our canons of literary excellence from becoming ossified.

In Chapter 14 Sheilagh Ogilvie shows how history and economic analysis can support and enhance one another. She takes the case of serfdom, analysing the range of choices and the background constraints involved in maintaining the system. Moving back and forth between the study of local conditions and more general economic reasoning, she illustrates the indispensability of historical analysis to explaining the entire phenomenon of serfdom: when and why it arose, why it flourished in some countries and not in others, and why it eventually declined.

An optimistic vision of intellectual collaboration likewise underlies Mira Siegelberg's discussion in Chapter 4 of how theorists of international relations are responding to the growing problem of migration induced by climate change. An excessively static image of the international order initially prevented the crisis from being adequately recognised. Of late, however, increasingly historicised models of international relations have begun to make a vital contribution to explicating the linked phenomena of climate migration and statelessness.

We round off our volume in Chapter 16 with an account of recent developments in social anthropology. Joel Isaac investigates what he describes as the turn to history among anthropologists, especially in the latter decades of the twentieth century. As Isaac shows, it was entirely through historical investigations that they were able to construct their widely influential accounts of how rivalrous groups of individuals can be held together in the absence of a politics centred on the state. It seems fitting to conclude our volume with Isaac's account of how the adoption of a wholeheartedly historical approach to this fundamental question had the effect of transforming a leading discipline in the social sciences.

References

Bambach, Charles R. 1995. *Heidegger, Dilthey, and the Crisis of Historicism.* Ithaca.
Beiser, Frederick C. 2011. *The German Historicist Tradition.* Oxford.
Bodin, Jean. 1945 [1566]. *Method for the Easy Comprehension of History*, trans. Beatrice Reynolds. New York.
Burckhardt, Jakob. 1979 [1905]. *Reflections on History.* Indianapolis.
Collingwood, R. G. 1993 [1946]. *The Idea of History*, ed. Jan van der Dussen. Oxford.

Grotius, Hugo 2005 [1625]. *The Rights of War and Peace*, ed. Richard Tuck. 3 vols. Indianapolis.

Hegel, G. W. F. 1977 [1801]. *The Difference between Fichte's and Schelling's System of Philosophy*. Albany.

1991 [1821]. *Elements of the Philosophy of Right*, ed. Allen W. Wood. Cambridge.

2018 [1807]. *The Phenomenology of Spirit*, ed. Terry Pinkard. Cambridge.

Heussi, Karl. 1932. *Die Krisis des Historismus*. Tübingen.

Hintze, Otto. 1927. 'Troeltsch und die Probleme des Historismus: Kritische Studien', *Historische Zeitschrift*, 135: 2, pp. 188–239.

Hirschman, Albert O. 1977. *The Passions and the Interests: Political Arguments for Capitalism before its Triumph*. Princeton.

Hobbes, Thomas. 2012 [1651]. *The Clarendon Edition of the Works of Thomas Hobbes, IV: Leviathan: The English and Latin Texts*, ed. Noel Malcolm. 3 vols. Oxford.

Hugo, Gustav. 1818 [1790]. *Lehrbuch der Geschichte des römischen Rechts*. Berlin.

Hume, David. 1985 [1742]. 'Of the Rise and Progress of the Arts and Sciences' in *Essays Moral, Political, and Literary*, ed. Eugene F. Miller. Indianapolis.

Iggers, Georg. 1968, rev. ed. 1983. *The German Conception of History: The National Tradition of Historical Thought from Herder to the Present*. Middletown, CT.

Isaac, Joel. 2012. *Working Knowledge: Making the Human Sciences from Parsons to Kuhn*. Cambridge, MA.

Kant, Immanuel. 1998 [1781]. *Critique of Pure Reason*, ed. Paul Guyer and Allen W. Wood. Cambridge.

Keedus, Liisi. 2015. *The Crisis of German Historicism: The Early Political Thought of Hannah Arendt and Leo Strauss*. Cambridge.

Machiavelli, Nicolò. 1989 [1521]. *Discourses on the First Decade of Titus Livius* in *Machiavelli: The Chief Works and Others*, trans. Allan Gilbert. 3 vols. Durham, NC.

Mannheim, Karl. 1968 [1924]. 'Historicism' in *Essays in the Sociology of Knowledge*, ed. Paul Kecskemeti. London.

Marx, Karl. 1975–2004. 'The Philosophical Manifesto of the Historical School of Law' (1842) in Karl Marx and Friedrich Engels, *Complete Works*. 50 vols. London.

Meinecke, Friedrich. 1972 [1936]. *Historism: The Rise of a New Historical Outlook*. London.

Menger, Carl. 2009 [1883]. *Investigation into the Method of the Social Sciences with Special Reference to Economics*. Auburn, AL.

de Montesquieu, Charles de Secondat, Baron. 1989 [1748]. *The Spirit of the Laws*, ed. Anne Cohler, Basia Miller and Harold Stone. Cambridge.

Pippin, Robert. 1989. *Hegel's Idealism: The Satisfactions of Self-Consciousness*. Cambridge.

Quine, W. V. 1953. 'Mr. Strawson on Logical Theory', *Mind*, 62: 248, pp. 433–51.

von Ranke, Leopold. 2011. 'On the Relations of History and Philosophy' in *Theory and Practice of History: Leopold von Ranke*, ed. Georg G. Iggers. London and New York.

von Savigny, Friedrich. 1831 [1814]. *Of the Vocation of the Age for Legislation and Jurisprudence*. London.

Schmoller, Gustav. 1888 [1883]. 'Zur Methodologie der Staats- und Sozialwissenschaften' in *Zur Literaturgeschichte der Staats- und Sozialwissenschaften*. Leipzig.

Schorske, Carl E. 1997. 'The New Rigorism in the Human Sciences, 1940–1960', *Daedalus*, 126: 1, pp. 289–309.

Smith, Adam. 1976 [1776]. *An Inquiry into the Nature and Causes of the Wealth of Nations*. 2 vols. Indianapolis.

de Staël, Germaine. 1800. *De la littérature considérée dans ses rapports avec les institutions sociales*. 2 vols. Paris.

Strauss, Leo. 1959 [1955]. 'What is Political Philosophy?' in *What is Political Philosophy?* Glencoe, IL.

Toews, John E. 2004. *Becoming Historical: Cultural Reformation and Public Memory in Early Nineteenth-Century Berlin*. Cambridge.

Troeltsch, Ernst. 1902. *Die Absolutheit des Christentums und die Religionsgeschichte*. Tübingen.

1922. 'Die Krisis des Historismus', *Die neue Rundschau*, 33: 1, pp. 572–90.

2008 [1922]. *Der Historismus und seine Probleme: Das logische Problem der Geschichtsphilosophie*, ed. F. W. Graf and M. Schloßberger. Berlin.

Weber, Max. 1984–. *Gesamtausgabe*. Tübingen.

2012 [1904]. 'The "Objectivity" of Knowledge in Social Science and Social Policy' in *Max Weber: Collected Methodological Writings*, ed. Hans Henrik Bruun and Sam Whimster. London and New York.

Windelband, Wilhelm. 1894. *Geschichte und Naturwissenschaft: Rede zum Antritt des Rectorats der Kaiser-Wilhelms-Universität* Strasburg.

1   Law and History, History and Law

Michael Lobban

Do lawyers and historians think differently about history? F. W. Maitland seemed to think so. In his inaugural lecture at Cambridge in 1888 he argued that when lawyers turn to history, it is to find authority for propositions about current law, whose 'true intent and meaning' can be teased out of what generations of jurists have said about the doctrine. Their aim is to find 'orthodox dogma' in history. 'From the historian's point of view,' Maitland said, this is 'almost of necessity a process of perversion and misunderstanding. ... If we try to make history the hand-maid of dogma, she will soon cease to be history.'[1] Maitland wanted to discourage this kind of history, and to invite lawyers to engage in 'deep historical research'.

The question whether lawyers and historians think differently about history has been revisited recently, in a debate between scholars of international law and intellectual historians. In this debate some lawyers have put forward a view of legal history which seems at odds with Maitland's, and which defends the idea that lawyers have a distinct method in using history. One of the prominent participants in the debate, Anne Orford, has written: 'Although international lawyers and historians at times look to the same texts from the past, the way the two disciplines approach such texts is quite different.' In her view, 'law is inherently genealogical, depending as it does upon the movement of concepts, languages and norms across time and even space'.[2] She therefore challenges what she calls 'the strong separation of past and present championed by the Cambridge school'[3] in its approach to reading texts in the history of political thought, rejecting the idea that 'present-day questions must not be allowed to distort our interpretation of past events'. She adds: 'If we want to understand the work that a particular legal argument is doing,

---

[1] Maitland 1911, p. 491.
[2] Orford 2012, pp. 2, 9.
[3] Orford 2017, p. 302. For a classic statement of the position criticised, see Skinner 2002a, p. 57.

we have to grasp both ... the way it relates to a particular, identifiable social context, and the way in which it gestures beyond that context to a conversation that may persist – sometimes in a neat linear progression, sometimes in wild leaps and bounds – across centuries.'[4] In her defence of a different kind of history, Orford asks, 'what kind of method is appropriate to a discipline in which judges, advocates, scholars and students all look to past texts precisely to discover the meaning of present *concepts*?' In a variant of the same sentence, she asks what method is needed to discover the 'nature of present *obligations*?'[5] Orford's suggestion here seems to be that in order to understand our present law, we need to approach it historically; but the kind of historical approach we must take is a distinctly *legal* one. It suggests that the lawyer uses historical scholarship not simply to know how present concepts emerged, but to understand how past concepts constitute present ones.

Despite the disagreements this debate has uncovered between lawyers and historians over both what the very study of history is for and what methods are appropriate for its study, it will be suggested in what follows that each side has much to gain from taking seriously the methods of the other, and that the disciplines are not engaged in fundamentally different exercises. Just as an understanding of law and legal doctrine can be enriched by historical research which seeks to understand the particular contexts in which legal ideas and practices developed, so an understanding of past societies is enriched by a better understanding of its juridical practices and techniques.

History and International Law

The debate to which Orford was contributing was occasioned by a disagreement over the interpretation of the works of Francisco Vitoria by Antony Anghie in his book *Imperialism, Sovereignty and the Making of International Law*.[6] In this debate, some intellectual historians criticised Anghie for making a 'retrospective construction' of Vitoria's intentions, which did not read the work in its proper context, and which evaluated it by using anachronistic criteria.[7] One of the historians who took part in the debate was Martti Koskenniemi, who (like Orford) defended the approach taken by Anghie. Koskenniemi questioned the intellectual historians' insistence that thinkers had to be read in their strictly

---

[4] Orford 2013, pp. 171, 176.
[5] Orford 2013, p. 171; Orford 2017, p. 302 (emphasis added).
[6] Anghie 2005.
[7] Cavaller 2008, p. 183; cf. Hunter 2010, p. 11; Brett 2011, pp. 14–15.

chronological context. The context in which a jurist is to be placed cannot (he argued) be limited to 'the chronological moment in which he lived and where his intentions and projects were formed'.[8] There are many other contexts in which the jurist could be placed, none of which have 'any *intrinsic* epistemological priority'. The point is a strong one, though one which would not necessarily trouble the historian interested in contextual study. Historians might very well wish to study how the works of jurists of one generation were made use of by later generations, who might have mis- or re-interpreted the original works and turned them to different uses. One might want to look for strands in earlier works which may not have been prominent in the original intentions of an author, but which over time made thinkable or legitimised actions the author never had in mind. This looks uncontentious, at least so long as care is taken not to mix up the intentions of an author with the subsequent uses made of his ideas. The context in which the historian puts an idea is not to be confused with the original author's own context(s).[9]

Koskenniemi does however point to a difference in the approach taken by lawyers, in arguing that 'the construction of the context ... is crucially dependent on what we now think international law "is" – its being today embodying likewise an account of what it is *for*'. He adds:

Historians of international law must accept that the validity of our histories lies not in their correspondence with 'facts' or 'coherence' with what we otherwise know about a 'context', but how they contribute to emancipation today. This is not to say that historiography should turn into propaganda, only that an understanding of a society – including our own – includes the perspective of its imagined future.[10]

This is to suggest that the historian of international law is a participant in a current practice, whose identity she wishes to elucidate, and whose future she wishes in some way to help shape. History is used to offer interpretations of the subject which might open up the possibility to develop it in different directions, or to reform it. Such an ambition is clearly different from the approach taken by most historians: while there are many historians who wish to write long-term histories of large topics, such as war or democracy, and draw conclusions about their nature, they do not tend to write from the view of engaged participants in the practice with an aim to shape its future development.[11] How far the position of the researcher as an engaged participant dictates the methodology of

---

[8] Koskenniemi 2014, p. 125.
[9] See Skinner 2002b, p. 116; Fitzmaurice 2018, p. 9; Brett 2021, p. 27.
[10] Koskenniemi 2014, p. 129.
[11] E.g., Armitage 2017.

the research itself is another question: if one's answers are too strongly dictated by one's questions, then it may turn into propaganda. While this does not seem to be a trap that historians such as Koskenniemi himself have fallen into,[12] there is always a danger that a lawyer's history will turn to presentism and anachronism. Any historical study will naturally involve a combination of uncovering evidence – which requires sensitivity to context – and interpreting its meaning – which entails the historian asking questions of the material informed by present preoccupations; but the more it loses its contextual bearings, the less robust can be its claims to be history.[13] There is a risk in particular that the jurist seeking to map out a historical trajectory to elucidate the meaning of present-day concepts may select as landmarks only those episodes that best fit the story intended to be told, while at the same time misunderstanding their original meanings.

Since the initial skirmishes between international lawyers and historians, there has been a proliferation of literature on the subject.[14] Much of this literature elaborates on the various approaches taken on both sides, though it is not clear how much progress has been made in effecting a rapprochement. Moreover, in some ways the terms of the debate appear to have changed. In her latest intervention Orford does not repeat the claim that lawyers seek to tease out the meaning of present concepts or obligations from historical materials by the use of a method particular to themselves. Instead, she draws a different distinction between the rival methods. In contrast to the method of lawyers, which is portrayed as a 'post-Realist' one stressing the contingent, contestable and political nature of law, the method of historians is described as an empiricism which makes claims to scientific standards of veracity and verifiability: 'history offers lawyers a vision of law in which it is possible to find a determinative source of truth about the law's meaning'.[15] The 'turn to history' is said to present dangers for the international lawyer, who may be tempted to think that 'we can use the work of historians to establish truths about international law' instead of 'fully accepting uncertainty and our responsibility for the politics of our legal arguments'.[16] Orford's latest argument is in many ways controversial. Few historians would claim to provide the level of scientific certainty described here: the writing of history is an interpretative enterprise, though the more rooted it is in

---

[12] Koskenniemi 2001.
[13] Fitzmaurice 2018, p. 12; Brett 2021, p. 30.
[14] See, e.g., Fitzmaurice 2018; Benton 2019; and Wheatley 2021.
[15] Orford 2021, p. 295.
[16] Orford 2021, p. 7.

careful, source-based research, which can be tested and evaluated by others, the more plausible its claims may be. Furthermore, the claim that historians purport to offer 'a non-partisan, objective account of "meaning", including the meaning of international law' – with the result that 'history has become a new foundation for formalism' – seems to lay the very kind of charge against historians which has been laid against the lawyers.[17]

Orford's latest work offers a sceptical view of the nature of law, arguing that 'there is no objective, impartial, or "verifiable" answer to the question "what is international law a history of?"'. For her, any history of international law is itself a 'creative and political work – "to see a pattern is to make a pattern"'.[18] Such a degree of scepticism may beg the question how, if there is no such thing as 'international law' to be sought, a study of its history could inform present understandings, one way or another. It also overlooks the point made by many jurists that law is not just a matter of patterns of behaviour, but imports normative attitudes or beliefs held within communities. Indeed, one of the criticisms of the Cambridge School made by scholars including Orford herself is that a contextual approach which focuses on the intentions of the authors of texts who sought to engage in particular debates cannot be applied straightforwardly to the study of bodies of law, which are articulated, bit by bit, over periods of time, by numerous actors who regard that law as normatively binding. In her latest work Orford does not address this question in detail, though it is one which has engaged the attention of other recent participants in this debate.[19] It is also a question which has long been considered by doctrinal legal historians. It is therefore noteworthy that, although Orford spends much time in her latest book critiquing the approach of the Cambridge School, there is no discussion of the approach to legal history pioneered in the same era by S. F. C. Milsom, which invited the historian to attempt to understand the law as contemporary lawyers and practitioners might have understood it, all the while accepting that it might be uncertain, ambiguous, contested and in flux.[20] In fact, the history of legal doctrine has not been much discussed

---

[17] Orford 2021, p. 284.
[18] Orford 2021, p. 256, quoting Karl Llewellyn.
[19] See esp. Wheatley 2021.
[20] Orford argues (unconvincingly) that Maitland's historical work was motivated by presentist concerns, and points out (correctly) that Maitland argued that only someone with training in modern law could understand the legal documents that made up the source material for much medieval history. It was this position that Milsom challenged, but arguing that one needed to attempt to recover the perspective of the historical lawyer: Orford 2021, pp. 115–19.

in these recent debates, perhaps because international law is less doctrinal than systems of municipal law, where legislation and courtroom precedents play a more central role.[21] However, the question of how history can be used to make sense of doctrine remains a pressing one, and it is to this that we now turn.

History and the Jurist

In recent years, lawyers in a number of other areas have also turned to history to rethink present understandings of their subject. Many of these have not claimed to be using a different form of 'lawyer's history' but have sought to build on bodies of research done by other historians. For instance, a number of criminal law theorists have drawn on the large body of historical work on crime and criminality to challenge some perceptions of current law. Criminal law is unusual in English law, in so far as there was very little doctrinal development in this area until the nineteenth century, when a new era of imprisonment and graduated punishments replaced the old system of execution and transportation. Much of criminal doctrine is consequently of relatively recent development, elaborated in an era when analytical jurisprudence encouraged jurists to take a very conceptual view of the law, which suggested that careful philosophical analysis could reveal timeless concepts.[22] Taking such a conceptual view, jurists developed a notion of criminal responsibility which is rooted in volitional and cognitive capacities. According to this view, to be held criminally responsible an actor must have made a subjective choice to perform the act in question – she must have had a 'guilty mind' – and must have had the capacity to make that choice (for instance, being of sound mind).[23]

This approach to understanding the nature of crime has been challenged by scholars who have looked to history. For instance, drawing on the work of historians of crime, Nicola Lacey has pointed out that before the nineteenth-century development of doctrine, judges and juries were more interested in evaluating the character of the defendant than in examining the nature of her guilty mind.[24] Before the arrival of lawyers in the courtroom and the development of rules of evidence, before the dislodging of the Bloody Code and the move to graduated

---

[21] For an intervention which stresses the importance of taking doctrine seriously see Fitzmaurice 2018.
[22] Smith 1998.
[23] See Hart 1968.
[24] Lacey 2016.

punishments, the operation of the criminal law looked very different. Lacey points out that the very kind of reasoning now seen as central to our understanding of criminal law is a product of the interplay of ideas, interests and institutions over time. Nor does she accept the idea that those who administered the eighteenth-century criminal justice system were simply unsophisticated, and were yet to discover the truths that later theorists have elaborated. Rather, she argues that responsibility is not a metaphysical essence, but needs to be understood in the contexts of its historical uses and social functions. This also allows her (and other jurists taking the same approach) to argue that the current dominant model does not explain all of criminal law (either past or present), but reflects a particular choice of what is to be regarded as the paradigm form. Jurists drawing on historical research can thereby show 'the existence of multiple, overlapping conceptions of responsibility', which have been excluded in the mainstream approach.[25] They can draw attention to features of the modern system of criminal justice in which the notion of *mens rea* plays a limited role, raising new questions about the uses and purposes of criminal law, and drawing the boundary between the different kinds of crime.

In a similar way, Lindsay Farmer's work on the evolution of the category of 'sexual offences' from the nineteenth century to the late twentieth shows that 'the harms or wrongs of sexual offences cannot be defined in terms of abstract values such as autonomy alone – or even sexual autonomy – but must also be contextualized in terms of the aims of the law, the kind of civil order that the law is trying to achieve, and the institutional capacity that it possesses to produce that order'.[26] Farmer shows that the notion of a distinct category of sexual offences only came into being in the second half of the twentieth century, under the influence of new models of social and scientific thought. As people began to think differently about the nature of the interest to be protected, so the way the law behaved was transformed. In the nineteenth century (Farmer explains) the law presumed consent to sex within marriage, but strictly regulated it outside marriage. By the late twentieth century, when sex was seen as a valued human activity which law ought to protect, the law became at the same time more liberal and more restrictive, particularly as jurists began to develop a much richer and more nuanced idea of what counts as consent. Writers such as these use history in order to challenge the way that current doctrine is understood and to debate how the very discipline should be seen. In the view of these criminal theorists, rather

---

[25] Lacey 2016, p. 190.
[26] Farmer 2016, pp. 293–4.

than seeing law as a closed autonomous analytical subject, it should be studied more broadly, using the tools not only of analytical philosophy but social theory, as well as history. If it is studied in terms of its institutions and their functions in maintaining systems of civil order, its normative principles and values can be better understood or rethought.

The scholars discussed hitherto, who draw on history to call into question current analytical orthodoxies, do not offer a different *lawyer's* version of history. Rather – in some ways like Sir Henry Maine – they make the point that a sensitivity to history can undermine overly ambitious conceptual claims.[27] Many of the jurists engaged in this endeavour do not claim to be producing historical scholarship, but draw 'on historical research to drive [the] interpretive project'.[28] At the same time, there are other jurists who seek a more ambitious kind of historical jurisprudence, whose methods might seem more distant from those of mainstream historians. To illustrate this, we can refer to the work of Martin Loughlin, who in his *Foundations of Public Law* engages with a large volume of historical material in arguing for a conception of 'public law' as a distinct branch of jurisprudence.[29] To put this enterprise in context, it may be noted that the dominant tradition in English legal theory has shown little interest in offering a theory of the state or of constitutions. This tradition is that of the so-called legal positivists, who take their cue from John Austin (who made no attempt to theorise the state) rather than from his mentor Jeremy Bentham (who did).[30] For the analytical jurists following the tradition of Austin, the state can be equated with the sovereign, who (or which) is the ultimate source of validity for the rules enforced by the legal system in the political community which accepts his sovereignty.[31]

Loughlin argues that, in taking this position, English jurists have missed something. In his view, the law that pertains to the constitution and operation of the state is different in kind from the ordinary law which the state enforces. It cannot be explained by the same concept of law which the positivists have articulated for ordinary law, which they explain simply in terms of a rule or habit which gives legal validity to all other rules in the system. It needs the elaboration of a different set of juristic principles, the kind of principles which French jurists call *droit politique* and German jurists call *allgemeines Staatsrecht*. In developing

---

[27] Maine 1875.
[28] Lacey 2016, p. 12.
[29] Loughlin 2010.
[30] Austin 1995; Rumble 1985; Freeman and Mindus 2013; Schofield 2006.
[31] English public lawyers such as Dicey, following Austin's lead, showed little interest in developing a legal theory of the state, beyond arguing that parliament was the supreme sovereign, the source of all valid rules. See Dicey 2013.

this argument, Loughlin draws on and engages with the work of a large number of jurists from different eras and different traditions. His aim is not to show the development of their thought and to situate them in their context, but rather to draw insights from their ideas when discussing particular concepts. Nor does he claim to be recovering a lost English tradition, for in his view the kind of concept of law he is seeking to elucidate 'has remained suppressed in British legal practice for much of the last 250 years ... because the British state has managed to present its governing arrangements as being so secure as to avoid the need for juristic investigation into its foundations'.[32] Instead, he argues that it is to be found in much continental legal theory and juristic work, and that engaging with these works can offer fruitful material for new juristic approaches. For Loughlin, if English jurists are to think afresh about the concept of the state, they might usefully begin with looking at traditions in which a distinctive notion of public law is to be found, and seek to develop ideas found there.

In presenting his own view of the nature of *droit politique*, Loughlin therefore builds on elements of thought which have hitherto had little purchase in English constitutional thought, such as the German *Staatslehre* tradition and the early twentieth-century French institutional scholars. For example, when discussing the relationship between constituent and constituted power, and the political dynamics at work in the constitutional ordering of the state, he comments in turn on the work of Lorenz von Stein, Carl Schmitt, Georg Jellinek, the Abbé Sieyes, Maurice Hauriou and Hermann Heller. In this process he uses ideas from historical figures who developed juristic theories of the state in building his own distinct theory, which sees public law as a site of negotiation and 'prudential judgement' in the public sphere. In so doing, he seeks to articulate an idea he often finds only hinted at in the work of earlier thinkers.[33]

History plays a part in Loughlin's theory, for he situates the origins of his idea of public law in a particular historical moment: the rise of the state in the early modern period, and the concomitant demise of a notion of fundamental law rooted in theology. This is a central moment for Loughlin, since his concept of public law rests on the notion of a

---

[32] Loughlin 2010, p. 3.

[33] For instance, he speaks of Stein as failing fully to bring out the distinction between positive law and *Staatsrecht* (Loughlin 2010, p. 209); and elsewhere he says that 'the notion of droit politique was widely – if only implicitly – understood around the turn of the twentieth century when a self-consciously modern idiom of public law was being advocated in many European regimes' (Loughlin 2010, p. 233).

state in which the people are perceived to come together to create a new autonomous political space.[34] At the same time, he aims to go further than those historians who speak of a conceptual revolution in early modern Europe, as a result of which 'the term *state* came to be accepted as the master noun of political discourse'.[35] He wishes to explore its philosophical or jurisprudential nature: following Foucault, Loughlin speaks of the state itself as a scheme of intelligibility – whereby institutions and actors are conceived of as elements of the state and are given meaning by it – which is revealed through public law. Public law is not simply the constitutional rules that determine the powers of the institutions: it encompasses the dialectical relationship between the constituent power (the people as an active political agency) and the constituted power (the institutional apparatus of the state).[36] Together, they make up the public sphere, which is itself 'constituted through a singular type of juristic discourse', made up of a 'set of customs and beliefs (ie, practices) that sustain this type of ordering'.[37]

In seeking to draw attention to a different tradition of *Staatslehre* to explain the juridical constitution of the state in ways not done in the English tradition, Loughlin opens up a new area of thought. This kind of approach, which invites the jurist to widen the concept of law to embrace broader questions of political debate and negotiation, may be particularly valuable at a time in the United Kingdom when older notions of a sovereign parliament are being called into question, in an era of devolved administrations and referendums. In developing this kind of historical jurisprudence, Loughlin's main aim is jurisprudential rather than historical. It assumes that there is a general conceptual problem which thinkers over a long period of time and in different places have wrestled with: the problem of how law is used to establish and maintain political authority. His interest is not in explaining the specific intentions of particular authors or in exploring how they used their ideas in their own contexts. Instead, the aim is to develop a theory of public law, in the light of how other thinkers have sought to do this in past debates. Historians might question Loughlin's reading of particular thinkers. They might also raise questions about how far it is possible to translate concepts from continental public law traditions into English terms, since so many of the idioms always depended on particular contexts: the very conceptualisation

---

[34] 'The concept of the state is nothing less than the *sine qua non* of public law': Loughlin 2010, p. 183.

[35] Skinner 2002c, p. 410.

[36] Loughlin 2010, pp. 228, 231.

[37] Loughlin 2010, pp. 231, 233.

of *Staatslehre* as law may itself be the product of a particular tradition and context which cannot be transposed. However, in so far as this does not claim to be a work of history, but one of theory, the acid test will not be the accuracy of its historical method, but whether it can offer a convincing theory.

Unlike Orford, Loughlin does not claim that history can uncover the meaning of present concepts or obligations. However, he does argue that there are common jurisprudential and philosophical problems which thinkers have debated over time – albeit in different ways and in different traditions – with which the contemporary jurist can usefully engage. Loughlin's work does not assume that the concepts are timeless – for, as has been seen, he roots his public law in the rise of the state – but neither does he accept that they are tied to their specific temporal and political contexts. As a consequence, he thinks that jurists can clarify their ideas of the nature and ambit of public law by reflecting on what other traditions have done.

History and the Lawyer

Let us turn now to consider whether history can be of use in elucidating the meaning of present legal concepts or obligations. Jurists in the positivist tradition have not tended to pay much attention to history. In this tradition, legal rules are identified by their pedigree. In the view made famous by H. L. A. Hart, where a rule is settled, the judge must follow it; and where its meaning is unclear, she has the discretion to develop the rule as she sees fit. In determining whether a rule is settled, the judge traces its pedigree to a recognised authoritative source which confers validity on the legal rule.[38] 'Historical jurisprudence', which seemed to offer a potent challenge to the Austinian vision in the hands of Sir Henry Maine, largely petered out in the early twentieth century[39] as English jurisprudence went down an analytical path, and American jurisprudence was reshaped under realist influences.[40] Scholarly work on legal history – of the kind pioneered by Maitland and reshaped by S. F. C. Milsom – did not seek to use history to answer present-day questions.[41] In this era, the analytical approach of Hart and his followers dominated.

However, the later twentieth century saw something of a revival of interest in history by lawyers concerned with current problems. Two kinds of

---

[38] Hart 2012.
[39] Rabban 2013.
[40] See Duxbury 1995; Duxbury 2004.
[41] Milsom 1981; Milsom 2003.

endeavour may be identified. The first is the endeavour to use history to inform the present about the substantive values found within the common law tradition. One root of this endeavour may be traced in the jurisprudence of Ronald Dworkin, who challenged Hart's 'model of rules'. Dworkin argued that when judges encounter novel or hard cases they do not have a simple discretion, but must develop the law according to the principles inherent in it. In his view, this is an interpretive exercise: the reasoning used by courts in adjudicating disputes considers that legal rules are coherent and are justified in the light of more abstract principles of political morality, which are found in a community's legal practice as it develops over time.[42] If this might suggest that legal reasoning is a deeply historical enterprise, in which the jurist looks to a historical *Volksgeist* underlying the law,[43] it is not an approach Dworkin himself applied in his jurisprudence, for he devoted little attention to actual history. However, some of his followers have been more interested in exploring the nature and development of the common law tradition. They are often attracted by the early seventeenth-century jurisprudence of Sir Edward Coke, with its view of judging as a distinctive form of forensic deliberation, which depends not merely on positive authorities but on a special kind of artificial legal reasoning.[44]

Using this kind of approach, some lawyers in the United Kingdom have looked to the common law tradition to identify a fundamental set of constitutional values which should be defended and developed by the judiciary. As one of the proponents of a theory of 'common law constitutionalism' has expressed it: 'The common law articulates the content of the common good, according to the society's shared values and traditions. The judges are its authoritative exponents because their role is to express the collective understanding, by interpretation of the precedents.'[45] Those who adopt this view often invoke *Dr Bonham's case*,[46] in which Coke famously (but ambiguously) stated that the common law would control Acts of Parliament and sometimes declare them void. Many defenders of the 'common law constitution' associate it with a liberal idea of the rule of law.[47] For its advocates, common law courts are the best legal vehicle for securing and advancing the rule of law: they are the ideal venue in which the rights of individuals are protected from unlawful state activity and in which the community's values are

---

[42] Dworkin 1977; Dworkin 1986.
[43] This approach is generally associated with F. C. von Savigny and his school, for which see Beiser 2011, ch. 5.
[44] See, for instance, Walters 2012. Cf. Walters 2008.
[45] Allan 1999, p. 239.
[46] *Dr Bonham's Case* (1610) 8 Co. Rep. 114.
[47] Allan 1999, pp. 233–9.

articulated and developed by the judges. In practice, however, the actual work done by historical investigation in uncovering the fundamental values of the British constitution has been rather slender. For many of its defenders the 'common law constitution' is associated more with a set of moral values than a particular history.[48] Rather than being a repository of precise answers to specific questions, history is used as the source of general 'principles' which reflect the 'fundamental values' of the community,[49] and which can be adapted in an evolutionary way as the common law 'evolves by reflection on experience'.[50] Rather than looking for precise answers to specific legal questions by historical investigation – in the manner of John Selden, for instance – it reflects a mixture of Sir Edward Coke's notion of the common law as a repository of timeless yet adaptable principles and Ronald Dworkin's idea of law-as-integrity.[51] It uses history more as ideology than as authority.

This might suggest that the jurist should be wary of using history to give answers to present-day problems;[52] and that the value of history might be negative, rather than positive, disproving assumptions about present authority rather than providing the answers to current questions.[53] There is a danger in allowing the jurist to claim to articulate the substantive values inherent in the common law on the basis of general assertions of what count as fundamental values. This does not, however, mean that there is no role for historical argument in contemporary legal reasoning. In recent years a number of jurists have engaged in a different kind of historical endeavour, making a careful and well-grounded use of history to illuminate the nature of particular rules and concepts, both to make sense of various areas of doctrine and to call into question assumptions about the coherence of current law.[54] In so far as the common law

---

[48] Laws 1996, discussed in Poole 2003. See also Poole 2005.
[49] As Allan puts it, the common law 'forms the chief source of values that together "constitute" the polity' and 'reflects the spontaneous order of society': Allan 2000, p. 21.
[50] Allan 1999, p. 241.
[51] By the 1620s Coke's own approach to history had proved unable to provide the kinds of answers to prerogative claims which the common lawyers desired, and a more exacting, source-based kind of history was used by other lawyers such as John Selden. See further Lobban 2007, chs. 2–3.
[52] See Holmes 1897, pp. 469, 474.
[53] An example may be seen in the recent debate over the nature of judicial review. Those who argued that the principle of *ultra vires* was not the foundational principle of the doctrine invoked historical arguments, examining the nature of the seventeenth-century prerogative writs which laid the foundations from which modern doctrine developed, in order to show that the courts were not as limited in their powers to develop the law as the proponents of the rival view held. However, this generated no answers to how judges should develop judicial review. On the debates see Allison 2013.
[54] See, for instance, Bently and Sherman 1999; and MacMillan 2010.

is a system which rests on the authority of precedents, it is necessary to attempt to understand what those who first articulated the precedent thought they were doing. In order to understand the rules and principles of the common law, we need to explore the particular techniques and procedures, or modes of argument, which have been used by lawyers over time, and the nature of the forum in which they were deployed.

In exploring this question, the lawyer needs to move beyond general assumptions about the nature of the values of the common law, and needs to be attuned to the specificities of its history. In particular, it needs to be borne in mind that the English system, in contrast to the continental civilian ones, was from its medieval beginnings more focused on remedies – the forms of actions and writs which gave litigants a 'ticket' into the king's courts – than on substantive rules of the kind which medieval continental jurists developed in their glosses and commentaries on the recently recovered *Digest* of Justinian. In this context, many of the rules which were articulated by the courts were linked to the particular procedures which were used to bring cases before them. The law which emerged often appeared inelegant, for the reason that it was shaped by litigants seeking to find whatever means of access to the king's justice they could, so that when they found one route blocked they would try another one. If the courts allowed the new form to work, a new strand of legal doctrine began to develop. Given the often haphazard nature of this casuistic development, it is often important to have an idea of the genealogy of a doctrinal idea to understand its nature and purpose. Matters are further complicated by the fact that until the Judicature Acts of 1873–5 there were two distinct systems of judicature, with the adversarial common law courts dealing with cases where parties brought their dispute to a single point at issue for decision by a jury (and where the parties were disqualified from giving evidence until the mid-nineteenth century) and the inquisitorial juryless Court of Chancery dealing with cases that might involve multiple parties and multiple questions, in a court whose procedure allowed the court to 'probe the conscience' of the parties through sworn answers. English lawyers have long recognised that 'common law' doctrine may differ from 'equitable' doctrine, even in a system where the two were procedurally merged in the later nineteenth century.

The different genealogies of different parts of the system may help explain their nature and purpose, and there can be pitfalls if one mistakes the genealogy. One recent example can be found in the way English courts in the 2010s approached the problem of rectifying mistakes made in the recording of contracts. The doctrine of rectification, whereby a court corrects a written contract to make it reflect the parties' underlying agreement, had its origin in the practice of the Court of Chancery.

It was this court which had the power to uncover the parties' true agreement – through its ability to 'probe their consciences' – as well as the power to direct them to correct the mistake in the written instrument. In exercising this jurisdiction, the court looked to what the parties subjectively thought they had agreed and only corrected it if both parties thought there had been a mistake in recording their agreement. In 2009, however, it was suggested in England's highest court that judges who were asked to rectify a contract should not look at what the parties subjectively thought they had agreed, but that they should read the written documents generated during contractual negotiations to see what an objective reading would suggest they had agreed to before the final contract was drawn up.[55] This was to take a 'common law' approach to the problem: for common law courts, in dealing with concluded contracts whose meaning was contested by the parties before them, refused to consider what the parties subjectively thought that the contract meant (for instance by admitting extraneous evidence to explain their understanding), but interpreted them from the 'objective' point of view of the 'reasonable person'.[56]

It was soon apparent that this new way of approaching the matter caused problems. It suggested that in cases where the parties had not subjectively come to an agreement on a particular matter before writing down their contract, the court could determine where the obligations pertaining to that matter should lie not by interpreting the words of the final contract concluded by the parties (which might place the burden on one of them) but by an objective reading of pre-contractual documents (which might put it on the other). This approach to rectification generated much controversy,[57] and in 2019 the Court of Appeal held that the objective test of rectification developed over the previous decade 'incorrectly states the law'.[58] In effect, the court found that earlier judges

---

[55] This was done only if it was clear that the parties had not purposely renegotiated the matter, but had simply assumed that nothing had changed during the course of negotiations. See *Chartbrook Ltd.* v. *Persimmon Homes Ltd.* [2009] UKHL 38; [2009] 1 A.C. 1101, followed in *Daventry District Council* v. *Daventry & District Housing Ltd.* [2011] EWCA Civ 1153; [2012] 1 W.L.R. 1333.

[56] 'If, whatever a man's real intention may be, he so conducts himself that a reasonable man would believe that he was assenting to the terms proposed by the other party, and that other party upon that belief enters into the contract with him, the man thus conducting himself would be equally bound as if he had intended to agree to the other party's terms': *Smith* v. *Hughes* (1871) LR 6 QB 597 at 607. Thus, a party contracting to buy 'oats' cannot avoid the contract by claiming that he subjectively thought he was buying old oats, rather than the new oats which were delivered.

[57] See, e.g., McLauchlan 2014; Davies 2016.

[58] *FSHC Group Holdings Ltd.* v. *Glas Trust Corporation Ltd.* [2019] EWCA Civ 1361 at para [176].

had erred in following the 'common law' approach to contract formation instead of the 'equitable' approach to rectification. In his judgment Lord Justice Leggatt spent some time discussing 'the traditional approach of courts of equity', and noted that 'the use of the term "intention" to refer to what an "objective" observer would reasonably have understood the parties' intention to be from their communications (irrespective of their actual states of mind) is, we believe, a comparatively recent legal artefact'.[59] As this example shows, judges who misread the genealogy of doctrines may find themselves developing the law in ways which may appear to lack coherence, and which need revision when the genealogy is remembered. A sensitivity to history can therefore be of practical utility to contemporary lawyers: but the history they need is one which seeks to understand how courts which developed particular doctrines in the past actually understood and handled them.

Legal History and the Historian

If a knowledge of the details of legal history can assist the contemporary lawyer better to understand the law, can the tools offered by legal scholarship be of use to the historian? It is evident that much of the subject matter studied by historians is concerned somehow or other with 'law' – whether the object of study is the legislation issued by kings or parliaments as tools of governance; the constitutions or rules which determine the powers of those in authority and how they are to exercise them; the ways in which communities resolve disputes or deal with anti-social behaviour; or the norms which determine family or gender relationships. It is difficult indeed to find any historical questions in which a consideration of law is not relevant in some way or other. But what are we to understand by the term 'law'? Can historians argue that they see 'law' differently from lawyers, just as some lawyers claim to see history differently from historians?

'Law' can be seen in a number of ways. One way to see it is as an instrument of power, the tool of those who (in Weber's phrase) lay claim to a monopoly of the legitimate use of violence.[60] From a Marxist perspective law can be seen as an instrument of the ruling class, which is used to confirm existing class power. In a colonial context it can be seen as 'an

---

[59] *FSHC Group Holdings Ltd.* v. *Glas Trust Corporation Ltd.* [2019] EWCA Civ 1361 at para [52].

[60] Skoda 2012, p. 50: 'Much historical analysis of legal developments is based on an underlying assumption that legalism's *raison d'être* must, in some sense, be power, even if not straightforwardly identified with state power.'

instrument of the power of an alien state and part of the process of coercion'.[61] From such a perspective, law is seen as the tools used by those in power to control others, ultimately through the use of violence. A second way to conceive of law is as the customary practices of a community, both in the way it regulates its conduct and in how it solves its disputes. Customary systems may operate without depending on strong systems of coercion, and without officials. A third way of conceiving of law is as something distinct from either power or practice: it may refer to norms that are distinct from practice – which are regarded as binding, rather than merely being matters of habit – and which are the subject matter of specialised knowledge, in so far as they generate rules which are generalised and reflected on.[62]

While historians have often looked at law from the viewpoint of power or practice (which is sometimes described as looking at law from an external point of view), jurists have often looked more at law as normative systems (which is sometimes described as looking at law from an internal point of view). From the jurist's point of view, it is necessary to do this in order fully to grasp what law is: to be able to identify what is regarded as lawful power or binding customary law, as opposed to lawless violence or mere habit. However, if we think of law in normative terms, we need to identify what rules are regarded in a community as normatively binding and justifying coercive enforcement. One approach in identifying these rules might simply be to count as law whatever mechanisms communities use to resolve disputes or coordinate behaviour, or to punish wrongdoers. The problem with such an approach would be that it would include any mechanism of social control, from the rules of particular religious groups to the rules of private associations to the enforcement of order by criminal gangs. This might be a good way of understanding the working of social control in a society, but it would fail to capture that part which might be regarded as distinct to 'law'.[63] It would overlook the distinction in kind which we perceive between (for instance) legal, religious and criminal forms of control. These differences are likely also to have been perceived by other societies in other times. If they have not been, that may be something worthy of observation which might be rendered impossible if we fail to make the distinction.

---

[61] Chanock 1985, p. 4. Cf. John Comaroff's definition of 'lawfare' as 'the effort to conquer and control indigenous peoples by the coercive use of legal means': Comaroff 2001, p. 306.

[62] See the definition of legalism in Dresch 2012, p. 2.

[63] John Griffiths therefore argued that since 'the words "law" and "legal" cannot be stipulatively purged of their associations with normative ideas about justice and legality' sociologists should abandon the expression '*legal* pluralism' and instead speak of 'normative pluralism' or 'pluralism in social control': Griffiths 2008, pp. 63–4.

We may find a more specific way to think of law as a distinct entity if we draw on the work of jurists who have sought to identify the concept of law. The most influential English theorist in this field has been H. L. A. Hart. Hart saw law as a system of rules, which are distinct from moral rules, but which are regarded as normatively binding from an 'internal' point of view, and are not simply followed from a fear of punishment. Hart distinguished between customary systems and legal systems, in so far as the former contain only 'primary' rules about social conduct, whereas the latter also contain 'secondary rules'. These are rules about rules: they determine how one recognises what is a valid rule, who adjudicates them, and how they can be changed.[64] In Hart's view, law is systematic. A law is valid by virtue of the fact that it derives from a source (such as a sovereign parliament) which is recognised as authoritative (via a 'rule of recognition'). Furthermore, the fact that a rule is recognised as valid within the legal system generates a reason for it to be accepted as normatively binding, regardless of its content.

Hart's theory has been much debated, and much criticised. Historians may find themselves unconvinced by a theory which refuses to recognise customary law as law, or which appears to seek a single authoritative source (or 'rule of recognition') of law. In response, other jurists – with an eye on the lessons of history, and with a greater awareness of legal pluralism – have looked for broader definitions. Brian Z. Tamanaha, for instance, argues that law 'is whatever people recognize and treat as law through their social practices'.[65] He argues that we should look for social institutions that are 'collectively recognised' as making a 'legal' system[66] applying 'norms that claim *authority*'.[67] For Tamanaha there is no exhaustive list of the features that identify a legal system. In his view, law is a 'folk' concept, which may connote one or more of the following: basic rules of social intercourse; institutionalised or organised enforcement by coercion; claims of justice and right.

Both of these jurists see law not simply as power or practice, but as something which needs to be understood by looking at the ideas and beliefs of different actors. However, both may have their shortcomings. Hart's definition of law in terms which look most suitable to twentieth-century nation-states may mean that its definition of law would not have

---

[64] Hart 2012.
[65] Tamanaha 2001, p. 167. Cf. p. 194: 'Law (and translations thereof) is whatever social groups conventionally attach the label "law" to.'
[66] Tamanaha 2017, p. 52.
[67] Tamanaha 2001, pp. 168–9.

been recognised by jurists in earlier eras as explaining what they did.[68] By contrast, Tamanaha's theory may not be precise enough in allowing us to identify the line between forms of social control which a community may regard as 'law' and those which it does not.[69] One solution might be to explore more deeply the notion of law as a special form of knowledge: considering more than Hart did who the 'officials' of the system are and how they operate, and considering who is consulted by the community in determining exactly what their 'law' was.

Rules derived from power or practice tend to become the objects of specialist knowledge once they have been enacted. Although law is often associated with the rules imposed by the will of a sovereign, the rules so imposed are not generally regarded as random or isolated, but as forming part of a body. They are not self-executing, but need to be interpreted and applied. The meaning of customary norms may equally be contested and open to interpretation. In this process many communities look to particular people to interpret or apply the rules. These need not be 'officials' in Hart's sense. They need not be trained jurists working in the institutional setting of law courts. The custom of a community might itself be the object of specialist knowledge, even before the evolution of what Hart would see as a legal system. For instance, in England, before the rise of the common law courts, disputes might be settled by those who were 'good men and knowledgeable in the law [*jurisperiti*]'.[70] Within the common law tradition, what began as community custom was transformed into technical law after the Angevin kings had created new forms of procedure to settle disputes. Law here became a specialist system precisely through the growth of a body of practices and precedents on how to resolve cases. In this tradition the law developed through the forensic process of adjudicating cases, for, as Coke put it, it was through 'solemn Argument' in the courtroom that 'Almighty God openeth and inlargeth the understanding of the desirous of Justice and Right'.[71] In the civilian tradition, the legal debates which drove the development of much law were also conducted by jurists. Here they occurred outside

---

[68] At the same time, since Hart's theory speaks of 'officials', rather than a coercive state, it does not 'suffice to distinguish legal systems from many other institutionalized normative systems, such as those regulating universities and trade associations and some competitive games and sports': Gardner 2010, p. 278.

[69] Simply asking what communities call law begs the question of translation.

[70] Van Caenegem 1990, No. 226, p. 192; cf. No. 135, p. 106 (Odo 'took good care to bring [the case] to all those whom he knew to be well versed in the laws and usages of the English realm'). Equally, in the continental tradition reference might be made by courts to those in the community who could best explain the custom: Ibbetson 2009, pp. 157–60.

[71] Coke 2003, I, p. 307.

the courtroom, in the universities, as the Glossators and Commentators discussed the meaning of the recently rediscovered *Digest* of Justinian.[72]

The matter about which these jurists are expert is generally the matter derived from those two great sources already mentioned: the custom of the community, derived from its practices; and the legislation imposed by those with political power. These sources generate the rules of social intercourse, backed by claims of justice or right and enforced with the power of the community to which Tamanaha's theory refers. However, it is often jurists who are recognised as the most authentic interpreters of that custom and legislation. If (as Tamanaha suggests) belief in the normativity of law must be rooted in the community, and not simply its officials (as Hart thought), the community will look to the advice of those learned in law not only to tell them what particular obligations the law imposes, but also to show them when things have gone wrong, as when rulers exceed their powers. This may suggest that an important aspect of the study of law and its history is to examine the languages used by the legal community, of lawyers, judges and jurists, and those citizens and political actors who self-consciously speak in that idiom.

This kind of study has often been criticised for looking at law in isolation from society, as a set of doctrines which develop autonomously and formally, without taking into account the influence of social, political and economic ideas on the legal system.[73] Critics of what is sometimes called 'internal legal history' argue that an 'external' perspective on law – one which looks at law from the point of view of society, rather than the viewpoint of the lawyers – can show that legal doctrine is much less autonomous than doctrinalists suppose.[74] The point is well made: those who focus on law as a specialist form of knowledge go awry if they ignore the purposes for which law is used, and its relationship to practice and power. Nonetheless, as E. P. Thompson famously reminded us in 1975, while law stands 'in a definite and active relationship with the social', it has 'its own characteristics, its own independent history and logic of evolution'.[75] Law may be a tool of power, but it is one which can also be used by the powerless.

This is to suggest that the history of legal doctrine has an important place in the study of history more generally. If we wish to understand the motives and intentions of past historical actors and to make sense of the

---

[72] See Bellomo 1995.
[73] See Gordon 1975.
[74] 'The [legal] system works like a blind, insensate machine. It does the bidding of those whose hands are on the controls': Friedman 1985, p. 18.
[75] Thompson 1975, pp. 260, 265.

meaning of social action in the past, we need to be able to grasp all the languages which were relevant to that action. This does not mean that every historian must be a legal historian, or a historian of legal doctrine, any more than it means that every citizen must be a lawyer. It does however mean that those historians who engage directly in matters where law was central to shaping social relations – in property relations or marital relations, for instance – need to take legal doctrine and its operations seriously.[76] If the study of history requires us to attempt to understand the languages of the past and their use, we must also be sensitive to the languages of law used in past societies. If we take too much of an external point of view, we may make assumptions about the effects and operation of law in particular contexts in ways which may be misleading. This can be seen from a recent study of a legal dispute which occurred in the context of Britain's imperial experience in China.

In an article of 2015, Elliot Young uses the 1871 case of a Chinese leader of a mutiny on a ship carrying indentured 'coolie' labour from Macau to Peru as a prism through which to explore how the British sought to use the language of human rights as a means to assert both their civilisational superiority over the Chinese and their jurisdictional right to intervene.[77] Law is here used as part of a larger story about the nature of British imperialism, and the history of human rights. In this case, Chief Justice John Smale refused to allow Kwok-a-sing to be extradited to China on the grounds that he had been effectively enslaved, and that the murder committed during the rising on board the ship was justified: so that no crime had been committed for which he could be extradited. A subsidiary ground for the refusal was that Kwok-a-sing might have been guilty of piracy under the law of nations, but that this was a matter over which the Hong Kong courts had jurisdiction, so that he could be tried there. Looking at these events, Young concludes that in this case 'the British defence of the natural rights to liberty of ... Chinese coolies trumped the sanctity of [Chinese] territorial sovereignty and they justified their imperial interventions with the idea that universal rights could only be protected by a nation as powerful as the British Empire'.[78] The defence of human rights as manifested in this particular litigation was thus used as an imperial tool to bolster Britain's power in the world.

As an argument about imperial power, and the British attempt to export its values, it seems compelling and contributes to a set of

---

[76] Economic historians and family historians have long taken legal doctrine seriously: see, e.g., Habakkuk 1994; Erickson 1993.
[77] Young 2015. See also Wells 2011.
[78] Young 2015, p. 147.

long-standing debates about the origin and nature of modern human rights. But does the legal story sustain the analysis? It should first be noted that the case was a habeas corpus application to challenge a decision to extradite Kwok-a-sing.[79] In refusing the extradition, Smale – who took the view that the coolie trade which was still permitted in Portuguese Macau constituted a form of slavery – invoked two precedents in which Britain refused to extradite suspects wanted by the United States government. The first (on the point of murder) was the case of John Anderson, a fugitive slave from Missouri who was wanted for killing a man who had attempted to recapture him during his escape. His extradition was refused, with the English Law Officers advising that Anderson's actions in defending his freedom could not constitute the offence of murder.[80] The second (on the point of piracy) was a case from 1864, in which the British refused to extradite confederate 'pirates' to the federal government during the American Civil War, on the grounds that piracy *jure gentium* was justiciable in England.[81] Smale's larger 'human rights' argument was controversial – and was opposed by the Colonial Office and Hong Kong's attorney-general – and was not accepted by the Privy Council. The latter court did however agree with the point on jurisdiction, insisting that Kwok-a-sing should be tried in Hong Kong. But if this showed that the British felt they could not trust the Chinese to conduct a fair trial in Kwok's case, it reflected a similar lack of trust in the American common law courts to give a fair trial for confederates. Rather than being a demonstration of legal imperialism – which showed that 'British legal authority literally had no limits' and which 'justified European and American empire, thus further exacerbating Chinese bondage'[82] – it may have reflected a reticence to extradite in politically sensitive cases. As Ivan Lee has noted, 'it is only by examining the case as being about extradition, and by historicising it as such, that we can understand the motivations of the officials involved and thus the real significance of their actions'.[83]

This is not to argue that the law was not often an instrument of imperial power, nor that it was not used to further particular and partial interests. However, we must be precise in establishing how and where and in

---

[79] For an excellent and critical discussion of the case of Kwok-a-sing as an extradition case see Lee 2019.

[80] Forsyth 1869, p. 373.

[81] *R v. Ternan and Others* (1864) 9 Cox CC 522.

[82] Young 2015, pp. 143, 126.

[83] Lee 2019, p. 112.

what ways it was used for those purposes. In other words, in exploring how and in what ways law could be a tool of power, we need to focus our attention not simply on those seeking to make use of the tool, but on the tool itself.

Conclusion

Historians and lawyers often assume that they deal with law and history in ways which differ because of the different needs and methods of their respective disciplines. Where lawyers generally focus closely on the technical 'internal' language of doctrine, many historians prefer to look at law from an 'external' perspective, as an instrument which reflects and reinforces wider power relations found in society. Where historians focus closely on the particular contexts in which ideas emerged or actions were taken, lawyers prefer to look at genealogies of concepts, seeking to 'understand the past for what it brought about and not for what it meant to the people living in it'.[84] Lawyers have their own visions of history, and historians their own vision of law. However, it has been suggested in this chapter that each discipline should pay more heed to the methods of the other: legal scholarship is enriched when jurists use the methods of historians when they turn to history, just as historical scholarship is enriched when historians use the tools of jurisprudence when dealing with matters of law.

As has been seen, how law is conceived of and applied is generally a matter of specialist knowledge and practice. In the course of their practice, these specialists – jurists – engage in theoretical reflection both about large foundational questions (about the nature of law and authority) and about analytical questions (about the nature of particular kinds of rights and obligations). The theoretical reflections of jurists on the nature of law can help the historian in identifying the matter of 'law' – or particular aspects of it, such as marriage, contract and property – in past societies. In taking this approach, it is certainly assumed that there are forms of social conduct in past societies which can better be understood by applying these concepts to them; but there is no concomitant assumption that the concepts suggested by contemporary jurisprudence are absolute or rigid. Since they are tools which can be used to sharpen our understanding of what we are looking for and finding in the past, they may need to be adapted. Nor is it assumed that other societies deal with questions of property, authority or punishment in the same way as

---

[84] Lesaffer 2007, p. 35.

modern (or other historical) societies. Nevertheless, asking questions about how they dealt with such matters may help us better understand what they did, and may also raise questions about our own concepts and their use.

Just as there are contemporary specialists of juridical thought, people can be found in past societies who also thought about such things as property, authority and punishment, and developed their own vocabularies to deal with them. These vocabularies often played a central role in the organising and functioning of past societies. If we do not try to understand the specialist normative systems which constitute 'law' in other societies, then we will fail to understand important aspects of their life. Furthermore, in order to understand the nature and workings of law in any society, historians should engage with the 'internal' history of law – the specialist vocabularies of the *jurisperiti* – without which its 'external' effects cannot fully be understood.

At the same time, while jurisprudential conceptual tools help us identify what we are looking for, they cannot dictate the answers we will find: it cannot be assumed that concepts of marriage, contract or property were the same in the past. To avoid anachronism, we must seek as far as we can to understand what past actors thought they were doing. This is of course the *métier* of the historian; but looking at past practices in this way can also can reap rich rewards for the contemporary jurist. To begin with, testing how well contemporary analytical concepts can explain past systems of law may reveal that the concepts are in need of revision or refinement. Scholars such as Lacey have shown how modern ideas may be tested by the acid-bath of history. Equally, as Loughlin's work suggests, an awareness of how jurists in other traditions thought about questions of the constitution of lawful authority may help modern jurists fashion better jurisprudential tools to deal with contemporary problems. Just as historians may draw on contemporary juridical concepts to set questions of the past without being tied to particular conceptual answers, concepts drawn from past thinkers may be suggestive about how to analyse modern society, without these past ideas dictating exactly how modern public law should be rethought.

These approaches rest on the jurist engaging with the methods of historians, or drawing on their actual work. What, then, of the claim that lawyers have a distinct method when dealing with historical texts and materials? Such claims are generally made by those who seek to understand the nature of present law not by tracing the genealogy of a particular concept, but by interpreting the broad historical tradition from which a whole body of law emerges. The claim that lawyers have a distinct historical method has been most clearly made in the field of international law, where critical historians have argued that the very structure of modern law has been shaped by its imperial past.[85] If it can be shown that the foundational concepts of international law derive from an exploitative colonial past, and that they continue to have exploitative effects, then those very concepts may be called into question. As Antony Anghie has put it:

> If ... the colonial encounter, with all its exclusions and subordinations, shaped the very foundations of international law, then grave questions must arise as to whether and how it is possible for the postcolonial world to construct a new international law that is liberated from these colonial origins. The question is an old one: can the postcolonial world deploy for its own purposes the law which had enabled its suppression in the first place?[86]

In some ways, this has echoes of Lacey's use of history to question current orthodoxies: but whereas Lacey argues that a resort to history – using the tools of the historian – may call into question conceptions regarded as timeless, the critical historians of international law contend that current conceptions are themselves the creation of history. They hold both that current law is made sense of by looking at its history and that its history needs to be rethought and revisited in order to rethink the (tainted) concepts and free future thought. Furthermore, in so far as the law derives authority from its history, challenges to the accepted beneficent histories of international law can raise questions about the legitimacy of the current system. However, for this approach to be effective it needs to be grounded in a secure historical method. Claims that 'a "universal" language of international law ... was devised specifically to ensure [the] disempowerment and disenfranchisement of colonized people'[87] need to be made good by showing when and how they were so devised. They cannot be made historically good by arguing that lawyers have a different way of reading history. For that different way may entail anachronistic readings, in which interpretations of the nature of present law are projected onto the past: and if present ideas shape one's interpretation of the past, it is hard to claim that it is that past which shapes present ideas and obligations. Instead of being properly historical claims, they may be as rhetorical as the claims made about the English legal tradition by 'common law constitutionalists', and may add little to the argument.

---

[85] As Anne Orford puts it, 'the past ... may be a source of present obligations. Similarly, legal concepts and practices that were developed in the age of formal empire may continue to shape international law in the post-colonial era': Orford 2012, p. 2.

[86] Anghie 2005, p. 8.

[87] Anghie 2005, p. 31.

References

Allan, T. R. S. 1999. 'The Rule of Law as the Rule of Reason: Consent and Constitutionalism', *Law Quarterly Review*, 115, pp. 221–44.
2000. 'Common Law Constitutionalism and Freedom of Speech' in *Freedom of Expression and Freedom of Information*, ed. J. Beatson and Y. Cripps. Oxford.
Allison, J. W. F. 2013. 'History to Understand, and History to Reform, English Public Law', *Cambridge Law Journal*, 72: 3, pp. 526–57.
Anghie, Antony. 2005. *Imperialism, Sovereignty and the Making of International Law*. Cambridge.
Armitage, David. 2017. *Civil Wars: A History in Ideas*. New York.
Austin, John. 1995. *The Province of Jurisprudence Determined*, ed. Wilfrid E. Rumble. Cambridge.
Beiser, Frederick C. 2011. *The German Historicist Tradition*. Oxford.
Bellomo, Manlio. 1995. *The Common Legal Past of Europe, 1000–1800*, trans. Lydia G. Cochrane. Washington, DC.
Bently, Lionel and Brad Sherman. 1999. *The Making of Modern Intellectual Property Law*. Cambridge.
Benton, Lauren. 2019. 'Beyond Anachronism: Histories of International Law and Global Legal Politics', *Journal of the History of International Law*, 21: 1, pp. 7–40.
Brett, Annabel S. 2011. *Changes of State: Nature and the Limits of the City in Early Modern Natural Law*. Princeton.
2021. 'Between History, Politics and Law: History of Political Thought and History of International Law' in *History, Politics, Law: Thinking through the International*, ed. Annabel Brett, Megan Donaldson and Martti Koskenniemi. Cambridge.
Cavaller, Georg. 2008. 'Vitoria, Grotius, Pufendorf, Wolff and Vattel: Accomplices of European Colonialism and Exploitation or True Cosmopolitans?', *Journal of the History of International Law*, 10: 2, pp. 181–209.
Chanock, Martin. 1985. *Law, Custom and Social Order: The Colonial Experience in Malawi and Zambia*. Cambridge.
Coke, Edward. 2003. *The Selected Writings of Sir Edward Coke*, ed. Steve Sheppard. 3 vols. Indianapolis.
Comaroff, John. 2001. 'Colonialism, Culture, and Law: A Foreword', *Law and Social Inquiry*, 26: 2, pp. 305–14.
Davies, Paul S. 2016. 'Rectification versus Interpretation: The Nature and Scope of the Equitable Jurisdiction', *Cambridge Law Journal*, 75: 1, pp. 62–85.
Dicey, A. V. 2013. *The Law of the Constitution*, ed. J. W. F. Allison, 2 vols. Oxford.
Dresch, Paul. 2012. 'Introduction Legalism, Anthropology, and History: A View from Part of Anthropology' in *Legalism: Anthropology and History*, ed. Paul Dresch and Hannah Skoda. Oxford.
Duxbury, Neil. 1995. *Patterns of American Jurisprudence*. Oxford.
2004. 'Why English Jurisprudence is Analytical', *Current Legal Problems*, 57: 1, pp. 1–51.

Dworkin, Ronald. 1977. *Taking Rights Seriously*. Cambridge, MA.
   1986. *Law's Empire*. Cambridge, MA.
Erickson, A. L. 1993. *Women and Property in Early Modern England*. London.
Farmer, Lindsay. 2016. *Making the Modern Criminal Law: Criminalization and Civil Order*. Oxford.
Fitzmaurice, Andrew. 2018. 'Context in the History of International Law', *Journal of the History of International Law*, 20: 1, pp. 5–30.
Forsyth, William. 1869. *Cases and Opinions on Constitutional Law*. London.
Freeman, Michael and Patricia Mindus. 2013. *The Legacy of John Austin's Jurisprudence*. Dordrecht.
Friedman, Lawrence M. 1985. *History of American Law*, 2nd ed. New York.
Gardner, John. 2010. *Law as a Leap of Faith*. Oxford.
Gordon, R. W. 1975. 'Introduction: J. Willard Hurst and the Common Law Tradition in American Legal Historiography', *Law and Society Review*, 10: 1, pp. 9–55.
Griffiths, John. 2008. 'The Idea of Sociology of Law and its Relation to Law and to Sociology' in *Law and Sociology*, ed. Michael Freeman. Oxford.
Habakkuk, John. 1994. *Marriage, Debt and the Estates System: English Landownership, 1650–1950*. Oxford.
Hart, H. L. A. 1968. *Punishment and Responsibility*. Oxford.
   2012. *The Concept of Law*, 3rd ed., ed. J. Raz and P. A. Bulloch. Oxford.
Holmes, Oliver Wendell. 1897. 'The Path of the Law', *Harvard Law Review*, 10: 8, pp. 457–78.
Hunter, Ian. 2010. 'Global Justice and Regional Metaphysics: On the Critical History of the Law of Nature and Nations' in *Law and Politics in British Colonial Thought: Transpositions of Empire*, ed. Shaunnagh Dorsett and Ian Hunter. New York.
Ibbetson, David. 2009. 'Custom in Medieval Law' in *The Nature of Customary Law: Legal, Historical and Philosophical Perspectives*, ed. Amanda Perreau-Sassine and James B. Murphy. Cambridge.
Koskenniemi, Martti. 2001. *The Gentle Civilizer of Nations: The Rise and Fall of International Law 1870–1960*. Cambridge.
   2014. 'Vitoria and Us: Thoughts on Critical Histories of International Law', *Rechtsgeschichte*, 22, pp. 119–38.
Lacey, Nicola. 2016. *In Search of Criminal Responsibility: Ideas, Interests, and Institutions*. Oxford.
Laws, John. 1996. 'The Constitution: Morals and Rights', *Public Law*, pp. 622–35.
Lee, Ivan. 2019. 'British Extradition Practice in Early Colonial Hong Kong', *Law & History*, 6, pp. 85–114.
Lesaffer, Randall. 2007. 'International Law and its History: The Story of an Unrequited Love' in *Time, History and International Law*, ed. Matthew Craven, Malgosia Fitzmaurice and Maria Vogiatzi. Leiden.
Lobban, Michael. 2007. *A History of the Philosophy of Law in the Common Law World, 1600–1900*. Dordrecht.
Loughlin, Martin. 2010. *Foundations of Public Law*. Oxford.
MacMillan, Catharine. 2010. *Mistakes in Contract Law*. Oxford.

Maine, Henry. 1875. *Lectures on the Early History of Institutions*. London.

Maitland, F. W. 1911. 'Why the History of English Law is not Written' in *The Collected Papers of Frederic William Maitland*, ed. H. A. L. Fisher, vol. I. Cambridge.

McLauchlan, David. 2014. 'Refining Rectification', *Law Quarterly Review*, 130, pp. 83–111.

Milsom, S. F. C. 1981. *Historical Foundations of the Common Law*, 2nd ed. London.

2003. *A Natural History of the Common Law*. New York.

Orford, Anne. 2012. 'The Past as Law or History? The Relevance of Imperialism for Modern International Law', Institute for International Law and Justice Working Paper 2012/2.

2013. 'On International Legal Method', *London Review of International Law*, 1: 1, pp. 166–97.

2017. 'International Law and the Limits of History' in *The Law of International Lawyers: Reading Martti Koskenniemi*, ed. Wouter Werner, Marieke de Hoon and Alexis Galán. Cambridge.

2021. *International Law and the Politics of History*. Cambridge.

Poole, Thomas. 2003. 'Back to the Future? Unearthing the Theory of Common Law Constitutionalism', *Oxford Journal of Legal Studies*, 23: 3, pp. 435–54.

2005. 'Questioning Common Law Constitutionalism', *Legal Studies*, 25: 1, pp. 142–63.

Rabban, David M. 2013. *Law's History: American Legal Thought and the Transatlantic Turn to History*. Cambridge.

Rumble, Wilfrid E. 1985. *The Thought of John Austin: Jurisprudence, Colonial Reform, and the British Constitution*. London.

Schofield, Philip. 2006. *Utility and Democracy: The Political Thought of Jeremy Bentham*. Oxford.

Skinner, Quentin. 2002a. 'Meaning and Understanding in the History of Ideas' in Q. Skinner, *Visions of Politics*, vol. I: *Regarding Method*. Cambridge.

2002b. 'Interpretation and the Understanding of Speech Acts' in Q. Skinner, *Visions of Politics*, vol. I: *Regarding Method*. Cambridge.

2002c. 'From the State of Princes to the Person of the State' in Q. Skinner, *Visions of Politics*, vol. II: *Renaissance Virtues*. Cambridge.

Skoda, Hannah. 2012. 'A Historian's Perspective on the Present Volume' in *Legalism: Anthropology and History*, ed. Paul Dresch and Hannah Skoda. Oxford.

Smith, K. J. M. 1998. *Lawyers, Legislators, and Theorists: Developments in English Criminal Jurisprudence 1800–1957*. Oxford.

Tamanaha, Brian Z. 2001. *A General Jurisprudence of Law and Society*. Oxford.

2017. *A Realistic Theory of Law*. Cambridge.

Thompson, E. P. 1975. *Whigs and Hunters: The Origin of the Black Act*. Harmondsworth.

van Caenegem, R. C. 1990. *English Lawsuits from William I to Richard I*. London.

Walters, Mark D. 2008. 'Legal Humanism and Law as Integrity', *Cambridge Law Journal*, 67: 2, pp. 352–75.

2012. 'Is Public Law Ordinary?', *Modern Law Review*, 75: 5, pp. 894–913.

Wells, Jennifer. 2011. 'Clashing Kingdoms, Hidden Agendas: The Battle to Extradite Kwok-a-sing and British Legal Imperialism in Nineteenth-Century China', *East Asia Law Review*, 7: 1, pp. 161–93.

Wheatley, Natasha. 2021. 'Law and the Time of Angels: International Law's Method Wars and the Affective Life of Disciplines', *History and Theory*, 60: 2, pp. 311–30.

Young, Elliott. 2015. 'Chinese Coolies, Universal Rights and the Limits of Liberalism in an Age of Empire', *Past and Present*, 227, pp. 121–49.

2 History, Law and the Rediscovery of Social Theory

Samuel Moyn

How historiography bears on legal scholarship presupposes some broader set of commitments about the intellectual framework we bring to both enterprises. In this chapter, I will try to gesture towards the need for both history and law to recommit to the broad tradition of social theory, in order for either to make progress on its own, let alone for one to plausibly reorient the other.

Before proceeding, let me explain my motivation and then turn to a proviso. It is common though usually unspoken for inhabitants of disciplines – including the discipline of history – to think that the ideal relationship of their knowledge to everyone else's is essentially a tutelary one. We historians know things, the thought goes, that are relevant to what non-historians are and ought to be doing. And that is often true, however self-serving it is for historians to say so.

But it is a short-sighted posture in two respects. For one thing, I doubt that the most effective way to propose to reform someone else's field is to tell them yours is indispensable to it. And more important, doing so distracts from how history, and not merely other disciplines, may stand in need of help, indeed of the same help as the others require. I want to propose that the tradition of social theory from the Enlightenment to the present can provide it. If historical consciousness is crucially vital to all disciplines, it has to be on terms that make social theory even more so.

Now the proviso. I will use law as my example of another discipline to which history is certainly relevant, even as it also requires the same kind of help from social theory as the historical discipline itself does. The field of history bears gifts for any of its neighbours, but all parties to the prospective exchange owe their ultimate value to their larger participation in social theory, the most distinctive and the master intellectual project of modern times. But I believe any other domain – art history or literary study or philosophy – might take the place of the law in the same argument.

Still, law is especially useful as an exemplary case study. Not least, it has always been pivotal in the tradition of social theory, whether one looks to Montesquieu, Émile Durkheim, Max Weber or, closer to the present day, Jürgen Habermas or Roberto Mangabeira Unger (who I think deserves much more attention in this regard, and to whom I shall therefore return again and again).

From the perspective of my argument for common need rather than cross-disciplinary largesse, it is not going to be good enough to suppose that contemporary historiography is already well positioned for relevance to other fields. In the last fifty years it has lost touch with the tradition of social theory, thanks to the linguistic and cultural turns and a certain fetishisation of contingent outcomes that have been emphasised in critical and genealogical sorts of history. In this chapter I will map three ongoing quandaries in social theory, since it is only within the discussion of each that – to my mind at least – the relationship of history to law takes on its significance.

These are (1) the dilemma of representations versus practices; (2) the reconciliation of contingency and determination; and (3) the quandary of the analytical and normative, both as something to explain in diverse past settings and what might motivate and orient present inquiry in the first place.

The Tradition of Social Theory

When I invoke the tradition of social theory, I have in mind the eighteenth-century discovery of the social by figures such as the baron Montesquieu and Giambattista Vico, as well as their nineteenth- and twentieth-century heirs and successors. What brings them together was the attempt to discern the changing principles of cohesion, meaning and value and, in a sense, the very existence of social order itself.

Louis Althusser characterised this in a classical way in his great pamphlet on Montesquieu and some of his successors in founding the tradition. According to Althusser, while the word society was new in its eighteenth-century usages, even more important was the move from 'society in general' to 'all the concrete societies in history'.[1] And, crucially, both theology and normativity were seen to be internal to the inventory of different social orders. They were part – and largely the products – of evolving social relations. How people live overall shapes the nature of their religious belief and habits, and their broader moral systems and practices.

---

[1] Althusser 1972, p. 20. As Richard Bourke points out to me, Althusser's claim is complicated by the fact (as I detail in regard to G. W. F. Hegel below) that Montesquieu's theory of relations had theological roots. See, e.g., Riley 2003.

The founders of social theory – Montesquieu or Vico – were not interested in origins of social order in will or reason – God's or a human social contract – because (as Althusser puts it) 'society always precedes itself'.[2] Social theory denies that anything comes before the social, and least of all God's almighty choices or nature's inbuilt norms. Intellectually, put in a different way, modernity consists in the repudiation of theism and Platonism alike. Instead, the optic was one that saw society as an artefact through and through, and the goal became to understand the conditions of the making, stabilisation and potential remaking of that creation.

And, of course, for Montesquieu these conceptual innovations were bound up with what Althusser calls 'a new theory of law'.[3] More broadly, we can say that, within the tradition of social theory, law was always of supreme importance as a theme but never in the sense of what God propounded or nature's ends, as it had been in earlier visions of a political life based on finding rather than making law. Modern social theory, in contrast, presupposed the collapse in intellectual credibility of those traditions. But if there were no antecedent lawgiver or external laws, there was no doubt that social theory could not do without an account of law in social form. What formal or informal laws there are express immanent social forces, not external divine will or pre-social natural constraint – and especially not the constraint of divine authority or that of an underlying human nature.

In modern social theory, law, and especially formal law, was generally assigned a parasitic relationship to accounts of society, the causal role of law normally doubtful and to be determined. It could enact change; more normally it accompanied or reflected broader transformations. In a certain sense, relative to earlier intellectual traditions, law was demoted in significance in the tradition of modern social theory. Theories of social cohesion and value generation were inextricably linked not with legislation but with the pre-eminence of an informal order of relations that law rarely enacted and usually reflected. 'The greatest change wrought by [the] Enlightenment in the field of social and historical thought [was] the perception of society as the movement towards "manners" or "*mœurs*"', J. G. A. Pocock once remarked. 'This keyword denoted a complex of shared practices and values, which secured the individual as social being and furnished the society surrounding him with an indefinitely complex and flexible texture; more powerfully even than laws, manners rendered civil society capable of absorbing and controlling human action and belief.'[4] Manners, or what we would now call norms, decentred law in social theory.

---

[2] Althusser 1972, p. 29.
[3] Althusser 1972, part 1, ch. 2.
[4] Pocock 1999, p. 20.

Much evidence substantiates Pocock's claim that modern social theorists placed law in a generally parasitic relationship. 'Manners are of more importance than laws', wrote Edmund Burke in *Letters on a Regicide Peace*. 'Manners are what vex or soothe, corrupt or purify, exalt or debase, barbarize or refine us, by a constant, steady, uniform, insensible operation, like that of the air we breathe in.'[5] '[The analysis of manners is] more crucial, for the laws to be promulgated will issue from manners, and will mirror them', the otherwise rather different figure of the Marquis de Sade agreed in *Philosophy in the Bedroom*: 'Frenchmen, you are too intelligent to fail to sense that new government will require new manners.'[6]

Nor was the demotion of law relative to the informal ordering of society a transient phenomenon. It helped define the tradition of modern social theory as such. An especially interesting case, fifty years on, is provided by the young Alexis de Tocqueville, who initially calls the 'principal aim' of *Democracy in America* 'to make known the laws of the United States', but eventually, even before the full-blown democratic social theory of volume II of that work, finds himself propounding the maxim that 'too much importance is attributed to legislation, too little to manners'.[7] It was for this reason that he portrayed majority tyranny as a much deeper syndrome than mere governmental or legislative despotism, despite concluding (perhaps optimistically) that 'laws, and especially manners, may exist which will allow a democratic people to remain free'.[8] It was not that law could never abet rather than reflect deeper customary movement, and Tocqueville cited as an example the abolition of primogeniture.[9] But this was an exception that proved the rule.

Over time, it is worth mentioning, some social theorists cultivated the belief that there were immanent 'laws' to the social, much like regularities of nature, while others contested this very proposition. The contrast of Karl Marx and Roberto Unger on this score is exemplary. One admired natural science enough to dedicate the second volume of *Capital* to Charles Darwin and liken the systemic evolution and crisis of 'capitalism' to a compulsive sequence governed by laws; the other hated naturalistic accounts so much that he ultimately argued that the laws of nature themselves have the plasticity of social arrangements.[10] But even for those like Marx discerning 'laws' of social life, they obtained neither

---

[5] Burke 1839, IV, p. 392.
[6] Sade 1965, p. 307.
[7] Tocqueville 1899, I, pp. 303, 323.
[8] Tocqueville 1899, I, p. 336.
[9] Tocqueville 1899, I, bk. 1, ch. 3.
[10] Smolin and Unger 2015, part I, esp. ch. 5 ('The mutability of the laws of nature').

because God propounded them nor because social laws depended on natural laws. And they underwrote society's legal order, in the literal sense. No one, least of all Marx, ever meant that the actual formal and informal legal systems of society were fundamental, however large a role they played in the stability of the social order.

There is much more to say about the contours of the once familiar tradition of social theory, but suffice it to add that nothing in the careers of Durkheim or Weber in the pivotal era of the invention of sociology or even in those of Habermas and Unger in the last great age of social theory in the 1970s and into the 1980s ever broke with any of the assumptions I have mentioned so far. All of them assumed in society as the intellectual quarry, in the parasitic relation of morals and law on norms or manners. The enterprise of understanding how humans construct their social orders was, for such figures, what integrated intellectual life across disciplines and as a whole.

If history is to provide perspective on the study of law (or any other field), historiography will have to restore its frayed relation with social theory first. In the 1960s and 1970s the two were loose allies, and historical sociology and sociologically informed history alike were in their heydays.[11] But since that time history has gone its own way – though one hopes that it is not too late to correct its wayward drift.

To suggest that this is the case, it will be most useful to concentrate on three dilemmas that the tradition of social theory after the Enlightenment elaborated but by no means fully overcame. Only if they are faced can the study of history come to the aid of the study of law – or, for that matter, any other field of inquiry.

Representations and Practices

By representations and practices I mean a somewhat different and more plausible version of the familiar dichotomy between the ideational and material. For a century social theory struggled with this problem, with historians in the mix, with the traditional correction of Marx by Weber the most memorable event.[12]

But this problem has not been prominent in historiography, including the historiography of political or legal thought, in our time. That it could have been is shown by looking back at the second series of Peter Laslett's edited collection on *Philosophy, Politics and Society* of 1962,

[11] For some reflection on this moment and its passing see Sewell 2005.
[12] Löwith 1982, ch. 4.

where one finds alongside Isaiah Berlin's investigation of whether political theory still exists and Pocock's 'methodological enquiry' into the history of political thought the essay by the late baron W. G. Runciman on the relation of social theory and political theory, anticipating his book *Social Science and Political Theory* of the next year.[13] But the first two interventions, by Berlin and Pocock, proved astonishingly more influential than Runciman's. Berlin's inquiry (in some sense an answer to Laslett's own earlier proclamation of the death of political theory) and especially Pocock's essay gave new life in the historiography of political thought.[14] Social theory, by contrast, was progressively abandoned among historians.

From a distance of six decades, the choice looks more or less catastrophic. The linguistic turn in its various forms displaced the project of social theory among historians, and it tended to privilege the representational over the practical, probably as a compensatory move in the aftermath of the failures of political radicalism of the 1960s. The linguistic turn came in a profusion of forms, of course, but Pocock's significance alerts us to one of the most important in the historical profession.

The founding gesture of the Cambridge School of the history of political thought (with which Pocock is associated) is often taken to be insistence on historical context against the commitment to sempiternity of concepts, problems and unit-ideas. In fact, 'context' came in some forms to the exclusion of others. As much as Arthur Lovejoy and Leo Strauss, the antagonists at the start were Karl Marx and Lewis Namier. The proposal in response was to study representations only, texts in their equally textual context, discourses or languages in their competing or successive relation to each other, and speech-acts as moves in argumentative games. Though we were all taught – I was – that the Cambridge School stands for context, from the first it was founded on an attack on the validity of 'contextual reading' and a defence of 'the independent life of ideas in history' (both phrases from Quentin Skinner's classic 1969 manifesto).[15]

But this attack on reductive approaches by asserting a contextualism based on texts is a non sequitur. As Claude Lefort, one member of the post-Marxist tradition in social theory that devised the notion of the social imaginary, put it at one point, 'To criticize Marx does not at all imply that we must assert the primacy of representation and fall back into the illusion, which he denounced, of an independent logic of

---

[13] Berlin 1962; Pocock 1962; Runciman 1962; Runciman 1963.
[14] Laslett 1956, p. vii.
[15] Skinner 1969, pp. 40, 42.

ideas.'[16] Over the years, important moves were made beyond the founding strictures of the Cambridge School, to my mind most promisingly by Skinner even before his landmark argument, as well as much later when he alluded to the post-Marxist notion of a social imaginary devised to overcome any crude dichotomy between representations and practices.[17] In another vein, Skinner's emphasis on how the theories vouchsafe legitimacy to institutional arrangements they do not entirely constitute performs similar work. Even so, the second generation of the Cambridge School intensified a commitment to solely textual forms of 'context' even more deeply.

In America, some voices were raised right away that the linguistic turn meant losing touch with the very social 'experience' that gave rise to the linguistic turn itself.[18] But I would venture to say that neither the Cambridge School (to the extent it existed) nor American versions of the linguistic turn in intellectual history have worked out what the overcoming of the dichotomy of representations and practices will look like, either in theory or in practice. Indeed, interest in working it out has not been prominent. We mainly know that there is a series of blind alleys – while in historiography an intellectualist textualism has generally prevailed, as if in prophylactic immunisation against 'vulgar' contextual reduction.

It is my own view that the crudeness of ascendant Marxism in many of its most famous applications (not to mention its crisis politically) authorised a very long hesitation among historians about the whole project of social theory and, in particular, an exemption from any felt need for scholars interested in representations to be part of that transdisciplinary project. Yet the intellectual situation seems to be undermining the plausibility of that defensive exemption – to the extent it ever was plausible.[19] In part, political events – not least the latest economic crisis of 2008–9 and its aftermath – have given Marxist intellectual traditions a new lease on life in recent years.[20] In part, alternative desires to reanimate social theory without the usual concessions to intellectualism have cropped up.

Either way, exemptions from social theory and hesitations to orient ourselves towards it are not going to be durable for much longer. Very quickly, the appeal to the social imaginary has come to feel as much the postponement of a theory of how to integrate representations with practices as it is a realisation of a plausible approach. Similarly, Skinner's

---

[16] Claude Lefort cited in Moyn 2008, p. 71.
[17] Skinner 1965; Skinner 2002, p. 102.
[18] Toews 1987. Ironically, the challenges to Toews's piece tended to ratify his point.
[19] See Moyn 2014.
[20] Consider, e.g., the founding of the journal *Critical Historical Studies* in 2014.

suggestion that only theory legitimises power omits both other roles for ideals and skirts engagement with the problem of how some practices ascend while others fail. And any permanent abstention from connecting the historical study of representations to that of practices is not theoretically plausible anyway.

Indeed, Lefort added, the point of the concept of the social imaginary was to overcome the entire distinction of representations from practices. There is no way to posit a realm of conceptual independence and juxtapose it to a domain of non-sapient practices allegedly separate from intellectual life. From the perspective of the social imaginary, Lefort noted, 'it turns out to be ... impossible to fix a frontier between what must be classed in the order of action and what must be classed in the order of representation'.[21] If that is right, then it is not just Marxists who need a more sophisticated theory of ideology; non- or post-Marxists need one too.

Another Cantabridgian, John B. Thompson, made a tremendous contribution to this goal as recently as the 1980s in his *Studies in the Theory of Ideology*.[22] And beginning the fulfilment of the need by eroding any distinction in principle between representation and action does not require any deep philosophy. All non-intellectual practices are shot through with conceptual meaning, intellectual life and language use are a kind of practice in the midst of practical worlds, and there is no way – except through an analytical legerdemain or a division of labour with benefits but also costs – to isolate 'thought' as an independent object of study. Saying that representation is itself a kind of action or may frame action for others begs the question of what precise relationship thinkers have to the whole world of practical activity in a place and time.

Now, the history of law is an ideal site – though, again, far from the only one – in which to return from abstraction to actual cases to explore how to address the dilemma of representations and practices in social theory. Indeed, examples of the attempts centred on law already make up some of the core of the tradition. It was what Durkheim did with primitive (so-called) criminal sanction in *The Division of Labor in Society*, as his chief example of how mechanical solidarity worked.[23] It was what Weber did with his stories of the emergence of all forms of law from tort and the necessities of intra-group dispute resolution, or of the rise in tandem of bureaucratisation and formal legality.[24]

---

[21] Cited in Moyn 2008, p. 72.
[22] Thompson 1986.
[23] See, e.g., Clarke 1976.
[24] See, e.g., Kronman 1983.

Not least, it was what Unger did in his *Law in Modern Society* (1976), rehabilitating a typological theory of the relation of law to changing forms of the social. 'Law seems a peculiarly fruitful subject of inquiry', Unger remarked, 'for the effort to understand its significance takes us straight to the heart of each of the major unsolved puzzles of social theory.'[25] But this did not predetermine the extent to which law merely described or mirrored antecedent processes of making social meaning or imposing social order, or explain by itself in which situations law brings about social outcomes more than it reflects them.

Not that the conceptual history of jurisprudence or various sorts of legal history are not valuable in their own right – but they are minor ones that themselves could not ultimately be hived off from the broader historiography of law as the institutionalisation of social order. Yet this is not how legal history's task has generally been seen of late. Much of the actual work tends to take the form of a history of doctrines or a neo-Marxist reductionism, more rarely exploiting the middle ground in which representations and practices are not treated as in a hierarchical relation or even distinctive from each other. The dilemma in social theory of how to relate representations and practices is thus a common difficulty. History and law stand not merely in need of mutual aid, but the same kind of external help.

Contingency and Determination

By contingency and structure (my second domain or problem) I refer essentially to the relationship in social theory between the insistence on room for manoeuvre and situated freedom of actors, and the determination attributed to entrenched potent relationships that, once set up, create the actors who reproduce them and who alter those relationships with difficulty, if at all.

As with the linguistic turn and the autonomy of representations, so with certain forms of thinking in the past decades about contingency: its prevalence in human affairs has been drastically overstated. Indeed, it seems like the height of ironies that a campaign against 'historical inevitability' led for a long time by Cold War liberals, and continued by some of their conservative followers even today, has taken root in a far wider community of scholarship than that group exclusively – sometimes obsessively – concerned with Marxian schemes.[26]

In the writing of legal history, the single most influential theoretician in the United States in the past thirty years, Yale Law School's Robert

---

[25] Unger 1976, p. 44.
[26] See Berlin 1955; Ferguson 1997.

Gordon (whose papers have recently been collected), has embedded the theme of contingency deep in the routines of professional legal historiography.[27] Gordon has been taken to argue that a sophisticated legal history must focus on the way law co-constitutes the social world, but always does so in ways that remain contingent: the law could have been otherwise. The possibility of contingent outcomes arises, for Gordon, both in the inception of some legal regime (which could always have been different) and especially in its application to concrete problems in judicial settings (in which judges must constantly choose among different interpretations of the legal regime). Law is constitutive and contingent – so runs the Gordonian mantra.

Yet both principles fit very poorly with the whole impulse of modern social theory. If not to demote the law, then to leave open how important it in fact is in social outcomes, has been the general pattern in the tradition of social theory, and understandably so. Perhaps those who present themselves as legal historians, in part to assert the importance of their field, have not particularly liked this lesson, for self-evident reasons: if the law is rarely constitutive and more often reflective, legal history is merely a study of effects determined elsewhere. But the lesson may all the same be true.

More important for this part of my argument, a commitment to discovering the contingency of outcomes cannot be exclusive or freestanding if it does not arise within some broader inquiry into structural determination. Constraint and room for manoeuvre are not intellectually separable in any account of the malleability of doctrine or law or of the situated freedom of actors within a legal system – for situated freedom is what human beings have to make choices for one legal regime or interpretation of a legal regime rather than another.[28] The field of legal history always requires reconstructing how law (though a minor constituent of results among others) both produces and restricts our freedom. That freedom, in turn, can be deployed to transform its conditions and thus contract or expand the agency of ourselves and others – never for the sake of full determination, but also making for situated forms of emancipation only, rather than a godlike autonomy without conditions or constraint. Even when it liberates, law can bear some interpretations but not others, and legal actors can make some moves but not others.

---

[27] See the essays collected in Gordon 2017, esp. part III.
[28] I take the term 'situated freedom' from Merleau-Ponty 2012: 'Man is a historical idea, not a natural species. ... Human existence will lead us to revisit our usual notion of necessity and contingency. ... All that we are, we are on the basis of a factual situation that we make our own and that we ceaselessly transform through a sort of *escape* that is never an unconditioned freedom' (p. 174).

Now, the emphasis on contingency in law and in society generally is most associated with Unger's stormy attack on *False Necessity*, the title of one of his books.[29] It certainly seems as if he believed that, in the intellectual setting of the mid-1980s, it was incredibly pertinent to insist – as Gordon did – that the constant temptation of social theory is to locate quasi-necessary systemic imperatives, as vulgar Marxism did in its time. (Unger also attributed this error to non-Marxist social theory in all its forms.) Consequently, Unger attacked the history of social theory for erring either in the direction of 'compulsive sequence' accounts (roughly, stadial views from the Scottish Enlightenment to the present of the evolution of the social, positing one track to modernity with no off-ramps) or 'closed list' accounts (in which possible variation was reduced to a set menu of options). And in response to these mistakes, it is certainly true that Unger thought it indispensable to insist on the creativity and spontaneity of human agency that social theory, he claimed, had consistently understated.

But today perhaps the reverse is the case. Our histories, and legal histories, consistently overstate rather than understate the contingency of outcomes, exaggerate the freedom that leads to legal regimes, and maximise the freedom that results. In the tradition Gordon established of legal history in the United States, in particular, it sometimes seems as if the same book is written over and over to show that some legal domain or other could have been different – and then the analysis is done. It is as if the analytic focus is therefore on accident and choice, with the often crushing structural determination that regularly makes actors their playthings entirely omitted, the freedom exercised on the margins treated as more effective than it in fact is.

I don't mean to deny the power of such enterprises, and have attempted one myself, in an old account of the origins of human rights meaningfully stressing their contingency as an operative language of global politics.[30] But when demonstrations that our world is contingent rather than necessary are all there is, something has gone dreadfully wrong. That legal arrangements are adventitious rather than eternal and could have been different does not explain the way they turned out, among the always plural but never infinite options, which get winnowed and then foreclosed. It is one thing to insist that things might have gone another way. But it is a highly partial endeavour not to explain why they went the way they did.

The truth is, in fact, that Unger's social theory was interested in recovering the relevance of contingency, but – like the whole tradition before

[29] Unger 1986.
[30] Moyn 2010.

it – without forgetting that the agenda of social theory is rightly defined by assessing the prevalence of structural determination in the fashioning of social order. Much as representations are not separate from practices, or freedom from situation, contingency is a function of a plausible theory of the making and transformation of social orders. Emphasising it is not to search for an exit from the project of social theory, but an attempt to perfect and reform it from within.

The closely allied work of Cantabridgian Geoffrey Hawthorn on counterfactuality was in a similar vein. Almost uncontrolled dreams and nightmares that answer the question 'what if things had been different?' in some historical situation or other have become prominent, even a new genre both of fiction and non-fiction.[31] But the intellectual uses of counterfactual reasoning, as Hawthorn explored them in *Plausible Worlds* (and as Unger had done in *False Necessity*), was not to indulge fantasies of how radically different things might have been. It was, instead, to assess the actual alternatives that concrete historical conjunctures allowed, the better to assess why they turned out the way they did.[32] But this agenda has not been pursued – certainly not in legal history, to the best of my limited knowledge. As legal theorist Susan Marks has rightly remarked in a classic paper entitled 'False Contingency', it was not Unger's intention to overemphasise the contingent. But it prevailed as a matter of his reception and as a major part of the legacy of critical legal studies – as Robert Gordon's career and much legal history as practised in the United States exemplifies.

This mistake occurred in a more general intellectual setting. As with the representational, the emphasis on the aleatory and contingent is probably a response to the disastrous failure of aspirations across the 1960s and 1970s to see political change.[33] In compensation, much like the overemphasis of the representational over the practical, for a generation accounts sought to show alternatives lurking beyond confirmed outcomes, fissures in apparent solidity, and play in seemingly ironclad systems. As a result of these developments in the humanities, I suspect it is fair to speak of a great divergence in our time. We have a group of historians and humanists who tend to have a bias for the contingent, even as a much larger victory has been won (on the model of economics, prestigious in spite of its analytical and predictive failures) by disciplines seeking out neo-positivistic laws of the social. We also have a new generation of Marxists offering their own compensatory overreaction to

[31] See the brilliant study Gallagher 2018.
[32] Hawthorn 1992.
[33] Felsch 2015.

their elders, with the aim of ratifying the determinative systemic powers of 'capitalism'.

But we cannot choose between the agenda of assessing determination and exploring the situated freedom that works within its setting. In this regard, too, existing historiography cannot come to the rescue without being rescued too. And the law, saved from its historians' own bias for contingency, is an attractive topic on which to fuse concerns for contingency and structure.

The Analytical and the Normative

The third dilemma is that social theory faced the challenge of authorising normative (moral and political) belief after claiming that it is unfailingly context dependent. A last reason historians cannot provide help to other disciplines is that, with their antiquarian biases, they need their own help endorsing normative grounds for intellectual life. And law is as good a terrain as any on which to face this difficulty.

Historians, even as they have slowly departed from the alliance with social theory that crested in the 1960s, have no particularly good responses to the dilemma of normative or political commitment on their own. Honourably, historians have wanted to be on guard against an instrumentalised history that plays tricks on the dead. But they also experience the countervailing imperative to be 'relevant' to their times. A good example is the fate of the Cambridge School, which has seen a more or less complete inversion from Skinner's original antiquarian suggestion to evade presentism in the history of political thought to David Armitage's recent embrace of it.[34]

A plausible compromise, endorsed by Skinner after he abandoned his more antiquarian pose, has been the genealogical move of claiming that the present could have been different, then leaving it up to contemporaries to choose whether to stick with the way history worked out. But aside from risking an implausible embrace of contingency – since it is not always clear how different the present could in fact have been, given structural determination all along – this stratagem results in an unhelpful division of labour. On this model, historians destabilise prevalent moral and political beliefs, but can play no role (as historians, at least) in guiding ethically and politically once their undermining of current beliefs is done.

For their part, social theorists have not done well either, most frequently clinging to the more or less relativist stance that normative

---

[34] Skinner 1969; Armitage forthcoming.

and political values are hostage to social conditions, not 'transcendent' norms that can guide them.[35] In the face of the antiquarian pose of professional historians, rooted deep in the superego of anyone formed in the discipline, the tradition of social theory at first appears to provide no help. It was essential, social theory held, to treat normative standards of judgement as social products rather than eternal truths that were divine or natural in origin. The same was true of political standards. No longer did political community answer to extra-human will or artificially build its cities in light of the non-constructed nature of human beings.[36] But if so, social theory appeared to be amoral and apolitical, discovering the conditions for diverse moral and political beliefs in particular societies. And if sceptics cannot live their scepticism, no one can simultaneously hew to normative beliefs while thinking them entirely an artefact of her place and time.

The most promising route to be followed for intellectual inquiry is to rediscover the lost path for social theory in the more explicitly action-guiding attempts of G. W. F. Hegel's immediate left disciples, intent as they were to recover the inbuilt ethical direction and potential of social evolution in order to further them.

This attempt to ally oneself with the direction of history was shared by Marx, of course, albeit in self-denying mode that called for liquidating ethical standards or even philosophy itself as bourgeois artefacts – in spite of the fact that his theory of the cause of proletarians was self-evidently shot through with moral passion, never the automatic and grim determinism his followers sometimes took it to be.[37] And in a lesser and less theorised form, the reliance on 'progress' was also (as John Burrow showed) the approach of much nineteenth-century thought that attempted to ally a theory of social evolution to an embrace of normative commitment as a condition of present action.[38] No doubt the risks of this appeal to the direction of history for the sake of guiding present and future action are serious, as generations of anti-Marxist commentators from Berlin to Tony Judt have tried to prove.[39] But then the alternative is an amoral and pseudo-scientific social theory that announces that it has no purchase on the present while – as in Durkheim and Weber – embedding normative prejudice it does not defend.[40]

---

[35] Turner 2010.
[36] See, e.g., Strauss 1964.
[37] For relevant interpretations see, e.g., Lukes 1987 or Brudney 2009.
[38] Burrow 1966.
[39] Berlin 1955; Judt 1992, ch. 6.
[40] Rose 1981.

In many of its forms, the normatively progressive approaches to social theory were thinly disguised versions of Christian providentialism. They attributed to the immanent direction of social order and structure in transformation what had once been located outside the system as a matter of God's will. (The phrase of one of the tradition's most distinguished members, 'the invisible hand', suggests as much.) The coming of social theory as an intellectual tradition, as many of its historians have insisted, was not possible apart from the complex departure from and re-embedding of reformist providentialism – ironically, among North European Protestants, most of all – so that progress was credible as a result of internal processes.[41] Not merely Hegel himself in his portrait of the cunning of reason in passionate history, but his predecessor Immanuel Kant in his treatment of the energy unsocial sociability afforded an eventually cosmopolitan history, and of course Marx himself with his historical materialism blazing the road to communism, trafficked in such notions too.

The price for the normative orientation this encrypted providentialism provided was high. In most of its forms it sapped agency and transferred choice to 'history', a mythology not merely of communists but reformist liberals who often insist that the arc of the moral universe bends towards justice. We can now see, as Unger argued, that when it takes the form of a theory of the compulsive sequence of historical forms or a set menu of structural options, the crypto-providentialism of this branch of the tradition of social theory not only understates the alternative pathways there were in the past and are in the present, once the proper balance of contingency and determination has been reckoned. Worse, a reliance on the workings of secular providence also liquidates the need for morally and politically justified choice among the available options.

The cure for this difficulty is, of course, by no means to refer to transcendent or universal moral criteria for choice, in spite of the popularity in recent decades of an outright moral realism (in a eudaimonistic spirit or on theological grounds) – as if the traditions of social theory had never been.[42] Rather, our thinking has to be insistent about how hostage our values, and even our reformist values, are to social organisation and structure, just as social theory dictates. Norms of ethics are parasitic on forms of society, not an opportunity to wishfully escape their significance. Our cherished ideals are captive to our historical setting to an extraordinary extent – if not totally. Interrogating how pervasively our

---

[41] For a range of perspectives on this development see Löwith 1949; Viner 1972; and Funkenstein 1986.
[42] See, e.g., Moyn 2018.

norms have been affected by their situation is therefore essential – not least to counteract the risk that what we cherish will turn out to be little more than an illicit secularisation of a pre-modern mythology, either of an enduring human nature or a God with a plan for humanity.

Fortunately, it strongly looks as if Hegel provided a credible normative orientation in supposing that reduction of ethics to circumstance is not all that social theory should accomplish. Whatever his own complex relationship to the Christian past, Hegel portrayed the emergence of universal freedom and equality of empowered human agents making and remaking themselves together as the immanent promise of modernising social organisation. To believe otherwise would yoke our intellectual work either to an emancipatory moral stance incompatible with the tradition of social theory or to the relativistic approach that equates the removal of transcendent guarantees that social theory accomplished with the result of an entirely contingent morality.

From the beginning to the end of his career, like so many in the tradition of social theory before him, Unger struggled with overcoming the divide between descriptive and prescriptive. In early works he tended to trace the quandary to modern liberalism.[43] In recent years, by contrast, he has elaborated a 'religion of the future' that accepts the importance of normative visions of humanity. Allowed like all ethical and political beliefs by history and social circumstance, such visions are not appeals outside the possibilities that social structure creates. Instead, they are insights into its potential transformations – in the nature of bets on the future that, if they affect enough people, can become self-fulfilling. Indeed, the realisation of any particular future may in some cases depend (among other things) on the hopes of agents anticipating imaginable structural change.[44]

In many ways this stance is in keeping with the tradition of German idealism that, even before Hegel, struggled to elaborate a theory of action orientation compatible with our post-metaphysical understanding of ourselves as the products of secular history. The difference is that Hegel and Unger's version is premised not merely on a rejection of knowledge beyond the bounds of sense or a commitment to establish a religion of human freedom within the limits of reason. It also accepts social theory's lesson that society is – has always been – what humans make it with the situated freedom they have had from place to place and era to era.[45]

---

[43] See esp. Unger 1975.
[44] See esp. Unger 2014.
[45] In Unger 2014, pp. 236–8 and 290–3, Unger argues for the viability of considering this secular quest a kind of religion.

While the difficulty of the analytical and normative in social theory is not an easy one to resolve, it is indispensable for historians who continually grapple with the dilemma of antiquarianism and presentism, in a generally more philosophically backward way. And since that dilemma pervades all of their work, there is reason to believe that law in general and legal history in particular offer a useful place in which to accept the lessons of social theory in a progressive historiography of legally instituted freedom.

Students of the past of the law embrace antiquarian diversion much more rarely than other historians, if only because they so often err on the side of generating crassly instrumental accounts of the past for present-day purposes of influencing the outcome of some case or other. The results of commonly instrumentalist and opportunistic legal history have, derisively and rightly, been called 'law office history'.[46] In compensation for this vice, however, law would appear to be so inexpungeably ethical and political a topic for historians as to require their commitment to some plausible approach to 'presentism'. If the choice is between antiquarian illusions and presentist distortions, at least the latter requires some admission that – as Benedetto Croce said – all history is contemporary history, with the virtue of normative orientation.

As noted above, historians of law are by no means immune to an addiction in recent writing to emphasising contingent outcomes – accounts of what might have been in the past, with unspecified implications for what law should now become. But the diminishing returns of such accounts that leave the present on its own, perhaps with the reminder of its plasticity, seem clear enough. If so, future legal historiography is an excellent place to work out the dilemma of the analytical and normative in communication with its most advanced form, which the tradition of social theory continues to provide, especially in its Hegelian model.

Conclusion

The present is a time of urgent need. Perhaps it has always been so, but the depredations of the end of European global empires and America's successor hegemony, the ravages of the policies of economic neo-liberalism, and the experience of worldwide pandemic have made this fact more graphic to transatlantic contemporaries than at any time since

---

[46] These arguments have clustered around the American constitution because of the rise of so-called originalist interpretations. For a range of comment see Kelly 1965; Kalman 1997; Kramer 2003; and Balkin 2020.

the crisis years of the 1970s or even the 1930s.[47] And of course, this is not even to mention the renaissance of exclusionary xenophobia and white nationalism that have haunted so many places in the global north.

As a matter of principle, the role that history writing plays cannot be an antiquarian one. The past produced this present of dereliction and dismay. For that reason, the reunion of history and law alike with social theory seems pressing. Historians have a lot to bring to the study of law, but less than the two together have to learn from a common search for plausible social theory of a modernity on the brink once again.

References

Althusser, Louis. 1972. *Politics and History: Montesquieu, Rousseau, Marx*, trans. Ben Brewster. London.

Armitage, David. forthcoming. 'In Defense of Presentism' in *The History of the Humanities and Human Flourishing*, ed. Darrin M. McMahon. Oxford.

Balkin, Jack. 2020. 'Lawyers and Historians Argue about the Constitution', *Constitutional Commentary*, 35, pp. 345–400.

Berlin, Isaiah. 1955. *Historical Inevitability*. Oxford.

1962. 'Does Political Theory Still Exist?' in *Philosophy, Politics and Society: Second Series*, ed. Peter Laslett and W. G. Runciman. Oxford.

Brudney, Daniel. 2009. *Marx's Attempt to Leave Philosophy*. Cambridge, MA.

Burke, Edmund. 1839. *Letters on a Regicide Peace* in *The Works of Edmund Burke*, 9 vols. New York.

Burrow, J. W. 1966. *Evolution and Society: A Study in Victorian Social Theory*. Cambridge.

Clarke, Michael. 1976. 'Durkheim's Sociology of Law', *British Journal of Law and Society*, 3: 2, pp. 246–55.

Felsch, Philipp. 2015. *Der lange Sommer der Theorie: Geschichte einer Revolte 1960–1990*. Munich.

Ferguson, Niall, ed. 1997. *Virtual History: Alternatives and Counterfactual*. London.

Funkenstein, Amos. 1986. *Theology and the Scientific Imagination from the Middle Ages to the Seventeenth Century*. Princeton.

Gallagher, Catherine. 2018. *Telling it Like it Wasn't: The Counterfactual Imagination in History and Fiction*. Chicago.

Gordon, Robert W. 2017. *Taming the Past: Essays on Law in History and History in Law*. Cambridge.

---

[47] Saved for the future is a contentious fourth matter, theorising the distinctively modern condition. I believe the kernel of truth in this bequest from social theory has to be rescued from the now plain verdict that its existing versions traffic in unacceptable Eurocentrism and primitivism. From Ronald Meek on we have known how indentured the tradition of social theory has been to civilisational and imperial accounts of what distinguishes modernity. See Meek 1978 and a vast successor literature.

Hawthorn, Geoffrey. 1992. *Plausible Worlds: Possibility and Understanding in History and the Social Sciences*. Cambridge.

Judt, Tony. 1992. *Past Imperfect: French Intellectuals, 1944–1956*. Berkeley.

Kalman, Laura. 1997. 'Border Patrol: Reflections on the Turn to History in Legal Scholarship', *Fordham Law Review*, 87, pp. 87–124.

Kelly, Alfred. 1965. 'Clio and the Court: An Illicit Law Affair', *Supreme Court Review*, 1965, pp. 119–58.

Kramer, Larry D. 2003. 'When Lawyers Do History', *George Washington Law Review*, 72, pp. 387–423.

Kronman, Anthony T. 1983. *Max Weber*. London.

Laslett, Peter. 1956. 'Introduction', in *Philosophy, Politics, Society*, ed. Peter Laslett and W. G. Runciman. Oxford.

Löwith, Karl. 1949. *Meaning in History*. Chicago.

1982. *Max Weber and Karl Marx*, trans. Hans Fantel. London.

Lukes, Steven. 1987. *Marxism and Morality*. Oxford.

Meek, Ronald L. 1978. *Social Science and the Ignoble Savage*. Cambridge.

Merleau-Ponty, Maurice. 2012. *Phenomenology of Perception*, trans. Donald Landes. London.

Moyn, Samuel. 2008. 'On the Intellectual Origins of François Furet's Masterpiece', *Tocqueville Review*, 29: 2, pp. 59–78.

2010. *The Last Utopia: Human Rights in History*. Cambridge, MA.

2014. 'Imaginary Intellectual History' in *Rethinking Modern European Intellectual History*, ed. Darrin M. McMahon and Samuel Moyn. Oxford.

2018. 'Human Rights in Heaven' in *Human Rights: Moral or Political?*, ed. Adam Etinson. Oxford.

Pocock, J. G. A. 1999. *Barbarism and Religion*, vol. II: *Narratives of Civil Government*. Cambridge.

1962. 'The History of Political Thought: A Methodological Enquiry' in *Philosophy, Politics and Society: Second Series*, ed. Peter Laslett and W. G. Runciman. Oxford.

Riley, Patrick. 2003. 'Malebranche and Natural Law' in *Early Modern Natural Law Theories: Contexts and Strategies in the Early Enlightenment*, ed. T. J. Hochstrasser and Peter Schröder. Dordrecht.

Rose, Gillian. 1981. *Hegel contra Sociology*. London.

Runciman, W. G. 1962. 'Sociological Evidence and Political Theory' in *Philosophy, Politics and Society: Second Series*, ed. Peter Laslett and W. G. Runciman. Oxford.

1963. *Social Science and Political Theory*. Cambridge.

de Sade, D. A. F. 1965. *Philosophy in the Bedroom* in *Justine, Philosophy in the Bedroom, and Other Writings*, ed. Richard Seaver. New York.

Sewell, William H. Jr. 2005. *Logics of History: Social Theory and Social Transformation*. Chicago.

Skinner, Quentin. 1965. 'History and Ideology in the English Revolution', *Historical Journal*, 8, pp. 151–78.

1969. 'Meaning and Understanding in the History of Ideas', *History & Theory*, 8: 1, pp. 3–53.

2002. 'Motives, Intentions, and Interpretation', in Quentin Skinner, *Visions of Politics*, vol. I: *Regarding Method*. Cambridge.

Smolin, Lee and Roberto Mangabeira Unger. 2015. *The Singular Universe and the Reality of Time*. Cambridge.

Strauss, Leo. 1964. *The City and Man*. Chicago.

Thompson, John B. 1986. *Studies in the Theory of Ideology*. Berkeley.

de Tocqueville, Alexis. 1899. *Democracy in America*, trans. Henry Reeve. 2 vols. New York.

Toews, John E. 1987. 'Intellectual History after the Linguistic Turn: The Autonomy of Meaning and the Irreducibility of Experience', *American Historical Review*, 92: 4, pp. 879–907.

Turner, Stephen P. 2010. *Explaining the Normative*. Cambridge.

Unger, Roberto Mangabeira. 1975. *Knowledge and Politics*. New York.

   1976. *Law in Modern Society: Toward a Criticism of Social Theory*. New York.

   1986. *False Necessity: Anti-Necessitarian Social Theory in the Service of Radical Democracy*. Cambridge.

   2014. *The Religion of the Future*. Cambridge, MA.

Viner, Jacob. 1972. *The Role of Providence in the Social Order: An Essay in Intellectual History*. Philadelphia.

3 The Uses of History in the Study of International Politics

Jennifer Pitts

Introduction

As Michel-Rolph Trouillot wrote in *Silencing the Past*, 'History is the fruit of power, but power itself is never so transparent that its analysis becomes superfluous. The ultimate mark of power may be its invisibility; the ultimate challenge, the exposition of its roots.'[1] The long-standing failings of historical understanding in the disciplines concerned with international politics – international relations and international law – have precisely been failures to reckon adequately with the global distribution of power and the hierarchical nature of the global order. The very disciplines that have prided themselves on the study of power have often been remarkably oblivious to global patterns in its exercise as well as to their own participation in the reproduction of these patterns. What sort of historical work, I want to ask in this chapter, enables a more adequate grasp of the global distribution of power past and present?

In the post-Second World War era, scholarship in international politics, whether carried out under the rubric of international relations (henceforth IR) or of international law, largely neglected historical study, even as stylised historical narratives played an important role in the self-understandings of both disciplines. In the case of international law, the narrative was, and often remains, of a march of progress towards an ever more rational and humane global order and of a universalisation of principles and practices that originated in Europe.[2] In IR, history has appeared

For comments on earlier versions of this chapter I am grateful to Richard Bourke and Quentin Skinner, to Adom Getachew, Joel Isaac, Emma Mackinnon, Tejas Parasher, Rose Parfitt, Mira Siegelberg and Lisa Wedeen, and to the participants in the History in the Humanities and Social Science workshop held at the University of Cambridge in July 2019.

[1] Trouillot 2015 [1995], p. xxiii.
[2] On the longer history of histories of the law of nations and international law see Koskenniemi 2012; he stresses the teleology, the providential view of history, that structured projects such as François Laurent's eighteen-volume history (Laurent 1851) and *Les origines du droit international* (1893) by his student Ernest Nys, 'the first professional historian of international law'.

mainly in the form of shadow-boxing between paradigms schematically identified with historical figures such as Grotius (standing for the English School), Hobbes (for realism), and Kant (for liberal institutionalism), which have dominated the field since Martin Wight invented them in the 1950s.[3] In 2001 the IR scholars Barry Buzan and Richard Little declared that 'International Relations has failed as an intellectual project', largely because of 'the prevalence of a-historical, even sometimes anti-historical, attitudes in formulating the concept of an international system'.[4]

This situation changed at precisely the moment that Buzan and Little were relegating their discipline to irrelevance, with what Duncan Bell called the 'dawn of a historiographical turn' in IR and David Armitage described as the closing of a 'fifty years' rift' between IR and intellectual history.[5] Both Bell and Armitage charted the reasons for and the costs of that long rift and welcomed the rapprochement between IR and intellectual history, even as they noted how much remained to be done to deepen the historicist turn in IR. As Armitage noted, the hold of the so-called traditions of IR – Hobbesian, Grotian and Kantian – was so tenacious that much of the new historical work was still wrestling with them.[6] If that is somewhat less true today than it was in the early years of this century, what has not changed is the imperviousness of much of mainstream American IR to this historical turn, partly because it is situated in Political Science departments under the spell of aspirations to positivist rigour, where large-n regressions, experiments, and now machine learning and computational models are the standards of knowledge production. The renaissance of historical work over the last two decades has been especially pronounced in international law, with an explosion of work first by lawyers, followed by political theorists and intellectual historians.[7]

Until the recent historiographical turn, historical work in both IR and international law, for all its failings, had been flawed most fundamentally,

---

[3] Wight 1966 [1959]; Wight 1991 (posthumously published work first delivered as lectures at the London School of Economics in the 1950s). When discussing mainstream IR, I refer primarily to security studies rather than international political economy (IPE); John Hobson and Branwen Gruffydd Jones, among others, have made related critiques with respect to IPE: Hobson 2019, p. 155; Gruffydd Jones 2013.

[4] Buzan and Little 2001, pp. 19, 24. Much historical work has been done in the last two decades to study the recent history of these disciplines and to account for their limitations with respect to both historical understanding and perspectives outside the USA. See, e.g., Devetak 2018; Acharya and Buzan 2019.

[5] Bell 2001; Armitage 2004. This turn has also involved disciplinary historiography: Schmidt 1998; Guilhot 2011. Some notable histories of international thought were published during the 'rift': e.g., Hinsley 1963; Hont 1983.

[6] Armitage 2004, p. 101.

[7] Craven, Fitzmaurice, and Vogiatzi 2007; Fassbender and Peters 2012; Armitage and Rasilla forthcoming.

I have suggested, in its failure to grasp patterns and structures of global domination. IR and international law have long contributed to these patterns, and have also occluded them. For this reason it is significant that the turn to history in international law over the last two decades has been so largely informed by post-colonial and Third World approaches. Thanks to this work, the revitalisation of historical interest in a field that had long lacked it has also entailed a challenge to international law's identity as an emancipatory project with an essentially European lineage.[8] The conjuncture between historical scholarship and post-colonial perspectives is less pronounced in IR but figures there as well, thanks to scholars such as Tarak Barkawi, Siba Grovogui, Branwen Gruffydd Jones, John Hobson, Sanjay Seth, Robbie Shilliam and Robert Vitalis, and those such as Duncan Bell and Jeanne Morefield who straddle political theory and IR. It is also no accident that contextual histories of international thought – in the work of Richard Tuck, James Tully, Anthony Pagden, Annabel Brett and David Armitage – have long centred on empire and colonisation, which were chief preoccupations of the historical figures in question, however forgotten that fact had been by IR theorists who thought in ahistorical and abstract terms only of states and the so-called state system. As we carry on this work, I want to suggest, contextual history of international politics will require greater attention to the playing out of imperial relations in diverse contexts around the world and not just in the centres of imperial power that have been the traditional objects of study in the history of political thought. We shall also need to attend more consistently to the interplay of economic forces with legal and political argument.

In what follows, I briefly discuss earlier critical histories of international politics, beginning with the work of W. E. B. Du Bois and others during the First World War and carrying through to the first generation of international lawyers from decolonising states – the forebears of the current renaissance of histories of international law and politics informed by post-colonial perspectives. I then suggest some of the insights to be gained from a style of history that integrates a contextual approach with the conjoined critique of imperialism, capitalism and white supremacy initiated by Du Bois.[9] Finally, I note failures of recent mainstream work

---

[8] E.g., Anghie 2005; Shilliam 2011; Becker Lorca 2014; von Bernstoff and Dann 2019; for reflections on this literature see Gathii 2013 and Gathii 2021.

[9] Emphasis on the persistence of a global order shaped by European and American imperialism arguably leaves such approaches ill-equipped to analyse other forms of imperialism: Du Bois was notoriously uncritical of Japanese imperialism in Asia (see Getachew and Pitts 2022), and the phenomenon of exploitative Chinese investment in Africa and South and South-East Asia likewise is not well accounted for by the idea of a global hegemony of liberal capitalism: Azeem 2019.

to attend to these new histories and the consequences of this failure for understanding international politics.

Critical International History: Du Bois and TWAIL

The recent post-colonial historiographical turn is indebted to a longer history. In the first few decades of the twentieth century, W. E. B. Du Bois, Alain Locke and other members of what Robert Vitalis has called the Howard School of International Relations were challenging mainstream white IR scholarship with historical accounts that traced the emergence in the modern world of a hierarchical global order structured by the interlinked phenomena of imperial power relations, capitalist exploitation and white supremacy. Vitalis's own book was written to challenge what he called 'two entwined myths of empire': that the United States is not and never was much of an imperial power; and that the discipline of IR has never shown much interest in the study of imperialism. He shows to the contrary 'the constitutive role of imperialism and racism in bringing an academic discipline [of IR] in the United States into existence'. Vitalis reminds us that 'in the first decades of the twentieth century in the United States, international relations meant race relations'. The discipline's first journal, founded in 1910, was the *Journal of Race Development*, renamed *The Journal of International Relations* in 1919, and, still later, *Foreign Affairs*, as it remains.[10] As he shows, the first American scholars of IR justified their new discipline on the basis of its scientific solutions to problems of imperial governance and the challenge of maintaining white racial dominance.

To the theories of so-called scientific racism and developmentalism that shaped the IR work of their white contemporaries, Locke and Du Bois, and then others, counterposed historical accounts of the global economic and political dynamics of the early twentieth century. In 'Science and empire', the chapter on the years 1894–1910 of his third quasi-autobiographical work, *Dusk of Dawn*, Du Bois recalled groping towards an adequate account of the world order. 'Above all', he wrote, 'it was the era of empire and while I had some equipment to deal with a scientific approach to social studies, I did not have any clear conception or grasp of the meaning of that industrial imperialism which was beginning to grip the world. My only approach to meanings and helpful study there again was through my interest in race contact.'[11] Du Bois's efforts to

---

[10] Vitalis 2015, pp. x, 1.
[11] Du Bois 2007b [1940], p. 27; and see Locke's 1916 lectures 'Race Contacts and Interracial Relations', in Locke 1992.

make sense of industrial imperialism evolved from his early preoccupation with racism as a matter 'simply [of] ignorance and ill will' to a belief, by the first decade of the twentieth century, that the colour line should be understood as the product of a four-century global history linking conquest, slavery, the 'income-bearing value of race prejudice' and the political uses of racism and imperial expansion within a democratising Europe.[12] This was in contrast to the approach taken by Hobson and Lenin, who both stressed the novelty of the connection between imperialism and the financial capitalism of the turn of the twentieth century, and also had little to say about the place of racism in that history.[13] Du Bois's critique bore on both ideas and material forces: white supremacy and European ideas of civilisation, together with the operations of global capital. Du Bois understood slavery as having been central to the origins of capitalism, and the modern world order as a global economic and political system shaped above all by the dynamics of imperial domination.

The phenomena he traced transcended state boundaries, and states for him were not always the decisive, much less the sole, agents. In 'The African roots of war', published in the *Atlantic Monthly* in 1915, Du Bois noted that it was with the rounding of the Cape of Good Hope that 'for the first time a real world-commerce was born' – a commerce that began 'mainly in the bodies and souls of men' – and that the 'present world war' was 'the result of jealousies engendered by the recent rise of armed national associations of labor and capital whose aim is the exploitation of the wealth of the world mainly outside the European circle of nations'.[14] Du Bois explained the First World War as the product of the rise of a modern racial capitalism with roots in slavery and imperial commerce that had taken a distinctive democratic form in the late nineteenth century. Imperial exploitation, in his words 'exploitation on an immense scale; for inordinate profit, not simply to the very rich, but to the middle class and the laborers', was 'no sudden invention but a way out of long, pressing difficulties' of revolutionary pressures among the European working classes.[15] White supremacy had, he wrote, 'worked itself through warp and woof of our daily thought with a thoroughness that few realize', legitimising, in European culture, in common habits of thought and speech, 'this vast quest of the dark world's wealth and toil'. Scholarly study was required to expose it and understand it. The flawed

[12] Du Bois 2007a, pp. 2, 65.
[13] Hobson 1902; Lenin 1917.
[14] Du Bois 1915, p. 711, repr. in Du Bois 2022; and see the discussion in Getachew and Pitts 2022.
[15] Du Bois 1917, pp. 439–41, repr. in Du Bois 2022.

historical understanding of his European contemporaries, he argued, such as the widespread assumption that the cause of the war lay in the Balkans, meant they were unequipped to understand both the true causes of the conflict and the economic and cultural or ideological transformations, of global capitalism and white supremacy, without which Europe would be doomed to repeat the war.[16] Du Bois made these arguments to the participants of the Paris Peace Conference in 1919 and again to the framers of the United Nations in San Francisco in 1945, after his disappointment at the failure of the earlier Dumbarton Oaks conference to address colonial matters.[17] When the discipline of IR remade itself during the Cold War as the theoretical (and supposedly race-blind) study of states under conditions of anarchy, both its mainstream history as a contribution to racial and colonial administration and the Howard School critique of imperial capitalism were forgotten.[18]

In international law, the first generation of lawyers representing the so-called New States beginning in the 1950s, the progenitors of the more recent Third World Approaches to International Law or TWAIL, undertook historical studies alongside their anti-colonial legal work: figures such as R. P. Anand, Mohammed Bedjaoui, T. O. Elias and C. H. Alexandrowicz.[19] Some of what these lawyers were doing with the history of international law would seem to bolster the recent insistence by some scholars of international law that lawyers must do history differently from historians.[20] They did mobilise historical argument explicitly to lay precedents for current law, sometimes stripping away historical context to leave in place portable principles. Alexandrowicz, for instance, made much of the invocation by the International Court of Justice in 1960 of a 1779 treaty between the Maratha and Portuguese

---

[16] 'We speak of the Balkans as the storm-centre of Europe and the cause of war, but this is mere habit. The Balkans are convenient for occasions, but the ownership of materials and men in the darker world is the real prize that is setting the nations of Europe at each other's throats today': Du Bois 1915, p. 711. Yet the Balkans, part of a European periphery, served as a 'site of experimentation for international legal techniques', tying its role in the outbreak of the war more closely than Du Bois acknowledged to the imperial phenomena he pointed to as the war's true cause: Tzouvala 2019. European Marxists including Lenin, Luxemburg and Bukharin also located the war's causes in imperialism; for discussion see Anievas 2015.

[17] Du Bois 1918; Du Bois 2007a; Lewis 2000, pp. 504–10.

[18] Vitalis 2015; for a description of the 'conventional view of the state as a unitary actor, constituted only by the competitive dynamics of the international system' see Reus-Smit 2002; on the shift in IR after the Second World War from 'scientific racism' to a 'subliminal Eurocentrism' that entailed proxy categories such as tradition versus modernity and failed states or quasi-states, see Hobson 2015.

[19] Anghie and Chimni 2003, pp. 79–87; von Bernstorff and Dann 2019.

[20] Orford 2013b; Orford 2021; and see below.

empires as 'a valid transaction in the law of nations'. This meant that the Maratha empire was 'in the sphere of international existence' in the eighteenth century, and consequently so were other Asian states, including Ceylon, Burma, the Mogul empire and Persia. That fact, in turn, meant that decolonised states in the 1960s were not new members of the international community whose admission into the club could be made conditional on their acceptance of European-made international law as it stood at the time of decolonisation. On the contrary, they were old states whose non-recognition in the nineteenth century was itself a violation of international law. Such an argument may flatten, in the service of legal reasoning in the present, many differences between eighteenth-century understandings of the law of nations and its scope of application, and the doctrine of state recognition developed by the new profession of international lawyers in the late nineteenth century. But legal historians such as Alexandrowicz also undertook contextual histories of legal argumentation in order to capture the distinctive concerns, for instance about dynastic legitimacy, of eighteenth-century thinkers like J. H. G. von Justi and Johann von Steck.[21] He traced patterns across global contexts in international law and diplomacy, particularly between India and his native Poland, dismembered by the great powers in the eighteenth century and once again recognised as an independent state in 1919.[22] If he flattened historical difference at some moments for the purposes of asserting legal precedent, he also scrupulously reconstructed the ways of seeing legal problems distinctive to particular contexts, and he did so with attention, as far as his sources and linguistic competence allowed, to transcontinental contexts such as the Indian Ocean trade. Since that post-war moment, imperial history has been mobilised by successive generations of self-described Third World international lawyers in service of critique and in the hope – often quite chastened – of contributing to a more emancipatory international law. Mohammed Bedjaoui took such an approach to the idea of the world as the common property of humankind in the history he wrote as part of the movement for a New International Economic Order or NIEO.[23]

The more recent surge of historical work in international law included the foundation of the *Journal of the History of International Law* in 1999 and the publication of the massive *Oxford Handbook of the History of International Law* in 2012, which took as among its key tasks the 'overcoming of Eurocentrism in the history of international law'. Martti Koskenniemi's

---

[21] 'Theory of recognition *in Fieri*' [1958], in Alexandrowicz 2017, pp. 384–9.
[22] Alexandrowicz 2017, pp. 152, 401–3.
[23] Bedjaoui 1979; also Weeramantry 1976.

The Gentle Civilizer of Nations (2002) and Antony Anghie's *Imperialism, Sovereignty and the Making of International Law* (2005) were among the most important inspirations and provocations to this outpouring of scholarship. The collection *Bandung, Global History, and International Law* (2017) revisits the 1955 Bandung Conference in an extensive, variegated and theoretically ambitious effort to set the conference in historical context, understand its antecedents and its own moment, and to explore the formation and subsequent meanings of the 'Bandung myth' and the idea of the 'Bandung spirit' of Afro-Asian solidarity in the sixty years since the conference.[24] In the wake of this dense and rich body of substantive work, methodological reflections and disputes followed so thick and fast that Gerry Simpson was able to ask, at a conference in Cambridge in 2016, 'what international legal history might look like "after method"', while he warned against overstating disciplinary divisions. As Simpson and others have pointed out, much of the historical work being done by international lawyers was self-consciously contextualist, and affinities between the work of historians and lawyers have been considerable. Simpson also warned against overstating disciplinary markers: some people, he ventured, may be prone to anachronism whatever their discipline, while on his view, following Marc Bloch, good work 'is just the ability or inclination to read the small print alongside the larger structural changes'. He noted that Anghie's book 'was, in a way, "unread"' when it first appeared; and that 'cross-methodological cross-hatching has reactivated the book – no longer a monument to be gingerly circumnavigated but part of a conversation about history and method'.[25]

Much ink has been spilled on the ostensible debate between international lawyers and historians over historical method, with some international lawyers, most prominently Anne Orford, protesting that so-called Cambridge School historians are concerned to police anachronisms in historical scholarship in a way that fails to recognise the distinctive way that lawyers do history, by looking to prior historical moments for usable precedents.[26] Koskenniemi himself first turned to historical scholarship in *The Gentle Civilizer of Nations* in a contextualist spirit, an effort to understand international law as, in his phrase, 'people with projects', an undertaking with clear affinities to Quentin Skinner's account of the historian's task as establishing what authors were doing in writing as they

---

[24] Eslava, Fakhri and Nesiah 2017.
[25] Simpson 2021.
[26] Orford 2013a; Orford 2013b; Orford 2017; Orford 2021; cf. Koskenniemi in Kemmerer, Koskenniemi and Orford 2015, pp. 2–3; for responses see Benton 2019; Fitzmaurice 2018.

did. In the case of the founding generation of international lawyers he called the 'men of 1873', the project was to express the 'legal conscience of the civilized world', central to which was the justification of European imperial expansion.[27] After avowing his affinities with contextual historical work, however, Koskenniemi retreated to a position of opposition, writing more recently that the 'validity of our histories lies not in their correspondence with "facts" or "coherence" with what we otherwise know about a context, but how they contribute to emancipation today' and proposing that all legal thinking is necessarily progressive and teleological. Contextualism, he now worries, 'encourages a historical relativism and ends up suppressing or undermining efforts to find patterns in history that might account for today's experiences of domination and injustice'.[28] Work by scholars such as David Scott, James Tully, Adom Getachew and Rose Parfitt, I argue below, suggests that these worries are misplaced. Rather than seeing them as being at odds, as Orford and (at times) Koskenniemi have done, we have much to gain from conjoining attention to theoretical arguments as ideological moves made in particular discursive contexts with attention to global patterns of domination in the modern era.

The 'fundamental concern' for historians of international thought, David Armitage has argued, should be 'How did we – all of us in the world – come to imagine that we inhabit a world of states?'[29] I would add that a fundamental concern for the study of international politics, one for which historical understanding is indispensable, is what role have ways of imagining the world – especially the view that we inhabit a world of states – themselves played in the practice of international politics, especially with respect to the violence, maldistribution and environmental catastrophe that have plagued the world in the modern period? Armitage's historical question is significant in part, that is, because of its implications for our understanding of domination in the present. I want to suggest, as a result, the complementarity of contextual history with history attentive to patterns of domination, in particular the value for contextual history of post-colonial and Marxian approaches to the history of international politics.

Contextual historical work and politically engaged thinking about global and international politics are usefully conjoined in David Scott's idea of problem-spaces, which he conceives drawing on R. G. Collingwood and Quentin Skinner. As he argues, a problem-space is 'an

---

[27] Koskenniemi 2002.
[28] Koskenniemi 2014, pp. 124, 129.
[29] Armitage 2013, p. 13.

ensemble of questions and answers around which a horizon of identifiable stakes (conceptual as well as ideological-political stakes) hangs'. What defines this context are 'the particular questions that seem worth asking and the kinds of answers that seem worth having'. It is a 'fundamentally temporal' concept: 'In new historical contexts, old questions may lose their salience', and answers to them may seem not so much wrong as irrelevant or 'lifeless'. As Scott shows, attention to the problem-spaces of historical figures or texts can help us to clarify our understanding of our own problem-space: it obliges us to ascertain 'whether and to what extent the questions [we are] trying to answer continue to be questions worth having answers to'.[30]

For Scott, those questions have to do with what he calls the tragedy of the post-colonial present, specifically the 'bankruptcy of postcolonial regimes' in the Caribbean and elsewhere, 'the acute paralysis of will ... the rampant corruption and vicious authoritarianism, the instrumental self-interest' and the 'collapse of the social and political hopes' of the anti-colonial struggle.[31] As a citizen not of a recently decolonised state but of a liberal global hegemon, I have found my own questions centring on the exercise of overwhelming power in the name of universal moral ideals. For Tully, the questions have to do with 'the ways peoples and subalternised states are subject to global imperial relationships of inequality, dependency and exploitation' and with what practices of civic freedom have emerged under those conditions.[32] Getachew's *Worldmaking after Empire* is similarly occupied by the question of how to secure non-domination in an international order structured by hierarchy rather than by the sovereign equality assumed by the dominant paradigms; her own framing of this problem is indebted to her history of anti-colonial thinkers of the Black Atlantic. Thanks to the assumption, widely shared in IR and international law, that we live in a world of states, anti-colonial leaders are remembered as having narrowly pursued nation-state sovereignty and are criticised for the failures of that project. Getachew's contextual history recovers in these figures – political actors and thinkers such as Kwame Nkrumah, Julius Nyerere, Michael Manley and others – more capacious visions of self-determination involving regional federation, a restructured global economy and the 'refashioning of the UN as a site of "postcolonial revolution"'. Recognising the practical limitations of these projects, she argues that 'even instances that appeared as moments of closure ... were occasion for reformulating the contours of

---

[30] Scott 2004, p. 4.
[31] Scott 2004, p. 1.
[32] Tully 2008, II, p. 4.

an anti-imperial future and enacting new strategies to realize this vision' and proposes that we see the fall of self-determination not merely as a dead end, but as a 'staging ground' for 'imagining an anti-imperial future' for ourselves.[33]

As I have been suggesting, the belief that we inhabit a world of states itself helps to shore up hierarchies by occluding them. One compelling answer to Armitage's question how we all came to share this belief is offered by Rose Parfitt in *The Process of International Legal Reproduction*. Parfitt offers an account of the political and economic dynamics that have contributed over the last 500 years to the reproduction of the 'self-governing' sovereign state, the patterns these dynamics have followed, and the costs of this process for so many of those who have been subjected to it. Parfitt seeks to do justice to the contingencies and particularities of the various cases she juxtaposes, while also bringing them together in order to propose that a logic of legal reproduction is repeatedly at work, with recognisably similar effects despite their distance from one another in time and space. In this sense her approach bears some resemblance to another aspect of Armitage's work, his argument for 'serial contextualism' as a way to analyse historical developments over a long period while remaining attentive to context in the various cases the historian brings together.[34]

Parfitt's core argument is that central to the 'doctrine and practice' of international law 'since its first stirrings in the late fifteenth century' has been a process of the 'gradual extension, consolidation, and reproduction' of a 'very specific constellation of rights and duties' that create the conditions for capital accumulation and secure participation in the market by the formally free but materially non-negotiable participation of both individuals and states.[35] Following other Marxian treatments of international law, including those of Evgeny Pashukanis, B. S. Chimni, Robert Knox and China Miéville, but offering contextual accounts of several episodes, she argues that the process by which states have been constituted as free and equal subjects of international law has been inextricable from the process by which individuals came to be constituted as free and equal bearers of rights, foremost among these property rights and rights to engage in commerce. The process is one that involved not only the imperial imposition of legal and property regimes on extra-European territories and polities as a condition of international membership but

---

[33] Getachew 2019a, pp. 178, 181.
[34] Parfitt cites Armitage with reference to 'the structuralist, *longue durée* history' of which she offers a 'modular' version: Parfitt 2019, p. 91.
[35] Parfitt 2019, p. 220.

also took place within Europe, where it occurred through less obviously coercive forms of inducement, often with an insistence on the formal consent of the states being brought into the international legal regime. Repeatedly, existing states conditioned (and continue to condition) their recognition of aspiring states first and foremost on the willingness and ability of those others to protect the property rights of people who were already constituted as legal subjects, namely their own citizens, the citizens of these existing (at first almost exclusively European) states. European subjects – traders, colonial officials, missionaries and so on – then served as a kind of bridgehead for the extension of the model of the liberal and capitalist subject to populations beyond Europe – an extension which offered the final proof of capacity for 'full' statehood. As Parfitt writes in reference to the nineteenth-century extension to China of international legal personality, 'formal equality and liberty could themselves prove to be the most precise instruments of domination, even when "freely" demanded by those struggling for emancipation'.[36] This is a history in which the abolition of slavery and the pursuit of profit through the exploitation of labour and resources in the colonies – and elsewhere – went hand in hand. These connections between international law's humanitarian and civilising missions and its replication of the legal structures of capitalism were patterned and recurrent but also varied across time and space, especially with respect to the role of racial ideologies.

The central case or episode in Parfitt's book is the so-called Abyssinian Crisis, in which Fascist Italy conquered Ethiopia and met with little resistance from other members of the League of Nations, despite Ethiopia's membership in the League as well as its long history of treaties with various European powers that explicitly recognised the Ethiopian kingdom's sovereign equality and independence. Ethiopia's encounter with international law, first in the nineteenth century and then by way of its partial integration into the League of Nations, serves as an illustration of the broader argument that 'the process through which the vast majority of the world's states were "emancipated" is one and the same process as that which ensures their ongoing subjection to a process of relentless resource extraction' unleashed in part through property-rights guarantees made first to European commercial agents and later to their local counterparts.[37] In her account of Ethiopia's subjugated incorporation into international law, Parfitt contextualises and juxtaposes what she calls the 'view from Geneva' alongside the 'view from Addis Ababa' in the 1930s. She analyses the split within the Ethiopian leadership about

---

[36] Parfitt 2019, p. 144.
[37] Parfitt 2019, p. 221.

the implications of their joining the Covenant of the League of Nations – over what was entailed by the commitment to a covenant or *Mäh'bar* with other Christian powers – and about whether Ethiopia would be more vulnerable to the inevitable European imperial pressures in the League or out of it. On the European side, Parfitt's account blends contextual and theoretical work to show how imperialism's civilisational and profit-seeking dynamics worked in tandem by creating, in part, myths of Christian affinity.

Among the questions such an approach helps to address is that of the role of race in international law, by attending to two phenomena that might seem in tension: the racialised nature of the late nineteenth- and twentieth-century international legal hierarchy, and the subjection of European communities and territories to related processes of discipline. In Europe as well as Africa, international legal personality has been made conditional on the willingness of vulnerable communities seeking to maintain their independence to protect property rights and more generally domestic legal regimes favourable to business, as Parfitt shows in a discussion of the constitution of Bosnia imposed by dominant international powers through the Dayton Accords in the 1990s.[38]

The book, in sum, illustrates the benefits of combining contextual interpretive work with an attention to 'international law's material dimensions and distributive implications'.[39] This combination enables the historian to identify patterns (such as the persistent centrality of property rights in international law, or the imposition of conditions on the full or partial recognition of new members of the 'international community') while also doing justice to the particular instantiations of those patterns at different historical moments, including our own, in the form of such discourses and disciplinary practices as 'good governance' and the Responsibility to Protect.[40]

Histories of international politics ignore imperial power and hierarchies in the international order at the risk of misunderstanding what many historical figures were doing in arguing as they did about the international order, even, and perhaps especially, when those hierarchies are not readily apparent in their language and conceptual categories. I have tried to make a case for one kind of historical approach that I think answers the critical demands of the moment, without suggesting that

---

[38] Parfitt 2019, p. 221. See the Preamble to Bosnia's externally imposed constitution: 'Based on respect for human dignity, liberty and equality. … Desiring to promote the general welfare and economic growth through the protection of private property and the promotion of a market economy' (Office of the High Representative 1994).

[39] Parfitt 2019, p. 389.

[40] Getachew 2019b.

it exhausts the possibilities for historical work to inform the study of international politics. Such an approach offers not just a diagnosis of domination, but also an understanding of how forms and techniques of domination change with changing historical conditions and political languages, and in the hands of different authors, and what forms and languages of resistance they have faced.

Empire in Mainstream IR and International Law

Despite this wealth of recent scholarship in IR and international law that builds on the insights of Du Bois, and of the first generation of post-colonial international lawyers, mainstream historical narratives in these disciplines still often ignore the history of racism and of European imperialism and their implications for contemporary global politics. Neglect of these dynamics takes a few distinct forms, of which I shall stress two. First, historical narratives that stand several removes from original sources are mobilised to bear out claims generated by theory, and register little sense of the scholar as mediator of historical material. Second, the phenomenon that Octave Mannoni calls disavowal – the gesture of 'je sais bien mais quand même' (I know very well, nevertheless …) – as Lisa Wedeen argues, undergirds 'status quo conventionality, perhaps particularly in moments when order is profoundly threatened'.[41]

Two recent books – John Mearsheimer's *The Great Delusion* and Oona Hathaway and Scott Shapiro's *The Internationalists* in international law – suggest the limited impact on mainstream scholarship of the historical and post-colonial turn in the study of international politics, and they illustrate some of the costs of failing to take its lessons on board, costs that come not from their altogether ignoring the history of empire and decolonisation, but rather from partial attention to its manifestation and implications. Each mobilises historical argument in ways that have long been typical of their respective disciplines. Both also rely on large-n political science research to support their arguments by amassing data over long periods of time but that, characteristically of this sort of political science research, ignores context and flattens particularity, as Stathis Kalyvas shows in his contribution to this volume.

The Great Delusion is a bracing critique of American foreign policy since the end of the Cold War as driven by a crusading liberal imperialism bent on spreading democracy and social welfare provision and protecting human rights and 'doing social engineering on a global scale'.[42]

---

[41] Wedeen 2019, pp. 141–2.
[42] Mearsheimer 2018, p. 231.

Mearsheimer's historical arguments have always run through the theoretical lens of IR realism, for which the only agents and purposes that matter are states seeking power, ultimately for the sake of their security. Such a lens makes it difficult to account for the motives of the USA after 1989, which according to the theory is a global hegemon whose security is assured in a unipolar global order. He concludes, reading the motives of powerful agents in the system off their own self-justificatory statements, that such a state will simply (but disastrously) indulge its 'liberal' penchant for remaking the world in its own democratic and humanitarian image.[43] IR scholarship in the USA, and realism in particular, has neglected the body of political economy literature on the international system that developed in the 1970s, world-systems and dependency theory, that challenged the very idea that 'sovereign states' ever existed in the Third World.[44] Mearsheimer's discontinuous history – in which the USA is driven first by Cold War power politics and then by liberal idealism – overlooks longer patterns of collaboration between capitalists' pursuit of profit, a liberal international order that secures individual rights, and the use by powerful states of a combination of strategies, including international law and institutions, to secure their global dominance and access to the rest of globe for their corporations. Those strategies have included formal imperial rule, other forms of military presence, the replication of favourable constitutional structures in other states and the creation of international institutions.

Hathaway and Shapiro's long and detailed intellectual history of the Paris Peace Pact of 1928, in contrast, illustrates the problem of disavowal, the 'I know very well, nevertheless'. Hathaway and Shapiro know very well the history of imperial conquest and domination that have structured the modern global order, but it proves largely inconsequential in their account of what they call the 'New World Order' that they claim was ushered in by the Kellogg–Briand Pact. *The Internationalists* argues that the Pact 'was among the most transformative events in human history, one that has, ultimately, made our world far more peaceful'. 'War has been outlawed for nearly a century, and the result has been a period

---

[43] Mearsheimer 2018, p. 170. Mearsheimer cites a 2004 op-ed by leading IR scholars Bruce Bueno de Mesquita and George Downs, which found that between the Second World War and 2004 'the US intervened more than 35 times in developing countries around the world' with 'a success rate of less than 3%'; but while his sources, in their more extensive 2006 study of interventions, conclude that democracy promotion could not have been the point of many of them, Mearsheimer presents the abysmal 'success rate' as evidence of the ineptitude of liberal imperialism. See Downs and Bueno de Mesquita 2004; and Bueno de Mesquita and Downs 2006.

[44] Thanks to Tejas Parasher on this point.

of unprecedented peace and cooperation between states.'[45] Typically
of narratives of disavowal, they make such claims despite acknowledging the many wars that succeeded the 1928 Peace Pact (Japan's invasion of Manchuria, Italy's invasion of Ethiopia, the Second World War,
Korea, Vietnam, Iraq, Afghanistan etc.). Their book tells a story very
traditional in form within international law, in which international law
is essentially Western and fundamentally emancipatory; expanding ever
outward, it tames power as it goes. In such stories, the substantial role
played by international law itself in the enforcement of coercive hierarchies is insufficiently acknowledged.[46] As Charlotte Peevers argued in
a keen review of *The Internationalists*, 'The capacity for great powers to
wage war otherwise made the prohibitions [on aggressive war] an illusory
and duplicitous promise.' Gunboat diplomacy of the older sort may have
ended, but 'the aims and purposes of such diplomacy – namely, coerced
agreements – did not magically disappear with the institutionalisation
of the prohibition on force'. Rather, the 'prohibitory framework' itself –
the prohibition of war – became an important technique of control by
powerful actors over the decolonising world.[47] Hathaway and Shapiro's
analysis, which essentially attributes decolonisation to a new iteration
of Western liberal internationalism in the Pact's outlawing of war, also
renders invisible the political agency of anti-colonial leaders and movements around the world.

For those who make states the prime objects of study, seemingly
important transformations in the state system – whether the proliferation
of new states with decolonisation or the end of the Cold War – obscure
continuities in global power asymmetries and in the flow of resources
from the global south to the global north. To return to Michel-Rolph
Trouillot, the problem is not that this scholarship neglects history but
more specifically that its narratives silence the operation of power through
international law and liberal foreign policy. Violence then looks like the
result of insufficient liberal internationalism, demanding redoubled
efforts to enforce it, rather than often being its predictable consequence.
Those who attend to these pathologies of liberal internationalism do not
thereby abandon the aspiration to a more just global order. Is this chapter then simply a call for a deeper liberal internationalism? The question
is one that TWAIL scholars have wrestled with productively, given their
generally shared hope that international law retains some emancipatory

---

[45] Hathaway and Shapiro 2017, pp. xiii, xxi.
[46] On the profound role of race and racial ideology in the global order see the essays in
Anievas, Manchanda and Shilliam 2015; and Bell 2019.
[47] Peevers 2018, pp. 315, 322.

potential despite being a 'child of imperialism'.[48] A full response is impossible here, but if this line of thinking can be considered an extension of liberal internationalism, it is one that will have to be informed both by histories of the ways in which seemingly emancipatory universalist ideals have been mobilised to justify domination and by the contextual study of particular instantiations of anti-colonial thought and practice.[49]

Conclusion

Indispensable as I hope to have shown post-colonial historical inquiries to be for international politics, we might ask why their influence on these disciplines has been modest. International lawyers' desire to see their enterprise as emancipatory makes it hard for many to come to terms with its complicity in domination; something similar is true for liberal institutionalists in IR such as John Ikenberry, who are determined to see the so-called Western liberal order as founded on principles of reciprocity, cooperation and mutual gain.[50] IR realists, on the other hand, tend not to admit to having normative commitments at all, while smuggling them in under the guise of timeless truths about power and security. More fundamentally, though, the nation-state framework that structures both disciplines and is implicit in the very term international hinders understanding of some of the most important forces in global politics. Du Bois, driven as he was by a desire to understand transnational and non-state phenomena such as the Atlantic slave trade and white supremacy, posed a challenge that these disciplines may be able to take up only by utterly reconceiving their object of study and their own identities.

References

Acharya, A. and B. Buzan. 2019. *The Making of Global International Relations: Origins and Evolution of IR at its Centenary*. Cambridge.

Alexandrowicz, C. H. 2017. *The Law of Nations in Global History*, ed. D. Armitage and J. Pitts. Oxford.

Anghie, A. 2005. *Imperialism, Sovereignty, and the Making of International Law*. Cambridge.

Anghie, A. and B. S. Chimni. 2003. 'Third World Approaches to International Law and Individual Responsibility in Internal Conflicts', *Chinese Journal of International Law*, 2: 1, pp. 77–103.

---

[48] Eslava and Pahuja 2012, p. 211.
[49] See, e.g., Getachew and Mantena 2021; and the essays in Shilliam 2011 and von Bernstorff and Dann 2019.
[50] Deudney and Ikenberry 1999, p. 179.

Anievas, A. 2015. 'Marxist Theory and the Origins of the First World War' in *Cataclysm 1914: The First World War and the Making of Modern World Politics*, ed. A. Anievas. Leiden.

Anievas, A., N. Manchanda and R. Shilliam. 2015. *Race and Racism in International Relations: Confronting the Global Colour Line*. London.

Armitage, D. 2004. 'The Fifty Years' Rift: Intellectual History and International Relations', *Modern Intellectual History*, 1: 1, pp. 97–109.

2013. *Foundations of Modern International Thought*. Cambridge.

Armitage, D. and I. Rasilla. forthcoming. 'The Most Neglected Province: British Historiography of International Law' in *The Cambridge History of International Law*, vol. I: *Introduction*, ed. R. Lesaffer and A. Peters. Cambridge.

Azeem, M. 2019. 'Theoretical Challenges to TWAIL with the Rise of China: Labor Conditions under Chinese Investment in Pakistan', *Oregon Review of International Law*, 20, pp. 395–436.

Becker Lorca, A. 2014. *Mestizo International Law: A Global Intellectual History 1842–1933*. Cambridge.

Bedjaoui, M. 1979. *Towards a New International Economic Order*. New York.

Bell, D. 2001. 'International Relations: The Dawn of a Historiographical Turn', *British Journal of Politics and International Relations*, 3: 1, pp. 115–26.

Bell, D., ed. 2019. *Empire, Race, and Global Justice*. Cambridge.

Benton, L. 2019. 'Beyond Anachronism: Histories of International Law and Global Legal Politics', *Journal of the History of International Law*, 21: 1, pp. 7–40.

Brett, A., M. Donaldson and M. Koskenniemi, eds. 2021. *History, Politics, Law: Thinking through the International*. Cambridge.

Bueno de Mesquita, B. and G. Downs. 2006. 'Intervention and Democracy', *International Organization*, 60: 3, pp. 627–49.

Buzan, B. and R. Little. 2001. 'Why International Relations has Failed as an Intellectual Project and What to Do About it', *Millennium: Journal of International Studies*, 30: 1, pp. 19–39.

Craven, M., M. Fitzmaurice and M. Vogiatzi. 2007. *Time, History and International Law*. Leiden.

Deudney, D. and G. J. Ikenberry. 1999. 'The Nature and Sources of Liberal International Order', *Review of International Studies*, 25: 2, pp. 179–96.

Devetak, R. 2018. *Critical International Theory*. Oxford.

Downs, G. and B. Bueno de Mesquita. 2004. 'Gun-Barrel Diplomacy has Failed Time and Again', *Los Angeles Times*, 4 February.

Du Bois, W. E. B. 1915. 'The African Roots of War', *Atlantic Monthly* (May), pp. 707–14.

1917. 'Of the Culture of White Folk', *Journal of Race Development*, 7: 4, pp. 434–47.

1918. 'Memoranda on the Future of Africa' in *Papers of Woodrow Wilson*, ed. A. Link. Princeton, vol. LIII, pp. 236–8.

2007a. *Color and Democracy* (1945) in *The World and Africa and Color and Democracy*, ed. Henry Louis Gates. Oxford.

2007b [1940]. *Dusk of Dawn: An Essay Toward an Autobiography of a Race Concept*, ed. Henry Louis Gates. Oxford.

2022. *International Writings*, ed. A. Getachew and J. Pitts. Cambridge.

Eslava, L., M. Fakhri and V. Nesiah, eds. 2017. *Bandung, Global History, and International Law: Critical Pasts and Pending Futures*. Cambridge.

Eslava, L. and S. Pahuja. 2012. 'Beyond the (Post)Colonial: TWAIL and the Everyday Life of International Law', *Verfassung und Recht in Übersee/Law and Politics in Africa, Asia, and Latin America*, 45: 2, pp. 195–221.

Fassbender, B. B. and A. Peters, eds. 2012. *The Oxford Handbook of the History of International Law*. Oxford.

Fitzmaurice, A. 2018. 'Context in the History of International Law', *Journal of the History of International Law*, 20: 1, pp. 5–30.

Gathii, J. 2013. 'TWAIL: A Brief History of its Origins, its Decentralized Network, and a Tentative Bibliography' in *International Law and New Approaches to the Third World: Between Repetition and Renewal*, ed. M. Toufayan, E. Toume-Jouannet and H. Ruiz Fabri. Paris.

2021. 'The Promise of International Law: A Third World View (Including a TWAIL Bibliography 1996–2019 as an Appendix' (ASIL Grotius Lecture 2020), *American Society of International Law Annual Meeting Proceedings*, 114, pp. 167–87.

Getachew, A. 2019a. *Worldmaking after Empire: The Rise and Fall of Self-Determination*. Princeton.

2019b. 'The Limits of Sovereignty as Responsibility', *Constellations*, 26, pp. 225–40.

Getachew, A. and K. Mantena. 2021. 'Anticolonialism and the Decolonization of Political Theory', *Critical Times: Interventions in Global Critical Theory*, 4, pp. 359–88.

Getachew, A. and J. Pitts. 2022. 'Democracy and Empire: An Introduction to the International Thought of W. E. B. Du Bois' in W. E. B. Du Bois, *International Writings*, ed. A. Getachew and J. Pitts. Cambridge.

Gruffydd Jones, B. 2013. 'Slavery, Finance and International Political Economy: Postcolonial Reflections' in *Postcolonial Theory and International Relations*, ed. S. Seth. New York.

Guilhot, N. 2011. *The Invention of International Relations Theory: Realism, the Rockefeller Foundation, and the 1954 Conference on Theory*. New York.

Hathaway, O. and S. J. Shapiro. 2017. *The Internationalists: How a Radical Plan to Outlaw War Remade the World*. New York.

Hinsley, F. H. 1963. *Power and the Pursuit of Peace*. Cambridge.

Hobson, J. A. 1902. *Imperialism: A Study*. London.

Hobson, J. M. 2015. 'Re-embedding the Global Colour Line' in *Race and Racism in International Relations*, ed. Alexander Anievas, Nivi Manchanda and Robbie Shilliam. London.

2019. 'What's at Stake in Doing (Critical) IR/IPE Historiography?' in *Historiographical Investigations in International Relations*, ed. B. C. Schmidt and N. Guilhot. Cham.

Hont, I. 1983. 'The Rich Country–Poor Country Debate in Scottish Classical Political Economy' in *Wealth and Virtue: The Shaping of Political Economy in the Scottish Enlightenment*, ed. I. Hont and M. Ignatieff. Cambridge.

Kemmerer, A., M. Koskenniemi and A. Orford. 2015. '"We Do Not Need to Always Look to Westphalia": A Conversation with Martti Koskenniemi and Anne Orford', *Journal of the History of International Law*, 17, pp. 1–14.

Koskenniemi, M. 2002. *The Gentle Civilizer of Nations: The Rise and Fall of International Law, 1870–1960*. Cambridge.

2012. 'A History of International Law Histories' in *The Oxford Handbook of the History of International Law*, ed. B. Fassbender and A. Peters. Oxford.

2014. 'Vitoria and Us: Thoughts on Critical Histories of International Law', *Rechtsgeschichte/Legal History*, 22, pp. 119–38.

Laurent, F. 1851. *Histoire de droit des gens et des relations internationales. Tôme premier: L'Orient*. Paris.

Lenin, N. [*sic*.]. 1917. *Imperialism: The Last Stage of Capitalism*. London.

Lewis, D. L. 2000. *W. E. B. Du Bois: The Fight for Equality and the American Century, 1919–1963*. New York.

Locke, A. L. 1992. *Race Contacts and Interracial Relations*, ed. Jeffrey C. Stewart. Washington, DC.

Mearsheimer, J. 2018. *The Great Delusion: Liberal Dreams and International Realities*. New Haven.

Office of the High Representative. 1994. *Constitution of Bosnia and Herzegovina*, www.ohr.int/laws-of-bih/constitutions-2/.

Orford, A. 2013a. 'On International Legal Method', *London Review of International Law*, 1, pp. 166–97.

2013b. 'The Past as Law or History? The Significance of Imperialism for Modern International Law' in *International Law and New Approaches to the Third World: Between Repetition and Renewal*, ed. M. Toufayan, E. Tourme-Jouannet and E. Ruiz Fabri. Paris.

2017. 'International Law and the Limits of History' in *The Law of International Lawyers: Reading Martti Koskenniemi*, ed. W. Werner, M. de Hoon and A. Galàn. Cambridge.

2021. *International Law and the Politics of History*. Cambridge.

Parfitt, R. 2019. *The Process of International Legal Reproduction: Inequality, Historiography, Resistance*. Cambridge.

Peevers, C. 2018. 'Liberal Internationalism, Radical Transformation, and the Making of World Orders (Review of Hathaway and Shapiro, *The Internationalists*)', *European Journal of International Law*, 29, pp. 303–22.

Reus-Smit, C. 2002. 'The Idea of History and History with Ideas' in *Historical Sociology of International Relations*, ed. Stephen Hobden and John M. Hobson. Cambridge.

Schmidt, B. 1998. *The Political Discourse of Anarchy: A Disciplinary History of International Relations*. Albany.

Scott, D. 2004. *Conscripts of Modernity: The Tragedy of Colonial Enlightenment*. Durham, NC.

Shilliam, R. 2011. *International Relations and Non-Western Thought: Imperialism, Colonialism, and Investigations of Global Moderninty*. London.

Simpson, G. 2021. 'After Method: International Law and the Problems of History' in *History, Politics, Law: Thinking through the International*, ed. A. Brett, M. Donaldson and M. Koskenniemi. Cambridge.

Trouillot, M. R. 2015 [1995]. *Silencing the Past: Power and the Production of History*. Boston.

Tully, J. 2008. *Public Philosophy in a New Key*. 2 vols. Cambridge.

Tzouvala, N. 2019. '"These Ancient Arenas of Racial Struggles": International Law and the Balkans', *European Journal of International Law*, 29: 4, pp. 1149–71.

Vitalis, R. 2015. *White World Order, Black Power Politics: The Birth of American International Relations*. Ithaca, NY.

von Bernstorff, J. and P. Dann. 2019. *The Battle for International Law: South–North Perspectives on the Decolonization Era*. Oxford.

Wedeen, L. 2019. *Authoritarian Apprehensions: Ideology, Judgment, and Mourning in Syria*. Chicago.

Weeramantry, C. 1976. *Equality and Freedom: Some Third World Perspectives*. Colombo.

Wight, M. 1966 [1959]. 'Why is there no International Theory?' in *Diplomatic Investigations: Essays in the Theory of International Politics*, ed. H. Butterfield and M. Wight. London.

    1991. *International Theory: The Three Traditions*, ed. G. Wight and B. Porter. Leicester.

4 International Relations Theory and Modern International Order: The Case of Refugees

Mira Siegelberg

Climate migration is surely one of the central political challenges of the coming decades. As many have rightly cautioned, catastrophising the anticipated scale of global migration risks strengthening far-right political parties that have built their platforms on the threat of mass immigration.[1] Facing up to statistical projections nevertheless holds out the arguably more urgent promise of prompting political solutions that head off the direst predictions. It is estimated, for example, that unless countries commit to immediate measures to curb carbon emissions, roughly 70 million people in search of safer and more habitable living conditions will be on the move in the coming decades. Barring intervention, the projected extent of these movements indicates that the effects of displacement will not be limited to regions directly impacted by the consequences of climate degradation.[2]

In other words, even if national politics ultimately dictates the shape of collective action to limit the human consequences of environmental transformation, comprehending the dynamics that generate mass migration and the wider consequences of the phenomenon depends

For comments on earlier versions of this chapter I am grateful to Richard Bourke and Quentin Skinner, to Jennifer Pitts and Duncan Bell and to the participants in the History in the Humanities and Social Science workshop held at the University of Cambridge in July 2019.

[1] On the political limitations of emphasising the general, global nature of the crisis see McAdam 2012, pp. 4–5. On the broader problem of politics and the future in relation to expectations of climate catastrophe see Forrester and Smith 2018.

[2] See https://features.propublica.org/climate-migration/model-how-climate-refugees-move-across-continents/. The terms 'forced migration' and 'forced displacement' used throughout this chapter encompass the movement of people, including those subject to the degradation of the environment due to climate change, who do not formally meet the criteria for recognition as refugees or stateless persons, the two main groups currently governed by international legal protection regimes. See esp. McAdam 2012 on the limits of current protection criteria. The importance of drawing conceptual and ethical distinctions between different causes of migration has been an important point of analysis in the political philosophy literature. See Kukathas 2016 and Fine and Ypi 2016.

on a form of analysis that seeks to encompass politics at a global scale. Scholars of international relations (IR) have therefore proposed that the theoretical frameworks and concepts available from this field of study can be productively drawn upon to intellectually comprehend the dimensions and implications of global migration. Most prominently, Alexander Betts and Gil Loescher argue that despite the often conflicting frameworks offered by various theories of IR – including realism, neo-realism, liberal institutionalism, analytical liberalism, the English School, constructivism and critical theory – these diverse approaches can be pluralistically drawn upon to provide a critical perspective on forced migration, and to assess how its causes and consequences relate to global politics.[3]

As I will argue in this chapter, evaluating the virtues of this scholarly agenda depends, as a first step, on interrogating the implicit theoretical and historical premises contained in the recent work in IR on forced migration and world politics. A striking feature of the most prominent work in this emerging field is their basic expectation that the mass numbers of people leaving their home countries in search of asylum and security represent a critical arena in which the integrity of national states faces the fundamental challenge of a rapidly shifting global order. According to these works, mass displacement represents an intrinsically transnational phenomenon that confronts a static world of states and international boundaries. This assertion rests therefore on the premise, shared for the most part with the dominant theoretical approaches in IR, that the mass movement of people within and across political borders, along with the rise of legal and institutional mechanisms that transcend states to address such transnational phenomena, have introduced novel questions about how the fundamental contours of the international system are transforming as a result of new dynamic forces.[4] Betts has particularly emphasised the role of refugees – defined in international law as individuals forced to flee their home countries as a result of persecution – in the proposed theoretical literature because their status implies that they have an immediate bearing on matters relating to state sovereignty and inter-state relations.[5] As Betts and Loecher have contended, IR theorists ignore forced migration at their peril since grappling with the phenomenon analytically is vital for updating accounts of global politics. They argue that whereas international politics used to be defined largely by Great Power conflicts, the immediate post-Cold War decades saw a diffusion

---

[3] Betts 2009; see also Betts and Loescher 2011.
[4] Betts and Loescher 2011; Betts 2009, p. 15.
[5] Betts 2009, p. 6.

of threats involving non-state actors and sources of conflict challenging the traditional ideal of bounded territorial sovereignty.[6]

The question taken up in this chapter, however, is how forced migration, broadly construed, came to be written out of the study of international politics in the first place. This development, I will argue, contributed to a fundamentally static vision of international order and has a significant bearing on the idea that IR possesses unique intellectual and conceptual resources to grapple with the challenges introduced by climate migration. In evaluating the larger proposal to draw on the resources of IR to comprehend forced migration generally, and the impact of climate migration in particular, the further question to consider, however, is what a revised historical account of international order implies for the proposal that theories of IR can illuminate present dynamics, particularly in relation to forced migration and global politics. The second task, then, will be to explore the emergence of a common enterprise among a subset of IR scholars and historians to historicise the dominant representations of international politics. As we shall see, a subset of scholars in IR have joined historians in privileging the study of the processes by which global order came to be what it is, and share a common conviction that knowledge of contemporary global order depends on how we understand how such an order originally emerged. The final matter to consider, then, is whether this common objective has merely deferred a more substantial reckoning between history and IR theory, which the challenge of grappling analytically with the causes and implications of climate migration acutely brings to light.

Much of the scholarly literature on refugees and international politics from recent decades has presented the plight of the displaced as a puzzling contradiction in the light of globalisation and the proliferation of non-state legal and moral orders in the later twentieth century. As the supremacy of 'Westphalian sovereignty' appeared to many observers to decline at the end of the twentieth century, theorists explored the puzzling tension between the expansion of rights beyond the state and the real condition of the politically homeless. The puzzle has been further reinforced by prominent interpretations of the emergence in the twentieth century of international legal regimes that established the terms of national responsibility towards anyone designated a refugee or a stateless person. According to the still-dominant view articulated by much of this literature, traditional conceptions of sovereignty inherited from the seventeenth century were only challenged in the wake of the Second

---

[6] Betts and Loescher 2011; Betts 2009, p. 15.

World War, when the individual was established as the nascent subject of international law. For example, in their study of refugees and IR theory, Betts and Loescher assume that the major shift in international law has been the move from a focus on the relationship between states to that between states and individuals, and that the rise of international human rights law and international refugee law signals a shift in the balance of power between state sovereignty and human rights. A critical premise of their study is that the founding of an international regime of refugee identification and protection after the Second World War demonstrates wide acknowledgement of how the 'significant and unprecedented human consequences of the Second World War and establishing a refugee regime was seen as a way of promoting values of human rights within the context of the emerging United Nations system. A refugee regime, it was believed, would ensure that all states made a collective contribution to overcoming what was a common humanitarian and political problem.'[7] Evidence of the contemporary deprivations experienced by those who lack the protection of their government therefore presents, at least according to this literature, a fundamental contradiction in the light of expectations about the emergence of an increasingly morally and legally unified world order.[8]

The approach to linking forced migration with the study of global politics proposed by these studies is thus intimately bound up with a particular reading of the past. However, though one particular historical narrative about the origins of the international refugee regime figures prominently in Betts and Loescher's account, they nevertheless grant the history of international refugee protection limited explanatory force in relation to the larger goal of analytically grasping contemporary forced migration and its relation to IR. They contend, in fact, that most studies of refugees in world politics have been excessively historical in their focus on reconstructing the archival record of how refugees became the object of international politics and have not drawn on the concepts offered by IR. Historical research on this subject, though important and necessary, provides the static backdrop against which IR can offer its conceptual interventions. While the literature on IR and forced migration argues that the displaced register the shifting dynamics of global order, this analysis

---

[7] Betts and Loescher 2011, p. 8.
[8] Betts 2009, p. 47. As Andrew Hurrell argues in his contribution to Betts and Loescher 2011, by the late twentieth century there was a dramatic increase in the scope and density of international rules. Yet 'when it comes to refugees, we remain closer to a pluralist world of Westphalian sovereignty, even at the level of proclaimed normative ambition. There has been little erosion of the state's political or legal authority to control borders and to exclude': Hurrell 2011, p. 93.

depends on a similar presumption about the fixed constancy of the political boundaries that have long defined the sphere of international politics. People on the move confront the stationary borders of countries of exit and entry, potentially destabilising given societies and social orders.[9]

In their fundamental assumptions about social and political closure as the presupposition of their scholarship rather than its object, these works in IR theory share a common basis with the post-war social sciences. As William Sewell has argued, the idea of the 'social' that lies at the base of the social sciences implicitly identifies society with the bounded nation-state and assumes 'that the social units and individuals that make up the society are themselves bounded units that are assembled into a structured whole'. Viewed collectively, post-war social science tended to assume the natural inevitability of the boundedness of groups and societies rather than treating evident boundaries as the object of investigation. More significantly for the purposes of this chapter, Sewell further contends that the theory of the social that underlies the post-war social science 'privileges stasis over process, implying that historical change, when it occurs, must be a consequence of conflicts or contradictions between already constituted groups, rather than an ever present process out of which groups are themselves precipitated, reshaped or dissolved'.[10] Intellectual historians of the human sciences have largely focused their attentions on the conceptions of 'science' developed by the various fields of the social sciences; however, as Sewell suggests here the notion of the social likewise demands deeper historical investigation.[11]

The history of the status of refugees in international politics in turn bears out Sewell's observation that the consolidation of the human sciences in the post-Second World War university tended to affirm the presumption of already existing closed societies, at a moment when the changing boundaries of international political order were bound up with forced migration. An intellectual and legal history of the legal frameworks that define what it now means to be a refugee or a stateless person, and the underlying turn to the social that underwrote the classifications, in turn reveals the connection between the history of the codification of the legal categories and the social closure enacted by the social sciences, as well as IR theory, in the same period. The question, then, is what the history of the legal frameworks reveals about the establishment of the political and legal boundaries of modern international order, and why understanding the meaning of these legal instruments is so important for

---

[9] Haddad 2009.
[10] Sewell 2005, p. 329.
[11] Isaac 2012; Moyn 2015.

the prospect of grasping forced migration as a critical feature of global politics.

The international regimes that regulate the lives of people who fall outside the protection of states developed in the context of global warfare and crisis precipitated by millions of people without a political home in the twentieth century. Vast numbers of people excluded from the protection of national governments after the First World War entered legal and political consciousness in a way that extended previous intellectual investigations of the nature of statehood and sovereignty – who are the actors or agents on the stage of international politics? When people without the formal protection of governments became the object of international politics at a novel scale in the years following the First World War, the boundaries and expectations of international order were being worked out in a variety of ways – conceptually, institutionally and militarily. At a time when the map of the world remained vigorously contested, the problem of statelessness – broadly defined to include those who would later be legally designated as 'refugees' – became bound up in international thought with debates about the foundations of political order.[12]

When we trace the history of the concept of statelessness from the moment when it became a recognised feature of the international and legal landscape, the post-Second World War international legal framework looks quite different from a more familiar narrative about the rise of transnational law and the legal revolution of human rights after 1945. As we shall see in more detail in a moment, more fundamental debates about the significance of mass displacement for international politics that crystallised following the First World War were eventually neutralised in and through the post-Second World War legal frameworks – bracketing an intrinsically collective phenomenon that had previously been understood to be bound together with the foundations of political order and the problem of how states and their boundaries are established in the first place. The history of modern international refugee identification and protection is therefore not simply an example of how international society has sought to transcend the limits of sovereignty to protect those who have lost the basic protection of their country. Understanding the conflicts that went into the making of categories of non-citizenship reveals one crucial part of the ideological legitimisation of states as the ultimate source of rights and how exactly the international constituted the boundaries of the national in the twentieth century.

---

[12] Siegelberg 2020.

It was in the sphere of international politics that a global settlement was achieved that marginalised statelessness as a critical problem for world order. The fundamental assumption underpinning the 1951 convention is that refugees 'already possess birthright citizenship – that is, they are not stateless'. The 1954 Convention on Statelessness in turn defines what it means to be stateless in fairly narrow terms: anyone who is 'not considered as a national by any state under the operation of its law'. The history of post-war category formation reveals the realpolitik calculations that went into the framing of the refugee convention and the separation of the refugee from the stateless person. In the post-war United Nations the original goal was to elaborate legal protections for both refugees and the stateless, and both were figured as part of the same conceptual equation and twin challenges for post-war order.[13] However, the US government supported the recommendation to designate the problem of people without a nationality as a separate legal phenomenon, and to instruct the UN's International Law Commission to draft a separate international convention designed to eliminate or reduce statelessness by working on resolving contradictory naturalisation legislation around the world. The convention, as the USA set out, would maintain the special interest of the UN in the field of refugees, and 'protect the position of the United States in insisting on a defined definition of refugees by not throwing it open to stateless people generally'. Stateless people who were not refugees would be covered by a separate agreement not tied to the UN's refugee machinery.[14]

The matter extended beyond the interest of certain governments to minimise future responsibility to legally designated groups. The separation of the stateless from refugees was a crucial part of the effort to stabilise the post-war international order by minimising the more fundamental issues provoked by the category of statelessness in international thought. The separation of the concept of the refugee from that of the stateless person was conditioned by the fact that statelessness relates to the state's sovereign power over membership and to the dynamism of state formation. The category of the refugee, and the idea of asylum, affirmed the efficacy of national communities with certain ethical or

---

[13] Patrick Murphy Malin argued that of the 2 million refugees and displaced persons, relatively few were legally 'stateless', but all effectively lacked legal and political protection, especially consular and diplomatic protection: Malin 1947. A different study from the previous year drew attention to the technical difference between refugees and the stateless but emphasised statelessness as an expansive category that should encompass both those without a formal connection to any state and those refugees who did not wish to return home: Carey 1946.

[14] United Nations 1950.

political obligations to the international community. It is of course true that the refugee regime after the Second World War compelled states to qualify their sovereign authority and created a specific regime of rights for refugees and allowed individuals to claim asylum.[15] The principle of *non-refoulement*, or the prohibition against expulsion or return, also became part of international law in the convention relating to the status of refugees in 1951. However, set in the context of the re-establishment of European states after the war, as well as the decolonisation of European empires, the regime of refugee protection strengthened international cooperation among agencies and relief workers and provided an argument for rebuilding strong states that could care for refugees.[16] The intended function of the regime, therefore, was not to mitigate or challenge the power of states to exert control over their membership, as much of the literature on refugees has supposed.

To fully comprehend, however, the stabilisation of the boundaries of international order, it is necessary to appreciate the intellectual justifications that authorised this separation, which are in turn only intelligible in light of the longer intellectual history of the problem of statelessness in international thought. Whereas the problem of statelessness in inter-war political thought was conceptually linked to the structure of international legal order due to the anomalous status of persons without a nationality, post-war debate emphasised more substantive moral considerations about the deprivation of statelessness and generally marginalised the virtues of the formal link between individuals and governments. The realist revolution in transatlantic intellectual history, which turned against formalist and abstract approaches to law and politics, in turn contextualises and clarifies the shift in how the problem of statelessness was conceptualised from the inter-war to the post-war era. Within the confines of the UN in the early 1950s, where legal scholars, international civil servants and representatives from member nations discussed the creation of an international agreement to outline the obligations of signatory states, the loss of nationality as a formal status was described as illegible and indeterminate from a moral perspective. Though these deliberations led to the international conventions that define what it means to be stateless in international law, the distinctions developed after the Second World War to define the stateless, to separate the concept from that of the refugee, were shaped by the emphasis placed on the substance of citizenship – and on the social and psychological experience of being a

---

[15] Barkan and Adelman 2011.
[16] Ballinger 2013.

stateless person – rather than on the protection afforded by bearing a formal legal connection to a state.

In line, therefore, with Sewell's observation about the foundation of the post-war social sciences, international thought and international law adopted the same expectations about the social closure implied by the boundaries of national states precisely at a moment when the legal boundaries of states and their citizens remained in a state of flux and political contestation. The turn from more formal to substantive sources of reasoning about the nature of the problem marked a turn in international thought and international law towards conceptualising national membership in social rather than formal legal terms. The arguments that justified the presumption that the boundaries of membership should be compatible with sociological and historical reality in turn contributed to the naturalisation of the boundaries of international legal order and international politics. Rather than focusing on the implications of statelessness for international legal order, the question posed in international courts, and within the UN, was how to understand the experience of statelessness, and why the loss of nationality represented a deprivation in moral terms. The emphasis on the social experience of citizenship and the loss of citizenship threatened to obscure the larger political significance of the loss of nationality in the global contexts of the mid-1950s. As post-colonial governments formed out of empires, the appeal to social reality in international settings, and the idea that citizenship should conform to a more fundamental social experience of belonging to a particular national political community, further facilitated the consolidation of national boundaries and the exclusiveness of national membership.[17]

The international legal frameworks established after the Second World War thus contributed to the expectation that global political order consists of a largely stable set of entities, covering over the dynamic process of state formation that rendered the creation of non-citizens and forced migrants a significant feature of international politics. Rather than comprehending the international system as a sphere defined by change and evolution as new states formed out of prior imperial polities, it was codified in international legal terms as static and unchanging. The conceptual formation of the category of the refugee, set in contrast to that of the stateless person, was therefore a crucial dimension of the marginalisation of non-citizens – including forced migrants – in international thought and explains how the boundaries of a world of states could be conceptualised by IR theorists as essentially static and unchanging for the purposes of theorising international politics.

[17] Siegelberg 2020.

The history of the formation of the central legal frameworks nevertheless supports the argument that the study of forced migration is vital for the study of global political order. As Betts argues, 'the causes, consequences, responses to refugees are all closely intertwined with world politics'.[18] However, without an understanding of how the study of international politics has, until recently, evaded this fact, theorists of IR will find it difficult to provide persuasive accounts of the contemporary implications of forced migration for global politics. Reconstructing how present arrangements emerged clarifies not just the contingency of present conditions, but also the relationship between ideological intentions and function – how, for instance, the separation of refugees from stateless persons neutralised the destabilising problem of how governments determine membership in the first place in the context of dynamic state formation. The history of international order in relation to refugees indicates that robust inquiry is not merely a matter of evaluating the efficacy of the existing frameworks for current problems. It is also a matter of reconnecting more fundamental political questions to the crisis of displacement and climate migration – the nature of borders and boundaries, the determination of national membership and the normative foundations of statehood. One can certainly argue about the relationship between the origins of concepts or legal categories and the work they do in the present – in other words, whether their application ever escapes their origins. It is nevertheless undoubtedly problematic to apply theories of IR to make sense of modern migration (forced or otherwise), and the existing legal and political frameworks that regulate it, without an understanding of how the institutions and conceptual and legal categories used to analyse it contributed to the making of the world that we have inherited. It is of course possible to err by mistaking historical function for contemporary function, but equally an understanding of the formation of the legal frameworks indicates what one might be missing in assessing present institutional arrangements without such knowledge. Failing to account for the origins of the modern regimes of international refugee identification and protection risks the depoliticisation of the question of how boundaries – including the conceptual boundary between the international and the national – were determined in the first place, which has a direct bearing on our understanding of the politics of forced migration. Legal and policy experts who are now assessing whether existing international legal frameworks and institutions will be able to accommodate the scale of migration and displacement ought to appreciate the successful bracketing of forced migration from international politics through

---

[18] Betts 2014, p. 60.

the creation of the post-war legal regimes that regulate the lives of non-citizens. By the same logic, IR theorists who wish to draw on the conceptual resources of the discipline will have to, at the very least, consider the limits of the historical narratives that implicitly structure their approach to the study of forced migration and global politics.

Beyond the particular limitations of the implicit historical narratives deployed by IR theorists of forced migration, the further issue to contend with is whether the ambition to apply IR theory to the global politics of migration stands in inevitable tension with the historicist goals established by a subset of the discipline since IR's historical, post-positivist, turn in recent years. In order to pursue this broader question, it is necessary to first establish the particular terms upon which a common terrain of historicist investigation about the constitution of modern international order has been established. When historical approaches resurfaced in IR (or at least expanded beyond the narrow spheres in which it had been quarantined since mid-century) towards the end of the twentieth century, it was in response to the particular challenge that the end of the Cold War, the onset of what was being called globalisation and the erosion of sovereignty, seemed to pose for how international politics had been represented. At that point, those who argued for better critical accounts of the constituent elements of international politics became not just allies in the epistemological battle between positivism and interpretivism, insisting on the relevance of comprehending meaningful human conduct, but also comrades in a broader revisionist project that encompassed historians of political thought, political theorists and international historians.[19] Together, these allies have argued that before anything can be said about the distinctiveness of the domain of international politics from a more theoretical standpoint, the origins of how the international has been represented and the concepts that have defined this arena such as the state, the state system, international law and, as David Armitage has argued, the basic distinction between the domestic and the international all have to be explored.[20] For these scholars, comprehending the domain of IR is inseparable from studying the historical development of the actors, institutions, strategic and normative principles and practices that came to define this sphere.[21] It is necessary, in other words, to

---

[19] Isaac 2012; Skinner 1985.
[20] Armitage 2013; Armitage 2015.
[21] Bukovansky, Keene, Reus-Smit and Spanu forthcoming; Teschke 2003; Bially and Zarakol 2016; Buzan 2004; Buzan and Lawson 2014; Buzan and Lawson 2015; Hobson 2012; Keene 2002; Phillips and Sharman 2015; Bain and Nardin 2017; Armitage 2014; Brett, Donaldson and Koskenniemi 2021.

begin by paying far more attention to how the entities that we associate with global or international politics were produced than to developing theories to characterise the relations among the constituent entities that result from the processes described.[22]

Viewed collectively, the common enterprise to revisit the orthodox representations of international politics, and to understand the role such representations have played in the constitution of modern international order, has prioritised responding to claims about globalisation and the erosion of sovereignty by historicising the terms that such claims have depended upon. Based on the concern that the dominant narrative about the end of the state and sovereignty obscures real present dynamics, one of the larger stakes of this project is the development of a capacity to correctly identify the patterns of political relations that characterise the contemporary world.[23] The revisionist accounts in turn broadly address three critical aspects of the orthodox theories of international politics: the relationship between state and non-state political order; the status of the 1648 Treaty of Westphalia in the formation of the domination dynamics of international relations; and the normative implications of a world of juridically sovereign and equal states.

To clarify the implications of this revisionist scholarship for the study of global politics, we must turn briefly to the theoretical premises that defined the formation of IR as a discipline. In a famed 1966 essay, Martin Wight defined 'international theory' as 'the tradition of speculation about relations between States, a tradition imagined as the twin of speculation about the State to which the name "political theory" is appropriated'. Wight emphasised, 'since the sixteenth century, international society has been so organized that no individuals except sovereign princes can be members of it, and these only in their representative capacity'.[24] Looked at through this particular lens, Wight concluded that it was difficult to find any evidence of such systematic reflection in the history of political thought. Was there any international theory before the First World War, when American philanthropists began spending vast sums of money to establish institutes for the study of peace and war? If it was to be found anywhere, Wight argued, it was in the field of international law and the speculations of international lawyers, as well as other sources including the writings of statesmen and diplomats.[25] Even before the positivist

---

[22] Berman 2019. On a post-structuralist approach to the study of how actors, entities and things are constructed see Walker 1992.

[23] On the philosophical value and validity of the genealogical study of concepts and of how the world has been represented see Srinivasan 2019.

[24] Wight 1966, p. 38.

[25] Wight 1966.

assumption that states are unitary actors with interests that are universal across time took hold in IR, mid-century theorists of IR had posited a basic opposition between ordered societies and disordered ones, and insisted that the nature of order depends on the possession of a monopoly of force. As a case in point, in a discussion of IR theory, Raymond Aron articulated the presumption that even if one begins with a premise about the essentially historical nature of international politics, any analysis of IR must begin with a sense of what differentiates relationships among politically organised communities from other social relationships, and he argued, echoing Max Weber, that the use of legitimate force is the defining trait.[26] Hedley Bull, the figure most identified with the English School of International Relations and its emphasis on the significant role played by norms, rules and institutions in international life, offered a similar line of demarcation in his major work, *The Anarchical Society*. Bull defined his subject in such a way as to prioritise independent political communities and to exclude 'entities that fall outside the purview of international relations' such as 'Germanic political communities of the Dark Ages in which rulers asserted supremacy over a population rather than a territory'; 'the kingdoms and principalities of western Christendom in the Middle Ages but not independent relative to the Pope or Holy Roman Emperor'; and 'parts of Africa and Oceania before the European intrusion, where independent political communities were held together by ties of kinship but there was no institution of government'.[27]

Against the presumption about the nature of political order articulated by this earlier generation, the historical turn in IR, especially among the descendants of the English School, has facilitated the rediscovery of earlier international (or inter-polity) thought which shows the variety of ways in which political order has been conceptualised and practised, and the consequent recentness of the world of states. This interpretive intervention resonates with the works of historians of international political thought who have argued for revisiting the texts that Wight referred to in his essay on the absence of international theory as 'scattered' and 'unsystematic', such as the Abbé de St Pierre on perpetual peace, or Hume on the balance of power. Shorn of the assumptions expressed by Wight, Aron and Bull about ordered as opposed to disordered societies, these texts reveal not the intellectual poverty that Wight diagnosed, but the disclosure of observations of inter-political and inter-imperial political order that became alien as disciplinary presumptions about a

---

[26] Aron 1967.
[27] Bull 1977, 8–9.

static world of states took hold. The second-generation English School theorists, though equally concerned with the principles that underwrite international orders, have likewise sought to expose how the generalisations and frameworks deployed by the English School theorists to comprehend international society, their focus on peace and war and on the move from systemic interaction to order, made it harder to grasp how hierarchies are introduced and sustained because their focus was on conflicts tearing society apart and was based on a limiting assumption about the nature of political order and international relations.[28] This argument has been further developed by the historian of political thought Jennifer Pitts, who has challenged scholars to consider the kind of historical work that can correct the failure to recognise hierarchy and to grasp patterns of domination in the sphere of the international. According to Pitts, IR has, until its recent historicist turn, rested on the myth that national states are the central agents of international politics and obscured the historical role of international law in the enforcement of coercive global hierarchies. As a corrective, international theory should return to an earlier appreciation of the role of race and empire in the formation of global order, which characterised work on international order by W. E. B. Du Bois and the Howard School of International Relations.[29]

By questioning the presumption about the nature of political and legal order, and the discovery of inter-political orders that do not conform to Wight's basic assumption, these authors thus pose a fundamental challenge to the narrative about how the end of the Cold War initiated new international political dynamics.[30] Historical accounts that have revised understandings of the Treaty of Westphalia, for example, and the idea and practice of sovereignty in the context of early modern imperial competition, have had profound implications for interpreting the post-Cold War world, especially narratives about globalisation, and a world of sovereign states giving way to a world unified morally and politically. The significance and status of various forms of non-state legal and political order depends on how one understands the trajectory of global politics. The identification of international order as 'post-Westphalian' has traditionally implied that economic globalisation has undermined the capacity of national states to control their economic destinies and that international institutions and human rights law since 1945 have set normative constraints on the exercise of sovereignty. However, an understanding of the 'Janus-faced' quality of the early modern state provides a different

[28] Keene 2002.
[29] See Pitts in this volume (Chapter 3); Pitts 2018; Parfitt 2019.
[30] Benton 2009.

perspective on the relationship between the proliferation of sovereignty and the emergence of what has been termed 'globalisation'. There is a meaningful conceptual difference, for example, between claiming that a Westphalian world has given way to one where a much larger range of agents impact global politics and questioning the historical validity of this representation in the first place.[31]

Historical accounts of the relationship between sovereignty and territoriality similarly undermine expectations about the erosion of state power in the late twentieth century. The typologies developed in Lauren Benton's *A Search for Sovereignty*, for example, designate ways of identifying the de-territorialised, non-national legal and economic orders that structure and discipline the globe and developed alongside the consolidation of the post-Second World War national state. In this work, Benton explores the implicit forms of ordering that sustained European empires as a global imperial system. Understanding the political and geographical imagination of European empire in turn illuminates the coexistence of territorial and non-territorial regimes of law and global governance in the twentieth and twenty-first centuries. By removing the blinkers of orthodox theories of sovereign power, Benton seeks to illuminate a world of alternative understandings of the rule of law and the nature of legitimacy in the age of European imperial expansion. One critical implication of this approach is the insight that uneven global spaces are continually produced; they are not just temporally and developmentally prior to territorial domination, and their history suggests that it is therefore a category error to speak of the erosion of sovereignty, as so many did in the decade after the Cold War.[32] The claim that control over territoriality matters less politically than it used to provides a very different perspective on contemporary global order than the argument that territorial and extra-territorial regimes have long coexisted and been mutually reinforcing.[33]

Besides the capacity to correctly identify the patterns of the present, there are normative implications to such reinterpretations of the representations of international politics. The effect of challenging the narrative that state sovereignty is eroding in the face of globalisation and neo-liberalism, the just-so story that builds on the idea that the most important development of the last millennium has been the sovereign state's triumph in Europe and its subsequent worldwide diffusion, reveals the model of the territorial sovereign state as one normative ideal for

---

[31] Armitage 2007; Christov 2015.
[32] On the origins of this approach in World-Systems Theory see Benton 1996.
[33] Ogle 2017. Compare Maier 2016.

political organisation that emerged in competition with other possibilities for global legal and political order.[34] The recovery not only of the formation of the units of international politics, and of the previously misunderstood significance of entities that had been written out of the story, but also of the more diverse and contested ways of conceptualising the inside and outside of political order, can also be portrayed as resources for grasping the contingency of present conditions and the possibility of evolving past them.[35] For example, for the historian Frederick Cooper, acknowledging the limits of the global citizenship revolution in the twentieth century, and recovering the forgotten histories of federalist post-imperial alternatives to national citizenship, introduces the possibility of envisioning new ways of organising humanity politically. According to Cooper, an emancipatory, more progressive collective future depends on appreciating that present conditions were not inevitable and that alternatives were foreclosed along the way.[36]

To return to my original question, then, how exactly does the cross-disciplinary project to revise the dominant representations of international politics challenge the proposal that theories of IR should be brought to bear to comprehend the nature of the coming migration crisis and its implications for world politics? As I have tried to suggest, the idea of a world of states that is in the process of being overcome by a different form of global order becomes a less secure ground from which to conceptualise modern political dynamics. Moreover, the shortened horizon for the history of a world of formally equal sovereign states as the norm of global political organisation changes the conceptual stakes for how to understand the rise of the displaced as a mass phenomenon, and the role of the distinct international legal categories defining non-citizenship in its formation and legitimisation. The collective project surveyed schematically here also calls attention to how the study of contemporary patterns of migration and displacement, as well as vulnerability to the effects of climate change, are inseparable from an understanding of the formation of global order with its current unevenness and inequality.[37]

---

[34] Explorations of the genealogical origins of IR theory, and in particular of realism, have been a critical dimension of the project to historicise the dominant representations of international politics. See Schmidt 1998. The foundations of the discipline naturalised and obscured the contingency of arrangements and contestations, as well as the fact that the study of IR had been a field based on the study of race and race relations. See Guilhot 2017; Vitalis 2015; Morefield 2020.

[35] Getachew 2018.

[36] Cooper 2018. For a critique of claims about the contingency of the mid-century national state see Moyn 2015. For a different critique of allowing present values to drive historical analysis see Bourke 2021.

[37] Achiumi 2019; Thomas 2016.

In considering the nature of the challenge set out by Betts and Loescher, it is nevertheless necessary to appreciate the particular terms upon which a common terrain of historicist investigation about the constitution of modern international order has been established.[38] Leaving aside shared criticisms of positivist approaches to comprehending international politics – approaches that may for example seek to extrapolate from historical particulars to develop general rules about topics such as ethnic power sharing, or civil war – what if anything distinguishes historicist, post-positivist, IR scholars from historians concerned with the history of international order? One suggestion is that the term 'modern international thought' encompasses the efforts of historians of political thought and historical approaches in IR theory.[39] Looked at from this perspective, there is no meaningful distinction between nominally distinct disciplines once both groups are engaged in the same general project; scholars are part of the same spectrum of empiricism, nominalism, those who are by habit more resistant to general, explanatory categories, even ones whose historical provenance is clearly mapped out, and those who argue that it is ridiculous to deny that concepts are necessary tools.

Yet the common endeavour to historicise dominant representations of international politics conceals division rooted in distinct disciplinary habits and practices. On closer inspection of the more recent literature on historical international relations, we find that different disciplinary habits inform whether scholars are comfortable with the use of broad categorisations to elucidate historical particulars.[40] Set in broad, abstract terms, a consideration of the relationship between IR and history necessarily introduces debates central to the philosophy of the social sciences with earlier precedents in the history of thought – questions such as, how are we to compare singularities with one another, if we do not see particulars as standing in relation? If we remove the disciplinary lens then we are left with more fundamental questions about selection and interpretation, choices that may more often come down to habits of mind rather than predetermined epistemological conviction. Historicist IR scholars who advocate viewing IR as a historical social science argue that it is necessary to establish a general ground from which to generalise international political dynamics. For example, does a nineteenth-century 'global transformation' provide a powerful causal framework to explain distinct phenomena?[41] The IR scholar Christian Reus-Smit has recently

---

[38] Gofas, Hamati-Ataya and Onuf 2018.
[39] Hutchings 2014.
[40] Bell forthcoming; Lawson 2018.
[41] Buzan 2015; Keene 2014.

argued for a fundamental overlap between contextualist approaches to the history of political thought and the 'constructivists' who followed the post-positivist interpretive turn in their approach to the study of international politics. As he points out, however, IR theorists tend towards comparative case studies and macro-histories that rely on ontological claims about the similarities underlying temporally disparate events.[42] When, in other words, is the historical imagination susceptible to transhistorical comparison, and how can such comparisons be justified methodologically? IR theorists have likewise challenged historians to be more explicit about their selection criteria and to more clearly thematise the actors and institutions that populate their narratives. They ask historians to be more reflective and explicit about the theoretical assumptions guiding historical research – a demand that runs against the narrative ambitions of a great deal of historical writing.[43]

By contrast, more radically historicist scholars directly avoid analysis of what Mark Bevir has called the 'aggregate concepts in the social sciences ... that point to an essence (including principles) that define the boundaries or development of relevant entities'. The result is, as Bevir describes, 'that radical historicism sometimes may seem opposed to all aggregate concepts and explanations'.[44] A more nominalist sensibility has implications for any generalisable claims, for instance about the role of international institutions in world politics and for the use of concepts as heuristic tools for organising research. For instance, Susan Pedersen's *The Guardians* establishes a persuasive case through thorough archival investigation that the institutional dynamic created by the existence of the League of Nations belies both IR realist and institutionalist claims about the role of international organisations in world politics. *The Guardians* suggests that the history of the League's oversight of the Mandate system cannot generate abstract insights about internationalism, international law, institutionalism or expertise, and that world history is not the stage on which theoretical insights about politics play out. Pedersen argues that the workings of the system have to be discovered through careful research, and that the results are not reproducible across time. Her research seeks to explain how the modern world of juridically sovereign, formally equal, states and actual economic hierarchy, inequality and domination was produced in the first place. In a truly nominalist

---

[42] Reus-Smit 2008. The question of whether studies that develop 'macro-histories' can explain causality is the subject of recent dispute over the explanatory power of the field of global history. See Drayton and Motadel 2018.
[43] Bukovansky, Keene, Reus-Smit and Spanu forthcoming.
[44] Bevir 2015, p. 230.

and historicist spirit, *The Guardians* implies that the critical resources to evaluate normative statehood derive from an understanding of the particular history of its formation.[45]

In terms of the historical analysis of the emergence of normative statehood, such nominalism nevertheless invites further questions about whether it is necessary to develop some form of heuristic distinction between empire and non-hierarchical forms of political order in order to obtain a critical perspective on the relationship between rulers and the ruled, and between imperial and non-imperial forms of governance.[46] Resistance to theory risks appearing like an evasion of the inevitable selection criteria deployed by historians. As Paul Veyne points out in his study of Foucault's hermeneutic method, it is possible to begin with a concept, or an ideal type, in order to then make variation explicit and visible or to make sense of past human conduct.[47] It is also difficult to deny that IR theory has provided the heuristic categories that set the agenda for a great deal of revisionist historical analysis of international and global order, even if historical analysis was then employed to qualify or challenge the categories and assumptions upon which the conclusions of IR rest. It is clear how historical analysis assists other fields to denaturalise, to appreciate that which is contingent and to identify and explain change over time. Less clear is how historians ground the use of concepts and analytic frameworks supplied by even the more methodologically historical IR scholarship.

Set in general epistemological terms, this characterisation of the different disciplinary habits that define each domain of inquiry does not meaningfully distinguish IR from the general contrast between social scientists and historians, who are not generally compelled to make their mental models explicit. It is helpful, therefore, at this point to consider how an earlier generation described the relationship between historical inquiry and IR theory. At the May 1954 Conference on International Politics hosted by the Rockefeller Foundation, in which IR theory was established as a distinct disciplinary project, we find a range of perspectives on the significance of history or historical inquiry for IR theory.[48] It is clear from these discussions that, prior to IR's historical, post-positivist turn after the Cold War, a more clear-cut division of labour between historical

---

[45] Pedersen 2015.

[46] Cooper 2005.

[47] Veyne 2012. See also Skinner 1997; Kleinberg, Scott and Wilder 2020.

[48] As historians of the discipline have recounted, history has always been central to the discipline of IR, though history and IR theory, particularly in the United States, began to part ways in favour of positivist approaches that could produce law-like generalisations in mid-century. See Armitage 2004; Bell 2001.

investigation and theorists of IR could be envisioned. At the conference, all of the participants stressed the role of the theorist in assisting practitioners in finding the right balance between knowledge of the constants of international politics and awareness of the contingent factors in history. Some participants such as Reinhold Niebuhr argued that knowledge of the very historical conditions of our selves and what we know constitutes the wisdom of historical understanding, which compels practitioners to confront the moral nature of the choices they face. Theorists assist practitioners to learn to 'play by ear' by developing the wisdom to become 'aware of the constants over against the unique events of the historical scene' – or to formulate the touchstones that enable the assembly of relevant facts.[49] According to Hans Morgenthau, another participant at the meeting, the theorists identify that which is uniform and typical and detect the general laws that animate the discrete facts of experience. Historians of IR organise their narrative according to an invisible theory (a 'skeleton', in his words), using narrative to demonstrate the theory. The theorist, meanwhile, renders the theory explicit, drawing on historical facts piecemeal to demonstrate the theory. Theorists then guide the statesman to see the particular issues that he confronts as 'special cases of general – that is theoretical – propositions'.[50]

A similar perspective on the division of labour between the work of the IR theorist and that of the historian animates the writings of the American diplomatic historian Paul Schroeder. Drawing on terms familiar from military and diplomatic history, Schroeder described a fruitful alliance between the fields, premised on the distinctive expertise supplied by each domain of knowledge. As Schroeder writes:

Historians can learn a lot from IR theory – it helps them avoid naïve empiricism, offers a wide variety of explanatory models and paradigms, compels them to think through their own methodological and epistemological presuppositions more carefully, helps them see repetitive patterns and analogies where they might otherwise have seen only unique particular circumstances and assists them in reaching broader and more convincing synoptic judgments.[51]

While historians are inclined to emphasise the discrete and distinctive, theory encourages them to identify meaningful repetitions and disparate moments that rhyme. In his most celebrated work on the significance of the Congress of Vienna for the history of international order, Schroeder demonstrated how careful historical analysis could challenge the generalisations of IR realism by showing how the transformation

---

[49] Niebuhr 2011 [1954], p. 241.
[50] Morgenthau 2011 [1954], p. 264.
[51] Schroeder 1997, p. 70

from a European inter-state order undermined claims about the enduring nature of balance-of-power politics. He argued that the interpretive study of international history contradicts the realist claim that international politics is best described as a competitive, conflictual game – the idea that the players change, the weapons change, but not the nature and purpose of the game itself. Instead, Schroeder drew inspiration from the English School theorists of IR, who argued that shared, historically grounded understandings of concepts such as war, or sovereignty, shape what the nature of the game is, how it is to be played and how it has changed or evolved. Schroeder's collection of essays on 'systems, stability, and statecraft' suggests that in so far as historical analysis yields transcendent wisdom, or eternal claims about politics, it is that choice matters and that order has been difficult to achieve, but beyond that there are no eternal truths about IR.[52]

Even with this profound historicism, however, Schroeder also articulated a supposition about the virtues of a general intellectual division of labour between theorists of IR and the work of diplomatic or international historians such as himself. Theorists produce the models that characterise how states interact, while historians can draw on these models to develop more richly textured accounts of systems of states, their dynamics and how such systems change over time. As he wrote in his more methodologically reflective essays, 'the main relationship between the two fields, however, should be an alliance, specifically conceived not primarily as a means of capability aggregation and joint security, but as a general instrument of restraint, influence, and management'.[53] While historians benefit from the models supplied by IR theory, theorists should endeavour to develop their models from careful engagement with the richness and nuance of historical writing, rather than drawing on potted histories found in other works of IR. Schroeder's argument about the relationship between the fields thus bears a resemblance to the claim that philosophy and history are, and should be, conceived as separate domains of inquiry since historians benefit by dipping into philosophers engaging in enduring philosophical questions and in doing so learn new ways of evaluating evidence and of formulating their investigations.[54]

---

[52] Schroeder 2004.
[53] Schroeder 1997, p. 74.
[54] See, e.g., the historian David Hollinger's response to the philosopher Ian Hacking in a symposium on the use and abuse of history in the human sciences. Hollinger described the power of 'autonomous' philosophical insight to sharpen historical analysis: Hollinger 1990, p. 370. For a similar perspective on the role that legal theory can play for the study of legal history see Del Mar and Lobban 2016.

As we have seen, the foundations of IR theory rest on doubtful premises about the nature of political order, and contributed to the foreclosure
of earlier analytical approaches to studying global order that prioritised
race and empire as the critical categories of analysis. It is nevertheless
worth considering whether the promise of a division of labour persists in
the aftermath of the common project to historicise the dominant representations of international politics. To echo Betts and Loescher's original question: what are the intellectual resources for grappling with the
importance of refugees and the stateless for global order? One possibility
outlined in the first part of this chapter is that understanding present
dynamics, including mass displacement and forced migration, involves
interpreting history, and the only debate is how to carve up and interpret the relevant parts of the past.[55] And as I referenced earlier, there
are also good reasons to approach climate migration through its local
manifestations and effects, and to avoid conflating the ultimately disparate motivations for migration.[56] Yet if one wishes to conceptualise the
phenomenon as unified and singular, then the disciplinary practice of
developing conceptual abstractions, theoretical frameworks and typologies that can account for 'the simultaneous existence of multiplicity and
interactivity' in the sphere of world politics remains important.[57] The
capacity to generalise and to develop heuristic categories of analysis in
order to comprehend particular dynamics and differences remains vital
in the light of the particular challenge of grasping the global dynamics
of climate migration. IR scholars are inclined by disciplinary expectation and habit to generalise to the level of the world – theorising politics
at the scale of global interaction and interdependence. Their tendency,
regardless of where they stand on the spectrum from nominalism to universalism, to search for broad patterns and to develop thematic categories to explain politics at particular scales of interaction re-introduces the
virtues of a division of labour, where the concepts, categories and generalisations generated by IR theorists provide significant frameworks from
which historians develop their inquiry, though the most productive end
result of such scholarship may be to challenge overgeneralisation and the
coarse-grained models that underwrite broad comparisons.[58]

---

[55] On the particular intellectual commitment to the idea, not held universally among
historians of political thought, that historical scholarship should inform contemporary understandings of politics, see Bell forthcoming.
[56] McAdam 2012.
[57] Go and Lawson 2017, p. 20.
[58] Nicholas Onuf has proposed that the craft of IR is located in the domain of concept
formation. 'Whatever else we do, we are wordsmiths': Onuf 2017. See also Smith
2017.

Even if we reject Betts and Loescher's proposal on the grounds that their pluralistic theoretical claims rest on an implausible historical account about the trajectory of international politics in the twentieth century, the challenge they pose persists, and underscores long-standing dilemmas relating to historical concerns about presentism and the application of historical understanding to contemporary political circumstances. My intention is not to deny the idea that grasping contemporary dynamics is inseparable from historical understanding and judgement, but to acknowledge the value and necessity of the theoretical ambition to comprehend politics at a global scale if we hope to comprehend the common threat posed by climate change and the collective responsibility to those most subject to the environmental desolation that will follow in its wake.

References

Achiume, Tendayi. 2019. 'Migration as Decolonization', *Stanford Law Review*, 71: 6, pp. 1509–74.

Armitage, David. 2004. 'The Fifty Years' Rift: Intellectual History and International Relations', *Modern Intellectual History*, 1: 1, pp. 97–109.

  2007. *The Declaration of Independence: A Global History*. Cambridge, MA.

  2013. *Foundations of Modern International Thought*. Cambridge.

  2014. 'The International Turn in Intellectual History' in *Rethinking Modern European Intellectual History*, ed. Darrin McMahon and Samuel Moyn. Oxford.

  2015. 'Modern International Thought: Problems and Prospects', *History of European Ideas*, 41: 1, pp. 116–30.

Aron, Raymond. 1967. 'What is a Theory of International Relations?', *Journal of International Affairs*, 21: 2, pp. 185–206.

Bain, William and Terry Nardin. 2017. 'International Relations and Intellectual History', *International Relations*, 31: 3, pp. 213–26.

Ballinger, Pamela. 2013. 'Impossible Returns, Enduring Legacies: Recent Historiography of Displacement and the Reconstruction of Europe after World War II', *Contemporary European History*, 22: 1, pp. 127–38.

Barkan, Elezar and Howard Adelman. 2011. *No Return, No Refuge: Rites and Rights in Minority Repatriation*. New York.

Bell, Duncan. 2001. 'International Relations: The Dawn of a Historiographical Turn?', *British Journal of Political and International Relations*, 3, pp. 115–26.

  forthcoming. 'International Relations and Intellectual History' in *The Oxford Handbook of Historical International Relations*, ed. Mlada Bukovansky, Edward Keene, Christian Reus-Smit and Maja Spanu. Oxford.

Benton, Lauren. 1996. 'From the World-Systems Perspective to Institutional World History: Culture and Economy in Global Theory', *Journal of World History*, 7: 2, pp. 261–95.

  2009. *A Search for Sovereignty: Law and Geography in European Empires 1400–1900*. Cambridge.

Berman, Nathaniel. 2019. 'Drama through Law: The Versailles Treaty and the Casting of the Modern International Stage' in *Peace through Law: The Versailles Peace Treaty and Dispute Settlement after World War I*, ed. Michel Erpelding, Burhard Hess and Hélène Ruiz Fabri. Luxembourg.

Betts, Alexander. 2009. *Forced Migration and Global Politics*. Chichester.

2014. 'International Relations and Forced Migration' in *The Oxford Handbook of Refugee and Forced Migration Studies*, ed. Elena Fiddian-Qasmiyah, Gil Loescher, Katy Long and Nando Sigona. Oxford.

Betts, Alexander and Gil Loescher, eds. 2011. *Refugees in International Relations*. Oxford.

Bevir, Mark. 2015. 'Historicism and Critique', *Philosophy of the Social Science*, 45: 2, pp. 227–45.

Bially, Mattern and Ayşe Zarakol. 2016. 'Hierarchies in World Politics', *International Organization*, 70: 3, pp. 623–54.

Bourke, Richard. 2021. 'European Empire and International Law from the Eighteenth to the Twentieth Century', *Historical Journal*, 64: 3, pp. 812–21.

Brett, Annabel, Megan Donaldson and Martti Koskenniemi, eds. 2021. *History, Law, Politics: Thinking through the International*. Cambridge.

Bukovansky, Mlada, Edward Keene, Christian Reus-Smit and Maja Spanu, eds. forthcoming. *The Oxford Handbook of History and International Relations*. Oxford.

Bull, Hedley. 1977. *The Anarchical Society: A Study of Order in World Politics*. New York.

Buzan, Barry. 2004. *From International to World Society? English School Theory and the Social Structure of Globalisation*. Cambridge.

Buzan, Barry and George Lawson. 2014. 'Capitalism and the Emergent World Order', *International Affairs*, 90: 1, pp. 71–9.

2015. *The Global Transformation: History, Modernity, and the Making of International Relations*. Cambridge.

Carey, Jane Perry Clark. 1946. 'Some Aspects of Statelessness since World War I', *American Political Science Review*, 40: 1, pp. 113–23.

Christov, Theodor. 2015. *Before Anarchy: Hobbes and his Critics in Modern International Thought*. Cambridge.

Cooper, Frederick. 2005. *Colonialism in Question: Theory, Knowledge, History*. Berkeley.

2018. *Citizenship, Inequality, Difference: Historical Perspectives*. Princeton.

Del Mar, Maks and Michael Lobban, eds. 2016. *Law in Theory and History: New Essays on a Neglected Dialogue*. Oxford.

Drayton, Richard and David Motadel. 2018. 'Discussion: The Future of Global History', *Journal of Global History*, 13: 1, pp. 1–21.

Fine, Sarah and Lea Ypi, eds. 2016. *Migration in Political Theory: The Ethics of Movement and Membership*. Oxford.

Forrester, Katrina and Sophie Smith. 2018. *Nature, Action and the Future*. Cambridge.

Getachew, Adom. 2018. 'The Limits of Sovereignty as Responsibility', *Constellations*, 26: 2, pp. 1–16.

Go, Julian and George Lawson, eds. 2017. *Global Historical Sociology*. Cambridge.

Gofas, Andreas, Inanna Hamati-Ataya and Nicholas Onuf, eds. 2018. *Handbook of the History, Philosophy, and Sociology of International Relations.* London.

Guilhot, Nicolas. 2017. *After the Enlightenment: Political Realism and International Relations in the Mid-Twentieth Century.* Cambridge.

Haddad, Emma. 2009. *The Refugee in International Society: Between Sovereigns.* Cambridge.

Hobson, John. 2012. *The Eurocentric Origins of International Relations.* Cambridge.

Hollinger, David. 1990. 'Reflections on the Jamesian Arch: A Response to Ian Hacking', *New Literary History*, 21: 2, pp. 365–71.

Hurrell, Andrew. 2011. 'Refugees, International Society, Global Order' in *Refugees in International Relations*, ed. Alexander Betts and Gil Loescher. Oxford.

Hutchings, Kimberly. 2014. 'Contribution to a Critical Exchange on David Armitage's Foundations of Modern International Thought', *Contemporary Political Theory*, 13: 4, pp. 387–92.

Isaac, Joel. 2012. *Working Knowledge: Making the Human Sciences from Parsons to Kuhn.* Cambridge, MA.

Keene, Edward. 2002. *Beyond the Anarchical Society: Grotius, Colonialism and Order in World Politics.* Cambridge.

    2014. 'The Standard of "Civilisation", the Expansion Thesis and the 19th Century International Social Space', *Millennium: Journal of International Studies*, 42: 3, pp. 651–73.

Kleinberg, Ethan, Joan Wallach Scott and Gary Wilder. 2020. 'Theses on Theory and History', *History of the Present*, 10: 1, pp. 157–65.

Kukathas, Chandran. 2016. 'Are Refugees Special?' in *Migration in Political Theory: The Ethics of Movement and Membership*, ed. Sarah Fine and Lea Ypi. Oxford.

Lawson, George. 2018. 'International Relations as a Historical Social Science' in *Handbook of the History, Philosophy, and Sociology of International Relations*, ed. Andreas Gofas, Inanna Hamati-Ataya and Nicholas Onuf. London.

Maier, Charles S. 2016. *Once Within Border: Territories of Power, Wealth and Belonging since 1500.* Cambridge, MA.

Malin, Patrick Murphy. 1947. 'The Refugee, a Problem for International Organization', *International Organization*, 1: 3, pp. 443–59.

McAdam, Jane. 2012. *Climate Change, Forced Migration, and International Law.* Oxford.

Morefield, Jeanne. 2020. 'Crashing the Cathedral: Historical Reassessments of Twentieth-Century International Relations', *Journal of the History of Ideas*, 81: 1, pp. 131–55.

Morgenthau, Hans. 2011 [1954]. 'The Theoretical and Practical Importance of a Theory of International Relations' in *The Invention of International Relations Theory: Realism, the Rockefeller Foundation, and the 1954 Conference on Theory*, ed. Nicolas Guilhot. New York.

Moyn, Samuel. 2015. 'Fantasies of Federalism', *Dissent*, 62: 1, pp. 145–51.

Niebuhr, Reinhold. 2011 [1954]. 'The Moral Issue in International Relations' in *The Invention of International Relations Theory: Realism, the Rockefeller Foundation and the 1954 Conference on Theory*, ed. Nicolas Guilhot. New York.

Ogle, Vanessa. 2017. 'Archipelago Capitalism: Tax Havens, Offshore Money, and the State, 1950s–1970s', *American Historical Review*, 122: 5, pp. 1431–58.

Onuf, Nicholas. 2017. 'What We Do: International Relations as Craft' in *Handbook of the History, Philosophy, and Sociology of International Relations*, ed. Andreas Gofas, Inanna Hamati-Ataya and Nicholas Onuf. London.

Parfitt, Rose. 2019. *The Process of International Legal Reproduction: Inequality, Historiography, Resistance*. Cambridge.

Pedersen, Susan. 2015. *The Guardians: The League of Nations and the Crisis of Empire*. Oxford.

Phillips, Andrew and J. C. Sharman. 2015. *International Order in Diversity*. Cambridge.

Pitts, Jennifer. 2018. *Boundaries of the International: Law and Empire*. Cambridge, MA.

Reus-Smit, Christian. 2008. 'Reading History through Constructivist Eyes', *Millennium: Journal of International Studies*, 37: 2, pp. 395–414.

Schmidt, Brian. 1998. *The Political Discourse of Anarchy: A Disciplinary History of International Relations*. Albany, NY.

Schroeder, Paul W. 1997. 'History and International Relations Theory: Not Use or Abuse, but Fit or Misfit', *International Security*, 22: 1, pp. 64–74.

2004. *Systems, Stability and Statecraft: Essays on the International History of Modern Europe*. New York.

Sewell, William. 2005. *Logics of History: Social Theory and Social Transformation*. Chicago.

Siegelberg, Mira. 2020. *Statelessness: A Modern History*. Cambridge, MA.

Skinner, Quentin. 1985. *The Return of Grand Theory in the Human Sciences*. Cambridge.

1997. 'Sir Geoffrey Elton and the Practice of History', *Transactions of the Royal Historical Society*, 7, pp. 301–16.

Smith, Sophie. 2017. 'The Nature of Politics', Quentin Skinner Lecture.

Srinivasan, Amia. 2019. 'Genealogy, Epistemology and Worldmaking', *Proceedings of the Aristotelian Society*, 119: 2, pp. 127–56.

Teschke, Benno. 2003. *The Myth of 1648: Class, Geopolitics, and the Making of Modern International Relations*. London.

Thomas, Chantal. 2016. 'Transnational Migration, Globalization, and Governance: Theorizing a Crisis' in *The Oxford Handbook of the Theory of International Law*, ed. Anne Orford and Florian Hoffmann. Oxford.

United Nations. 1950. Report of the Ad Hoc Committee on Statelessness – Position Paper. ECOSOC SD/E/448, box 3, RG59 General Records of the Department of State, National Archives and Records Administration, 10 June.

Veyne, Paul. 2012. *Foucault: His Thought, his Character*. Malden, MA.

Vitalis, Robert. 2015. *White World Order, Black Power Politics: The Birth of American International Relations*. Ithaca, NY.

Walker, R. B. J. 1992. *Inside/Outside: International Relations as Political Theory*. Cambridge.

Wight, Martin. 1966. 'Why is there no International Theory?' in *Diplomatic Investigations: Essays in the Theory of International Politics*, ed. Herbert Butterfield, Martin Wight and Hedley Bull. London.

5   The Delphi Syndrome: Using History in the Social Sciences

Stathis N. Kalyvas and Daniel Fedorowycz

Introduction

In his famous science fiction book *Foundation*, Isaac Asimov described 'psychohistory' as a science combining history, sociology and mathematical statistics that provides the ability to make general predictions about future collective behaviour.[1] Though not stating their future-seeking ambition in such bold terms, social scientists are increasingly combining history, sociology and statistics to identify generalisable causal laws that can inform policies in the present and predict future trends. However, this ambition comes with significant, and often overlooked, requirements.

Studying the past is a pursuit motivated to a substantial degree by the desire to better understand the present and glimpse into the future. Yet, although historians did not reject the idea that the lessons of the past could be transferred to the present and the future,[2] they have been always extremely cautious about the modalities and scope of such a transfer. As E. H. Carr put it, and Gaddis summarised, 'If we can widen the range of experiences of others who've had to confront comparable situations in the past, then – although there are no guarantees – our *chances* of acting wisely should increase proportionately.'[3] And it goes without saying that, for historians, understanding the present was not the fundamental justification for studying the past; rather, the past was studied for its own sake and on its own terms. It is in this sense that historians can be said to have aspired to primarily idiographic knowledge.

In contrast, many social scientists increasingly view history as the ticket to becoming or being perceived as modern oracles. This 'Delphi syndrome' drives them to view the past primarily, if not exclusively, as a

We are grateful to Matthias Dilling, Marcus Kreuzer and the editors for their incisive comments. The usual caveat applies.
[1] Asimov 1951.
[2] See, e.g., Hobsbawm 1981.
[3] Gaddis 2002, p. 9.

massive repository of data and an experimental laboratory that can help them decode the fundamental structures and patterns of human action and comprehend the basic laws of social behaviour. Hence, the key difference between generalisability for social scientists and 'transferability' for historians lies in the degree of contextualisation and conditionality surrounding causal claims: compared to historians, social scientists feel much freer to roam beyond the boundaries of their historical data. This nomothetic aspiration is dominant in the social sciences and accounts for how social scientists use, and sometimes misuse, history.

To argue our point, we concisely review how three social science disciplines (economics, sociology and political science) approach history. In particular, we focus on sophisticated statistical methodologies that initially emerged from economics with the aim of extracting general causal laws from historical data, before spreading to sociology and political science. We argue that the tension between the promise and requirements of using history in a nomothetic way has far-reaching ramifications for the validity of its findings. We highlight the enormous, often unrealistic, demands that recent methodological advances place on the historical capacity of social scientists, and we note that *using* history increasingly requires *doing* history as well, in the minimal sense of adhering to the best practices of historians. We argue that this requirement includes an extensive engagement with historical processes, deep attention to temporal effects, and a commitment to descriptive rather than just causal inference. We conclude by arguing that a way forward requires an understanding of the relation between nomothetic and idiographic research principles as approximating a continuum rather than an opposition.

The History of Economists

The idea that history can be used as a repository of data entered the discipline of economics via economic history, which sought to apply standard historical methods to the study of economic processes. The influential Historical School of Economics that emerged in Germany in the nineteenth century initially rejected nomothetic economic theories and quantitative analysis. Instead, proponents of this school, notably Gustav von Schmoller, believed that understanding a country's economy requires understanding its specific historical and political context; economic theories were not, according to this school, generalisable. Economic historians at that time were trained either in history or economics, and the methods used were largely historical, not quantitative. It was not until the inter-war years, especially in the United States, that the quantitative trend in economics proper began to influence economic history.

In 1920 the National Bureau of Economic Research began measuring the first official estimates of national incomes. The years after the Second World War saw the height of economic history's quantification: economic histories of the USA and other developed countries were used to draw lessons on development. More specifically, at the end of the 1950s a methodological revolution known as 'new economic history', 'econometric history' or 'cliometrics' took place, igniting a polemic on the use of the scientific method in history. Though it is less so today, in the 1950s and 1960s it was popular for cliometricians – economic historians who applied econometric/quantitative methods to the study of history – to systematically test hypotheses put forward by historians.

The most controversial topic examined by cliometricians was probably the institution of American slavery during the late antebellum period (1840–60). It garnered mainstream attention, far beyond specialised debates between academics. Using economic theory and quantitative analysis, Fogel and Engerman's *Time on the Cross* sought to revise the history of slavery in the American South, challenging the idea that slavery was an unprofitable and overwhelmingly cruel institution.[4] Fogel and Engerman were trained economists and statisticians – not historians – and their conclusions were based largely on statistical estimations. At the core of their argument was the contention that slavery was a rational business in which the interests of slave owners and slaves often converged. Using quantitative analysis, Fogel and Engerman attempted to demonstrate that slavery was an efficient, profitable and far less vicious enterprise than historians had claimed it to be. They argued that slaves were rarely abused, enjoyed relatively stable family lives, and had living standards that were good by contemporary standards. In fact, following emancipation, they argued, freed slaves' life expectancy decreased sharply. The implications of their conclusions were controversial, spurring intense debate among historians and economists about the limitations of applying quantitative analysis to understanding history.[5] The separation between history and economics, which began in the twentieth century, finally reached a point at which most historians, largely as a result of cliometrics, refused to engage with the new economic history and the use of quantitative methods in history. Conversely, the cliometric revolution raised the prestige and perceived legitimacy of economic history by moving it closer to the methodological standards of economics and, in their view, leaving at the wayside their colleagues in history proper.

[4] Fogel and Engerman 1974.
[5] David 1976; Gutman 1975.

As a result, historians and economists largely went their separate ways. This separation led Deidre McCloskey to lament that 'economists bemused by revolutions in the substance and method of economics neglected the reading of history in favor of macroeconomics, mathematics, and statistics'.[6] More than three decades later Robert Whaples echoed McCloskey's sentiment, arguing that economic history 'is a neglected field, one on the margins, caught between history and economics'.[7] He argued that the emphasis in mainstream economics is on technicality over substance and context; technical mastery of mathematical models and complex statistical estimation techniques, rather than in-depth knowledge of context and causation, is considered a key indication of 'cleverness'.[8] Seen from this perspective, history is only occasionally useful, and archival work certainly is not 'clever'. As such, economists today are largely trained to think of history, when they think of it at all, in utilitarian terms.[9] Or, as pointed out by Mokyr in response to Whaples, history's use is limited to telling an anecdote to decorate the first paragraph of an otherwise technical paper.[10] McCloskey, also in response to Whaples, charged that quantitative social scientists 'don't get the point of the humanities', and that

many social scientists, and especially those trained as economists, believe adamantly that, as Lord Kelvin put it in 1883, 'when you cannot express it in numbers, your knowledge is of a meager and unsatisfactory kind; it may be the beginning of knowledge, but you have scarcely in your thoughts advanced to the state of *Science*'. The young economists nowadays believe so fervently that rather than deviating from their faith they insist on collecting sometimes quite meaningless numbers.[11]

In the last two decades, however, as increasing amounts of historical data became available for quantitative analysis, many mainstream economists (rather than economic historians) turned their attention to the past, to empirically test a wide variety of theoretical conjectures. Remarkably, economists broke free from the shackles of economic questions and began to study a broad range of phenomena – economic, social, political, even cultural – ranging across space and time. This trend is particularly visible in the study of historical persistence – that is, the causal impact of the past on the present. In a survey of this rapidly growing body of

---

[6] McCloskey 1976, pp. 434, 439.
[7] Whaples 2010, p. 18.
[8] Whaples 2010, p. 18.
[9] Whaples 2010, p. 17.
[10] Mokyr 2010, p. 23.
[11] McCloskey 2010, p. 22.

research, Nunn surveys a large number of studies which attempt to precisely estimate the reverberating effects that historical events have had on the present, using cases from across the globe and over remarkably long time horizons; he concludes that cultural traits and formal institutions have a considerable long-term impact on present behaviour, but also recognises that the causal mechanisms driving these effects remain for the most part underspecified.[12]

In particular, colonialism and its legacies have emerged as an especially popular topic among contemporary economists searching for this type of effect. For example, Dell, Lane and Querubin focus on Vietnam to show that areas exposed to Dai Viet administrative institutions for a longer period prior to French colonisation have experienced better economic outputs over the past 150 years.[13] Similarly, Dell and Olken turn to the impact of nineteenth-century Dutch sugar factories in Java to demonstrate that villages forced to grow sugar cane in the mid-nineteenth century are richer and better educated today than areas without such factories.[14] Moving on to Peru and Bolivia, Dell finds that children living in areas subject to the *mita*, a forced mining labour system extensively used in Peru and Bolivia between 1573 and 1812, are stunted in their growth by about 6 per cent, compared with areas not subjected to *mita* centuries previously.[15] Moving further into the past and away from economic institutions, Voigtländer and Voth report that medieval pogroms against Jews during the Black Death (1348–50) reliably predict anti-Semitism 600 years later, including violence against Jews in the 1920s, votes for the Nazi Party, deportations after 1933, attacks on synagogues, and letters to *Der Stürmer* – although Gingerich and Vogler find that areas in Germany that experienced high levels of exposure to the Black Death exhibit significantly lower levels of electoral support for the Nazis compared to areas that had low levels of exposure.[16] Indeed, a cottage industry has emerged investigating the long-term effects of the Black Death on all kinds of contemporary outcomes, from urbanisation to electoral behaviour.[17]

This approach signals a highly significant transition in terms of analytical focus and, hence, research strategy, from the study of the 'causes of effects' to that of the 'effects of causes'. The former privileges multi-causal explanations of specific (and sometimes unique) outcomes of

---

[12] Nunn 2014.
[13] Dell, Lane and Querubin 2018.
[14] Dell and Olken 2020.
[15] Dell 2010.
[16] Voigtländer and Voth 2012; Gingerich and Vogler 2020.
[17] Gingerich and Vogler 2020.

political, social or economic import that could be conditionally generalised, whereas the latter searches for a single causal factor which, everything else equal, accounts for outcomes that recur across time and space. In the 'causes of effects' framework we might ask, 'Why does Switzerland regulate citizenship the way it does?',[18] whereas in the 'effects of causes' framework we would have asked instead, 'What is the effect of national origin on the outcomes of citizenship referenda in Switzerland?' This analytical transition has taken place in both sociology and political science.

In sum, the relationship between economics and history has followed a path whereby economists have moved simultaneously closer to and further away from history. On the one hand, they draw on historical data using increasingly complex statistical methods to understand the present and predict and shape the future; but on the other hand, their treatment of history is becoming more superficial: they do not delve too deeply into the historical context that produced the data they use, and they tend to bypass the mental world of historical actors, assuming that certain mental states remain constant across time and space. In other words, they *use* history without *doing* history the way historians do. Again, this tendency reverberates in the two other disciplines.

The History of Sociologists

Sociology was born with history at its core. In 1844 Auguste Comte's 'Lecture on the Positivist Outlook' proposed the name 'sociology' for the general science of society. His conception consisted 'largely of analyzing the development of humanity through historical stages'.[19] The classics of sociology are thus dominated by historically informed thinkers who blurred the lines between the social and human sciences. By the mid-twentieth century the development of Marxism as a political programme based on the 'scientific' understanding of history took this relationship to unprecedented heights: sociological history became a way to peek into the future via the laws of history, but also a tool to assist or accelerate the movement of societies on their preassigned historical course. At the same time, the failures of the Marxist paradigm and of 'real socialism' sealed its scholarly fate. It was not long before sociology took an ahistorical turn and became more about studying living individuals than the laws of history.

---

[18] Pepinsky 2019, p. 201.
[19] Tilly 2001, p. 6753.

Sociology's scientific aspirations are based on imitating the method of the physical, 'hard' sciences, and identifying causality. Regulative principles such as John Stuart Mill's methods of induction, Carl Hempel's deductive-nomological model and Karl Popper's concept of falsificationism were introduced as *the* scientific methods from which sociologists derived their scientific legitimacy.[20] Hence, sociology is methodologically no different from economics; it is just broader in its ambition, being firmly committed to a 'causes of effects' rather than an 'effects of causes' framework. The difficulty of applying these methods to historical data, however, led sociology to take an ahistorical turn after the Second World War.[21] The nomothetic principle was incompatible with the idiographic demands of historical research. As Tilly notes:

From these contrasting bases of intellectual organization sprang a number of mutual misunderstandings between historians and sociologists, including the sociologists' common presumption that sociology is an explanatory, generalizing science and history a descriptive, particularizing science fated to provide raw material for sociologists' generalizations. Historians returned the compliment by complaining that the present studied by sociologists was itself a narrow historical moment with no claim to universal significance, and that to pluck examples from history without thorough knowledge of the relevant sources, languages, and institutions courted intellectual disaster.[22]

The ahistorical turn in sociology was challenged in the 1970s with the introduction of comparative historical analysis, a method used for developing explanations of macro-historical phenomena of which there are inherently only a few cases – effectively an application of the hypothetico-deductive method and a substitute for multivariate statistical analysis.[23] This method was successfully applied by scholars such as Barrington Moore, Charles Tilly and Reinhard Bendix, followed by Theda Skocpol, William Sewell, Andrew Abbott and others, giving rise to a sub-field known as 'historical sociology'.

Comparative historical analysis seeks to identify the causes of major social phenomena, such as revolutions and political regimes. The standard template for macro-causal analysis is largely derived from Barrington Moore's *Social Origins of Dictatorship and Democracy*, an influential study comparing the histories of France, England, the United States, Japan, China and India, with reference to Germany and Russia, to understand how societies transform from agrarian to modern

---

[20] Burawoy 1989, p. 759.
[21] Tilly 1980, p. 55.
[22] Tilly 2001, p. 6753.
[23] Skocpol 1979, p. 36.

industrial.[24] The methodological template set out by Moore and picked up by several others since involves identifying cross-sectional variation of some sort of macro-phenomena, such as types of nation-states, revolutions or broad regime outcomes. The historical processes that produced the variation in macro-outcomes in each case are retraced, and abstract typologies and generalisable conclusions are drawn. Unlike many studies of historical persistence discussed above, this type of analysis focuses on a small number of cases, therefore entailing a much more in-depth type of engagement with historical context. Nevertheless, comparative, macro-historical causal analysis rests on the assumption that history is a set of structures that, when correctly identified, can be used potentially to forecast future trends since even rare social phenomena such as revolutions and regime change recur. However, this assumption about history turned out to be the Achilles heel of historical sociology.

In the time that has elapsed since the publication of the classic works of historical sociology, the field arguably has lost some of its lustre. The main blow was administered by the successful call for an increase in the number of observations (the 'N') along with the application of econometric techniques to ostensibly raise the standards of causal inference.[25] Indeed, using a combination of game theoretic models and statistical analysis both political scientists[26] and economists[27] have claimed the mantle of Barrington Moore's research agenda.

The History of Political Scientists

Political scientists have integrated history into their work in many ways, liberally borrowing research methods from economics, sociology and history proper. Hence, the debates taking place within political science echo those in economics and sociology.

Traditionally, political scientists used history without aiming to make broad causal claims or to craft general theories. This conception most closely parallels the kind of history practised by historians, with each studied case considered more or less unique and conclusions did not need to 'travel' to many other cases as a condition of their scholarly value. In so far as this type or research was associated with the study of particular world regions or countries, it came under the purview of what is known as 'Area Studies'. Gradually, however, and reflecting the

---

[24] Moore 1966.
[25] King, Keohane and Verba 1994, pp. 208–9.
[26] See, e.g., Boix 2003.
[27] See, e.g., Robinson and Acemoglu 2006.

broader trends of social science, this idiographic approach gave (total) way to the nomothetic imperative. This development took place in three phases.

At first, political scientists ploughed through a vast repository of historical research, built specialised datasets (mainly using electoral data) and used the narrative form to articulate and provide empirical validation for grand theories of global political change. Landmark works by V. O. Key, Stein Rokkan or Juan Linz and Alfred Stepan stand out in a well-populated field.[28] As with historical sociology, comparative historical analysis is still practised in political science,[29] but no longer enjoys its former prominent position. It was first superseded by quantitative studies that sought to multiply the number of cases studied, usually via cross-national datasets, to achieve more rigorous empirical validation.[30] This type of research, which posited a fundamental interchangeability of cases across historical time and geographical space, became the bread and butter of the political science sub-field of comparative politics, sometimes with the addition of game-theoretic models that helped account for the link between explanatory and outcome variables.

The next iteration arose from a devastating econometric critique of the standard statistical cross-national model, known as the 'credibility revolution'.[31] This critique ushered in the era of field experiments and experimental techniques more broadly. Historical data – which is observational par excellence – was deemed suspect with few exceptions. One of those was its transformation into quasi-experimental, that is, data produced through the random assignment of 'treatment' and 'control' groups in a way unintentionally mimicking actual experiments. Natural experiments (or quasi-experiments) held the promise of that holy grail of social scientific research, the rigorous identification of causation.

An example of this type of research is provided by Ferwerda and Miller, who sought to estimate differences in levels of native resistance against foreign occupiers and native rulers.[32] As is usually the case, their paper is framed very broadly, despite an extremely narrow empirical footprint: it examines a small slice of territory located on either side of the boundary (the 'demarcation line') separating German-occupied France and the Vichy regime during a short period, between November 1942 and September 1944. The authors justify their choice by claiming

---

[28] Key 1949; Rokkan 1970; Linz and Stepan 1978.
[29] See, e.g., Mahoney and Rueschemeyer 2003; Mahoney and Thelen 2015.
[30] See, e.g., Boix 2003.
[31] Angrist and Pischke 2010.
[32] Ferwerda and Miller 2014.

that the Germans randomly drew the boundary between the two sides. Using data on resistance incidents compiled by French historians, they find that there was more resistance on the German side of the boundary than on the French one, thus concluding that foreign rule caused higher levels of resistance. The authors conclude that their results 'provide causal evidence that the devolution of authority in the context of foreign occupation can be an effective strategy for staving off or reducing armed resistance'.[33] Their prediction is that foreign occupation regimes are likely to face higher levels of native resistance and, correspondingly, their policy recommendation is that foreign powers seeking to control alien territories ought to rely on native rule.

Misuses of History in the Social Sciences

In their quest to discover broadly applicable causal laws, social scientists in all three fields discussed in this chapter are increasingly turning to history – a trend sometimes referred to as a 'historical turn'. We note, however, that although many practitioners of this historical turn are analysing historical data using increasingly sophisticated statistical methods, they often fail to heed the best practices of historians. This tendency is most obvious when the intricacies and nuances of historical understanding are overlooked because they interfere with the nomothetic imperative. Less obviously, the spread of quasi-experimental methodologies in contemporary social sciences introduces historical demands that are extremely hard to satisfy.

We identify three such practices: an extensive engagement with historical processes; a deep understanding of temporality; and a commitment to anchoring causal inquiry on solid descriptive inference. Ignoring them leads to serious problems with far-reaching implications for research validity. Below, we discuss all three.

Limited Engagement with Historical Processes

Economists such as Melissa Dell can leap from Peru and Bolivia, to Vietnam, to Java, and to different historical time periods – an intellectual feat no historian would dare attempt – because, like most modern economists, they view history as a storehouse of data and an opportunity to test hypotheses about the present and the future. The underlying aspiration of this research lies not in understanding the past but in

---

[33] Ferwerda and Miller 2014, p. 659.

analysing it to come up with 'evidence-based' policy making that would transform the future. This preoccupation with crafting practical policies based on scientifically sound evidence (the term used is 'evidence-based policy'), however, largely comes at the expense of a serious engagement with the historical context that produced that evidence – assuming, in other words, that these data are reliable and straightforwardly interpretable. Unlike historians, economists relying on historical data to identify causal effects are not expected to demonstrate in-depth knowledge of the historical context they study. Obviously, this hands-off attitude comes with considerable risks: the most sophisticated analysis is as good as the data it is based on. Perhaps most troubling, and reflecting McCloskey's lament four decades ago, rather than meeting at a halfway point, economists have drifted away from historians, while at the same time seeing themselves as having substituted them, simply because they use data from the past. The irony is that often this 'historical economics' or 'historical political economy'[34] is about neither history nor economics.

Despite a deeper engagement with historical material, historical sociology has not been immune to this problem. John H. Goldthorpe developed a similar critique of historical sociology, arguing that sociologists are better off bypassing historical data.[35] He observes that history and sociology are different disciplines largely because of the way they generate and use evidence. Historians rely on physical relics, such as artefacts and various documents that have survived the past. They are thus limited to a finite and incomplete stock of historical 'facts'. One cannot accurately assess how representative surviving relics are of a given historical period or setting because what was destroyed will never be known. Sociologists, on the other hand, have a methodological advantage because they can generate their own data based on rigorous methods of inference. They should therefore only turn to historical data when they absolutely must. If possible, Goldthorpe advises, a research question is best addressed through collecting and generating data in the present. That is not to say that Goldthorpe believes sociological research methods to be superior to historical ones; rather, he judges that sociologists have a methodological advantage that should be recognised and not discounted without good reason. Goldthorpe acknowledges, however, that there are circumstances in which it is justifiable for sociologists to use historical data, but in such cases they must recognise the limitations of these data and accept that certain questions, sometimes critical ones, could remain unanswered due to the incomplete nature of the historical

---

[34] Cironne 2020.
[35] Goldthorpe 1991.

data. He specifically criticises the use of history by historical sociologists who defer to secondary literature rather than carry out primary research, because their approach relies on the interpretation of a second-order kind and often leads to cherry-picking, a point also stressed by Lustick.[36] The result, according to Goldthorpe, is a '*tenuous* and *arbitrary*' connection between argument and evidence in grand historical sociological studies, quite often to an 'unacceptable degree'.[37]

Lastly, the same problem is visible in political science where, with the gradual replacement of books by journal articles, longer historical narratives have given way to capsule illustrations. Kreuzer has painstakingly documented the often-cavalier attitude towards history exhibited in cross-national research that relies on historical data, convincingly showing how an incomplete or erroneous understanding of historical context can result in misinterpretation and miscoding of data, resulting in misleading or plainly false conclusions.[38] He concludes that 'the limited engagement with historians, and with contextual information more generally, contributes to a loss of historical knowledge that can undermine the validity of quantitative analysis'.[39]

Paradoxically, this problem has been exacerbated by the introduction of quasi-experimental approaches using the past as a laboratory. Let us return to Ferwerda and Miller, a study that was the object of a particularly trenchant critique by Kocher and Monteiro.[40] Their conclusion that foreign devolution of authority in the context of foreign occupation can be an effective strategy for staving off or reducing armed resistance primarily rests on the random design of the demarcation line in German-occupied France. But was this line randomly drawn? Clearly, their conclusion hinges on this claim, and this claim alone. Drawing on extensive historical research, Kocher and Monteiro revisited this paper and demonstrated that its key claim was, in fact, incorrect: the demarcation line was designed to ensure that important double-track railways were located on the German side of the boundary.[41] It is thus hardly surprising that many resistance actions, which were mostly related to rail sabotage, took place on the German side.

This example suggests that validating a natural experiment requires researchers to thoroughly reconstruct the historical data-generation process and investigate the causal pathway linking potential causes

---

[36] Lustick 1996.
[37] Goldthorpe 1991, p. 222.
[38] Kreuzer 2010.
[39] Kreuzer 2010, p. 369.
[40] Ferwerda and Miller 2014; Kocher and Monteiro 2016.
[41] Kocher and Monteiro 2016.

with outcomes by delving deeply into history. They must uncover, in other words, the intentions, deliberations and decisions of the actors whose actions the data record. Historians have long stressed the importance of a solid understanding of context in the process of interpreting historical events. In fact, the validity of inferences drawn from historical data hinges on a deep understanding of the processes that generated these data in the first place. Typical problems here include ahistoricism or presentism, or the tendency to project our assumptions about human behaviour backwards. In his examination of the ancient Graeco-Roman social practice of 'euergetism', civic benefaction by local nobles (which is not to be conflated with charity), Paul Veyne argues that nobles, defying rational expectations, derived pleasure from spending fortunes on lavish public spectacles: 'The oligarchs had no rational need to make themselves popular. They did not have to be loved by the plebs in order to hold onto their power. But they could not help themselves – they wanted to be loved.'[42] To understand the behaviour of nobles in the early Hellenistic period requires a firm grasp of their mental world, which, in turn, requires a deep knowledge of the countries and time periods under investigation. However, many social scientists lack the time, expertise or perhaps interest for this kind of engagement. This is the source of a well-known pathology, sometimes referred to as 'historical tourism'.[43]

Herein lies a great paradox: it is precisely because quasi-experimental designs hinge to such an enormous extent on the process of treatment assignment that social scientists must effectively become historians – indeed, they must dig even deeper than many historians do. Because causal claims derived from quasi-experimental designs depend on random assignment, their validation frequently hangs from incredibly esoteric historical details that even the most antiquarian historians would probably find impossible to substantiate. The question of the precise location of double-track railways in occupied France is far from unique in that respect. For example, to establish the causal impact that the 2010 riots in the Kyrgyz city of Osh had on subsequent levels of trust among the Uzbek, Hager, Krakowski and Schaub had to establish that the Soviet army had placed its garrisons randomly around the city.[44] Likewise, to justify their causal claim about the long-term effect that the Spanish Civil War had on present-day levels of trust, Tur-Prats and Valencia Caicedo needed to prove that the Spanish insurgents' decision

---

[42] Veyne 1990, p. 261.
[43] Kreuzer 2020, p. 152.
[44] Hager, Krakowski and Schaub 2019.

to reach Madrid through Badajoz rather than through the Despe-
ñaperros pass was unexpected.[45] Sometimes the necessary evidence is
extremely hard to come by and controversial to interpret; at others, it
might simply be non-existent.

The fact that essentially ahistorical social scientists must effectively
demonstrate extraordinary historical knowledge was also noted by Jon
Elster in his critique of 'deductive history', an attempt to interpret past
events using game-theoretic models and insights.[46] Elster argued that the
imputation of rationalist models of individual action on historical actors
clashed with the way they actually made decisions given their mental
states; he also criticised the assumptions made about their mental states
because they were merely stipulated rather than actually verified. Altogether, he expressed scepticism about the possibility of attaining that
standard, arguing that 'deductive history will forever remain impossible.
First, the micro mechanisms, if and when we find them, are likely to be
very fine grain. Second, however assiduously we search the historical
record, the evidence is unlikely ever to match the fineness of grain of the
mechanisms.'[47]

Perhaps the most radical way to deal with the non-availability of certain types of historical evidence (including evidence related to unrealised
historical outcomes) is the emerging prospect of historical simulation
through the method of 'synthetic control'.[48] This method raises the
promise (or is it the spectre?) of 'artificial history'. The goal is to do
away with the drawbacks of historical comparisons, where 'the selection
of the comparison units is not formalized and often relies on informal
statements of affinity between the units affected by the event or intervention of interest and a set of comparison units'. In a path-breaking paper,
Abadie and Gardeazabal explored the economic effects of conflict by
focusing on terrorism in the Basque country.[49] Using data from various Spanish regions, they constructed a 'synthetic' Basque country that
resembles the real one prior to the outset of the conflict in the 1970s.
They then compared the economic trajectory of the Basque country to
that of their artificial counterfactual Basque country which did not experience terrorism, and reached the estimate that terrorism cost the Basque
country 10 percentage points in terms of per capita GDP. As it turns out,
artificial history is highly dependent on an accurate assessment of real

---

[45] Tur-Prats and Valencia Caicedo 2020.
[46] Elster 2000.
[47] Elster 2000, p. 694.
[48] Abadie 2021.
[49] Abadie and Gardeazabal 2003.

history: 'The validity of synthetic control estimators depends on important practical requirements,' Abadie warns.[50] 'Perfunctory applications that ignore the context of the empirical investigation and the characteristics of the data may miss the mark, producing misleading estimates.'[51] In other words, bad real history can only result in misleading artificial history. History can't be bypassed.

Neglect of Temporal Effects

Traditionally, historians have explored patterns of change and continuity by using narrative to represent and interpret the past, which allows them to use temporality as a way to simplify multiple causal pathways into a single coherent story. A narrative is not just a mechanical threading of events, but a sophisticated theoretical enterprise, even when done implicitly. Social scientists have mostly done away with narrative, a reflection of their tendency to neglect temporal effects and assume that the observations they study are both equivalent (despite enormous temporal lags) and independent from each other (effectively assuming learning and diffusion processes away).[52] Kreuzer describes this and related tendencies as 'temporal illiteracy'.[53]

Nowhere perhaps is time more visible than in recent studies of historical persistence. Clearly, the bigger the chronological distance between purported causes and effects and the larger the geographical area covered, the harder it is to explore the role of time. Yet by showing that some effects linger on despite the passage of time, these studies suggest that time matters. However, despite the significance they attach to the passage of time, these studies appear to suffer from an inability to actually engage with time. First, in contrast to the rigour characterising the statistical estimation of long-term causal effects, the mechanisms causally linking these historically distant processes to present phenomena tend to be the object of speculation, 'just-so stories' or superficial capsule narratives. Second, even if it is plausible to think that the past can cast extremely long shadows, showing that this is really the case is much harder than many of these studies make it sound. After re-analysing the results of twenty-eight papers published in top economic journals that examine long-term persistence, Kelly found them to be extremely sensitive to simple robustness checks; indeed, most of these findings disappear

---

[50] Abadie 2021, p. 391.
[51] Abadie 2021, p. 391.
[52] Hanson and Kopstein 2005.
[53] Kreuzer 2020, p. 38.

once spatial controls are introduced, suggesting that they might just be artefacts of 'spatial noise'.[54] Lastly, this literature appears vulnerable to macro-level distortion through massive publication bias since it tends to report only instances of long-term historical persistence rather than historical continuity.

In a parallel critical vein, Sewell pointed out how classic works of historical sociology neglected or distorted temporality in favour of a deterministic teleology.[55] In Sewell's words, teleological temporality is

the attribution of the cause of a historical happening neither to the actions and reactions that constitute the happening nor to concrete and specifiable conditions that shape or constrain the actions and reactions but rather to abstract transhistorical processes leading to some future historical state. Events in some historical present, in other words, are actually explained by events in the future.[56]

In short, the potential of historical sociology, he argued, had been blunted by its use of fallacious versions of temporality, which he believed fell back on either teleological or experimental timing, neither of which sufficiently addressed the complexity of historical time. Sewell argues that a similar teleological perspective underlies the classic historical sociological work of Charles Tilly and Immanuel Wallerstein. He claims that Theda Skocpol's work, on the other hand, is driven by experimental temporality. In *States and Social Revolutions* Skocpol extends the standard 'scientific' methodology of sociology to history.[57] Her analysis attempts to use comparative natural experiments to identify the causal factors that explain the occurrence of social revolutions. The fundamental logic of this enterprise, according to Sewell, 'rests on two fundamental assumptions: a uniformity of causal laws across time and a causal independence of every sequence of occurrences from previous and subsequent occurrences'.[58] Her analysis requires us, in Burawoy's words, to 'freeze history' and assume that the revolutions in Russia, China and France are independent cases.[59] This leads Skocpol to ignore the ways in which revolutions interact over time because her assumption is that revolutionary moments in history – the structures she analyses – are interchangeable units, independent and not influenced by one another.

---

[54] Kelly 2019; Kelly 2020.
[55] Sewell 2005.
[56] Sewell 2005, p. 84.
[57] Skocpol 1979.
[58] Sewell 2005, p. 100.
[59] Burawoy 1989, p. 782.

Primacy of Causal over Descriptive Inference

The belief in the superiority of nomothetic over idiographic principles establishes the primacy of causal over descriptive inference in social science research. Descriptive inference is, thus, marginalised. However, this marginalisation is associated with two problems: misleading causal claims and historical distortion.

First, as our discussion of quasi-experimental designs, deductive history and artificial history made clear, the relation between causal and descriptive inference is one of mutual dependence: without solid, reliable descriptive inference, causal inference fails. Kocher and Monteiro point out that because the validity of natural experiments depends on the historical validation of the process of treatment assignment and administration, 'there is no good reason for natural experiments to be considered epistemically superior to historical research'.[60]

Second, and more overlooked, is the fact that the primacy of causal over descriptive inference might distort our understanding of the very phenomena that we are trying to explain through causal inference. Going back to Ferwerda and Miller, their goal to causally identify the (transhistorical) effect of occupation on resistance ended up producing a distorted account of French resistance as a historical phenomenon – and in so doing, undermined their causal enterprise as well.[61] How? Kocher and Monteiro point out that, in order to identify the causal effect of an occupation regime on levels of resistance, Ferwerda and Miller had to rely on a tiny and highly unrepresentative sample of all French resistance actions – those that took place in a small period of time and in a minuscule band of territory surrounding the demarcation line, namely those occurring during the first thirty-four months of the German occupation of France, when differences in the structure of authority between the occupied and unoccupied zones were starkest.[62] However, during this period sabotage was virtually non-existent in this area. In fact, although this period accounts for two-thirds of the entire duration of the occupation it saw less than 5 per cent of all resistance actions. As a result, the study missed how the larger strategic context helped produce violent resistance action, including within the area studied. It also led to the neglect of spillover effects between the two zones of occupation and the effective dismissal of actual chains of command operating independently of territorial distinctions. In short, prioritising the identification of

---

[60] Kocher and Monteiro 2016, p. 952.
[61] Ferwerda and Miller 2014.
[62] Kocher and Monteiro 2016.

a causal effect led to a distorted understanding of French resistance as a historical phenomenon.

Another example is supplied by a paper that explores the effect of slave ownership and personal wealth on the likelihood of joining the Confederate Army during the American Civil War, generalising its findings to the role of material incentives for fighting in civil wars more broadly.[63] Wealthy Southerners could avoid fighting, yet they were disproportionately slave owners who had a material incentive to fight. Using a dataset of roughly 3.9 million free citizens in the Confederacy along with a randomised land lottery held in 1832 in Georgia, this study shows that slave owners were on average more likely to enlist than non-slave owners. Following a battery of tests, the authors conclude that the propensity to enlist in the Confederate Army was lowest for those households owning no slaves; being a slave owner is associated with an increased contribution of 0.12 soldiers, while owning one additional slave is associated with an increase of 0.017 soldiers. This effect might be small, they argue, but it is distinguishable from a null association. They also find similar effects for household wealth, but wealth was produced mainly by slave ownership. At the same time, the authors observe that the overwhelming majority of Confederate Army soldiers were not slave owners: 410,646 compared to 193,785. Material self-interest via the preservation of slavery clearly did not motivate the bulk of the men who joined the army. How do the authors deal with this important fact? They effectively dismiss it by arguing that it biases us: the 'prevalence of non-slaveowners in the army may have led some observers to infer that non-slaveowners were just as likely, if not more likely, than slaveowners to fight. Instead, non-slaveowners' rate of fighting in the Confederate Army was substantially lower.'[64] They conclude, therefore, that 'wealthier people joined the Confederate Army at higher rates than poorer people, probably because they had the most to gain from preserving a system of slavery that prioritized their own well-being over the freedom and well-being of others, and the most to lose from the system's destruction'.[65] However, it is far from obvious that the goal of understanding and explaining the motivations of the men who joined the Confederate Army requires us to privilege the differential rate of participation of slave-owner and non-slave-owner households compared to their base rate participation. Put differently, this study dismisses a large and striking fact to showcase a potentially interesting but small causal effect, whose validity is further weakened by both the failure to

---

[63] Hall, Huff and Kuriwaki 2019.
[64] Hall, Huff and Kuriwaki 2019, p. 664.
[65] Hall, Huff and Kuriwaki 2019, p. 672.

explore potential alternative explanations of joining, such as peer effects, ideology or norms of honour, and the inflation of its external validity, since the American Civil War shares very little with contemporary guerrilla wars. In sum, by prioritising causal over descriptive inference, this study fosters a distorted view of the composition and, therefore, nature of the Confederate Army.

Our critical review suggests three related corrective moves: a deeper engagement with historical processes; a better integration of temporality in the analysis; and the rehabilitation of descriptive inference. We bypass the call 'to take not only history, but also historians seriously'[66] because it has received extensive attention,[67] and we focus on the remaining two.

First, causal claims could be formulated in a more conditional way, informed by a temporality that is less teleological or experimental. In other words, historical causality entails a careful sequencing of events and processes and is not easily or automatically reduced to the effect of treatments on outcomes. We heed Sewell in recommending a return to the 'logics of history – fatefulness, contingency, complexity, eventfulness, and causal heterogeneity'.[68] He reminds us of the 'eventful temporality' that recognises the power of events in history along with contingency and individual agency, admits the transformation of structures by events, and allows for a heterogeneity of causal laws: different outcomes can happen at different times, and the outcome of one event can have an impact on the outcome of a subsequent event, which challenges the structural experimental view of history. But doesn't a constant preoccupation with contingency and eventful temporality undermine the effort to produce nomothetic knowledge? Wouldn't this deny the very possibility of a social science?

The answer is negative. Accepting the messy and contingent nature of historical processes is not incompatible with theoretical abstraction and empirical generalisation. Isaiah Berlin reminds us that 'the nature of men, however various and subject to change, must possess some generic character if it is to be called human at all'.[69] Nevertheless, we feel that the balance between the drive to understand the past on its own terms and the desire to use this understanding in order to shape the present and predict the future requires an adjustment.

Among several existing possibilities, a first one is the systematic study of the micro-foundations of critical historical phenomena. Ermakoff

---

[66] Kreuzer 2010, p. 383.
[67] See, e.g., Costalli and Ruggeri 2019; Gasparyan 2019; and Møller 2019.
[68] Sewell 2005, p. 280.
[69] Berlin 1980, p. 96.

suggests focusing on critical breaks in patterns of social relations and analysing the role played by individual agency by using methods such as event structure analysis to reconstruct and disaggregate sequences of events and identify junctures that are both indeterminate *ex ante* and consequential *ex post*.[70] By identifying its specific properties in a systematic and rigorous way, such a positive conception of contingency aims to move us beyond its characterisation as purely chaotic.[71] A second possibility is theorising contingency via path dependence, as suggested by Capoccia and Kelemen; they argue that contingency is the key element of critical junctures because change is then substantially less constrained than it is under normal circumstances.[72] To identify and validate these critical junctures one needs to establish detailed sequences and their plausible counterfactual scenarios, based on sound theoretical intuition and empirical evidence. A third possibility consists in modelling processes of multiple causation along the lines suggested by Capoccia and Ziblatt, who remind us that democracy did not emerge as a singular coherent whole from a single uni-causal process, but rather as a set of different institutions from a variety of conflicts – the result of 'crooked lines' rather than linear processes.[73] Lastly, a fourth possibility calls for a more sustained study of diffusion processes.[74] An example of an argument whose causal logic is based on the sequence of events is offered by Chandra and García-Ponce, who explain why some districts in India suffered chronic Maoist violence while others avoided it: where subaltern-led parties in India emerged before revolutionary armed organisations did, they crowded Maoist groups out, thus avoiding their violence.[75] This type of explanation is often challenged as subject to infinite regress and the accompanying charge of spurious causation. However, such critiques also assume that contingency always must be superficial and epiphenomenal to deeper, structural causes; they can be addressed through the study of historical antecedents that permit or limit such sequences.[76] In general, the study of temporality is not exempt from the standards of rigour that apply across the social sciences.

Second, it makes a lot of sense to rehabilitate descriptive inference. Social scientists prize causal inference above everything else, but it is often as useful, if not more, to explore patterns that challenge our priors and

---

[70] Ermakoff 2019; Ermakoff 2015.
[71] Ermakoff 2019, p. 592.
[72] Capoccia and Kelemen 2007, p. 368.
[73] Capoccia and Ziblatt 2010, p. 958.
[74] See, e.g., Marsh and Sharman 2009.
[75] Chandra and García-Ponce 2019.
[76] Slater and Simmons 2010; Kalyvas 1996.

measure key quantities of interest more precisely.[77] For example, Thomas Piketty's acclaimed *Capital in the Twenty-First Century* derives a great deal of its power from a descriptive analysis of long-term changes in patterns of wealth.[78] So does a widely discussed study by Chetty, Hendren, Kline and Saez of American social mobility in historical perspective, or Ferrie's analysis on the geographical and occupational mobility of more than 75,000 Americans from the 1850s to the 1920s.[79] Others look at the very long run: Clark and Clark, Cummins, Hao and Vidal use family names to measure socio-economic status over several generations in contexts ranging from Sweden to Qing-dynasty China, demonstrating that surname distributions can be used to measure rates of social mobility in contemporary and historical societies.[80] Rehabilitating descriptive inference will push us to approach causality in a more nuanced way. Deaton reminds us that

as John Stuart Mill noted long ago, the 'method of differences', which compares two groups, one treated, one not, is only one among many ways of making causal inference. Finding out the cause of a plane crash does not involve differences (or at least we might hope not), and the hypothetico-deductive method, which is how physicists say they work, does not involve differences, simply the making and checking of predictions.[81]

Careful process tracing, for example, can help establish that a potential cause preceded its effect, thus helping to address a type of reverse causation haunting social scientists, in a non-statistical way.

Conclusion

As we hope to have made clear in this chapter, history is becoming increasingly attractive to economists, sociologists and political scientists. Historical data hold tremendous promise, yet properly using such data is very hard. Social scientists in thrall to the Delphi syndrome often disregard the best practices of historians.

We have described some of the problems that arise when social scientists plunge into the past to discover causal laws as the result of using history without doing history. We do not advocate, however, that social scientists become historians – clearly, there are good reasons and many benefits behind the existing disciplinary division of labour. Rather, we wish to highlight the very significant demands that accompany the

---

[77] Paglayan 2019.
[78] Piketty 2014.
[79] Chetty, Hendren, Kline and Saez 2014; Ferrie 2005.
[80] Clark 2014; Clark, Cummins, Hao and Vidal 2015.
[81] Deaton 2020, p. 15.

equally significant promise of using historical data. One way of bypassing these demands, consistent with Goldthorpe's suggestion, is for social scientists to avoid using history unless they absolutely must, and to concentrate more on data that can be generated in the present, under highly controlled conditions. However, we believe that it would be a real shame to sacrifice the unique insights that history offers for understanding our world, even when historical data cannot fully conform to the requirements of quasi-experimental techniques.

What gives, then? Rather than bending history in favour of the Delphi syndrome, we could temper our nomothetic principles instead. A different way of stating this point is to say that idiographic and nomothetic principles are not stark opposites but extreme points on a continuum. Although it might prove impossible to specify the necessary and sufficient conditions under which a recurrent causal nexus will obtain in the future, accepting that we are unlikely to predict a given outcome does not mean that it must remain a total mystery. We are, in this regard, better off understanding under what conditions certain phenomena are potentially more likely to occur, rather than attempting to predict their occurrence.[82] This ultimately entails accepting that social-scientific generalisations are likely to remain highly conditional. Put differently, we might have to accept that our ability to conditionally account for the past does not necessarily extend into the future. But this would be a fatal predicament only in Isaac Asimov's psychohistory world.

References

Abadie, A. 2021. 'Using Synthetic Controls: Feasibility, Data Requirements, and Methodological Aspects', *Journal of Economic Literature*, 59: 2, pp. 391–425.

Abadie, A. and J. Gardeazabal. 2003. 'The Economic Costs of Conflict: A Case Study of the Basque Country', *American Economic Review*, 93: 1, pp. 113–32.

Angrist, J. D. and J. Pischke. 2010. 'The Credibility Revolution in Empirical Economics: How Better Research Design is Taking the Con out of Econometrics', *Journal of Economic Perspectives*, 24: 2, pp. 3–30.

Asimov, I. 1951. *Foundation*. New York.

Berlin, I. 1980. 'Alleged Relativism in Eighteenth-Century European Thought', *British Journal for Eighteenth-Century Studies*, 3, pp. 89–106.

Boix, C. 2003. *Democracy and Redistribution*. New York.

Burawoy, M. 1989. 'Two Methods in Search of Science: Skocpol versus Trotsky', *Theory and Society*, 18: 6, pp. 759–805.

---

[82] Kuran 1995.

Capoccia, G. and R. D. Kelemen. 2007. 'The Study of Critical Junctures: Theory, Narrative, and Counterfactuals in Historical Institutionalism', *World Politics*, 59: 3, pp. 341–69.

Capoccia, G. and D. Ziblatt. 2010. 'The Historical Turn in Democratization Studies', *Comparative Political Studies*, 43: 8–9, pp. 931–68.

Chandra, K. and O. García-Ponce. 2019. 'Why Ethnic Subaltern-Led Parties Crowd Out Armed Organizations: Explaining Maoist Violence in India', *World Politics*, 71: 2, pp. 367–416.

Chetty, R., N. Hendren, P. Kline and E. Saez. 2014. 'Where is the Land of Opportunity? The Geography of Intergenerational Mobility in the United States', *Quarterly Journal of Economics*, 129: 4, pp. 1553–1623.

Cironne, A. 2020. 'Historical Political Economy of Parliaments' in *Handbook of Parliamentary Studies: Interdisciplinary Approaches to Legislatures*, ed. C. Benoît and O. Rozenberg. Cheltenham.

Clark, G. 2014. *The Son Also Rises*. Princeton.

Clark, G., N. Cummins, Y. Hao and D. D. Vidal. 2015. 'Surnames: A New Source for the History of Social Mobility', *Explorations in Economic History*, 55: 1, pp. 3–24.

Costalli, S. and A. Ruggeri. 2019. 'The Study of Armed Conflict and Historical Data', *APSA-CP Newsletter*, 29: 2, pp. 58–63.

David, P. A. 1976. *Reckoning with Slavery: A Critical Study in the Quantitative History of American Negro Slavery*. New York.

Deaton, A. 2020. 'Randomization in the Tropics Revisited: A Theme and Eleven Variations', NBER Working Paper 27600.

Dell, M. 2010. 'The Persistent Effects of Peru's Mining "Mita"', *Econometrica*, 78: 6, pp. 1863–1903.

Dell, M., N. Lane and P. Querubin. 2018. 'The Historical State, Local Collective Action, and Economic Development in Vietnam', *Econometrica*, 86: 6, pp. 2083–2121.

Dell, M. and B. A. Olken. 2020. 'The Development Effects of the Extractive Colonial Economy: The Dutch Cultivation System in Java', *Review of Economic Studies*, 87: 1, pp. 164–203.

Elster, J. 2000. 'Review: Rational Choice History: A Case of Excessive Ambition', *American Political Science Review*, 94: 3, pp. 685–95.

Ermakoff, I. 2015. 'The Structure of Contingency', *American Journal of Sociology*, 121: 1, pp. 64–125.

2019. 'Causality and History: Modes of Causal Investigation in Historical Social Sciences', *Annual Review of Sociology*, 45: 1, pp. 581–606.

Ferrie, J. P. 2005. 'History Lessons: The End of American Exceptionalism? Mobility in the United States since 1850', *Journal of Economic Perspectives*, 19: 3, pp. 199–215.

Ferwerda, J. and N. L. Miller. 2014. 'Political Devolution and Resistance to Foreign Rule: A Natural Experiment', *American Political Science Review*, 108: 3, pp. 642–60.

Fogel, R. W. and S. L. Engerman. 1974. *Time on the Cross: The Economics of American Negro Slavery*. Boston.

Gaddis, J. L. 2002. *The Landscape of History*. Oxford.

Gasparyan, O. 2019. 'The Importance and Peculiarities of Archival Work in Political Science', *APSA-CP Newsletter*, 29: 2, pp. 5–11.

Gingerich, D. W. and J. P. Vogler. 2020. 'Pandemics and Political Development: The Electoral Legacy of the Black Death in Germany', Working Paper, University of Virginia.

Goldthorpe, J. H. 1991. 'The Uses of History in Sociology: Reflections on Some Recent Tendencies', *British Journal of Sociology*, 42: 2, pp. 211–30.

Gutman, H. G. 1975. *Slavery and the Numbers Game: A Critique of* Time on the Cross. Urbana.

Hager, A., K. Krakowski and M. Schaub. 2019. 'Ethnic Riots and Prosocial Behavior: Evidence from Kyrgyzstan', *American Political Science Review*, 113: 4, pp. 1029–44.

Hall, A. B., C. Huff and S. Kuriwaki. 2019. 'Wealth, Slaveownership, and Fighting for the Confederacy: An Empirical Study of the American Civil War', *American Political Science Review*, 113: 3, pp. 658–73.

Hanson, S. E. and J. S. Kopstein. 2005. 'Regime Type and Diffusion in Comparative Politics Methodology', *Canadian Journal of Political Science/ Revue Canadienne de Science Politique*, 38: 1, pp. 69–99.

Hobsbawm, E. 1981. 'Looking Forward: History and the Future', *New Left Review*, 125: 1, pp. 3–19.

Kalyvas, Stathis N. 1996. *The Rise of Christian Democracy in Europe*. Ithaca and New York.

Kelly, M. 2019. 'The Standard Errors of Persistence', UCD Centre for Economic Policy Research, Working Paper 19/13.

2020. 'Understanding Persistence', UCD Centre for Economic Policy Research, Working Paper 20/23.

Key, V. O. 1949. *Southern Politics in State and Nation*. New York.

King, G., R. O. Keohane and S. Verba. 1994. *Designing Social Inquiry: Scientific Inference in Qualitative Research*. Princeton.

Kocher, M. A. and N. Monteiro. 2016. 'Lines of Demarcation: Causation, Design-Based Inference, and Historical Research', *Perspectives on Politics*, 14: 4, pp. 952–75.

Kreuzer, M. 2010. 'Historical Knowledge and Quantitative Analysis: The Case of the Origins of Proportional Representation', *American Political Science Review*, 104: 2, pp. 369–92.

2020. *The Grammar of Time: Using Comparative Historical Analysis to Investigate Macro-Historical Questions*. New York.

Kuran, T. 1995. 'The Inevitability of Future Revolutionary Surprises', *American Journal of Sociology*, 100: 6, pp. 1528–51.

Linz, J. J. and A. Stepan. 1978. *The Breakdown of Democratic Regimes*. Baltimore.

Lustick, I. S. 1996. 'History, Historiography, and Political Science: Multiple Historical Records and the Problem of Selection Bias', *American Political Science Review*, 90: 3, pp. 605–18.

Mahoney, J. and D. Rueschemeyer. 2003. *Comparative Historical Analysis in the Social Sciences*. Cambridge.

Mahoney, J. and K. A. Thelen. 2015. *Advances in Comparative-Historical Analysis*. Cambridge.

Marsh, D. and J. C. Sharman. 2009. 'Policy Diffusion and Policy Transfer', *Policy Studies*, 30: 3, pp. 269–88.

McCloskey, D. N. 1976. 'Does the Past Have Useful Economics?', *Journal of Economic Literature*, 14: 2, pp. 434–61.

2010. 'One More Step: An Agreeable Reply to Whaples', *Historically Speaking*, 11: 2, pp. 22–3.

Mokyr, J. 2010. 'On the Supposed Decline and Fall of Economic History', *Historically Speaking*, 11: 2, pp. 23–5.

Møller, J. 2019. 'Feet of Clay? How to Review Political Science Papers that Make Use of the Work of Historians', *PS: Political Science & Politics*, 53: 2, pp. 253–7.

Moore, B. 1966. *Social Origins of Dictatorship and Democracy: Lord and Peasant in the Making of the Modern World*. Boston.

Nunn, N. 2014. 'Historical Development' in *Handbook of Economic Growth*, ed. P. Aghion and S. Durlauf, vol. II. Amsterdam.

Paglayan, A. 2019. 'We Have History – and How it Changed me', *APSA-CP Newsletter*, 29: 2, pp. 18–25.

Pepinsky, T. 2019. 'The Return of the Single-Country Study', *Annual Reviews of Political Science*, 22, pp. 187–203.

Piketty, T. 2014. *Capital in the Twenty-First Century*. Cambridge, MA.

Robinson, J. A. and D. Acemoglu. 2006. *Economic Origins of Dictatorship and Democracy*. Cambridge.

Rokkan, S. 1970. *Citizens, Elections, Parties: Approaches to the Comparative Study of the Processes of Development*. Oslo.

Sewell, W. H. 2005. *Logics of History: Social Theory and Social Transformation*. Chicago.

Skocpol, T. 1979. *States and Social Revolutions: A Comparative Analysis of France, Russia, and China*. Cambridge.

Slater, D. and E. Simmons. 2010. 'Informative Regress: Critical Antecedents in Comparative Politics', *Comparative Political Studies*, 43: 7, pp. 886–917.

Stone, L. 1979. 'The Revival of Narrative: Reflections on a New Old History', *Past and Present*, 85: 1, pp. 3–24.

Tilly, C. 1964. *The Vendée*. Cambridge, MA.

1980. 'Historical Sociology' in *Current Perspectives in Social Theory*, ed. S. G. McNall and G. N. Howe, vol. I. Greenwich, CT.

2001. 'Historical Sociology' in *International Encyclopedia of the Behavioral and Social Sciences*, vol. X. Amsterdam.

Tur-Prats, A. and F. Valencia Caicedo. 2020. 'The Long Shadow of the Spanish Civil War', unpublished paper.

Veyne, P. 1990. *Bread and Circuses: Historical Sociology and Political Pluralism*. London.

Voigtländer, N. and H.-J. Voth. 2012. 'Persecution Perpetuated: The Medieval Origins of Anti-Semitic Violence in Nazi Germany', *Quarterly Journal of Economics*, 127: 3, pp. 1339–92.

Whaples, R. 2010. 'Is Economic History a Neglected Field of Study?', *Historically Speaking*, 11: 2, pp. 17–20.

6   Power in Narrative and Narratives of Power in Historical Sociology

Hazem Kandil

> To study history, one must know in advance that one is attempting something fundamentally impossible, yet necessary. ... To study history means submitting to chaos and nevertheless retaining faith in order and meaning. It is a very serious task ... and possibly a tragic one.
>
> Herman Hesse, *The Glass Bead Game*

Using history to make sociological arguments has been integral to the discipline from the start. This tradition never abated, but was often contested, and sometimes submerged, by methodologies hoping to make sociology more scientific by making it less historical. Perhaps this is why historical sociology, as a research programme, was born with a chip on its shoulder, always fending off accusations of reducing sociology to storytelling. Historical research, it defensively insisted, can provide causal explanations as scientific as those of structuralism, rational choice and purely quantitative methods. Historical sociologists were not amateur historians trying to figure out the what, when, where and who of history. They pursued the question historians tend (or pretend) to avoid: why.[1]

Sociologists construct narratives around a causal chain of events to reveal the social power driving it through. And whereas many historians avoid explicit theorisation, sociologists are guided by one of various theories of causality to identify that power, whether economic class, cultural currents, social identity groups, state institutions, geopolitics, or a combination thereof. This commitment to locate power in narrative made sense methodologically. Unless the narrative is anchored to a specific power (or set of powers) that cause it to unfold in an explicable (perhaps predictable) way, it might drift into a narration of accidents and contingencies.

---

[1] 'History tells us *what*, but if we ask her *why*, she can only answer by giving us more of the *what*': Cobban 1961, p. 4. Hence, the sociological caricature of historians as 'theory-dreading, fact-worshiping, data-collecting antiquarians, concerned with just about everything but the question "Why do human beings behave as they do?"': Nisbet 1999, p. 91.

But the way sociologists perceive modernity strained this method to the limit. Few theorists today would draw a fixed boundary between traditional and modern societies. Yet it does seem that power is becoming more diffuse. Tocqueville made this point emphatically. He was not the only nineteenth-century author to start his analysis with the breakdown of old hierarchies. However, his contemporaries believed that fluidity would lead, through polarisation, to new forms of social consolidation: vigorous class struggle working its way to the dictatorship of the proletariat and its withering away into classless society (Marx); stratification along class, party and status lines gradually overshadowed by hyper-rationalised bureaucracy (Weber); the teething problems of transitioning from traditional to modern society easing with the development of organic solidarity (Durkheim). Tocqueville, by contrast, envisaged a perpetual proliferation of power. Power players were multiplying as new sources of power were becoming available and more social positions were opening up for competition. In this fervid condition, power relations could only spiral upwards towards higher levels of complexity. And as they get hopelessly entangled, narratives with clear lines of causality become terribly difficult. Pierre Bourdieu and Andrew Abbott subscribed to this view. While not spinning their theories out of the old Tocquevillean yarn, they still produced remarkably systematic accounts of society as a nexus of ever more intricate power relations.

So how can we deal with this methodologically? Most historical sociologists went for multi-causal narratives, placing causality at the cross-current of several power streams. Michel Foucault despaired of nailing down specific power players and opted for a genealogy of power itself. What I propose instead is an entirely different type of narrative – not narrative as a form of causal explanation, but a heuristic for capturing complex social interactions. In other words, shifting from narrative as a means of uncovering a determinative power in action to narratives of power representing power relations as experienced by social actors.

This requires modifying how we study power. Sociologists start with a given definition of power. A better alternative is to dispense with scholarly definitions and consider how social actors themselves comprehend and measure power; how they exercise it and for what purpose. Do they believe power operates through coercion or consent? Is it competitive or cooperative? Concentrated or constantly circulating? People seldom care to formally disentangle this bundle of meanings. Yet their understanding of power reveals itself in action. A sociological account can therefore begin with this array of perspectives and practical dealings. It can swap a single causal narrative for a finely textured fabric of social narratives.

A good place to start is Carl von Clausewitz. Often pigeonholed as a theorist of war, Clausewitz was a keen historian with original reflections on method. Among those was his concept of 'narrative as re-enactment'. Narrative here is a pedagogical tool that replicates rather than explains reality. It educates readers not by telling them why things happened, but by allowing them to experience how reality unfolded for themselves. This requires an exhaustively detailed knowledge of the facts. But above all, it demands an extraordinary amount of empathy with social actors, and a lyrical sensibility in recounting their interactions. The key for Clausewitz is to internalise the practical experience of others faithfully enough to be able to reproduce it. Among contemporary sociologists who struggled with this quest were Robert Nisbet in his *Sociology as an Art Form* (1976) and Abbott in *Processual Sociology* (2016), along with Bourdieu's piercing insights into the epistemological breaks necessary for scholars to access reality and represent it with some fidelity.

Let us first lay out the logic behind causal narratives, which still dominate historical sociology, and discuss their limitations as power becomes more diffuse, before exploring the possibility of an alternative sort of narrative, one better suited to a society constantly in flux.

The Reason Why: Narrative as Explanation

Historical sociology owed its resurgence to the pioneering works of sociologists committed to historical research, and historians adopting a sociological approach – a broad church with scholars as diverse as Perry Anderson, Michael Mann, Theda Skocpol, Charles Tilly and, later, Jack Goldstone, Philip Gorski and James Mahoney. It was institutionalised in the 1980s with edited books, such as the landmark *Vision and Division in Historical Sociology* (1984), specialised publications, including the *Journal of Historical Sociology* (founded in 1988), and a section at the American Sociological Association. A critical onslaught followed. Sociologists eager to deduce generalisable laws that uphold the scientific credentials of their discipline dismissed those travelling in the opposite direction. Historical sociologists reminded them that sociology was always historically grounded, but accepted their detractors' basic premise: that sociologists must produce causal explanations.

Skocpol famously treats history as a data pool for testing causal hypotheses. She distinguishes sociologists from historians by their commitment to 'why' questions.[2] The agenda-setting *Comparative Historical*

---

[2] Skocpol 1984, pp. 365–85.

Analysis in the Social Sciences (2003) seconds that. Historical sociology is essentially concerned with explaining causal configurations.[3] Narratives are only important because causality relies on sequence. Yet sociologists are no mere narrators. They build causal narratives using sophisticated techniques, such as methodical comparisons, process tracing, path dependence and event-structure analysis.

Even less methodologically anxious historical sociologists still adhere to causal narratives. Tilly's work demonstrates the effect of structural variables on society. Anderson, a master at delineating empirical variations, is keen to uncover structural laws. Mann's highly pluralistic model operates through refining causal hypotheses in repeated skirmishes with historical data. Indeed, he complains, 'I find historians far less sophisticated when generalizing about the societies they are studying. I also find annoying the ... piling on [of facts] without trying to arrange their evidence in more systematic ways.' Sociologists, in contrast, find causal chains that historians miss because 'theory leads us to ask questions of the data which historians have not asked'.[4] And when society proves messier than our causal models, we must devise more flexible ones 'suited to dealing with the mess'.[5]

Doubtless, seeking causal explanation is a worthy endeavour that remains central to historical sociology. However, there are good reasons to add a new form of narrative to our arsenal. Society has not only become extremely complicated, but presses onwards in that direction.

The Age of Power Diffusion

One of the founding views of sociology is that people seek power for ideal or material aims. Mann restates that with a practical twist: 'human beings are restless ... striving to increase their enjoyment of the good things of life and capable of choosing and pursuing appropriate means for doing so'. And if this might not apply to everyone, 'enough of them do this to provide the dynamism that is characteristic of human life'.[6] These are not philosophical musings on human nature. Sociologists believe that behaviour is conditioned by society, not inherent or immutable.[7] So, let us consider how people responded to one of the most sweeping changes to their reality.

[3] Mahoney and Rueschemeyer 2003, p. 11.
[4] Mann 1994, pp. 37–43.
[5] Mann 1986, p. 4.
[6] Mann 1986, p. 4.
[7] Nisbet 1966, p. 88.

The overriding concern of early sociologists was the breakdown of traditional communities due to historical trends that came to fruition during the nineteenth century. As hierarchies gave way to fluctuating groups, there was a release of long-pent-up energy and a dispersion of power. Freed from old communal settings, unanchored individuals sought new associations. And the banishment of formal barriers to advancement whetted their appetite. This scrambling for better positions made modernity essentially an arena for 'unending and agonizing competition among individuals'.[8]

This was, at least, how Tocqueville comprehended the changes he lived through. Modern societies might not be that different from traditional ones. However, one of their central preoccupations is the levelling of ranks. And liberation from traditional authority drove individuals into more complex power relations. The same equality that obliterated the privileges of the few opened up society to universal competition. All now faced each other as equals desiring the same things. Uniformity overcrowded the field, leaving individuals little room for manoeuvre, while giving free rein to their aspirations. Each individual now 'tries to insinuate himself into the sphere above him, [and] fights relentlessly against those working up from below'.[9] Rivalries as old as time intensified. Ironically, then, the same modern equality that drew people closer together gave them fresh reasons to resent each other 'so that with mutual fear and envy they rebuff each other's claims to power'.[10] It is impossible to improve upon Tocqueville's depiction. Hunger for power intoxicates those without it, and the dread of losing it torments those who have it. It is never attained without strain; never enjoyed without apprehension. People feel equal, but never to the extent they desire.

[Their ambition] retreats before them without getting quite out of sight, and as it retreats it beckons them on to pursue. Every instant they think they will catch it, and each time it slips through their fingers. They see it close enough to know its charms, but they do not get near enough to enjoy it, and they will be dead before they have fully relished its delights.[11]

Abbott conveys the same effect by inverting our customary concern with scarcity and arguing that 'excess and overabundance' are also problematic. In our attempt to alleviate poverty, we often forget the downside of a society of plenty. Excess of options inspires an excess of aspiration – the ancient verity that the more you have, the more you

[8] Nisbet 1966, pp. 180–3.
[9] Tocqueville 1969, p. 566.
[10] Tocqueville 1969, p. 15.
[11] Tocqueville 1969, pp. 531–8.

desire. Chateaubriand called it *le mal de l'infini*. What intensifies conflict, obviously, is not excess in itself, but the type of uniformity that steers everyone in the same direction – paradoxically, creating scarcity.[12]

For Nisbet, conflict is not necessarily a bad thing. It drives social change. 'Sometimes this conflict is passive, awakening only vague sensations of tension. ... At other times it may be fierce and overt, reflected in widespread mass upheaval.' He soberly admits, however, that such conflicts do not 'resolve themselves inevitably into systems of new coherence and order'.[13] This is because modernity shifted the axes of social conflict. While traditional communities knew conflict between institutions or other well-defined groups, modern society is dominated by power contests on all levels. In socially mobile, impersonal settings, where traditional authority has been successfully subverted, the burden of securing status falls upon individuals, creating a permanent condition of status anxiety.[14] This is why Abbott highlights the fact that an ordered society is one with working traditions – an inconvenient fact to those who relish subverting tradition.[15]

Bourdieu takes a similar view, attributing the relative stability of traditional community to the 'quasi-perfect coincidence between ... expectations and the objective chances of realizing them'.[16] And, like Tocqueville, he knows there is no way back. Power no longer inhabits particular loci: the absolutist monarchy, the ecclesiastical order, the feudal dominion. It spreads continuously through society, producing networks of interlocking power fields, both autonomous and interdependent, competitive and complementary. Individuals belong to one or more fields, and their ceaseless interaction reproduces, subverts or totally destroys these fields. The subordinated wish to rise; the dominant hope to persist; and the ferment extends across fields – as even the dominant quarrel over 'the dominant principle of domination and the "exchange rate" between ... different kinds of power', and their strife creates opportunities for usurpers to replace them and rewrite the rule book.[17]

Corresponding to Bourdieu's fields are Abbott's ecologies. An ecology is composed of social actors located in specific spaces and interacting with others in neighbouring ecologies. Each ecology is the ground for competition and collaboration amongst members, and a springboard for similar interactions across ecological boundaries. The various ecologies constrain

---

[12] Abbott 2016, pp. 123–44.
[13] Nisbet 1999, pp. 189–93.
[14] Nisbet 1999, p. 123.
[15] Abbott 2016, pp. 217–18.
[16] Bourdieu 2000a, p. 147.
[17] Bourdieu 2000b, pp. 102–3.

and contest each other. Society is basically a codification of linked ecologies that struggle, overlap, merge, divide and build alliances.[18]

Nisbet, Bourdieu and Abbott – like Tocqueville – are therefore primarily concerned with the diffusion of power, in itself a reason to transcend the narrow focus on why certain actors are dominant to a wider inquiry into how it all happens.

From Why to How: Narrative as Re-Enactment

When historians think about re-enactment, it is R. G. Collingwood who comes to mind. For Collingwood, re-enactment is less a method than a philosophy. Realists insist that the past is what really happened. Collingwood disagrees. The past is unknowable. Historians have no direct knowledge of it. They can only re-enact it in their minds.[19] Slightly carried away by his anti-realism, Collingwood identifies re-enactment of the past with 'the past itself' because it is all we can know about it[20]– hence, the accusation of relativism.

But what is being re-enacted? It is the thought of social agents. Collingwood accepts that historians investigate actions. However, he declares that action has an exterior and interior: outside, the concrete conditions; inside, the mental aspect. Historians commence by detailing external aspects, but the crux of their work is 'to discern the thought of the agent'. It is not enough to determine the circumstances under which Caesar crossed the Rubicon. Proper history requires rethinking what went through Caesar's mind.[21] And Collingwood is quite exacting. Copying or imitating will not do; 'to know another's act of thought involves repeating it for oneself'.[22] How is that possible if the scholar inhabits a different context from the subject? Collingwood believes we can have similar thoughts without experiencing the same situation. We can 'rethink the process of thought by which Archimedes reached his famous discovery' without feeling the bath water rising or his sense of elation.[23] In other words, historians do not have to replicate the emotions or sensations of agents to access their thoughts.

Collingwood's re-enactment may be invaluable to intellectual history. After all, he announced, in another rhetorical flourish, that 'all history is the history of thought'.[24] But his application diverges sharply

---

[18] Abbott 2016, pp. 35–50.
[19] Collingwood 1993, p. 282.
[20] Collingwood 1993, p. 450.
[21] Collingwood 1993, pp. 213–15.
[22] Collingwood 1993, p. 288.
[23] Collingwood 1993, p. 297.
[24] Collingwood 1993, p. 215.

from what is proposed here. Actions are indeed the object of study. And some are expressions of thought, although a great many remain pre-reflective. However, rethinking thoughts is infinitely more speculative than reimagining lived experiences. Most scholars know what it is like to be afraid or angry. They are familiar with pain and pleasure, hunger and sleep deprivation. They can conceive these feeling in amplified form. With a stretch of the imagination, they can simulate those emotions and sensations within themselves to empathise with social actors. This requires reconstructing material circumstances: the weight of a soldier's backpack, the length of the march, the harshness of terrain and weather, the frequency of ambushes. Such tangibles help approximate a soldier's condition. Inhabiting his consciousness and rethinking the same thoughts is murkier business, especially when it comes to evidence. Of course all historians contend with the unreliability of memory and testimonies. But corporeal experiences rank higher than retrospective reasoning. In war memoirs, an account of how an officer reached a certain decision might be greeted with scepticism. Descriptions of how panic loosened his bowels, or how frost paralysed his limbs, are more readily accepted.

More important, Collingwood is again concerned with causality. He makes the controversial claim that ascertaining people's thoughts explains their actions. 'When the historian knows what happened, he already knows why it happened.'[25] It was a bit too much even for a sympathetic reader such as William Dray. Collingwood's 'equivalence of the "what" and "why", although accepted by many of his apologists, I find quite indefensible'.[26] Fortunately, Clausewitz offers an alternative approach to re-enactment.

Two-thirds of Clausewitz's work is historical studies. *On War*, which takes up the rest, is a theoretical meditation grounded in history. His approach emphasises how rather than why things happen. He has little patience with the 'plain narrative of a historical event, which merely arranges facts one after another, and at most touches on their immediate causal links'. But he also worries that those fixated on locating causality may overstretch facts. Outcomes result from concurrent causes, some unknown, others difficult to assess. His proposition is to dig deeper. Without recovering the specific circumstances surrounding an action, it becomes 'like an object seen at a great distance ... it looks the same from every angle'.[27] Only by 'painstakingly assembling the specific details of

---

[25] Collingwood 1993, p. 214.
[26] Dray 1999, p. 38.
[27] Clausewitz 1984, pp. 156–74.

certain episodes' can we 're-create the events for ... readers'.[28] A Clause-witzian narrative, in other words, attempts 'to approximate, if not repli-cate, actual experience'. This historical re-enactment, the recreating of past reality in all its practical details, is meant to substitute for experi-ence. It bestows upon readers a certain 'sensibility rather than a form of knowledge'.[29]

There are affinities with Tocqueville, according to one Clausewitz scholar. Not only did they both write comparative-historical sociology, but their literary styles moved from abstract analysis to realistic portraits that captured complex social interactions.[30] History, for Tocqueville, did not impart lessons. But immersing readers in particulars allows them to develop a sense of how things work.[31] Almost all chapter titles of his *Ancien régime* start with 'How'. Craig Calhoun is sympathetic. Those who explain things by showing how they work, rather than just what caused them, move beyond explaining to understanding. They delineate the 'practical orientations' of social actors rather than 'external causal linkages'.[32]

Bourdieu never attempted such narrative himself, but prescribes it. Criticising those who pursue single lines of causality, he urges sociolo-gists to 'track multiple lines and levels of causation to whatever extent is practically possible' in order to 'reconstruct a web of causal inter-dependence'.[33] And like Clausewitz, Bourdieu does not believe in causal laws, only sensitising concepts, or thinking tools that render complex sequences intelligible.[34] Yet he comes closest to Clausewitz in declar-ing: 'My entire scientific enterprise is indeed based on the belief that the deepest logic of the social world can be grasped only if one plunges into the particularity of an empirical reality ... with the objective of [re]con-structing it'[35] – described elsewhere as the actualisation or reactivation of social reality.[36]

Abbott ploughs deeper still. He compares causal and narrative accounts to two paths through the same garden. You see the same things but from different angles. In the causal view, variables govern society. 'Variables do things' to social subjects.[37] From a narrative perspective,

---

[28] Clausewitz 1992, p. 104.
[29] Sumida 2008, pp. 189–95.
[30] Clausewitz 1992, pp. 143–53.
[31] Winthrop 1981, pp. 88–9.
[32] Calhoun 1998, p. 864.
[33] Gorski 2013, pp. 356–7.
[34] Gorski 2013, p. 328.
[35] Bourdieu 1998, p. 2.
[36] Bourdieu 2000a, p. 88.
[37] In Calhoun's vivid image, causes are like doctors treating patients. People are objects not actors (Calhoun 1998, pp. 851, 864).

the social world is constituted of social actors who do things to each other. Their interactions are the building blocks of narrative. So while causal analysts might dress up their arguments in narrative style to make their variables appear livelier, narrativists believe the social process itself can only be revealed through narrative.[38] For example, a causal account concludes that a revolution was caused by a structural variable such as class struggle, or shifts in the international power balance, and then tells it like a story. Narrativists, by contrast, attribute revolution to a series of interactions whose inherent logic could only be captured by a carefully constructed narrative. Those who rely on causal variables protest, rightly, that 'reality is too complex to do otherwise'. Abbott admits as much, yet urges them to embrace complexity, not shun it through abstraction. Society consists of actors who interact in complicated ways. Causality exists, but it flows differently depending on the type and order of their interaction. Consequently, some causal factors might count in one situation but not others; they remain 'bubbling in the background'. The effect of education on income, for instance, cannot be generalised. It depends on how interactions occurred in real time. In the narrative approach, therefore, reality is not directly produced by causal variables, but social interactions that alter the value of these variables. 'Such a view directly contravenes the views of most social scientists,' Abbott concludes. 'The physical science model on which social scientists try to operate makes no allowances for causes that appear and disappear.'[39]

Not only that. Causal studies are only concerned with events that happen. Good narratives are not similarly restricted. Just because we know how the tale ends does not mean we forget that most events do not occur – though they could have. Narratives preserve those counterfactuals. Social interactions are open to various realisations, not just the one that occurred. For readers to fully comprehend reality, they must 'hear the whisper of possibility and the sigh of passage'.[40] They must feel how in the 'succession of presents ... everything in the social structure is at risk', everything is on the brink of change.[41] Actors here are no longer the unwilling servants of structure. They are not simply reflections of social forces beyond their control: class, identity, institutions. They might be shaped or constrained by them but still make moment-to-moment choices that either reproduce or modify these structures.

[38] Here is how Calhoun puts it (Calhoun 1998, p. 857): causal narratives are constructed by first identifying causal factors that then intrude into and direct the narrative.
[39] Abbott 1990, pp. 140–7.
[40] Abbott 2007, pp. 86–90.
[41] Abbott 2016, p. 14.

The focus on social actors owes something to Tocqueville's preference for methodological individualism in explaining history over structural entities, such as class (Marx) or social facts (Durkheim), which have autonomous explanatory power.[42] But Tocqueville's individuals are not the rational actors of economics or game theory, but rather are involved in concrete social settings. Not atomised, abstract individuals, but kinfolk, workers, politicians, soldiers, intellectuals and people who wear several hats at once. Neither should the readmission of individuals into history, as Abbott puts it, lead to a return to the Great Man theory. It is rather a rejection of the view of the world as a place where 'large social forces push little individuals around'. Individuals are not clean slates on which social structures inscribe their logic. They are the nexus of the historical connection between past and future. They carry the past literally in their bodies and memories as they move forward. And they do it better than structures or even institutions, where tradition and experience are scattered in thousands of minds, documents and half-forgotten rituals.[43] This conception resolves the byzantine debate on agents versus structure. Here agents embody structure.

Tocqueville was an early advocate of this two-way interaction between what sociologists call micro and macro levels of society. The micro does not shape society from the bottom up. Nor does the macro act in reverse. The micro embodies the macro, then goes on to reproduce or change it.[44] Bourdieu calls it structured agency. Outcomes result from the meeting of two histories: the objective factors of social structure (field); and the particular dispositions of social actors within those structures (habitus). Social interactions reflect both an actor's 'feel for the game and the game itself'. Causal factors, such as economic or cultural hegemony, count only if and to the extent that they imbue social actors with specific dispositions. And these dispositions, in turn, 'do not lead in a determinate way to a determinate action; they are revealed and fulfilled only in appropriate circumstances'.[45] In other words, only through social interactions in practical situations does causality reveal itself. Like Bourdieu, Nisbet is interested in people making choices. Action is based on people's knowledge of their social world. And the essence of this knowledge is practicality: not academic knowledge about society, but common-sense knowledge gained through trial and error and direct experience of society.[46] Causal relations cannot be found outside the realm of social interactions.

---

[42] Elster 2009, p. 6.
[43] Abbott 2016, pp. 3–7.
[44] Elster 2009, pp. 182–3.
[45] Bourdieu 2000a, pp. 149–51.
[46] Nisbet 1986, pp. 30–2.

Events are where these interactions occur. Society is a flow of events, made and navigated by people, who are themselves lineages of events. People experience their lives narratively through the stories they tell about who they are, what happened to them, why they behave this way. And these events are knotted into bundles of social relations, which in turn present new constraints and opportunities. Abbott sums it up eloquently: just as 'Personalities are made up of shreds of social life. So also is social life itself merely the interaction of shreds of persons.'[47]

No wonder Abbott is among the few singled out for praise in William Sewell's otherwise disparaging exposé of historical sociologists. Embarrassed to confront their scientifically minded discipline with something as contingent as events, they seek sturdier scaffolding for their historical research. One is teleology – adhered to in spirit long after the term became anathema. Here narratives are propelled by underlying processes, such as state building or progress towards social justice. Another is experimental induction, a favourite of comparativists, whereby fragments from one historical narrative are carved up for comparison with fragments from another, allowing the testing of the determinative power of structural factors such as class struggle, military competition or political institutionalisation. Sewell exhorts sociologists to shed their timidity and embrace an eventful sociology. Social life is a series of interactions. Most reproduce existing patterns. Some modify, subvert or transform them. These are the events worth studying. 'An eventful historical sociology', he concludes, 'would come to resemble history ever more closely.'[48]

Indeed, sociologists distinguish themselves from historians based on how they treat events. According to Nisbet, sociologists are interested in events as signifiers of change. Historians, meanwhile, see events as building blocks of the past not milestones to the future. But sociology can become historical without losing its preoccupation with change, by reorienting its research from structural forces that cause change to how disparate events come together to render several options for change possible. Nisbet is not asking historical sociologists to apply the same narrative framework of historiography. They just need to focus on specific events rather than built-in determinants of change.[49]

It is events that show which social relations had weight and which remained irrelevant; which choices were determined by rigid structures and which demonstrated a degree of flexibility. The narrative approach is therefore not just historical, but fundamentally empirical. Society is not

---

[47] Abbott 2016, p. 246.
[48] Sewell 2005, p. 111.
[49] Nisbet 1999, pp. 92–8.

an abstract space governed by causal laws. It is always a specific time and place, always historically contingent. This should not reduce events to a laundry list of contingencies. Well-crafted narratives allow for patterns to emerge: not general laws, but causal mechanisms at work here and there. This is how Clausewitz understood war: not as a social phenomenon governed by universal laws, but the realm of shared mechanisms, such as friction, that feature somehow in most wars. Some of these mechanisms are exportable, enabling sociologists to draw on knowledge acquired in one setting to understand another. Hence, Tocqueville's study of democracy in America shed light on contemporaneous tendencies in France.

A narrative can therefore go beyond why democracy succeeded in America, or Waterloo ended in French defeat, to how social interactions coalesced in actual events to make this happen. And the knowledge generated therefrom can prove generally useful in studying other democracies and wars. However, it is not a matter of mastering a new research technique. This type of narrative requires changes in the researcher's attitude towards the subject and purpose of research.

Breaking with Scholastic Fallacies

In *Recollections*, Tocqueville contrasts intellectuals with practical folk: 'the former see general causes everywhere, whereas the latter, spending their lives amid the disconnected events of each day, freely attribute everything to particular incidents and think that all the little strings their hands are busy pulling daily are those that control the world's destiny. Probably both of them are mistaken.'[50] Scholars cannot bridge the gap, Tocqueville continues, by spinning out theories and fitting everyday practices into them. Practice must come first.[51] Clausewitz is similarly put off by great minds with 'much intelligence and cultivation, but wholly ignorant of real life'. To transcend 'false conflicts between theory and practice', he urges them to discard 'artificial and learned theorizing' and 'empty phraseology', and allow themselves to be 'stimulated by the force of immediate circumstance', just like their subjects.[52]

Empathy is therefore the key: internalising other logics of action than our own. Calhoun presses sociologists to pursue empathetic understanding of their objects of study because social practice cannot be sufficiently explained in terms of causal conditions.[53] But empathy presents a moral challenge. It demands that most elusive of research goals: impartiality.

[50] Tocqueville 1987, p. 62.
[51] Winthrop 1981, pp. 96–7.
[52] Clausewitz 1992, pp. 104–15, 134–5.
[53] Calhoun 1998, p. 852.

To get around this problem, W. G. Runciman recommends a multi-tiered attitude to understanding. Reporting actions accurately furnishes primary understanding. Explaining why actors acted this way elevates that to secondary understanding. A third level still is to appreciate what it was like for them. And this understanding triad stands separate from evaluating the merits of action, morally or otherwise.[54] Runciman is quite clear on the distinction between reportage and explanation. Reports must be plain enough to be 'accepted as factual by rival observers, even from different theoretical schools' and not preclude alternative explanations.[55] Describing, however, is trickier. It can get lost in the 'ill-charted territory between matters of palpable fact and of palpable value'.[56] When referring to illiterate voters, are we reporting their lack of education, describing what their lives are like, or scorning their intellectual inferiority?

Still, impartial understanding is achievable. Impartiality is often confused with objectivity, and the latter is indeed beyond the pale. In tracing the history of both concepts, Lorraine Daston distinguishes between impartiality, which means not taking sides, and objectivity, which implies value-neutrality. Impartiality is not indifference. 'On the contrary, the aim of historical impartiality was to reach sound conclusions ... much as the aim of judicial impartiality was to reach a just verdict.'[57] Like Runciman, she accepts that passing judgement cannot precede even-handed understanding. Sociology provides many early examples.

It was remarkable of a dry methodological analyst of Tocqueville's work to praise him so passionately for fairness.[58] Indeed, Tocqueville writes in a letter to his slightly biased English translator, 'I beg you earnestly to struggle against yourself ... to preserve my book its character, which is a veritable impartiality.'[59] He reminds his brother that: 'Personal opinion adds nothing to the strength of reasoning, and can harm it to the extent that the perfect impartiality that inspires confidence is no longer seen in the author. ... The reader must be allowed to judge.' His ambivalence grew from a deep-seated conviction that searching for certainty in a world of approximations was a disease that intellectuals must cure themselves from. Suspending judgement during research is more becoming of a scholar than applause or condemnation.[60] And he does not achieve this in the pedantic fashion of presenting conflicting views on

---

[54] Runciman 1983, p. 1.
[55] Runciman 1983, p. 95.
[56] Runciman 1972, pp. 380–8.
[57] Daston 2015, p. 28.
[58] Smelser 1973, p. 40.
[59] Tocqueville 1969, p. xi.
[60] Adler 2019, p. 54.

every topic. Instead, he unsettles readers by conveying how perplexing reality appears to social actors, taking them behind the scenes, exposing them to irresolvable paradoxes and circumstances alien to their own.[61]

Clausewitz also stands out for his attempt at impartiality. Like Tocqueville, his critical analysis of his own society was so fair-minded, it sometimes felt cold.[62] Even in histories of military campaigns he personally participated in, his tone is 'detached and impersonal'. In fact, one of the reasons why Wellington agreed to respond to his study of Waterloo was because his friends described Clausewitz as 'an honest writer seeking the truth, rather than one with a personal or national ax to grind', a writer free from 'prejudices and nonsense'.[63] Clausewitz is invariably empathic to his subjects. When considering the actions of Napoleon, his bitter enemy, he often repeats, 'But we must also consider matters as they appeared from Bonaparte's perspective.'[64] His analysis of the 1812 Russian campaign, through which he personally suffered, is notable for trying to reconstruct the circumstances of various actors, from princes to army privates. Clausewitz is convinced that understanding practices requires one 'to recapture the way things appeared at the time, rather than impose retrospective judgments or values'.[65] He tells readers, 'my entire merit will perhaps be found in ... the eradication of prejudices ... to allow you a clear view of the issue so you will soon be in a position to draw your own conclusions'.[66]

By contrast, many contemporary sociologists fall below par. In surveying recent sociological writings, Abbott finds far too many infused with indignation, disgust, moral outrage. Their aim is to rub noses in repugnant or otherwise offensive actions rather than place them in perspective.[67] And this inspired his drive for a more humanist sociology.

Regardless of method, topic or normative views, a researcher must treat social actors with humane sympathy.[68] Abbott invokes the golden rule. 'We too will be studies in our time, and it behooves us to study others as we would be studied.'[69] His tone becomes personal. 'Any subject I study is a human being, deserving the same dignity and care I would

---

[61] Smelser 1973, pp. 46–7.
[62] Paret 1976, p. 256.
[63] Bassford 2015, pp. 6–8.
[64] Clausewitz 1992, p. 204.
[65] Moran 2015, pp. 240–5.
[66] Clausewitz 2015b, p. 20.
[67] Abbott 2007, pp. 93–4.
[68] By sympathy Abbott actually means empathy: 'Sympathy here has the literal sense of "feeling with" another, not the common modern one of "providing emotional support for" another' (Abbott 2016, p. 286).
[69] Abbott 2016, p. 231.

take in understanding myself.' And this is why, he concludes, 'a human-ist sociologist is hesitant'. Sociology as a vocation strives to grasp how people behave when caught up in the force of immediate circumstances and the merciless flow of events. It does not brandish weapons such as false consciousness and hidden biases to imply that scholars know people better than they know themselves. Sociologists can code variables and classify actors for analytical purposes. But they must remain mindful of how this violates their subjects. Just as sociologists modify their meth-ods to make them more scientific, they should also make them more humane. People must be understood on their own terms, not reduced to the plaything of presumptuous researchers.[70] 'I've always been struck by the incoherence reigning in one and the same soul', Tocqueville remarks in a letter, on 26 September 1840, 'and I've often heartily laughed seeing historians force themselves to make a single piece out of a being com-pletely composed of retrieved bits.'[71]

Naturally, sociologists blink when they encounter behaviours they dis-approve of, especially 'strange and frightening things'. Nonetheless, they ought to remember that these form part of a social reality that must be 'humanely understood in order to be avoided'.[72] Bourdieu also endorses the search for the *raison d'être* of the seemingly most illogical or derisory human behaviors ... rather than condemning or mocking them, like the "half-learned" who are always ready to "play the philosopher"'.[73]

Humane sympathy certainly does not mean that to understand all is to pardon all – like sociological approaches that shift responsibility from individuals to social structures. It simply prioritises understanding the world over changing it. This is where Abbott parts company with Michael Burawoy and other campaigners for public sociology. He rejects what he sees as their narrow-minded belief that moral people must change soci-ety. Understanding society is 'inherently a moral project, whether we go on to exercise our undoubted political right to urge change or not'. Either way, sociology must begin with understanding, 'itself based on humane sympathy, and not on any particular judgment'. Otherwise, the author is 'a politician masquerading as a scientist' or a peddler of 'ideology masquerading as truth'.[74]

Abbott, in short, rejects the distinction between politically commit-ted sociologists and detached, professional ones, arguing that these are

---

[70] Abbott 2016, pp. 287–9.
[71] Tocqueville 2018, p. 149.
[72] Abbott 2016, pp. 287–9.
[73] Bourdieu 2000a, p. 2.
[74] Abbott 2016, pp. 279–90.

different types of 'sociological encounters with the normative side of the social process: the political one, which emphasizes attempts to change a social process perceived as unjust; and the moral or humanist one, which emphasizes the attempt to understand the complexities and varieties of the social "for themselves", as they are'.[75] Improving knowledge is itself a great moral project. Indeed, Nisbet describes the discovery of what was previously unknown or scarcely imaginable as a 'marvelous tonic to not only university professors but people in all walks of life'.[76]

This does not appeal to many academics who, as Bourdieu caustically remarks, relish the illusion that their writings are some sort of political action. Bourdieu himself was often repelled by heroic postures, rolling with every new fad. The sociologist's duty, he writes, 'is to tell about the things of the social world ... the way they are'.[77] He might have found solace in Clausewitz's assertion that 'critical analysis exists only to discover the truth, not to sit in judgment'.[78]

It probably helps that Clausewitz and Tocqueville are realists who distrust ideology.[79] So is Bourdieu, who knew his colleagues found his social realism disenchanting. Scholars, who are overwhelmingly idealistic, 'will be quick to denounce the cynical realism of a description of how things really work'. Nonetheless, Bourdieu continues, if one is not to 'indulge in an irresponsible utopianism, which often has no other effect than to procure the short-lived euphoria of humanist hopes, almost always as brief as adolescence ... it is necessary ... to return to a "realistic" vision of the universe'.[80] Alas, 'humankind cannot bear too much reality', as T. S. Eliot laments.

But the challenge to empathy is not just moral but also scientific attitudes. The typical epistemic posture of social scientists is to rise above reality to see it better; to gain perspective through distance. The scholar occupies a fixed and higher position. Subjects down there in the muddle are cut out of the dense texture of their lives using analytical frames to become interchangeable props representing whatever causal forces are projected onto them. Scholars then pour their theories into the heads of actors, explaining practices according to whichever causal model is currently in favour.[81] People become figments of our scientific imagination.

The problem with this all-too-common procedure is that, unlike social actors, researchers do not have skin in the game. They are as sheltered as

[75] Abbott 2016, p. 268 n. 7.
[76] Nisbet 2013, p. 211.
[77] Bourdieu 2000a, pp. 2–5.
[78] Clausewitz 2015a, p. 123.
[79] Paret 1992, p. 153 n. 22.
[80] Bourdieu 2000a, p. 127.
[81] Bourdieu 2000a, pp. 51–4.

their subjects are exposed. And this inhibits their ability to come to terms with the practical logic of those whose bodies, emotions, livelihoods and reputations are at stake, and are therefore forced to take life seriously. Social actors feel 'at home in the world because the world is in [them]'. Scholars, on the other hand, inhabit a transcendent universe, observing social life from afar.[82] Bourdieu, in fact, identifies the scholastic situation or *skholè* as freedom from real-life urgencies.[83]

Scholars, moreover, do not just observe subjects from a safe distance, but also operate in a different time zone. Social actors are *in* time, constantly caught up in the immediate present or, at most, the imminently forthcoming. Researchers approach time from the outside. Actions under study are either in the past or recent history.[84] Abbott notes how sociologists treat events as markers of the flow of time towards a preconceived outcome. Actors embedded in time experience events as open-ended.[85] This is why Tocqueville distinguishes between time in the objective sense and as perceived by social actors, always prioritising subjective time in explaining behaviour.[86] Abbott goes further. Research should not be oriented towards outcomes because the 'social process doesn't have outcomes. It just keeps on going.'[87] Historical sociology erroneously 'envisions a timeline and slides a window of investigation along the line, cutting out a segment for investigation'. It then uses narrative to create the illusion of self-contained events with a beginning and an end. In reality, 'Any moment can be an end; any moment can be a beginning. Outcome is simply the state of affairs in some arbitrary time period.'[88] Socially authentic narratives must be attuned to the continuity of social life: how past interactions determine present relations, setting the stage for future rounds – how everything remains in transit.

Finally, it is crucial to recognise how the moral and scientific elements of the scholastic attitude are related. It is only because researchers and their subjects occupy parallel realities, the motionless and transcendent one versus the fluid here and now, that they are tempted to judge them. The 'abstracted sociologist outside the situation' can neither appreciate nor 'recreate for the reader' the immediacy and tensions engulfing social actors. Crafting such narratives requires scholars to cross the chasm between their reality and those of their subjects, to stretch their

[82] Bourdieu 2000a, pp. 140–51.
[83] Bourdieu 2000a, p. 1.
[84] Bourdieu 2000a, pp. 206–7.
[85] Abbott 2007, p. 85.
[86] Elster 2009, p. 184.
[87] Abbott 2016, p. 4.
[88] Abbott 2016, pp. 181–6.

sociological imagination in order to comprehend the lives of others. Abbott wishes them to be 'curious without exoticism, sympathetic without presumption, and thoughtful without judgment'.[89] Bourdieu's remedy is quite similar. Acknowledge the repressed distinction between the scholarly and ordinary worlds, then 'reverse the movement … return to the world of everyday existence … armed with a scientific thought that is sufficiently aware of itself and its limits to be capable of thinking practice without destroying its object'.[90] To be able to place yourself in the position of those immersed in situations alien to your own is the necessary first step towards understanding the world. And then comes the problem of communication.

On Artistic Style

'Hitherto you have experienced truth only with the abstract intellect. I will bring you where you can taste it like honey,' wrote C. S. Lewis. Clausewitz has little faith in the ability of language to convey meaning: 'words, being cheap, are the most common means of creating false impressions'.[91] Rather than explaining things to the intellect, language should transmit a mental and emotional state. It should embody experience and invite readers to relive it. And this acquired sensibility, Clausewitz believes, is the basis of sound knowledge. One interpreter speculates that the Prussian theorist might have been influenced by the Passions, musical re-enactments of the final days of Christ that provide listeners with intuitive understanding of suffering. Clausewitz and his wife were involved in Mendelssohn's campaign to revive Bach's *St Matthew Passion* after half a century of neglect. It was performed in Berlin in 1829 as Clausewitz honed his views on narrative.[92] Clausewitz wants language to stimulate readers by simulating reality.

A student of Tocqueville, Judith Adler, attributes the longevity of his influence to style as much as content. The pallid language of contemporary social science contrasts poorly with his 'vivid, dramatically gripping vocabulary that invites intimate identification and … private introspection'. Without affectation, he treats writing as an art, refining its rhythm, emotional tone and variation on themes, borrowing devices from music and the visual arts. A jot on the margins of one of his manuscripts reminds him to convey a certain idea using 'a precise and particular image'. In

---

[89] Abbott 2007, pp. 93–5.
[90] Bourdieu 2000a, p. 50.
[91] Clausewitz 1984, p. 202.
[92] Sumida 2008, p. 197.

another, he notes that 'the pace should be quickened'. When circulating drafts, he often solicits advice on how to make his prose 'sensible to the imagination'. He wants to endow readers with 'a sense of intimate mimetic participation' in the reality being described through 'bodily participation in the text: seeing, breathing, vocalizing, hearing'. And indeed, in one Wagnerian paragraph he breaks sentences into clauses 'cut to the measure of a human breath ... breathing slows as the clauses ascended, in a series of suspended aspirations, before coming to rest'. This is how he diverges from most sociologists today. 'Tocqueville aims to *move* his readers', Adler concludes, '*not* as an expert, critic, preacher, or opinion writer but as a courteous conversant.'[93]

Nonsense, Skocpol scowls on behalf of sociologists. These narratives, 'like a good Flaubert novel', convey through colourful detail an 'impression of fullness much more readily than works of historical sociology'.[94] However, sociologists persuade by revealing causation not recreating the past.[95] Bourdieu, that great admirer of Flaubert, returns the compliment. Sociological interpretations that claim to be more scientific than rich narratives remind him of bad novels where heroic forces control events – 'totally unrealistic representations of ordinary action'.[96] He also frets about widening the gap between scholastic and practical logics by substituting everyday language with the 'socially neutralized and controlled language that prevails in scholastic universes'.[97] Perhaps this is why Tocqueville insists on employing 'everyday words of self-evident, stable meaning'.[98] Runciman dares go further, permitting sociologists to use 'terms so unscientifically elastic that they can be stretched' because description is particularly hard. Runciman invokes Wittgenstein's challenge to underline the difficulty: Can anyone describe the aroma of coffee? The success of a description hangs on its communicative effect. It does not inform or solicit approval, it rather makes readers feel how things felt. A good pastoral symphony is the one that transports listeners to the idyllic countryside.[99]

Indeed, none of this is alien to classical sociology. It is true that Tocqueville's analytical accounts are not presented in the form of sustained historical narration, yet they are peppered with snippets of portraits, metaphors and vignettes. So are many classic accounts. Marx's portrayal

---

[93] Adler 2019, pp. 47–55.
[94] Skocpol 1984, p. 371.
[95] Skocpol 1987, p. 27.
[96] Bourdieu 2000a, pp. 137–8.
[97] Bourdieu 2000a, p. 32.
[98] Adler 2019, p. 52.
[99] Runciman 1972, pp. 380–8.

of factory life is positively Dickensian. Simmel's stranger comes alive on the page as much as that of Camus. And few watch Puccini's *La Bohème* without recalling Tocqueville's depiction of nineteenth-century intellectuals.

Nisbet and Abbott famously champion artistic style in sociology. Nisbet's mentor, F. J. Teggart, notes that the reconstruction of reality requires a sensibility 'which is the very essence of art'.[100] Nisbet first broaches the topic in his presidential address to the Pacific Sociological Association in 1962, later published as an article, then a book in 1976. Sociology is both art and science. For its scientific findings to amount to more than a 'sandheap of empiricism', it should draw on artistic forms and modes of discovery.[101] Nisbet distinguishes between science, as the systematic study of something, and its reduction to causal hypothesis-testing, which he calls 'scientism', not science. Sociologists labour under the misconception that science uncovers reality and art beautifies it. Yet both strive to understand reality by capturing its chaos in a lucid representation.[102] And indeed, forms of representation, such as portraiture, landscaping and techniques conveying motion, can be employed in sociology, as much as in painting, musical composition and literature.[103] A portrait of a soldier relays features common to an entire social group, making the universal concrete. In contrast, an urban landscape distils in a single snapshot a multitude of social variations.[104] Literary pace and musical tempo transmit the dynamic buzz of social life.[105]

Likewise, Abbott's advocacy of lyrical sociology is not about embellishing explanatory narratives to render them more pleasing to the eye. He echoes Nisbet's belief that sociology is concerned with scientific knowledge, but that its roots and aims lie in the humanities.[106] Abbot, however, is also interested in what style tells us about authors, not just subjects. Style restores the process of discovery that begins when a sociologist is overpowered by the dazzling complexity of a certain social situation, then tries to 'awaken those feelings in the minds – and even more the hearts – of his readers'. He offers the example of an urban sociologist of Chicago who transmutes with his subjects: socialising with elites, feeling lonely with urbanites, wistful with bohemians, listless with immigrants. Lyric here is not about elegant prose. It sets the mood. In

---

[100] Teggart 1916, p. 123.
[101] Nisbet 1962, p. 67.
[102] Nisbet 2017, pp. 3–15.
[103] Nisbet 2017, p. 110.
[104] Nisbet 2017, pp. 68–70, 43.
[105] Nisbet 2017, p. 6.
[106] Abbott 2016, p. 277.

E. P. Thompson's classic on the working class, one glimpses both the workers' passionate radicalism and the author's reaction to it. This is how lyricism differs from its 'avatar in the social sciences – explanation'. Causal narrators explain outcomes through causally arranged events. Lyrical ones relay their powerful reaction to events through tone and images that sweep the reader along.[107]

To conclude, discovering and ascertaining facts is the point of departure for any historical research. But where do we go from here? Historical sociologists commonly provide causal explanations of why things happened. And they do so by identifying one or more powers that determine social outcomes, and construct a narrative around that. This is usually an abstract variable: class, culture, social identity groups, state institutions, geopolitics, or a mixture. However, the diffusion of power in society continues to muddy the waters. An alternative method begins with understanding social interactions through the accounts that people give of themselves and how they recognise and practise power. For whatever else it may be, power is a relational phenomenon that reveals itself in action. Re-enacting narratives that capture how reality unfolded from the viewpoint of social actors might be preferable to neat chronologies with a solid line of causation shot right through. Prerequisites for weaving these bottom-up narratives of power are two: an empathetic sensibility that internalises other people's experiences; and a literary style that vividly portrays their situation. Above all, a scholarly disposition that embraces social complexity rather than settling for the simplification of underlying processes and structural factors.

References

Abbott, Andrew. 1990. 'Conceptions of Time and Events in Social Science Methods: Causal and Narrative Approaches', *Historical Methods: A Journal of Quantitative and Interdisciplinary History*, 23: 4, pp. 140–50.

2007. 'Against Narrative: A Preface to Lyrical Sociology', *Sociological Theory*, 25: 1, pp. 67–99.

2016. *Processual Sociology*. Chicago.

Adler, Judith. 2019. 'Tocqueville Mortal and Immortal: Power and Style' in *The Anthem Companion to Alexis de Tocqueville*, ed. Daniel Gordon. London.

Bassford, Christopher. 2015. 'Introduction' in *On Waterloo: Clausewitz, Wellington, and the Campaign of 1815*, ed. Christopher Bassford, Daniel Moran and Gregory W. Pedlow. Clausewitz.com (bicentennial paperback ed.).

Bourdieu, Pierre. 1977. *Outline of a Theory of Practice*. Cambridge.

---

[107] Abbott 2007, pp. 70–82.

1988. *Homo Academicus*. Paris.

1998. *Practical Reason*. Cambridge.

2000a. *Pascalian Meditations*. Stanford.

2000b. *Practical Reason: On the Theory of Action*. Stanford.

Calhoun, Craig. 1998. 'Explanation in Historical Sociology: Narrative, General Theory, and Historically Specific Theory', *American Journal of Sociology*, 104: 3, pp. 846–71.

von Clausewitz, Carl. 1984. *On War*. Princeton.

1992. *Historical and Political Writings*, ed. and trans. Peter Paret and Daniel Moran. Princeton.

2015a. 'The Campaign of 1815: Strategic Overview of the Campaign of 1815' in *On Waterloo: Clausewitz, Wellington, and the Campaign of 1815*, ed. Christopher Bassford, Daniel Moran and Gregory W. Pedlow. Clausewitz .com (bicentennial paperback ed.).

2015b. *On Small Wars*, ed. and trans. Christopher Daase and James W. Davis. New York.

Cobban, Alfred. 1961. 'History and Sociology' in *Historical Studies III*. London.

Collingwood, R. G. 1993. *Idea of History*, ed. Jan van der Dussen. Oxford.

Daston, Lorraine. 2015. 'Objectivity and Impartiality: Epistemic Virtues in the Humanities' in *The Making of the Humanities*, vol. III: *The Modern Humanities*, ed. Rens Bod et al. Amsterdam.

Dray, William. 1999. *History as Re-enactment: R. G. Collingwood's Idea of History*. Oxford.

Elster, Jon. 2009. *Alexis de Tocqueville: The First Social Scientist*. Cambridge.

Gorski, Philip. 2013. *Bourdieu and Historical Analysis*. London.

Mahoney, James and Dietrich Rueschemeyer. 2003. 'Comparative Historical Analysis: Achievements and Agendas' in *Comparative Historical Analysis in the Social Sciences*, ed. James Mahoney and Dietrich Rueschemeyer. Cambridge.

Mann, Michael. 1986. *The Sources of Social Power*, vol. I: *A History of Power from the Beginning to AD 1760*. New York.

1994. 'In Praise of Macro-Sociology: A Reply to Goldthorpe', *British Journal of Sociology*, 45: 1, pp. 37–54.

Moran, Daniel. 2015. 'Clausewitz on Waterloo: Napoleon at Bay' in *On Waterloo: Clausewitz, Wellington, and the Campaign of 1815*, ed. Christopher Bassford, Daniel Moran and Gregory W. Pedlow. Clausewitz.com (bicentennial paperback ed.).

Nisbet, Robert. 1962. 'Sociology as an Art Form', *Pacific Sociological Review* 5: 2, pp. 67–74.

1966. *The Sociological Tradition*. New York.

1986. *Conservatism: Dream and Reality*. Minneapolis.

1999. *Tradition and Revolt*. New Brunswick, NJ.

2013. *Teachers and Scholars: A Memoir of Berkeley in Depression and War*. London.

2017. *Sociology as an Art Form*. New York.

Paret, Peter. 1976. *Clausewitz and the State*. Princeton.

1992. *Understanding War: Essays on Clausewitz and the History of Military Power*. Princeton.

Runciman, W. G. 1972. 'Describing', *Mind*, New Series, 81: 232, pp. 372–88.

1983. *A Treatise on Social Theory*, vol. I: *The Methodology of Social Theory*. Cambridge.

Sewell, William. 2005. *Logics of History: Social Theory and Social Transformation*. Chicago.

Skocpol, Theda. 1984. 'Emerging Agendas and Recurrent Strategies in Historical Sociology' in *Vision and Division in Historical Sociology*, ed. Theda Skocpol. New York.

1987. 'Social History and Historical Sociology', *Social Science History*, 11: 1, pp. 17–30.

Smelser, Neil. 1973. 'Alexis de Tocqueville as a Comparative Analyst' in *Comparative Methods in Sociology: Essays on Trends and Applications*, ed. Ivan Vallier. Berkeley.

Sumida, Jon. 2008. *Decoding Clausewitz: A New Approach to On War*. Lawrence, KS.

Teggart, Fredrick. 1916. *Prolegomena to History: The Relation of History to Literature, Philosophy, and Science*. Berkeley.

de Tocqueville, Alexis. 1969. *Democracy in America*, ed. J. P. Mayer, trans. George Lawrence. London.

1987. *Recollections: The French Revolution of 1848*, ed. J. P. Mayer and A. P. Kerr. New York.

2018. *Oeuvre completes d'Alexis de Tocqueville, XV, 1*. Paris.

Winthrop, Delba. 1981. 'Tocqueville's Old Regime: Political History', *Review of Politics*, 43: 1, pp. 88–111.

7 History and Normativity in Political Theory: The Case of Rawls

Richard Bourke

Moral and Political Philosophy

Over the past generation an approach to political philosophy has emerged that views its task as vindicating fundamental principles in support of projected institutional arrangements. Its focus has been normative rather than causal in nature: it has been less concerned to account for existing social relations than to justify an alternative scheme of values. John Rawls has been the decisive influence on this development. In 1951 he proposed that justification was the 'principal aim' of ethics; and, twenty years later, in the original preface to *A Theory of Justice*, he described his project as one of establishing the 'moral basis' for 'a democratic society'.[1] An approach to ethics had been extended into the domain of political philosophy. Rawls then anchored political philosophy in a conception of justice, which in turn provided a 'standard' against which society could be assessed.[2] Yet, at the same time, it is usually acknowledged that norms of justice should be practicable as well as justifiable in theory.[3] John von Neumann famously commented that mathematics becomes 'baroque' when divorced from empirical inquiry.[4] In this spirit, it is generally conceded that political thought becomes utopian when dissociated from practicality.[5] The practicality of an arrangement presupposes its viability. In politics this implies that it can be instituted and sustained; it must be historically feasible and enduring. In political philosophy, therefore, judgements of value and judgements of prudence ought to be reconciled; normativity and history should optimally be combined.

I am grateful to Claudia Blöser, Andrew Chignell, Stephan Eich, Katrina Forrester, Jakob Huber, Ira Katznelson, Quentin Skinner, Paul Weithman and Allen W. Wood for discussion of the arguments developed here.

[1] Rawls 1951, pp. 9–10; Rawls 1971a, p. viii.
[2] Rawls 1971c [rev. 1999], p. 8.
[3] The point is pressed throughout Dunn 1985 and Waldron 2016.
[4] Von Neumann 1947, p. 196.
[5] There have of course been varying conceptions of utopia. See Bloch 1918; Mannheim 1929; Shklar 1965; Manuel and Manuel 1979.

Given this conclusion, it would be strange, and indeed unfortunate, if one of these requirements should be explored without a systematic awareness of the other. Often, however, they are taken to constitute mutually indifferent domains of inquiry. G. A. Cohen wrote that once political philosophy takes off, 'it leaves the ground of fact behind'.[6] Yet what is philosophy's role before and after this ascent? There is something incongruous about a style of practical philosophy that is impractical as a matter of principle. In the introduction to the *Critique of the Power of Judgment* Kant distinguished sharply between philosophy in its theoretical and practical roles. All questions of skill and prudence, he argued, involve technical applications of theoretical principles dependent on human understanding. These include familiar problems of statecraft and political economy. For Kant these concerns were entirely distinct from what he termed 'practical' philosophy proper, which was concerned with the moral law applied through the faculty of freedom.[7] With this verdict, political philosophy was pegged to an exclusively normative enterprise in a way that would have made no sense to any of Kant's predecessors. Yet, as will become clear in the final section of this chapter, a coherent moral science still depended for Kant on what he termed its practical 'possibility'.[8] Moreover, a complete programme of ethics had to be applicable to behaviour, which entailed an empirical (or anthropological) component.[9] Ultimately it would require the development of a philosophy of history, including an account of the transition from existing conditions to improved moral aptitudes.[10]

Kant's impact on the thought of the nineteenth and twentieth centuries has yet to be written, but it is clear that he did not directly determine the character of political philosophy.[11] This is partly because figures such as Hegel and Marx transformed the elements they absorbed from his thinking, while others such as Weber and Kelsen relied on neo-Kantian epistemology without recourse to Kant's political ideas.[12] It was only with Rawls that Kant really came to matter for political philosophy.

It is debatable at what point Kant impacted on Rawls. Certainly his commitment to Christian ethics pre-dated any all-encompassing

---

[6] Cohen 2008, p. 232n.
[7] Kant 2000 [1790], AA 5: 167–73. Cf. the version of the argument in the 'First Introduction', AA 20: 196–201. Page references in Kant throughout are to the *Akademie Ausgabe* (AA).
[8] Kant 2015 [1788], AA 5: 142.
[9] Kant 2012 [1785], AA 4: 388; Kant 2017 [1797], AA 6: 216–17.
[10] Kant 2007 [1784], AA 8: 15–31.
[11] The best continuous narrative covering part of the story is Beiser 2014.
[12] Toews 1981; Schnädelbach 1984.

investment in Kant.[13] However, equally, Kantian ethics played a role in Rawls's earliest thinking, and he increasingly used Kant's ideas to frame some of his basic principles, although naturally we need to be alert in registering his mature departures from pure Kantianism.[14] In his under-graduate senior thesis Rawls invoked the principle of humanity as laid out by Kant in the second formulation of the categorical imperative to capture his support for the idea of persons as 'ends', even if his essential point is traceable to doctrines associated with reformed theology.[15] Two decades later Rawls identified the 'sense of justice' with the Kantian category of the 'good will'.[16] This does not entail any kind of Kantian orthodoxy on Rawls's part, but it does serve to highlight his enduring commitment to a vision of ethics as devoted to securing the possibility of morality. The purpose of this chapter is to analyse the implications of that commitment, above all to ascertain how the possible relates to the actual in practical reasoning.

Thirteen years before *A Theory of Justice* appeared, Rawls presented the possibility of subscribing to just principles as resting on a capacity for self-constraint that was 'analogous' to subjection to 'morality' as such.[17] That capacity assumed a facility for strict or narrow rationality, construed as the ability to pursue one's long-term interests consistently. But it also assumed an aptitude for reciprocity based on reasonableness. Here Rawls departed self-consciously from a Hobbesian conception of reason, which at that point he placed in a 'contractual' tradition stretching back to the Sophists.[18] On such a model of reasoning, Rawls contended, justice is conceived as 'a pact between rational egoists'.[19] However, for his own part he believed that it was possible to establish normative principles 'impartially'. He would later distinguish this brand of impartiality from the scheme of impartial judgement developed by Hume and refined by Smith, which he thought of as in fact a form of impersonation requiring benevolence.[20] Properly understood, impartiality could deliver a 'fair'

---

[13] Bok 2017a; Forrester 2019, p. 8.
[14] On the role of Kant in Rawls's thought see Darwall 1976; O'Neill 2002; Pogge 2007, pp. 188–95; Gališanka 2019, ch. 8.
[15] Rawls 2009 [1942], p. 195: for commentary see Adams 'Introduction'; Gregory 2007; Nelson 2019.
[16] Rawls 1963, p. 115. Cf. Rawls 1958, p. 48n.
[17] Rawls 1958, p. 54. Rawls relied on Gardiner 1955.
[18] Rawls 1958, p. 55. At this point Rawls's view of this 'tradition' depended on Gierke 1939 and Gough 1957.
[19] Rawls 1958, p. 56. Rawls 1993 [rev. 1996], pp. 51–2, associated this understanding with Gauthier 1986.
[20] Rawls 1980, pp. 335–6; Rawls 1971c [rev. 1999], pp. 24, 161–6; Rawls 2000, pp. 67, 88; Rawls 2007, pp. 185–7.

equilibrium between persons based on a mutual acknowledgement of principles. Thus, from almost the start, Rawls identified the limitations of a game-theoretic approach to behaviour: he recognised that we might usefully seek to analyse large areas of human interaction on the model of a game, but morality was a 'game' of 'a special sort'.[21] It was special because it required reasonableness as well as rationality, and consequently principled reciprocation. By the 1960s Rawls equated the facility for reciprocity with an idea of contract that he now associated with a rejection of Hobbes and the Sophists: that is, with Locke and, above all, Rousseau.[22] Joint subordination to reciprocal rules was founded on a mutual acknowledgement of personality. It offered a means of achieving true community.[23]

Rawls's work has inspired sympathetic critics as well as imitators, with partisans distributed across Europe, the United States and beyond. A vast array of commentary is now available, scrutinising the import of his arguments and charting his debts to precursors. This has all served to commend a model of political philosophy dedicated to unearthing basic values by reference to which prevailing structures should be reformed: existing social and political conditions are judged against the standards set by what Rawls termed 'ideal theory'.[24] This conception has been dubbed an 'ethics first' approach – or, more disparagingly, presented as an exercise in 'moralism'.[25] These depictions have seemed to many to miss the intricacy of the original programme. Rawls himself was explicit: 'justice as fairness is not applied moral philosophy'.[26] This comment was made in revising *A Theory of Justice* itself. What Rawls meant was that the ideal of justice as fairness did not cover the whole domain of social value but was only applicable to 'political' fundamentals – to the system of rights and the structure of distribution.

This ideal, Rawls was at pains to insist, should not be an empty ambition. It had to be, as he made the point in self-consciously modal terms, 'possible'.[27] It was by this emphasis on the importance of tangible possibility that Rawls distinguished his theory as 'political' and not merely 'moral'. As Rawls saw it, pure moralism need not adjust to actual circumstances: 'a moral conception may condemn the world and human

---

[21] Rawls 1958, p. 58.

[22] Rawls 1963, p. 74n already highlighted the importance of Rousseau. For Rawls's response to Rousseau see Brooke 2015 and Spector 2016. For the role of Locke in this context see Rawls 2007, pp. 88, 107, 172–3, 187.

[23] Rawls 1971b, pp. 212–13.

[24] On this widely discussed aspect of Rawls see Valentini 2012.

[25] Dunn 1996, pp. 92–3; Geuss 2005, p. 16; Williams 2005, p. 2; Geuss 2008, p. 8. See also Waldron 1992.

[26] Rawls 1989, p. 482.

[27] For his long-standing interest in the modal operator see Rawls 1958, p. 59.

nature as too corrupt to be moved by its precepts and ideals'.[28] This stance was not conducive to political philosophy proper: 'the political conception must be practicable, that is, must fall under the art of the possible'.[29] This defence of the possibility of normative justification is standardly regarded as having revived political theory. But what exactly was being revived? How was normative possibility to be conditioned by historical viability? Rawls, we have just seen, invoked the 'art of the possible', yet we have to drill down deeply into his work to understand what this involved. On Rawls's own reckoning, nothing in political philosophy could be more important, yet the details of his position on the topic are sparse. Even so, it was on the basis of his analysis of normative possibility, not his account of actual practicality, that Rawls was credited with inaugurating the rebirth of a field.[30] As will become clear, ultimately his work elides the difference between the two.

The standard view is that political philosophy declined in the generation of Russell, Moore and Wittgenstein, with the slump persisting into the age of Ayer, Ryle and Austin. Yet this conclusion sits oddly with the fact that H. L. A. Hart's *The Concept of Law*, first delivered as a set of lectures in 1952, was published in 1961. It further assumes that the mode of inquiry with which we associate Rawls was categorically different from the concerns of G. E. M. Anscombe, Richard Brandt, William Frankena, Kurt Baier, Roderick Firth or Philippa Foot – a perception that Rawls himself never shared. In fact, he oriented himself with reference to precisely these figures, as well as Peter Strawson, Geoffrey Warnock, Stuart Hampshire, Gilbert Ryle and Isaiah Berlin.[31] This situates Rawls in the midst of a mid-century renaissance in moral philosophy as the impact of logical positivism on ethical theory waned, although it is right that he came to focus less on meta-questions in personal morality and addressed himself instead to the evaluation of social norms. However, to think of this development as resuscitating a discipline passes in silence over well-known monuments of political reflection that appeared across the careers of Russell and Austin – work by Weber, Kelsen, Schmitt, Lukács, Hayek, Oakeshott and Arendt.

This list of names makes the idea of a 'strange death' of political philosophy – first articulated by Alfred Cobban and Peter Laslett and then repeated from Brian Barry to David Miller – look misguided, or at best parochial.[32] What died, perhaps, was sustained engagement with

---

[28] Rawls 1989, p. 486.
[29] Rawls 1989, p. 486. Cf. Rawls 1987, p. 447.
[30] Gutman 1989; Ball 1995; Nussbaum 2001.
[31] Pogge 2007, p. 16; Bok 2017b; Forrester 2019, p. 18.
[32] Cobban 1953; Laslett 1956; Barry 1980; Miller 1990.

political theory in the philosophy departments of Oxford and Cambridge between the wars, and by extension in departments on the North American continent that still fell under their spell. Partly as a result of this, after the Second World War there was a protracted anglophone debate about the future of political theory, but from this we do not need to conclude that the enterprise was moribund.[33] There was no abatement in systematic reflection on politics, though there were new emphases in moral philosophy that encouraged a parting of the ways between ethics and politics, giving rise to claims that the former was independent of the latter.[34] The impact of Moore's *Principia Ethica* promoted the insulation of moral reasoning from an examination of social and political structures. Although Moore saw himself as simply building on Sidgwick's *Methods of Ethics*, in practice he aligned the subject more closely with analysis of the meaning of ethical terms, creating in effect a free-standing field of inquiry.[35] In addition, the idealism against which he rebelled had increasingly turned from the theory of the state in Green and Bosanquet to problems in logic and metaphysics in McTaggart and Mure. It is also relevant to note that Collingwood's sole political work – *The New Leviathan* – only appeared in 1942, at the end of his career. Taken together, these developments helped encourage the migration of the study of politics from philosophy to political science.

Rawls himself was sensitive to this change. In the preface to the first edition of *A Theory of Justice* he noted that, by comparison with the current state of the field, the ethics of Hume, Smith, Bentham and Mill had serviced a comprehensive vision of politics. The catch-all term 'utilitarianism' that Rawls used to categorise these thinkers was procrustean and distorting. In fact sometimes, on reflection, Rawls himself exempted Hume and Mill from the utilitarian creed.[36] But the important point is that these figures were regarded by him as 'social theorists and economists of the first rank' and not just labourers in some sub-field of a sub-discipline such as meta-ethics.[37] By comparison, the tradition of moral theory as it had unfolded since the nineteenth century had become hermetic. Hume, for example, had worked out ideas, including a basic moral doctrine, in order to develop what Rawls described as a 'comprehensive

---

[33] Plamenatz 1960; Berlin 1962; Germino 1967; Runciman 1969. For discussion of this moment see Forrester 2011, pp. 595–7.
[34] The selections in Sellars and Hospers 1952 are indicative of this tendency.
[35] Compare Sidgwick 1899 with Moore 1903, ch. 2. On the autonomy of ethics see Darwall 2006, p. 19.
[36] Rawls 1958, pp. 48n, 51n; Rawls 1971b, p. 231n; Rawls 1971c [rev. 1999], pp. 28–9, 439–40.
[37] Rawls 1971a, p. vii.

scheme'.[38] The scope of his thought embraced government, trade, social relations and religion as well as morals. Yet, as Rawls saw it, over the course of the first half of the twentieth century ethics had grown more isolated in the humanities and social sciences, just as its questions had become more limited and recondite. The situation Rawls observed was partly a product of disciplinary specialisation, but not completely so. Since the eighteenth century, full-time scholarly activity had increasingly been confined to universities, and the academic division of labour became sub-partitioned and professionalised. Yet the development of philosophy, including the rise of moral theory, is not altogether reducible to this larger process. Understandings internal to the discipline have also shaped its trajectory.

In terms of approaches specific to moral philosophy in the 1950s, utilitarianism and intuitionism dominated the field, with theorists often blending elements of both.[39] In response, Rawls hoped to revive the fortunes of moral theory, and extend the parameters of its concerns to encompass public institutions. Yet despite this extension, there was no suggestion that he wanted to resuscitate the large-scale social-scientific ambition of Hume and Smith. His aim was to construct a moral framework for modern democracy, not to explain how a society of the kind came into being or analyse the components that enabled it to function. However, to set out the practicability of normative possibility stood in need of precisely such an account. Meanwhile, over the course of the twentieth century, political philosophy had prospered elsewhere, sometimes in university departments – most often in Politics, Sociology, Economics and History – and occasionally outside the academy. To the catalogue of personalities above one might add the following names as significant innovators writing before the appearance of *A Theory of Justice*: Dewey, Laski, Wallas, Schumpeter, Ritter, Gramsci, Sartre, Aron, de Beauvoir, Lefort and Shklar. The group of figures here is purely indicative; we can all add to the list.

While a more synoptic view of the landscape clarifies Rawls's goals, it would be wrong to conclude that his first book did not radically change the way things stood. It was, to begin with, an extraordinary intellectual achievement. What was new was an analytically trained philosopher tackling a major theme in ethical–political theory sustained over the course of a large and original study. The last time such a feat had been attempted by an anglophone thinker was in the days of Green and Sidgwick, although it might be mentioned that these figures had in addition published between

[38] Rawls 1971a, p. vii.
[39] For a retrospective see Urmson 1974–5.

them in the fields of history, economics and politics. Given this distance from the Victorian era, Rawls's achievement sparked admiration among fellow ethical theorists, giving rise to a community of philosophical debate, and in due course producing a stream of followers, variously qualified to take up positions in Philosophy, Law or Government departments. This did not amount to a wholesale recrudescence exactly. It was not the rebirth of a discipline that had been under threat, since political philosophy in the past was not confined to normative inquiry, although moral theory had always played an essential role. To Hegel, Tocqueville, Marx or Mill the study of ethics in isolation from politics would have appeared problematically circumscribed; it would have seemed an artificial constriction to Aristotle, Machiavelli and Locke too. An approach that projects from moral foundations to possible worlds is better understood as a new departure altogether, shaped by the requirements of Philosophy departments as these expanded over the course of the twentieth century.

After academic disciplines had been reformed in the nineteenth century, and then institutionalised in the research universities of the twentieth, philosophy was obliged to carve out a space that was neither experimental science, theology, history, sociology, economics, psychology nor anthropology. 'Philosophy in an important sense has no subject-matter', Wilfrid Sellars wrote in 1962. It ought to operate, therefore, with an 'eye on the whole'.[40] How it might do this was naturally a matter of dispute. On one model its best prospects lay in presenting itself as the arbiter of other enterprises. Philosophy was neither mathematics nor natural science, yet it might account for how their characteristic forms of judgement were possible; it was not theology, although it might assess the claims of religious argument; it did not investigate known forms of politics, however it might evaluate the underlying principles used to justify them. These various options did not exhaust the potential applications of philosophy: Heidegger and Wittgenstein had entertained still different visions of the subject. But for Sellars himself, philosophy should secure the means of 'knowing one's way around with respect to the subject-matters of all other special disciplines'.[41]

For all Sellars's usual care and discretion, this was an exceptionally ambitious goal. Its objectives have hardly been met in practice. Six years before Sellars's programmatic statement, Morton White sought in *Toward Reunion in Philosophy* to bring branches of the discipline together by uncovering commonalities.[42] But this only encompassed science,

[40] Sellars 2007, pp. 370, 371.
[41] Sellars 2007, p. 370.
[42] White 1956, p. xi.

logic and ethics, not the full gamut of learning that Sellars's vision comprised. The example of White, along with a shared admiration for Quine, spurred Rawls on to see how moral claims might be tested on the model of empirical validation, thereby similarly trespassing across boundaries.[43] The idea was that the methods of epistemology and ethics might prove reciprocally enlightening. Yet while granting this, Rawls went on in 1975 to clarify how the two domains should be provisionally separated, leading in effect to the 'independence' of moral inquiry.[44] He thought that a Cartesian model of deductive justification could not plausibly govern philosophical procedure, and so moral philosophy might usefully occupy a quasi-autonomous realm while ultimately standing in a relationship of mutual dependence with other sub-specialisms.[45] In addition, Rawls saw scope for creating a specific compartment of 'moral theory' inside the overarching unit of moral philosophy. Moral theory, in this limited sense, was essentially empirical: it covered the study of existing moral conceptions, spanning perfectionism, utilitarianism, intuitionism and so on. In the end these conceptions would have to be adjudicated, and values would need to be approved at the level of moral philosophy. But meanwhile, different principles and structures of argument among leading doctrines in the history of moral consciousness could be assembled. These assorted worldviews could then be compared with 'fixed points' – or abiding convictions – in our moral sensibility, such as the injunction to treat like cases equally or the opposition to slavery.[46] A moral framework could then be established by means of 'reflective' adjustments between general principles and particular judgements.[47] Since rival normative perspectives had developed across time, they were not all equally applicable at every historical moment. To be viable, a given conception would have to be matched with contingent beliefs. This ambition would force Rawls to address the plurality of moral attitudes and the stability of just arrangements.

Stability and Pluralism

The issue of contingency is complicated in Rawls. The resort to prevailing conceptions of morality drawn from the history of ethical

---

[43] Rawls 1971a, p. 509n.
[44] Rawls 1975, p. 286.
[45] Rawls 1975, p. 302.
[46] Rawls 1971c [rev. 1999], p. 507.
[47] Rawls 1971c [rev. 1999], pp. 17–19.

thought is an appeal to attitudes about appropriate conduct and arrangements. This amounts to recourse to contingent opinion. Yet, in the larger theory, opinion is used to construct a fair agreement on basic justice through the device of the original position. Moral beliefs are thereby subject to impartial evaluation. The theory in effect matches levels of agreement between prevailing conceptions, impartially selected principles and particular convictions in order to generate a model of a well-ordered society against which real-world arrangements can be judged. In this way, an ideal scheme is constructed out of consensus-based judgements developed from different points of view. As an ideal arrangement, Rawls's well-ordered society presents a counterfactual state of affairs, a world that would obtain if appropriate agreements could be secured. Yet it is essential for Rawls that this counterfactual realm be 'feasible'.[48] Ideal time has to operate in real time.

Politics in the ordinary sense plays no clear role in establishing feasibility in Rawls. For this reason, despite the disclaimers already entered, Rawlsian political philosophy, operating even within an expansive understanding of ethics, exhibits some of the narrowing of focus characteristic of the twentieth-century developments outlined above by comparison with earlier, more capacious accounts of government, society and economy. Although Rawls included economic analyses of rational behaviour in his theory, he did not factor in economic processes. He assumed a basic contrast between peasant, feudal and commercial societies, but paid little attention to the dynamics of economic change.[49] His interest in government was similarly based on static modelling. We find no treatment of perverse effects from unintended consequences in realising values in institutions, nor any appreciation of practical jeopardy as familiarly encountered in worldly affairs.[50] Rawls understood his feasibility criterion in terms of a stability equilibrium rooted in moral attitudes, not in the mechanisms sustaining political and economic relations.[51] This picture of stability bears a strong resemblance to Hume's idea of convention as a system of self-enforcing iterated behaviour. The durability of a well-ordered society of justice as fairness was not conditional, as in

---

[48] Rawls 1971c [rev. 1999], p. 508.
[49] On peasant societies see Rawls 1971c [rev. 1999], p. 472, and on feudal hierarchies p. 479. On Rawls's assumptions about economic productivity see Rodgers 2011, pp. 184, 198–9. Rawls did entertain a theoretical contrast between growth-based and stationary economies as part of a critique of consumerism. On this see Forrester 2019, p. 202; and Eich 2021.
[50] On these effects in politics, critically examined, see Hirschman 1991.
[51] Rawls 1971c [rev. 1999], pp. 400, 434–5.

Hobbes, on coercive constraints. Stability would instead be secured by opinion in the form of convention.[52]

In his *Lectures on the History of Moral Philosophy* Rawls claimed that Hume was 'the first to see that in a small society natural obligation suffices to lead people to honor the conventions of justice'.[53] As Rawls realised, this meant that, under the right conditions, justice and the rules of property could, for Hume, be sustained by convention on its own without enforcement by government. Rawls of course rejected the Humean account of moral deliberation, so he further believed that conventions would have to be endorsed 'for the right reasons' – that is, approved on the basis of principle rather than passion.[54] But another major departure from Hume is more telling still. The load that Hume expected the convention of justice to bear in enabling cooperation only obtained in what Rawls (paraphrasing Hume) termed 'small' societies: namely, prior to the accumulation of riches. This was under conditions of comparative simplicity with sparse population levels such as could be found, Hume noted, among 'the *American* tribes' beyond the pale of British colonial settlement in the eighteenth century.[55] These tribal arrangements included only the most rudimentary division of labour. Association was based on immediately affective bonds. A mere convention could never maintain order under a more complex system of property depending on the fulfilment of contractual relations among strangers. For Hume, social relations under these circumstances – in 'large and polish'd societies' – might be accepted by convention but the efficacy of the rules presupposed arbitration by government.[56]

We find in Rawls the notion of 'private society' loosely constructed from a Smithian conception of market relations under an unequal property regime. Rawls likened the condition to Hegel's idea of 'bourgeois' or 'civil' society (*bürgerliche Gesellschaft*) in which individuals pursue their competing objectives without the intention of cooperation.[57] Under such an arrangement, Rawls argued, 'the actual division of advantages is determined largely by the balance of power and strategic position resulting from existing circumstances'.[58] In private society in a modern context

---

[52] On the contrast between Hobbes and Hume see Sagar 2018. For Rawls's rejection of Hobbesian stability see Weithman 2010.
[53] Rawls 2000, p. 63.
[54] Rawls 1993 [rev. 1996], p. xl.
[55] Hume 2000 [1739], p. 346.
[56] Hume 2000 [1739], p. 348.
[57] Rawls 1971c [rev. 1999], p. 457, invoking Smith 1976 [1776], I, p. 456 and Hegel 1991 [1821], §§ 182–7. Rawls also finds the category in Plato 2000, 369a1–372d1.
[58] Rawls 1971c [rev. 1999], p. 457.

we also typically find 'variations in men's prospects' – or, an unequal division of resources, often to a considerable extent.[59] In this situation, Rawls conceded, stability requires 'sanctions': cohesion is not possible on the basis of convention, let alone convention supported for the right reasons.[60] In a well-ordered society of justice as fairness, by comparison, inequalities would still obtain. In fact, here we could find even 'large' disparities, although fair institutions, including the tax regime, should keep these below the levels found in the private societies typical of capitalist states.[61] However, inequalities would be for the sake of less favoured groups, and the ethos of the polity would be different. The division of interests would be compensated by a collaborative spirit fostered by equal rights, fair opportunities and the difference principle. A durable equilibrium would be secured by principled acclamation alone, without the need for 'stabilizing institutional devices'.[62]

It was always an essential part of Rawls's project to present his well-ordered society as a realistic prospect. This realism, we now see, was not based on structures of power. What Rawls rejected was a vision of a possible society formed from expectations of wholesale moral conversion. The world could not be adjusted to fit a fanciful view of behaviour. But it could be reformed in a way that would be 'realistically utopian'.[63] This realism was grounded on normative convention governed by a balance of motives. Rousseau had outlined his purpose in the *Social Contract* as one of seeking to reconcile 'right' (*le droit*) and 'interest' (*l'intérêt*), thereby harmonising justice and utility under a government of laws.[64] In *A Theory of Justice* Rawls pursued the analogous objective of rendering the motive of morality (or justice) congruent with the incentive to promote the good (or utility). Under the influence of what Rawls called the 'Aristotelian principle', the goal of utility was interpreted in terms of higher-order interests, associated with the development of more discerning capacities, including our moral faculties.[65] Following Humboldt, Rawls also thought that the individual cultivation of complex aptitudes would be experienced in a well-ordered society as a general benefit.[66] At the same time, Rawls further surmised that the moral ideals that underwrote justice as fairness could be smoothly integrated into a corresponding plan

---

[59] Rawls 1971c [rev. 1999], p. 470.
[60] Rawls 1971c [rev. 1999], p. 459.
[61] Rawls 1971c [rev. 1999], p. 470.
[62] Rawls 1971c [rev. 1999], p. 458.
[63] Rawls 2001b, p. 4. Cf. Rawls 1999, p. 14.
[64] Rousseau 1964 [1762], p. 351.
[65] Rawls 1971c [rev. 1999], pp. 364, 375 ff.
[66] Rawls 1971c [rev. 1999], pp. 221 ff.

of life, thus making our long-term regulative interests a part of the trigger motivating the adoption of the principle of justice. This reconciliation between right and utility was licensed by what Rawls termed the 'Kantian interpretation' which proposed that moral principles could be made an object of rational choice. This delicate architecture was given further ballast by the operation of supplementary moral sentiments such as guilt and shame.[67] Altogether, Rawlsian stability as presented in 1971 was based on an intricate web of mutually supporting components that were normative in origin yet purportedly realistic in character.

It is well known that Rawls soon abandoned his idea of congruence between the right and the good on the grounds that the account was not realistic after all.[68] It was implausible to expect that any democratic society would uniformly embrace a Kantian understanding of the good of morality. On the contrary, liberal democracy presupposed a plurality of legitimate ends. Agreement might be reached on principles of justice, but still a well-ordered society would be 'divided and pluralistic' given the diversity of goals that were reasonably pursued individually and within associations.[69] This conclusion extended Rawls's commitment to a doctrine of pluralism already sketched in *A Theory of Justice*. There he had described a just polity as a 'social union of social unions' in which diverse ends were pursued by members, alone and in affective groups, without subjecting the range of aspirations to a subordinating purpose.[70] This vision of diversity was indebted to forms of pluralism that Rawls had encountered at Oxford, above all in the work of H. A. Prichard, W. D. Ross and Isaiah Berlin. Prichard and Ross had argued for the irreducibility of values to a common measure, depicting ethics as a field in which a plurality of primary moral reasons reigns.[71] Rawls's defence of the indexical priority of the right over the good was intended to modify this radical conclusion, though he still retained an opposition to unmitigated 'monism' under which assorted social goals were all equally regulated by an exhaustive design. Influenced by Berlin, he argued that his model of a well-ordered society did not establish 'a dominant end' from which all social values were derived.[72]

However, it was not until *Political Liberalism* that a version of Berlinian pluralism came to play a leading role in Rawls's thought. In a series

---

[67] Rawls 1971c [rev. 1999], pp. 225, 386 ff.
[68] The fullest treatment is in Weithman 2010.
[69] Rawls 1980, pp. 326–7. Cf. Rawls 1982, p. 360.
[70] Rawls 1971c [rev. 1999], pp. 462–3.
[71] Prichard 1912; Ross 1930. Williams 1995 labels this doctrine 'methodological' intuitionism in order to distinguish it from its 'epistemological' counterpart.
[72] Rawls 1971c [rev. 1999], p. 463.

of works published in the 1950s and 1960s Berlin had advanced a thesis about diversity with four parts. First, he proposed that not all values were equally compatible, that many of them were liable to conflict, and that there could be no sure means of reconciling these differences.[73] Second, he believed, following ideas found in Herder and Mill, variety was itself intrinsically worthwhile, even if there was a limit to accommodating all social goods.[74] Third, he observed that pluralism was a historical phenomenon that arose in Europe in opposition to rationalism towards the end of the eighteenth century.[75] And, finally, he contended that the specific ideals of liberty and equality were prone to collide.[76] For his part, Rawls accepted the existence of incommensurable values, and the fact that there was insufficient room to accommodate all ideals. He also celebrated the benefits of variety over uniformity. However, he still insisted that certain apparently divergent goals could be harmonised, including liberty and equality. Lastly, unlike Berlin, Rawls traced the rise of pluralism to the Reformation.

The practical question for any pluralistic scheme of social organisation concerns the point at which constructive competition yields to conflict. Berlin, largely interested in defending liberal multiplicity against totalitarian uniformity, never faced this issue. Rawls, on the other hand, was acutely conscious of the potential for fundamental disputes in modern societies, although his primary interest lay in whether this eventuality could in theory be avoided. Everything ultimately turns in Rawls on the theoretical possibility of avoiding this potential outcome. But a more immediate target was what he took to be Michael Walzer's complacency about the ready availability of 'shared political understandings' in communities under modern conditions.[77] Division in society was pervasive, Rawls believed, and the evident threat of collision was a consequence. Among the deepest contests, he conceded to Berlin, was the battle between liberty and equality. Since controversies of the kind were practical rather than epistemological or metaphysical, the idea of the depth of disagreement presumably referred to the historical longevity of the problem. This discord between values, Rawls thought, was as old as Locke and Rousseau, a dissonance famously stylised by Benjamin Constant as a standoff between the freedom of the ancients and the moderns.[78] It

---

[73] Berlin 1962, pp. 151–2; Berlin 1958, pp. 167 ff.
[74] Berlin 1960, pp. 18–20; Berlin 1959, p. 194.
[75] Berlin 1956, p. 89.
[76] Berlin 1956, p. 96.
[77] Rawls 1993 [rev. 1996], p. 44, criticising Walzer 1983 in line with Cohen 1986.
[78] Rawls 1980, p. 307; Rawls 1985, pp. 391–2; Rawls 1993 [rev. 1996], pp. 4–5.

was one of the jobs of philosophy, as Rawls saw it, to repair the breach.[79] Its chief resource in this role was what he designated 'abstraction', which in practice entailed finding common ground on which the disparity between differences could be narrowed.[80]

The formula of justice as fairness was Rawls's leading philosophical abstraction designed to accommodate divergent preferences, rooted in rival traditions, regarding the substance and priority of liberty and equality. Here, at least, was one 'deep' dispute that Rawls was sure was amenable in principle to resolution. Yet he recognised that this hardly meant that conflicts were always open to settlement. In general, while natural science seemed to yield agreement about the empirical world, divergence of opinion in the field of morals was endemic. This was a consequence, Rawls argued, of the 'burdens of judgment'.[81] The very conditions of normative evaluation bred controversy. This leaves the following question for political philosophy, as Rawls posed it: 'How is it possible that there may exist over time a stable and just society of free and equal citizens profoundly divided by reasonable though incompatible religious, philosophical, and ethical doctrines?'[82] With justice as fairness in place as a free-standing module that could command agreement, the chief mechanism for accommodating residual conflicts in *Political Liberalism* was a scheme of toleration.[83] Liberal societies will inevitably generate contradictory beliefs, yet such divergence among reasonable views is compatible with concord where toleration is practised between them. The resulting profusion of tolerated doctrines can contribute to political collaboration where each disparate outlook 'overlaps' with a consensus on the fundamental ideal of justice. The question for any reader of Rawls must be to what extent his programme of justice is really proof against systematic dissent, and how robust his model of toleration is for accommodating reasonable pluralism.

Historical Judgement and Practical Belief

To understand the specific pressure introduced by pluralism, Rawls contrasted ancient with early modern societies. In the early modern case, Christianity gave rise to a clerically enforced ecclesiastical faith based on salvationist and expansionist principles. With the Reformation, rival

---

[79] Rawls 2001b, p. 2.
[80] Rawls 1993 [rev. 1996], pp. 45–6, following Scanlon 1985 on Hampshire 1984.
[81] Rawls 1993 [rev. 1996], pp. 54–8.
[82] Rawls 1993 [rev. 1996], p. xviii.
[83] Rawls 1985, pp. 388–90. Toleration likewise underpins equal liberty in *A Theory of Justice*: see Rawls 1971c [rev. 1999], p. 180n.

accounts of salvation instigated internecine struggle.[84] By comparison, on Rawls's telling, a civic religious culture grounded on public practice in the ancient Greek cities avoided conflict with philosophical sects.[85] Of course, it is in actual fact inaccurate to assume that there was no clash in classical Athens. Instead, with the conspicuous exception of Socrates, the point is that strife did not tend to engage the forces of the polis. In any case, in contrast with his picture of the ancients, it is interesting that Rawls ascribes the sources of modern discord to the 'transcendent element' added by Christian religions to conceptions of the good.[86] This element, he argued, brooks no compromise and so pushes disagreements towards hostilities. One weakness in this account is that it derives from a strand of Enlightenment thinking about the Reformation, rather than constituting an uncontroversial fact. Another is that it omits the role of the state in the relevant disturbances. Rawls was right to argue that 'stability' is 'fundamental to political philosophy'.[87] But the plausibility of any analysis of political stability depends on the rigour of its accompanying theory of conflict. Naturally, for Rawls, the credibility of his approach does not simply rest on his view of ancient Athens or Reformation Europe. More important is his understanding of the contemporary West, the United States in particular. However, his considered position was that early modern disputes over religion offered a template for interpreting 'the basic historical questions'.[88] Solutions derived from past contestation could then be mapped onto later instances, ranging from conflict over slavery to civil rights.

Rawls's template was more capacious still. It could apparently encompass dissension over 'race, ethnicity and gender'.[89] The same applied to culture, nationality and class.[90] In fact, every one of these complex grounds for dispute could, according to Rawls, be comprehended under the concept of rights and so resolved by the application of justice as fairness. Where grievances turned on legal inequality and lack of opportunity, they would be addressed by the principle of equal liberty; where they turned on the allocation of resources, they could be met by distributive fairness. Most striking is Rawls's expectation that in an appropriately just society contention over merit would not upset consensus over

---

[84] Rawls 1993 [rev. 1996], p. xxiii.
[85] Rawls 1993 [rev. 1996], pp. xxi–xxii, based on a reading of Burkert 1985, pp. 254–60, 273–5 and Irwin 1989, ch. 2.
[86] Rawls 1993 [rev. 1996], p. xxvi.
[87] Rawls 1993 [rev. 1996], p. xvii.
[88] Rawls 1993 [rev. 1996], pp. xxvii–xxix. Cf. Rawls 1971c [rev. 1999], p. 193.
[89] Rawls 1993 [rev. 1996], p. xxviii.
[90] Rawls 1993 [rev. 1996], p. lviii, citing Tamir 1993 on nationalism.

justice. Despite protestation to the contrary, this amounts to hoping for a moral conversion or change of heart. He expressed this by predicting that social jealousy, spite and envy would wither under correctly well-ordered arrangements.[91] The scale of this assumption is worth contemplating. From Aristotle to Hobbes, anxiety about desert was taken to drive the demand for justice, yet Rawls anticipates that such worries will retreat under justice as fairness and, with this, rancour and resentment directed at the social structure will dissolve.[92] For Rawls, injustice in Aristotle was a function of greed (*pleonexía*), which could be managed by imposing appropriate restraints.[93] The challenge for Aristotle, however, was securing agreement on these restraints since people systematically diverged on what they considered due to them. The sticking point was the estimation of worth (*axía*), from which 'quarrels and complaints arise'.[94] To subtract this cause of complaints, as Rawls does, is to abstract the feeling of desert from the sense of justice. To adapt the language of Rousseau, this results in a picture of laws as they 'can be' (*qu'elles peuvent être*) with no regard for people as 'they are' (*qu'ils sont*).[95] Ironically, it presents a world, as Rawls said of Marx, 'beyond justice'.[96] It is beyond justice because it is exempt from the conditions that require justice.

One reason for Rawls's confidence in the promise of his ideal of justice as a means of dissipating resentment is his reliance on a view of likely behaviour in suitably adjusted circumstances. Society under justice as fairness, much like society under existing capitalism, would largely be made up of what Rawls termed 'noncomparing groups'.[97] The absence of comparison across extremes of wealth and station would reduce the incidence of discontent. Yet while it is right that in elaborately stratified societies comparisons are often confined within particular socio-economic brackets, surely it is untrue that limited discrepancies are less irksome. Average experience suggests that minor differences are galling since it is marginal disparities that frustrate aspirations. As Hume noted, the proximate success of another provokes more grudging distress than remote and therefore incomparable advantage. Take Hume's example: common 'hackney scribblers' rarely resent truly eminent writers – they envy their peers.[98]

---

[91] On envy in Rawls see Luban forthcoming.
[92] Rawls 1971c [rev. 1999], pp. 464 ff. On Rawls's place in the history of ideas of justice see Fleischacker 2004, pp. 109 ff.
[93] Rawls 1971c [rev. 1999], pp. 9–10, presumably referring to Aristotle 1926, 1129b1–5.
[94] Aristotle 1926, 1131a20–25.
[95] Rousseau 1964 [1762], p. 351.
[96] Rawls 2007, p. 321, though the point applies differently to Rawls himself.
[97] Rawls 1971c [rev. 1999], p. 470.
[98] Hume 2000 [1739], p. 243.

Despite all this, assuming with Rawls that altercation over rights can be resolved by justice as fairness, we are still left with conflicts in the 'background culture' over religious, philosophical and moral doctrines.[99] Typically, in the context of liberalism, these competing visions of the good do not directly clash with one another. Instead, they are liable to collide on the level of national politics. Historically, Rawls accepted, there have been many instances in which consensus has been thwarted by politically subversive doctrines or, more subtly, inadvertently compromised by dissenting ideologies. Discontent, acrimony, malice, exasperation or resentment might pit a given community against the institutions of the state. Yet the crucial point for Rawls was that accord was at least possible: 'We must start with the assumption that a reasonably just society is at least possible.'[100] Otherwise, Rawls thought, we are liable to embrace the kind of cynicism that had doomed the Weimar constitution.[101] However, we need more than the threat of adverse consequences to justify an appeal to alternative possibilities. 'It is possible that the Turkish Sultan becomes Pope,' observed Hegel sardonically of discussions of modality.[102] The point was: an outcome that is merely thinkable provides little information regarding its probability. In other words, logical possibility can provide no guidance in assessing the likely course of affairs. So we have to assume that Rawls was interested in real possibility as conditioned by the limits of the empirical world.

Given these constraints, and Rawls's vintage, it is notable that he showed little inclination to assess the various frameworks that have been used to characterise modern societies. More significantly, he paid no obvious attention to the actual make-up of countries, such as the United States, that he hoped to reform. Explicit debate about the character and merits of cultural pluralism pre-dated Berlin by decades in America, though it played no role in the thought of Rawls.[103] Political scientists and sociologists who had taken up the subject of social structure in US democracy – such as R. M. MacIver, David Truman, Seymour Martin Lipset, William Kornhauser, Gabriel Almond and Robert Dahl – are never discussed in his writings.[104] Within a few

---

[99] Rawls 1993 [rev. 1996], pp. 14, 135.

[100] Rawls 1993 [rev. 1996], p. lx.

[101] Rawls 1993 [rev. 1996], pp. lix–lx, taking issue with Schmitt 1985 [1923, rev. 1926], preface to the second ed. and ch. 2.

[102] Hegel 2010 [1830], p. 214.

[103] Kallen 1924; Myrdal 1944; Park 1950; Gleason 1964; Higham 1975. The early Rawls had been interested in pluralism as a resource against the concentration of state power, but that is another subject, on which see Forrester 2019, p. 2.

[104] Some, such as Dahl 1956, appear fleetingly, for instance in Rawls 1971c [rev. 1999], p. 317n, but only to be dispatched.

years of Rawls's first publication, Will Herberg's classic study, *Protestant, Catholic, Jew*, appeared.[105] The title conveyed the author's sense of the dominant cleavages in American society. However, where the divisions in fact lay was already controversial, and assumptions would soon be comprehensively revised. Throughout the period from 1918 to 1951, there were anthropological and historical literatures on assorted rifts caused by a history of large-scale immigration that complicated patterns of religious diversity and political participation.[106] As is well known, over the course of the 1960s and 1970s these schemes of analysis were challenged and updated: new fractures appeared, minority consciousness proliferated, opposition to discrimination spread, and doubts about assimilation to the 'American creed' increased.[107] Since the 1970s consensus about the American way of life has come under pressure from other directions, engendering new tensions over race, abortion, prayer, sexuality, gender and the family.[108] The results are found in churches, law courts, schools, universities, the media and public administration, and the issues have spawned new polarities across religious divides. They have also created new alliances that cut across the old denominations.[109]

Faced with this, there are reasons to doubt Rawls's Reformation analogy, above all the ability of his illustrative template to capture American antagonisms. The religious schisms of early modern Europe were succeeded by collisions over Enlightenment, Revolution and the aftermath of both, none of which are explicable in the terms of the preceding age. In the USA, on the other hand, the principle of the free exercise of religion has underpinned relations between the federal government and churches since 1791. The American pattern of conflicts is therefore poorly served by a European interpretative grid. The history of these disagreements demands context-sensitive analysis if their character and potency are to be weighed. The applicability of the categories on offer needs to be surveyed, the shifting balance of forces has to be assessed, and the politicisation of social movements requires sociological and historical study. Only on that basis can we realistically hope to determine the possibility of resolving current strains by introducing the modifications stipulated by the ideal of justice.

Rawls described philosophy in *Political Liberalism* as a species of 'apologia'. It offers a defence of a specific kind: it seeks to vindicate 'rational

[105] Herberg 1955.
[106] Thomas and Znaniecki 1918–20; Handlin 1951.
[107] Glazer and Moynihan 1963; Ture and Hamilton 1967; Arendt 1970; Millett 1970.
[108] Hunter 1991; Rodgers 2011; Hartman 2015.
[109] Wuthnow 1988.

faith'.[110] This goal was self-consciously Kantian in character, and the form of rationality involved was avowedly practical. In his *Lectures on the History of Moral Philosophy* Rawls identified the theme of practical faith as one of the three leading topics in Kant's ethics.[111] Similarly, he described his own project as 'practical' in nature, though the term in his hands had a different meaning from Kant's.[112] For Rawls it signalled something more like empirical viability. The 'limits of the practical' were determined, he stipulated, by 'what the conditions of our social world in fact are' – or, 'the general facts of the political sociology of democratic regimes'.[113] By implication, as Rawls himself put it, the credibility of a programme of ideal justice had to take account of the 'forces' – psychological, social and political – that determine how the venture is 'likely to be realized'.[114] But if Rawls placed his faith in the near availability of an adjusted world comprising renovated liberalism, Kant was altogether more sober about a realm of morals being rendered actual even within millennia.[115] To complicate matters, there are several objects of practical faith or belief (*Glaube*) in Kant. Rawls found only one of them pertinent to his own project: belief in a moral commonwealth or kingdom of ends.[116] This, Rawls thought, was the Kantian equivalent of his own belief in the possibility of true democratic justice. Understanding the scope and basis of belief is therefore vital for an evaluation of both thinkers.

Belief in Kant had broad significance, ranging in meaning from trust in historical testimony and fidelity in daily transactions to acceptance of the existence of life on distant planets.[117] However, for the most part, Kant understood belief as a propositional attitude adopted for the purpose of action.[118] Because of the kind of merit licensing the affirmation, Kant contrasted belief on the grounds of action with other forms of epistemic assent (such as knowledge, opinion and persuasion). The force of assent in the field of action depended on the nature of the undertaking.

---

[110] Rawls 1993 [rev. 1996], pp. 101, 172. See also Rawls 1987, p. 448. For discussion see Weithman 2016, ch. 2.
[111] Rawls 2000, pp. 15–16, 319, 321.
[112] Rawls 1993 [rev. 1996], p. 9.
[113] Rawls 2001b, p. 5; Rawls 2007, p. 321.
[114] Rawls 1993 [rev. 1996], p. 164.
[115] See Kant 2007 [1784], AA 8: 27, where he invokes a kind of philosophical 'chiliasm', but only expected 'from afar' (*von weitem*).
[116] Rawls 2000, p. 319.
[117] Kant 1998 [1781, rev. 1787], A824/B853–A825/B853; Kant 1992 (Blomberg), AA 24: 242–3.
[118] Wood 1970, ch. 1; Chignell 2007; Pasternack 2011; Wood 2020; Abaci 2022. On the relation of belief to hope see Blöser 2020.

Action could either be pragmatic (*pragmatisch*) or practical (*praktisch*). Pragmatic action always has a cognitive element. We decide to pursue an objective with the aid of information: when to reap or sow, how to treat a patient, whether to strike a bargain.[119] Sometimes the decision is based on sound opinion, sometimes on mere persuasion driven by a will to believe. By comparison, practical belief, which for Kant accompanies morally necessary action, does not require empirical input to justify assent. To be coherent, acting from duty depends on postulating certain objects of belief. Yet these objects are not themselves affirmed on the basis of evidence. For Kant, belief in certain moral and supersensory ideas – such as immortality, perpetual peace or the highest good – is necessary to render ethical behaviour rational: for example, we *must* believe there is a point to fulfilling our duty even though we lack theoretical knowledge of the goal to which it leads.[120] While lacking knowledge, we possess moral certainty.[121]

Consideration of the extent to which moral certainty in Kant can remain secure in the absence of empirical confirmation is beyond the scope of this chapter. Yet belief in Rawls's regime of justice certainly needs supporting evidence. What he set out to justify was a form of 'hope' in a possible object of experience. The hope rested on 'the belief that the social world allows at least a decent political order, so that a reasonably just, though not perfect, democratic regime is possible'.[122] In a Kantian idiom it is possible to hold an opinion (*Meinung*) about such an eventuality, or even speciously persuade oneself about its likelihood – if, for example, one really *wanted* to assert that it *could* come about in order to motivate oneself.[123] Yet neither form of assent is strictly a case of moral (or practical) belief. Consequently, we need to clarify how Rawls might justify his hope for a decent democratic order. Since this involves projecting a future state of the world, justification requires an account of feasibility and an explanation of how we might get there. Writing on Rousseau, Rawls billed these requirements as the need for sustainability and the problem of 'historical origins'.[124] Rawls's feasibility assessment is based on an interpretation of how moral motivation would function

---

119 Kant 1992 (Vienna), AA 24: 852–3, (Jäsche), AA 9: 68–9; Kant 2012 [1785], AA 4: 416 ff.
120 Kant 2015 [1788], AA 5: 142–6.
121 Kant transformed the meaning of moral certainty in distinguishing it from pragmatic certainty, for example in judicial reasoning: see Kant 1992 (Dohna-Wundlacken), AA 24: 734. For the pre-Kantian idiom see van Leeuwen 1961.
122 Rawls 2001b, p. 4.
123 Kant 1992 (Jäsche), AA 9: 73–4.
124 Rawls 2007, pp. 238–41.

under a regime of justice, while plotting a route to this outcome is to envisage a probable course of development. The former is a counterfactual hypothesis, the latter a theory of transition.[125] We have already considered whether Rawls's counterfactual assumptions are plausible. This involved adopting what he called political philosophy's 'longest view' by looking to society's 'permanent historical and social conditions'.[126] In this regard, we questioned whether Rawls's psychological assumptions made sense, asking if systemic disagreements over merit could be reasonably expected to recede as a well-ordered society emerged. Now we need to consider his idea of a passage to a better world by tackling, in conclusion, the issue of transition.

Ever since the Enlightenment, the notion of transition has been associated with stages of historical progress. Philosophers, social scientists and historians have forecast transitions that have proved disturbingly erroneous, so there is a premium on circumspect prediction. Baseless hope is at least as dangerous as dogmatic fatalism. While the capitalist stage of production did not lead to a communist one as Marx anticipated, a number of predominantly peasant societies did, prompting Ernest Gellner to observe of this inversion of stages that 'Marxist revolutions precede, and do not follow, industrial development'.[127] By comparison with Marx, Rawls's expectations were modest. Given the reality of diversity under liberalism, we should find it 'remarkable', he once commented, that concord is possible at all: 'historical experience suggests that it rarely is'.[128] Likewise, an overlapping consensus 'may not be possible under many historical conditions'.[129] Yet Rawls also claimed that the record points to the success of toleration: contingent accommodation based on mutually strategic interest has led to a principled reconciliation of differences.[130] By historical analogy, Rawls surmised, the affirmation of a just basic structure could evolve into a political agreement and lay the foundations for a stable consensus supported for the right reasons.[131] This prognosis is empirical in nature: it must be possible, not as a matter of practical belief in Kant's sense, but according to judgement about 'the laws and tendencies of the social world'.[132]

---

[125] For the relevance of counterfactual judgement in social prediction see Elster 1978; Hawthorn 1991.
[126] Rawls 1982, p. 447.
[127] Gellner 1964, p. 137.
[128] Rawls 1993 [rev. 1996], p. 4.
[129] Rawls 1993 [rev. 1996], p. 126.
[130] Rawls 1993 [rev. 1996], pp. 140, 142–3.
[131] Rawls 1993 [rev. 1996], p. 168; Rawls 2001b, p. 194.
[132] Rawls 2001b, p. 4.

A principal guide to these tendencies is the record of history, which should help direct the course of reform 'over generations'.[133] Rawls found that record encouraging because of the angle from which he viewed it. To facilitate this vision, he could have drawn on a long tradition of reflection on the unique path of American evolution towards a benign future.[134] In any case his perspective was shaped by assumptions he made about the march of moral progress, a trajectory he dubbed the 'movement of thought'.[135] This involved the steady advance of the principle of toleration. He insisted that this development was not simply a matter of 'historical good fortune'; it was determined by the trend of democratic ideas.[136] Rawls once applauded Mill for recognising this trend in a discussion of his theory of civilisation: as society moves forward, morality improves, until the common interest becomes the prevailing criterion of justice.[137] This forward momentum was traced by Rawls's student Thomas Nagel. For him, Rawlsian liberalism represented the 'logical conclusion' of earlier doctrines that variously promoted the cause of liberty and equality. It was, he argued, the 'latest stage in the long evolution in the content of liberalism' that began with Locke.[138] The arc of the moral universe was bending towards justice. But the story here is based on a blinkered narrative of the past which foregrounds moral achievements with no analysis of their causes or assessment of their costs. In contrast with the actual course of events, process is governed by principle and historical development is stripped of irony. Unintended consequences are replaced by moral impulses.

In the same vein, hope in Rawls depends on faith in the benign complexion of 'inherent long-run' tendencies.[139] For him, the passage to a better place is realised in 'steps' or 'stages'.[140] But the steps do not lead in sequence from where we are to where we would like to be: first Rawls 'supposes' that a reasonably just regime has come about, and then conjectures likely scenarios that might explain its possible endorsement from assorted pluralistic perspectives.[141] The key initial stage in the process of transition – the mechanism that transports us from existing arrangements to ideal conditions – is missing. Consequently, the only process Rawls entertains

---

[133] Rawls 2001b, p. 193. Cf. Rawls 1999, p. 58, for appeal to the historical record.
[134] The tradition is recounted in Ross 1991.
[135] Rawls 1982, p. 437.
[136] Rawls 1982, p. 446.
[137] Rawls 1971c [rev. 1999], p. 439.
[138] Nagel 2003, p. 63.
[139] Rawls 1971c [rev. 1999], p. 217; Rawls 1993 [rev. 1996], pp. 250–1.
[140] Rawls 1993 [rev. 1996], p. 164.
[141] Rawls 1987, pp. 440–4; Rawls 1993 [rev. 1996], pp. 164–8.

is the development of support for his ideal as a 'moral object' based on self-interest to its approval on 'moral grounds'.[142] Faith in a process of the kind is not a matter of practical belief as Kant understood the concept, but something more like a will to believe ratified by an appeal to history. Judging the character of a possible future on the evidence of the past can only ever be a matter of opinion; it cannot deliver moral certainty.[143] Nonetheless, this is not to downgrade the importance of opinion. In point of fact, we have nothing else to go on, though not all opinions are equally credible. Coolly sifting the evidence of the past is thus an essential facet of judgement, the only legitimate basis for prudential reasoning. Philosophy is right to interrogate our moral faculties and speculate about a better future, but its work is undone by wilful beliefs about how things ought to be.

References

Abaci, Uygar. 2022. 'Kant's Enigmatic Transition: Practical Cognition of the Supersensible' in *The Sensible and Intelligible Worlds: New Essays on Kant's Metaphysics and Epistemology*, ed. Nicholas Stang and Karl Schafer. Oxford.

Arendt, Hannah. 1970. *On Violence*. New York.

Aristotle. 1926. *Nicomachean Ethics*, trans. H. Rackham. Cambridge, MA.

Ball, Terence. 1995. *Reappraising Political Theory*. Oxford.

Barry, Brian. 1980. 'The Strange Death of Political Philosophy', *Government and Opposition*, 15: 3–4, pp. 276–88.

Beiser, F. C. 2014. *The Genesis of Neo-Kantianism, 1796–1880*. Oxford.

Berlin, Isaiah. 1956. 'Equality' in *Concepts and Categories*.

   1958. 'Two Concepts of Liberty' in *Four Essays on Liberty*. Oxford.

   1959. 'John Stuart Mill and the Ends of Life' in *Four Essays on Liberty*.

   1960. *Vico and Herder* in *Three Critics of Enlightenment*.

   1962. 'Does Political Theory Still Exist?' in *Concepts and Categories*.

   1969. *Four Essays on Liberty*. Oxford.

   1978. *Concepts and Categories: Philosophical Essays*. London.

   2000. *Three Critics of Enlightenment: Vico, Hamann, Herder*. Princeton.

Bloch, Ernst. 1918. *Geist der Utopie*. Munich.

Blöser, Claudia. 2020. 'Hope in Kant' in *The Moral Psychology of Hope*, ed. Claudia Blöser and Titus Stahl. New York.

Bok, Mackenzie P. 2017a. 'To the Mountaintop Again: The Early Rawls and Post-Protestant Ethics in Postwar America', *Modern Intellectual History*, 14: 1, pp. 153–85.

   2017b. '"The Latest Invasion from Britain": Young Rawls and his Community of American Ethical Theorists', *Journal of the History of Ideas*, 72: 2, pp. 275–85.

---

[142] Rawls 1987, p. 422.
[143] Kant 1996 [1793], AA 8: 312.

Brooke, Christopher. 2015. 'Rawls on Rousseau and the General Will' in *The General Will: The Evolution of a Concept*, ed. David Lay Williams and James Farr. Cambridge.

Burkert, Walter. 1985. *Greek Religion: Archaic and Classical*. Oxford.

Chignell, Andrew. 2007. 'Belief in Kant', *Philosophical Review*, 116: 3, pp. 323–60.

Cobban, Alfred. 1953. 'The Decline of Political Theory', *Political Science Quarterly*, 67, pp. 321–37.

Cohen, G. A. 2008. *Rescuing Justice and Equality*. Cambridge.

Cohen, Joshua. 1986. 'Review of *Spheres of Justice*', *Journal of Philosophy*, 83: 8, pp. 457–68.

Dahl, Robert. 1956. *A Preface to Democratic Theory*. Chicago.

Darwall, Stephen L. 1976. 'A Defense of the Kantian Interpretation', *Ethics*, 86: 2, pp. 164–70.

2006. 'How Should Ethics Relate to (the Rest of) Philosophy?' in *Metaethics after Moore*, ed. Terry Horgan and Mark Timmons. Oxford.

Dunn, John. 1985. *Rethinking Modern Political Theory: Essays 1979–1983*. Cambridge.

1996. *The History of Political Theory and Other Essays*. Cambridge.

Eich, Stefan. 2021. 'The Theodicy of Growth: John Rawls, Political Economy, and Reasonable Faith', *Modern Intellectual History*, 18: 4, pp. 984–1009.

Elster, Jon. 1978. *Logic and Society: Contradictions and Possible Worlds*. New York.

Fleischacker, Samuel. 2004. *A Short History of Distributive Justice*. Cambridge.

Forrester, Katrina. 2011. 'Hope and Memory in the Thought of Judith Shklar', *Modern Intellectual History*, 8: 3, pp. 591–620.

2019. *In the Shadow of Justice: Postwar Liberalism and the Remaking of Political Philosophy*. Princeton.

Gališanka, Andrius. 2019. *John Rawls: The Path to a Theory of Justice*. Cambridge, MA.

Gardiner, Patrick. 1955. 'On Assenting to a Moral Principle', *Proceedings of the Aristotelian Society*, 55, pp. 23–44.

Gauthier, David. 1986. *Morals by Agreement*. Oxford.

Gellner, Ernest. 1964. *Thought and Change*. London.

Germino, Dante. 1967. *Beyond Ideology: The Revival of Political Theory*. New York.

Geuss, Raymond. 2005. *Outside Ethics*. Princeton.

2008. *Philosophy and Real Politics*. Princeton.

von Gierke, Otto. 1939. *The Development of Political Theory*, trans. B. Freyd. London.

Glazer, Nathan and Daniel P. Moynihan. 1963. *Beyond the Melting Pot: The Negroes, Puerto Ricans, Jews, Italians, and Irish of New York City*. Cambridge, MA.

Gleason, Philip. 1964. 'The Melting Pot: Symbol of Fusion or Confusion?', *American Quarterly*, 16, pp. 20–46.

Gough, J. W. 1957. *The Social Contract*. Oxford.

Gregory, Eric. 2007. 'Before the Original Position: The Neo-Orthodox Theology of the Young Rawls', *Journal of Religious Ethics*, 25, pp. 179–206.

Gutmann, Amy. 1989. 'The Central Role of Rawls's Theory', *Dissent*, 36, pp. 338–42.

Hampshire, Stuart. 1984. *Morality and Conflict*. Oxford.

Handlin, Oscar. 1951. *The Uprooted: The Epic Story of the Great Migration that Made the American People*. Boston.

Hartman, Andrew. 2015. *A War for the Soul of America: A History of the Culture Wars*. Chicago.

Hawthorn, Geoffrey. 1991. *Plausible Worlds: Possibility and Understanding in History and the Social Sciences*. Cambridge.

Hegel, G. W. F. 1991 [1821]. *Elements of the Philosophy of Right*, ed. Allen W. Wood. Cambridge.

   2010 [1830]. *Encyclopedia of the Philosophical Sciences in Basic Outline, Part I: Science of Logic*, trans. Klaus Brinkmann and Daniel O. Dahlstrom. Cambridge.

Herberg, Will. 1955. *Protestant, Catholic, Jew: An Essay in American Religious Sociology*. New York.

Higham, John. 1975. *Send These to Me: Jews and Other Immigrants in Urban America*. New York.

Hirschman, Albert O. 1991. *The Rhetoric of Reaction: Perversity, Futility, Jeopardy*. Cambridge, MA.

Hume, David. 2000 [1739]. *A Treatise of Human Nature*, ed. David Fate Norton and Mary J. Norton. Oxford.

Hunter, James Davison. 1991. *Culture Wars: The Struggle to Define America*. New York.

Irwin, Terence. 1989. *Classical Thought*. Oxford.

Kallen, Horace. 1924. *Culture and Democracy in the United States: Studies in the Group Psychologies of the American Peoples*. New York.

Kant, Immanuel. 1900–. *Kants gesammelte Schriften: Ausgabe der königlich preußischen Akademie der Wissenschaften* [AA]. Berlin.

   1992. *Lectures on Logic*, ed. J. Michael Young. Cambridge.

   1996 [1793]. 'On the Common Saying: That may be Correct in Theory, But is of no Use in Practice' in *Practical Philosophy*, ed. Mary J. Gregor and Allen Wood. Cambridge.

   1998 [1781, rev. 1787]. *Critique of Pure Reason*, ed. Paul Guyer and Allen W. Wood. Cambridge.

   2000 [1790]. *Critique of the Power of Judgment*, ed. Paul Guyer. Cambridge.

   2007 [1784]. 'Idea for a Universal History with a Cosmopolitan Aim' in *Anthropology, History, and Education*, ed. Robert B. Louden and Günter Zöller. Cambridge.

   2012 [1785]. *Groundwork of the Metaphysics of Morals*, ed. Mary Gregor and Jens Timmerman. Cambridge.

   2015 [1788]. *Critique of Practical Reason*, ed. Mary Gregor and Andrews Reath. Cambridge.

   2017 [1797]. *The Metaphysics of Morals*, ed. Lara Denis. Cambridge.

Laslett, Peter. 1956. 'Introduction' in *Philosophy, Politics and Society*, ed. Peter Laslett, first series. New York.

Luban, Daniel. forthcoming. 'Rawls on Envy', working paper.

Mannheim, Karl. 1929. *Ideologie und Utopie*. Bonn.

Manuel, F. E and F. P. Manuel. 1979. *Utopian Thought in the Western World.* Cambridge, MA.

Miller, David. 1990. 'The Resurgence of Political Theory', *Political Studies,* 38: 3, pp. 421–37.

Millett, Kate. 1970. *Sexual Politics.* New York.

Moore, G. E. 1903. *Principia Ethica.* Cambridge.

Myrdal, Gunnar. 1944. *An American Dilemma: The Negro Problem and Modern Democracy.* New York.

Nagel, Thomas. 2003. 'Rawls and Liberalism' in *The Cambridge Companion to Rawls,* ed. Samuel Freeman. Cambridge.

Nelson, Eric. 2019. *The Theology of Liberalism: Political Philosophy and the Justice of God.* Cambridge, MA.

Nussbaum, Martha. 2001. 'The Enduring Significance of John Rawls', *Chronicle of Higher Education,* 47: 45, B7–B9.

O'Neill, Onora. 2002. 'Constructivism in Rawls and Kant' in *The Cambridge Companion to Rawls,* ed. Samuel Freeman. Cambridge.

Park, Robert E. 1950. *Race and Culture.* Glencoe, IL.

Pasternack, Lawrence. 2011. 'The Development and Scope of Kantian Belief: The Highest Good, the Practical Postulates and the Fact of Reason', *Kant-Studien,* 102: 3, pp. 290–315.

Plamenatz, John. 1960. 'The Use of Political Theory', *Political Studies,* 8, pp. 37–47.

Plato. 2000. *The Republic,* ed. G. R. F. Ferrari. Cambridge.

Pogge, Thomas. 2007. *John Rawls: His Life and Theory of Justice.* Oxford.

Prichard, H. A. 1912. 'Does Moral Philosophy Rest on a Mistake?' *Mind,* 21, pp. 21–37.

Rawls, John. 1951. 'Outline of a Decision Procedure for Ethics' in *John Rawls: Collected Papers.*

1958. 'Justice as Fairness' in *John Rawls: Collected Papers.*

1963. 'Constitutional Liberty and the Concept of Justice' in *John Rawls: Collected Papers.*

1971a. *A Theory of Justice.* Cambridge, MA.

1971b. 'Justice as Reciprocity' in *John Rawls: Collected Papers.*

1971c [rev. 1999]. *A Theory of Justice.* Rev. ed. Oxford.

1975. 'The Independence of Moral Theory' in *John Rawls: Collected Papers.*

1980. 'Kantian Constructivism in Moral Theory' in *John Rawls: Collected Papers.*

1982. 'Social Unity and Primary Goods' in *John Rawls: Collected Papers.*

1985. 'Justice as Fairness: Political not Metaphysical' in *John Rawls: Collected Papers.*

1987. 'The Idea of an Overlapping Consensus' in *John Rawls: Collected Papers.*

1989. 'The Domain of the Political and Overlapping Consensus' in *John Rawls: Collected Papers.*

1993 [rev. 1996]. *Political Liberalism.* New York.

1999. *Law of Peoples.* Cambridge, MA.

2000. *Lectures on the History of Moral Philosophy,* ed. Barbara Herman. Cambridge, MA.

2001a. *John Rawls: Collected Papers,* ed. Samuel Freeman. Cambridge, MA.

2001b. *Justice as Fairness: A Restatement*. Cambridge, MA.

2007. *Lectures on the History of Political Philosophy*, ed. Samuel Freeman. Cambridge, MA.

2009 [1942]. *A Brief Inquiry into the Meaning of Sin and Faith*. Cambridge, MA.

Rodgers, Daniel T. 2011. *Age of Fracture*. Cambridge, MA.

Ross, Dorothy. 1991. *The Origins of American Social Science*. Cambridge.

Ross, W. D. 1930. *The Right and the Good*. Oxford.

Rousseau, Jean-Jacques. 1964 [1762]. *Du contrat social* in *Oeuvres complètes*, vol. III, ed. R. Derathé et al. Paris.

Runciman, W. G. 1969. *Social Science and Political Theory*. Cambridge.

Sagar, Paul. 2018. *The Opinion of Mankind: Sociability and the Theory of the State from Hobbes to Smith*. Princeton.

Scanlon, T. M. 1985. 'Local Justice', *London Review of Books*, September, 7: 15, pp. 17–18.

Schmitt, Carl. 1985 [1923, rev. 1926]. *The Crisis of Parliamentary Democracy*. Cambridge, MA.

Schnädelbach, Herbert. 1984. *Philosophy in Germany: 1831–1933*. Cambridge.

Sellars, Wilfrid. 2007. 'Philosophy and the Scientific Image of Man' (1962) in *In the Space of Reasons: Selected Essays*, ed. Kevin Sharp and Robert B. Brandom. Cambridge, MA.

Sellars, Wilfrid and John Hospers. 1952. *Readings in Ethical Theory*. New York.

Shklar, Judith. 1965. 'The Political Theory of Utopia: From Melancholy to Nostalgia', *Daedalus*, 94: 2, pp. 367–81.

Sidgwick, Henry. 1899. 'The Relation of Ethics to Sociology', *International Journal of Ethics*, 10: 1, pp. 1–21.

Smith, Adam. 1976 [1776]. *Inquiry into the Nature and Causes of the Wealth of Nations*, ed. R. H. Campbell and A. S. Skinner. Oxford.

Spector, Céline. 2016. 'Rousseau at Harvard' in *Engaging with Rousseau: Reaction and Interpretation from the Eighteenth Century to the Present*, ed. Avi Lifschitz. Cambridge.

Tamir, Yael. 1993. *Liberal Nationalism*. Princeton.

Thomas, William I. and Florian Znaniecki. 1918–20. *The Polish Peasant in Europe and America*. 5 vols. Boston.

Toews, John. 1981. *Hegelianism: The Path toward Dialectical Humanism*. Cambridge.

Ture, Kwame [Stokely Carmichael] and Charles V. Hamilton. 1967. *Black Power: The Politics of Liberation*. New York.

Urmson, J. O. 1974–5. 'A Defense of Intuitionism', *Proceedings of the Aristotelian Society*, New Series, 75, pp. 111–19.

Valentini, Laura. 2012. 'Ideal vs. Non-Ideal Theory: A Conceptual Map', *Philosophy Compass*, 7: 9, pp. 654–64.

van Leeuwen, Hendrik Gerrit. 1961. 'The Problem of Certainty in English Thought from Chillingworth to Locke', PhD thesis, State University of Iowa.

von Neumann, John. 1947. 'The Mathematician' in *The Works of the Mind*, ed. R. B. Heywood. Chicago.

Waldron, Jeremy. 1992. 'Justice Revisited: Rawls Turns towards Political Philosophy', *Times Literary Supplement*, 18 June, pp. 5–6.

2016. *Political Political Theory: Essays on Institutions*. Cambridge, MA.

Walzer, Michael. 1983. *Spheres of Justice: A Defense of Pluralism and Equality*. New York.

Weithman, Paul. 2010. *Why Political Liberalism: On John Rawls's Political Turn*. Oxford.

2016. *Rawls, Political Liberalism and Reasonable Faith*. Cambridge.

White, Morton. 1956. *Toward Reunion in Philosophy*. Cambridge, MA.

Williams, Bernard. 1995. *Making Sense of Humanity and Other Philosophical Papers, 1982–1993*. Cambridge.

2005. *In the Beginning was the Deed: Realism and Moralism in Political Argument*. Princeton.

Wood, Allen W. 1970. *Kant's Moral Religion*. Ithaca, NY.

2020. *Kant and Religion*. Cambridge.

Wuthnow, Robert. 1988. *The Restructuring of American Religion*. Princeton.

8   Political Philosophy and the Uses of History

Quentin Skinner

A generation ago there was widespread agreement, at least among anglophone scholars, about the relationship between political philosophy and its history. Political philosophy was said to be preoccupied with a distinctive set of questions, among which the most central were taken to be about the grounds and limits of political obligation, and hence about such topics as sovereignty, liberty, obligation and rights.[1] The task of the historian of political philosophy was viewed as that of focusing on a canon of classic texts in which these topics had duly been foregrounded. The special value of the canon was claimed to stem from the fact that it provides us with insights of enduring relevance. The proper approach to the canonical writers was consequently held to be that of investigating what each of them said about the concepts fundamental to political life. We were enjoined to treat their answers as if they had been written by contemporaries. It was indeed held to be essential to approach them in this way. We were warned that, if we instead allow ourselves to become side-tracked into investigating the social conditions or the intellectual contexts out of which the canonical texts arose, we shall run the danger of losing sight of their relevance, thereby losing contact with the value and purpose of studying them.[2]

During the 1960s and 1970s a younger generation of scholars began to challenge this orthodoxy in what came to be called a 'historicist' style.[3] The historicists enlarged the range of texts usually studied by historians of political philosophy, focusing not merely on canonical texts but on broader political ideologies. Viewed from this perspective, the works of

For reading and commenting on drafts I am indebted to Adrian Blau, Richard Bourke, Hannah Dawson, John Dunn, Andrew Fitzmaurice, Susan James, James Tully and Melissa Williams.

[1] See, e.g., Berlin 1962, p. 7.
[2] For a list of works containing these arguments see Skinner 2002a, p. 57.
[3] For this term see Tarlton 1973; Kelly 2011, pp. 23, 26–8; Muller 2014, p. 87; Whatmore 2016, pp. 97–9. For statements of the historicist case in the 1960s see Pocock 1962; Dunn 1968; Skinner 1969. For some recent discussions see Klosko 2011.

the canonical writers began to appear less as general and abstract statements of political principles and more as interventions in local political
debates. This shift in focus in turn led the historicists to a characteristic preoccupation with attempting to recover the underlying intentions
and purposes that individual writers may have had in mind when making such interventions, thereby seeking to identify what they may have
meant by what they said, what they may have been doing in saying it.

From this approach a picture emerged of the political philosopher as
someone typically preoccupied with attacking or defending contentious
policies or points of view, or providing advice and warnings about different courses of action, or sometimes merely satirising and ridiculing
the passing political scene. The project in which such writers were basically taken to be engaged was that of seeking to legitimise (or delegiti-
mise) some prevailing political value, institution or practice. The final
outcome of adopting the historicist approach was thus to question any
strong distinction between ideology and political philosophy. The classic
texts began to look less like systematic treatises above the political battle
and more like participants in the battle itself.

These commitments are worth underlining, if only because there has
been a tendency among recent critics of the historicist approach to complain that it sees 'nothing determinative outside texts except other texts',
and consequently views 'the discursive surroundings of texts as the sole
potential source of historical explanation'.[4] This is a surprising misunderstanding. The post-structuralist contention that there is no *hors-texte*
was precisely the perspective that most historicists explicitly rejected,
emphasising instead that the problems addressed by political theorists
generally arise from political life itself, and that this is where the quest
for explanations must begin.

The philosophical commitments underpinning the historicist approach
owed much to the work of Wittgenstein and his disciples, especially
those who had derived from Wittgenstein's arguments about meaning
and use the more general claim that we need to distinguish two separable dimensions of language.[5] We obviously need to investigate the sense
and reference of terms, but we also need to recognise that language is
a form of social action. The project of understanding utterances must
therefore include an attempt to grasp what Wittgenstein had called the
specific *Sprachspielen* in play. This pivotal term was generally rendered
into English as 'language games'. But J. L. Austin noticed that, if we

[4] Moyn 2014, p. 113. On the concept of 'context' see Boucher 1985; Blau 2017,
pp. 245–50.
[5] The classic studies are Austin 1962 and Searle 1969.

wish to translate the term more literally, we ought instead to speak of the specific speech-performances being enacted. To focus on speech-acts is to acknowledge that concepts are tools (or weapons, as Nietzsche had preferred to say): as well as using words to say things, we use them to do things. To grasp the use of a concept involves understanding what it is for, what can appropriately be done with it. This requires us to comprehend not merely the meanings of the terms used to express the concept, but also the specific context of their use, from which we can alone hope to identify the range of speech-acts being performed. The implication is that the project of attempting to interpret any utterance, especially such immensely complex utterances as philosophical texts, can only proceed historically. We must try to re-enter the different intellectual and political worlds in which each individual text constituted an intervention in an existing debate if there is to be any prospect of understanding them.

I next want to try to give a more precise sense of what the historicist approach looks like in practice. To do so I shall examine, briefly and schematically, one specific example. I shall focus on a text that has invariably been treated as central to the canon of anglophone political philosophy, Thomas Hobbes's *Leviathan* of 1651. Hobbes's treatise perfectly exemplifies the requirements of canonicity as traditionally understood. He focuses on questions about political obligation, and he goes on to connect them with questions about rights and liberty in precisely the approved style. As his point of departure, he attempts to persuade us that any attempt to live our lives in our natural condition of equal liberty would inevitably degenerate into an endless war 'of every man, against every man'.[6] This pessimistic vision of human nature prompts him to insist that we have no alternative but to relinquish our natural rights and subject ourselves to an absolute form of sovereign state that can hope to protect us from the violence of humankind. The inference he draws is that we have an obligation to obey the state if and only if it succeeds in protecting us. He goes so far as to declare in the conclusion of *Leviathan* that he composed the book 'without other designe, than to set before mens eyes the mutuall Relation between Protection and Obedience'.[7]

If protection requires obedience, what becomes of the unbounded liberty we enjoyed in the state of nature? When we agree to turn ourselves into the subjects of a state, Hobbes replies, we remain free to act according to our own will only to the extent that we are not obliged by the coercive force of law to act otherwise. Liberty can thus be defined as an absence of any such interference. Natural liberty consists in our

[6] Hobbes 2012 [1651], II, p. 192.
[7] Hobbes 2012 [1651], III, p. 1141.

power to act without 'externall Impediments of motion'.[8] Civil liberty consists in our retained power to act without legal impediments, and largely depends on 'the Silence of the Law'.[9] Where we find that 'the Sovereign has prescribed no rule', there 'the Subject hath the Liberty to do, or forbeare, according to his own discretion'.[10] A free person is someone who, in respect of actions they are capable of performing, is not hindered from performing them.[11]

During the middle decades of the twentieth century a large exegetical literature gathered around this Hobbesian treatment of obligation, liberty and rights. A number of distinguished studies appeared in which Hobbes's analysis of these concepts was dissected, and the grounding of his argument on his beliefs about the character of the laws of God and nature was explored.[12] To the historicists of the younger generation, however, this seemed far from sufficient. They wanted to know what Hobbes was doing in analysing obligation in terms of protection and defining liberty as absence of interference. What kind of intervention was he making? What political commitments was he championing, or alternatively placing under attack? What sort of political stance was he aiming to legitimise?

As Hobbes himself had indicated, one of his principal aims in connecting obedience with protection had been to sever any links between the obligation of subjects and the supposed rights of rulers and states. If a state is invaded by a foreign power, or collapses into civil war, and if its military forces suffer a final defeat, then 'there is no farther protection of Subjects in their loyalty'.[13] There is consequently no further obligation to obey the state. Hobbes concedes that 'the Right of a Soveraign Monarch cannot be extinguished by the act of another', because we agree to treat the decisions of our sovereign as our own authorised acts when we covenant to institute a state.[14] But the obligation of subjects is undoubtedly rescinded, because 'the end of Obedience is Protection', and 'he that wants protection, may seek it any where'.[15]

If we now ask in historicist vein what political stance Hobbes may have been attempting to legitimise by making this case, we find that

---

[8] Hobbes 2012 [1651], II, p. 324.
[9] Hobbes 2012 [1651], II, p. 340.
[10] Hobbes 2012 [1651], II, p. 340.
[11] Hobbes 2012 [1651], II, p. 324.
[12] See, e.g., Warrender 1957; Hood 1964; Goldsmith 1966; McNeilly 1968; Gauthier 1969.
[13] Hobbes 2012 [1651], II, p. 518.
[14] Hobbes 2012 [1651], II, p. 518, and cf. pp. 264–6.
[15] Hobbes 2012 [1651], II, pp. 344, 518.

beneath the surface of his argument there lies an eirenic commitment to vindicating the new republican government of England. The supporters of King Charles I had condemned his trial and execution in 1649 as a blasphemous and illegal act of usurpation on the part of the conquering forces in the civil war. One response from the protagonists of the new regime had been to concede that an act of conquest had admittedly taken place, while insisting that conquest can be a means of acquiring political authority even in the absence of consent.[16] Hobbes challenges both parties, insisting that all such questions about right and lawfulness are beside the point. The only question is whether the new regime is providing the people with protection and peace. If it is successfully doing so, then they have a duty to obey, even if they happen to disapprove of the way in which the civil war was brought to an end.

There remains the related question of what Hobbes was doing in arguing that civil liberty should be defined in terms of the silence of the law. To speak once more in historicist vein, what kind of intervention was he making? And what political commitments was this argument designed at once to legitimise and set aside? Here we need to be aware that the leading parliamentarian opponents of Charles I, especially such legal theorists as Henry Parker, had defended their attacks on the crown with the claim that the king was exercising an arbitrary and hence an enslaving form of absolute power. Drawing on Roman- and common-law assumptions about freedom and servitude, Parker had maintained as early as 1640 that the crown's policies on taxation presupposed that 'the meere will of the Prince is law', and that 'he may charge the Kingdome thereupon at his discretion, though they assent not'.[17] But any sovereign who claims this degree of power is making his subjects dependent on his arbitrary will, thereby despotically turning them into 'the most despicable slaves in the whole world'.[18]

This argument was in turn used to sustain the revolutionary claim that individual liberty can be upheld only under conditions of popular sovereignty. Unless every citizen can see their will embodied, at least by representation, in the dictates of the law, the law will confront them as nothing better than an arbitrary will to which they are subject. It is true that this predicament need not necessarily have the effect of impeding any of their choices or actions. But they will be choosing and acting subject to the will and hence the permission of someone else. As Parker and others insisted, however, this is the very definition of slavery. The

---

[16] Skinner 2002b, pp. 230–1.
[17] [Parker] 1640, pp. 5, 17.
[18] [Parker] 1640, p. 21.

conclusion they drew is that it is possible to live as a free person, and at the same time as the subject of a state, if and only if you live in what they liked to describe as a free state. You need to live, that is, as a member of a body politic in which – as with the individual body of a free person – the body is moved exclusively by its own will, which in the case of a body politic can only mean the will of the people as a whole.

Hobbes was not a royalist, but he was emphatically a monarchist, strongly devoted to the belief that the instituting of absolute authority in one person as the representative of the state is the best means of providing security and peace. But what of the objection that this is to institute arbitrary domination and servitude? Here Hobbes made perhaps his most original intervention in the politics of the English revolution. The underlying aim of his argument is to show that the juridical analysis of liberty in terms of freedom from subjection is conceptually confused. It is not necessary to the upholding of liberty, Hobbes retorts, that we should be free from the possibility of interference from the arbitrary will of others. Hobbes's epoch-making contention is that it is sufficient if we are not in fact impeded in our choices and actions. To speak of a free person is merely to describe someone who is not hindered from doing what they have a will to do.[19]

If we ask, finally, about the nature of the political commitment that this redefinition was designed to legitimise, we find that it enabled Hobbes to repudiate, and to dismiss as confused, the entire case in favour of popular sovereignty put forward by those whom he was later to stigmatise as the democratical gentlemen in the English Parliament.[20] If freedom is nothing more than absence of interference, the question of the extent to which we enjoy civil liberty has nothing to do with forms of government. The question is not who makes the laws, but simply how many laws are made. The fewer the laws, the less the interference, and hence the greater the liberty. 'Whether a Common-wealth be Monarchicall, or Popular, the Freedome is still the same.'[21]

Viewed from this perspective, Hobbes's *Leviathan* no longer appears mainly or even primarily as a general analysis of the concepts of liberty, obligation and rights. Rather, it emerges as a vehemently polemical tract in which an immediate and almost paradoxically complex political message is being conveyed, a message in which the enemies of the Stuart monarchy are denounced while the duty to obey the new republican government is upheld. The moral of the historicist story is that, if we

---

[19] Hobbes 2012 [1651], II, p. 324.
[20] Hobbes 2010 [1682], pp. 141, 158.
[21] Hobbes 2012 [1651], II, p. 332.

wish to understand Hobbes's *Leviathan*, what we need to appreciate is the overwhelming degree to which it was a tract for the times.

By the opening years of the present century the approach I have been exemplifying had gained a sufficient ascendancy for a number of political philosophers to observe that 'the turn to history' had become a new orthodoxy.[22] By then, however, it had also been subjected to a number of critical assaults. Some objections levelled against it were admittedly hyperbolical, notably the postmodern assertion that intentions and purposes are irrecoverable.[23] Others took the form of abuse rather than argument, especially the attempt during the heyday of social history to dismiss the study of ideas as a marginal and perhaps even a suspicious activity.[24] But in recent years two more serious criticisms have been widely put forward, and no analysis of the role of history in the study of political philosophy can now fail to take account of them.

Some political philosophers, as well as international relations theorists, began to denounce what they saw as an increasing 'tyranny of history'.[25] They repudiated what they took to be 'a reduction of meaning to historical context',[26] the effect of which was to make it a cardinal sin to retrieve past texts and make use of them as a present resource.[27] One objection to this 'policing of anachronism' was that it exercised a constricting and conservative influence on legal and political theory by cutting us off from a usable past.[28] A more general objection was that it embodied an unwarranted refusal to acknowledge that some political philosophers have advanced 'general claims about political phenomena' that are 'universal in scope'.[29] The claim here was that there are 'transhistorical dimensions of the meaning of philosophical texts' that enable them to be appraised 'from the perspective of universal reason' and deployed in contemporary debates.[30] By contrast, the historicist approach leaves us with nothing of relevance to our current concerns, and consequently amounts to a form of enquiry of little more than dusty antiquarian interest.[31]

---

[22] Ball 2011; Kelly 2011, pp. 14–22; Blau 2017, p. 245.
[23] See, e.g., Harlan 1989. For responses see Richter 2001, pp. 61–4; Skinner 2002a, pp. 90–2, 120–2.
[24] As noted in McMahon 2014, pp. 17–21; Armitage 2014, pp. 235–6.
[25] Kelly 2011, p. 15.
[26] Kelly 2011, pp. 24, 31. See also LaCapra 1980, and for a discussion see Gordon 2014, esp. pp. 40–2.
[27] Orford 2017, pp. 297, 301–2. For a critical response see Leader Maynard 2017, p. 313.
[28] Orford 2017, pp. 301, 304, 309.
[29] Kelly 2011, p. 26.
[30] Kelly 2011, pp. 19–20, 24.
[31] See, e.g., Tarlton 1973; Graham 2011.

There seem to be two distinct arguments here, and it is worth try-ing to disentangle them. The accusation of antiquarianism has been a persistent one, but there are good reasons for rejecting it outright. The effect of adopting a historicist approach is to raise the possibility that even the most central concepts we currently use to evaluate our political world may have been decisively shaped by the contingencies of political life. To recur to the example I have examined, the claim that civil liberty can be defined as absence of interference remains an article of faith in many influential works of political philosophy, John Rawls's *A Theory of Justice* being only the most prominent example.[32] As I have argued, however, the original articulation of this particular reading of the con-cept was powerfully influenced by a desire to offer an anti-egalitarian response to the growing popularity of theories of popular sovereignty. Whatever may be said for and against this claim, it cannot be dismissed as merely antiquarian. Rather the underlying suggestion is one of consid-erable philosophical significance: that the distinction between ideology and political philosophy is difficult to mark, and may not be a categorical distinction at all. To entertain this possibility is to think differently not just about our philosophical heritage but about ourselves.

The objection to the tyranny of history at first sight looks more serious, but on closer inspection turns out to be based on a misunderstanding. It must be admitted that this partly arose from some early misstatements by the historicists themselves, some of whom began by insisting on a complete separation between past and present.[33] But no historicist would nowadays wish to speak of a reduction of meaning to historical context. It is not the meanings of texts that the historicist takes to be recoverable only from their context, but a recognition of what their authors may have been doing in writing them. What cannot be recovered except by historical excavation is the range of intentions with which any given text may have been written, and hence a comprehension of how the text was meant or intended to be taken and understood.[34]

This commitment in no way denies that a given text may bear a mean-ing, and a possible philosophical significance, that transcends the original context out of which it arose. Within the Western tradition of thinking about politics there have undoubtedly been some striking continuities in the use of particular concepts, and many corresponding stabilities in the vocabulary in which they have been expressed. As a result, there may be considerable scope for returning to past thinkers in order to help us

[32] For Rawls's articulation of this claim see Rawls 1971.
[33] This is true of my own attempt to state the historicist case in Skinner 1969.
[34] See Blau 2020.

restate and even to improve our prevailing understanding of the concepts involved.[35]

Consider, for example, Hobbes's way of thinking about the concept of liberty. As we have seen, Hobbes defines liberty as absence of interference, and few anglophone political philosophers would nowadays disagree with him. He also had a distinctive way of thinking about the concept of interference. Believing that our wills are always expressed in whatever actions we undertake, he inferred that coercion must be viewed as a source of motivation rather than a constraint.[36] This further commitment yielded the conclusion that 'Feare, and Liberty are consistent', and thus that freedom is limited only by physical impediments.[37] These contentions have lately caught the attention of some distinguished legal and political philosophers, notably Ian Carter and Matthew Kramer, both of whom have defended the thesis that the antonym of liberty is interference in the specific sense understood by Hobbes. While they have refined and extended Hobbes's argument, they have explicitly acknowledged his inspiration and made it clear that he directly influenced the formulation of their own case.[38]

Faced with this example, no historicist will wish to deny that here we have an instance of an argument escaping from its original context and surviving to make a contribution to contemporary philosophical debate. There are I think only two caveats to be entered. The first is about the nature of the debt that, in the example I have given, Carter and Kramer may be said to owe to Hobbes. No historicist is in a position to object in principle to their conclusion that Hobbes's argument provides us with the most illuminating and persuasive way of thinking about the concept of liberty. But any historicist will baulk at the further claim that some critics have been especially anxious to add: that Carter and Kramer, in reaffirming a version of Hobbes's theory, are not only appraising its meaning and significance independently of its original context, but may be speaking from 'the perspective of universal reason', defending a view of liberty that anyone may be said to have a good reason to endorse.[39] The most that any historicist will feel able to concede is that Hobbes's view of liberty may be susceptible of rational defence. No historicist can fail to feel doubtful about the additional contention that 'a turn to history undermines the claims of political reason by reducing them to local

---

[35] As noted in Floyd 2011, pp. 46–8.
[36] Hobbes 2012 [1651], II, pp. 324–6.
[37] Hobbes 2012 [1651], II, p. 326.
[38] Carter 1999, pp. 1, 150, 212, 284; Carter 2008, pp. 61–4; Kramer 2003, pp. 17–18, 25–40, 46–60, 66–70; Kramer 2008.
[39] See, e.g., Kelly 2011, pp. 19, 20–1, 26.

prejudices'.[40] The historicist is far more likely to perceive a danger of endowing local prejudices with the undeserved status of universal truths.

The other caveat that a historicist will want to enter is a more specific and less speculative one. Whatever we may think of the conclusions to which Carter and Kramer have been drawn in part by their engagement with Hobbes, we must not confuse their project with that of seeking to understand Hobbes's theory of liberty. The fundamental claim to which the historicist is committed is that meaning and understanding are not correlative terms. The quest for understanding requires us not merely to recover the meanings of utterances but also to grasp what the given speaker or writer may have been doing in uttering them. But this is not a question that Carter or Kramer addresses.

Some critics have retorted that no such 'intrinsic epistemological priority' can be assigned to the moment at which any writer lived and wrote, and hence at which their intentions and projects were formed.[41] A historicist is bound to reply that, if our aspiration is to understand what they were doing as well as what they were saying, then such a priority cannot be denied. No one, for example, can be said to understand what Hobbes is telling us about what it means to be free if they fail to recognise that he is aiming to discredit the belief, virtually unquestioned in his time, that freedom can be defined as absence of subjection to the arbitrary will of others. This is what Hobbes is doing in arguing that liberty consists in nothing more than an absence of hindrances to action. Nor can anyone be said to understand Hobbes's argument without recognising that the move he is making was designed to legitimise the possession of absolute sovereignty, and thus to undermine the contention that it is possible to live as a free person only in a self-governing state. The moral that a historicist will always want to draw is that the project of understanding a text of any kind, by contrast with merely elucidating its meaning, will always to some degree be a historical task.

I turn to the other and more pervasive doubt that has recently been voiced about the project of attempting to reconstruct the inherited themes and styles of our political thinking in their own terms. One question now frequently raised is whether this heritage remains worthy of such close attention at all. It is possible to distinguish two different versions of this doubt. The more radical stems from the complaint that 'it is difficult for most of us to see ourselves in "the canon" and to feel that our stories are being represented'.[42] The right conclusion to draw, it is

[40] Kelly 2011, p. 17.
[41] Koskenniemi 2014, p. 125.
[42] Bird 2018.

suggested, is that because the most pressing political problems of our age now centre on such topics as race and gender, we should concentrate on studying those issues rather than cleaving to a tradition in which they tended to be silenced or marginalised.[43]

This line of criticism is somewhat outdated in so far as it objects to the omission of historical voices that deserve to be heard. Many successful efforts have been made in recent years to remedy this deficiency, especially by way of foregrounding the writings of women philosophers and those who have spoken on behalf of disadvantaged groups.[44] But my main objection is that the criticism seems insensitive to one of the most valuable ways in which we can hope to learn from the past. If we are willing to turn to our inherited traditions of thinking only in quest of what may help us to reaffirm our existing values and identities, we shall cut ourselves off from the possibility of using the past as a critical resource, a means of challenging and enlarging our current beliefs rather than merely underpinning and celebrating them. While our inherited traditions contain striking continuities, there are also some radical discontinuities stemming from the fact that many of our basic concepts have been reformulated or even jettisoned over the course of time. If we are not to become lost in self-regard, we need to remain alive to the possibility that the exploration of these abandoned intellectual pathways may be of more value to us here and now than some ways of thinking that we currently endorse or even take for granted.

As I have already intimated, there is a strong case for saying that these considerations apply to the current way of thinking about the concept of liberty.[45] There is much to be gained from reflecting on the suggestion that freedom is always taken away by subjection to the will of others. As soon as we consider the implications of this claim, it is hard to avoid the conclusion that our abandonment of this way of thinking has directed us along some morally questionable paths.[46] We have been encouraged to treat as free agents a large number of people who are currently deprived of liberty in significant domains of their lives. Consider, for example, the extent to which de-unionised workforces increasingly live at the mercy of employers with power to dismiss them at will. Or consider how far the disproportionately frequent economic dependence of women leaves them vulnerable to partners whom they lack the resources to escape. The loss of liberty suffered in such circumstances need never be due to any

---

[43] Laursen 2013, p. 88, reporting a conversation.
[44] For two important anthologies see Lloyd 2002 and Broad and Detlefsen 2017.
[45] For a classic exposition of this claim see Pettit 1997. See also Skinner 1998.
[46] Here I draw on Skinner 2022.

overt acts of intimidation or interference; it already stems from the mere fact of living under arbitrary power, and the resulting impossibility of arguing on equal terms.

The rejection of this way of thinking has also rendered us insensitive to some silent threats to our liberty.[47] Consider the current business models of digital and social media companies. They provide free services that enable them covertly to acquire swathes of data about our personal preferences. This in turn allows them to engage in a systematic policy of surveillance, predicting our behaviour and making use of the resulting information for undisclosed purposes. We are left subject to an unaccountable form of power that may or may not be employed for our benefit, and over which we have no control.

The relevance of this analysis to our present concerns will I hope by now be clear. If we persist in thinking of freedom as a predicate of actions rather than a status of agents, we can hardly hope to perceive, still less to ameliorate, many forms of subjection that currently disfigure our societies. The alternative tradition of thinking about freedom that we have largely abandoned helps us to see that what primarily matters in thinking about civil liberty is what it means to be a free person, and how that status can be equally secured and upheld. Rather than continuing to ignore this line of thought, it might be more fruitful if we were to exorcise the ghost of Hobbes and redirect our attention towards this alternative tradition of thought.

I end by turning to the second and related doubt that has recently been voiced. The study of the Western canon, it is increasingly argued, currently enjoys an unwarranted prominence, and needs to be supplemented by a broader and comparative investigation of the political understandings that have evolved in different parts of our increasingly globalised world.[48] We are consequently urged to decolonise our research projects,[49] to provincialise Europe,[50] to deparochialise our curricula and the discipline as a whole.[51]

There seems every reason to welcome this so-called global turn. Some political issues have become inherently worldwide, most obviously those stemming from the climate crisis, and need to be addressed in correspondingly wide-ranging terms. Even if we confine ourselves to writing

---

[47] For examples of this rejection see Patten 1996; Goodin 2003; Podoksik 2010.
[48] See Dallmayr 2010; Freeden and Vincent 2013; Moyn and Sartori 2013; Kapila 2014; Ackerly and Bajpai 2017; Kapust and Kinsella 2017; Dunn 2018; and for a more critical recent survey see Charette and Skjönsberg 2020.
[49] Mills 2015.
[50] Chakrabarty 2000.
[51] Tully 2014; Tully 2020; Williams and Warren 2014; Obregón 2017.

a global history of political theory, as opposed to a history of globalised issues, we can hope to gain at least two related academic as well as broader benefits. If we can learn to see ourselves in a more anthropological spirit as one tribe among others, we can hope not merely to enlarge our range of knowledge, but at the same time our self-awareness, and hence potentially our capacity for tolerance and our range of sympathies.[52] Meanwhile those who continue to focus on Western traditions in political philosophy can expect to benefit as well. As many recent studies have shown, a more global perspective can help us to acquire a clearer perception of many elements in these traditions that have long been neglected or sanitised.[53]

This is an inspiring vision, but one obvious and I hope uncontentious caveat needs to be entered. The project of moving beyond the post-colonial as well as the imperial age in order to create a genuinely global history will be an immense and inter-generational enterprise. A daunting range of linguistic expertise will be required, together with exceptional sophistication in the understanding of unfamiliar concepts and how they fit together to create distinctive cultural systems. Unless these exacting requirements are met, there will be an unavoidable danger – as many exercises in global history already illustrate – that superficial and celebratory forms of scholarship will all too easily come to dominate the field.[54] To avoid this risk, it may be wise to cultivate a certain modesty. We need to keep asking ourselves (in the words of Frederick Cooper's classic study) what the concept of globalisation is good for. We may need to pay more attention to the fact that, as Cooper argued, the channels through which ideologies spread are shaped less by geography than by power, and that this tends to limit as well as determine the extent of their global reach.[55]

We must also take care not to throw the baby out with the bathwater. Due to the impact of Western imperialism, the history of political thinking in many areas of the world has been intertwined ever since the early modern period with Western values and attitudes. Until the time comes when we judge these influences to have run their course, the project of understanding politics on a global scale will need to be pursued hand in hand with the study of Western political thought. If the study of Western traditions now begins to be neglected, there will be a corresponding decline in our understanding of how a number of political concepts

---

[52] Dunn 2018; Tully 2018.
[53] For a discussion see Blau 2017, pp. 258–9.
[54] For these warnings see Pocock 2019; Fleischer, Kafadar and Subrahmanyam 2020.
[55] Cooper 2001.

and values in our globalised world came into existence, and hence in our understanding of those concepts themselves. Nor should we think of the future study of Western political philosophy as having a value merely in relation to these broader interests. The pre-globalised world of individual states persists everywhere. For those of us who live in anglophone or European communities it will remain important to acquaint ourselves with, and think critically about, the history and current value of the concepts we use to guide our local institutions and behaviour.[56]

Finally, it is obvious that, if a global history of political philosophy is to have any value, it will need to follow the best available canons of historical practice. My main aim in what I have been arguing has been to defend and exemplify the view that, in the study of textual traditions, these canons require us to recognise that meaning and understanding are not correlative terms. The acquisition of understanding always involves something other than grasping the meaning of what has been said; it requires that textual interpretation should ask and answer questions about the range of things that speakers or writers may have been doing in saying what they said. I can hardly avoid concluding on a dogmatic note. If our new and more globalised histories of political philosophy are to be satisfactory as history, there will be a continuing need to adopt and follow the kind of historicist principles I have here been trying to exemplify and defend.

References

Ackerly, Brooke and Rochana Bajpai. 2017. 'Comparative Political Thought' in *Methods in Analytical Political Theory*, ed. Adrian Blau. Cambridge.

Armitage, David. 2014. 'The International Turn in Intellectual History' in *Rethinking Modern European Intellectual History*, ed. Darrin McMahon and Samuel Moyn. Oxford.

Austin, J. L. 1962. *How to Do Things with Words*. Oxford.

Ball, Terence. 2011. 'The Value of the History of Political Philosophy' in *The Oxford Handbook of the History of Political Philosophy*, ed. George Klosko. Oxford.

Berlin, Isaiah. 1962. 'Does Political Theory Still Exist?' in *Philosophy, Politics and Society*, second series, ed. Peter Laslett and W. G. Runciman. Oxford.

Bird, Gemma. 2018. 'I'll Pass on Plato', *Times Higher Education*, 1 November, p. 31.

Blau, Adrian. 2017. 'Interpreting Texts' in *Methods in Analytical Political Theory*, ed. Adrian Blau. Cambridge.

2020. 'Meanings and Understandings in the History of Ideas', *Journal of the Philosophy of History*, 14, pp. 232–56.

---

[56] As emphasised in Pocock 2019.

Boucher, David. 1985. *Texts in Context: Revisionist Methods for Studying the History of Ideas*. Dordrecht.

Broad, Jacqueline and Karen Detlefsen, eds. 2017. *Women and Liberty 1600–1800: Philosophical Essays*. Oxford.

Carter, Ian. 1999. *A Measure of Freedom*. Oxford.

    2008. 'How are Power and Unfreedom Related?' in *Republicanism and Political Theory*, ed. Cécile Laborde and John Maynor. Oxford.

Chakrabarty, Dipesh. 2000. *Provincializing Europe: Postcolonial Thought and Historical Difference*. Princeton.

Charette, Danielle and Max Skjönsberg. 2020. 'State of the Field: The History of Political Thought', *History*, 105, pp. 470–83.

Cooper, Frederick. 2001. 'What is the Concept of Globalisation Good for? An African Historian's Perspective', *African Affairs*, 100, pp. 189–213.

Dallmayr, Fred. 2010. *Comparative Political Theory: An Introduction*. New York.

Dunn, John. 1968. 'The Identity of the History of Ideas', *Philosophy*, 43, pp. 85–104.

    2018. 'Why we Need a Global History of Political Thought' in *Markets, Morals, Politics: Jealousy of Trade and the History of Political Thought*, ed. Béla Kapossy, Isaac Nakhimovsky, Sophus Reinert and Richard Whatmore. Cambridge, MA.

Fleischer, Cornell, Cemal Kafadar and Sanjay Subrahmanyam. 2020. 'How to Write Fake Global History', *Cromohs*, 10, https://oajournals.fupress.net/index.php.cromohs/debate.

Floyd, Jonathan. 2011. 'From Historical Contextualism, to Mentalism, to Behaviourism' in *Political Philosophy versus History?*, ed. Jonathan Floyd and Marc Stears. Oxford.

Freeden, Michael and Andrew Vincent, eds. 2013. *Comparative Political Thought: Theorising Practices*. London.

Gauthier, David P. 1969. *The Logic of Leviathan: The Moral and Political Theory of Thomas Hobbes*. Oxford.

Goldsmith, M. M. 1966. *Hobbes's Science of Politics*. New York.

Goodin, Robert E. 2003. 'Folie Républicaine', *Annual Review of Political Science*, 6, pp. 55–76.

Gordon, Peter. 2014. 'Contextualism and Criticism in the History of Ideas' in *Rethinking Modern European Intellectual History*, ed. Darrin McMahon and Samuel Moyn. Oxford.

Graham, Gordon. 2011. 'Political Philosophy and the Dead Hand of its History' in *Political Philosophy versus History?*, ed. Jonathan Floyd and Marc Stears. Oxford.

Harlan, David. 1989. 'Intellectual History and the Return of Literature', *American Historical Review*, 94, pp. 581–609.

Hobbes, Thomas. 2010 [1682]. *Behemoth or the Long Parliament*, ed. Paul Seaward. Oxford.

    2012 [1651]. *Leviathan*, ed. Noel Malcolm. 3 vols. Oxford.

Hood, F. C. 1964. *The Divine Politics of Thomas Hobbes: An Interpretation of Leviathan*. Oxford.

Kapila, Shruti. 2014. 'Global Intellectual History and the Indian Political' in *Rethinking Modern European Intellectual History*, ed. Darrin McMahon and Samuel Moyn. Oxford.

Kapust, Daniel and Helen Kinsella, eds. 2017. *Comparative Political Theory in Time and Place*. New York.

Kelly, Paul. 2011. 'Rescuing Political Theory from the Tyranny of History' in *Political Philosophy versus History?*, ed Jonathan Floyd and Marc Stears. Oxford.

Klosko, George, ed. 2011. *The Oxford Handbook of the History of Political Philosophy*. Oxford.

Koskenniemi, Martti. 2014. 'Vitoria and Us: Thoughts on Critical Histories of International Law', *Rechsgeschichte*, 22, pp. 119–38.

Kramer, Matthew. 2003. *The Quality of Freedom*. Oxford.

2008. 'Liberty and Domination' in *Republicanism and Political Theory*, ed. Cécile Laborde and John Maynor. Oxford.

LaCapra, Dominick. 1980. 'Rethinking Intellectual History and Reading Texts', *History and Theory*, 19, pp. 245–76.

Laursen, John. 2013. 'Five Questions' in *Intellectual History: Five Questions*, ed. Morten Jeppesen, Frederik Stjernfelt and Mikkel Thorup. London.

Leader Maynard, Jonathan. 2017. 'Ideological Analysis' in *Methods in Analytical Political Theory*, ed. Adrian Blau. Cambridge.

Lloyd, Genevieve, ed. 2002. *Feminism and the History of Philosophy*. Oxford.

McMahon, Darrin. 2014. 'The Return of the History of Ideas?' in *Rethinking Modern European Intellectual History*, ed. Darrin McMahon and Samuel Moyn. Oxford.

McNeilly, F. S. 1968. *The Anatomy of Leviathan*. London.

Mills, Charles. 2015. 'Decolonizing Western Political Philosophy', *New Political Science*, 37, pp. 1–24.

Moyn, Samuel. 2014. 'Imaginary Intellectual History' in *Rethinking Modern European Intellectual History*, ed. Darrin McMahon and Samuel Moyn. Oxford.

Moyn, Samuel and Andrew Sartori, eds. 2013. *Global Intellectual History*. New York.

Müller, Jan-Werner. 2014. 'On Conceptual History' in *Rethinking Modern European Intellectual History*, ed. Darrin McMahon and Samuel Moyn. Oxford.

Obregón, Liliana. 2017. 'Martti Koskenniemi's Critique of Eurocentrism in International Law' in *The Law of International Lawyers*, ed. Wouter Werner, Marieke de Hoon and Alexis Galan. Cambridge.

Orford, Anne. 2017. 'International Law and the Limits of History' in *The Law of International Lawyers*, ed. Wouter Werner, Marieke de Hoon and Alexis Galan. Cambridge.

[Parker, Henry]. 1640. *The Case of Shipmony briefly discoursed*. London.

Patten, Alan. 1996. 'The Republican Critique of Liberalism', *British Journal of Political Science*, 26, pp. 25–44.

Pettit, Philip. 1997. *Republicanism: A Theory of Freedom and Government*. Oxford.

Pocock, J. G. A. 1962. 'The History of Political Thought: A Methodological Enquiry' in *Philosophy, Politics and Society*, ed. Peter Laslett and W. G. Runciman, Oxford.

2019. 'On the Unglobality of Contexts: Cambridge Methods and the History of Political Thought', *Global Intellectual History*, 4, pp. 1–14.

Podoksik, Efraim. 2010. 'One Concept of Liberty: Towards Writing the History of a Political Concept', *Journal of the History of Ideas*, 71, pp. 219–40.

Rawls, John. 1971. *A Theory of Justice*. Oxford.

Richter, Melvin. 2001. 'A German Version of the "Linguistic Turn": Reinhart Koselleck and the History of Political and Social Concepts' in *The History of Political Thought in National Context*, ed. Dario Castiglione and Iain Hampsher-Monk. Cambridge.

Searle, John. 1969. *Speech Acts: An Essay in the Philosophy of Language*. Cambridge.

Skinner, Quentin. 1969. 'Meaning and Understanding in the History of Ideas', *History and Theory*, 8, pp. 3–53.

1998. *Liberty before Liberalism*. Cambridge.

2002a. *Visions of Politics*, vol. I: *Regarding Method*. Cambridge.

2002b. *Visions of Politics*, vol. III: *Hobbes and Civil Science*. Cambridge.

2022. 'On Neo-Roman Liberty: A Response and Reassessment' in *Rethinking Liberty before Liberalism*, ed. Hannah Dawson and Annelien de Dijn. Cambridge.

Tarlton, Charles. 1973. 'Historicity, Meaning and Revisionism in the Study of Political Thought', *History and Theory*, 12, pp. 307–28.

Tully, James. 2014. *On Global Citizenship: James Tully in Dialogue*. London.

2018. 'Reconciliation Here on Earth' in *Resurgence and Reconciliation: Indigenous–Settler Relations and Earth Teachings*, ed. Michael Asch, John Borrows and James Tully. Toronto.

2020. 'Deparochializing Political Theory and Beyond: A Dialogue Approach to Comparative Political Thought' in *Deparochializing Political Theory*, ed. Melissa S. Williams. Cambridge.

Warrender, Howard. 1957. *The Political Philosophy of Hobbes: His Theory of Obligation*. Oxford.

Whatmore, Richard. 2016. 'Quentin Skinner and the Relevance of Intellectual History' in *A Companion to Intellectual History*, ed. Richard Whatmore and Brian Young. Oxford.

Williams, Melissa S. and Mark E. Warren. 2014. 'A Democratic Case for Comparative Political Theory', *Political Theory*, 42, pp. 26–57.

9 The Relationship between Philosophy and its History

Susan James

There is nowadays a widespread consensus that, whilst some philosophical enquiry is historical and some is not, advocates of the two approaches can work together harmoniously. Writing in 2005, Gary Hatfield observed that contextually oriented historians of philosophy no longer needed to worry about being marginalised, and had no reason to complain of 'a lack of appreciation from ahistorical colleagues'.[1] More recently, Christia Mercer has argued that historians of philosophy should avoid wasting their energies on internal squabbles about method. It is now widely accepted, she claims, that the quality of philosophical work 'has less to do with any specific method we use and more to do with the proper fit between the projects we select for study and the skills we apply to them'.[2]

These ecumenical reassurances aim to forge a symbiosis between philosophy and its history, and largely reflect the status quo; but, despite their wish to rise above disagreements that might sully the relationship between historically and ahistorically minded philosophers, disagreement has not entirely disappeared. Some hostility remains, and continues to generate a degree of suspicion. One of the clearest manifestations of this mistrust is what I shall call the Separation Thesis: the view that the study of philosophy and the study of its history are distinct forms of enquiry. This position has a number of active advocates. In Timothy Williamson's estimation, for example, a historian of philosophy puts forward an account of 'what some philosopher held', while philosophy consists in 'putting a theory forward as true'.[3] Or, as Michael Huemer provocatively contends, historians who interpret texts tell us 'what

I am grateful for the many helpful comments on an earlier draft that I received at the conference associated with this project, and at the Work in Progress Seminar of the Philosophy Department, Birkbeck College. For extremely useful suggestions on the final draft I thank Alexander Douglas and the editors of this volume.

[1] Hatfield 2005, pp. 88–9.
[2] Mercer 2019, p. 530.
[3] Williamson 2018, p. 99.

philosopher P meant by utterance U', but 'this is of no philosophical import', because we still do not know whether P's claim is true.[4] Defenders of the Separation Thesis are thus an exception to the ecumenical rule. Rather than accepting that one can do philosophy historically, they view the history of philosophy as an appendage. Rather than embracing a historical approach, they isolate philosophy from its past.

The claim that there is just one thing philosophers do, namely putting forward theories as true, and just one thing that lies within the purview of the history of philosophy, namely telling us what past philosophers have said, will undoubtedly amaze a great many recent and contemporary practitioners, historically minded or not.[5] Where is the exploration of alien points of view, or the development of two sides of a case, that are part and parcel of philosophical investigation? Where is the critical reflection on canon formation or the interpretation and assessment of reasons that are integral to studying the subject? To uphold a bare distinction between affirmation and reportage, these and many other aspects of philosophical creativity have to be suppressed. Yet, according to Williamson, historians of philosophy must respect the boundaries he lays down for them. Reporting what earlier thinkers have said possesses some value, and is even 'part of philosophy'; but although historians are free to dig around in the past, they must not delude themselves into believing that they are contributing to philosophy proper. The fruits of their research are no more than a series of footnotes, which rarely if ever advance the subject. Few modern developments, Williamson claims, 'have been directly inspired by much earlier work. Even when older precedents were clear in retrospect, the new ideas often had to be discovered independently before the similarity was realised.'[6] Even where past thinkers anticipated our philosophical ideas, we can reach their conclusions for ourselves without drawing on their arguments. It is therefore not essential to examine them.

The Separation Thesis seeks to legitimise a certain view of philosophical authority. The only way to make a contribution to the subject, its supporters claim, is to affirm philosophical truths in your own voice, and this is the criterion by which philosophers should be judged: 'the test of a good major is that s/he does good philosophy, not good history of philosophy'.[7] Underlying this view there is also, perhaps, a resentful suspicion, mischievously voiced by Huemer, that philosophising in

---

[4] Huemer 2020.
[5] See, e.g., Rorty 1984.
[6] Williamson 2018, p. 109.
[7] Scriven 1977, p. 233.

this fashion is more difficult than doing historical research, and deserves greater respect. 'If you're a historian ... you're not arguing that any philosophical thesis is *true*. You're just saying that some philosophical thesis is *supported by the texts*. That makes life simpler and easier.'[8] It is not hard to see how this ordering of significance and skill embodies a bid for status. By marginalising the history of philosophy, the Separation Thesis elevates research that answers to a particular conception of what philosophy is, and endows people who do this kind of work with philosophical authority.

Since these aspects of the Separation Thesis open it to the charges of arrogance and dogmatism, it is not particularly surprising that it has relatively few committed advocates. Why, then, should we bother to discuss it? Why worry about an extreme and combative position that can only stir up trouble? In many contexts the Separation Thesis is probably best ignored; but in relation to our present purposes it remains significant, because it continues to shape our understanding of the relationship between philosophy and history, and fuels some of the residual disagreement that surrounds it. If we want to understand why this relationship remains somewhat uneasy, and deepen our understanding of what the uneasiness is about, we cannot simply set the Separation Thesis aside. On the contrary, we need to interrogate it. In the next section I identify three ways in which the Separation Thesis continues to haunt contemporary discussions of the relation between philosophy and its history. However, if we only concentrate on its current effects, I go on to suggest, the grounds of its influence remain obscure and we cannot adequately explain why it remains a force to be reckoned with. To address this question, I argue in the third section, we need to take a historical approach to the Separation Thesis itself. By considering how philosophy has traditionally set itself apart from history, we can get a fuller sense of what drives contemporary philosophers to defend the Separation Thesis, and what they hope to gain by doing so. I conclude by arguing that the Separation Thesis enacts a fantasy about philosophy's unique and transformative power, and answers to some of our deepest desires. To acknowledge the interdependence of philosophy and history we need to set this fantasy aside; but before we can do so we must examine it.

Many of the methodological issues that absorb historians of philosophy are internal to their practice. When, for example, should one study the genealogy of concepts, reconstruct the arguments of individual texts or trace their reception? What can we learn by examining the conditions in which people are prepared to fight for a philosophical doctrine, or the

---

[8] Huemer 2020.

circumstances in which systems of ideas become tools of oppression? Immersed in questions such as these, researchers rarely pause to consider why the history of philosophy as such is worth studying. Confident of its value, and operating within a historical frame of reference, they focus on the problems to which it gives rise. Asked to explain what their work contributes to non-historical forms of philosophy, these historians often adopt a defensive posture. Shifting onto the back foot, they take it on themselves to show that at least part of what makes their research valuable is its contribution to our understanding of contemporary philosophical issues. Contrary to the claim made by the Separation Thesis, they argue, the history of philosophy is not distinct from, or subordinate to, its ahistorical counterpart. Quite the opposite, it plays a role in the putting forward of philosophical truths.[9]

In following out this line of argument, historians largely accept the Separation Thesis on its own terms. Much as they oppose its attitude to history, they bow to its assumption that it falls to them to justify their activities in terms their non-historical colleagues can accept, rather than the other way around. Taking on the burden of self-legitimisation, they set out to show how the history of philosophy enriches philosophy proper. This is a powerful approach to take. As an extensive literature demonstrates, there are many ways in which historians can advance ongoing philosophical debates. But not all historians find this response to separatism satisfying. As some of them object, it already concedes too much to the Separation Thesis, and in doing so loses sight of the real reasons for studying the history of philosophy. Reconstructing the meaning of texts is not, as the Separation Thesis claims and some conciliatory historians seem to allow, a subordinate task allocated to philosophy's historical handmaidens; on the contrary, it is an undertaking in its own right. Furthermore, it embodies its own standards of success, which cannot be assimilated to the norms governing the assessment of philosophical truths. If we try to evaluate the history of philosophy in the terms laid down by the Separation Thesis, we are bound to sell it short. Better, then, to embrace the separatist view that philosophy and the history of philosophy are different projects, and agree that the history of philosophy aims to interpret what past philosophers have said.[10]

The attempt to face down the separatist implication that the history of philosophy is not only different from, but subordinate to, philosophy proper has obvious polemical force. Given that it would be regarded as unreasonable to expect contemporary epistemologists, for example, to

[9] Yolton 1986; Curley 1986; Antognazza 2015.
[10] Garber 2005; Laerke 2013.

conduct their research in such a way as to promote historical enquiry, 'why', Mogens Laerke asks, 'should the reverse be the case?'[11] But the strategy is also costly. While it releases historians from the subordinate position to which the Separation Thesis consigns them, it simultaneously cuts them off from the philosophical practice of assessing positions for their truth or falsehood, and for many historians this is too high a price to pay. As one can see from their continuing efforts to show that their research contributes to the process of articulating truths, they are not ready to exclude themselves from philosophising as separatists construe it.

I now turn to two further attempts to engage with the Separation Thesis, one of which focuses on its tendency towards conservatism, the other on its unduly narrow conception of philosophical enquiry. When challenging the Separation Thesis, historians of philosophy regularly argue that philosophers need to draw on the ideas of historical figures to form and test hypotheses.[12] Without knowing what positions earlier authors have taken and how they have defended them, contemporary thinkers run the risk of overlooking objections to their own proposals, reinventing the wheel, or attacking straw men. By way of reply, a separatist might argue that philosophers are only contingently dependent on history, since the past is not their only source of potential counter-arguments and objections; they can also draw on their intuitions – that is to say, on their existing beliefs – to assess the truth of a claim, and adjust their positions in the light of thought experiments. By imagining a range of hypothetical scenarios, for example, one can exclude claims with implausible implications; and the method of reflective equilibrium provides a means to test one intuition against another.

Michael Della Rocca has recently described these appeals to intuition as attempts to tame philosophy.[13] Why, he asks, should we assume that beliefs we find intuitively acceptable are more likely to be true than those we find counter-intuitive? Why should we exclude possibilities that are at odds with, and might revolutionise, our current outlook? In the course of this critique Della Rocca also points out that a commitment to saving our intuitions has implications for the history of philosophy. It shapes a philosopher's approach to history by directing their attention away from historical ideas they happen to find unconvincing. Rather than looking to the wild side of history for challenges that might alter their thinking, they will tend to appeal to the past to shore up their existing beliefs.

[11] Laerke 2013, p. 9.
[12] Cottingham 2005; Wilson 2005.
[13] Della Rocca 2013, p. 187.

Although he does not put it this way, Della Rocca's analysis serves as a further illustration of the continuing influence of the Separation Thesis. Advocates of the intuitive approach defend a form of philosophising that purportedly has nothing substantial to learn from the past. Our existing beliefs supplant the need to seriously engage with historical points of view that do not already strike us as convincing; and to find out what questions are of philosophical interest, it is enough to study the prevailing practice of the subject. Philosophers can therefore rely on non-historical resources. Although an issue may have been discussed for thousands of years, our present knowledge and powers of reasoning give us our best means of assessing its truth. Any contribution that the history of philosophy may make to this self-contained form of philosophising is non-essential, and can be set aside.

The dependence on intuition that Della Rocca criticises points to one limitation of the Separation Thesis: by excluding historical work from the realm of properly philosophical activity, and favouring intuition as a means of testing philosophical claims, the thesis narrows the horizons of philosophical investigation. But a further accusation of narrowness comes from critics who voice a different objection: that the Separation Thesis arbitrarily limits the range of questions that count as philosophical. Even if separatists are right to claim that some philosophical problems can be addressed in non-historical terms, there are other problems, including a number of reflexive issues about philosophy itself, that demand historical treatment. For example, to address the question 'What is philosophy?' we need to consider what philosophy has been. To find out whether any philosophical questions are eternal we need to examine the ruptures that have occurred within the philosophical tradition. In short, we need to adopt a historical approach.[14]

A possible reply might be that questions such as these are not after all philosophical. But it is hard to see how this could be more than a stipulation. Once issues about the character of philosophy as a practice are acknowledged to be integral to the study of the subject, the Separation Thesis emerges as one view among others. It offers an account of what philosophy does and where its limits lie. But what of the contrasting Nietzschean proposal that philosophy proceeds genealogically as the repressed seek to discredit the ideologies of those who dominate them?[15] What of the view that philosophy, like science, hangs onto faltering paradigms long after the available evidence has ceased to support

---

[14] Vermeir 2013, p. 54.
[15] Nietzsche 1994.

them?[16] What of the view that philosophy is more malleable than either of these models implies, and changes in response to a broad array of cultural pressures? In order to treat any of these proposals as subjects of philosophical investigation one must abandon the separatist view that truly philosophical research does not encompass historical enquiry into philosophy's past.

The criticisms of the Separation Thesis that I have offered seem to me to hit their mark. One might therefore expect some concessions from the separatist side. But as far as I am aware, none have been forthcoming. Why should this be? While the refusal to give way might merely be the fruit of philosophical obstinacy, I believe it has a more interesting explanation. Even when the Separation Thesis is put under the pressures we have so far charted, its advocates are not willing to abandon it. Something else about it, which the criticisms do not touch, continues to strike them as importantly right, and sustains their commitment to it. To get a deeper appreciation of the separatist's hostility to history we need to try to understand what this is, and in the remainder of the chapter I offer a hypothesis. To grasp what is at stake, I shall argue, we need to take a historical approach to the Separation Thesis itself and consider how, historically speaking, philosophy has differentiated itself from history.

When advocates of the Separation Thesis claim that philosophers put forward theories as true, they have a particular kind of truth in mind. Lepidopterists, after all, put forward truths about butterflies. The distinctive feature of philosophy, as Williamson sees it, is that it aims to answer 'questions of stupendous generality'.[17] It is often far from obvious how contemporary philosophical research answers to this description – many of the issues it addresses are extremely specific. But the view that philosophy deals in general problems remains a commonplace, and derives its authority, I shall suggest, from the history of the subject. For all that writers such as Williamson aim to dissociate philosophy from its history, that very history inflects their conception of what philosophy is.

The claim that philosophical truths are distinguished by their generality is rooted in the classical view that philosophy aspires to comprehend Being in its entirety. Since the truths it aims to uncover apply to all beings, they are universal rather than particular; and because they capture the unchanging essences of things, they are eternal rather than temporal. These features are held to distinguish philosophy, which alone deals in knowledge that is entirely general, from other forms of enquiry. At the same time, however, other features of philosophy add

---

[16] Kuhn 1962; Rorty 1979, pp. 322–56.
[17] Williamson 2018, p. 5.

to its distinctive character. To gain philosophical understanding one must employ specific methods, usually described as forms of reasoning, which deliver an indefeasible and compelling kind of knowledge that can in turn be used to assess knowledge of other kinds. Alongside these epistemological traits, philosophising also has a theological aspect; as we grasp philosophical truths, we come to share some of God's knowledge, and in doing so participate in the divine. To some extent, our understanding of the elements and structure of Being mirrors that of God. Finally, this process transforms us. As Socrates intimates in the *Timaeus*, the more philosophers immerse themselves in knowledge of the eternal, feel its force and live as it dictates, the more joyful they become.[18] The contemplation and enactment of philosophical truth generates intense and enduring happiness, and constitutes the greatest perfection of which human beings are capable.

This ancient conception of philosophy as a form of understanding unlike any other reappears throughout the history of the subject. In some of its reincarnations the four aspects we have identified are all reaffirmed, and philosophy is again represented as the transformative route to a quasi-divine and supremely joyful way of life. In others, priority is given to one or other aspect, as Williamson gives priority to the generality of philosophical truths. Even then, however, the other traits continue to hover in the wings, posing questions of their own. What is it like to comprehend truths of stupendous generality? What intellectual or practical skills does it require? And how does it change our lives? Each aspect of the view I have outlined, which I shall call the Classical Conception, continues to resonate more or less audibly, even as new metaphysical and moral outlooks inform successive accounts of philosophical enquiry.

To trace the Classical Conception from the ancient world to the present would be to write an entire history of philosophy, and is far beyond the scope of a single chapter. To illustrate the way this conception has endured, and show how it has continued to legitimise the separation of philosophy and history, I shall focus on a single example. Early modern philosophers were, as Aaron Garrett points out, 'extremely (and sometimes overtly) eclectic'. They were 'acutely aware that they were not ancients, at the same time that they appropriated from the ancient schools'.[19] Thanks in part to the work of Pierre Hadot[20] and Michel Foucault,[21] we are alert to the extent to which authors writing during

---

[18] Sedley 1999, p. 312; Plato 1965, *Timaeus* 90b–c.
[19] Garrett 2013, p. 232.
[20] Hadot 1995.
[21] Foucault 1997.

this period continue to advocate an ancient view of philosophy as an art of living, a form of knowledge manifested in a harmonious way of life. Whilst many early modern thinkers defend versions of this stance, one of its clearest exponents is Spinoza, who blends a strong commitment to the Classical Conception with a revolutionary philosophical system. Spinoza's metaphysics and his resulting ideal of human liberation do not align precisely with the claims of any of his predecessors; but taken as a whole, his philosophical vision reaffirms the Classical Conception of philosophy and provides a basis for distinguishing philosophy from history.

Spinoza organises his conception of philosophical knowledge around a distinction between imagining and reasoning. Rather than working with the confused ideas we derive from imagination, that is to say, from our everyday experience, philosophical enquirers reason their way to adequate ideas of the essential natures of things. At one level of generality they grasp the natures of particular types of things such as bodies or minds, and at a still higher level they come to understand the nature of an individual thing as such.[22] By reasoning, they come to understand the universal truth that the essence of an individual thing is its power to persevere in its being or go on existing as the individual it is. At the same time, reasoning as Spinoza portrays it alerts philosophers to a contrast between the temporal features of an individual and its unchanging essence. In our day-to-day lives we take it that individuals come into being and endure for a certain length of time; but, once reasoning allows us to 'perceive things under a certain species of eternity',[23] we view them in a different light. Not only are the natures or essences of individual things eternal; it is also an eternal or atemporal truth that the essence of an individual thing is its power to persevere in its being.

We find here the first two features of the Classical Conception of philosophy: by reasoning, philosophers can arrive at an understanding of universal and eternal truths. With these conclusions in hand, Spinoza goes on to embrace the conception's two remaining features. First, rational understanding makes us joyful. As our philosophical knowledge of the essential natures of things extends, we become better able to judge what is good for us and what we can achieve. Guided by these insights, we become less prone to act self-destructively, and take pleasure in our resilience. The more we develop ways of life that enable us to live in the light of our knowledge, the happier we become. Finally, as Spinoza continually stresses, philosophy has a theological dimension. As our understanding advances, its focus shifts from the natures of

---

[22] Spinoza 1985a, IIp40s2.
[23] Spinoza 1985a, EIIp44 Corr.2.

individual things to their ultimate dependence on the single substance that Spinoza calls God or nature.[24] At this level of abstraction we know individual things through their place in the natural order. In the words of the *Ethics*, 'the more we understand singular things, the more we understand God'[25] and experience 'the greatest satisfaction of mind that there can be'.[26] In its highest reaches, then, philosophising enables us to see beyond the temporal features of things to their universal and unchanging natures. In doing so, it increases our understanding of our place in nature and empowers us to live more joyfully. During the earlier stages of this process many of the changes we undergo reflect our existing desires. But the radical transformation of outlook that Spinoza envisages at the end of the *Ethics* is harder to imagine. Focusing on the nature of God alters us in ways that are beyond our current comprehension. A distinctive feature of philosophy is therefore its power to transform almost out of recognition what we know, what we value and what we are.

By situating the separatist assertion that philosophy puts forward general claims as true in the broader context of the Classical Conception, we have perhaps made it easier to see what gives the Separation Thesis its appeal. Part of its attraction derives from its place in an enduring and ambitious account of what philosophy can achieve. However, it is still not clear why philosophy, thus understood, should exclude historical research, and here again the Classical Conception can help us. When authors such as Spinoza delineate this conception, they explain what philosophy is. At the same time, however, they define the boundaries that set it apart from other kinds of enquiry. Philosophy's capacity to make general truths intelligible, to unite us with God and to generate supreme happiness is, as they see it, not shared by other subjects, which are consequently excluded from the philosophical realm. To put it another way, the Classical Conception incorporates a series of Separation Theses, of which the divide between philosophy and history is one.

Perhaps the most persistently contested of the boundaries around philosophy is the one dividing it from poetry – the boundary between the generalising mode of thought that characterises philosophical reflection and the mimetic practices of poetic imagination. Where philosophical truths are the fruit of reasoning, poetry draws on the imagination to create images, metaphors and personifications. The relationship between the two is widely acknowledged to be close; according to Aristotle, for

---

[24] Spinoza 1985a, Vp29s.
[25] Spinoza 1985a, Vp24.
[26] Spinoza 1985a, Vp27.

example, poetry imagines what philosophy then goes on to understand. But whether they can remain distinct is not so clear. Perhaps, as Aristotle seems to suggest, a philosopher who initially depends on poetic devices to imagine the liberating force of philosophical understanding can eventually leave them behind; or perhaps, as Plato's representation of Socrates intimates, the two are so intertwined that philosophy can never free itself from its dependence upon poetry, and is not autonomous after all. On the one hand, Socrates condemns poetry for dragging us downwards, away from the world of Forms. On the other hand, he appeals to myths and narratives to convey the pleasures of philosophical knowledge. The underlying worry, as Stephen Halliwell argues, is that, while poetry can convey the beauty of rational understanding, philosophy cannot capture it by means of discursive reasoning.[27] Only with poetic support can it generate the intense joyfulness that is a hallmark of the Classical Conception.

In an early modern context this challenge to separatism is expressed in Philip Sidney's claim that poetry, rather than philosophy, is the monarch of the sciences.[28] Unless philosophical arguments are 'illuminated or figured forth by the speaking picture of poesy',[29] their truths 'lie dark before the imaginative and judging power' and are incapable of moving us either to reason further or to act on our rational understanding.[30] Without 'the images of virtues, vices and what else, with that delightful teaching that must be the right describing note to know a poet by' there can be no successful philosophising.[31] In short, philosophy as the Classical Conception defines it cannot manage without imagination in the form of poetry.

Plato's Socrates is not alone in entertaining this suspicion. We also find it in Spinoza, who, rather than spelling out the content of philosophical understanding, personifies the transformation it brings about in an image or exemplar of the free man. To illuminate the benefits of philosophising, the *Ethics* describes the outstanding powers that flow from the free man's understanding, and encourages us to imagine what it would be like to possess them.[32] By thinking ahead to what we might become, identifying with the free man's powers, and doing our best to imitate them, we strengthen our sense of what understanding can achieve and motivate ourselves to go on philosophising.

[27] Halliwell 2011, p. 106.
[28] Sidney 1952, p. 124.
[29] Sidney 1952, p. 115.
[30] Sidney 1952, p. 119.
[31] Sidney 1952, p. 116.
[32] Spinoza 1985a, Vp27.

Spinoza does not draw attention to this poetic dimension of philo-sophical practice, or acknowledge it as problematic. Commentators are divided between the view that, like Aristotle, he sees it as a temporary support from which philosophers can eventually break free, and the view that he takes poetry and philosophy to be inextricably intertwined. On either reading, the tension between the imaginative and rational aspects of his analysis of philosophising illustrates the general problem with which we are concerned: the uneasy relationship between philosophy and other forms of enquiry. In the case of poetry, it suggests, separatism may not be an easy position to defend. Despite the allure of the Classical Conception, the aspiration to represent philosophy as an autonomous practice is difficult to sustain.

A comparable challenge besets the boundary between philosophy and history. As we have seen, contemporary separatists claim that studying the history of philosophy is distinct from studying philosophy, and are unimpressed by historians' objections to their view. However, once we situate their position in the context of the Classical Conception, we get a clearer sense of what they are excluding. According to Aristotle, both history and philosophy aim at truth; but whereas history tries to cap-ture truths about particular types of phenomena, philosophical truths are general. The Classical Conception agrees: since philosophical truths are truths of the utmost generality, philosophy is not fundamentally con-cerned with truths about particulars. That is to say, it is not concerned with the very truths that are traditionally identified as historical. History is therefore separate from philosophy.

This contrast continues to echo through early modern debate. We find it, for example, in the *Advancement of Learning*, where Francis Bacon dis-tinguishes several types of history, each concerned with particular things or events. Chronicles, lives and narrations deal with 'a time, or a person, or an action',[33] natural histories are about creatures, marvels or arts, and mechanical histories focus on manual arts and artefacts.[34] Whereas philosophy moves from universal principles to general conclusions, his-torians build up inductively grounded knowledge of their subject matter, based on their experience of particulars.

Spinoza was deeply critical of many aspects of Bacon's philosophy, as he explained in a letter to Henry Oldenburg.[35] But he shared Bacon's view of history. Whether one is trying to write a history of nature or Scripture, his *Theological-Political Treatise* affirms, one must derive one's

[33] Bacon 1996, p. 179.
[34] Bacon 1996, pp. 176–7.
[35] Spinoza 1985b, p. 167.

conclusions from a systematic study of the particular phenomena concerned. Natural historians, for example, infer definitions of natural things
from the data at their disposal, while historians of Scripture ground their
interpretations of the text on a comprehensive study of its particular features including the language in which it is written and the meanings
of individual words.[36] Thus far, Spinoza's conception of the difference
between philosophy and history is consonant with the Classical Conception and the boundary it implies. While philosophical reasoning yields
knowledge of the eternal natures of things, historians infer conclusions of
limited generality from the particular ideas they have acquired through
experience. Furthermore, the fact that historical investigations are rooted
in time and place prevents them from illuminating the unchanging nature
of God, and cuts them off from the supreme joyfulness that comes with
philosophical understanding. History and philosophy are distinct.

As in the case of poetry, however, this official view does not go unquestioned. Even an author such as Spinoza, who is largely sympathetic to
the Classical Conception, allows that philosophy is dependent on history
and concedes that the boundary between them is porous. To be sure, he
envisages a kind of understanding that transcends particulars; but he also
recognises that, in the process of acquiring it, philosophers draw on their
knowledge of individual things. As our experience grows, we gradually
refine our inadequate ideas of the world around us into a richer and more
reliable vision, and generate the concepts on which some of our most
fundamental insights are grounded. By this means, for example, we can
arrive at the ideas of motion and rest that are the basis of physics.[37] In
addition to adopting a synthetic method and working from the universal
to the particular, philosophers also need to take an analytic or historical
approach and work in the other direction. To put the point another way,
history plays a part in the acquisition of philosophical knowledge.

As before, some commentators hold that historical enquiry functions
for Spinoza as a form of scaffolding. It allows philosophers to reach a
certain level of insight, but as they immerse themselves in rational and
intuitive knowledge they cease to depend on it. This is partly because the
balance of their thinking tips away from the historical and they become
increasingly preoccupied with universal ideas.[38] But it is also because, as
philosophers reflect on the general ideas they have derived from experience, they recognise them as universal ideas of the eternal natures of
things. Their historical grasp of these ideas becomes philosophical. This

[36] Spinoza 2016, p. 171.
[37] Spinoza 2016, p. 176.
[38] Spinoza 1985a, EVp20s5.

is a puzzling transition, and Spinoza does not say much about it. On one interpretation, the historical process through which an idea was reached is entirely superseded when its universal nature becomes clear. On another interpretation, however, the history of an idea is carried along with it, so that even our most purely philosophical ideas of the natures of things bear traces of the historical processes by which they were formed. On this account, history penetrates so deeply into philosophical understanding that the autonomy of philosophy is undermined.

Spinoza's analysis of the relationships between philosophy, poetry and history implicitly concedes that philosophy may be more dependent on the other two than the Classical Conception allows. Poetry challenges the presumption that purely philosophical understanding is motivating, and competes with it as a source of joyfulness. History, meanwhile, challenges philosophy's claim to be the unique route to knowledge of the universal natures of things. Increasingly, philosophy emerges as part of a cooperative intellectual undertaking in which all three play a part. Spinoza refuses to risk the supremacy of philosophical enquiry by openly acknowledging that it is inherently historical, and the image of understanding in which the *Ethics* culminates sets particularity aside. Nevertheless, the tension between his two accounts of philosophical knowledge as both unified with and distinct from its historical counterpart suggests that unqualified defences of the Separation Thesis may involve an element of denial. To maintain a firm and impermeable boundary between philosophy and history, one may have to ignore or suppress the extent to which philosophical understanding is concerned with the historical, that is to say with the inductively based study of particular things.

In the preceding section I identified a historical strand of philosophical thinking about philosophy itself. The Classical Conception, I proposed, runs through the philosophical tradition and informs debate about what philosophy is. Contested though it has always been, it defends a vision of philosophy as an autonomous enquiry, firmly separated from history and able to proceed without historical support. It is clear from the examples I have discussed that this outlook remained influential in the early modern era, where it underwrote an ambitious vision of what philosophy could and should aspire to achieve. But the idea that it might continue to define our current understanding of philosophy and cast light on recent or contemporary forms of separatism may seem absurd.[39] According to Hadot, for example, philosophy has long since ceased to be a potentially transformative practice and has become a type of discourse – an enquiry

---

[39] Thomasson 2017.

into truths that, even when they are truths about human life, are meant to inform us rather than alter the way we live.[40] Nowadays, it might seem, the Classical Conception of philosophy has itself been transformed and has become irrelevant.

Hadot's diagnosis arguably fails to do justice to a revival of interest in philosophising as a way of life, for which his own work is partly responsible.[41] All the same, there is no doubt that, particularly within the analytic tradition, the pursuit of philosophical knowledge is on the whole no longer regarded as a way to transform ourselves. With some exceptions, it does not aim to unite us with God or generate unparalleled joyfulness.[42] At certain points in its history, however, analytic philosophy has continued to echo some of the Classical Conception's defining commitments. Writing in 1914, for example, Bertrand Russell argued that philosophical propositions 'must be applicable to everything that exists or may exist' and 'are concerned with properties of things that are true in every possible world, independently of facts that can only be discovered by our senses'.[43] In line with the Classical Conception, one of the defining features of philosophical truths is their universality. In addition, they are independent of the particular facts we derive from experience and thus of historical knowledge. 'Too often', Russell continues, 'we find in philosophical books arguments based on the course of history, or the convolutions of the brain, or the eyes of shellfish. Special and accidental facts of this kind are irrelevant to philosophy, which must make only such assertions as would be equally true, however the actual world were constituted.'[44]

Like other defenders of the Classical Conception, Russell here insists that philosophy is distinct from history. At the same time, he also upholds the boundary between philosophy and poetry. Philosophy, he contends, is indistinguishable from logic. It provides 'an inventory of abstractly tenable hypotheses',[45] a definitive dissection of propositions that would set out clearly all their connections and remove all possibilities of misunderstanding. By abandoning natural language and mapping the world in logical terms, Russell's atomism not only aspired to eradicate the linguistic ambiguity on which poetry thrives, but set out to remove philosophy's dependence on imagination. Rather than relying on images or

---

[40] Hadot 1995, pp. 20–1.
[41] Nehamas 1998; Sellars 2013; Tanesini 2017.
[42] Jantzen 1998.
[43] Russell 1963 [1914], p. 84.
[44] Russell 1963 [1914], p. 84.
[45] Russell 1963 [1914], p. 85.

exemplars, it presented itself as utterly transparent to reason. Perhaps surprisingly, then, some of the most formative analytic interpretations of philosophy have been shaped by the Classical Conception; and as we saw at the beginning of the chapter, this legacy has not entirely disappeared. Whether or not its exponents are fully aware of it, contemporary defences of the Separation Thesis are indebted to the Classical Conception and reiterate some of its defining commitments.

When philosophers such as Plato or Spinoza portray the joyful and empowering understanding to which philosophising gives rise, they are surely seeking, among other things, to assuage a desire. By dividing philosophy from history they release themselves from a messy domain of particular facts into an orderly realm of general truths. Putting aside the frustrations that arise from the incompleteness of experience and the endless proliferation of counter-examples, they cultivate a reassuringly secure form of knowledge that grows step by step. Breaking free of the finite human imagination, they encounter the world and themselves as they fundamentally are. Even if one does not share these aspirations, it is hard to be entirely deaf to their appeal. They answer to an intelligible longing to achieve what Thomas Nagel calls the view from nowhere, and grasp the whole of Being in its unchanging entirety.[46] They hold out the prospect of a superhuman power to live in the light of truth and free oneself from sadness.[47]

Contemporary separatists would almost certainly dismiss this image as a fantasy. Like the great majority of philosophers nowadays, they would view it as an imaginative projection of real but unrealisable desires. It is arguable, however, that traces of these desires explain their continuing commitments. The determination to elevate philosophical truth to a level of 'stupendous generality' manifests an anxiety about our human finitude that is integral to the Classical Conception and brings with it the wish for a philosophy divided from the particular. To concede that philosophical investigation is part of history in the sense that its conclusions reflect the cultural limitations of time and place and fall short of complete universality would be to give up the hope of this transcendental form of knowledge and settle for a more mundane conception of philosophical practice. Unwilling as they may be to avow a desire for transcendence – indeed, much as they may reject it – separatist philosophers continue to yearn for it. Endowing philosophy with autonomy and an outstanding form of power remains important to them and is reflected in the way they characterise their own activity.

---

[46] Nagel 1986.
[47] Lloyd 1984; Lloyd 1993.

I began by proposing that, despite a widespread pluralism, the place of history of philosophy within philosophical enquiry remains uneasy. As the debate between separatists and their opponents shows, the history of philosophy is and is not regarded as fully philosophical. One reason for this, I have suggested, is the continuing influence of the Classical Conception of philosophy, together with the desires it expresses. To render philosophy and history entirely harmonious, we need to recognise the view of philosophy that the Classical Conception defends for the fantasy that it is. We cannot transcend the historical traditions that have given us our contested conceptions of philosophy, and our philosophising must take them into account.

References

Antognazza, Maria Rosa. 2015. 'The Benefit to Philosophy of the Study of History', *British Journal for the History of Philosophy*, 23: 1, pp. 161–84.

Bacon, Francis. 1996. 'The Advancement of Learning' in *Francis Bacon*, ed. Brian Vickers. Oxford.

Cottingham, John. 2005. 'Why Should Analytic Philosophers do History of Philosophy?' in *Analytic Philosophy and History of Philosophy*, ed. T. Sorell and G. A. J. Rogers. Oxford.

Curley, Edwin. 1986. 'Dialogues with the Dead', *Synthese*, 67: 1, pp. 33–49.

Della Rocca, Michael. 2013. 'The Taming of Philosophy' in *Philosophy and its History*, ed. Mogens Laerke, Justin E. H. Smith and Eric Schliesser. Oxford.

Foucault, Michel. 1997. 'The Ethics of the Concern of the Self as a Practice of Freedom' in *Ethics: Subjectivity and Truth*, ed. Paul Rabinow. New York.

Garber, Daniel. 2005. 'What's Philosophical about the History of Philosophy?' in *Analytic Philosophy and History of Philosophy*, ed. T. Sorell and G. A. J. Rogers. Oxford.

Garrett, Aaron. 2013. 'Seventeenth-Century Moral Philosophy: Self-Help, Self-Knowledge and the Devil's Mountain' in *The Oxford Handbook of the History of Ethics*, ed. Roger Crisp. Oxford.

Hadot, Pierre. 1995. *Philosophy as a Way of Life*, ed. Arnold Davidson, trans. Michael Chase. Oxford.

Halliwell, Stephen. 2011. *Between Ecstasy and Truth*. Oxford.

Hatfield, Gary. 2005. 'The History of Philosophy as Philosophy' in *Analytic Philosophy and History of Philosophy*, ed. T. Sorell and G. A. J. Rogers. Oxford.

Huemer, Michael. 2020. 'Against History', http://fakenous.net/?p=1168.

Jantzen, Grace M. 1998. *Becoming Divine. Towards a Feminist Philosophy of Religion*. Manchester.

Kuhn, Thomas. 1962. *The Structure of Scientific Revolutions*. Chicago.

Laerke, Mogens. 2013. 'The Anthropological Analogy and the Constitution of Historical Perspectivism' in *Philosophy and its History: Aims and Methods in the Study of Early Modern Philosophy*, ed. Mogens Laerke, Justin E. H. Smith and Eric Schliesser. Oxford.

Lloyd, Genevieve. 1984. *The Man of Reason: 'Male' and 'Female' in Western Philosophy*. London.
    1993. 'Maleness, Metaphor and the "Crisis of Reason"' in *A Mind of One's Own. Feminist Essays on Reason and Objectivity*, ed. Louise M. Anthony and Charlotte Witt. Boulder.
Mercer, Christia. 2019. 'The Contextualist Revolution in Early Modern Philosophy', *Journal of the History of Philosophy*, 57: 3, pp. 529–48.
Nagel, Thomas. 1986. *The View from Nowhere*. Princeton.
Nehamas, Alexander. 1998. *The Art of Living: Socratic Reflections from Plato to Foucault*. Berkeley.
Nietzsche, Friedrich. 1994. *On the Genealogy of Morality*, ed. Keith Ansell-Pearson, trans. Carol Diethe. Cambridge.
Plato. 1965. *Timaeus and Critias*, ed. Desmond Lee. Harmondsworth.
Rorty, Richard. 1979. *Philosophy and the Mirror of Nature*. Princeton.
    1984. 'The Historiography of Philosophy: Four Genres' in *Philosophy in History*, ed. R. Rorty, J. B. Schneewind and Q. Skinner. Cambridge.
Russell, Bertrand. 1963 [1914]. 'On Scientific Method in Philosophy' (Herbert Spencer Lecture, Oxford 1914) in *Mysticism and Logic*. London.
Scriven, Michael. 1977. 'Increasing Philosophy Enrollments and Appointments through Better Philosophy Teaching', *Proceedings and Addresses of the American Philosophical Association*, 50, pp. 232–44.
Sedley, David. 1999. 'The Ideal of Godlikeness' in *Plato 2: Ethics, Politics, Religion and the Soul*, ed. Gail Fine. Oxford.
Sellars, John. 2013. *The Art of Living: The Stoics on the Nature and Function of Philosophy*. London.
Sidney, Philip. 1952. 'An Apology for Poetry' in *Criticism: The Major Texts*, ed. Jackson Bate. New York.
Spinoza, Benedict. 1985a. *Ethics* in *The Collected Works of Spinoza*, ed. Edwin Curley, vol. I. Princeton.
    1985b. *Correspondence 1661–3* in *The Collected Works of Spinoza*, ed. Edwin Curley, vol. I. Princeton.
    2016. *Theological-Political Treatise* in *The Collected Works of Spinoza*, ed. Edwin Curley, vol. II. Princeton.
Tanesini, Alessandra. 2017. 'Doing Philosophy' in *The Cambridge Companion to Philosophical Methodology*, ed. Giuseppina d'Oro and Søren Overgaard. Cambridge.
Thomasson, Amie L. 2017. 'What Can we Do When we Do Metaphysics?' in *The Cambridge Companion to Philosophical Methodology*, ed. Giuseppina d'Oro and Søren Overgaard. Cambridge.
Vermeir, Koen. 2013. 'Philosophy and Genealogy: Ways of Writing History of Philosophy' in *Philosophy and its History: Aims and Methods in the Study of Early Modern Philosophy*, ed. Mogens Laerke, Justin E. H. Smith and Eric Schliesser. Oxford.
Williamson, Timothy. 2018. *Doing Philosophy*. Oxford.
Wilson, Catherine. 2005. 'Is the History of Philosophy Good for Philosophy?' in *Analytic Philosophy and History of Philosophy*, ed. T. Sorell and G. A. J. Rogers. Oxford.
Yolton, John. 1986. 'Is There a History of Philosophy? Some Difficulties and Suggestions', *Synthese*, 67: 1, pp. 3–21.

10 When Reason Does Not See You: Feminism at the Intersection of History and Philosophy

Hannah Dawson

In *What Does it all Mean?* Thomas Nagel declares that he is providing an account of some core 'philosophical problems, each of which can be understood in itself, without reference to the history of thought'. This declaration makes explicit a characteristically dismissive attitude towards history from within philosophy – or at least from within the analytic approach to philosophy that dominates anglophone universities. With a brush of the hand, the philosopher sweeps aside the past, and applies the steady eye of reason to perennial questions. 'The center of philosophy', Nagel goes on, 'lies in certain questions which the reflective human mind finds naturally puzzling, and the best way to begin the study of philosophy is to think about them directly.'[1] In this vision of the discipline, the enquirer together with the object of enquiry are universalised. They are abstracted from time and place, and operate in a 'natural' intellectual zone, beyond culture. It is as if all the specifics of life fall away and, as the years rush by, thinkers are fixed on the same, given, ideas. Flanked on one side by the impersonal, impartial machinery of logical argument and on the other by the pristine insights of natural intuition, the philosopher analyses concepts – such as knowledge, justice and freedom – and comes to see them clearly, even objectively, for what they are.

History, by contrast, is definitionally interested in change, and difference, through time and geography. It is, especially since the cultural turn that still pervades the discipline, interested in the excavation of meaning rather than truth.[2] It envisages concepts as constructs of culture and power, as contingent and shifting ways of seeing – and making – the

I thank the anonymous peer reviewers from Cambridge University Press for their helpful comments on this chapter, and Mary Starkey for her exemplary copy-editing. I am indebted to Richard Bourke and Quentin Skinner for their invaluable editorial feedback, and for the series of workshops that brought all of us in this volume together in person, and that carved out time to develop our ideas in conversation – in lecture halls, in candlelight and stretched out in the sunshine beside the mill pond.
[1] Nagel 1987, p. 4.
[2] See, e.g., Hunt 1989, pp. 1–22; Clark 1997, pp. 3–10.

world. It thinks of words and ideas as constituent parts of specific modes of social organisation – as weapons, consolations, markers of identity, as well as semantic vessels of leaky content. In the historian's vision, human minds – or rather, human beings – are not interchangeable, natural or isolable, but diverse, embodied creatures of society, and thickly situated in political structures that privilege some and disadvantage others, so that, for example, there is no straightforward or uniform answer to the question 'do human beings have free will?' This question has little purchase on the historian's object of enquiry, which is susceptible to neither general nor static understanding. The historian is sensitive to the perspectival and plural nature of reason; indeed, to the thundering of unreason, to the ways in which motivations and events are often obscure to the actors involved, to the malleability of perception and memory, and to the constructions of hindsight.

These are caricatures, of course. There are branches of history and philosophy that grow in entirely different directions to the two outlined above. Within each discipline there are deep, reflexive critiques of their own methodologies, and many practitioners would baulk at the dichotomy I have sketched above.[3] After all, one of the founding stories of the discipline of history is that it should show us *wie es eigentlich gewesen* (and Ranke's ambition here was arguably philosophical), and most historians take themselves to be saying something that is, at least, persuasive about the past and grounded in evidence, even as they might acknowledge that there are multiple truths and perspectives to be uncovered, and cringe at the idea of objectivity.[4] Few historians are in the profession because they think they are simply making things up.

Equally, many philosophers, most obviously those working in the continental tradition, embed history at the heart of their practice – and indeed, continental philosophy was and continues to be deeply influential for the cultural turn in history, such as through the work of Michel Foucault. Philosophy has taken many historical turns. Ludwig Wittgenstein arguably took one in his own lifetime, and, pertinently in relation to this chapter, philosophers in the long eighteenth century such as

---

[3] For a classic historicist critique of philosophy from within philosophy see, e.g., Rorty 1979; cf. Rorty 1967. For two powerful recent examples of works that bring political philosophy into dialogue with history see Moyn 2010 and Forrester 2019.

[4] Evans 1997 gives a particularly robust defence of history, e.g. 'Through the sources we use, and the methods with which we handle them, we can, if we are very careful and thorough, approach a reconstruction of past reality that may be partial and provisional, and certainly will not be objective, but is nevertheless true ... the stories we tell will be true stories, even if the truth they tell is our own, and even if other people can and will tell them differently' (pp. 249–50). See also Novick 1988.

Giambattista Vico and Jean-Jacques Rousseau began to theorise human nature as intrinsically historical. As I write, anglophone philosophy is opening itself up ever wider to interdisciplinary approaches, many of which include historicist elements, and looking to – and from – for example, law, critical race theory, standpoint theory and genealogy.[5] This chapter I hope fits into these commitments to disciplinary dialogue and relaxation, to an unbolting of the gates.

There are, in short, schools and individuals – historicist philosophers and philosophical historians – many of whom are in this volume, who move seamlessly between the two arenas, for whom, perhaps, there is properly speaking only one arena. I wager, however, that anyone who has spent any time in departments of Philosophy and History in British and North American universities will still recognise my caricatures. Certainly, having taught in both departments, I can testify to the distinctive feel of each. I once taught a course on the philosophy of law with a moral philosopher who, when I proposed putting Aquinas and Hobbes on the syllabus, asked why we would bother with people who had got it wrong. In his view, philosophy proceeded by sloughing off the mistakes and carrying forward the bits people had got right.

This chapter is about one historicist critique of philosophy from within philosophy: that of feminism. I argue that feminist thought is often, perhaps inherently, a historicist practice that uses both history and historicist methodology to expose not only what it regards as the delusions of philosophy but also the sexism of these delusions.[6] In connecting sexism to an archetypal philosophical outlook, it suggests that the two reside within, and reinforce, each other. But feminism itself is not immune from the lure of philosophy – from the sensations of perspicuity and truth, especially when those sensations are charged with the conviction of speaking truth to power. Feminist thinkers have exercised their philosophical reflexes not just against patriarchy, but against each other, resulting in further historicist pushback and philosophical reassertion. Feminist thought therefore operates as, and exemplifies, a tight hinge between history and philosophy, bringing the force of each to bear on the other.

---

[5] For examples of discipline-transforming work see Crenshaw, Gotanda, Peller and Kendall 1996; Levy 2014; Stanley 2015; O'Connor, Bright and Zucker 2019; Srinivasan 2019; and Táíwò 2020.

[6] Feminist philosophy is a diverse field, and while I am focusing on its historicist dimensions, it shoots out in many different disciplinary directions, e.g. Young 2011 brings it into direct dialogue with post-modernism; Haslanger 2012 brings it together with critical race theory and ameliorative analysis; Manne 2019 draws on literature and anecdote alongside conceptual analysis.

I will begin by illustrating the ahistoricism of philosophy, and then turn to feminism's breaking – or strengthening – of the spell.

Very Common Ideas that All of us Use

Nagel's best-selling introduction to philosophy, with which I began, is worth returning to. First published in 1987, and still routinely set for first-year undergraduates, it crisply delineates the disciplinary standpoint and, relatedly, the rejection of history – where 'history' encompasses both (and overlappingly) the history of philosophy and the human past. While the problems of philosophy have, on Nagel's account, 'been written about for thousands of years', the 'raw material comes directly from the world and our relation to it, not from writings of the past. That is why they come up again and again, in the heads of people who haven't read about them.' It is not just the history of philosophy that is shelved here, but the notion that either philosophers or their objects – 'the heads of people' and 'raw material', the mechanism and the matter of philosophy – might be part of a fractured history. The ideas that it is the 'main concern of philosophy' to understand are the 'very common ideas that all of us use every day without thinking about them'. Note the blithe erasure of any specificity of thinker or thought, the easy subsumption of particular individuals under 'all of us'. Nagel's philosopher is expressly interested in transcending the empirical. 'Unlike science', Nagel says, philosophy 'doesn't rely on experiments or observation, but only on thought'. Whereas 'a historian may ask what happened at some time in the past … a philosopher will ask, "What is time?"'[7]

High up in this rarefied air, 'the reflective human mind' seems to have no gender, race or class. It flies over the centuries. It pushes 'our understanding of the world and ourselves a bit deeper'. The teeming specificities and ruptures of experience evaporate; the 'world' appears as the same for all, and the philosopher's 'I' emerges as a sleight of hand, since 'we' are apparently all the same.

In his suggestively titled *The View from Nowhere* (1986), Nagel himself addresses the gap between the first person perspective and 'an objective view'. While his intention here is, in part, to insist on the irreducibility of subjectivity, he is also interested in demonstrating where 'the perspective of a particular person inside the world' might be 'combined', indeed 'unified', 'with an objective view of that same world'. In a way that he

---

[7] Nagel 1987, pp. 4–5. Again, I want to note that many philosophers *are* interested in doing interdisciplinary work: see, e.g., Smith 2013 on the productive collaboration between philosophy and science.

hopes the reader will find 'natural', he sets out to defend 'the pursuit of objectivity' and 'the pursuit of truth', and to explain how a human creature can 'transcend its particular point of view and ... conceive of the world as a whole'.[8] Moreover, when Nagel does write explicitly from an individual's point of view, it is a light-footed, asocial and unencumbered positionality. For example, embarking on the general question of whether people have free will or not, Nagel wonders whether you could have chosen the peach rather than the cake.[9]

These tropes – the buoyant, unsituated, first person that slides unreflectively into 'we'; the putative naturalness of what makes sense, of what seems right; the commonality and panoramic scope of the philosopher's viewpoint; the imperial roaming over the concepts to be understood; the givenness of those concepts; the totalising clarity of reason; the mind as a window onto the world, onto ideas, onto truth – all these punctuate the discipline of philosophy. One can spot them in *The Problems of Philosophy* laid out by Bertrand Russell, father of the analytic tradition, in 1912, and his claim that 'philosophy is merely the attempt to answer ... ultimate questions'; there they variously are in G. E. Moore's 'intuitions' and 'common sense', in Edward Craig's three 'basic philosophical questions, namely: what should we do? ... what is there? ... how do we know?', in the 'clarity, precision, and rigour' that Michael Beaney says are the hallmark virtues of analytic philosophy, in the 'fundamental issues' that, according to Jonathan Cohen, 'analytic philosophy' aims to resolve, and in the 'intuitions' that are 'the data' of 'categorical philosophical reasoning'.[10]

Cohen's account of intuition in *The Dialogue of Reason: An Analysis of Analytical Philosophy* (1986) shows how analytic philosophy dreams that it can short-circuit history and throw a direct light on the untarnished glass of the universalised human mind. Intuitions are presented as capable of providing 'the ultimate premises of philosophical argument' because they are not 'conclusions of further reasoning', and therefore not interfered with by possibly prejudicious thoughts. Saved from error by being 'immediate and unreflective', having 'an independent standing and authority', they furnish philosophers with 'prima-facie data' with which to make their way over the rock-solid stepping stones of reason.[11]

---

[8] Nagel 1986, pp. 3, 7, 9.
[9] Nagel 1987, p. 47.
[10] Russell 1998, p. 1; Moore 1922, p. x; Moore 1925; Craig 2002, p. 1; Beaney 2017, p. 1; Cohen 1986, pp. 1, 73.
[11] Cohen 1986, pp. 76–7.

Beaney, writing in 2017 in his *Analytic Philosophy: A Very Short Introduction*, is self-conscious about the rejection of history, and the assumption of the timelessness of philosophical problems. Beaney says that one good reason to avoid history is that it is hard for generation upon generation of philosophers to make 'conceptual innovations' if they are 'overawed by tradition'.[12] This is an endearing explanation of why analytic philosophers ignore history, but I am not sure that it is because they feel 'overawed'. As Robert Nozick writes in *The Nature of Rationality* (1993), 'what philosophers really love is reasoning'. 'Rationality', he elaborates, 'provides us with the (potential) power to investigate and discover anything and everything.' It is the profession's 'tool for discovering truth, a potentially unlimited one'. In response to the objection that rationality might be '*biased* because it is a class-based or male or Western or whatever notion', Nozick briskly retorts that it is the job of reason to 'notice' and 'correct' biases, and anyway, 'charging a bias in existing standards does not show that one exists'.[13] Reason, it seems – that pure, impersonal capacity of mankind – knows best. It is the supreme court, and the philosopher is judge in his own cause.

A Gigantic Oversight

I now turn to the ways in which feminist thinking uses history to undermine the philosophical house from inside – not only through its explicit attention to the past but also through its broader historicist sensibilities. Feminism is not one thing, but core to many of its articulations is the view that gender relations are – in many if not all ways – not given in nature but rather made and remade through time.[14] As Beauvoir wrote in 1949, 'One is not born, but rather becomes, woman.'[15] In revealing that there is little, if anything at all, that is fixed or essential about being a woman or a man – or indeed a human being, that our most basic concepts are carved out at least in part by culture, and into our subjectivities – feminism destabilises the philosopher's easy invocation of a bedrock of concepts and his neutral distance from those concepts. There is no mental

---

[12] Beaney 2017, pp. 110–12.
[13] Nozick 1993, pp. xi–xii.
[14] For an account of the vast history of overlapping and conflicting feminisms see Dawson 2021, pp. xix–l. On 'the seeming ahistoricity of patriarchy', and the challenge for historians of thinking through a phenomenon that is 'everywhere, but ... not everywhere the same', see Bennett 2006, pp. 54–81.
[15] Beauvoir 2011, p. 293. On the importance of history for feminism as a way to 'break open the daily naturalism of what surrounds us' see Riley 1988, p. 5. On xenofeminism, a recent articulation of feminism as 'an anti-naturalist endeavour', see Hester 2018, p. 19. Cf. Cuboniks 2018.

space that does not bear the imprint of our manufactured intellectual architecture, that is not angled or embodied within structures of power. There is no perspective that is transparent either to itself or to 'reality'. The dissolution of the gendered bifurcation of the world exposes our concepts as historical acts of smoke and mirrors, as functions often of brute force and ignorance. It reveals the universalised first person as a land grab, unearthing instead diverse and clashing viewpoints, some of which come from places of greater strength than others. Feminists are sensitive to the partialities, privileges and prejudices of what passes for truth and objectivity, to the blind spot that occludes half of humankind.

When Emmeline Pankhurst went to Hartford, Connecticut in 1913 to deliver her 'Freedom or Death' speech, she stressed the baffling nature of her task: to bring into view what seemed to her to be obvious. If she were a man, she said, a male taxpayer, standing in front of her audience, deprived by his government of his representative rights, it would be self-evident to them that he were entitled to take up arms against that government. After all, Americans had done it. 'We women,' she said, 'in trying to make our case clear, always have to make as part of our argument, and urge upon men in our audience the fact – a very simple fact – that women are human beings. It is quite evident you do not all realise we are human beings or it would not be necessary to argue with you that women may, suffering from intolerable injustice, be driven to adopt revolutionary methods.'[16] In 1999 Catharine A. MacKinnon was still asking 'When will women be human? When?'[17]

Feminism remains in large part the project of making the invisible visible, of pointing out the perceptual sediments that have built up over the years in the fabrication of social reality.[18] It lays bare the erasures and exclusions – the temporal constructedness – of reason. It is about what happens, and what it feels like, when reason does not see you.

The most blatant way in which philosophical reason does not see women is through its default-male setting. In his preface to *The Dialogue of Reason*, having thanked Pat Lloyd, who 'typed and retyped and re-retyped' his manuscript, for 'all her work', Cohen proceeds to spell out that 'unless there are contextual reasons to suppose otherwise, the pronoun 'he' is to be understood in the text as meaning 'he or she', the pronoun 'him' as meaning 'him or her' and the pronoun 'his' as meaning 'his or hers'.[19] While the stipulation that 'man' should stand for men and

---

[16] Pankhurst 2019, p. 6.
[17] MacKinnon 2007, p. 43.
[18] E.g., Threadcraft 2016 makes visible the occlusions of American 'justice' and 'equality'.
[19] Cohen 1986, preface.

women is not confined to philosophers, and is a dying habit across the board, it was a striking stipulation for people professionally interested in language and truth, since 'he' does not mean 'he or she'. There is no gender neutrality in male pronouns.

The occlusion of women in philosophy is adumbrated in Craig's 2002 *Very Short Introduction* to the discipline. Characterising philosophy as humanity's ongoing attempt to recover from the shock of complex consciousness, he asks, 'Can reeling *homo sapiens* think his way back to the vertical?'[20] If we turn to the book's index we find an entry on 'women' slotted in between Wittgenstein, Ludwig and Woolston, Thomas, and when we turn to that section in the text we find women elucidated through John Stuart Mill. 'Since it would be strange to draw attention only to something written by a man', says Craig, he goes on to cite Beauvoir. She, says Craig, writes a sentence that 'could almost have been written by Mill', and ends up with a similar position to him, which 'almost makes you think they might be right'. After dealing with 'Women', the book moves on to consider 'Animals'.[21]

In David Miller's *Political Philosophy: A Very Short Introduction* (2003) he wonders why gender relations were historically 'routinely ignored in treatises of political thought'. 'It is tempting', he says, 'to see this either as some kind of gigantic oversight, or else to argue that dominant groups in society kept such issues off the agenda.' He concludes that while the men writing political philosophy 'took it for granted that the subordination of women to men was a natural fact', the reason they took it for granted was that 'nobody was arguing the opposite case'. The ongoing problem, according to Miller, is that while 'we live in societies that are founded on commitments to freedom and equality', these societies 'have failed so far to live up to these commitments in the case of women and people from minority cultures'.[22] There is a lot going on here: the sharp distinction between theory and practice, as though normative commitments are not themselves entrenched in practice, as though theories of freedom and equality that tacitly or expressly exclude women, or enslaved people, or poor people, are getting it 'right'; the gliding over what it means, philosophically, to take the subordination of women 'for granted' – what the analysis is of the kind of collective spell that captivates philosophers into thinking this a 'natural fact'; the claim that the perception of women's inferiority is explained by the absence of opposition to this view, not least when there were men and women arguing for equality; the summary

---

[20] Craig 2002, p. 8.
[21] Craig 2002, pp. 132, 111–14.
[22] Miller 2003, p. 93.

dismissal of the thought that 'dominant groups' might have been trying to stifle the issue.[23] A historicist–feminist critique of philosophy drills into the 'facts' that are naturalised, the taken-for-granted beliefs and the 'reasons' that make them intelligible. It is interested in how what now seems unreasonable to us could have correlated with Enlightenment reason. It is wary of an easy separation between sense and nonsense, between ideas and ideology, conceiving instead of regimes of truth. It is alert to what reason does not notice, or suppresses.

They Say it is Love

The calling out of the universalised/male philosophical gaze, and its concomitant vision of an extra-historical human subject, is integral to various traditions of feminist philosophy. Marxist feminists, for example, pointed out the ways in which women were invisible to Marxism. Women are workers too, both paid and, even less visibly, unpaid – an insight that grounded the Wages for Housework campaign in the 1970s. As Selma James explained in *The Power of Women and the Subversion of the Community* in 1972, women's isolation behind closed doors hid the fact and value of their work, and 'the fact that it brought no wage had hidden that it was work'.[24] Looking all the way down the rabbit hole, James articulated the most fundamental work that women do: the production of labour power itself. 'So-called Marxists', she wrote, 'could not see that women in the home produced' – and that the commodity they produced was nothing other than 'the living human being – "the laborer himself"'. 'First', James explains,

[the labourer] must be nine months in the womb, must be fed, clothed, and trained; then when it works its bed must be made, its floor swept, its lunchbox prepared, its sexuality not gratified but quietened, its dinner ready when it gets home, even if this is eight in the morning from the night shift. This is how labor power is produced and reproduced when it is daily consumed in the factory or the office. *To describe its basic production and reproduction is to describe women's work.*[25]

---

[23] As this chapter will show, there were many philosophers 'arguing the opposite case', but the following are two early seventeenth century examples: *À la Reyne, l'égalité des hommes et des femmes* by Marie le Jars de Gournay in 1622; and *Dissertatio de Ingenii muliebris ad Doctrinam, & meliores Litteras aptitudine* by Anna Maria van Schurman in 1641. See also Weil 1999 on the centrality of debates about gender in political debates in England in 1680–1714; cf. Hughes 2012; Becker 2020.

[24] James 2012, p. 45. See also Silvia Federici's pioneering analysis, such as in *Wages against Housework* (1975): 'They say it is love. We say it is unwaged work' (Federici 2021, p. 15).

[25] James 2012, p. 51.

While Marx had made wage-slavery visible as a site of partial robbery, where the capitalist creams off surplus value, James revealed the home as a site of total theft: a machine line where the worker has her labour valued at nought.

Feminist philosophers have also shone lights into the hollows of liberalism. In *Justice, Gender, and the Family* (1989) humanist Susan Moller Okin expressed her incredulity at the political philosophy that had flourished since 'the late 60s', placing social justice at its heart, but ignoring the 'justice crisis' in gender, in particular, in the heteropatriarchal family – a hidden harbour for inequality.[26] Marriage harms women, she argued, not only in obvious ways, such as through the unequal division of unpaid labour, but also in so far as this division is assumed, and thereby reinforced, as a matter of 'natural necessity' – when in reality it persists due to 'the historically, socially constructed differentiation between the sexes that feminists have come to call *gender*'.[27] The failure to see gender injustice by philosophers of justice is 'remarkable', says Okin. It seems 'inexplicable', in philosophical terms at least, but it starts to make sense if one thinks in a more historicist way; if one thinks, that is, about 'reason' not, or not just, in terms of crystalline propositions but also as buried inheritances of collective discourse. Philosophical blind spots become intelligible, inevitable even, if one reconceives of intuitions as concoctions of custom rather than emanations of primordial truth.[28] When you probe the grand theories of justice that promise justice and liberty for all, you find, says Okin, that they, 'like those of the past, are about men with wives at home'.[29] Some philosophers, she says, such as Bruce Ackerman, Ronald Dworkin and William Galston, do not discuss the family at all. John Rawls does at least address it, but proceeds with his own 'unexplained assumption that family institutions are just'.[30] Okin wants a theory of justice that exhumes the historical premises.

Writing more resolutely within liberalism, Martha Nussbaum queries its blank treatment of sovereign human subjects, whose choices are 'simply given'.[31] In *Sex and Social Justice* (1999) she points to the ways in which history forms particular subjectivities not only over generations

---

[26] Okin 1989, p. 7. See also Matsuda 1986 for a feminist critique of Rawls's assumptions about human nature.
[27] Okin 1989, p. 5.
[28] Okin 1989, p. 8.
[29] Okin 1989, p. 12.
[30] Okin 1989, pp. 21–2. For a fascinating series of papers that bring history to bear on Rawls himself see Smith, Bejan and Zimmermann 2021.
[31] Nussbaum 1999, p. 11. Cf. Chambers 2008 on the self-harming choices women make, and liberalism's problematic focus on autonomy.

but also in the course of lifetimes. Men may be aggressive, and women may be fearful, 'because they have been formed to be that way'.[32] Nussbaum cites Mill on the fantasy of the 'natural', and the sapling that is half bathed in vapour and half caked in snow, so that one half thrives and the other shrivels. By the same token, 'the nature of male and female sexuality has been shaped by long habits of domination and subordination'.[33] Even those aspects of ourselves that seem most raw and untutored have their own genealogies. Even our desires are contingent. Liberalism falters when it seeks simply to promote freedom of choice, because our personal choices – what we dare to want – are themselves a function of socio-historic advantage and disadvantage. People from particular groups may 'fail to form desires for things their circumstances have placed out of reach'.[34] Human agency has structural dimensions that philosophical arguments about liberty often miss.

Challenging airy Enlightenment invocations of the human subject from another direction, drawing explicitly on communitarianism and postmodernism, Seyla Benhabib takes aim at all 'givens'.[35] In *Situating the Self* (1992) she seeks to dispel 'the illusions of a self-transparent and self-grounding reason, the illusion of a disembedded and disembodied subject, and the fantasy of having found an Archimedean standpoint, situated beyond historical and cultural contingency'.[36] Benhabib, Nussbaum and Okin are just three examples from the rich assembly of recent feminist philosophers who have brought a broadly historicist critique to bear on their discipline. Of course, it is not only feminism, nor indeed only history, that has developed ideas of construction and denaturalisation, and indeed feminists and historians are part of and indebted to the broader critical practice of the humanities, notably sociology and anthropology. It is nonetheless striking that long before twentieth-century eruptions, feminist philosophers were chipping away at the 'Systems of universal nature' of 'wise men'.[37]

Who Made Man the Exclusive Judge?

Spooling back through the years, we find early modern feminists brandishing history, and a historicist sensibility, against the beam of

---

[32] Nussbaum 1999, p. 12.
[33] Nussbaum 1999, p. 13.
[34] Nussbaum 1999, p. 11.
[35] Benhabib 1992, p. 5.
[36] Benhabib 1992, p. 4.
[37] Astell 1996, p. 61.

philosophical reason and the categorical truths it wielded.[38] In his *Discours physique et moral de l'égalité des deux sexes, où l'on voit l'importance de se défaire des préjugez* (1673) François Poulain de la Barre unpicks the intergenerational construction of 'reason' that defends the subjection of women. Philosophers, he says, merely recycle 'common opinion'. They swallow prejudices when they are children, before reaching 'the age of reason', and then take these prejudices as veracious, because they feel profound and immemorial, and 'criminal' to question. The inequality of men and women seems to bubble up from a natural well of truth. And since 'common folk' assume that philosophers have done the hard thinking and know best, they bow to authority, and the prejudices are recycled. Moreover, when they do exercise their minds, says Poulain, philosophers do not study 'the real nature of things', but rather 'trifles and entities that are constructed by reason'.[39] If they thought even a little about the actual bodies of men and women, they would conclude that 'the mind has no sex'.[40] Instead, they pile inherited assumption upon inherited assumption, and busy themselves with insubstantial enquiries into 'imaginary spaces' and the divisibility of dust motes.[41] Reason spins abstractions, and cannot, will not, slip the loop of prejudice.

This critique of reason as a cover for the historical accumulations of bigotry, together with the accusation of attending to *verba* not *res*, were staples of anti-scholastic new philosophy, and early modern feminists drew on the standard modes of refutation. They built on attacks not only on the cynicism of bad-faith sophistry, but also on the more or less innocent reproduction of unreason through our personal and collective chronicles. Mary Wollstonecraft, for example, points to both the malicious mobilisation of the non-negotiable authority of reason and the unconsciousness of biases that are handed down time out of mind. This is a killer combination that is used to deprive women of their natural rights. 'Men, in general', she declares in *A Vindication of the Rights of Woman* (1792), 'seem to employ their reason to justify prejudices, which they have imbibed, they can scarcely trace how, rather than to root them out.'[42] No one is immune to the intellectual sickness of our foremothers and fathers. 'Deeply rooted prejudices', explains Wollstonecraft, 'have

---

[38] There is a rich and still burgeoning literature on early modern feminism: see, e.g., Offen 2000; Knott and Taylor 2005; O'Brien 2009; Broad and Green 2009; Green 2014; Broad and Detlefsen 2017. On Astell specifically see Broad 2015; Bejan 2019. On Wollstonecraft see Taylor 2003; Halldenius 2015; Tomaselli 2021.

[39] Poulain de la Barre 2013, pp. 153–4.

[40] Poulain de la Barre 2013, p. 157.

[41] Poulain de la Barre 2013, p. 154.

[42] Wollstonecraft 1995, p. 79.

clouded reason.'[43] 'Many ingenious arguments' justify 'the tyranny of men'.[44] Even Rousseau's eye could not pierce 'through the foggy atmosphere' as he remained fixed on male superiority, and imagined women 'like a fanciful kind of *half* being'.[45] 'The page of genius', mourns Wollstonecraft, has 'always been blurred by the prejudices of the age.'[46]

Early modern feminists enrich a wider contemporary anxiety about scarcely traceable dogma by slotting it into a broader analysis of structural oppression. They connect punitive 'rational' norms to the laws and practices that subjugate women in a system that draws sustenance from history. They are sensitive to the ways in which power operates through prejudice that passes for reason – as both a function and a mechanism of historical domination. Regimes of truth, on the early modern account, operate not only over women but in them, and between them, too. As they grow up, girls internalise the maxims that they are weak and passive, and valuable only as sexual and docile objects. If you are told that your value lies in your appearance then not only will you believe it, but you will pour yourself into this telos. 'Taught from their infancy that beauty is woman's sceptre,' writes Wollstonecraft, 'the mind shapes itself to the body, and, roaming around its gilt cage, only seeks to adorn its prison.'[47] Women, like men, 'see things through a false medium'.[48] One might even say that they think with a false consciousness.

In addition to inducing women to constrain themselves, the dictates of reason constrain women directly. They keep her in a subordinate place, as Mary Astell explains in *Reflections upon Marriage* (1706 edition): while there is 'nothing in the Reason of Things' to indicate 'the natural Inferiority of our Sex', it is nonetheless laid down by 'our Masters ... as a Self-Evident and Fundamental Truth'.[49] They – who 'make worlds and ruin them' – write the conceptual schemes that define women. 'All that a wise Man pronounces is an Oracle', bemoans Astell.[50] Perhaps the most direct assault of patriarchal reason on women is its denial of their capacity for reason itself. Catharine Macaulay, writing in 1790, quotes Chesterfield: '"Women," says his Lordship, "are only children of a larger growth".' They lack '"solid reasoning"'.[51] As Wollstonecraft

---

[43] Wollstonecraft 1995, p. 79.
[44] Wollstonecraft 1995, p. 87.
[45] Wollstonecraft 1995, pp. 86, 110.
[46] Wollstonecraft 1995, p. 113.
[47] Wollstonecraft 1995, p. 116.
[48] Wollstonecraft 1995, p. 113.
[49] Astell 1996, p. 9.
[50] Astell 1996, p. 61.
[51] Macaulay 2014, p. 209.

asks, 'Who made man the exclusive judge, if woman partake with him the gift of reason?', indicating the circular horror of women's eviction from rationality.[52]

While later feminists argued that reason was implicitly coded male, that the supposedly universal eye of philosophy was in fact a man's eye, many early modern (male) philosophers explicitly excluded women from reason. They maintained that women were not rational, or that they were not sufficiently rational. Wollstonecraft quotes from Rousseau's *Emile* to show what her sex is up against: 'Researches into abstract and speculative truths' are 'not the proper province of women', she reads; 'women observe, men reason'.[53] The absence, or inferiority, of a woman's reason was the mainstay of the argument in favour of the subjection of women: if women were not rational, or were less rational than men, then women could not govern themselves, and needed the government of men. This was legitimate rule for the common good. As Locke puts it in his *Two Treatises of Government* (1689), 'Rule' in a marriage 'naturally falls to the man's share' as the 'abler and the stronger' party.[54] As William Nicholls expresses it in *The Duty of Inferiours towards their Superiours* (1701), the 'higher State of natural Perfection' in men puts them 'in a just Claim of Superiority' over 'the female Sex'; their superiority is 'a perfect Government and Rule'.[55]

Early modern feminists accordingly spent a lot of time fighting over the territory of reason, trying to show that it belonged to them, too.[56] If women were rational, then they had rights. If women were rational, then men's power over them was illegitimate. One cannot simply claim power over equals, over beings to whom God has given the capacity – and therefore the duty and the right – to rule themselves. This is a 'usurpation', in Wollstonecraft's formulation, in the specious name of utility. She challenges the framers of the new constitution in France who want to deny women 'a voice' to prove that women 'want reason'.[57] If they cannot, then they, the proponents of *liberté*, are themselves tyrants, exercising power without right.

Here we see feminist philosophers prising open concepts, challenging their fixedness and givenness – and trying to squeeze women into

---

[52] Wollstonecraft 1995, p. 69.
[53] Wollstonecraft 1995, pp. 110–11. See Lloyd 1993 for a pioneering study of 'the historical maleness of Reason' (p. xix).
[54] Locke 1988, p. 321.
[55] Nicholls 1701, Discourse IV, pp. 88, 91.
[56] On early modern feminism's fight to claim reason see Dawson 2018. See Fricker 2007 for a contemporary philosophical account of the epistemic injustice women face, in particular the lack of credibility that is afforded them as speakers, and the disadvantages they suffer as knowers.
[57] Wollstonecraft 1995, p. 69.

the orbit of 'reason'. Relatedly, they want to establish their place in the concept of 'mankind' – a term Wollstonecraft fought to be seen as truly 'comprehensive'. She urged philosophers to reconsider 'females' not so much as 'women' as 'human creatures'. Everyone should aim 'to obtain a character as a human being, regardless of the distinction of sex'. She also sought to untether masculinity from maleness, indeed, to sidestep maleness; in response to contemporary 'exclamations' about her ushering in a tribe of 'masculine women', she doubled down, explaining that in so far as 'masculinity' is associated with virtue and a noble 'human character', we should be glad for women to become masculine. Indeed, a true 'philosophic eye' would wish for this.[58] In blurring the distinction between the sexes, Wollstonecraft pushes at conceptual boundaries, exposes the partial vision of philosophy, and prods 'reason' on its illicit throne.

Early modern feminists associate dogmatic, myopic reason – and its exclusionary concepts – with violence. Mary Astell reels off an ironic list of 'reasons which demonstrate the superiority and pre-eminence of the men'. In addition to 'Immemorial Prescription' and the fact that 'Our Fathers have all along Taught and Practis'd Superiority over the weaker Sex', men have legal and political power, and 'not only the sharpest Sword, but even all the Swords and Blunderbusses'. They have, that is to say, a monopoly on force and the threat of force – which is, in Astell's suggestive phrase, 'the strongest Logic in the World'.[59] Logic, the art of reason, folds into aggression and subjugates women.

Logical disputation – the backbone of early modern philosophy – was itself explicitly framed by its male participants in schools, universities and the public sphere, as a form of combat, a kind of fencing, as Locke puts it in his *Essay Concerning Humane Understanding* (1689), where the ambition is to a win an argument rather than submit to truth.[60] A logic of violence was therefore embedded in the practice of reason that itself buttressed violence in the world – a bewildering, all-encompassing assault that the author who called herself Jane Anger also points out. In her resonantly titled *Her Protection for Women* (1589), Anger dons her visor and enters the disputatious fray – the designated cultural space for reason – and in so doing tries to bring her own reason into being, and to oppose

---

[58] Wollstonecraft 1995, pp. 74–7. For a classic analysis of the omission of women from the social contract in the history of political thought see Pateman 1988. Smith 2002 shows how this exclusion of women from the universal 'human' was developed in the English Revolution. On the development of the meaning of sexual difference to accommodate the inequality of women following the French Revolution see Fraisse 1994.

[59] Astell 1996, pp. 28–9.

[60] Locke 1975, pp. 677–8.

it to the brutal 'reason' of men, to prove that it is in fact men who have 'unreasonable minds' while mustering reason's empty name to harass and shame women.[61] Arming herself with the weapons of logic, she sets out to turn the upside-down world the right way up, to cut through the falsehoods about women lacking virtue, and demonstrate that things are the other way around. She argues, for example, that true reason sees that a woman who trusts a man is analogous to 'a goose standing before a ravenous fox'.[62] She depicts her opponents as snarling at her, 'barking out' their 'reason'.[63] Reason does not just perorate, it growls and bites.

A large part of early modern feminism's insurgency against what it saw as the joint empire of philosophy and patriarchy was its insistence on the historical constructedness and contingency of 'nature' – nature fixed in concepts that were mobilised to box in women, as well as to justify their subjection. Astell, for example, read Nicolas Malebranche, who tried to naturalise women's inferior minds. Due to the 'delicacy' of their 'brain fibres', he explains in *De la recherche de la verité* (1674), 'everything abstract is incomprehensible to them', and 'they consider only the surface of things'; this is why only 'grown men', whose brains are hardest and strongest from 'thirty to fifty years', are suited to the search after truth.[64] More prosaically, William Nicholls asserts that 'Natural Dignity' 'is discernable in the Man beyond the Woman. There is more of natural imbecility in the Woman, than in the Man, as well in respect of her Bodily, as in her Intellectual Capacities.'[65]

Most differences between men and women, retorted feminists, are not prearranged in nature, but manufactured in time and systems of domination – and might therefore be subject to scrutiny and change. Feminist philosophers therefore both acknowledged the binding spell of the past and tried to break it. They confronted the fallacy that facts are values, that the way things are and always have been is the way things must be. As Astell explains, it is 'the Custom of the World' that 'has put Women, generally speaking, into a State of Subjection' – 'but the Right can no more be prov'd from the Fact, than the Predominancy of Vice can justifie it'. Just because a man might look after pigs for a living, she elaborates, this does not mean he was 'Made' for the task.[66] Wollstonecraft echoes the thought, arguing that it is not 'nature' that 'has made a great difference between man and man', but rather 'civilization' which 'has been

---

[61] Anger 1985, p. 36.
[62] Anger 1985, p. 37.
[63] Anger 1985, p. 39.
[64] Malebranche 1997, pp. 130–1.
[65] Nicholls 1701, Discourse IV, p. 87.
[66] Astell 1996, pp. 10–11.

very partial'.[67] In her 1790 essay 'On the Equality of the Sexes', Judith Sargent Murray also wonders whether 'nature' is as partial as the discrepancies between men and women suggest, and concludes it is rather 'opportunity' that causes the disparity.[68] In *An Essay in Defence of the Female Sex* (1696) the anonymous author whom we now know as Judith Drake reminds her readers of the way in which power shapes selfhood when she remarks that women are not 'by Nature' less able but only so due to 'the Usurpation of Men, and the Tyranny of Custom (here in *England* especially)'.[69] In peeling away the idea of nature, feminist philosophers gesture to the ubiquity and discipline of culture, and the inseparability of history and reality.

It is certainly the case, they concede, that many women do, de facto, have weaker minds than men, but this is due to personal and collective histories; there is nothing de iure, inevitable or natural about it. The most obvious external circumstance that wrings inward difference is education. As Wollstonecraft puts it, one cause of the unhealthy state of women's intellects is 'the neglected education of my fellow-creatures'.[70] While 'Boys', explains Astell, 'have much Time and Pains, Care and Cost bestow'd on their Education, Girls have little or none'.[71] A woman's education, says Mary Hays in her *Appeal to the men of Great Britain in behalf of women* (1798), is designed to keep her 'in a state of PERPETUAL BABYISM'.[72] Murray gives a vivid account of just how absolutely the 'source' of inequality lies in 'the difference of education, and continued advantages'.[73] If a girl were given the same instruction as her brother, her mind would expand too. Were she to be taught astronomy, 'she might catch a glimpse of the immensity of the Deity'.[74] How can you appreciate the heavens unless you are directed to look up, and given a telescope? Only by being allowed to see, will your mind receive an imprint of the stars.

The historical construction of human subjects is effected far beyond the classroom. Early modern feminists offer a holistic critique of the interlinking affective, psychological and material ways in which women and men are grown between generations. Murray describes the unhappiness that comes with feeling 'the want of a cultivated mind', and next

---

[67] Wollstonecraft 1995, p. 74.
[68] Murray 1995, pp. 4–5.
[69] Drake 1696, p. 3.
[70] Wollstonecraft 1995, p. 74.
[71] Astell 1996, p. 28.
[72] Hays 1798, p. 97.
[73] Murray 1995, p. 5.
[74] Murray 1995, p. 6.

to this sensation of self-lack, the 'mortifying consciousness of inferiority' that comes from being tied to a man whose 'education hath set him so far above her'.[75] Wollstonecraft widens the definition of education to encompass the 'opinions and manners' that shape centuries as well as individuals.[76] She explains how 'notions of passive obedience' are 'early imbibed' and passed on through vicious circles of mothers and daughters.[77] It is not just what girls are 'told from their infancy', but the 'example of their mothers' that communicates what they should embody – 'cunning ... softness ... *outward* obedience ... a puerile kind of propriety' and beauty – if they are to win their only hope in life: 'the protection of man'.[78]

Wollstonecraft goes deeper still in her analysis of the fabrication of subjectivities when she reflects on the ways in which bodies and minds are mutually disciplined. Both 'the limbs and faculties' of girls, she says, are 'cramped with worse than Chinese bands'. While boys run about in the fresh air, girls are 'condemned to sit for hours together listening to the idle chat of weak nurses, or ... attend at her mother's toilet', which they in turn 'imitate' on a 'lifeless doll' until they come to repeat the cycle, generating a succession of animate mannequins.[79] Woman, says Wollstonecraft, 'was created to be the toy of man, his rattle', ordained to 'jingle in his ears whenever, dismissing reason, he chooses to be amused'.[80] Macaulay had chimed in with the insistence that the 'foibles and vices' of women emanate not from some 'unalterable law of female nature', but rather from their 'situation and education only'.[81] These, as she says, 'corrupt and debilitate both the powers of mind and body'. 'From a false notion of beauty and delicacy', for example, their 'system of nerves is depraved before they come out of their nursery'.[82] Hays adverts to the psychological confinement of a woman's life: in contrast to the many roads open to a man, women find their 'part in life already prescribed for them ... they find themselves enclosed in a kind of magic circle, out of which they cannot move, but to contempt or destruction'. This circle is, says Hays, a 'prison of the soul'.[83]

---

[75] Murray 1995, p. 6.
[76] Wollstonecraft 1995, p. 89.
[77] Wollstonecraft 1995, p. 104.
[78] Wollstonecraft 1995, p. 87.
[79] Wollstonecraft 1995, p. 113.
[80] Wollstonecraft 1995, p. 104.
[81] Macaulay 2014, p. 206.
[82] Macaulay 2014, p. 207.
[83] Hays 1798, p. 111. Cf. Achille Mbembe's account of 'Black reason', which he describes as 'like a kind of giant cage': Mbembe 2017, p. 10.

Women, then, become 'women', and men become 'men', and the concepts in turn come to fit and fix reality. Human agents do not spring fully formed – or deformed – into the world but are forged in particular social structures and situations. Minds are moulded in systems of biopower, and, as Murray says, picking up a common trope, 'custom becomes *second nature*'.[84]

Early modern feminists further unsettle the idea of universal human nature when they envisage female subjectivity as hollowed out in inverse proportion to the male ego. As Astell says, men 'are their own Centres', whereas a wife 'must follow all his paces, and tread in all his unreasonable steps'.[85] Macaulay lays out the dialectical relation: 'the highest honour' for women, their '*summum bonum*', is that they should win 'the admiration of the other sex'.[86] Their selfhood is tilted outside themselves. Wollstonecraft attacks Rousseau and other 'male writers' for setting this down in philosophical scripture. They 'warmly inculcate', she says, 'that the whole tendency of female education ought to be directed to one point: – to render [women] pleasing'.[87] This endeavour – to placate men – is 'the mighty business of female life'.[88] A woman's energy flows outward. A man becomes someone as she loses herself.

This process of othering, this production of radically differentiated and variously empowered human agents, is precipitated by and gives succour to the structural relation between the sexes which early modern feminists articulate as slavery. In expressing this view, they draw on the neo-Roman theory of liberty that Quentin Skinner has shown prevailed in early modernity.[89] According to this theory, you are unfree not only if your freedom of action is directly constrained, but also if you simply find yourself dependent on the will of another. You are unfree, that is, not only if you are physically controlled, or coerced, but if you live subject to the arbitrary power of someone else. In this case, your master might let you do everything you want, but if you do it at their mercy, then you are a slave. Early modern feminists thought that this precisely described the predicament of women. It evinced the way in which a wife was unfree even when she suffered no actual interference. It also hooked onto what I have argued above was early modern feminism's sensitivity to structural oppression – the way in which systems of concepts and practices interlock to dominate and disadvantage particular groups of people. These

---

[84] Murray 1995, p. 6.
[85] Astell 1996, pp. 45, 47.
[86] Macaulay 2014, p. 208.
[87] Wollstonecraft 1995, p. 96.
[88] Wollstonecraft 1995, p. 282.
[89] Skinner 1998.

systems hold women in a state of uncertainty, precarity and dependence. These systems are not real in the way that prison bars are real, but they nonetheless exert an iron force. They cannot be pointed to like trees or birds; they are not easily seen by the perpetrators and beneficiaries – indeed, they are easily denied – but they are palpable in their effects and in patterns of life.

Early modern women were dependent on men at many interwoven personal and political levels, very explicitly in the institution of marriage. Under the system of coverture in English common law, a wife's rights and identity were covered by those of her husband, so that, for example, he in fact owned everything that was hers, including the ring he had given her.[90] Astell evinces the abjection that follows from a wife's dependence when she explains that 'the Woman has in truth no security but the Man's Honour and Good-nature'. He might pledge kindness and freedoms, but he can whip these away at a stroke and she has no redress. 'Being absolute Master', Astell elaborates, 'she and all the Grants he makes her are in his Power.' The promises he advances, 'like Laws in an Arbitrary Government, are of little Force, the Will of the Sovereign is all in all'.[91] Sarah Chapone, in *The Hardships of the English Laws in Relation to Wives* (1735), goes so far as to say that the law puts wives 'in a worse Condition than *Slavery* itself'.[92] A wife, in Wollstonecraft's words, is 'the humble dependent of her husband'; marriage is 'slavery', and, more generally, women are 'the slaves of power'.[93] Macaulay suggests that the 'state of abject slavery' in which 'the female species' finds itself has roots in men's historical abuse of their physical strength.[94]

Astell calls out male philosophers who pronounce in supposedly universal terms on supposedly universal mankind, and talk boldly of freedom, while not seeing half of mankind, nor the harm they cause it. 'If *all men are born free*,' she demands, 'how is it that all Women are born slaves?'[95] Although – indeed, because – Astell herself is a Tory, and no fan of Whig freedom or the resistance it legitimises, she marvels at the hypocrisy of Whigs who beat their emancipatory drum while condemning women, by their own logic, to be slaves – as women must be, says Astell, 'if the being subjected to the *inconstant, uncertain, unknown, arbitrary Will*

[90] Gowing 2012, p. 45. Cf. Gowing 2003 on the vulnerabilities of early modern women's bodies.
[91] Astell 1996, pp. 51–2.
[92] Chapone 2018, p. 28.
[93] Wollstonecraft 1995, pp. 99, 248, 259. On Wollstonecraft's feminist republicanism see Halldenius 2015.
[94] Macaulay 2014, p. 206.
[95] Astell 1996, p. 18.

of Men, be the *perfect Condition of Slavery?* And if the Essence of Freedom consists, as our Masters say it does, in having a *standing Rule to live by?*'[96] Astell is quoting Locke here, who was rehearsing the unmistakable notes of the neo-Roman theory of liberty to resist the absolute power of Charles II, but could not see that he endorsed in one instance the very thing he criticised in another.

This feminist critique of the blind spots of philosophical reason shines light on the importance of differentiating and situating human beings, and disrupts the uniformity and fixity of subjects and objects. It overturns any neat, unitary understanding of freedom, not only by opening up the chasm identified by Skinner between freedom as non-interference (the liberal view) and freedom as non-dependence (the neo-Roman view), but also by drilling into freedom as non-interference. Hobbes, who Skinner has shown was an ancestor of the liberal view, defined freedom in *Leviathan* (1651) as the absence of external impediments to motion; you are free so long as you are not stopped from exercising your will; you are free so long as you can exercise *choice*, so long as you consent.[97] But Astell, like later feminists, queries this valorisation of choice and consent. When explaining why it is problematic to blame a wife for having chosen an abusive husband, she writes: 'A Woman indeed can't properly be said to Choose, [when] all that is allow'd her, is to Refuse or Accept what is offer'd.'[98] bell hooks would go on to frame the point as follows: 'Being oppressed means the *absence of choices.*'[99]

Early modern feminists complicate the concepts of freedom and agency by throwing into doubt the possibility of an overarching account of free will. If you are dependent on men for your security and well-being, if you are rewarded for performing a certain role for them, then you will start to play by their rules, to chase and relish the only wins you are allowed. Astell describes how dependence works on the psyche: women, she says, 'are for the most part Wise enough to Love their Chains, and to discern how very becomingly they set'.[100] Wollstonecraft repeats the trope, reflecting on the way in which willing servitude is 'transmitted to posterity': 'Considering the length of time that women have been dependent, is it surprising that some of them hug their chains, and fawn like the spaniel?'[101] The general question of whether

---

[96] Astell 1996, pp. 18–19. Cf. Locke 1988, p. 284.
[97] Hobbes 2012, II, p. 145.
[98] Astell 1996, p. 43.
[99] hooks 2000, p. 5.
[100] Astell 1996, p. 29.
[101] Wollstonecraft 1995, pp. 161–2.

human beings have free will or not, as beloved of philosophers now as it was in the seventeenth century, forgets, or refuses to see, the particular ways in which people's wills are moulded in history and by power. Our will – what we really want, what we ought to want, what would be good for us – is often opaque to us, and goes against us. Any normative theory of freedom that stops at simply ensuring that we are able to act according to our will fails to see the tight corners, the prisons of the soul, that form our will and (mis)inform our consent.

This feminist complication of freedom and the will also spills into concepts of reason and intuition. As we saw Astell indicate above, there is 'wisdom' in self-abasement. Wollstonecraft gestures at the rationality, the good sense, of servility, if you depend completely on a man's will. There is method in simpering, in flattering, in keeping quiet. Degraded by prejudice and dependency, it is a woman's 'reason, her misty reason!' that 'is employed rather to burnish than to snap her chains'.[102] 'Reason', then, is not fixed, but finds its levels, its constituents, in the tunnels of power.

Ain't I a Woman?

Just as feminists have brought history to bear on philosophy, to point out the partiality and plurality of reason, and the contingency and constructedness of concepts and human minds, so have they yearned themselves to occupy philosophical ground – to claim for themselves the pinnacle of reason, to lay down their own superior truths.[103] Wollstonecraft believes in reason, and she believes in a universal rational human subject; she just does not think that philosophers or society have got there yet. While she is critical of philosophy as it is practised in her time, therefore, she has the same utopian hopes for the discipline as her forefathers. Her project is in line with the spirit of philosophy: to dispel the mists before our eyes and see more clearly. In *The Christian Religion* (1705) Astell goes so far as to reject history in favour of the art of reason as the proper subject of study for a woman. She is frustrated by men who recommend that women read history; in part, this is because history is written by men, is

---

[102] Wollstonecraft 1995, p. 184.
[103] It should be noted that while I have in this chapter focused on early modern feminism's critique of and fight over reason, early modern feminists and indeed modern feminist commentary on early modern philosophy also explore the vast scope of extra-rational, imaginative and affective modes of understanding; see, e.g., Gilby 2019 on the porous relation between passion, poetics and reason in Descartes; Gatens and Lloyd 1999 on the importance of the imagination in Spinoza's philosophy; Gatens 2009 for a collection of feminist essays on Spinoza.

about men, and erases women from the record – except when their greatness is too obvious to be ignored, in which instances they are said to have '*acted above their sex*'. But Astell's preference for logic is also grounded in her desire 'to learn the weakness and strength of our minds; to form judgments, and to render them always just; to know how to discover false reasonings, and to disentangle truth from those mazes of error into which men have hunted her'.[104] In *A Serious Proposal to the Ladies* (1694) Astell invites women to form an intellectual monastic order, where they might obtain 'right Ideas' and cultivate their intelligent souls. It is to be a refuge for the 'Female Virtuoso'.[105] Her philosophical ambition could not be more absolute, nor more recognisable. 'Reason and Truth', she avows, 'are firm and immutable, she who bottoms on them is on sure ground'.[106]

Twentieth- and twenty-first-century feminist philosophers are also, albeit on different metaphysical and epistemological premises, committed to the rightness, the rational strength, of their positions, and some even pursue a renovated universalism. Recalling the philosophers I mentioned above, for example, Nussbaum argues for a feminist liberalism, Okin for a theory of justice that truly attends to '*everyone's* point of view' and Benhabib for, as she puts it, a shift 'from a substantialistic to a discursive, communicative concept of rationality' and 'the reconciliation of the universal and the concrete other'.[107] In *Decolonising Universalism: A Transnational Feminist Ethic* (2019) Serene J. Khader proposes a 'non-ideal universalism' that at once decolonises feminism while retaining its normative agenda.[108]

Sometimes feminist theorists bring the same exclusionary energy to their analyses that they object to in patriarchal thought. Astell, along with a long line of white feminists who have defined marriage as slavery, did not reflect on the enslaved men and women who were kidnapped from Africa and shipped to the Americas, or brought to London by their owners. Her reasoning, like that of Locke – who himself had close links to colonisation and the slave trade – did not extend to human beings in literal chains, but rather to aristocratic white women in Chelsea, and (in Locke's case) well-fed white gentlemen in the English countryside.[109]

---

104 Astell 1705, p. 293.
105 Astell 2002, p. 78.
106 Astell 2002, p. 71. On Astell's soaring ambition see Bejan 2019.
107 Nussbaum 1999; Okin 1989, p. 15; Benhabib 1992, p. 5; Benhabib 2011, p. 48.
108 Khader 2019, p. 7. See also Fraser 1997 on the integration of the 'politics of recognition' and the 'politics of redistribution'; Allen 2004 on the politics of talking to strangers.
109 Wollstonecraft 1995, p. 235 acknowledges 'African slaves'.

Black feminists have shown the implicit or explicit exclusion of black women from the category of woman. It lay behind Sojourner Truth's question to the Women's Rights Convention in Akron, Ohio, in 1851. 'Ain't I a woman?' she asked, in a formulation that has become a rallying cry for women of colour ever since.[110] In *A Voice from the South by a Black Woman of the South* (1892) Anna Julia Cooper described what it was like to see white women helped off the train by the conductor, who then turns his back on her, and on the platform, to look up and see two signs – one 'FOR LADIES' and one 'FOR COLORED PEOPLE', and to feel herself falling between concepts, to find herself unconsidered, non-existent, without any place to call her own.[111] Campaigning for a reform of American manners, Cooper appeals to 'American Women ... the exponents of woman's advancement, the leaders in woman's thought' to teach the nation to show courtesy to 'all'. 'The "all"', however, she muses, 'will inevitably stick in the throat of the Southern woman. She must be allowed, please, to except the "darkey" from the "all"; it is too bitter a pill with black people in it.'[112] White feminism's universal was (and is) not universal.

The fight for conceptual inclusion is ongoing, together with the ambition for cut-glass clarity in analytic philosophy. Kathleen Stock locates herself in the tradition of 'conceptual analysis', which she describes as 'concerned with how concepts *should be* and not just how how they *are*'.[113] In *Material Girls: Why Reality Matters for Feminism* (2021) Stock argues that 'if trans women are women, they are not "women" in the same sense in which adult human females are "women"'. 'Ideally', she goes on, 'we should have phonetically different terms to refer to each', but if that is not possible, 'we should at least be clear that TRANS WOMAN, TRANS MAN, WOMAN and MAN are four different concepts, each with different membership conditions'.[114] In the 'debate' over who counts as a woman, Stock argues against 'changing the concept of "woman" to include self-declared trans women'.[115]

Trans people respond that they are not a debate. They exist. In *The Transgender Issue: An Argument for Justice* (2021) Shon Faye writes, 'we

---

[110] Truth 2021, p. 42. On the racism of 'the women's movement' and its reclamation see, e.g., Lee Maracle's 1988 text *I am Woman*: 'We are part of a global movement of women in the world, struggling for emancipation. ... Until white women can come to us on our own terms, we ought to leave the door closed' (Maracle 2021, p. 477). See also Bay 2015.

[111] Cooper 2021, p. 80.

[112] Cooper 2021, p. 81.

[113] Stock 2021, p. 147.

[114] Stock 2021, p. 175.

[115] Stock 2018. Cf. Stock 2019.

are not an "issue" to be debated and derided'.[116] She lays out 'the reality of the issues facing trans people today' – the discrimination, violence and oppression – and argues that 'the central demands of trans liberation are not merely aligned with, and no threat to, gay rights and feminism, but are synonymous with the goals of those movements'.[117] Faye wonders 'why a theoretical framework for understanding trans people should be the prime concern for any feminist' when 'sexism, misogyny and transphobia' are being entrenched by populist and authoritarian regimes around the world, and she suggests that 'theory should only ever play second fiddle to the practical work of movement building, resource-allocation, care and solidarity. Political coalitions rarely achieve full mutual understanding of every facet of one another's reality.'[118]

When life exceeds our conceptual categories, when experience recoils under conceptual policing, when our concepts are causing harm, it is time to rethink our concepts, and to embrace that rethinking – not just in order to reflect the multitudinous complexity of the world, but as a matter of justice, with a view to abundant liberation for all, with a view, as Faye puts it, to 'the possibility of living more fully and freely'. 'Our existence', concludes Faye, 'enriches this world.'[119] For Christa Peterson the '"gender critical" movement ... tries to make the fact' of gender identity 'disappear through *conceptual analysis*'.[120] Intersectional, transinclusive feminism is open to the intricacy of sex/gender and listens to the voices at the margins of power.[121] '"Woman" has never been a coherent group, it has always been a shifting category', writes Lola Olufemi; '"woman" is frequently coded as cis, white and heterosexual. But it belongs to no one.'[122] In Emi Koyama's words in *The Transfeminist Manifesto* (2001) 'there are as many ways of being a woman as there are women'.[123]

Angela Davis points to the imperative of being open to conceptual change and, relatedly, to history. Speaking in 2013, she looked back to the twentieth century and the 'debates about how to define the category "woman"', at the 'numerous struggles over who got included and who

---

[116] Faye 2021, p. 268.
[117] Faye 2021, pp. xiv, xv.
[118] Faye 2021, pp. 260–1.
[119] Faye 2021, p. 268.
[120] Peterson 2021.
[121] See, e.g., Butler 1990; James 2003; Moi 2005, p. 4; Manne 2019, pp. 24–5; Olufemi 2020, pp. 49–66; Phipps 2020, pp. 104–8; Srinivasan 2021, pp. xi–xii.
[122] Olufemi 2020, p. 65. Cf. Long Chu 2019 for a dazzling account of femaleness; Riley 1988, p. 5 on 'women' as an 'unstable category'.
[123] Koyama 2020, p. 87.

was excluded from that category'. She remembers the feminist movement 'as a struggle for white middle-class women's rights, pushing out working-class and poor women, pushing out Black women, Latinas, and other women of color'.[124] She remembers the transformative World Conference on Women in Nairobi in 1985, and thinking then that what was needed 'was to expand the category "women" so that it could embrace Black women, Latina women, Native American women, and so forth'.[125] What she did not foresee, she says, 'was that we would have to rewrite the whole category'.[126]

In working with trans women of colour, Davis feels the echoes of her own fight for inclusion and transformation, which themselves echo earlier struggles against the patrolling of categorical boundaries and the invocation of fixed or given concepts. We cannot know all, nor can we speak for everyone, nor see round our own corners. Davis encourages us to be curious about concepts that do not seem to make sense, especially when those concepts come from intersections of oppression. It is there that the greatest insights into justice and injustice are likely to be found. She urges us to be alert to the philosophical productiveness of taxonomic rupture, confusion and surprise, rather than sticking to what we know. Addressing 'the academics in the house', Davis celebrates a 'feminism that urges us to be flexible, one that warns us not to become too attached to our ... objects of study ... don't even become too attached to the concept of gender ... the more closely we examine it, the more we discover it is embedded in a range of social, political, cultural, and ideological formations. It is not one thing. There is not one definition.'[127]

Don't Give Me your Lukewarm Gods

Feminism injected history and a historicist sensibility into philosophy. It faced up to the philosopher colossus who stood above time and used the penetrating light of his universal reason to understand human minds and perennial concepts. It replied that nothing and no one is outside time or circumstance, that reason is embodied, positional, plural, and that, when wielded with power, it can be punitive, that it tends either not to see women, or gender, or difference, or to naturalise, justify and reinforce patriarchy. It insisted that human beings, like concepts, are contingent constructs.

---

[124] Davis 2016, p. 95.
[125] Davis 2016, p. 96.
[126] Davis 2016, p. 96.
[127] Davis 2016, pp. 100–1.

But just as history showed that women and men are made in time, not given in nature, nor intelligible with pristine intuition, so it also offered the promise that human beings might be remade and rethought – that they might remake and rethink themselves. Feminism therefore holds onto the vestiges of the ambitions of philosophy, while combining them with a sensitivity to multiple perspectives, and the ways in which these are rooted in historical structures of domination and resistance. Gloria Anzaldúa articulates the combination of the rejection and the reinvention of philosophy in her 1984 book *Borderlands: La Frontera*:

> So, don't give me your tenets and your laws. Don't give me your lukewarm gods. What I want is an accounting with all three cultures – white, Mexican, Indian. I want the freedom to carve and chisel my own face, to staunch the bleeding with ashes, to fashion my own gods out of my entrails. And if going home is denied me then I will have to stand and claim my space, making a new culture – *una cultura mestiza* – with my own lumber, my own bricks and mortar and my own feminist architecture.[128]

Anzaldúa's desires also point to another reason why feminism might want to recollect philosophy: to let women climb, if not to the light outside the cave, or to the panoramic mountain top (which will always be epistemic fantasies), then to higher ground, where the air is fresher, the burdens lighter and the horizon wider. Part of the difficulty for women thinking is that they are tethered down, not only by invisible labour and in invisible spaces, but also in relation to how they are perceived. When they speak of abstract things, they are not heard as doing so. As Chris Kraus says in *I Love Dick* (1997), the gendered world is divided into 'poet-men, presenters of ideas, and actress-women, presenters of themselves'.[129] While Locke and Rousseau have no difficulty entering the canon, Wollstonecraft still struggles not to be reduced to her life. Allowing women a philosophical voice gives them a share of the privilege.

References

Allen, Danielle. 2004. *Anxieties of Citizenship since Brown v. Board of Education*. Chicago.

Anger, Jane. 1985. *Her Protection for Women* in *The Women's Sharp Revenge*, ed. Simon Shepherd. New York.

Anzaldúa, Gloria. 2012. *Borderlands: La Frontera: The New Mestiza*. San Francisco.

Astell, Mary. 1705. *The Christian Religion*. London.

---

[128] Anzaldúa 2012, p. 44.
[129] Kraus 2015, pp. 161–2.

1996. *Reflections upon Marriage* in *Political Writings*, ed. Patricia Springborg, Cambridge.

2002. *A Serious Proposal to the Ladies*, ed. Patricia Springborg. Peterborough, Ont.

Bay, Mia. 2015. 'The Battle for Womanhood is the Battle for Race: Black Women and Nineteenth-Century Racial Thought' in *Toward an Intellectual History of Black Women*, ed. Mia Bay, Farah J. Griffin, Martha S. Jones and Barbara D. Savage. Chapel Hill.

Beaney, Michael. 2017. *Analytic Philosophy: A Very Short Introduction*. Oxford.

de Beauvoir, Simone. 2011. *The Second Sex*, trans. Constance Borde and Sheila Malovany-Chevallier. New York.

Becker, Anna. 2020. *Gendering the Renaissance Commonwealth*. Cambridge.

Bejan, Teresa M. 2019. '"Since All the World is mad, why should not I be so?" Mary Astell on Equality, Hierarchy, and Ambition', *Political Theory*, 47: 6, pp. 781–808.

Benhabib, Seyla. 1992. *Situating the Self: Gender, Community and Postmodernism in Contemporary Ethics*. New York.

2011. 'Concrete Universality and Critical Social Theory: Dialogue with Alfredo Gomez-Muller and Gabriel Rockhill' in *Politics of Culture and the Spirit of Critique*, ed. Gabriel Rockhill and Alfredo Gomez-Muller. New York.

Bennett, Judith M. 2006. *History Matters: Patriarchy and the Challenge of Feminism*. Philadelphia.

Broad, Jacqueline. 2015. *The Philosophy of Mary Astell: An Early Modern Theory of Virtue*. Oxford.

Broad, Jacqueline and Karen Detlefsen, eds. 2017. *Women and Liberty, 1600–1800: Philosophical Essays*. Oxford.

Broad, Jacqueline and Karen Green, eds. 2009. *A History of Women's Political Thought in Europe, 1400–1700*. Cambridge.

Butler, Judith. 1990. *Gender Trouble*. New York and London.

Chambers, Clare. 2008. *Sex, Culture, and Justice: The Limits of Choice*. University Park, PA.

Chapone, Sarah. 2018. *The Hardships of the English Laws in Relation to Wives*, ed. Susan Paterson Glover. London.

Clark, Stuart. 1997. *Thinking with Demons: The Idea of Witchcraft in Early Modern Europe*. Oxford.

Cohen, L. Jonathan. 1986. *The Dialogue of Reason: An Analysis of Analytic Philosophy*. Oxford.

Cooper, Anna Julia. 2021. Extract from *A Voice from the South by a Black Woman of the South* (1892) in *The Penguin Book of Feminist Writing*, ed. Hannah Dawson. London.

Craig, Edward. 2002. *Philosophy: A Very Short Introduction*. Oxford.

Crenshaw, Kimberlé, Neil T. Gotanda, Gary Peller and Kendall Thomas. 1996. *Critical Race Theory: The Key Writings that Formed the Movement*. New York.

Cuboniks, Laboria. 2018. *The Xenofeminist Manifesto*. London.

Davis, Angela. 2016. *Freedom is a Constant Struggle*. Chicago.

Dawson, Hannah. 2018. 'Fighting for my Mind: Feminist Logic at the Edge of Enlightenment', *Proceedings of the Aristotelian Society*, 118: 3, pp. 275–306.
2021. *The Penguin Book of Feminist Writing*. London.
Drake, Judith. 1696. *An Essay in Defence of the Female Sex*. London.
Evans, Richard. 1997. *In Defence of History*. London.
Faye, Shon. 2021. *The Transgender Issue: An Argument for Justice*. London.
Federici, Silvia. 2021. *Revolution at Point Zero: Housework, Reproduction, and Feminist Struggle*. Oakland, CA.
Forrester, Katrina. 2019. *In the Shadow of Justice: Postwar Liberalism and the Remaking of Political Philosophy*. Princeton.
Fraisse, Geneviève. 1994. *Reasons's Muse: Sexual Difference and the Birth of Democracy*, trans. Jane Marie Todd. Chicago and London.
Fraser, Nancy. 1997. *Justice Interruptus: Critical Reflections on the 'Postsocialist' Condition*. London and New York.
Fricker, Miranda. 2007. *Epistemic Injustice: Power and the Ethics of Knowing*. Oxford.
Gatens, Moira, ed. 2009. *Feminist Interpretations of Benedict Spinoza*. University Park, PA.
Gatens, Moira and Genevieve Lloyd. 1999. *Collective Imaginings: Spinoza, Past and Present*. London.
Gilby, Emma. 2019. *Descartes's Fictions: Reading Philosophy with Poetics*. Oxford.
Gowing, Laura. 2003. *Common Bodies: Women, Touch and Power in Seventeenth-Century England*. New Haven and London.
2012. *Gender Relations in Early Modern England*. Harlow.
Green, Karen. 2014. *A History of Women's Political Thought in Europe, 1700–1800*. Cambridge.
Halldenius, Lena. 2015. *Mary Wollstonecraft and Feminist Republicanism*. London.
Haslanger, Sally. 2012. *Resisting Reality: Social Construction and Social Critique*. Oxford.
Hays, Mary. 1798. *Appeal to the Men of Great Britain in behalf of Women*. London.
Hester, Helen. 2018. *Xenofeminism*. Cambridge.
Hobbes, Thomas. 2012. *Leviathan*, ed. Noel Malcolm. Oxford.
hooks, bell. 2000. *Feminist Theory: From Margin to Center*. London.
Hughes, Ann. 2012. *Gender and the English Revolution*. Abingdon.
Hunt, Lynn, ed. 1989. *The New Cultural History*. Berkeley.
James, Selma. 2012. *The Power of Women and the Subversion of the Community* in *Sex, Race and Class: The Perspective of Winning: A Selection of Writings, 1952–2011*. Pontypool.
James, Susan. 2003. 'Feminisms' in *The Cambridge History of Twentieth-Century Political Thought*, ed. Terence Ball and Richard Bellamy. Cambridge.
Khader, Serene J. 2019. *Decolonizing Universalism: A Transnational Feminist Ethic*. Oxford.
Knott, Sarah and Barbara Taylor, eds. 2005. *Women, Gender and Enlightenment*. Basingstoke.
Koyama, Emi. 2020. *The Transfeminist Manifesto* in *Burn it Down! Feminist Manifestos for the Revolution*, ed. Breanne Fahs. London.

Kraus, Chris. 2015. *I Love Dick*. London.

Levy, Jacob T. 2014. *Rationalism, Pluralism, and Freedom*. Oxford.

Lloyd, Genevieve. 1993. *The Man of Reason*. London.

Locke, John. 1975. *An Essay concerning Human Understanding*, ed. Peter H. Nidditch. Oxford.

1988. *Two Treatises of Government*, ed. Peter Laslett. Cambridge.

Long Chu, Andrea. 2019. *Females*. London.

Macaulay, Catharine. 2014. *Letters on Education*. Cambridge.

MacKinnon, Catharine A. 2007. *Are Women Human? And Other International Dialogues*. Cambridge, MA.

Malebranche, Nicolas. 1997. *The Search after Truth*, ed. Thomas M. Lennon and Paul J. Olscamp. Cambridge.

Manne, Kate. 2019. *Down Girl: The Logic of Misogyny*. London.

Maracle, Lee. 2021. An extract from *I am Woman* in *The Penguin Book of Feminist Writing*, ed. Hannah Dawson. London.

Matsuda, Mari J. 1986. 'Liberal Jurisprudence and Abstracted Visions of Human Nature: A Feminist Critique of Rawls' Theory of Justice', *New Mexico Law Review*, 16: 3, pp. 613–30.

Mbembe, Achille. 2017. *Critique of Black Reason*, trans. Laurent Dubois. Durham, NC, and London.

Miller, David. 2003. *Political Philosophy: A Very Short Introduction*. Oxford.

Moi, Toril. 2005. 'What is a Woman? Sex, Gender, and the Body in Feminist Theory' in *Sex, Gender and the Body*. Oxford.

Moore, G. E. 1922. *Principia Ethica*. Cambridge.

1925. 'A Defence of Common Sense' in *Contemporary British Philosophy*, ed. J. H. Muirhead. London.

Moyn, Samuel. 2010. *The Last Utopia: Human Rights in History*. Cambridge, MA.

Murray, Judith Sargent. 1995. *On the Equality of the Sexes* in *Selected Writings of Judith Sargent Murray*, ed. Sharon M. Harris. Oxford.

Nagel, Thomas. 1986. *The View from Nowhere*. Oxford.

1987. *What Does it all Mean? A Very Short Introduction to Philosophy*. Oxford.

Nicholls, William. 1701. *The Duty of Inferiours towards their Superiours*. London.

Novick, Peter. 1988. *That Noble Dream: The 'Objectivity Question' and the American Historical Profession*. Cambridge.

Nozick, Robert. 1993. *The Nature of Rationality*. Princeton.

Nussbaum, Martha C. 1999. *Sex and Social Justice*. Oxford.

O'Brien, Karen. 2009. *Women and Enlightenment in Eighteenth-Century Britain*. Cambridge.

O'Connor, Cailin, Liam Kofi Bright and Andrew Zucker. 2019. 'Vindicating Methodological Triangulation', *Synthese*, 196: 8, pp. 3067–81.

Offen, Karen. 2000. *European Feminisms 1700–1950: A Political History*. Stanford.

Okin, Susan Moller. 1989. *Justice, Gender, and the Family*. New York.

Olufemi, Lola. 2020. *Feminism, Interrupted: Disrupting Power*. London.

Pankhurst, Emmeline. 2019. *Freedom or Death*. n.p.

Pateman, Carole. 1988. *The Sexual Contract*. Cambridge.

Peterson, Christa. 2021. 'Kathleen Stock, OBE', www.praile.net/post/kathleen-stock-obe.

Phipps, Alison. 2020. *Me, not You: The Trouble with Mainstream Feminism*. Manchester.

Poulain de la Barre, François. 2013. *A Physical and Moral Discourse concerning the Equality of Both Sexes* in *The Equality of the Sexes*. Oxford.

Riley, Denise. 1988. *'Am I That Name?' Feminism and the Category of 'Women' in History*. Basingstoke.

Rorty, Richard, ed. 1967. *The Linguistic Turn*. Chicago.

1979. *Philosophy and the Mirror of Nature*. Princeton.

Russell, Bertrand. 1998. *The Problems of Philosophy*. Oxford.

Skinner, Quentin. 1998. *Liberty before Liberalism*. Cambridge.

Smith, Barry. 2013. 'Philosophical and Empirical Approaches to Language' in *Philosophical Methodology: The Armchair or the Laboratory?*, ed. Matthew Haug. London.

Smith, Hilda. 2002. *All Men and Both Sexes: Gender, Politics, and the False Universal in England 1640–1832*. University Park, PA.

Smith, Sophie, Teresa Bejan and Annette Zimmermann, eds. 2021. *The Historical Rawls*, a special issue of *Modern Intellectual History*.

Srinivasan, Amia. 2019. 'Genealogy, Epistemology and Worldmaking', *Proceedings of the Aristotelian Society*, 119: 2, pp. 127–56.

2021. *The Right to Sex*. London.

Stanley, Jason. 2015. *How Propaganda Works*. Princeton.

Stock, Kathleen. 2018. 'Changing the Concept of "Woman" Will Cause Unintended Harms', *The Economist*, 6 July.

2019. 'Sexual Orientation: What is it?', *Proceedings of the Aristotelian Society*, 119: 3, pp. 295–319.

2021. *Material Girls: Why Reality Matters for Feminism*. London.

Táíwò, Olúfémi O. 2020. 'Being-in-the-Room Privilege: Elite Capture and Epistemic Deference', *The Philosopher*, 108, p. 4.

Taylor, Barbara. 2003. *Mary Wollstonecraft and the Feminist Imagination*. Cambridge.

Threadcraft, Shatema. 2016. *Intimate Justice: The Black Female Body and the Body Politic*. Oxford.

Tomaselli, Sylvana. 2021. *Wollstonecraft: Philosophy, Passion, and Politics*. Princeton.

Truth, Sojourner. 2021. 'Ain't I a Woman?' in *The Penguin Book of Feminist Writing*, ed. Hannah Dawson. London.

Weil, Rachel. 1999. *Political Passions: Gender, the Family and Political Argument in England 1680–1714*. Manchester and New York.

Wollstonecraft, Mary. 1995. *A Vindication of the Rights of Woman* in *A Vindication of the Rights of Men and A Vindication of the Rights of Woman*, ed. Sylvana Tomaselli. Cambridge.

Young, Iris Marion. 2011. *Justice and the Politics of Difference*. Princeton.

11 On (Lost and Found) Analytical History in Political Science

Ira Katznelson

> Social scientists who try to escape history because they do not wish to be classified as humanists who can never be certain of their inferences are fleeing from the places where the richest treasures are buried.
>
> Kagan 2009, p. 174

This chapter reflects on history's uneven but requisite role for political science. I consider the character of their borders; costs and gains brought about by different degrees of proximity and distance; and prospects for creative joining within the ambit of what the historian Richard Hofstadter designated as 'analytical history', a productive but uneasy scholarly site marked by diverse sensibilities, contending orientations and competing ways of working.[1]

An intellectual discipline is a constellation of people, ideas and institutions. During the closing decades of the nineteenth century, the very interval when pioneering research sensibilities and arrangements began to transform leading universities on both shores of the Atlantic, history and political science were discernible tendencies and emergent specialisations, but mutually constitutive and only gently distinct. Scholars on each side of their flexible and permeable frontier shared questions, orientations and identities more than differences. They composed a single, if variegated, epistemic community.

Though this degree of imbrication did not last, it is useful to recall the terms of connection and the effects of separation, not all negative, less in the spirit of an elegy than as means to advance encouraging opportunities. Such possibilities, past and present, are underpinned by the reality that, not being gods, both historians and political scientists cannot capture the full complexity of an inexhaustible actual world. We are constrained to represent and simplify reality by creating shadow worlds of structures, actors and causal mechanisms. These models are both

---

[1] Hofstadter 1956.

analytical and descriptive, along a spectrum from literal particularity to broader abstraction as they apprehend the motion of historical developments. About structures, we need to specify the circumstances actors are in. About actors, we should know their attributes, what they want and why, based on their experiences and dispositions. About mechanisms, we need to comprehend how they shape structures, actors and patterns of meaning, how they mobilise interests, preferences and ideas, and how they can be deployed in narratives that combine periodisation with choices about concepts that make sense of the character and rhythms of historical time.[2]

Origins

Political science, of course, is an ancient craft. Methodical reasoning about political authority fills many pages in biblical as well as ancient Chinese, Indian, Greek and Roman writing, then in medieval, early modern and modern Western texts. Nonetheless, something novel regarding the quest for political knowledge happened in the late nineteenth and early twentieth centuries: the birth of organised academic disciplines and the restructuring of higher education. The character of leading universities was transformed by new facilities built to advance systematic study and prospects for serendipity, by disciplinary organisation, by new practices such as peer review, by hiring academic staff committed to systematic research, and by initiating graduate training, especially in Germany and America, as the principal pathway to academic careers.

A central hallmark in the United States at this juncture was the creation of a constellation of organised scholarly associations as a means to construct networks, develop and police standards, and establish patterns of validation and communication. When political science was born in the United States as an organisationally autonomous discipline, its founders, then all members of the American Historical Association (AHA), visibly separated from the established profession to which they had belonged.[3] These AHA members had acquired the sense of inhabiting a zone for inquiry that no longer could, or should, be subsumed within the extant

---

[2] Hedström and Swedberg 1998.
[3] At just that moment, US historians were moving decisively away from Teutonic theories of organic human development. Students of American history were developing a more national, continental account of their country's distinctiveness, signified by Frederick Jackson Turner's frontier thesis that placed the implications of America's westward torque at the centre of understanding. This thrust proved to be quite distant from the subjects most pursued by the AHA members who left to found the American Political Science Association. See Turner 1893.

historical craft. Concerned less with the nature of the past than with the character of political challenges under ever more complex and vexing conditions, they identified presentism as a value rather than a vice.

Starting with 204 members in 1903, and growing rapidly to 1,462 by 1915,[4] the American Political Science Association (APSA; followed, in 1906, by the field-defining *American Political Science Review*) was led by persons who distinguished their new domain in three dimensions: by topics, especially the standing of constitutional democracy; by policy objectives, primarily governmental reform; and by research methods, many inspired by positivist trends pioneered in sociology by such figures as Auguste Comte and Émile Durkheim.

The aspiring political scientists who embarked on a self-conscious effort to develop a professional domain for the study of politics were not bare-bones empiricists. They were motivated principally by the wish to comprehend the development of the modern state and the capacities of political liberalism to both restrict and orient constitutional and legal arrangements as instruments to guard and advance such regimes.

One key American figure, Westel Willoughby, wrote a theory of the state.[5] Another, Charles Merriam, soon to be a pioneer political behaviourist, wrote a doctoral thesis on the history of political ideas that concern sovereignty.[6] What they insisted on, sometimes explicitly, was how the moment of modernism was producing a break in human affairs whose political dimensions must urgently invite deep inquiry on behalf of fragile liberal democracies.

Withdrawing from organised history but not quite, and not yet, from the craft, these individuals were keen to forge a distinctive set of American contributions to a larger conversation present in Britain and on the European Continent (especially in Germany, where many had been trained), about the role of the state, the character of public law and the institutional and psychological qualities of public affairs, and do so based on claims to science and rationality.[7]

The decision to secede from the organised history profession almost certainly surprised many, perhaps most, active members of the AHA. The official historical discipline was still small enough that every member was known to many, perhaps most, or in some cases even all. The AHA had been fashioned in 1884 as the first professional academic association in the United States, with a population of university scholars

[4] Adcock and Bevir 2010, p. 72.
[5] Willoughby 1911.
[6] Merriam 1900.
[7] Katznelson 1986, pp. 17–47.

quite distinct from the non-academic amateurs of the American Social Science Association, launched in 1865 at the close of the Civil War. Like the AHA, the new APSA was an explicitly professional organisation, different from the American Academy of Political and Social Science, founded in 1890, that had '[brought] together industrialists, financiers, clergymen, government officials and educators to discuss topical political and economic issues'.[8]

As a society of professionals at a time when the ethos of science was on the rise, many AHA members were not averse, especially in light of the motivating example of Leopold von Ranke, to advance the very values of science and objectivity that later came to dominate political science and would become a good deal more controversial within history. It was Ranke who had established history from the 1820s as a discipline with archive-based methods, and the ability to move methodically on the basis of the critical appraisal of sources and imaginative movements from the particular to the universal. It was Ranke, above all, who effectively first distinguished the craft of history from studies of religion and philosophy within which it had been embedded. It was he who rigorously distinguished speculative abstraction from accurate knowledge of the particular, which he considered to be building blocks, writing that 'the discipline of history – at its highest – is itself called upon, and is able, to lift itself in its own fashion from the investigation and observation of particulars to a universal view of events, to a knowledge of the objectively existing relatedness'.[9] Following Ranke, 'Science ("objective science", "the scientific fact")', Peter Novick observed in his account of the contested status of objectivity among historians, 'was never more highly regarded in the United States, was never more of a cult, than in the late nineteenth and early twentieth centuries'.[10]

The very year APSA recruited its first members, the characterisation of history as a science was articulated in J. B. Bury's influential January 1903 Inaugural Address as Regius Professor of Modern History at the University of Cambridge, a post that, following Lord Acton, Bury would occupy for a quarter of a century. He displayed an affinity not only

---

[8] Bowen 1983, p. 18.
[9] Cited in Stern 1956, p. 59.
[10] Novick 1988, p. 31. Unlike the currently oriented and hypothesis-driven science that later became a hallmark of political science, the historians' 'model of scientific method', Peter Novick noted, was 'rigidly factual', characterised by shunning hypotheses and by maintaining a scrupulous neutrality, signalling a distinctive pattern of professionalisation within the new research university setting. At the time, there were greater similarities: Novick 1988, pp. 37, 56, 67.

with the key systematic ambitions of the scholars who were at work fashioning APSA, but with some of their themes, as he announced the wish to deploy history as a tool 'for shaping public opinion and advancing the cause of intellectual and political liberty'.[11]

It was this sensibility and preference for a systematic and cumulative knowledge that had undergirded the tight integration of history with political science in prior decades. The sense of building a systematic social and historical science traversed what later became a yawning gap. This impulse provided the premise for the proclamation by Columbia's John Burgess at the 1896 annual meeting of the AHA that 'Political Science must be studied historically and history must be studied politically in order to have a correct comprehension of either. Separate them, and one becomes a cripple, if not a corpse, the other a will-o'-the-wisp.'[12]

It was with this orientation that a diverse group of leading figures, including Herbert Baxter Adams, Woodrow Wilson and Burgess, worked to advance what they designated as 'historico-political studies', a term first used by the German émigré Francis Lieber. Their scholarship identified an intellectual world in which more than one boundary was still indistinct – not only dividing history from political science, but the frontiers distinguishing political science and, respectively, sociology, psychology, law and economics. Writing in 1884, Adams (who had earned a PhD at Heidelberg before joining the faculty at Johns Hopkins) underscored this quality when he celebrated the Columbia School of Political Science, then in its fifth year, as being 'great' for the manner 'in which Economics, History, and Sociology find their proper place, all in harmony with ... Law'. Also taking note of emerging intellectual life at Cornell, Harvard, Michigan and Wisconsin, Adams observed how all 'these subjects have been intimately associated', on the model of his home institution, where, from the founding of graduate history and social science education in 1876, these subjects, he wrote, 'have never

---

[11] Bury acknowledged the emerging existence of separate spheres uneasily. Revealingly, he felt the need to caution his historian colleagues not to become 'the handmaid of social science' when performing the 'very important function' of supplying 'material for social and political science': Bury 1903, pp. 41, 14. Before the nineteenth century, Bury argued, history had yet to be scientific. By the early twentieth it had exited the constraints of imaginative literature to enter the domains of fact and cause. Despite 'a vague cloud half concealing from men's eyes her new position in the heavens,' he famously opined, 'history has really been enthroned and ensphered among the sciences' based on the centrality of reason, critical doubt, a quest for objectivity and systematic methods based on a scrupulous pursuit and validation of historical fact (p. 9). Like that generation's political scientists, he traced the origins and inspiration for this development to academic Germany.

[12] Burgess 1897, p. 211.

been divided'.[13] Tellingly, the frontispiece of the *Johns Hopkins University Studies* series of publications prominently displayed a locution of Edward Augustus Freeman, Regius Professor of History at Oxford, drawn from his 1880 opening address in Birmingham to the UK Historical Society: 'History is past Politics and Politics present History.'[14] This conjunction was something of a truism for scholars on both sides of the Atlantic. As a study of the politics curriculum in the late nineteenth century to the early twentieth century at the University of Cambridge concluded, 'What is, perhaps, most striking of all about the various courses in political science is the extent to which the kind of political knowledge they offered the student was historical.'[15]

Emblematic was how so many courses of study featured Thucydides. Late nineteenth-century scholars assigned *The Peloponnesian War* not only for its riveting, impossible-to-put-down character, but for the text's model of systematic history to which integrated orientations to knowledge aspired.

Charged with such big puzzles as why Athens went to war, and how, given the balance of power, that city could have held off defeat by Sparta for nearly three decades, *The Peloponnesian War* is self-conscious in method, referring to 'exact knowledge'. Thucydides contrasted his work's analytically controlled evidence and argument with what he believed to be a less rigorous and less logical orientation to historical narration in Herodotus's *The Histories*. *The Peloponnesian War* is characterised by a regime typology, a systematic interplay between global realism and justice and between power and moral passion. What the investigation calls its 'archeology' – a consideration of the remote Greek past – opens the presentation of what, throughout, is compelling diagnostic political history. The study combines material situations with discursive orientations. It is interested in the systematic relationship of words and deeds. It climbs up and down a ladder of abstraction, ranging from the crucial role and speech-acts of proper-named leaders to conceptual considerations of power. It is rich in variables, mechanisms and hypotheses. It cares about dimensions and qualities of measurement. It appraises ethics and self-interest together. It combines the analysis of internal politics, including democratic factionalism, with matters of empire, war and foreign policy. And it conjoins painstakingly detailed description with explanation and

---

[13] Adams 1894, pp. 194, 195. At its beginning in 1880, Columbia's School of Political Science had indeed included not just history but sociology and economics, not yet separate disciplines.
[14] Johns Hopkins 1883–4.
[15] Collini, Winch and Burrow 1983, p. 359.

causal claims. Not just a narrative of the summer and winter seasons of war, the text is a deeply probing analytical – one might say scientific – account. As a result, in the pre-APSA world of the AHA, no other text was understood to be more foundational for an integrated scientific history and political science. The agenda and example of this great work, I argue below, endures as arguably the most compelling guide to the practice of analytical history within political science.

Together and Apart

In short, during the last quarter of the nineteenth century the academy's later matrix of specialisation did not yet exist.[16] Political science and history were entwined, inspired in the United States by the German university model dedicated to systematic *Wissenschaft* and secondarily motivated by features of the philosophical approach to politics at Oxford and the portmanteau form that characterised the curriculum in the Moral Sciences Tripos in Cambridge since 1851, 'involving papers in mental and moral philosophy, logic, psychology, history and political philosophy, political economy and jurisprudence'.[17]

Robert Adcock has designated this moment's impulse as 'a single ordered field of knowledge', a vision of integration, with the central commitments of history to context and temporality in the leading role.[18] As an indicator, *Political Science Quarterly*, the first modern American journal of political science, founded in 1886 and housed at Columbia, was devoted not to a free-standing science of politics but to all the substantive dimensions of political studies, most notably including history. Nearly all its early contributors identified as historians. And most were devoted to a common, if broad and not fully specified, scientific commitment.

At first, the new APSA, sharing many dispositions and principled dispositions with the older unit, initiated what seemed to be a noncontentious separation, not a hostile divorce. In practical terms, the separation of APSA from the AHA did not immediately bring about an end to a still-vibrant set of intellectual intersections. But the early situated unity did not last.

There had been harbingers. Heralding the division that soon would come, one colleague at the 1901 AHA meeting, H. Morse Stephens, a Cornell-based historian who had arrived from Scotland two years prior, specified his 'astonishment amounting to somewhat of a disgust, that

---

[16] Higham 1979.
[17] Collini, Winch and Burrow 1983, p. 345.
[18] Adcock 2003, p. 483.

history [in the United States] was regarded ... rather as a handmaid of political science than as a subject of study for its own sake'.[19] A report of that year's meeting took note of the dissatisfactions of some political scientists along these lines, even as it complacently concluded that there is 'no danger of disruption of the larger body'.[20] Just then, the president of the AHA, Charles Francis Adams, was warning colleagues that developments being promoted in history were isolating and marginalising political scientists. 'That politics should find no place at its meetings, I believe', he stated, has become 'the unwritten law of this association; and by politics I refer to the discussion of those questions of public conduct and policy for the time uppermost in the mind of the community.'[21]

Two years later the creation of APSA put a decisive end to a comprehensive AHA. By 1908, an American Political Science Association committee accurately reported, as the proceedings of the 1909 meeting record, the distinction between historians and political scientists had grown: 'their points of view, aims and their methods are distinct now and getting more so'.[22]

Unity fell victim to situational, institutional and intellectual trends. At a moment characterised in the United States by charged conflict and division – by industrial development and labour unrest, rapid urban growth, mass immigration, the institutional elaboration of mass political participation, racial violence and the emergence of a Jim Crow South, Native Indian warfare in the west, and the conquest of Puerto Rico and the Philippines – the organicist understanding that once had joined the disciplines came to seem simple to the point of *naïveté*. Institutionally, as the research university model deepened and proliferated – signified by Columbia's move to a capacious campus in Morningside Heights and by the founding of the University of Chicago, which quickly adopted a departmental structure – great pressure was put on the prospects of any conjoined organisational, or intellectual, site for history and political science.

Though the founders of APSA intended a division of labour within a common ethos, they initiated significantly more, a process that soon began to fashion a discipline with ever stronger borders, and with an emergent character at odds with central commitments of the history profession. Yet not until the exit from the tribulations of the Second World War did the gap grow so wide as to seem nearly impossible to bridge.

---

[19] Cited in Burgess 1897, p. 212.
[20] Meeting of the AHA 2003.
[21] Adams 1902, p. 203.
[22] Cited in Adcock 2003, p. 507.

That degree of separation, still familiar today, was the product of a process lasting a generation. Though officially, even doggedly, non-partisan, the new political science was charged with normative purpose: not just to understand but to secure and advance liberal democracy, less by understanding the lineage of regimes than by focusing on policy solutions to problems, and, by the mid-1920s, by developing scientific approaches to human political behaviour in the here and now.[23]

The scope of the discipline thus became both deeper and more restricted. Studies of the state turned pragmatist, and narrowed to studies at a lower, more realistic, level of abstraction, dominated by methodical considerations of power, governance, decisions and mass as well as elite conduct. The centre of gravity moved from the east coast to the University of Chicago, where organised empirical research thrived together with experimentation with new kinds of quantitative methods and data, and where the new Social Science Research Council was first nourished into existence before moving to New York City. Exactness about data and method began to reign in the study of political parties, interest groups, public opinion, voting behaviour and other institutional loci of political behaviour. The task was to discern how liberal democracy actually worked rather than how it had been imagined. As such, modern American political science pursued a project Woodrow Wilson had identified as early as 1886: the wish to understand how the state could be controlled and tamed by political actions in and by civil society, balancing effective administration with popular sovereignty;[24] in short, by the wish to comprehend and affect the relationship between liberalism and democracy, not simply in the realm of ideas, but inside the domain of institutions where these ties actually exist.

By today's disciplinary standard, rules of evidence and procedures for inference within political science in that period were primitive, yet the direction of ambition was clear. As the Ohio State political scientist Walter James Shepard wrote approvingly and optimistically in 1925, the discipline was making 'distinct progress toward a really scientific character'.[25] The key, as *The Process of Government* by Arthur Bentley had underscored in 1908 and David Truman's *The Governmental Process* would stress in 1951, was precisely the challenge of developing a

---

[23] A Finnish scholar characterises this effort in four overlapping phases, which correspond to the formation of mass representative democracies between 1880 and 1930; the crisis of representative democracies between 1900 and 1940; the behavioural and pluralist solution to the problems of democracy between 1920 and 1965; and the crisis of pluralist democracy, starting in 1945 to the present: Berndtson 1983, p. 95.
[24] Wilson 1887, pp. 197–222.
[25] Shepard 1925, p. 427.

realistic, empirically grounded understanding of practices within liberal democracy – arrangements for voting, interest representation, public opinion and legislative behaviour; knowledge not in or for itself, but to advance prospects for regimes based on a robust interaction between active citizens and their government.

A dance of distance followed the 'migration out of history' by political scientists and the reciprocal isolation of historians.[26] Certainly by the 1940s the division between history and political science had started to be significantly more pronounced. The disciplines began to mesh more fitfully, engage more warily, and collaborate only uncommonly. Historians and political scientists learned to cherish demotic control over different impulses and values. Passionate about historiography and the identification and control of sources, historians came to underscore complexity, contingency and temporal variability, privileging the particularity of situations as Kitson Clark emphasised when he stated that 'the most important principle of historical scholarship' is 'the importance of context'.[27] Portable hypotheses were suspect; narrative the dominant form; causality a matter of judgement and plausibility.

By contrast, political scientists placed a tighter control on procedures, and developed more explicit conceptualisation while elevating standards to validate causal claims. For Bury, 'science' had implied differentiation from literature. For many political scientists, the scientific dimension designated a search for trans-historical mechanisms identified either by deductive models or empirically investigated conjectures and hypotheses that would have made Bury uncomfortable. As many political scientists worked with historical data, such as congressional roll calls, they often treated each observed behaviour as equivalent in time series analysed by

---

[26] Novick 1988, p. 69. The disciplines in the United States developed in phases. During the first two decades of the century political scientists thrust themselves into public debate while historians tended to withdraw. From the 1920s there was something of a reversal, as some political scientists came to interpret objectivity as neutrality at just the moment at which progressive historians such as Charles Beard and Vernon Parrington placed their historical scholarship within conflict between the people and the elite to identify with the democratising movements of the former. Later, as policy-distant objectivity was revived within history, political scientists renewed a strong policy orientation. Later still, as bottom-up history thrived, many political scientists turned to state-centred analyses. Yet later, down to the present, history's social engagement and purposes grew in tandem with the retreat of numerous political scientists into the more arcane reaches of advanced statistical methods, with a passion to nail down causality sometimes surpassing interest in real-world situations.

[27] Kitson Clark 1967, p. 25. A striking example can be found in an essay by Bin Wong (Wong 2012, pp. 27–54). Contrasting social movements against taxation in Europe and China, the essay shows variation due to shifts in the parameters of meaning. Similar causal chains, he shows, can be embedded in quite different patterns of meaning, thus altering outcomes.

workhorse regression techniques that failed to consider the very features of analysis historians always place front and centre: questions of temporality, sequence, context and, in statistical language, the importance of shifts to parameters.

This new situation was signified by the bifurcation of what once had been a quite unified orientation to studies of the modern sovereign state, an approach that had underscored regime issues of sovereignty and law, constitution and representation, global conflict and its remedies in international agreement, and a normative and practical quest for a broadly liberal political order characterised by consent, rule of law and a state guaranteeing individual and collective rights while being permeable to the preferences of citizens in civil society.

We can observe how this shift proceeded in a short book of 1934, *The State as a Concept of Political Science* by Frederick Mundell Watkins, who went on to a significant career at Yale as a student of the collapse of Weimar and of the character of political liberalism. Originating as a graduate student paper in a Harvard seminar taught by Carl Friedrich on 'The Scope of Methods in Political Science', the volume, a manifesto favouring a behavioural turn within political science, is organised in two parts. The first presents a tight and compelling history of state making and sovereignty dating back to medieval and early modern Europe. Having displayed a mastery of the subject through this powerful condensed history, worthy, say, of later work on the sovereign state by Barrington Moore, Perry Anderson, Charles Tilly and Theda Skocpol,[28] Watkins moved to make his primary programmatic point. He counselled a deep and profound shift in subject and method by advancing a present-centred 'realistic political science' that would focus on 'the data of political experience'. Political scientists, he argued, should advance 'the progress of the science' based on a wide arc of curated social and political data regarding a wide range of private as well as public associations. Orienting the discipline to questions of power and action, he underlined psychological motivation and the examination of persuasion and coercion as sources of actual behaviour within the polity. For the organised discipline, he argued, such an orientation 'for the first time' would 'verify the hypotheses of political science against a truly adequate and sufficiently available body of social experience. In this direction', he concluded, 'lies the future development of a systematic political science.'[29]

In short, speculation should yield to observation, ideas to facts. By the mid-twentieth century this orientation came to characterise the most

---

[28] Moore 1966; Anderson 1974; Tilly 1975; Skocpol 1979.
[29] Watkins 1934, pp. 5, 81, 82, 84.

assertive and influential political science scholarship, not only at Yale, but at other major centres. Most notable was the University of Chicago. There, such leading faculty as Charles Merriam, Harold Gosnell, Leonard White, Quincy Wright and Harold Lasswell produced studies of voting, political psychology, public opinion, the administrative state, city politics (including African American politics) and the causes of war that demonstrated the capacities of rigorous observational political science. This cohort soon trained a luminous next generation that included V. O. Key Jr., Herman Pritchett, David Truman and Gabriel Almond.[30] It was in the Social Science Building in Hyde Park that the most familiar aspects of contemporary political science took shape, where scholars conducted early randomised field experiments, used factor analysis and multiple regression, and combined statistical methods with ethnographic field research.[31] In political studies, history lost its commanding height.

The goal of this intellectual turn, as Merriam had put things in a 1921 programmatic essay, was the creation of a more unified, more precise, pragmatic body of work. His call, in Tocquevillean language, for 'a new science of politics', favoured drawing on the practices of the biological sciences for the creation of theory and the natural sciences for methods based on rigorous observation both in the field and in research labs where team research could flourish. Merriam further counselled that students of politics should learn from scientists how to achieve targeted practical effects on human problems. These various goals, Merriam argued, would best be advanced by the refinement and use of targeted statistical methods, the social science version of the telescope or microscope.[32] He had come quite a distance from his 1900 doctoral thesis in the history of political thought that had surveyed writings about sovereignty by Bodin, Althusius, Grotius, Hobbes, Pufendorf, Locke and Rousseau.[33]

This programme led to a bifurcation in American political studies. With the close of the Second World War, leading political scientists deepened understanding of political behaviour in the United States through uncommonly rich, sustained empirical work about a small set of connected subjects, each tightly woven into the fabric of liberal democracy:

---

[30] Heaney and Hansen 2006; Tsou 1951.

[31] Heaney 2007, p. 753.

[32] Merriam 1921, pp. 173–85. An earlier version of these hortatory themes can be found in the recommendations in Lowell 1910, pp. 1–15.

[33] Merriam 1900. The PhD thesis, published in the Columbia University Press dissertation series Studies in History, Economics, and Public Law, volume 12I, no. 4, was followed by his first book, *A History of American Political Theories*, 'a description and analysis of the characteristic types of political theory that have from time to time been dominant in American political life': Merriam 1903, p. viii.

the behaviour of interest groups, the strategies of political parties, the actions of members of Congress, patterns of mass political psychology and the making and shape of public opinion with a type of focus on power, agency and choice in the here and now that reflected the research project Watkins had advanced.[34] At their best, they achieved a concerted effort of political theory, institutional analysis and what Bury would have applauded as scientific investigation of human action.

American political history remained dominated by a far more traditional narrative form. In stinging critiques, the historian Thomas Cochran lamented how 'the past fifty years of progress in the development of social science methods and hypotheses have had surprisingly little effect on historical interests, content, of forms of synthesis'. At mid-century, historical thinking seemed stuck on 'synthesis in terms of great men and a sequence of important unique events'. For historians of the United States, the dominant mode continued to be the presidential synthesis.[35] In the main, their best political histories, including Arthur Schlesinger's Pulitzer Prize-winning *The Age of Jackson*, published in 1945, and his three-volume *The Age of Roosevelt*, appearing between 1957 and 1960, advanced but did not break with this long-established approach to periodisation and interpretation.[36]

Openings

History, for political scientists, had become a source of facts and a repository of qualitative and quantitative data, not a place to look for analytical imagination. In that context, the early work of Richard Hofstadter proved galvanising across disciplinary lines. By altering and deepening the contours of the political history of the United States, Hofstadter inspired both historians and political scientists to take up his call for analytical history.

Hofstadter's books on Social Darwinism and the Progressive Era, provocative critical assessments of key figures in the eighteenth, nineteenth and twentieth centuries, and bracing essays on then-current themes

---

[34] Of course the literature is massive. Consider as emblematic Truman 1951; Truman 1959; Key 1955; Key 1961; Key 1966.

[35] Cochran 1948, pp. 748–59; Cochran 1956, p. 348. In political history, Cochran ruefully mused, 'fifty years of rapid growth in the social sciences have had surprisingly little effect'. The primary structure of narrative that had characterised the profession at the turn of the century is 'still securely in place'. And, by the standards and orientation of the social sciences, he judged the presidential synthesis to be a failure: Cochran 1948, p. 748.

[36] Schlesinger 1945; Schlesinger 1957–60.

ranging from Southern Jim Crow to what he designated as pseudo-conservatism, each assertively thematic, burst onto the scene both as exciting ways to practise the historical craft and as public interventions that reprised the strong hope for current relevance that had character-ised the aspirations of many political scientists ever since the founding of APSA a half-century earlier. Manifestly, Hofstadter's writings consti-tuted a visible break with more familiar historiographical traditions, and suggested pathways for historians to renew ties with the social sciences and for political scientists to engage with this type of history.[37]

What Hofstadter took in from social scientists and how he would become a figure of influence within the social sciences were shaped by his membership at Columbia in an informal study group that called itself 'A Seminar on the State'. Meeting from the mid-1940s to the mid-1950s, the members of this workshop included a small number of top-tier historians (William Leuchtenburg, Fritz Stern and Karl Wittfogel, in addition to Hofstadter) and an all-star cast of social scientists (including sociologists Daniel Bell, Robert K. Merton, C. Wright Mills and Sey-mour Martin Lipset, and political scientists William T. R. Fox, David Truman, Richard Neustadt, Gabriel Almond, Julian Franklin and Franz Neumann). This cohort was drawn to behavioural studies of politics not as an alternative, Watkins style, to considerations of the state, but as means to more deeply understand the central unit of sovereignty's char-acter and effects both within and outside the liberal tradition.[38]

The dominant mode of their work was reflected in a hortatory essay written by Hofstadter for a volume about the varieties of history edited by Stern. Writing in the mid-1950s, Hofstadter called for 'the develop-ment of a somewhat new historical genre, which will be a mixture of traditional history and the social sciences' that, among other virtues, would firmly enlarge the place of historical inquiries within political science. Designating this approach as *analytical history*, he explained how

It will differ from the narrative history of the past in that its primary purpose will be analytical … [and] will focus on types of problems that the monograph has all too often failed to raise. It will be informed by the insights of the social sciences and at some point will make use of methods they have originated. Without pretending to be scientific, it may well command more reciprocal interest and provide more stimulation for social scientists than a great deal of the history that is now being written.[39]

---

[37] Hofstadter 1944; Hofstadter 1948; Hofstadter 1949; Hofstadter 1954–5; Hofstadter 1955; Hofstadter 1965.
[38] For a discussion of the Seminar on the State see Katznelson 2003b, pp. 107–51.
[39] Hofstadter 1956, p. 363.

'Authors of narrative histories', he regretted, 'rarely hesitate to retell a story that is already substantially known, adding perhaps some new information but seldom in systematic fashion or with a clear analytical purpose', while 'many a monograph ... leaves its readers, and perhaps even its author, with misgivings as to whether that part of it which is new is truly significant'.

Hofstadter asked historians to be more open-minded about the social sciences as 'a special kind of opportunity' to gain more rigour by broadening their toolkit to include 'such techniques as panel studies ... content analysis ... more sophisticated sampling, an increased use, where it is possible and appropriate, of measurement – all of them methods in which the social sciences have gone far ahead'.[40] He further observed that the social sciences offer the chance to engage with 'new problems which the historian has usually ignored', including issues central to political science. 'It seems inevitable', he wrote, 'that some of the discoveries made ... about current mass political behavior and political influence will revise some of the historian's assumptions about political behavior in the past.'[41]

As it turned out, both concurrently and since, analytical history began to thrive in more than one genre and in more than one discipline. Just as Hofstadter was advocating a new historical genre, the historian of Venice Frederic C. Lane was offering more detailed methodological advice. He highlighted how investigations of the past can be oriented to identify key points of historical inflection, what social scientists who were soon to call themselves historical institutionalists later named as critical junctures, moments characterised by discontinuity and marked by significant alterations to structure, experience, disposition and behaviour. This approach, as recommended by Lane, also entailed a search for causal explanations of such large-scale temporal breaks, and a concern for systematic approaches to temporality and sequence, often designated as considerations of path dependency that were taken up by advocates

---

[40] Hofstadter 1956, pp. 359, 362, 364.
[41] Hofstadter 1956, p. 364. Reciprocally, Hofstadter thought history had much to offer the social sciences, which must learn, he believed, to transcend their penchant for trans-historical generalisation in their search for explanations of variation. The relationships connecting history and the social sciences had been explored in essays by seven historians commissioned by the Social Science Research Council (1954). A review by the historian David Potter observed how a great many historians 'still remain antagonistic to the use of the findings of economists, sociologists, psychologists, anthropologists, political scientists, and demographers'. He lamented this resistance because, like Hofstadter, he believed traditional historical methods to be inadequate. But he was even more critical of social scientists who 'suppose both that they understand history and that they do not need it': Potter 1955, pp. 79, 81.

within political science who were developing new approaches to analytical history.[42]

Just over a decade after Hofstadter's call, J. P. Nettl published 'The State as a Conceptual Variable', an article that sought to reverse the shift Watkins had advocated to move political science away from the state as the discipline's central conceptual pivot towards power as the fulcrum of analysis. Opening by taking stock of a thirty-year trend, Nettl observed that 'the concept of state is not much in vogue in the social sciences right now', while announcing the goal of developing an approach 'which offers a means of integrating the concept of state into the current primacy of social science concerns and analytical methods'.[43]

Lane and Nettl helped instigate a profound turn to analytical history in political sociology and political science, an emphasis especially concerned to grapple with large-scale political change and connections between military violence and state formation. There were other programmatic calls, including Charles Tilly's *Big Structures, Large Processes, and Huge Comparisons* and the Social Science Research Council volume, edited by Peter Evans, Dietrich Rueschemeyer and Theda Skocpol beseeching scholars to advance *Bringing the State Back In.*[44]

Much superb substantive scholarship burst onto the scene in this period, including Barrington Moore on the origins of dictatorship and democracy, Perry Anderson on the trajectory towards modernity, Immanuel Wallerstein on the rise of a Europe-dominated market system in the sixteenth century, Tilly on European state formation and Skocpol on comparative revolutions.[45] Strikingly, these influential works were not written by persons then in departments of History or Political Science (Tilly and Skocpol only later would have joint appointments). None was located at the centre of history or political science as professional disciplines. Large-scale analytical history had outsider status.

For political science, this circumstance altered with the rise of Historical Institutionalism (HI) as an orientation within the discipline. Its hallmarks, Paul Pierson and Skocpol identified in an early 2000s state-of-the-discipline volume, included interrogating significant

---

[42] Lane 1955; Mahoney and Thelen 2015; Pierson and Skocpol 2002; Orren and Skowronek 2002; Katznelson and Milner 2002; Smith 1997.
[43] Nettl 1968, p. 559.
[44] Tilly 1984; Evans, Rueschemeyer and Skocpol 1985.
[45] Moore 1966; Wallerstein 1974; Tilly 1975; Skocpol 1979.

real-world puzzles about political economy, demography, the welfare state, the character of regimes and ethnic identities as historical processes more systematically than was common in scholarship by historians. More specifically, HI has taken up Lane's approach to temporality, including the focus on path dependence, sequences and conjunctures, and the analysis of institutional development and its effects in context.[46] A tandem effort also has developed, if at a slower pace, within a form of rational choice concerned to develop analytical narratives that engage intensively with historical evidence and specific events.[47]

Historical Institutionalism inspired students of US politics, long the centre of present-oriented behavioural studies, field experiments and deductive modelling, to offer a counter-current under the rubric of American Political Development (APD). When, in 1986, the political scientists Karen Orren and Stephen Skowronek launched, as founding editors, *Studies in American Political Development*, they were able to identify 'a turn by political scientists to history' in the form of a 'new institutionalism' as the foundation for the work of the new journal. This scholarship, they wrote, 'has used the work of the ... past as a new point of departure from which to specify more closely the complex patterns of state-society relations. History', they added, 'provides the dimension necessary for understanding institutions as they operate under varying conditions. Beyond that, it is also the natural proving ground for the claim that institutions have an independent and formative influence on politics.'[48]

Within history, such statements would have been banal. Within mid-1980s political science they constituted a clarion call for a change in relative emphasis, a shift away from dominant features of their discipline.

Taking stock of this subfield nearly two decades later, Orren and Skowronek identified APD's institutional orientation, a concern for the systematic appraisal of temporality, attention to values in American political culture, especially the liberal tradition, and an interest in patterns of governance and policy, with attention to how substantive policy outcomes affect subsequent possibilities.[49]

With these initiatives, we can observe an ironic outcome to Hofstadter's summons to analytical history. The assertive trends of HI and APD in political science have not been matched, in the main, within his

[46] Pierson and Skocpol 2002.
[47] Bates et al. 1998.
[48] Orren and Skowronek 1986, p. vii.
[49] Orren and Skowronek 2002.

own discipline, notwithstanding some organised efforts, most conspicuously the creation of the Social Science History Association in 1976, an effort that aimed explicitly to bring various social science tools, including quantification, to the craft of social, cultural and political history, and the growth of global history, efforts at micro- and macro-quantitative history, even the emergence of ambitious Big History, each responsive to Hofstadter's appeal in its own way.[50]

The comparatively successful achievements and effects of the historical turn inside political science should not be exaggerated, however. Large-N statistical analyses, field experimentation, game theory and deductive modelling with history serving as illustration dominate. There has been an intensification in the prioritisation of causal identification in deep tension with the complexity of causation and the inevitability of endogeneity in the historical experience.[51]

In all, within political science, the historical orientation plays in a minor key, often at some distance from these more dominant registers, a rather different situation from the prevailing orientation to political knowledge that had characterised the second half of the nineteenth century and the opening of the twentieth. What we can observe, however, are non-trivial openings that have proved particularly important for the historical study of politics within political science in tandem with something of a return to political history by historians after the long moment when cultural and social history marginalised political history as too enclosed, too traditional, too elitist.

All the same, present circumstances in political science and history might be conducive to a re-engagement on the terrain of analytical history. Both disciplines share an unprecedented degree of ontological and epistemological pluralism. Their centre has not held. Intense sub-groups within each discipline distinctively combine substance and method, often with mutual incomprehension. Strikingly, a recent excellent overview of the current state of the history profession is organised not by a matrix of time and place, the familiar way the discipline records its variety, but both by 'themes and structures', including population, gender, ethnicity, ideas, culture, science, religion, commerce and power, and by 'writing history', including the status of historical knowledge and causation. Somewhere, Hofstadter is smiling.

The combination of deep pluralism and the growth of corresponding orientations opens prospects for those of us who would wish to help fashion an overlapping consensus on behalf of analytical history that does

[50] Katznelson 2003a.
[51] Wawro and Katznelson 2020.

not require historians and political scientists to perfectly align, only to discern a location for collaborative endeavours.[52]

How, then, in the light of more than a century of intellectual distancing and not a little mutual suspicion, can analytical history achieve a supple, determined and effective role within political science by designating strategies that join ordered narratives of events in time to analyses of structures, dispositions and choices without erasing or eliding disciplinary differences, but by mobilising the strengths of each? Could we do just that without over-corrections that would lose important disciplinary achievements, including literary excellence in outstanding histories and demanding causal reasoning in excellent political science?

Despite and in part as a result of their mostly separate development, the two organised disciplines today inquire better, know more, and have widened their arcs of topics and questions a good deal more than at the start of the last century. What is required are forms of friendly reciprocity, collaboration across disciplines, methods and ideas but not an erasure of difference or a return to the type of 'single ordered field of knowledge' that Adcock identified as the hallmark of the late nineteenth-century hybrid of history and social science.

Parameters

In that spirit, I should like to reflect on how analytical history might come to thrive more successfully inside political science, not as the dominant mode of inquiry but with more standing than having either an antiquarian or a peripheral status, thus not as an exception but as integral to the discipline's kitbag of tools. Among other issues, this ambition requires thought about analytical narration, terms of collaboration and degrees of abstraction in models of reality, together with the designation of analytical history as a layered set of choices: from art to science; from structures to events; from tight to configurative causality; and from the local to the grand in time, space and scale.

---

[52] As I write, I am thinking of two very different but outstanding instances of actual and promising conjunction. First is by Abram de Swaan (1988), a leading Dutch social scientist, who deploys strategic tools drawn from theories of collective action and comparative historical social science of the kind written by Moore and Tilly to probe, at a deep historical level, why and how the modern sovereign state in Britain, France, Germany, the Netherlands and the United States accumulated responsibilities for education, assistance to the poor, public health and social insurance that once belonged to religious and civil society institutions. Second is the essay devoted to 'Power' by Christopher Clark (2012). This tight contribution is rich with suggestions, most implicit, about how to (re)connect the political spheres of state and power that Watkins divided at the onset of the behavioural revolution in political science.

I very much like the imagery the historian John Lewis Gaddis uses to explain how we can best organise understanding of the landscape of history through the science and art of map making. The main goal of a map is legibility. By thinking about making history as the creation of maps, analytical historians in any disciplinary location, he points out, can learn from cartographers how to 'permit varying levels of detail, not just as a reflection of scale', and how to verify by '*fitting* representation to reality', tasks that require both critical imagination and logic, and decisions about the type of information and data being mapped. Maps, moreover, can be layered one on the other. Like the blueprints architects generate to guide building, charting to represent reality helps make possible inferences about configurations of causes as constellations that order complexity.[53]

Gaddis also identifies a significant tension in how historians and social scientists often go about their work. Generalising, he observes differing habits of mind and craft that divide these intellectual communities even when the social scientists are deeply engaged with historical evidence. The historians, devoted to contextualisation and chronology, usually embed generalisations as mechanisms within, and that propel, their narratives; whereas social scientists, devoted to theory and causation, typically embed narratives within generalisations. Historians tend to prefer contingent and experience-near causation; social scientists search for reasons and foundations that are more categorical and experience distant. Historians risk having complexity override the ability to discern driving forces while social scientists risk the danger of excessive simplification. Historians are diffident about showing the methods they use to connect causes to outcomes, while social scientists are compelled to do just that in a display of formal methodologies. And they are likely to value parsimony in different places, in consequences or cause.[54]

These are not hard-and-fast contradictions, but unavoidable tensions. Each mode of working contains its own distinct power, each with ways of mapping that advance understanding. Analytical history as a good in itself, and markedly when this type of work is placed within political science, requires self-conscious choices about each of these matters. That is not a problem at all, but a reminder that such work, to be persuasive, must combine art and science in acts of systematic recovery to persuasively and creatively mobilise and make sense of historical fact and evidence. After all, work in analytical history evokes degrees of uncertainty and probability, whether in prospective or retrospective accounts,

[53] Gaddis 2002, pp. 32–4, 52–62 (emphasis in original).
[54] Gaddis 2002, pp. 52–65, 92, 95, 105.

the first repressing knowledge of outcomes, the second making that the point of departure, a different balance of bafflement and knowledge.

'Sometimes an art' is how Bernard Bailyn has characterised the historical craft.[55] Perhaps he might have added, 'Sometimes a science', in the same sense that Frederic Lane was concerned with developing systematic work on temporality. The mix of artistic and scientific orientations is best judged by how their combinations of imagination and rigour produce fresh understanding by linking diverse elements together in causal stories. Not just the what, but the why and the how.

When Hofstadter invited historians and social scientists to the feast of analytical history, he did so without much specification of means and difficulties. These are foreseeable. A passion for detail can feed narrative overconfidence. A passion for structure can lead to excessive simplification in the 'search for explanations in terms of a relatively limited set of enduring, entrenched, and causally powerful features of the social world'. The search for less exaggerated and productive combined efforts, the historian and political scientist William Sewell has contended, should lead us to view events not just as facts but as 'significant happenings'. What analytical history is challenged to do is to connect happenings to structures, processes and contexts, large, medium and small, rather than treating them as matters of fate and contingency. This orientation approaches temporality in ways that move beyond descriptions of experience and that seek to avoid the seductions of teleology.[56]

In crafting scholarship at the juncture where history meets political science, data does not always come in the neat bundles that appear when political scientists methodically create evidence through polling, experiments, regression analysis and other means with which to study such subjects as elections, legislative roll calls, budgets and the size of armies, in which each unit of observation can be made to count as the other. Analytical history demands systematic attention to the meaning of such data, especially quantitative data, by using methods that pay particular attention to variations to parameters, thus meeting historians on the ground of temporality and context. Further, in terms of method, most historical evidence presents limitations we can try to turn to advantage. First, we need to restrict the level of causal claiming to what might be called simplified plausibility. Second, we can compensate for the irregularity of

---

[55] Bailyn 2015.
[56] Sewell 2005, pp. 11–14, 8, 81–112. For a characterisation of the structural imperatives in work by a leading analytical historian within sociology and political science see Tilly 1984, pp. 123–43, with particular attention to what he calls encompassing comparisons.

evidence by oscillating perspectives, not investing exclusively in a single methodological or substantive basket, but by rotating axes of analysis. We can also compensate by engaging with the full range of historiographical treatments of the same case materials, and with the full range of tools they might usefully appropriate from the social sciences.

In sum, there exists a vibrant set of promising prospects and ways of proceeding to recover an active role for analytical history within political science; nothing like a fixed formula, but a set of sensibilities and orientations. This pursuit might well return us to the same great text that inspired research and teaching during the late nineteenth century: *The Peloponnesian War*. All the elements identified by Hofstadter and Lane are here, not least an astonishing narrative with a sense of the tragic, a secular history carried along through a temporal structure with key choice points and moments of critical inflection. Here we find extraordinary literature, including chilling depictions of atrocities, and rigorous exposition based on methodological choices that are made explicit. The text identifies a balance between chance and necessity, and moves fluidly between the local and the global; between reality and signification; among levels of uncertainty and decision; accounts of the conditioning qualities of political regimes; matters of political psychology; the powers of rhetoric; the distinction between friends and enemies – and all this embedded within theories of motivation and a structural account of empire, global power and international relations realism. The work is both a contemporary history and timeless. It is committed to objectivity, accuracy, truth and fact based on rigorous observation and evidence. And it selects out the most powerful causes from among many possibilities. Ambition, interest, honour, fear and power are linked in what essentially is an institutional and political account of cause and effect. The text also contains what seem like very modern considerations of democracy versus oligarchy and the dangers of tyranny associated with both. Doing all this, Thucydides demonstrates command over the complexity and vulnerability of the human condition.[57]

One more guide, perhaps more surprising, as I close. Consider the three Cubist portraits painted by Picasso in 1910, whose subjects were his three most important art dealers: Daniel Henry Kahnweiler, Wilhelm Udhe and Ambroise Vollard. As portraits of actual persons, each much photographed and each much portrayed by other artists, these three images result from exacting decisions about the degree of abstraction that should be present in each representation.

---

[57] Mynott 2013, pp. xv–xl; Zagorin 2005.

For analytical history, it is the portrait of Vollard that offers the most compelling model. What attracts is its methodological equilibrium between history and social science. In this image, the facet planes are more delicate and complex, the passages increase between the facets; it most keeps a resemblance to the actual man. It decentres less and centres more. By reducing the weight of abstraction, it makes fewer claims to portability. Its acts of simplification, its modelling and its shadow depiction of structure and agency – its social science, as it were – are more like the world historians portray.

Simply put, when Picasso painted Vollard, he showed what a particular kind of social science could become. Unlike the organicist formulas that first linked political science and history in the middle to late nineteenth century, this Cubist portraiture makes ample room for variety and contradiction, and different levels of abstraction, all the while demonstrating that decomposing history into facets and elements that can be causally recombined is not just a matter of science but of quite striking art.

Would that we could convene an analytical history seminar moderated by Hofstadter, attended by Frederick Watkins, and addressed by Thucydides and Picasso!

References

Adams, C. F. 1902. 'An Undeveloped Function', *American Historical Review*, 7: 2, pp. 203–32.

Adams, Herbert B. 1895. 'Is History Past Politics?', *Johns Hopkins University Studies in Historical and Political Science*, 13th series, 3–4, pp. 67–81.

Adcock, Robert. 2003. 'The Emergence of Political Science as a Discipline: History and the Study of Politics in America, 1875–1910', *History of Political Thought*, 24: 3, pp. 481–508.

Adcock, Robert and Mark Bevir. 2010. 'Political Science' in *The History of the Social Sciences since 1945*, ed. Roger E. Backhouse and Philippe Fontaine. Cambridge.

Anderson, Perry. 1974. *Lineages of the Absolutist State*. London.

Bailyn, Bernard. 2015. *Sometimes an Art: Nine Essays on History*. New York.

Bates, Robert H. et al. 1998. *Analytic Narratives*. Princeton.

Berndtson, Erkki. 1983. 'Political Science and Democracy: Four Phases of the Development in American Political Democracy' in *Exploring the Basis of Politics: Five Essays on the Politics of Experience. Language, Knowledge, and History*, ed. Ilkka Heiskanen and Sakari Hänninen. Tampere.

Bowen, Norman. 1983. 'Professionalism, Reform and Organic Theory in the Founding of the Social Sciences', *Revue française d'études américaines*, 16, pp. 11–22.

Burgess, J. W. 1897. 'Political Science and History' in *Annual Report of the American Historical Association for the Year 1896, Volume I*. Washington.

Bury, J. B. 1903. *The Science of History: An Inaugural Lecture Delivered in the Divinity School Cambridge on January 26, 1903*. Cambridge.

Clark, Christopher. 2012. 'Power' in *A Concise Companion to History*, ed. Ulinka Rublack. Oxford.

Cochran, Thomas C. 1948. 'The "Presidential Synthesis" in American History', *American Historical Review*, 53: 4, pp. 748–59.

1956. 'The Social Sciences and the Problem of Historical Synthesis' in *Varieties of History*, ed. Fritz Stern. New York.

Collini, Stephan, Donald Winch and John Burrow. 1983. *The Noble Science of Politics: A Study in Nineteenth Century Intellectual History*. Cambridge.

de Swaan, Abram. 1988. *In Care of the State*. New York.

Evans, Peter, Dietrich Rueschemeyer and Theda Skocpol, eds. 1985. *Bringing the State Back In*. Cambridge.

Gaddis, John Lewis. 2002. *The Landscape of History: How Historians Map the Past*. New York.

Heaney, Michael T. 2007. 'The Chicago School that Never Was', *PA: Political Science and Politics*, 40: 4, pp. 753–8.

Heaney, Michael T. and John Mark Hansen. 2006. 'Building the Chicago School', *American Political Science Review*, 100, pp. 589–96.

Hedström, Peter and Richard Swedberg, eds. 1998. *Social Mechanisms: An Analytical Approach to Social Theory*. Cambridge.

Higham, John. 1979. 'The Matrix of Specialization' in *The Organization of Knowledge in America, 1860–1920*, ed. Alexandra Oleson and John Voss. Baltimore.

Hofstadter, Richard. 1944. *Social Darwinism in American Thought, 1860–1915*. Philadelphia.

1948. *The American Political Tradition*. New York.

1949. 'From Calhoun to the Dixiecrats', *Social Research*, 26 (June), pp. 135–50.

1954–5. 'The Pseudo-Conservative Revolt', *The American Scholar*, 24 (Winter), pp. 9–27.

1955. *The Age of Reform: From Bryan to F.D.R.* New York.

1956. 'History and the Social Sciences, in *Varieties of History*, ed. Fritz Stern. New York.

1965. *The Paranoid Style in American Politics*. New York.

Johns Hopkins University Studies in Historical and Political Science. 1883. Series 1–2. Baltimore.

Kagan, Jerome. 2009. *The Three Cultures*. Cambridge.

Katznelson, Ira. 1986. 'Knowledge about What? Policy Intellectuals and the New Liberalism' in *States, Social Knowledge, and the Origins of Modern Social Policies*, ed. Dietrich Rueschemeyer and Theda Skocpol. Princeton.

2003a. 'The Possibilities of Analytical History' in *The Democratic Experiment: New Directions in American Political History*, ed. Meg Jacobs, William J. Novak and Julian Zelizer. Princeton.

2003b. *Desolation and Enlightenment: Political Knowledge after Total War, Totalitarianism, and the Holocaust*. New York.

Katznelson, Ira and Helen Milner, eds. 2002. *Political Science: State of the Discipline*. New York.

Key, V. O., Jr. 1955. 'A Theory of Critical Elections', *Journal of Politics*, 17: 1, pp. 3–18.

1961. *Public Opinion and American Democracy*. New York.

1966. *The Responsible Electorate: Rationality in Presidential Voting, 1938–1960*. Cambridge, MA.

Kitson Clark, G. 1967. *The Critical Historian*. London.

Lane, Frederic C. 1955. Review of *The Social Sciences in Historical Study*, *Journal of Economic History*, 15, pp. 65–67.

Lowell, A. 1910. 'The Physiology of Politics', *American Political Science Review*, 4, pp. 1–15.

Mahoney, James and Kathleen Thelen, eds. 2015. *Advances in Comparative Historical Analysis*. New York.

'The Meeting of the American Historical Association in Philadelphia'. 2003. *American Historical Review*, 8: 3, p. 421.

Merriam, Charles Edward. 1900. *History of the Theory of Sovereignty since Rousseau*. New York.

1903. *A History of American Political Theories*. London and New York.

1921. 'The Present State of the Study of Politics', *American Political Science Review*, 15, pp. 173–85.

Moore, Barrington, Jr. 1966. *Social Origins of Dictatorship and Democracy: Lord and Peasant in the Making of the Modern World*. Boston.

Mynott, Jeremy. 2013. 'Introduction' in Thucydides, *The War of the Peloponnesians and the Athenians*. Cambridge.

Nettl, J. P. 1968. 'The State as a Conceptual Variable', *World Politics*, 20: 4, pp. 559–92.

Novick, Peter. 1988. *That Noble Dream: The 'Objectivity Question' and the American Historical Profession*. New York.

Orren, Karen and Stephen Skowronek. 1986. 'Editors' Preface', *Studies in American Political Development*, 1, pp. vii–viii.

2002. 'The Study of American Political Development' in *Political Science: State of the Discipline*, ed. Ira Katznelson and Helen Milner. New York.

Pierson, Paul and Theda Skocpol. 2002. 'Historical Institutionalism in Contemporary Political Science' in *Political Science: State of the Discipline*, ed. Ira Katznelson and Helen Milner. New York.

Potter, David M. 1955. 'Review', *American Quarterly*, 7, pp. 78–81.

Schlesinger, Arthur M., Jr. 1945. *The Age of Jackson*. Boston.

1957–60. *The Age of Roosevelt*. 3 vols. Boston.

Sewell, William H., Jr. 2005. *Logics of History: Social Theory and Social Transformation*. Chicago.

Shepard, Walter James. 1925. 'Political Science' in *The History and Prospects of the Social Sciences*, ed. Harry Elmer Barnes. New York.

Skocpol, Theda. 1979. *States and Social Revolutions: A Comparative Analysis of Social Revolutions in Russia, France, and China*. New York.

Smith, Rogers M. 1997. 'Still Blowing in the Wind: The American Quest for a Democratic, Scientific Political Science' in *American Academic Culture in Transformation*, ed. Thomas Bender and Carl E. Schorske. Princeton.

Social Science Research Council. 1954. *The Social Sciences in Historical Study: A Report of the Committee on Historiography*. Bulletin 64.

Stern, Fritz, ed. 1956. *Varieties of History*. New York.

Tilly, Charles, ed. 1975. *The Formation of National States in Western Europe*. Princeton.

Tilly, Charles. 1984. *Big Structures, Large Processes, and Huge Comparisons*. New York.

Truman, David B. 1951. *The Governmental Process: Political Interests and Public Opinion*. New York.

1959. *The Congressional Party: A Case Study*. New York.

Tsou Tang. 1951. 'A Study of the Development of the Scientific Approach in Political Studies in the United States, with Particular Emphasis on the Methodological Aspects of the Works of Charles E. Merriam and Harold D. Lasswell'. PhD thesis, University of Chicago.

Turner, Frederick Jackson. 1893. 'The Significance of the Frontier in American History' in *Annual Report of the American Historical Association*. Washington.

Wallerstein, Immanuel. 1974.*The Modern World System*. New York.

Watkins, Frederick Mundell. 1934. *The State as a Concept of Political Science*. New York.

Wawro, Gregory J. and Ira Katznelson. 2020. 'American Political Development and New Challenges of Causal Inference', *Public Choice*, 185, pp. 299–314.

Willoughby, Westel. 1911. *Examination of the Nature of the State: A Study in Political Philosophy*. New York.

Wilson, Woodrow. 1887. 'The Study of Administration', *Political Science Quarterly*, 2, pp. 197–222.

Wong, Bin. 2012. 'Causation' in *A Concise Companion to History*, ed. Ulinka Rublack. Oxford.

Zagorin, Perez. 2005. *Thucydides: An Introduction for the Common Reader*. Princeton.

12   Making History: Poetry and *Prosopopoeia*

Cathy Shrank

'What is Literature?' asks Terry Eagleton in the introduction to his *Literary Theory*. Discarding definitions of literature as 'fiction', as '"imaginative" writing', as '"non-pragmatic" discourse' or as texts that 'intensif[y] ordinary language, deviat[ing] systematically from everyday speech', Eagleton settles on a classification of literature as a work which 'belongs to the *type* of writing' which is 'highly valued', his emphasis on 'type' allowing even texts deemed stylistically 'inferior' to retain a literary status.[1] A definition dependent on value judgements is, of course, volatile, as Eagleton admits. Drawing on John M. Ellis's conceptualisation of 'literature' as a label like 'weed', Eagleton therefore argues that both are '*functional* rather than *ontological* terms. ... They tell us about the role of a text or a thistle in a social context', 'not about the fixed being of things'.[2]

If literature is a weed, the academics who pick through it are best described as magpies, regularly and habitually borrowing from a wide range of disciplines. 'The intellectual range and diversity of approaches in English open it up to the knowledge and practices of other subjects,' note the subject benchmarks produced by the UK's Quality Assurance Agency for Higher Education (QAA).[3] History is just one among a long list of subjects that comprise (amongst others) philology, philosophy and anthropology. The connections with history are, however, particularly close, as can be seen from institutional contexts in which English literature emerged as an academic discipline in the nineteenth century. King's College London was one of the earliest institutions to teach and examine English literature: the former from its establishment in 1831; the latter from 1859.[4] The relevant chair was in English Literature and History, the early holders of which further reveal the multi-disciplinary roots of those in charge of the subject. The theologian F. D. Maurice was elected

---

[1] Eagleton 2012, pp. 2, 7, 9–10.
[2] Eagleton 2012, p. 8, responding to Ellis 1977.
[3] QAA 2019, p. 34.
[4] Bacon 1986, p. 591.

to the chair in 1840; four years previously he had 'allowed himself to be named as a candidate for the chair of political economy at Oxford'.[5] His predecessor, Thomas Dale, was a clergyman, a translator of Sophocles, and first chair of English Language and Literature at University College, London.[6] His successor, Sir George Webbe Dasent, was one-time assistant editor at *The Times*, a translator of Norse sagas, and in 1852 – the year before taking up the post – had been called to the bar.[7] Nor was the combination of literature and history a quirk of King's: other pioneering departments (including Queen's University, Belfast, and University College of South Wales, Cardiff) followed suit when establishing their chairs; when Cambridge University launched its English Tripos in 1917, the Modern Languages Board decreed that 'literature should be studied with close reference to the history and the actual conditions under which it has grown up'.[8]

This interrelation of the two disciplines continued well after English literature had been accepted as a field of academic study. When the numbers of institutions of higher education increased in the 1960s, those new universities had the opportunity of 'designing a course from scratch'.[9] The models adopted by institutions such as the Universities of East Anglia (UEA), Sussex and York all embedded the historicised study of literature through a range of methods: compulsory modules (UEA); co-teaching (Sussex); and period papers (York).[10] Bonamy Dobrée describes such period papers as being designed 'to actualise the historical imagination', or – in Philip Brockbank's words – 'to keep us fully alive to the energies and values of the past'.[11] The historicist ambitions of the degree remain. According to subject benchmarking in the twenty-first century, the first 'aim' of an English degree is 'inspiring ... an appreciation of its [English's] past'.[12]

The focus on history – then and now – is accompanied by an emphasis on textual analysis: training in 'critical reading' which, by the mid-twentieth century, owed much to the Cambridge mode of 'practical criticism'.[13] 'We do it rather in the Cambridge manner,' David Daiches breezily explains of the methods adopted at Sussex.[14] For the Cambridge

---

[5] Reardon 2006.
[6] Burns 2010.
[7] Seccombe and Haigh 2016.
[8] Cited in Townsend 1967, p. 131.
[9] Lawlor 1962, p. 46.
[10] Watt et al. 1962.
[11] Dobrée 1962, p. 55; Brockbank 1962, p. 55.
[12] QAA 2019, p. 3.
[13] Townsend 1967, p. 129.
[14] Daiches 1962, p. 50.

scholar F. R. Leavis a crucial purpose of this training was to cultivate 'evaluative judgement', inculcating 'sensibility' and 'intelligence' that would inoculate students against naive enthusiasm for A. E. Housman's *A Shropshire Lad* or the comic prose of P. G. Wodehouse.[15] The animus is less exclusionary now, and most literary critics tend to be open to widening or even deconstructing the canon, rather than restricting it, but the language of reading 'closely and critically' is still embedded in the discipline, taking pride of place as the first item in QAA's list of subject-specific skills.[16]

Close, critical reading might be the defining disciplinary skill, yet even it cannot exist in a monodisciplinary vacuum. Literature is shaped by, and for, the time and culture in which it was composed (as well as by the time and culture in which any analysis is conducted): convincing textual analysis requires significant levels of contextual knowledge. I want to demonstrate this by providing a close and 'literary' reading of the inscription to and opening stanzas of 'Who lyst his welthe and eas Retayne' by the Henrician courtier, poet and diplomat Thomas Wyatt, a piece almost certainly written in the later 1530s:

> .*V. Innocentia*
> *Veritas Viat Fides*
> *Circumdederunt me inimici mei*
> *W*

> Who lyst his welthe and eas Retayne,
>   hym selffe let hym unknowne contayne[.]
>   Presse not to[o] Fast in at that gatte
>   wher the Retorne standis by desdayne[,]
>   for sure, circa Regna tonat[.]

> The hye montayns ar blastyd oft
>   when the lowe vaylye ys myld and soft[.]
>   Fortune with helthe stondis at debate[.]
>   The Fall is grevous Frome Aloffte[,]
>   and sure, circa Regna tonat[.][17]

In the inscription, the Latin version of Wyatt's name (Viat) is flanked by Innocence, Truth and Faith. Oddly, though, the final line – adapted from Psalm 17 (16 in the Vulgate and Great Bible), one of the psalms of

---

[15] Leavis 1948, pp. 38–9.
[16] QAA 2019, p. 5.
[17] Trinity College Dublin, MS 160, fol. 183r. When citing texts in original spelling (as opposed to modernised editions), u/v and i/j have been standardised and contractions (e.g. *y* for th-) have been silently expanded. Where necessary for sense, punctuation has been added [in square brackets].

David – announces that 'Myne enemyes [have] compasse[d] me rounde about'.[18] This reworks the psalm in a way that typifies Wyatt's translations, through its reluctance to deploy explicitly religious language: in the biblical verse, foes surround David's *anima* (soul/spirit). Further to that, it also potentially shifts our perspective on innocence, truth and faith, suggesting that the poetic speaker is at risk because of these qualities, rather than despite them.[19]

The lines that follow loosely paraphrase the final chorus of Seneca's *Phaedra*, a source to which Wyatt also turned for another anti-court lament, 'Stond whoso list'.[20] Here, that debt is highlighted by the retention of the Latin tag 'circa Regna tonat' ('around thrones it thunders').[21] The relatively short octosyllabic lines and frequent enjambment (where syntactic units run over the line-endings) keep propelling readers on towards that refrain, the rhyme it makes with the third line of every stanza ensuring that its threatening rumble is threaded through the poem, whilst the linking phrase ('for/and sure') emphasises its grim certainty. In this fickle world, Stoic self-reliance is the only available remedy (as it so often is in Wyatt's poetry): a message encapsulated in that opening couplet, its self-reflexivity epitomised by the repetition of the pronoun ('hym') and the self-completing nature of the rhyme.

Despite the seemingly autobiographical nature of the poem established by the inscription (which has versions of Wyatt's name/initials running through it), the poem opens in a curiously impersonal mode, offering advice to a generalised 'Who'. As well as avoiding references to identifiable people or situations, this stylistic decision increases the sense of jeopardy: the dangers incurred by proximity to the throne are presented as universal and inevitable, not the result of individual choices or failings. The impersonal strain of these opening stanzas is then accentuated by the way abstract qualities are transformed into allegorical figures, akin to those that populate John Skelton's satire *The Bowge of Court*:[22] Disdain appears like a doorkeeper hindering the courtier's retreat; Fortune tussles with Health (well-being), before the following line evokes the ever-turning wheel of Fortune and alters its meaning from 'success, prosperity' to 'chance'.[23] Words too prove unstable.

Even without addressing the biographical circumstances of the poem and the way it reflects the often deadly politics of the Henrician court

---

[18] The Byble in Englyshe 1539, Psalm 16:9.
[19] Compare Stamatakis 2012, p. 48.
[20] Seneca 2018, lines 1123–40.
[21] Seneca 2018, line 1140.
[22] Skelton 1499.
[23] 'health', *OED*, sense 5a; 'fortune', *OED*, senses 4, 1.

in the 1530s and 1540s, the analysis undertaken here – with its focus on metre, rhyme, syntax, diction and literary tradition – cannot exist in a purely formalist bubble. It has required knowledge of the history of philosophy (the reception of Stoic thought in Henrician England); of sixteenth-century orthographic practices (including the need to discount inconsistent use of capitalisation); and of changing pronunciation between then and now (whereby '-at' can make a full rhyme with 'gate' and 'debate'). Pushing further to unravel the reasons behind Wyatt's paraphrastic choices would lead to an investigation of his habits as a translator, and the way his semantic decisions are often prompted by the sound, rather than the exact sense, of a word in the original.[24] This in turn would lead back to the Henrician court, not as it is usually remembered as a site of tyranny and fear, but as a nexus for cutting-edge humanist scholarship, as found in the production of the first large-scale Latin–English dictionary, compiled by Wyatt's contemporary Thomas Elyot in the late 1530s (printed 1538), using books from the king's library, and sponsored by Wyatt's own patron and protector, Thomas Cromwell. Certainly, some of the English vocabulary that Wyatt uses in his Senecan translations match the definitions found in Elyot's *Dictionary*.[25] Literary studies, then, has fuzzy boundaries, and it is often unclear where 'text' ends and 'context' begins. The analysis conducted above is of a piece with C. S. Lewis's insistence that students (and critics) of literature pay attention to 'the whole context of a work: the historical and intellectual framework of its time, the conventions of its genre, and the expectations of its audience', an endeavour which includes 'the work's semantics, its hard words, especially ones that had changed their meaning over time'.[26]

The chapter that follows argues for the proximity of history and literature, and the challenges, and even the undesirability, of disaggregating the underpinning skills and techniques of the two disciplines. It does so from a quite particular perspective. As noted above, 'literature' is a capacious subject, which regularly draws on other disciplines. As someone who self-identifies in research terms as either a 'literary historian' or – by period, rather than discipline – as an 'early modernist', my affiliations are patently historicist. There are also very different traditions of teaching and approaching literature in different linguistic cultures, as can be seen in the way that – when setting up the English Literature Tripos in Cambridge in the 1910s – Arthur Quiller-Couch celebrated a degree that would signal 'the end of the old German method of teaching modern

---

[24] Shrank 2016, pp. 592–3.
[25] Shrank 2016, p. 592.
[26] Quoted in Barbour 1999, p. 441.

languages, the method inseparably bound up with philology, with the dead moulding bones of sound changes, syntactical form, and all the rest of it'.[27] My focus is therefore necessarily narrow, restricted to English literature, and – for the most part – drawing on sixteenth-century examples: a period when there is only an emergent concept of literature as *belles lettres*, and much of whose writing has been subject to critical disfavour and scorn. Witness C. S. Lewis's labelling of the mid-sixteenth century as 'Drab': 'an earnest, heavy-handed, commonplace age', the deficiencies of which are exemplified by Thomas Peend and Alexander Neville, both deemed 'very, very bad' poets.[28]

'Literature' before 1600 meant, not 'fiction' or 'creative writing', but what the *Oxford English Dictionary* defines as a more general 'familiarity with letters or books' and the 'knowledge acquired from reading or studying books, esp[ecially] the principal classical texts associated with humane learning'.[29] We can see the early moderns starting to feel their way towards a conception of what we now call 'literature' – that is, 'a body of literary works', particularly 'written work valued for superior or lasting artistic merit' – when Philip Sidney observes *circa* 1582 in his *Defence of Poesy* that 'one may be a poet without versing, and a versifier without poetry'.[30] Sidney uses 'poetry' – not to indicate verse – but as a way of defining a body of fictive writing. The use of the suffix *-ive* here encapsulates that sense of nascency or hybridity: 'having a tendency to', rather than 'being'.[31]

Much of Sidney's *Defence* seeks (tongue-in-cheek) to set poetry above the rival disciplines of philosophy and history. His endeavours, however, soon blur the boundaries between them, as he demonstrates the indebtedness of those other arts to poetry: 'the philosophers of Greece durst not a long time appear to the world but under the mask of poets'; 'historiographers, although their lips sound of things done, and verity be written in their foreheads, have been glad to borrow both the fashions, and perchance weight of Poets'.[32] Nor is 'history' as 'captived to the truth' as Sidney contends.[33] The primary meaning of the term – 'a narration of incidents' – does not guarantee its grounding in fact, as the frequent and often misleading need to assert that something was a 'true' history suggests.[34] This more fictional meaning of 'history' can be seen in Bernard

---

[27] Cited in Townsend 1967, p. 131.
[28] Lewis 1954, pp. 250, 255.
[29] 'literature', *OED*, sense 1.
[30] 'literature', *OED*, senses 3a, 3b; Sidney 2004 [1580], p. 32.
[31] '-ive', *OED*.
[32] Sidney 2004 [1580], p. 5.
[33] Sidney 2004 [1580], p. 21.
[34] 'history', *OED*, sense 1b.

Garter's *Tragicall and true history that happened between two English Lovers*, an imitation of Arthur Brooke's *Tragicall historie of Romeus and Juliet*, or Thomas Lodge's *Famous, true and historicall life of Robert second Duke of Normandy*,[35] which recounts the transformation of its protagonist from problem-child (the first of whose many violent acts is to bite off the Lady of Sancerre's nose as she croons over him in his cradle) into the quasi-saint-like figure who saves Rome from Saracen hordes: a life-history bearing scant resemblance to the biography of the actual second duke, Robert the Magnificent (1000–35).

Unlike Sidney's *Defence*, *The Art of English Poesy* (printed in 1586 and usually attributed to George Puttenham) does adopt a formal definition of poetry (as verse). Nonetheless, it shares Sidney's fluid approach to disciplinary boundaries; throughout the volume 'poem or history' form a synonymous pairing.[36] This expansive view of 'poetry' is further evidenced by the opening chapters, which chart its earliest usages, claiming that:

It is written that poesy was the original cause and occasion of [humans'] first assemblies, when before the people remained in the woods and mountains, vagrant and dispersed like the wild beasts, lawless and naked, or very ill-clad, and of all good and necessary provision for harbour or sustenance utterly unfurnished, so as they little differed for their manner of life, from the very brute beasts of the field.[37]

Puttenham here appropriates for poetry a civilisation myth which attributes to the power of eloquence the founding of cities and establishing of laws: a myth that can be traced back through Cicero's *De Inventione* to Plato and Isocrates. Puttenham thus makes poetry synonymous with rhetoric and with composition more broadly, as poets are declared 'the first priests', 'the first prophets', 'the first lawmakers', 'politicians', 'philosophers', 'astronomers and historiographers', 'orators and musicians': proof, should any be needed, that – in the sixteenth century at least – '"non-pragmatic" discourse' does not work as a definition of literature.[38] Indeed, for Puttenham the function of poetry is primarily didactic: a means of conveying important information in a memorable form. 'The chief and principal [use] is the laud, honour and glory of the immortal gods,' he writes. 'Secondly the worthy gests [deeds] of noble princes, the memorial and registry of all great fortunes, the praise of virtue and

---

[35] Garter 1565; Brooke 1562; Lodge 1591.
[36] Puttenham 2004 [1589], pp. 77, 79, 92, 94.
[37] Puttenham 2004 [1589], p. 60.
[38] Puttenham 2004 [1589], pp. 60–2; the term '"non-pragmatic" discourse' is used in Eagleton 2012, p. 7.

reproof of vice, the instruction of moral doctrines, the revealing of sciences natural and other profitable arts, the redress [aid] of boisterous and sturdy courages by persuasion.'[39] Poetry thus encapsulates a range of disciplines, from moral philosophy to history, and is designed to meet various purposes, from teaching to inspiring action. It is only 'finally' that Puttenham arrives at the 'recreation[al]' use of poetry: 'the common solace of mankind in all his travails and cares of this transitory life. And in this last sort, being used for recreation only, may allowably bear matter not always of the gravest, or of any great commodity or profit'.[40]

This sliding notion of poetry/literature, and its relationship to history, is not merely espoused by apologists for the literary arts in sixteenth-century England; it is also evident in its historiography. Composed in 1553 and printed posthumously in 1570, Roger Ascham's *Report and discourse of the affaires and state of Germany* provides an account of the 'great stirs' in the Holy Roman Empire in the early 1550s, when Ascham was serving as secretary to one of England's ambassadors. Citing his historical models, Ascham lists Livy, Caesar, Polybius, Philippe de Comines and Thucydides; but he also joins these bona fide historians with Homer and with 'our *Chaucer*', whose only claim to something resembling 'historical' poetry is his romance *Troilus and Criseyde*, where Chaucer self-consciously plays with ideas of 'truth' by concocting a fictional source ('Lollius') for his narrative, which is in fact derived from Boccaccio's poem *Il Filostrato*.[41] Ascham's choice of Chaucer as a vernacular exemplar (over chroniclers, such as Edward Hall, whom he might have mentioned) is perhaps explained by his view of history as 'character in action'.[42] Chaucer's poem provides a model for Ascham's historiographical method because it gives expression, and therefore access, to the inner workings of its characters in a way that chronicle habitually does not. Ascham's *Report* confidently ascribes motivation to its historical agents – as when Pope Julius III 'gave good eare to this talke, for he spied that hereby should be offered unto him, a fit occasion to set the Emperour and *Fraunce* together by the eares' – or delineates their emotions, such as the 'wonderfull gelousy' towards Albert, duke of Prussia, conceived 'in the Emperours head'.[43] Similarly, Ascham's narrative recounts, not just words that have been said (to which he has not been witness), but how those words have been pronounced: 'earnestly',

---

[39] Puttenham 2004 [1589], p. 76.
[40] Puttenham 2004 [1589], p. 76.
[41] Ascham 1570, sig. A4r.
[42] Ryan 1963, p. 171.
[43] Ascham 1570, sigs. C2r, E4v.

'roundly and plainly', 'smiling', 'gently and quietly'.[44] At times, for additional immediacy, such speeches are given in direct, not indirect, speech, as when Albert 'soddenly brast out into a fury saying: what devill? will the Emperour never leave strivyng with God in defacyng true Religion and tossyng the world in debarryng all mens liberties?'[45]

Here – as Ascham adopts Albert's voice – we see him deploying the rhetorical device of *prosopopoeia*: a 'figure ... that to stirre and moove affection, attributeth speech to dead men, or to wals & such like'.[46] *Prosopopoeia* is one of the rhetorical figures that feature prominently, not just in the works of the classical poets, but also the classical historians studied, and emulated, as part of the humanist curriculum that dominated western Europe from the end of the fifteenth century. As Sidney writes in the *Defence*, the ancient Greek historian Herodotus 'and all the rest that followed him, either st[o]le or usurped of poetry their passionate describing of passions, the many particularities of battles which no man could affirm, or ... long orations put in the mouths of great kings and captains, which it is certain they never pronounced'.[47] In *How to Write History*, the second-century rhetorician Lucian strives to draw distinctions between the composition of poetry and history, particularly regarding the latter's use of passages of purple prose. He attacks those misguided historians who 'seem unaware that history has aims and rules different from poetry and poems'.[48] Concise expression is commended: 'Rapidity is everywhere useful, especially if there is no lack of material; and one must look to the subject matter to provide this rather than to the words and phrases.'[49] Outbreaks of evocative prose merit his particular disdain. 'You need especial discretion in descriptions of mountains, fortifications, and rivers, to avoid the appearance of a tasteless display of word-power and of indulging your own interests at the expense of the history,' he cautions.[50] Nonetheless, despite his call for a stripped-back style, Lucian gives historians a notably freer rein when deploying *prosopopoeia*: 'If a person has to be introduced to make a speech, above all let his language suit his person and his subject, and next let these also be as clear as possible. It is then, however, that you can play the orator and show your eloquence.'[51] Lucian thus treats this rhetorical figure

---

[44] Ascham 1570, sigs. C1v, E4v, F1r, F3r.
[45] Ascham 1570, sig. F2v.
[46] Anon 1598, sig. *2v.
[47] Sidney 2004 [1580], p. 6.
[48] Lucian 1959, p. 8.
[49] Lucian 1959, p. 56.
[50] Lucian 1959, p. 57.
[51] Lucian 1959, p. 58.

differently from the figures of *topographia* (description of place) and *pragmatographia* (description of action), granting *prosopopoeia* a privileged place in the historian's toolkit.

Unsurprisingly, considering its centrality to both classical literature and history, *prosopopoeia* was a rhetorical figure that was taught and rigorously practised in the early modern classroom. The role of imitation and the use of models for developing pupils' linguistic style are well established in the historiography of Renaissance education.[52] John Brinsley's *Ludus Literarius* was printed in 1612 in response to the rapid increase in the number of schools by the early seventeenth century, and the subsequent strain that placed on recruiting sufficient numbers of suitably trained masters. Brinsley's dialogue is not revolutionary in method but is rather designed to help inexperienced and provincial teachers (the 'younger sort', and those of 'the poore Countrey schooles') by disseminating good practice gleaned from the author's own career and from consultation with 'happily experienced Schoolemasters'.[53] As such, it provides a useful guide to standard schoolroom practice in this period. Brinsley's spokesperson, Philoponus, puts great emphasis not just on reading *prosopopoeia* but also on its oral performance. After construing and parsing dialogic texts, such as Evaldus Gallus's *Pueriles confabulatiunculae* (1565) or Mathurin Cordier's *Colloquia scholastica* (1564), pupils should then 'talk together; uttering every sentence pathetically one to another'.[54] The inclusion of the adjective 'pathetically' is important. Students are not simply required to go through the motions, droning out the words on the page: they are expected to pronounce the words in such a way as to evoke appropriate emotions in their auditors. Doing so demands an act of imagination on the speaker's part. 'Cause [your pupils] to utter every dialogue lively, as if they themselves were the persons which did speake in that dialogue,' Philoponus urges, '& so in every other speech, to imagine themselves to have occasion to utter the very same thing.'[55] The practice of impersonation thus begins with these very basic schoolroom colloquia: Gallus and Cordier are simple texts, designed for the early stages of language learning. Nevertheless, it is an approach that pupils were expected to continue and refine as they proceeded up the school: 'So after when they shall come to Virgils Eclogues,' Philoponus instructs,

---

[52] See, e.g., Boswell 1986, pp. 109–11; Halpern 1991, esp. pp. 19–60.
[53] Brinsley 1612, sigs. ¶1r, *1r, ¶3r.
[54] Brinsley 1612, sig. 2F1r.
[55] Brinsley 1612, sig. 2E3r.

cause them yet still more lively, in saying without booke, to expresse the affections and persons of sheepeheards or whose speech soever else, which they are to imitate. Of which sort are the Prosopopeyes of Jupiter, Apollo, and others in Ovids Metamorphosis, Juno, Neptune, AEolus, Aeneas, Venus, Dido &c. [in] Virgils AEneids.[56]

Processes of impersonation that began with the elementary colloquies are consequently carried over into the performance and interpretation of other, more complex works, and, from there, into the pupils' own compositions: the sort of exercise (giving voice to the dead) that we can see being conducted in surviving school notebooks, such as the one compiled by a young William Badger, around 1565, which – amongst other exercises – contains a scene between the emperor Nero and his mistress Poppaea.[57] *Nero et Poppaea simul loquuntur* reads the heading ('Nero and Poppaea talk together').

For Lucian, 'history' (ἱστορία) 'has one task and one end – what is useful – and that comes from truth [ἀλήθεια] alone'; to history belongs 'the publication of the truth'.[58] The trouble is that the historical record is inevitably incomplete: voices are missing, which is perhaps why Lucian gives more leeway to historians when crafting speeches than he does to other linguistic 'embellishments' (ὑπερβολή).[59] It is in response to the fragmentary nature of the historical record that we see *prosopopoeia* being deployed by the mid-Tudor writers behind the *Mirror for Magistrates*, a collection of verse complaints published in ever-expanding editions from 1559, in which the assembled poets 'take upon [themselves] the ... person[s]' of various figures from fourteenth- and fifteenth-century English history.[60] Like early modern schoolboys, the poets are shown delivering these prosopopeys orally: they gather to read out their compositions to the rest of the group. The project, coordinated by the printer-poet William Baldwin, is intensely aware of the partiality of history: its incompleteness, but also its concomitant biases. The prose-frame, in which the poets discuss each other's efforts and the endeavour in hand, recurrently draws attention to the gaps in the record and the contingent nature of historical 'truth'. 'I wyll so far as my memorie and judgement serveth, sumwhat further you in the truth of the story,' states George Ferrers.[61] His reference to the limits of his memory and judgement qualify the possibility of arriving at the 'truth' even as he promises to help to do so.

[56] Brinsley 1612, sig. 2E3r.
[57] British Library Add. MS 4379, fols. 143r–145r.
[58] Lucian 1959, p. 9.
[59] Lucian 1959, p. 8.
[60] Baldwin et al. 1938 [1559], p. 71.
[61] Baldwin et al. 1938 [1559], p. 71.

The work thus foregrounds the subjectivity of history and its self-perpetuating incompleteness, as when the contributors comment on the dearth of information about Richard, duke of Cambridge, who is 'litle favoured of wryters, for our Cronicles speake very little of him'.[62]

The *Mirror* spawned two important literary legacies: it was a source for Elizabethan history plays (notably Shakespeare's) and a model for the verse complaints, particularly female-voiced complaint, in vogue in the 1590s, as witnessed by works such as Samuel Daniel's *Complaint of Rosamond* (1592), Thomas Lodge's *Elstred* (1593), or Michael Drayton's *Matilda* (1594). The women in these poems demand that their poet-auditors rescue them from the 'blacke oblivion' that 'hath too long concealed them', writing down their stories, which other pens have 'overpasse[d]'.[63] By the end of the sixteenth century the popular re-telling of history – through drama and poetic complaint – consequently relied on *prosopopoeia* and writers imagining their way into different voices: exactly the sort of exercise practised by generations of humanistically educated schoolboys, such as Daniel, Drayton, Lodge and Shakespeare. The development of English literature is explained, in part, by the history of education. *Prosopopoeia* becomes a means of making space for and commemorating not just major figures (such as Richard II or Owen Glendower) but also those 'overskipped' by historians and chroniclers.[64] These are people like the blacksmith Michael Joseph who helped lead the 1497 Cornish Rebellion, or Edward IV's paramour, Mistress Shore (whose first name remains lost to history, so that her identity is forever tied to the men in her life). As the historical novelist Hilary Mantel observes, some 450 years later: 'Many writers of historical fiction feel drawn to the untold tale. They want to give a voice to those who have been silenced.'[65]

Mantel reserves for fiction the ability (or even the right) to 'give a voice to those who have been silenced'. However, 'the gaps, the erasures, the silences' which she encountered, and which 'made [her] into a novelist', are a challenge for historians too.[66] It is striking that the use of *prosopopoeia* is witnessing a resurgence in the writing of twenty-first-century public-facing history, where it is once again both a means of bringing the past 'alive' for non-specialists and a response to lacunae in the available evidence, often with a social or gendered agenda, glimpsed,

---

[62] Baldwin et al. 1938 [1559], p. 142.
[63] Drayton 1594, sig. B1r; Daniel 1592, sig. I1v.
[64] Baldwin et al. 1938 [1559], p. 219.
[65] Mantel 2017b, p. 6.
[66] Mantel 2017a, p. 5.

in embryonic form, in the *Mirror*'s complaints of the Blacksmith and Shore's Wife, which seek to retrieve the perspective and experiences of figures otherwise marginalised from the historical record due to their class and/or gender.

The seventeenth-century antiquarian John Aubrey was all too aware of the transience and subsequent incompleteness of historical evidence. He witnessed the razing of monastic ruins; the use of old manuscripts as endpapers or scrap; and he describes his *Brief Lives* as the detritus of a shipwreck: *tanquam tabulata naufragii*, a phrase he recycles in the preface to his life of Thomas Hobbes.[67] Kate Bennett's edition preserves the imperfections of his manuscripts: the spaces he left to fill later but never returned to; the cropped marginalia; the erasures (for example, signalling excised leaves with blank pages).[68] When researching Aubrey's biography, Ruth Scurr had to work with information about Aubrey's life that was just as fragmentary; her solution was to turn to *prosopopoeia*, constructing a diary for Aubrey, written in the first person, 'us[ing] as many as possible of his own words'.[69] Her introduction lays out her reasoning:

When I was searching for a biographical form that would suit the remnants of his life, I realised that he would all but vanish inside a conventional biography, crowded out by his friends, acquaintances and their multitudinous interests. Aubrey lived through fascinating times and has long been valued for what can be seen through him; there is no shortage of scholars who appreciated the use that can be made of him. But the biographer has other purposes: to get as close to her subject and his sensibility as possible; to produce a portrait that captures at least something of what that person was like.[70]

Scurr explicitly distinguishes what she does from the historical novelist; unlike them, she does not permit herself to 'invent scenes', but the form that she adopts – *prosopopoeia* – is nonetheless a fictive one: a literary technique that allows the historical subject (in Scurr's words) to 'liv[e] vividly', paradoxically achieving a version of 'truth' that sticking to the letter of the record cannot.[71]

Scurr also implicitly differentiates the task of the biographer from that of the more 'conventional' historian (her author's note lists these as two separate roles). For Scurr, the biographer's task goes beyond reconstructing and narrating events in their subject's life and the times in which they lived: key to the work of the biographer is the excavation,

[67] Aubrey 1898, pp. 9, 18.
[68] Aubrey 2015.
[69] Scurr 2015, p. 12.
[70] Scurr 2015, p. 11.
[71] Scurr 2015, p. 12.

and reanimation, of their subject's personality. *Prosopopoeia* therefore provides a useful way of recovering voices, and persons, whose experience otherwise remains un- or only partially documented. Miranda Kaufmann's 2017 *Black Tudors*, the subtitle of which announces that it is 'the untold story', is a case in point. In the vignettes that preface each chapter, we see an event imagined through the eyes of each of these 'Black Tudors'; we hear their thoughts, as well as the words they exchange with others:

Diego ran headlong through the gunshot towards the boats on the beach. 'Are you Captain Drake's?' he cried. He had to get on board.[72]

There, she was ready. What did the French character in that old play call the black maid? A 'black swan, silk'ner then Signet's plush'.[73]

In the process, Kaufmann mingles *prosopopeia* with other literary techniques, not least the combination of focalisation – the perspective from which events are related – and free indirect discourse associated with modernist prose.

The 'Sheffield Lives' walking trail is more conventionally prosopopoeic, but equally invested in salvaging neglected voices, in this case those of women and the 'lower sorts': the non-elite voices that are often 'overskipped' by history (to echo the *Mirror* poets embarking on a similar mission of recuperation). The route recovers early modern Sheffield, much of which has been effaced by the industrial city which developed after 1800, by tracing a chronological journey through the sixteenth- and seventeenth-century city. Walkers pause at significant sites to hear 'audio tales from characters, based on real historical figures': people such as Kelham Homer (the city's armourer); Widow Revell, who operated the city mills during the Civil War in the mid-seventeenth century; an anonymous almswoman describing the destruction wreaked during the siege of Sheffield (1644); or the three Shore brothers who guarded the roof of Sheffield Castle during its demolition to stop people stealing the lead. Their stories make tangible the intellectual agenda of the 'new' social history, and its desire – from the 1960s onwards – to reclaim the experience of non-elites and to write history 'from below'.[74]

The format of both these prosopopoeic projects functions rather like twenty-first-century practices of heritage restoration, which leave the new repairs clearly distinguishable from the old and 'authentic': devices alert readers/auditors to the fictive nature of these endeavours, be it

---

[72] Kaufmann 2017, p. 56.
[73] Kaufmann 2017, p. 219.
[74] Wrightson 2003, pp. 9–16. See also Sheffield Lives 2022.

through Kaufmann's use of italic, distinguishing the vignettes from the biographies that follow, or Sheffield Lives's description of the figures it features as 'characters'. Nonetheless, for all the artifice, these are historical projects, and not 'just' biographical ones: they vocalise, and thus animate, previously muted historical figures in order to restore missing pieces of the past. Enabled by literary techniques, these individual stories are a way of telling a larger national (or even global) story.

If literary techniques of composition have a role to play in historiography and in conceptualising the purpose of history (as an act of restoration), then so too do literary texts and modes of analysis. When arguing for 'the importance of reading and interpreting complex texts' (i.e., literature) as part of historical investigation, Dominick LaCapra differentiates between the 'worklike' and the 'documentary' aspects of texts.[75] For LaCapra, a 'work' is a sustained composition which, requiring artifice to shape it, 'supplement[s] empirical reality by adding to and subtracting from it'.[76] 'Works' consequently comprise 'non-literary' texts as well as 'literary' ones (I am here using 'literary' in the dominant modern sense): Hegel's exploration of consciousness, *The Phenomenology of Mind*, as well as Dostoyevsky's novel *The Brothers Karamazov*. 'Documents', meanwhile, are constituted by texts such as tax rolls, wills and registers of inquisitions. However, LaCapra soon breaks down the distinction between the modes, just as Sidney's division of poetry and history proved unsustainable in his *Defence*. As LaCapra states, 'the work is situated in history in a way that gives it documentary dimensions, and the document has worklike aspects'. Analysing a 'work' in a 'purely formalistic way' produces a partial reading, by neglecting its documentary elements – what it can tell us about the past – just as overlooking the worklike dimensions of a document risks 'filter[ing]' out' 'its relations to sociopolitical processes'.[77] For instance, Lodge's *Life of Robert second Duke of Normandy* (mentioned earlier) will help little in terms of retrieving information about Robert the Magnificent, William the Conqueror's father, but its erasure or downplaying of the ritualistic or supernatural elements found in the source material (such as almsgiving or angelic visitations) and its generic status as a conversion narrative can tell us something about the pressures of being a Catholic convert (as Lodge was) in post-Reformation England. Form matters as well as content. To give another, more recent – and more personal – example of interactions between literature and history and the interpretative value of acknowledging literary convention: my

---

[75] LaCapra 1983, pp. 15, 30.
[76] LaCapra 1983, p. 30.
[77] LaCapra 1983, p. 31.

childhood reading in the 1970s and 1980s was dominated by material about resisting totalitarian regimes or surviving apocalyptic forces (pandemics; nuclear holocaust; alien invasion) that had wiped out the way we live now and, in most cases, all but a few teenagers. This mode of writing was clearly, on one level, a response to the Cold War, but it is equally part of a tradition of children's fiction whose young protagonists attain autonomy because of the absence of their parents, be it through their death or, less drastically, genre (fantasy) or location (boarding school; the summer holidays). An old formula, found in late nineteenth- and early twentieth-century fiction, such as E. Nesbit's *The Phoenix and the Carpet* (1904), Frances Hodgson Burnett's *The Secret Garden* (1911) or Arthur Ransome's *Swallows and Amazons* series (1930), is reapplied to new, more politicised contexts.

When interpreting a text in its context, the literary critic's task shares much with that of the historian. Both need what R. G. Collingwood calls '*a priori* imagination', which 'bridg[es] the gaps between what our authorities tell us'.[78] Without that deductive process there would be 'no narrative to adorn'.[79] However, the 'act of interpolation' – of filling the gaps – comes with risks.[80] To return to Wyatt. My earlier analysis of 'Who lyst' skirted round one of the ways in which his poetry is frequently read, namely, biographically, and above all in regard to his rumoured relationship with Anne Boleyn before her attachment to Henry VIII. Wyatt's poems are undoubtedly characterised by a forceful sense of the first person. In part, this is the result of many of them being translated from inflected languages such as Latin and Italian, which require embedded pronouns to be extrapolated into English, increasing their prominence (so, for example, the Italian verb 'trovo' becomes 'I find'). However, Wyatt also maximises this linguistic effect, turning poems addressed to a second-person other into poems exploring a first-person experience, intensifying that sense of self-examination, as in Wyatt's 'Though I my self be bridled of my mind', translating Petrarch's *rima* 98 ('Orso, al vostro destrier' ('Orso, on your charger')).[81]

Nevertheless, for all their seeming confessional nature, Wyatt's poems are also typically opaque. This tendency is perhaps best illustrated through his Petrarchan translations. Wyatt's versions are free-standing poems, extracted from the narrative of the *Rime Sparse*, which encourages readers to equate every description of a pale-skinned, blonde-haired beauty

---

[78] Collingwood 1994 [1946], p. 241.
[79] Collingwood 1994 [1946], p. 241.
[80] Collingwood 1994 [1946], p. 240.
[81] Petrarch 1979 [1327–74].

with Petrarch's poetic muse, the virtuous Laura. Wyatt also systematically strips his translations of allusions that would tie them to identifiable figures and situations: a feature evident in *rima* 98 (cited above), where the address to the Roman nobleman Orso dell' Anguillara is transformed into remonstrance with the poetic speaker's own self. When critics interpret Wyatt's 'Who so list to hount' – a version of *rima* 190 ('Una candida cerva' ('A white doe')) – as reflecting on the loss of Anne Boleyn, or 'The piller pearisht is' (translating *rima* 269, 'Rotta e l'alta colonna e 'l verde lauro' ('Broken are the high Column and the green Laurel')) as a tribute to Thomas Cromwell, these are readings that have been imposed on the poems. These interpretations – these 'act[s] of interpolation', in Collingwood's words – may well be correct. Nevertheless, they remain purely circumstantial. As W. K. Wimsatt and M. C. Beardsley, advocates of formalist analysis, note, 'even a short lyric poem is dramatic, the response of speaker ... to a situation. We ought to impute the thoughts and attitudes of the poem immediately to the dramatic *speaker*, and if to the author at all, only by a biographical act of inference.'[82] Further to that, there is also value in respecting and acknowledging Wyatt's silences and omissions: in their cultivated, cautious circumspection these are as potentially revealing about Henrician court culture and politics as *roman-a-clef* readings tying his poems to specific historical figures and situations.

The contexts – the 'histories' – that inform a work (or even a document, to continue with LaCapra's terminology) are often as much 'textual' as 'actual'. In LaCapra's words, 'The context or "real world" is itself "textualized" in a variety of ways. ... Social and invidual life has in part a textual structure and is involved in textual processes.'[83] By way of conclusion, the final section of the chapter illustrates this by returning to the early modern schoolroom. We have already seen how sixteenth-century pedagogic practices shaped how 'history' was conveyed to a play-going and poetry-reading public. By the middle of the sixteenth century, and on through the seventeenth, education in England was fairly standardised. From Canterbury to Carlisle, schoolboys read the same set of (mainly Latin) texts, in a similar order, and were drilled in similar practices of parsing, reciting, double translation (translating from Latin to English and back again), disputing and opposing. 'There are adaptations to circumstances' (such as the number of masters), T. W. Baldwin explains, 'yet the same fundamental routine evidently continues in these schools and others throughout the sixteenth century and beyond'.[84] This form of

---

[82] Wimsatt and Beardsley 1946, p. 470.
[83] LaCapra 1983, p. 50.
[84] Baldwin 1944, I, p. 435.

education was also designed to instil a sense of public duty. As Richard Mulcaster, head of Merchant Taylors School (1561–86), writes, the ultimate end of education is that former schoolboys, post-university, might 'serve abrode in publik functions of the common weal'.[85] We can see the methods inculcated during this schooling shaping the habits of many of its former (probably the more assiduous) students in later life. The imprint of such a humanist education can be glimpsed, amongst other places, in the memoranda drawn up question-and-answer style (peril and remedy) by William Cecil when deliberating on paths of action, or when Gabriel Harvey and his acquaintances turn to classical history for the light it might cast on present circumstances, their pragmatic readings recorded in the margins of Harvey's copy of Livy.[86] The ideological import of this training – supposedly equipping schoolboys for a life of virtuous action – can also be traced in the way former pupils frequently reacted against it, using their pens, not in service of the common weal, as Mulcaster would have it, but to expose and question the humanist assumption that reading and writing should be morally instructive. Unlike his equivalent in the source material, Lodge's Robert cites Ovid as he murders his schoolmaster with a pen-knife (an essential piece of writing equipment), and the works of what Richard Helgerson calls this 'prodigal' generation frequently depict young men using their rhetorical skills, not in service of the state, but to seduce women into their beds.[87]

A humanist schooling, in other words, moulded the practices, actions, works and documents of its one-time students. At the same time, this mode of education was – in essence – a textual one, based on books. If we are what we eat, then we are also what we read. When thinking about the methods and materials we use when trying to understand the past, it is not just LaCapra's works and documents, or Sidney's poetry and history, that operate on a spectrum and which are not necessarily easily divisible: the same can be true of text and practice. 'Literature' is made by history, but it can also work the other way around.

References

Anon. 1598. *The riddles of Heraclitus and Democritus*. London.
Ascham, Roger. 1570. *A report and discourse written by Roger Ascham of the affaires and state of Germany*. London.

---

[85] Mulcaster 1582, sig. ¶2v.
[86] Haynes 1740, p. 588; Jardine and Grafton 1990.
[87] Lodge 1591, sig. C1v; Helgerson 1976; for examples of persuasive seduction see Sidney 1591 [*c*.1580] and Marlowe 1598.

Aubrey, John. 1898 [last quarter of seventeenth century]. *Brief Lives*, ed. Andrew Clark. Oxford.

2015. *Brief Lives*, ed. Kate Bennett. 2 vols. Oxford.

Bacon, Alan. 1986. 'English Literature Becomes a University Subject: King's College, London as Pioneer', *Victorian Studies*, 29, pp. 591–612.

Baldwin, T. W. 1944. *William Shakspere's Small Latine & Lesse Greeke*. 2 vols. Urbana.

Baldwin, William et al. 1938 [1559; rev. 1563]. *The Mirror for Magistrates*, ed. Lily B. Campbell. Cambridge.

Barbour, Brian. 1999. 'Lewis and Cambridge', *Modern Philology*, 96, pp. 439–84.

Boswell, Grant M. 1986. 'The Rhetoric of Pedagogy: Changing Assumptions in Seventeenth-Century English Rhetorical Education', *Rhetoric Society Quarterly*, 16, pp. 109–23.

Brinsley, John. 1612. *Ludus Literarius*. London.

British Library Add. MS. 4379. c. 1565. William Badger's school notebook.

Brockbank, Philip. 1962. 'English at York', *Critical Survey*, 1, pp. 52–5.

Brooke, Arthur. 1562. *The tragicall historie of Romeus and Juliet*. London.

Burns, Arthur. 2010. 'Dale, Thomas (1797–1870)' in *Oxford Dictionary of National Biography*, www.oxforddnb.com.

The Byble in Englyshe. 1539. London.

Collingwood, R. G. 1994 [1946]. *The Idea of History*, ed. Jan van der Dussen, rev. ed. Oxford.

Daiches, David. 1962. 'English Studies at the University of Sussex', *Critical Survey*, 1, pp. 48–51.

Daniel, Samuel. 1592. *Delia. Containing certaine sonnets: with the complaynt of Rosamond* [London]. STC² 6243.3.

Dobrée, Bonamy. 1962. 'The Teaching of English Literature: A Personal Confession', *Critical Survey*, 1, pp. 55–7.

Drayton, Michael. 1594. *Matilda*. London.

Eagleton, Terry. 2012 [1983]. *Literary Theory: An Introduction*, anniversary ed. Hoboken, NJ.

Ellis, John M. 1977. *The Theory of Literary Criticism: A Logical Analysis*. Berkeley.

Garter, Bernard. 1565. *The tragicall and true history that happened between two English Lovers*. London.

Halpern, Richard. 1991. *The Poetics of Primitive Accumulation: English Renaissance Culture and the Genealogy of Capital*. Ithaca, NY.

Haynes, Samuel, ed. 1740. *A Collection of State Papers [...] Left by William Cecil, Lord Burghley*. London.

Helgerson, Richard. 1976. *Elizabethan Prodigals*. Berkeley.

Jardine, Lisa and Anthony Grafton. 1990. '"Studied for Action": How Gabriel Harvey Read his Livy', *Past and Present*, 129, pp. 30–78.

Kaufmann, Miranda. 2017. *Black Tudors: The Untold Story*. London.

LaCapra, Dominick. 1983. *Rethinking Intellectual History: Texts, Contexts, Language*. Ithaca, NY.

Lawlor, John. 1962. 'English at Keele', *Critical Survey*, 1, pp. 46–8.

Leavis, F. R. 1948. *Education and the University: A Sketch for an English School*. London.

Lewis, C. S. 1954. *English Literature in the Sixteenth Century Excluding Drama*. Oxford.

Lodge, Thomas. 1591. *The famous, true and historicall life of Robert second Duke of Normandy*. London.

Lucian. 1959. *How to Write History*, trans. K. Kilburn. Loeb Classical Library 430. Cambridge, MA.

Mantel, Hilary. 2017a. 'The Day is for the Living', BBC Reith Lectures, Lecture 1, http://downloads.bbc.co.uk/radio4/reith2017/reith_2017_hilary_mantel_lecture1.pdf.

2017b. 'The Iron Maiden', BBC Reith Lectures, Lecture 2, http://downloads.bbc.co.uk/radio4/reith2017/reith_2017_hilary_mantel_lecture2.pdf.

Marlowe, Christopher. 1598. *Hero and Leander*. London.

Mulcaster, Richard. 1582. *The first part of the elementary*. London.

Petrarch, Francesco. 1979 [1327–74]. *Lyric Poems*, ed. and trans. Robert Durling. Cambridge, MA.

Puttenham, George. 2004 [1589]. *The Art of English Poesy* in *Sidney's 'The Defence of Poesy' and Selected Renaissance Literary Criticism*, ed. Gavin Alexander. London.

Quality Assurance Agency for Higher Education (QAA). 2019. *Subject Benchmark Statement: English*, www.qaa.ac.uk/docs/qaa/subject-benchmark-statements/subject-benchmark-statement-english.pdf.

Reardon, Bernard M. G. 2006. 'Maurice, (John) Frederick Denison (1805–72)' in *Oxford Dictionary of National Biography*, www.oxforddnb.com.

Ryan, Lawrence. 1963. *Roger Ascham*. Stanford.

Scurr, Ruth. 2015. *John Aubrey: My Own Life*. London.

Seccombe, Thomas and John D. Haigh. 2016. 'Dasent, Sir George Webbe (1817–96)' in *Oxford Dictionary of National Biography*, www.oxforddnb.com.

Seneca. 2018. *Phaedra* in *Tragedies*, trans. John G. Fitch. Loeb Classical Library 62. Cambridge, MA.

Shrank, Cathy. 2016. 'Finding a Vernacular Voice: The Classical Translations of Sir Thomas Wyatt (c. 1503–1542)' in *The Oxford History of Classical Reception*, vol. I, ed. Rita Copeland. Oxford.

Sheffield Lives. 2022. https://situate.io/sheffieldlives/.

Sidney, Philip. 1591. *Syr P. S. His Astrophel and Stella*. London.

2004 [c.1580]. *The Defence of Poesy* in *Sidney's 'The Defence of Poesy' and Selected Renaissance Literary Criticism*, ed. Gavin Alexander. London.

Skelton, John. 1499. *The Bowge of Court*. London.

Stamatakis, Chris. 2012. *Sir Thomas Wyatt and the Rhetoric of Rewriting: 'Turning the Word'*. Oxford.

Townsend, R. C. 1967. 'The Idea of an English School', *Critical Survey*, 3, pp. 129–44.

Trinity College Dublin, MS 160. 'The Blage Manuscript'.

Watt, Ian et al. 1962. 'The Idea of an English School', *Critical Survey*, 1, pp. 39–60.

Wimsatt, W. K. and M. C. Beardsley. 1946. 'The Intentional Fallacy', *The Sewanee Review*, 54, pp. 468–88.

Wrightson, Keith. 2003 [1993]. *English Society, 1580–1680*, rev. ed. London.

13 Reloading the British Romantic Canon: The Historical Editing of Literary Texts

Pamela Clemit

The literary canon may appear to be timeless, but it is shaped by history. Until the last two decades of the twentieth century, the canon of British Romantic authors established by the Victorians looked fixed, though its boundaries were debated. It gave primacy to six poets (Blake, Wordsworth, Coleridge, Byron, Shelley and Keats), the most significant modern adjustment being the replacement of Sir Walter Scott (a Victorian favourite) by the tradesman-class visionary Blake. Consensus about the canon was broken in the 1970s and 1980s by successive waves of structuralism, post-structuralism, Marxism, feminism, deconstruction and other theoretical approaches. But it was not enough to read beyond the canon: its substance could be changed only by editorial recovery of neglected writings.

Marilyn Butler, the most eminent British Romantic scholar in recent decades, opened the canon to peripheral figures by placing them in their localised historical contexts. Her intervention kicked off a new historical turn in textual editing, which is still rotating. Editing, properly done, is a mode of historical thinking. The practice of editing as a form of historical enquiry may be exemplified by the scholarly rehabilitation of the polymathic intellectual William Godwin, a figure once regarded as not quite canonical, whose writings are undergoing comprehensive editorial recovery. Editing Godwin captures history in the making. It enables us to track the development of his two principal works – each of which went through two sets of revisions in the fast-moving 1790s – and to recover and contextualise a rich trove of unpublished letters, augmenting the canon of his writings.

The Historicist Revolution

The historicist revolution in British criticism of Romantic-era texts began in the 1970s. Butler broke away from earlier critical schools which

Thanks to John Barnard, Louise Gordon, Paul Hamilton, James B. Lewis, Jenny McAuley, Avner Offer, Michael Rossington and Richard Whatmore for helpful comments on various drafts.

treated texts as self-contained aesthetic objects – notably the practical criticism of I. A. Richards (in the 1930s) and American New Criticism (in the 1940s and 1950s).[1] She also took issue with influential anthologists and canon makers associated (from the 1960s) with Cornell and Yale Universities: M. H. Abrams, Geoffrey Hartman, Harold Bloom and their colleagues and pupils. They interpreted the revolutionary turn in Romantic writing in spiritual and aesthetic terms, taking Wordsworth's *The Prelude* (first published in 1850) as their chief example.[2]

Butler thought that they had installed the wrong canon. She insisted that literature is 'powerfully conditioned by social forces, what needs to be and what may be said in a particular community at a given time'.[3] In *Romantics, Rebels, and Reactionaries* (1981), she reconfigured the field by placing literary works in their historical settings, and made canonical authors more understandable by reading them alongside their lost peers. She rejected the notion that experience was something that goes on entirely in the head, and showed that Romantic authors took their own society and its culture as their proper subject.

The British historicist approach was quite different from New Historicism, which was introduced in America around the same time by Stephen Greenblatt, a scholar of the English Renaissance.[4] New Historicism was not historical. It drew on the writings of Michel Foucault, for whom history was not a sequence of temporal cause and effect, but a phenomenological 'archaeology', in which discursive traces of the past were examined in order to write a history of the present.[5] New Historicists characteristically drew together a bricolage of historical sources from unlikely provenances which purported to get to the essence of literary works. The propagation of transcendental experience in British Romantic writing attracted their critical scrutiny. They berated scholars and critics of Romanticism for being themselves Romantic.[6] New Historicists claimed to place Romantic literary works in the cultural contexts of their time, but in practice their readings were often coloured by Foucauldian discourse analysis.

The historicist revolution in Britain was empirical and materialist. It began in the archive, often close to home, and was theorised retrospectively. Butler herself wrote her first book using the unpublished papers of the Anglo-Irish novelist Maria Edgeworth, her husband's

---

[1] Robey 1986.
[2] Abrams 1971.
[3] Butler 1981, p. 9.
[4] Hamilton 1996, pp. 150–75.
[5] Hamilton 1996, pp. 134–44.
[6] McGann 1983, p. 1.

great-great-aunt.[7] In *Jane Austen and the War of Ideas* (1975), she positioned Austen's conservative novels in the context of British partisan literature of the 1790s, wresting her from the clutches of the New York intellectual Lionel Trilling, who had idealised her as a timeless moral authority.[8] In *Peacock Displayed* (1979), she examined the satirical novels of Thomas Love Peacock in relation to the literary and political controversies of his times.[9] *Romantics, Rebels, and Reactionaries* shifted attention from solitary authorship to social engagement. For many years it appeared to be the fullest expression of her thought. All the while, in essays and conference papers, she was investigating a group of eighteenth-century writers – including Thomas Gray, James Macpherson, Thomas Chatterton and William Blake – who made use of primitive British mythology to invent oppositional narratives of the past. She identified with antiquaries of humble origins who sought to recover local roots, and sometimes to invent them: the ballad collector Joseph Ritson, a native of Stockton-on-Tees, who began his career as a lawyer's clerk; and the Glamorgan stonemason, Welsh-language poet and literary forger Edward Williams (pseud. Iolo Morganwg). This research culminated in her posthumously published book, *Mapping Mythologies* (2015).[10]

What did Butler mean by writing as she did? A theoretical case for historical criticism was slow to emerge, since most historical critics were inclined to embed their methodological principles in their research practice, rather than provide a conceptual rationale. Butler's reflections on historical method came out of her empirical work, and had an explicit agenda. Her work challenged the North American disregard for English history that dominated post-war literary criticism. She regarded Northrop Frye, an early exponent of archetypal criticism, as beginning the process of 'de-Englishing the English Romantics'.[11] The canon as established in the second half of the twentieth century by Abrams, Hartman and Bloom, among others, reflected their own intellectual genealogy as first- or second-generation American immigrants of central European Jewish origin or descent. They had their history too – Hartman, a Kindertransport refugee from Germany, attributed his lifelong engagement with Wordsworth to his childhood years in Britain.[12] They held to central European intellectual traditions, while espousing American liberal Cold War values. Kant, Hegel, Nietzsche and Freud formed

---

[7] Butler 1972; Leask 2017, p. 90.
[8] Butler 1987; Trilling 1955.
[9] Butler 1979.
[10] Butler 2015.
[11] Butler 1983, p. 18.
[12] Redfield 2006, pp. 11–13, 56.

part of their repertoire, alongside Blake, Wordsworth, Coleridge, Shelley and American transcendentalists such as Emerson. These Ivy League Romanticists were distant heirs of Coleridge, who had introduced German transcendentalism to Britain. Their approaches were diverse, but, for the empiricist Butler, all of them stripped out the local circumstances that drove the performative function of a particular work.

Butler did not establish a school or affiliate herself to any other historical approach to the study of literature. Nonetheless, her particularised historical method had much in common with the practices of the Cambridge School of intellectual historians (Peter Laslett, J. G. A. Pocock, Quentin Skinner, John Dunn and others) from 1960 onwards. Though each had distinct interests, they all worked to place the canonical texts of political thought in their immediate historical contexts – an enterprise that Skinner defined as 'essentially linguistic'.[13] Butler saw the advantages of this mode of investigation for literary study, and praised Skinner and Pocock for not letting their theory get the better of their practice. But she did not become an acolyte: 'A method each has arrived at independently could be the formula a lot of people are looking for.'[14]

Butler had a closer affinity with the left-wing social historian E. P. Thompson. He was a literary scholar too, whom she described as 'one of the most significant, persuasive models for how to write on the literature of the past'.[15] They had many values in common. Each was roused to protest by the political crises of 1956, the Anglo-French invasion of Suez and the Soviet invasion of Hungary, and each supported the Campaign for Nuclear Disarmament from its inception in 1957.[16] Butler was early associated with Oxford's New Left, a student group which in 1957 founded the *Universities and Left Review*, later merged with Thompson's *The New Reasoner* (1957–9) as the *New Left Review*. They shared a dislike of critical theory. Both embarked on the practical task of recovering forgotten writers and non-elite discourse from 'the enormous condescension of posterity',[17] with particular attention to English religious nonconformity. Both were fascinated by the artisanal traditions

---

[13] Skinner 1969, p. 49. This essay, later described by Skinner as a manifesto, was originally entitled 'The Unimportance of the Great Texts in the History of Political Thought' (Pallares-Burke 2002, pp. 218–19; Goldie 2006, p. 8).

[14] Butler 1986, pp. 45, 37. The Cambridge School had more direct literary descendants in John Barrell and Nigel Leask, who drew on Pocock's investigation of the political languages of Renaissance civic humanism to contextualise, respectively, the classic English art theorists of the late eighteenth century and Coleridge's critical thought (Pocock 1975; Barrell 1986; Leask 1988).

[15] Butler 1995b, p. 72.

[16] Butler 1987, p. xiii; Leask 2017, p. 88.

[17] Thompson 1968, p. 12.

of Blake, the self-taught visionary of the 1790s, with which Butler began *Romantics, Rebels, and Reactionaries* and ended *Mapping Mythologies*.[18] Thompson's last book, *Witness Against the Beast: William Blake and the Moral Law* (1993), was a revisionist study inspired by the archive of the last member of the Muggletonian sect.[19] For Thompson and Butler, literary excavation was also a way of connecting with deep native roots.

The Editorial Turn

Once canonicity was recognised as the product of an elite interest group, there was a push to extend the field to outlying figures. 'Why is it that some literary works survive to become part of the accepted canon, while others, just as successful in their own time, are forgotten?'[20] To answer this question, the neglected writings of the past had to be made available in the classroom. An editorial revolution began to take shape, driven by two external forces: feminism and the New Left. The Ivy League canon (like its Oxbridge counterpart) was almost entirely male, with university programmes dominated by the 'Big Six' Romantic poets.[21] In contrast, the Women's Liberation Movement of the 1970s sent feminists into the archives in search of heroines, leading to a revival of interest in many women writers eminent in their own day, who had since dropped out of sight. Around the same time, veterans of the counter-culture and the New Left in the expanding universities embarked on a quest for antecedents, leading to a new wave of interest in the radical writers of the 1790s. Yet political commitment alone could not bring back the extended oeuvres of authors such as Mary Wollstonecraft and William Godwin. Scholarly editions were needed, 'not only to grasp the internal dynamics of an individual career, but to understand its group dynamics, its inter-relations with society and history'.[22] The real grassroots historicist revolution took place in textual editing.

Editions dedicated to maintaining the status of the Ivy League canon were already under way. They included the magisterial Cornell Wordsworth (1975–2007), produced under the general editorship of Stephen M. Parrish, a former US wartime code-breaker. Texts were drawn from Wordsworth's original poetical manuscripts, over 90 per cent of which were preserved in the family archive at Dove Cottage in Grasmere.

[18] Butler 1981, pp. 39–53; Butler 2015, pp. 162–88.
[19] Thompson 1993, pp. 115–19.
[20] Thomas 1988, p. 20.
[21] Cantor 1989, p. 708.
[22] Butler 1995a, p. 274.

Helen Darbishire, one of the editors of the Clarendon Press edition of Wordsworth's *Poetical Works* (1940–9), sought to protect the Dove Cottage archive from destruction in the event of a nuclear war.[23] She had the collection microfilmed and the reels stored in a Canadian bank vault. Another set was deposited at Cornell, where it became available to Abrams, Parrish and their colleagues. They became convinced of the need for a comprehensive new edition based on the earliest complete versions of Wordsworth's poems.

The Cornell effort was ambitious and well funded, provoking resentment among impoverished British cousins who felt that their cultural heritage had been appropriated.[24] The editors overrode Wordsworth's own preference for 'following strictly the last Copy of the text of an Author',[25] and printed early manuscript versions of many poems which he either never published, or published towards the end of his career in a heavily revised form, relegating the authorised texts to the back of the volumes. By the 1980s and 1990s, a revised Wordsworth canon was in place. It included many poems reconstituted from manuscript, which for several generations of university students took precedence over the published work that had made Wordsworth famous in the first place.[26] Some scholars complained that, however authentic the recovered texts might be, they did not represent the Wordsworth that his contemporaries read.[27] The balance was redressed only when Nicholas Halmi published his Norton Critical Edition, *Wordsworth's Poetry and Prose* (2014), which reconstructs Wordsworth's poetic career as it unfolded before contemporary readers in his published works from 1798 to (roughly) 1815. The 'textual primitivism' of the Cornell edition was originalist, not historical, though it facilitated genuine historical studies.[28]

Once historicist critics got down to work, they found themselves in unfamiliar terrain. Their empirical discoveries changed the shape of the field, replacing a top-down perspective with a bottom-up one. On university reading lists, some authors traditionally consigned to the 'background' section came to the fore. Charlotte Smith, whose *Elegiac Sonnets* (1784) went through nine (frequently augmented) editions by 1800, was rediscovered as the originator of the Romantic-era revival of the sonnet form, who inspired up-and-coming figures such as Wordsworth and

---

[23] Butler 1997, p. 96.
[24] Graver 2015, pp. 826–7.
[25] Wordsworth to Alexander Dyce, [19 April 1830], in Wordsworth 1979, p. 236.
[26] Gill 1983, pp. 185–90; Graver 2015, pp. 831–2.
[27] Stillinger 1989.
[28] Stillinger 1989, p. 4; e.g., Roe 1988 (a second edition appeared in 2018).

Coleridge.[29] Mary Shelley was recognised as an author in her own right on the strength of *Frankenstein* (1818), which shot to prominence on American undergraduate survey courses on British Romanticism.[30] Dorothy Wordsworth, invisible in her own day – her journals were published posthumously – was brought out of her brother's shadow,[31] and many others appeared in the teaching canon for the first time.

The historian's chronology of Romantic literature would always be different from that of the literary critic. William St Clair's quantitative analysis of nineteenth-century readerships led him to propose a contemporaneous canon made up of the eight most admired male poets: Byron, Campbell, Coleridge, Moore, Rogers, Scott, Southey and Wordsworth.[32] However, except for Byron and Scott, the most commercially successful verse writers were not the same as St Clair's canonical eight. Best-selling authors included the labouring-class poet Robert Bloomfield, whose *The Farmer's Boy* (1800) sold over 25,000 copies within two years; the Anglican clergyman George Crabbe, whose verse tales documented the seamy side of rural life; and Felicia Hemans, 'the first poetess of the day', who celebrated British military valour abroad and Anglican domestic pieties at home.[33]

Not all of the writers rediscovered by historicist critics became available for modern critical scrutiny. Why were some texts reprinted in scholarly or classroom editions, and not others? The true canon makers were publishers. William Rees-Mogg identified a business opportunity. In 1983 he established Pickering & Chatto (Publishers) Limited, with himself as chairman. His policy was to republish complete or near-complete editions of the works of out-of-copyright authors distinguished in their own day, but rarely reprinted, in handsome multi-volume sets for sale to scholarly libraries. The firm specialised in economic and financial history, but capitalised on the growing market created by historicist literary scholarship. *The Works of Mary Wollstonecraft*, edited by Janet Todd and Marilyn Butler, brought together Wollstonecraft's entire oeuvre for the first time.[34] Further landmark editions included the works of William Godwin, Mary Shelley, William Hazlitt, Maria Edgeworth, Charlotte Smith and Mary Robinson, together with facsimile collections of pamphlets and documents relating to the reform societies of the 1790s, the 1792–4 Treason Trials and the popular radical press of the

---

[29] Robinson 1996.
[30] Shelley 1994; St Clair 2004, pp. 360–1; Linkin 1991.
[31] Wordsworth 1991.
[32] St Clair 2004, pp. 210, 216–19.
[33] St Clair 2004, pp. 582, 595–6, 607–8; Anon. 1826, p. 518.
[34] Wollstonecraft 1989.

Regency era. Some of these topics may seem surprising for a publisher who, around the same time, co-wrote several mass-market primers on right-wing economics.[35] Rees-Mogg had his eyes on Japan, the firm's second-largest outlet after the USA,[36] where the survival of academic Marxism made scholars keen to access original radical texts.

Pickering & Chatto provided the foundations for much of the historical contextualisation of lesser-known authors in British Romantic scholarship over the last thirty years. Yet the firm's high prices, combined with its policy of selling full sets, meant that it did not satisfy the need for classroom editions. Feminist critics shouted loudest for cheap reading copies. Academics at Brown University established the Women Writers Project in the late 1980s in order to provide accurate electronic editions of all printed texts by women in English from 1400 to 1850.[37] The British publisher Virago Press (established 1973), the first mass-market publisher of women's books, resurrected eighteenth- and early nineteenth-century titles. Pandora Press issued Dale Spender's Mothers of the Novel series (1986–8), comprising raw texts of twenty women's novels from 1749 to 1834. Broadview Press, an independent Canadian academic publisher (established 1985), led the market in well-edited classroom editions of lesser-known works, which included contemporaneous primary source materials. Penguin Books and Oxford World's Classics raised their game. The 1818 text of Mary Shelley's *Frankenstein*, edited by Butler with full scholarly apparatus and originally published in Todd's Pickering Women's Classics series, was reissued in Oxford World's Classics in 1994, and has now superseded the revised 1831 edition as the standard text. In 1995 Penguin produced what remains the only series of Austen's novels based on the texts of the first editions, with scholarly annotations embedding each work in its distinct historical context.

Recontextualising *Political Justice* and *Caleb Williams*

Editing is not just about making new texts available, but is itself a form of historical enquiry. It raises questions about textual identity, textual meaning and textual function. A scholarly edition provides the methodological apparatus for answering them, building up an incremental understanding of a writer's oeuvre in its particular historical moment. This idea is best worked out through a case study of a single author. The

---

[35] See, e.g., Davidson and Rees-Mogg 1987.
[36] Rees-Mogg 2011.
[37] Jakacki 2017. The project moved to Northeastern University in 2013.

radical political philosopher and novelist William Godwin was brought back to prominence by the combined pressure of feminist criticism – which focused attention on his first wife, Mary Wollstonecraft, and their daughter, Mary Shelley – and the historical recovery of English radicalism. Godwin is of particular interest to historically minded editors for two reasons: the textual complexity of his two most famous works; and the preservation of a large personal archive, which includes around 1,500 mostly unpublished items of correspondence.

Godwin rose to fame as the author of *An Enquiry Concerning Political Justice* (1793), a work of iconoclastic social theory which reinvigorated the British reform movement as the French Revolution entered its darkest phase. In 1794 he published *Things as They Are; or, The Adventures of Caleb Williams*, a fictional exploration of his philosophical ideas, which confirmed his reputation. He wrote five more full-length novels, works of educational theory, children's books, plays, philosophical biographies, essays, political pamphlets and a four-volume *History of the Commonwealth of England* (1824–8). Godwin knew or corresponded with almost everyone of note on the political left from the era of the French Revolution to that of the Great Reform Bill (1832), including nearly all the major literary figures of the age. He documented his social contacts in his diary and kept many of his letters. These habits of personal record-keeping may be attributed to his upbringing and education in English religious nonconformity.[38]

Individual works do not provide definitive statements of Godwin's philosophy, but represent what he thought and judged it possible to say at a particular historical moment. He did not revise his texts as compulsively as Wordsworth,[39] but revisited the same preoccupations throughout his writing life. From 1794 to 1797 he revised and reformulated his philosophical principles in successive editions of his two major works, each pulling the other along. From May to October 1795 he revised *Political Justice* for a second edition (1796), after which he spent two months revising *Caleb Williams* for a second edition (1796); from January to March 1797 he revised *Caleb Williams* again for a third edition (1797) while simultaneously revising *Political Justice* for a third edition (1798), which was completed in July 1797.[40] In the pamphlet *Thoughts Occasioned by the Perusal of Dr Parr's Spital Sermon* (1801), Godwin remarked: 'The human intellect is a sort of barometer, directed in its variations by the atmosphere which surrounds it.'[41] He was alluding to those who

[38] Clemit 2011, pp. xxvi, xxxv–xxxvii.
[39] Gill 2011.
[40] Godwin 2010.
[41] Godwin 1993, II, p. 170.

originally welcomed *Political Justice*, and later changed their minds –
but the statement also reflects his own mental flexibility. In the second
and third editions of *Political Justice*, Godwin modified the rational and
individualistic doctrines of the first edition and placed a new emphasis
on the role of sympathy and feeling in moral judgements,[42] which he
had first explored through his dramatisation of the psychological effects
of inequality in *Caleb Williams*. A justification for such flexibility may
be found in the Dissenting belief in the duty of ceaseless enquiry. To
commit oneself to following truth, 'whithersoever thou leadest',[43] was to
embark on an open quest for moral and spiritual enlightenment. When
further exploration or insight reveals the inadequacies of one's professed
views, revision becomes a moral duty.[44]

Mark Philp set out in *Godwin's Political Justice* (1986) to reconstruct
the intellectual and political contexts in which *Political Justice* was written and revised. He was interested not just in the changing meanings
of *Political Justice* but in the broader question of what Godwin, in Skinner's phrase, was '*up to*, what he may have *meant* by writing as he did',
in each of the three editions.[45] There was no modern scholarly edition
to help him. F. E. L. Priestley's 1946 edition reproduced a facsimile of
the third edition, the conventional choice as the last edition corrected by
the author, with variants from the first and second editions in a separate
volume.[46] Isaac Kramnick's 1976 Penguin Classics edition was based
on the text of the third and final lifetime edition.[47] Philp went back to
the original eighteenth-century editions, then accessible only in research
libraries. He argued that the evolution of Godwin's thought needed to
be understood in the light of metropolitan Rational Dissent, its relations
to the extra-parliamentary movement for reform of the political franchise
in the early 1790s, and its decline in the wake of a sustained government
campaign against radical intellectuals in the second half of the decade.
The first edition best captured the discursive contexts of Rational Dissent and revealed Godwin as a perfectibilist rather than a utilitarian.[48]
Changes made to subsequent editions, especially the increased emphasis
on feeling as the basis of human action, reflected Godwin's engagement
with British moral sense philosophy and the literature of sensibility.[49] He

---

[42] Philp 1986, pp. 142–59, 202–13.
[43] Godwin 1993, VI, pp. 173, 219.
[44] Fitzpatrick 1982, pp. 17–18.
[45] Pallares-Burke 2002, p. 224.
[46] Godwin 1946.
[47] Godwin 1976.
[48] Philp 1986, pp. 80–98.
[49] Philp 1986, pp. 159–67.

remained committed to the Dissenting ideal of private judgement, which was not merely a matter of principle but also a way of life. Philp's leap from social context to intellectual orientation was unacceptable to some readers, who noted that Godwin wrote in other idioms besides Dissent.[50] Nonetheless, Philp's book set the trend for subsequent scholarship. The next step had to be an annotated scholarly edition which would capture Godwin's 'text on the move' and make it available for further study.

Political Justice was not Godwin's only 'text on the move'. The textual instability of *Caleb Williams* was complicated by his writing, immediately after completing the manuscript, a new ending which transformed the novel's meaning and appeared in the published work. Following the rediscovery of the original manuscript ending,[51] most editors of *Caleb Williams* have published it as an appendix to the main text. From the 1970s onwards, *Caleb Williams* was widely studied as the most successful English 'Jacobin novel',[52] but editorial scholarship did not keep pace with critical developments. The 1970 Oxford English Novels edition (republished in Oxford World's Classics in 1982) presented an eclectic text based on the surviving portions of the original manuscript and the first published text of 1794, silently incorporating substantive revisions in later editions.[53] Editions published by Penguin Classics (1988) and Broadview (2000) adhered to the last edition corrected in the author's lifetime (1831), but presented it, misleadingly, alongside contextual materials from the 1790s.[54] In my monograph *The Godwinian Novel* (1993), which anchored *Caleb Williams* in the historical currents of the 1790s, I, following Philp, used the original first edition.[55]

What type of edition would convey the textual complexity of Godwin's two most celebrated works? The Pickering editions of Godwin's *Collected Novels and Memoirs* (1992) and of his *Political and Philosophical Writings* (1993), both under the general editorship of Mark Philp, provided answers.[56] They broke with tradition in their treatment of *Political Justice* and *Caleb Williams*, providing, in each case, a clean text of the first edition, together with variants from the manuscript and subsequent lifetime editions. The first editions were preferred because they represented Godwin's original intentions and philosophical baseline, and were the texts that established his fame. They captured the historical moment of

[50] Claeys 1987, p. 764.
[51] Dumas 1966.
[52] Kelly 1976 coined the term.
[53] Godwin 1970.
[54] Godwin 1988; Godwin 2000.
[55] Clemit 1993.
[56] Godwin 1992a; Godwin 1993.

his intervention in the pamphlet war over the French Revolution and made it possible to define his position in the spectrum of debate. The variants from later editions – which occupied an entire volume in the case of *Political Justice* – presented a record of his changing ideas which could be studied separately. In providing a register of what was sayable to different readers at different times, they are 'as useful as the many volumes that print the 1805 and 1850 versions of *The Prelude* on facing pages'.[57] The first editions reached a mass audience when Oxford World's Classics published the 1794 text of *Caleb Williams*, with variants (withdrawing their final lifetime edition), and the 1793 text of *Political Justice*, minus variants.[58]

Philp's reset Pickering edition was not the first modern publication of the 1793 text of *Political Justice*. In 1992 Jonathan Wordsworth published the first edition, in its original two-volume quarto format, in his Woodstock Facsimile series.[59] This facsimile reprint was a timely reminder that texts must be read as books if we are to recover their contemporaneous significance. The expansive typographical layout of the quarto *Political Justice*, and its apparatus of marginal glosses and appendices, conveyed authority. Its high price of 36 shillings signalled its distance from the 'dangerous portability' of the occasional pamphlet.[60] Historical recovery involves not only discursive contexts but also material forms.

Recovering Godwin's Letters

Godwin's letters were as constrained by materiality as *Political Justice*. In my Oxford University Press edition I am collecting his 1,500 or so surviving letters, drawn from repositories all over the world, in a uniform scholarly format. These letters represent texts at many different stages of composition: holograph sent letters; drafts in various hands; and copies. What a sent letter looked like was determined by the cost of postage, which increased five times between 1784 and 1812. Postage was charged (to the recipient) per sheet and, outside the Greater London area covered by the Penny Post (Twopenny Post after 1801), according to the distance travelled.[61] Godwin's letters were usually written on single sheets of paper folded in half to create four pages. The middle section of the fourth page

---

[57] Bromwich 1994, p. 9.
[58] Godwin 2009; Godwin 2013.
[59] Godwin 1992b.
[60] Sutherland 1994, p. 45. In contrast, when part 2 of Thomas Paine's *Rights of Man* was published in February 1792, both it and the reprinted part 1 (1791), initially priced at 3 shillings, became available in sixpenny editions (Sutherland 1994, p. 19).
[61] Robinson 1948, pp. 154–7, 137.

was left blank to accommodate the address, so that the sheet could be folded and sealed. If the text required more space, Godwin would write across the top and bottom of the fourth page, or in the margins. Shorter letters were written on half-sheets, with the address on the other side; brief, informal notes might be written on scraps of paper. Sometimes salutations and signatures would be omitted to save space (or for prudential reasons).

Keith Thomas has written: 'If we are to understand the minds of people in the past, to go on reading until we can hear them talking, it is partly to literature that we must turn.'[62] We might also turn to letters, which may be the closest we can get to the unmediated voices of the past. In trying to understand what these interpersonal communications are saying, the editor's task is to present them as faithfully to the original utterance as possible. My aim is to provide a text of each letter which represents exactly what Godwin wrote and what his correspondent read. But establishing an authoritative text is only part of the work of editing letters. Letters are compositions, however spontaneous they may appear. They are written according to specific conventions and carry signals that are crafted uniquely for the recipient.[63] How might an editor recapture those signals and convey their power to a modern reader?

Scholarly annotation builds a bridge to the past with contextual information. It may be argued that an annotated text can never resemble what authors of the past intended or first readers encountered. But a raw Godwin letter, spanning modern disciplinary categories, cannot be read today in the same way that it was by the original recipient. The editor provides knowledge that the first reader would have taken for granted. For example, to understand Godwin's financial dealings with patrons, publishers and tradespeople, it is necessary to be familiar with contemporary instruments of credit. To grasp the significance of Godwin's intervention in the 1794 Treason Trials (those indicted included personal friends), the reader needs historical guidance. To calibrate the urgency of his journeys to, say, Bath (to court Harriet Lee), Norfolk (to visit his dying mother) or Edinburgh (in quest of a publisher's advance to keep him out of jail), the reader must know about the modes of transport and staging places that shaped each route. Good annotation does not provide interpretation, but 'position[s] the reader on the brink of interpretation'.[64] The choice of what to annotate is never neutral: different annotations make the same text available in different ways.[65] In

---

[62] Thomas 1988, p. 19.
[63] Clemit 2019.
[64] New 1984, p. 21.
[65] Hanna 1991.

The Letters of William Godwin, annotation relevant to the particular historical crux addressed is necessarily a multi-disciplinary undertaking.

Explanatory and textual notes, when read together, give access to broader and more enduring modes of historical understanding. Godwin's letters may be read as an extension of his published writings. In *Political Justice*, Godwin envisaged a future society of autonomous moral agents, in which the rule of law would be superseded by the rule of reason. If people exercised impartial judgement in every action of their lives, they would gradually free themselves from the constraints of government. Institutions would become redundant, and would slowly wither away. Godwin acknowledged that some elements in human nature and society obstructed this process, but insisted that such elements would, in time, be governed by reason. The chief instrument of moral progress was private conversation: 'If there be such a thing as truth, it must infallibly be struck out by the collision of mind with mind.'[66] Through 'free and unrestricted discussion',[67] existing political society, with all its divisions and inequalities, would eventually be transformed into a community of rational men and women seeking the good of all.

Godwin's letters reveal his efforts to put his principles into practice in daily life, charting his responses to situations in which his key philosophical commitments were put to the test. The main challenge came from the rising generation, to whom Godwin, a former Dissenting minister, felt a special duty. For example, in the early 1790s his protégés included Thomas Abthorpe Cooper, his second cousin and a future star of the American stage, whom he educated at home from the age of twelve to sixteen, and George Dyson, a translator and amateur painter, who was a few years older than Cooper.[68] When on 20 March 1792 the two young men quarrelled and Dyson struck Cooper, Godwin seized the opportunity for moral instruction by writing a letter to Dyson:

You say, you struck him from a feeling uncorrected by philosophy, & supported by an opinion that such modes of reproof were necessary for minds like his ... & what good did you intend to his mind by striking him? ... A blessed government will this be of philosophers who are to deal their blows whenever it shall please their high mightinesses to be in a passion. You have already perhaps done an irreparable injury to T's mind, who, like all young people is very apt to judge of philosophy or any set of principles by the conduct of those who profess them. Ought we to beat our fellow mortals for our own sakes or for theirs? If for theirs, we ought at least maturely to deliberate in each instance whether

---

[66] Godwin 1993, III, p. 15.
[67] Godwin 1993, III, p. 115.
[68] Godwin 2011, p. 50 n. 1, p. 70 n. 1.

beating be precisely the best mode of reforming their characters & meliorat-
ing their minds. The doctrine of beating is a very comfortable one, because
it indulges all our indolent propensities ... Not to add that as in your case it
teaches us to indulge our passions, & persuades us that there is no reason for us
to be very anxious to subdue the brutality of our nature.[69]

This letter may be read in the context of the unfolding history of emotional norms. It shows the dilemmas that arose when Godwin's role as
self-appointed arbiter of one young man's moral conduct was complicated by the presence of another. The overt lesson, conveyed in forthright
Rational Dissenting style, is that philosophers should not get angry – or
should at least not lash out if they do. Yet Godwin himself is angry (with
Dyson) and fiercely protective of the younger man (Cooper). Emotions
are not to be so easily subdued.

A further dimension to this episode is brought to light by codicologi-
cal analysis. The sole surviving text of the letter is preserved in a draft
in Cooper's hand with Godwin's autograph corrections, indicating that
it was dictated to the person who forms its subject.[70] Godwin evidently
wished Cooper as well as Dyson to be instructed by his intervention.
Moreover, the letter includes a postscript bringing in a fourth party,
Thomas Holcroft, Godwin's friend and intellectual mentor: 'Mr Holcroft has read what I have written[;] perhaps it would be of use to you to
converse with him while the impression is fresh on his mind.'[71] The letter enacts a Godwinian scene of instruction and exemplifies the ideal of
collective moral supervision advocated in *Political Justice*.[72] Yet it makes
it hard for Dyson to do anything but admit he was in the wrong. A range
of editorial skills is needed to decode this letter, and thereby reveal the
tensions between theory and practice arising from attempts to live out
the principles of *Political Justice*.

When individual letters are brought together in a uniform scholarly
format, they gain deeper historical significance from cross-referencing
and interconnection. Familiar letters are thrown into new relationships
when placed in sequence with less familiar ones, and new layers of meaning are revealed where the replies survive. For example, in 1812 Godwin
wrote to another wayward protégé in need of guidance, Percy Bysshe
Shelley. His letters have long been known to scholars, but chiefly as footnotes to Shelley's letters to him. Shelley had been drawn to Ireland by
the new phase of agitation for Catholic emancipation and the repeal of

---

[69] Godwin 2011, p. 69.
[70] Godwin 2011, p. 70.
[71] Godwin 2011, p. 70.
[72] Godwin 1993, III, pp. 448–9, 456.

the 1800 Act of Union, led by Daniel O'Connell.[73] In December 1811 he wrote a pamphlet, *An Address, to the Irish People* (1812), intended 'to awaken in the minds of the Irish poor, a knowledge of their real state', in which he urged them to assemble to discuss their grievances.[74] In February 1812 he went to Dublin to have it printed for mass distribution. On 24 February he dispatched a copy to Godwin, who responded by invoking his strictures against political associations in *Political Justice*.[75] Shelley wrote again, enclosing a newspaper report of his speech at an Aggregate Meeting of the Catholics of Ireland and an extract from a second pamphlet, *Proposals for an Association of Philanthropists* (1812), in which he exhorted the Irish people to take the redress of grievances into their own hands 'with energy and expedition'.[76]

Shelley had found meanings in *Political Justice* that Godwin did not intend, and was about to cross the line between 'informing the people and inflaming them'.[77] Godwin did not hold back. He compared Shelley's impatience to that of the French revolutionaries:

Auspicious and admirable materials were working in the general mind of France, but these men said, as you say, "when we look on the last twenty years, we are seized with a sort of moral scepticism,—we must own we are eager that some thing should be done;" and see what has been the result of their doings! He that would benefit mankind on a comprehensive scale, by changing the principles and elements of society, must learn the hard lesson, to put off self, and to contribute by a quiet, but incessant activity, like a rill of water, to irrigate and fertilise the intellectual soil.[78]

The reproof had the desired effect. In his next letter Shelley conceded that his plan had been 'ill-timed' (but defended the efficacy of political associations), promised to withdraw the two pamphlets from circulation, and announced that he was about to leave Ireland.[79]

This episode has been studied extensively by Shelley scholars, who have often read Godwin's side of the correspondence in isolation as the utterances of an ageing, reactionary fireside philosopher, out of touch with Irish politics.[80] However, when Godwin's letters are taken out of the footnotes of Shelley's letters and treated as texts in their own right,

---

[73] Fisher 2009, VI, pp. 525–6.
[74] Shelley 1993, pp. 8, 30.
[75] Shelley 1964, I, p. 258; Godwin 1812a; Godwin 1993, III, pp. 117–23.
[76] Shelley 1964, I, pp. 266–8; Shelley 1993, pp. 296–8, 41–5 (at 42).
[77] Godwin 1993, III, p. 115.
[78] Godwin 1812b, fol. 43r–v.
[79] Shelley 1964, I, p. 276.
[80] E.g., Cameron 1951, p. 154; McNiece 1969, p. 110; Foot 1984, p. 206; O'Brien 2002, p. 123.

alongside his other letters on Ireland, his response may be seen as far from pusillanimous, and the depth of his understanding of Irish affairs becomes clear.

Godwin's warning was based on personal experience. Twelve years before his exchange with Shelley, he had spent six weeks in Ireland as the guest of John Philpot Curran, the defence counsel of choice for United Irishmen prosecuted for treason before and after the 1798 Rebellion, whom Godwin later described as 'the sincerest friend I ever had'.[81] Curran had written to Godwin in June 1800 inviting him to witness the state of Ireland at the time of the passing of the two parallel Acts of Union between Great Britain and Ireland (2 July and 1 August respectively), which both men opposed: 'You would think that slavery is no such fearful thing as you have supposed in theory ... our trees and our fields are as green as ever.'[82] What Godwin took away from the visit was stories of the atrocities of 1798, which he reported in letters home to his friend James Marshall.[83] Through Curran, Godwin met figures across the spectrum of Irish revolutionary politics. Henry Grattan, whom Godwin visited at his country house at Tinnehinch, introduced him to a local man who had been 'twice half-hanged' by English troops during the Rebellion.[84] When Curran took him to the Carlow assizes, the two men stayed overnight at Hacketstown, 'late distinguished for its flourishing streets, but of which every house but two, including the church & the barracks, was reduced to a heap of ruins by the late rebellion'.[85] The intensity of these experiences accounts for Godwin's remark when Shelley yielded to his admonishment in 1812:

I can now look upon you as a friend. Before I knew not what might happen. It was like making an acquaintance with Robert Emmet, who I believe, like yourself, was a man of a very pure mind; but respecting whom I could not have told from day to day, what calamities he might bring upon his country ... & what premature & tragical fate he might bring down upon himself.[86]

Robert Emmet became active in regrouping the United Irishmen after their defeat in 1798 and led an unsuccessful rising against British rule in

---

[81] Godwin 1992a, VI, p. 4.
[82] Quoted in Godwin 2014, p. 149 n. 4. Godwin arrived in Dublin on 2 July, the date on which the Union with Ireland Act 1800 was passed by the British Parliament and entered into statute (39 and 40 Geo. 3 c. 67); the Act of Union (Ireland) 1800 was passed by the Irish Parliament and entered into statute (40 Geo. 3 c. 38) on 1 August; Godwin left Ireland on 12 August (Godwin 2010). The Act of Union (combining these two parallel Acts) was implemented on 1 January 1801.
[83] Godwin 2014, pp. 147–50, 153–65.
[84] Godwin 2014, pp. 158, 161 n. 15.
[85] Godwin 2014, pp. 162, 164–5 n. 9.
[86] Godwin 1812c, fol. 44r–v; for speculations on Godwin's degree of acquaintance with Emmet see Webb 2007, pp. 115–16, 132.

1803, for which he was hanged. He and Godwin represented opposing methods of effecting social change. Shelley, oscillating between the two, had come down on the right side.

Godwin's engagement with Irish affairs did not begin or end with his 1800 visit. As early as 1786, he had published an open letter to the people of Ireland warning of the dangers of a trade union with Britain.[87] In the 1790s and early 1800s, he had many contacts among the Irish in London, ranging from working-class radicals through members of the post-Union migrant community to Whig lawyers and politicians.[88] He was plugged in to a network of Irish Patriot exiles and émigrés well into the 1820s.[89] This discursive community, which was kept together by writing letters, may have been as significant for Godwin's later published writings as Rational Dissent was for *Political Justice*. These letters, properly contextualised, change our view of Godwin's treatment of Ireland in his later published writings. He depicts the history of Ireland as inseparable from that of England, with Ireland serving as a testing-ground for English colonial practices. His novel *Mandeville: A Tale of the Seventeenth Century in England* (1817) opens with a dramatisation of the Anglo-Irish protagonist's childhood experience of the Irish Catholic uprising of 1641.[90] In *Of Population* (1820), he accounts for mass Irish emigration to North America by highlighting the subjugation of Irish Catholics by English colonists since the mid-seventeenth century.[91] In *History of the Commonwealth*, his account of the Cromwellian reconquest of Ireland (1649–53) is based on his dogged tracking of repressive legislation through the English statute book.[92] His personal letters reveal the complexities of his engagement with Irish history, and capture the historical investigator as well as the author and social thinker at work.

Conclusion

The editorial turn in Romantic-era literary studies brings literary scholars onto the same terrain as historians. Textual editing may be the most faithful way of capturing the precise historical context of literary texts. This is not an original observation. In the field of intellectual history,

---

[87] Godwin 1993, I, pp. 297–303.
[88] O'Shaughnessy 2012; on late eighteenth-century metropolitan Irish identities see O'Shaughnessy 2015.
[89] Godwin 2010.
[90] Godwin 1992a, VI, pp. 9–23.
[91] Godwin 1820, pp. 386–7; Godwin 1819, fol. 56r.
[92] Godwin 1824–8, I, pp. 213–44, 245–84, III, pp. 140–62, 322–32; Godwin 1827a; Godwin 1827b.

Peter Laslett's edition of Locke's *Two Treatises of Government* (1960), which showed that the work had been written ten years before the English Revolution of 1688 it had traditionally been held to justify,[93] was a catalyst for the methods of the Cambridge School.

Editorial practice, like historical research, answers theory with evidence. Editors are engaged by the materiality of literary creation and production. Empirical research makes it possible to define the identity, function and meaning of particular texts. This process enables the editor to construct the precise circumstances in which, say, Godwin's *Political Justice* and *Caleb Williams* were written, and to account for the successive series of revisions of each work. In editing his letters, judgements need to be made on a case-by-case basis in order to recover the historical context of each text and the social practices in which it is embedded. Godwin's letters show him to be a more complex figure than literary history has allowed, and may ultimately prove more significant than his published writings for understanding what he was '*up to*'.[94] Viewed collectively, they create a whole that is greater than and different from the sum of the parts.

The editorial turn is expanding the literary canon in all directions, but is of special value in the recovery of Romantic-era letters. The letters of Byron, Coleridge and Keats have long been considered canonical. To understand an extra-canonical figure such as Godwin, it is necessary to treat his letters with the same rigour and precision as any works by the 'Big Six' poets. The literary texts brought to light by the editorial turn feed back into historical understanding of an extended revolutionary era.

References

Abrams, M. H. 1971. *Natural Supernaturalism: Tradition and Revolution in Romantic Literature*, New York.

Anon. 1826. Review of Felicia Hemans, *The Forest Sanctuary, and Other Poems*, *Literary Chronicle*, 379, pp. 518–19.

Barrell, John. 1986. *The Political Theory of Painting from Reynolds to Hazlitt: 'The Body of the Public'*. New Haven.

Bromwich, David. 1994. 'Perfection without Consolation: William Godwin and the Divinity of Reason', *Times Literary Supplement*, 20 May, pp. 7–9.

Butler, J. A. 1997. 'The Cornell Wordsworth Series', *The Wordsworth Circle*, 28, pp. 96–8.

Butler, Marilyn. 1972. *Maria Edgeworth: A Literary Biography*. Oxford.
1979. *Peacock Displayed: A Satirist in his Context*. London.

---

[93] Laslett 1988, pp. 45–66.
[94] See note 45.

1981. *Romantics, Rebels, and Reactionaries: English Literature and its Background, 1760–1830*. Oxford.

1983. 'Three Feet on the Ground', *London Review of Books*, 5, pp. 18–19.

1986. 'Against Tradition: The Case for a Particularized Historical Method' in *Historical Studies and Literary Interpretation*, ed. Jerome J. McGann. Madison.

1987. *Jane Austen and the War of Ideas*, 2nd ed. Oxford.

1995a. 'Editing Women', *Studies in the Novel*, 27, pp. 273–83.

1995b. 'Thompson's Second Front', *History Workshop Journal*, 39, pp. 71–8.

2015. *Mapping Mythologies: Countercurrents in Eighteenth-Century British Poetry and Cultural History*. Cambridge.

Cameron, Kenneth Neill. 1951. *The Young Shelley: Genesis of a Radical*. London.

Cantor, Paul. 1989. 'Stoning the Romance: The Ideological Critique of Nineteenth-Century Literature', *South Atlantic Quarterly*, 88, pp. 705–20.

Claeys, Gregory. 1987. 'Godwinian Enthusiasms', *Historical Journal*, 30, pp. 759–64.

Clemit, Pamela. 1993. *The Godwinian Novel: The Rational Fictions of Godwin, Brockden Brown, Mary Shelley*. Oxford.

2011. 'Introduction' in *The Letters of William Godwin. Volume I: 1778–1797*, ed. Pamela Clemit. Oxford.

2019. 'The Signal of Regard: William Godwin's Correspondence Networks', *European Romantic Review*, 30, pp. 353–66.

Davidson, James Dale and William Rees-Mogg. 1987. *Blood in the Streets: Investment Profits in a World Gone Mad*. London.

Dumas, D. Gilbert. 1966. 'Things as they Were: The Original Ending of *Caleb Williams*', *Studies in English Literature, 1500–1900*, 6, pp. 575–97.

Fisher, D. R., ed. 2009. *The History of Parliament: The House of Commons 1820–1832*. 7 vols. Cambridge.

Fitzpatrick, Martin. 1982. 'Toleration and Truth', *Enlightenment and Dissent*, 1, pp. 5–31.

Foot, Paul. 1984. *Red Shelley*, 2nd ed. London.

Gill, Stephen. 1983. 'Wordsworth's Poems: The Question of Text', *Review of English Studies*, n.s. 34, pp. 172–90.

2011. *Wordsworth's Revisitings*. Oxford.

Godwin, William. 1812a. Letter to Percy Bysshe Shelley, 4 Mar. [ms.]. Bod. MS Abinger c. 19, fols. 37–41. Bodleian Library, Oxford.

1812b. Letter to Percy Bysshe Shelley, 14 Mar. [ms.] Bod. MS Abinger c. 19, fols. 42–3. Bodleian Library, Oxford.

1812c. Letter to Percy Bysshe Shelley, 30 Mar. [ms.] Bod. MS Abinger c. 19, fols. 44–5. Bodleian Library, Oxford.

1819. Letter to William Henry Curran, 9 June. [ms.] Bod. MS Abinger c. 12, fols. 55–6. Bodleian Library, Oxford.

1820. *Of Population: An Enquiry Concerning the Power of Increase in the Numbers of Mankind*. London.

1824–8. *History of the Commonwealth of England. From its Commencement, to the Restoration of Charles the Second*. 4 vols. London.

1827a. Letter to Henry Augustus Dillon-Lee, Viscount Dillon, 8 June. [ms.] Pforz. MS G 0152. New York Public Library, New York.

1827b. Letter to [William Henry Curran], 19 Dec. [ms.] Bod. MS Abinger c. 20, fol. 9. Bodleian Library, Oxford.

1946. *Enquiry Concerning Political Justice and its Influence on Morals and Happiness*, ed. F. E. L. Priestley. 3 vols. Toronto.

1970. *Caleb Williams*, ed. David McCracken. Oxford English Novels. Oxford.

1976. *Enquiry Concerning Political Justice and its Influence on Modern Morals and Happiness*, ed. Isaac Kramnick. London.

1988. *Things as They Are, or, The Adventures of Caleb Williams*, ed. Maurice Hindle. Penguin Classics. Harmondsworth.

1992a. *Collected Novels and Memoirs of William Godwin*, gen. ed. Mark Philp. Pickering Masters. 8 vols. London.

1992b. *An Enquiry Concerning Political Justice and its Influence on General Virtue and Happiness*. Woodstock Facsimile. 2 vols. Oxford.

1993. *Political and Philosophical Writings of William Godwin*, gen. ed. Mark Philp. Pickering Masters. 7 vols. London.

2000. *Caleb Williams*, ed. Gary Handwerk and A. A. Markley. Broadview Literary Texts. Peterborough, Ont.

2009. *Caleb Williams*, ed. Pamela Clemit. Oxford World's Classics. Oxford.

2010. *William Godwin's Diary*, ed. Victoria Myers, David O'Shaughnessy and Mark Philp, http://godwindiary.bodleian.ox.ac.uk/index2.html.

2011. *The Letters of William Godwin. Volume I: 1778–1797*, ed. Pamela Clemit. Oxford.

2013. *An Enquiry Concerning Political Justice*, ed. Mark Philp. Oxford World's Classics. Oxford.

2014. *The Letters of William Godwin. Volume II: 1798–1805*, ed. Pamela Clemit. Oxford.

Goldie, Mark. 2006. 'The Context of the Foundations' in *Rethinking the Foundations of Modern Political Thought*, ed. Annabel Brett et al. Cambridge.

Graver, Bruce E. 2015. 'Editing Wordsworth' in *The Oxford Handbook of William Wordsworth*, ed. Richard Gravil and Daniel Robinson. Oxford.

Hamilton, Paul. 1996. *Historicism*. London and New York.

Hanna, Ralph. 1991. 'Annotation as Social Practice' in *Annotation and its Texts*, ed. Stephen A. Barney. New York.

Jakacki, Diane K. 2017. 'The Women Writers Project', *Early Modern Women*, 11, pp. 140–4.

Kelly, Gary. 1976. *The English Jacobin Novel, 1780–1805*. Oxford.

Laslett, Peter. 1988. 'Introduction' in *Locke: Two Treatises of Government*. Cambridge.

Leask, Nigel. 1988. *The Politics of Imagination in Coleridge's Critical Thought*. Basingstoke.

2017. 'Marilyn Speers Butler, 1937–2014', *Biographical Memoirs of Fellows of the British Academy*, 16, pp. 85–106.

Linkin, Harriet Kramer. 1991. 'The Current Canon in British Romantics Studies', *College English*, 53, pp. 548–70.

McGann, Jerome J. 1983. *The Romantic Ideology: A Critical Investigation*. Chicago.

McNiece, Gerald. 1969. *Shelley and the Revolutionary Idea*. Cambridge, MA.

New, Melvyn. 1984. 'At the Backside of the Door of Purgatory' in *Laurence Sterne: Riddles and Mysteries*, ed. Valerie Grosvenor Myer. London.

O'Brien, Paul. 2002. *Shelley and Revolutionary Ireland*. London.

O'Shaughnessy, David. 2012. '*Caleb Williams* and the Philomaths: Recalibrating Political Justice for the Nineteenth Century', *Nineteenth-Century Literature*, 66, pp. 423–48.

2015. 'Introduction: "Tolerably Numerous": Recovering the London Irish of the Eighteenth Century', *Eighteenth-Century Life*, 39, pp. 1–13.

Pallares-Burke, Maria Lúcia G. 2002. 'Quentin Skinner' in *The New History: Confessions and Conversations*. Oxford.

Philp, Mark. 1986. *Godwin's Political Justice*. London.

Pocock, J. G. A. 1975. *The Machiavellian Moment: Florentine Political Thought and the Atlantic Republican Tradition*. Princeton.

Redfield, Marc. 2006. 'Wordsworth, Poetry, Romanticism: An Interview with Geoffrey Hartman' in *Geoffrey Hartman and Harold Bloom: Two Interviews*, ed. Orrin N. C. Wang, http://romantic-circles.org/praxis/bloom_hartman/toc.html.

Rees-Mogg, William. 2011. 'The Fault Line beneath our Nuclear World', *Mail on Sunday*, 20 March.

Robey, David. 1986. 'Anglo-American New Criticism' in *Modern Literary Theory: A Comparative Introduction*, ed. Ann Jefferson and David Robey, 2nd ed. London.

Robinson, Daniel. 1996. 'Reviving the Sonnet: Women Romantic Poets and the Sonnet Claim', *European Romantic Review*, 6, pp. 98–127.

Robinson, Howard. 1948. *The British Post Office: A History*. Princeton.

Roe, Nicholas. 1988. *Wordsworth and Coleridge: The Radical Years*. Oxford.

St Clair, William. 2004. *The Reading Nation in the Romantic Period*. Cambridge.

Shelley, Mary. 1994. *Frankenstein, or, The Modern Prometheus: The 1818 Text*, ed. Marilyn Butler. Oxford World's Classics. Oxford.

Shelley, Percy Bysshe. 1964. *The Letters of Percy Bysshe Shelley*, ed. F. L. Jones. 2 vols. Oxford.

1993. *The Prose Works of Percy Bysshe Shelley. Volume I*, ed. E. B. Murray. Oxford.

Skinner, Quentin. 1969. 'Meaning and Understanding in the History of Ideas', *History and Theory*, 8, pp. 3–53.

Stillinger, Jack. 1989. 'Textual Primitivism and the Editing of Wordsworth', *Studies in Romanticism*, 28, pp. 3–28.

Sutherland, Kathryn. 1994. '"Events … Have Made Us a World of Readers": Reader Relations 1780–1830' in *The Penguin History of Literature*, vol. V: *The Romantic Period*, ed. David B. Pirie. Harmondsworth.

Thomas, Keith. 1988. *History and Literature: The Ernest Hughes Memorial Lecture Delivered at the College on 7 March 1988*. Swansea.

Thompson, E. P. 1968. *The Making of the English Working Class*, 2nd rev. ed. Harmondsworth.

1993. *Witness Against the Beast: William Blake and the Moral Law*. Cambridge.

Trilling, Lionel. 1955. '*Mansfield Park*' in *The Opposing Self: Nine Essays in Criticism*. London.

Webb, Timothy. 2007. 'Missing Robert Emmet: William Godwin's Irish Expedition' in *Reinterpreting Emmet: Essays on the Life and Legacy of Robert Emmet*, ed. Anne Dolan, Patrick M. Geoghegan and Darryl Jones. Dublin.

Wollstonecraft, Mary. 1989. *The Works of Mary Wollstonecraft*, ed. Janet Todd and Marilyn Butler. Pickering Masters. 7 vols. London.

Wordsworth, Dorothy. 1991. *The Grasmere Journals*, ed. Pamela Woof. Oxford World's Classics. Oxford.

Wordsworth, William. 2014. *Wordsworth's Poetry and Prose*, ed. Nicholas Halmi. Norton Critical Editions. New York.

Wordsworth, William and Dorothy Wordsworth. 1979. *The Letters of William and Dorothy Wordsworth. Volume V: The Later Years: Part II: 1829–1834*, ed. Alan G. Hill, 2nd rev. ed. Oxford.

14   Economics and History: Analysing Serfdom

Sheilagh Ogilvie

Introduction

Economists and historians are often pictured as fundamentally separate clans – sometimes even as warring tribes. In the one camp, economists are believed to fetishise abstract models, assume narrowly materialistic motivations, posit perfectly functioning markets innocent of coercion or institutions, rely exclusively on quantitative evidence drawn from huge homogeneous datasets and construct baroque statistical edifices in an obsession with identifying causal relationships. On the other side, historians are supposed to reject abstraction, focus on non-material desires, regard the market as an ahistorical modern concept, privilege qualitative and narrative sources, reject statistics and – in extreme cases – repudiate causal explanations altogether.[1]

Are the two disciplines indeed so antithetical? Are they doomed to sever future links as they dig deeper into their trenches? Quite the contrary, this chapter will argue. The space between economics and history consists not of no man's land but rather of common ground which benefits both communities and enriches the wider scholarly world.

Economics, as this chapter seeks to show, offers theoretical tools for thinking logically about goal-maximising action, but adopts no a priori definition of what people's goals might be, incorporating preferences for leisure, altruism, security and social bonds alongside pecuniary and material interests. Economics does not restrict itself to well-functioning markets but also analyses market imperfections, information asymmetries, entry barriers, institutions, coercion and crime. Economists often analyse quantitative data, but also use qualitative evidence (e.g., on institutions) where this is most appropriate for investigating the phenomena at hand. Economics has certainly developed advanced statistical approaches, and some of these focus on identifying causal relationships,

---

[1] See Fogel and Elton 1983 for illustrative arguments to this effect, though also for strong similarities of approach unanticipated by the authors.

but it also uses a wide array of other techniques to address bias, data gaps, selection problems, sample composition issues and multivariate associations – empirical issues that also perturb historians.

History, conversely, does not recoil from grand theory. Nor does it intrinsically restrict itself to focusing on intricate nuances and cultural features. Precisely because historians seek a comprehensive understanding of the societies they study, they have been at the forefront in uncovering markets operating in far-flung times and places. Much history does not rely solely on qualitative and narrative evidence, but rather seeks out all possible sources of information, including quantitative ones. Historians may not typically use advanced statistical approaches, but some do. Many historians count, measure, compare, and use quantitative information to test and refine their hypotheses. Finally, few historians wholly abjure questions of causation.

Economic and historical approaches, as will be argued here, are not substitutes but complements. This chapter will build its case in the first instance by exploring an example, showing how economics and history together provide complementary approaches to analysing a specific historical institution: serfdom. To draw out general implications of such disciplinary complementarities, it will scrutinise three scholarly controversies about serfdom: how it shaped peasant choices; how it constrained these choices; and how it affected entire societies. To resolve these controversies, economics and history each brings special expertise, which proves most productive when used jointly. The chapter uses these specific debates about serfdom to draw out general implications concerning the mutually reinforcing capacities of economics and history. It concludes that, by working together, economics and history have improved our understanding of pre-modern society to a much greater extent than either discipline could have achieved in isolation.

Serfdom

Serfdom is the shorthand term for an institutional system in which a landlord was legitimately entitled to restrict the choices of people living on his lands, including binding them to his territory, compelling them to work for him and limiting many of their other economic and demographic decisions.[2] Serfdom prevailed in most European societies in various forms between around 800 and around 1350. After the Black Death (1346–52) serfdom gradually declined in some societies, especially in north-western Europe, but survived for much longer in others.[3]

---

[2] Ogilvie 2014a; Ogilvie 2014b; Ogilvie 2014c; Ogilvie and Carus 2014.
[3] Brenner 1976.

Then, beginning in the sixteenth century, it intensified across much of central, eastern and south-eastern Europe in a development known as the 'second serfdom'. This early modern manifestation of serfdom was abolished in some societies (such as Bohemia) as early as the 1780s but survived in others (such as Russia and Poland) into the 1860s.

Typically, a serf was legally tied to his landlord and had to get that lord's consent to migrate, marry (or stay single), head a household independently (especially if female), sell or bequeath land or buildings, get education or training, practise a non-agricultural occupation, sell goods, lend or borrow money, and make many other economic, demographic, social and cultural choices. In numerous societies under serfdom a large percentage of rural people were personally unfree, were obliged to perform coerced labour for their lords, and were forbidden to move away to escape these burdens.

In pre-modern societies the rural economy employed most of the population and produced almost all output, so where serfdom prevailed it affected the overwhelming majority of people and activities.[4] This makes it important to understand how serfdom worked.[5]

Individual Agency

A central question about serfdom concerns peasant choice. Much traditional scholarship assumed that pre-modern rural people were unwilling or unable to choose what they produced or consumed.[6] Peasants were thought to lack key concepts, such as cost or profit, which were prerequisites for making choices. Instead, peasants were risk averse to such an extent that they were oblivious to the possibility of choosing among opportunities. Peasants were also believed to lack any desire to choose new forms of work or consumption. Rather, they defaulted to traditional norms of subsistence and leisure. These assumptions about peasant choice implied that economic stagnation was caused by distinctive mentalities and thus that policies to reform institutions would be futile.[7]

But how realistic were these assumptions? In recent decades, studies combining economic and historical approaches have generated a more differentiated understanding of peasant decision making.[8] From the

[4] Allen 2001; Broadberry and Gardner 2015.
[5] Ogilvie 2014a; Ogilvie 2014b.
[6] Chayanov et al. 1966 [1925]; Redfield 1956; Polanyi 1957; Brunner 1968; Wolf 1969; Shanin 1971; Scott 1976; Figes 1989; Mironov 1990; Hoch 1996; Pallot 1999.
[7] Little 1982.
[8] Popkin 1979; Wunder 1985; Enders 1995; Ogilvie 2001; Hatekar 2003; Dennison 2011.

perspective of basic microeconomics, it emerged that key components of 'peasant mentalities' are in fact normal for us all.

'Risk aversion', for instance, is a universal feature of economic decision making. Uncertainty has a cost, so reducing it has benefits. Incentives to avoid risks are stronger in poor economies: production is poorly diversified, credit and insurance are lacking, information is scarce, and more people live close to subsistence where risk can mean starvation. Risk aversion is higher in Ethiopia than India, and inside Ethiopian villages it is higher among labourers than farmers. But even rich people in rich economies pay to reduce risks. There is nothing distinctive about risk aversion among unfree peasants.

The same is true of 'leisure preference'. We all choose some combination of consuming goods and consuming leisure. We stop working at the point where the cost of giving up an extra hour of leisure exceeds the benefit. In poor economies, people may choose more leisure because non-subsistence consumer goods are scarce or wage rates are institutionally suppressed. In economies lacking insurance or welfare, people invest in sociability (which may resemble leisure) to create and sustain a social safety net. But even rich people in rich economies consume some leisure. There is nothing specific to serfs about leisure preference.

Historical research on serf societies has upheld, extended and refined this analysis. Archival sources such as court records, land transfers, serf petitions and rent rolls make it possible to analyse serf choices both quantitatively and qualitatively.[9] Serfs rejected innovations when the risk–return ratio was high, but adopted new practices when information was available and risks could be diversified. Serfs were indolent when performing coerced demesne services or forced labour at legally capped wages, but industrious when they themselves received the yield. When their own well-being was at stake, serfs displayed impressive agency, keenly transacting in markets, negotiating for higher pay and haggling for better prices. Serfs bought, sold, rented and leased land, openly seeking good bargains, and calculating the higher price for which a farm might sell because of 'improvement' from clearing and fertilising. Quantitative analyses show that this behaviour was accentuated among poorer serfs, who bought and sold land more frequently than richer ones and transacted more often with strangers.[10] Serfs themselves ascribed inability to assess land values not to the absence of a concept of 'price' but to

---

[9] Among many other studies see Cerman 1996; Hagen 2002; Ogilvie 2005; Dennison and Ogilvie 2007; Dennison 2011.

[10] Štefanová 1999.

youth, inexperience and deficient information.[11] Serfs also had a clear concept of 'profit', 'advantage' and 'utility', engaging in enterprises they thought would make money and trading 'upon profit and loss'.[12] Serfs paid cash to commute coerced labour services, hired other serfs to perform their services, charged and paid interest on loans, paid rebates to borrowers for early repayment, and rented out cattle and land to fellow serfs. Serfs showed a clear understanding of money, bargained for more of it from lords, stole it from one another, detected when it was counterfeit, recorded it in their inheritance inventories, and easily calculated exchange rates between parallel currency systems. Serfs – including females – developed reputations as keen traders and showed a clear appreciation of supposedly 'modern' economic concepts such as the 'opportunity cost of time'.[13] Even in leisure, serfs presented cash to girlfriends, gambled for it over bowls or cards, and carefully apportioned the collective beer tab by head. Despite grinding poverty, serfs even chose to spend their cash on the occasional silk ribbon, illicit pamphlet or cheap portrait of Joseph II.

Basic economic reasoning, therefore, proffered alternative explanations of serfs' actions, in terms of external constraints on their choices rather than internal mental models precluding choice. The explanations stemming from economic analysis were internally consistent and theoretically credible. But whether they indeed explained serfs' behaviour was an empirical question. The expertise of historians made it possible to test and improve these hypotheses by identifying relevant documentary sources, engaging with texts critically, interrogating them for bias (e.g., whether they included women and the poor), and understanding the wider social framework within which economic activity took place, including information sources, kinship relations, property rights, credit links, labour markets, seigneurial coercion, religious conviction and many more features. Together, the logical reasoning of the economist and the rigorous research of the historian generated stronger and more differentiated explanations of serf behaviour. These were based not on patronising assumptions about 'peasant mentalities', but on consistent, plausible and empirically documented patterns of action by serfs themselves. Unfree rural people, it emerged, exercised agency to make the best choices for themselves and their families within a framework of high risks, low information, limited opportunities and institutionalised coercion. Serf agency existed.

[11] Ogilvie 2001, pp. 439–40.
[12] Ogilvie 2001, p. 441.
[13] Ogilvie 2001, pp. 436–7.

Institutional Constraints

The recognition that serfs made choices did not resolve all controversies about serfdom. Rather, it opened up an even livelier debate. Did serfdom matter?

'Serf agency' began to be interpreted as implying that the constraints of serfdom did not seriously affect rural people. Superficially, this seemed to be borne out by micro-level evidence. Historians had suddenly realised that serfs made a colourful array of goal-maximising choices, in many cases without apparent manorial intervention. Many transfers of serf holdings took place with the landlord's consent recorded only in a formulaic phrase, or not at all. Serf marriages were frequently formalised with no obvious record of landlord interference. Serfs migrated from farm to farm, village to village, and sometimes outside the landlord's domain altogether. Serfs hired labourers, earned wages, borrowed and loaned money at interest. They bought and sold food, raw materials, craft wares and proto-industrial manufactures, sometimes trading them far beyond the estate to which they were formally tied.

Do such observations imply that landlord powers were ineffectual and therefore serfdom did not matter? Is the fact that serfs were able to make some choices without visible interference sufficient to conclude that they could make all their choices autonomously, without taking landlord intervention into account, and thus that serfdom did not impose any binding constraints?

Basic economic reasoning can help us assess this argument. The fact that people are observed making choices does not imply that the restrictions on those choices have exercised no effect. People make choices subject to the constraints they face: resources, prices, technology and the institutions of their society – including serfdom. If someone makes a choice that violates socially defined rules, they face the risk of incurring a penalty. This risk does not have to be 100 per cent in order to have a non-zero expected value. Imagine that in seventeenth-century Bohemia migrating without the lord's consent carried a 10-*Schock* fine. Even if the chance of detection was only one in two, the expected monetary cost of illegally migrating would be half of 10 *Schock*, i.e. 5 *Schock*. Even if there was only a 10 per cent change of detection, the expected cost would be 1 *Schock*. In some cases the expected cost would exceed the expected benefit. On the margin, some serfs would refrain from migrating at this expected cost, even while others would go ahead. The same theoretical reasoning applied to transferring one's farm without the lord's consent, defying manorial commands to marry, weaving linen without paying one's loom dues or buying beer from a supplier other than the lord's brewery. All carried penalties of fines, imprisonment or burdens on one's family; and for all there was at least some risk of detection. As a result, the expected cost of engaging in that action was non-zero, and there would therefore be some marginal migraters, land sellers, marriers, linen weavers and even beer drinkers who would refrain from making that choice (which they would otherwise have made), even while others would go ahead. Only if the penalty or the risk of detection for violating manorial restrictions were zero would no one's choices be affected. The fact that some people can be observed making particular choices does not logically imply, therefore, that the institutional rules governing those choices had no effect.

The economics of crime provides further insights.[14] Serfdom entitled lords to impose a system of rules on serfs, and to designate violations of those rules as crimes. Under this legal system the actions taken by both criminals (serfs) and prosecuting authorities (lords) can be analysed as individual choices, influenced by perceived consequences. This analytical framework predicts that we should not necessarily expect to observe lordly enforcement being exercised very frequently. For one thing, regulation was costly in terms of time and personnel, and lords were only interested in forms of intervention that yielded benefits for themselves; this reduced the frequency of intervention to those cases in which serf violations seriously threatened landlord interests and exceeded the costs of enforcement. Second, the existence of lords' power to impose penalties and the desire to avoid attracting such sanctions deterred serfs from even trying to take certain actions. Situations in which serfs refrained from making certain choices because the expected penalty outweighed the expected benefit would, by definition, not be detectable – because nothing happened. But serfdom would still have affected their choices. The institutional constraints of serfdom still make a difference even if some people violate them.

Economic reasoning alone can tell us what is logically possible, but not what actually happened. Here again the expertise of the historian steps in. If serfdom exercised no effect on peasant choices, there should have been arenas of decision making that were off-limits to lordly intervention. Migration, marriage and landholding are three of the most important choices serfs could make and were crucial to the functioning of the rural economy. Investigating them is thus a good way of finding out whether serfdom mattered for peasant decisions.

---

[14] Becker 1968; Cook et al. 2013.

Mobility restrictions were a key component of serfdom.[15] Geographical mobility is now a recognised characteristic of rural societies in the past. Unfree serfs, like free peasants, had many reasons to seek to migrate – in order to work, trade, marry, find a vacant farm, learn a craft, visit kin, practise their religion, and many more. But in deciding whether to migrate in practice, serfs had to take into account the constraints of serfdom. In most serf societies, permanent emigration from the lord's estate required an emancipation certificate showing that one had been 'released in goodwill'.[16] Lords typically granted consent only to low-value serfs whose temporary or permanent absence would not harm manorial interests. The most frequent type of serf migration therefore involved landless or land-poor labourers who could not get jobs on the home estate, craftsmen who could not find vacant workshops locally, journeymen whose guilds obliged them to go on the tramp, or soldiers conscripted by the monarch. Even such temporary migration by low-value serfs required securing lordly consent, paying fees, relinquishing inheritance claims, proving that one had carried out one's prescribed adolescent demesne servanthood, finding a new holder to take responsibility for one's farm and manorial dues, providing personal or financial 'pledges' to guarantee ultimate return, or satisfying some combination of these conditions.[17]

Lacking such consent, not only was the serf legally obliged to stay on his lord's estate, but other lords were breaking the law if they tolerated that serf's illicit presence on their estates. Illegal emigration involved sufficient penalties that many serfs were willing to pay substantial fees for migration permits. Those who migrated without permission were penalised by fining, whipping, gaoling, being put in the stocks or being ordered into forced service on the demesne. On larger estates under the same overlord, movement within the estate from one village to another was in principle permitted, but in practice was prohibited when it threatened manorial interests, for instance by leaving a holding vacant in a thinly settled village, thereby threatening its collective ability to render dues, labour services and taxes. In early modern Bohemia a serf could even be ordered to stay on a particular farm if the lord regarded him as essential to ensure that his village could render coerced labour and other manorial payments.[18] In eighteenth-century Poland, lords forcibly

---

[15] Hatcher 1981; Ogilvie 2005; Ogilvie 2014a; Ogilvie 2014b; Dennison 2011; Klein 2014.
[16] Ogilvie 2005, p. 93.
[17] Smith 1974; Dyer 1980; Hatcher 1981; Whittle 1998; Ogilvie 2005.
[18] Ogilvie 2005, p. 96.

relocated serf families from one holding to another in order to ensure the allocation of serf labour in the interests of the landlord.[19]

This does not mean that all enserfed peasants who wanted to migrate (or wanted not to migrate) were deprived by their lords of any choice in the matter. But it did mean that, before making decisions about their own mobility, those subject to serfdom had to take into account whether they would be allowed to move, how much they would have to pay for a permit, what the penalty would be if they migrated without consent, and what was the risk of being detected migrating illegally. Not every medieval English serf who migrated paid the manorial fine required for permission to move, 'but this does not undermine the point that they were liable to be charged because of their father's tenure and status'.[20] Quantitative approaches have added substance to such arguments. Analysis of 3,644 Bohemian serf petitions between 1652 and 1682, for instance, found that only 25 per cent of applications for migration permits were granted, 21 per cent were denied outright, and all others were deferred or made dependent on satisfying conditions imposed by the lord.[21] As soon as the decision to migrate was made more costly, in terms either of money or of fulfilling other conditions, every serf's migration choices were circumscribed and the marginal migrater was deterred – thus confirming the predictions of the economic models of crime and punishment referred to above. There may have been important types of choice made autonomously by serfs without lordly intervention. But in most serf societies, migration was not one of them.

The same applies to marriage. Peasant nuptiality was influenced by a wide array of factors other than serfdom – individual preferences, family strategies, economic conditions, community pressures – and in most cases there is no record of lordly interference. But the fact that other factors influenced marriage choices and that lords did not frequently intervene does not mean that serf marriage was unconstrained by serfdom. On the contrary: micro-studies show that serfdom constrained marriage choices in far-reaching ways.[22] In most serf societies serfs could not marry without lordly consent: a permit cost money and could be refused. Lords imposed special controls on marriages of orphans, requiring them to pay higher fees and prove that they had been released from forced service on the lord's demesne. Lords also made marriage permits conditional on the couple proving they could support themselves, in order to ensure

[19] Kula 1972; Plakans 1973, Plakans 1975; Freeze 1976; Czap 1978.
[20] Whittle 1998, p. 46.
[21] Ogilvie 2005, p. 81.
[22] Whittle 1998; Ogilvie and Edwards 2000; Ogilvie 2005; Dennison 2011.

that farms were occupied by 'capable holders' who would reliably deliver forced labour, rents and taxes.[23] Lords carefully controlled marriages by their serfs to spouses from outside their estates, since such mixed marriages could create incentives to abscond and uncertainty about the servile status of offspring. Consent was made conditional on settling within the estate, payment of extra fees, promise of future reciprocity by the outside lord, relinquishment of property, debts or inheritance entitlements, and guarantees that offspring would be subject to local servility.

The obligation to obtain the lord's consent imposed costs on serfs wishing to marry and thus constrained their choices. The fees medieval English serfs had to pay lords for marriage permits were sufficiently costly that 'these sums were a burden, and peasants had to adjust their budgets to afford them, and in bad years they would cause real hardship'.[24] Failure to obtain a permit was even more costly. In early modern Bohemia, for instance, those who married without manorial consent were punished with fines, gaoling, and even forcible separation and the deportation of one partner.[25] Denial of a manorial marriage permit led to betrothals being dissolved, illegitimate pregnancies not being legitimised, and serfs eloping. Although such cases may have been rare, it is hard to believe that they did not deter serfs from attempting to undertake marriages likely to attract manorial opposition.

Lords had the power not only to prevent serf marriage but to compel it. In a number of serf societies lords ordered widows, spinsters and bachelors to marry, in order to fill all land with couples that would deliver forced labour and beget new serfs.[26] Even in medieval England, where serfdom was enforced more leniently than in most parts of early modern eastern Europe, lordly pressure on spinsters and widows to marry was not rare.[27] In early modern Bohemia overlords regarded widows as poor fiscal risks and put considerable pressure on them to remarry or vacate their farms. Female household headship was much lower in serf than non-serf societies across Europe, and an econometric analysis of its determinants in rural Bohemia from 1591 to 1722 found that, controlling for other potential influences, female headship was strongly affected by the strategies and policies of the specific manorial regime.[28]

Variants of serfdom in which landlords merely charged fees for marriage permits undeniably constrained peasant choices much less than those in which landlords prohibited certain marriages and compelled

[23] Ogilvie and Edwards 2000, pp. 983–98.
[24] Dyer 2007, p. 74.
[25] Ogilvie 2005.
[26] Hatcher 1981; Ogilvie and Edwards 2000; Ogilvie 2005.
[27] Hatcher 1981.
[28] Ogilvie and Edwards 2000.

others.[29] Not every medieval English serf's daughter who married paid the manorial fine, but that does not alter the fact that they were liable to do so, and thus that serfdom mattered.[30] Although the letter of the law was not always enforced, analysis of medieval English manors indicates that 'the weight of monetary exactions could in itself constitute a grave restriction of freedom'.[31] Likewise, variants of serfdom in which land-lords were unsystematic in requiring serfs to obtain marriage permits, or granted applications in most circumstances, were less restrictive than those in which manorial marriage regulation was comprehensive and applications were often denied. But even when the lord typically only imposed conditions or demanded a fee, he constrained serfs' marriage choices and increased their costs.

Analysis of serf land transfers yields similar findings. Most serf societies reveal much elective action by serfs in buying, selling or bequeathing real property – so much so that it is sometimes claimed that although overlords enjoyed the legal right to limit serf property rights, they seldom did so in practice.[32] The main empirical support for this argument is the fact that village registers seldom record cases in which a land transfer was prohibited by the lord. The problem with this argument is that register-ing a transfer was unlikely to take place before manorial consent had been granted. Problematic transfers were stopped at an earlier stage or even deterred altogether (as with migration and marriage) by the aware-ness, on the part of both individual serfs and the serf commune, that the lord opposed certain types of transfer.

This is borne out by evidence from micro-studies. In almost every serf society a peasant had to obtain permission from the lord before trans-ferring his holding, and the documents testify that the requirement was enforced in practice.[33] Manorial consent could be refused if the new holder was not regarded as a 'capable holder' who would reliably ren-der manorial dues, or if he or she had other undesirable characteristics such as subjection to a different lord or a poor reputation.[34] In a num-ber of rural societies under serfdom, lords blocked land transfers that threatened the impartibility of holdings, since lords regarded impartibil-ity as a guarantee that a holding would be viable in rendering mano-rial dues and services.[35] Quantitative analysis of serf petitions on one

---

[29] Hatcher 1981; Ogilvie 2005.
[30] Whittle 1998.
[31] Hatcher 1981, p. 14.
[32] Melton 1988; Štefanová 1997; Cerman 1999.
[33] Hatcher 1981; Campbell 1984; Whittle 1998; Ogilvie 2005; Van Bavel 2008.
[34] Levett 1938; Homans 1941; Hilton 1975; Ogilvie 2005; Cerman 2008.
[35] Ogilvie 2005; Van Bavel 2008; Cerman 2008.

seventeenth-century Bohemian estate shows that 26 per cent of applications for land-transfer permits were granted, another 26 per cent were denied, and the remainder were deferred or made conditional on satisfying conditions imposed by the lord.[36] Even where lords usually granted permission for land transfers, they were often entitled to collect a fee from both seller and buyer. These fees were not merely symbolic but in many regions amounted to substantial sums that restricted the choices of both seller and buyer.[37] In most medieval English manorial courts such entry fines constituted the largest sums paid into the court, would have sent many incoming serfs to money-lenders to obtain the cash, and 'must sometimes have discouraged them from buying a piece of land'.[38]

Such restrictions affected peasants' choices about land allocation, their ability to borrow money in times of need, their inheritance strategies, the options open to non-inheriting offspring, the stratification of rural society, the development of wage labour and servanthood, the importance of the bond between family and land, kinship behaviour and household structure.[39] Even manorial rules that were violated affected peasant choices by shifting land transfers into the informal sector where risks were high, contract enforcement poor and exploitation rife.[40] The powers of landlords under serfdom created rigidities and rent seeking throughout the whole rural economy, disorted factor and product markets, and prevented serfs from expanding their entrepreneurial activities beyond certain institutionally circumscribed boundaries.[41]

The interplay between economics and history has flowed in both directions as scholars have sought to assess whether and how serfdom constrained peasant choice. A surprising finding to emerge from historical microstudies, for instance, was that manorial restrictions on migration, marriage and land transfers were often enforced not by the lord or his officials, but by serf families and village communities.[42] Family members appeared in the lord's manorial court to report the illegal emigration of relatives, dispute land transfers and prosecute young people who married (or stayed single) to disoblige their kin. Serf communes hunted down absconding villagers, reported illegitimate land transfers to the manorial court, and put formal and informal pressure on village members to marry or remain single.

---

[36] Ogilvie 2005, p. 81.
[37] Van Bavel 2008.
[38] Dyer 2007, pp. 80–1.
[39] Razi 1980; Razi 1993; Raftis 1996; Whittle 1998; Campbell 2005.
[40] Ogilvie 2005.
[41] Campbell 2005; Dennison 2011.
[42] Hatcher 1981; Ogilvie and Edwards 2000; Hagen 2002; Ogilvie 2005; Dennison and Ogilvie 2007; Dennison 2011.

Why would serf families and communities act in this way? Surely one would expect serfs and lords to work against one another when it came to enforcing the constraints of serfdom? Economic reasoning provides an explanation. In the absence of an effective local policing and administrative system, enforcement costs are high. This creates incentives for the authorities to use other mechanisms to enforce costs. One method is to require offenders to name personal guarantors, usually family members, who will be penalised if the suspect violates the lord's regulations. A second enforcement mechanism is to threaten that an individual serf's offence will bring punishment on the offender's whole family or community, which will therefore have an incentive to police compliance. A third approach is for the central authorities (the lord) to devolve enforcement to local authorities (serf communes and families) in return for favourable treatment in future transactions.

Micro-historical research in serf societies as various as Prussia, Bohemia and Russia has revealed precisely such mechanisms in action.[43] If manorial officials believed a serf to be at risk of absconding or violating other rules of serfdom, they required him or her to name groups of 'pledges', usually male relatives, as a bond on compliance. Serf families and serf communes were penalised by the lord if one of their members violated manorial rules, on the grounds that 'it was impossible ... that there was no knowledge of it in the community'.[44] Threats of collective reprisals induced relatives and neighbours to exert familial and communal pressure on individual serfs to comply with restrictions. Finally, lords systematically granted favours to male householders and village oligarchs in return for their help in enforcing manorial regulations on the local level.[45]

Societal Effects

A final question remains. We now know that serfs were able and willing to make rational economic choices, so that slow rural development was probably not caused by distinctive peasant mentalities.[46] We also know that serfdom imposed binding constraints, so that even though serfs exercised agency, there were some choices they would have liked to make but could not.[47] On the level of individual serfs, therefore, serfdom

[43] Hagen 2002; Ogilvie 2005; Dennison and Ogilvie 2007; Dennison 2011.
[44] Quoted in Dennison and Ogilvie 2007, p. 535.
[45] Dennison and Ogilvie 2007, pp. 526–30.
[46] Little 1982; Ogilvie 2001.
[47] Dennison 2006; Ogilvie 2014a; Ogilvie 2014b.

mattered. But did it matter for the whole economy? And, if so, how much did it matter?

In recent decades a revisionist school has contended that serfdom, while oppressing some serfs, did not harm the wider economy.[48] These scholars point to wide variations across serf economies, with only some being notably underdeveloped, while others were more prosperous. Some serfs in eastern Europe, they point out, were materially better off than some freemen in western Europe. Such arguments are adduced to rebut the claim that serfdom had harmful economic effects. Serfdom, it is concluded, was perfectly compatible with economic growth.[49]

There are three linked problems with this argument. The first is that we cannot compare serf with non-serf economies without systematic measures of economic activity as opposed to impressionistic examples. The second problem is that the presence or absence of serfdom is only one of many possible influences on the level and growth rate of economic activity, so that in seeking to identify the effect of serfdom it is necessary to control for other, potentially confounding variables. Finally, even if one detects an association between serfdom and some measure of economic activity, further analysis is necessary to identify whether this reflects a causal relationship. Together, economics and history have tackled these problems.

First we need to find out the facts. If we want to compare economic performance between serf and non-serf societies, we need to start by establishing 'macroeconomic indicators' – information about overall economic activity in a society – for regions that were and were not subject to serfdom. It might be thought that establishing such indicators for historical economies, especially in the period before modern government statistics, would be impossible. Working together, however, economics and history have made significant progress.

Historical national income accounting is a first major sphere of cooperation. Economics provides techniques for calculating national income accounts from underlying data in pre-statistical societies, while history supplies expertise with archival sources and the understanding of how historical societies operated. Such interdisciplinary projects have generated plausible estimates of macroeconomic indicators for an array of societies reaching back before the Black Death.

Figure 14.1 shows estimates of one of these indicators, real per capita GDP, for the 1300–1850 period, during which serfdom vanished in some European societies and survived in others. These estimates show that the

---

[48] Moon 1996; Hagen 2002; Cerman 2012; Stanziani 2014a; Stanziani 2014b.
[49] Hagen 2002, pp. 597–601; Cerman 2012, pp. 6–9, 95–123.

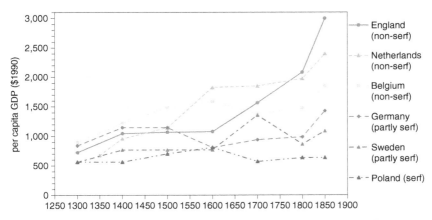

Figure 14.1 Per capita GDP ($1990) in different parts of Europe, *c.*1300–*c.*1850.
Source: Broadberry 2016, table 2; Broadberry, Guan and Li 2018, table 7.

survival of serfdom was associated with diverging economic trajectories, although they do not show that it caused such economic divergence. Among societies in which serfdom survived into the nineteenth century, Poland is the only one whose per capita GDP has been reconstructed over the medieval and early modern periods. Figure 14.1 shows that per capita GDP in Poland was very low, grew very slowly from 1400 to 1600, and declined noticeably from 1600 to 1800. The two partially enserfed societies for which estimates exist are Sweden and the German lands, where serfdom declined in some regions in the late medieval period, but intensified in others from around 1500 to around 1800 under the 'second serfdom'.[50] These societies also had quite low per capita GDP and slow growth, except in Sweden around 1700 and in Germany after about 1800 (the period during which German serfdom was progressively abolished). Among societies in which serfdom disappeared very early, per capita GDP has been estimated for the Netherlands (where serfdom never prevailed), Belgium (where it declined from the twelfth century) and England (where it declined from the fourteenth century). In these societies in the medieval period, per capita GDP was higher than in Sweden or Poland but about the same as Germany. But from around 1400, Belgium and the Netherlands (which were largely free of serfdom by that time) saw consistent economic growth, followed by England after around 1600.

---

[50] Ogilvie 2014a; North 2014; Rasmussen 2014; Jensen et al. 2018; Seppel 2020.

Figure 14.1 thus shows a rough association between an early decline of serfdom and better economic performance, although this association is quite approximate and not necessarily causal – an insight from economics which must be emphasised, as it has greatly strengthened historical argumentation. What these figures do is to establish a factual basis for comparing overall economic performance in a systematic way, a first step towards assessing the possible societal effects of serfdom.

Estimating historical per capita GDP figures requires dedicated work by interdisciplinary research teams combining the expertise of historians and economists.[51] Generating accurate estimates requires the expertise of the historian to examine the underlying sources rigorously with a view to source quality, alternative interpretations, consistency with other findings, and a comprehensive understanding of how the society functioned. It requires the expertise of the economist to ensure that quantities, prices and growth rates of different sectors and production factors are based on realistic assumptions, follow plausible trajectories, and are consistent with one another. Macroeconomic estimates must always be regarded as current best guesses, which rule out obviously impossible or nonsensical values but are constantly revised as new research becomes available. Without the expertise of both historians and economists, we would not even have such good guesses as we do. But even substantial revisions are unlikely to overturn the general patterns in Figure 14.1.

A second macroeconomic indicator for historical societies is the percentage of the population working in agriculture, which reflects the productivity of farming, the degree of economic specialisation, the security of the food supply and the resilience of the economy to growth reversals.[52] Figure 14.2 shows estimates of this indicator for the period during which serfdom vanished in some European societies and survived in others. The Netherlands, Belgium and England, where serfdom was weak or non-existent, already had less than 60 per cent of the population working in agriculture by 1400, falling to less than 50 per cent by 1700. Poland, Germany and Austria-Hungary-Bohemia, where large regions remained wholly or partly enserfed into the nineteenth century, had 75 per cent of their populations working in agriculture until 1500, and still around 65 per cent in 1700. It took serf economies until about 1800 to attain the same degree of agricultural productivity, sectoral specialisation and resilience to growth reversals as non-serf economies had achieved around 1400 – a development delay of four centuries. Again, it must be emphasised that this is just a descriptive association between serfdom

---

[51] See, e.g., Broadberry et al. 2015.
[52] Allen 2000; Broadberry and Gardner 2015.

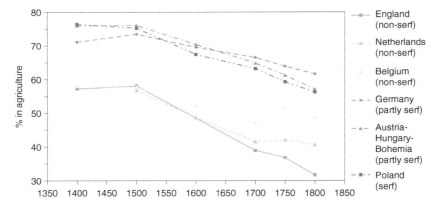

Figure 14.2 Percentage of population in agriculture in different parts of Europe, *c*.1400–*c*.1800.
Source: Allen 2000, pp. 8–9; Broadberry and Gardner 2015, p. 25.

and underdevelopment, whose possible causal dimensions are discussed below.

Economists and historians have worked together to generate a number of other indicators that establish the existence of economic differences between serf and non-serf societies. Urbanisation and agricultural productivity rates were lower in eastern than western Europe from the late medieval period onwards.[53] Real wages were much lower in eastern than western Europe between 1500 and 1800, which economists and historians ascribe to lower productivity in the primarily serf economies of the east.[54] By the early nineteenth century, human heights were around 3 cm lower in the serf societies of Hungary, Galicia and Prussia than in the non-serf societies of England and the Netherlands, despite English and Dutch urbanisation, which systematically reduced human stature because children lacked access to milk.[55] Army recruits from Prussia's eastern territories (where serfdom was more restrictive) were shorter than those from its western territories (where serfdom was mild or non-existent), again despite much higher western urbanisation.[56] Rural female household headship – an indicator of women's autonomy – was substantially lower in eastern than in western Europe during the late

[53] Allen 2000.
[54] Broadberry and Gupta 2006.
[55] Coppola 2010.
[56] Coppola 2010.

medieval and early modern period, averaging around 5 per cent in the east and 15 per cent in the west.[57]

Together, therefore, economists and historians have succeeded in calculating a variety of systematic measures of economic and social activity in serf and non-serf societies. Their findings establish that, as a pure matter of fact, serf and non-serf economies differed on most measures of economic development. This provides a minimal test of whether serfdom harmed the economy. Had serf economies turned out to be characterised by better development measures than non-serf ones, it would have falsified that hypothesis and suggested that serfdom was indeed perfectly compatible with economic growth.

However, as has been emphasised, the link between serfdom and poor development indicators is just an association. To establish whether serfdom exercised a negative economic impact, we need to devise ways of testing for causal effects. Economists and historians have tackled this question in complementary ways, as can be seen from their efforts to investigate widely theorised causal mechanisms by which serfdom was likely to cause economic harm. One such mechanism operated via labour coercion, a central feature of serfdom. Forced labour for the lord involved the extraction of a non-trivial share of a serf family's main resource – as much as three to six days' work every week.[58] This was harmful not only for serfs, but for the wider economy. When labour is coerced, and is thus inadequately rewarded, it creates incentives for the labourer to 'shirk', in the term used by labour economists – to work slowly and unproductively. Extracting forced labour from serfs meant that a non-trivial share of the most important input in the economy – human labour – was deployed unproductively.

Qualitative evidence from contemporaries appears to substantiate that shirking was a major problem with serf labour. In societies as various as medieval England and early modern Bohemia, serf workers were described as so unproductive that it was sometimes worth replacing them with wage workers despite the extra cost.[59] In early nineteenth-century Hanover, Thomas Hodgskin observed of forced serf workers that 'if the landlord had to hire labourers, he might have his work tolerably well performed, but it is now shamefully performed, because the people who have it to do have no interest whatever in doing it well, and no other wish but to perform so little as possible within the prescribed time'.[60] Yet serf

---

[57] Ogilvie and Edwards 2000.
[58] Ogilvie 2014b; Klein 2014.
[59] Stone 1997, p. 641; Himl 2003, p. 87; Klein 2014.
[60] Hodgskin 1820, p. 85.

societies continued to extract forced labour from serfs, even though the incentives created by coercion meant that human time was used unproductively and thus went to waste. This raises the question of whether it might be possible to provide more systematic evidence of a causal link between serfdom and reduced economic productivity.

Historians have tackled this challenge through detailed analysis of archival documents and mobilisation of contextual information on work organisation in serf societies. Stone, for example, made a direct comparison of the productivity of free and forced labour on the fourteenth-century English manor of Wisbech Barton.[61] He analysed a variety of agricultural tasks, including mowing, making hay, weeding, reaping and binding grain. In all cases he found a strong negative relationship between the use of coerced serf workers and the quantity of output per worker. On this demesne alone, for instance, it would have taken coerced serf workers 69–115 more man-days to reap and bind the annual grain harvest than it took free wage workers. Aggregated over the entire economy, this implies that a very large quantity of human labour was wasted by being used in the coerced, and therefore unproductive, institutional setting of serfdom. In analysing the productivity of coerced serf labour compared to free wage labour, Stone gave careful consideration to other variables that might affect productivity, including weather fluctuations, soil fertility, the size of labour inputs, the strength and skill required for different tasks, possible remuneration as a share of the yield, and the potential for theft. Although he could not quantify these confounding variables, he assessed them using contextual evidence and concluded that labour coercion was the main causal factor in accounting for the reduction in productivity.

Economists have tackled the issue of establishing causation very differently, using econometric (i.e., statistical) approaches directed at estimating the effect of serfdom on variations in economic outcomes across time and space, controlling for other possible influences. Such statistical approaches have been applied to a panel of Russian provinces in order to analyse the effect of the abolition of serfdom in 1861 on a range of outcomes, including agricultural productivity, industrial output and peasant nutrition.[62] To deal with the possible influence of confounding variables, variations among provinces in pre-existing characteristics and post-abolition developments were controlled for. The study also used the econometric techniques of difference in differences and instrumental variables to identify whether the associations they found between

---

[61] Stone 1997.
[62] Markevich and Zhuravskaya 2018.

serfdom and economic outcomes were indeed causal relationships. The conclusion was unambiguous: the abolition of serfdom had a positive causal effect on economic outcomes, substantially improving grain productivity, industrial output and industrial employment. Abolishing serfdom improved demographic outcomes, causing peasant mortality to fall by 5.6 per 1,000. The abolition of serfdom had a particularly marked effect in provinces where serfs had previously been obliged to deliver forced labour, leading to a 1.6 cm increase after 1861 in peasant heights, reflecting better nutritional status. The main mechanism by which the disappearance of serfdom improved agricultural performance was by changing the incentives of peasant workers, leading to greater effort, adoption of better agricultural practices and improved exploitation of local agronomic conditions.

Conclusion: Economics and History

Where does this take us in thinking about economics and history? This chapter began by posing three questions about serfdom. Did serf mentalities preclude goal-maximising action? Does serf agency imply that serfdom did not constrain serfs' choices? And did serfdom affect aggregate economic and social outcomes? Alone, neither economics nor history could answer these questions. Together, they are doing so. Neither discipline has dominated. Instead, each contributes distinctive expertise, which complements and enhances the productivity of the other discipline.

Economics spells out the concepts and preferences that constitute economic agency, clearly defining what historians must look for to determine whether serfs engaged in goal-maximising action, what their goals were, and hence whether historical underdevelopment can be ascribed to serf mentalities that precluded economic volition. Economics also clarifies the logic of making choices within a structure of constraints – the fundamental toolkit of microeconomics. This makes it possible to distinguish conceptually between the preferences of serfs on the one hand and the constraints they faced in pursuing those preferences on the other. Economics provides tools to reconstruct per capita GDP, occupational structure and other indicators, making it possible to assess not just whether serfdom was associated with poorer development outcomes, but how large this association was. Finally, economics contributes econometric approaches directed at multivariate analysis and identifying causal relationships. This makes it possible to control for confounding variables and even, in some cases, to establish definitively that the association between serfdom and underdevelopment was a causal effect.

History provides complementary expertise. Historians identify innovative sources of evidence shedding light on the concrete enforcement of serfdom, widening our empirical purview beyond official estate accounts, rent rolls and elite correspondence to village records, manorial court minutes, serf petitions, village land transfer registers and community listings which illuminate the aspirations of serfs and the obstacles impeding their achievement. History provides expertise to interpret sources critically, interrogating them for biases imposed by the literate elites who wrote them, the village oligarchs who enjoyed lordly favour and the adult males who usually spoke for subordinate household members. History contributes its disciplinary ethos of tenaciously seeking to establish exactly what happened and taking into account the widest possible range of contributory factors. History provides its own expertise in approaching the tricky question of establishing causal links, identifying concrete situations recorded in the documents showing how productivity differed between coerced serf labour and free wage labour. History supplies the recognition that however important serfdom might have been, it operated in a wider institutional framework which also has to be taken into account. Finally, history furnishes the intuitive grasp (*Verstehen*) of the whole society which supplies hypotheses to investigate, interpretations for quantitative findings and plausibility tests for conclusions.[63]

Cooperation between economics and history has been crucial to advancing our understanding of serfdom, a critical institution in the development of pre-modern Europe. Serfdom was virtually universal throughout the Middle Ages, and its decline in some societies and survival in others is strongly associated with economic and political divergence between eastern and western Europe from the late medieval period until long past 1800. Precisely because economics and history have not behaved like warring tribes, but instead engaged in peaceful exchange, the realm of scholarship has been enriched.

References

Allen, R. C. 2000. 'Economic Structure and Agricultural Productivity in Europe, 1300–1800', *European Review of Economic History*, 4: 1, pp. 1–25.
2001. 'The Great Divergence in European Wages and Prices from the Middle Ages to the First World War', *Explorations in Economic History*, 38: 4, pp. 411–47.
Becker, G. S. 1968. 'Crime and Punishment: An Economic Approach', *Journal of Political Economy*, 76: 2, pp. 169–217.

---

[63] Carus and Ogilvie 2009.

Brenner, R. 1976. 'Agrarian Class Structure and Economic Development in Pre-Industrial Europe', *Past & Present*, 70, pp. 30–75.

Broadberry, S. 2016. 'When and How Did the Great Divergence Begin?', paper presented to the Fifth Asian Historical Economics Conference, Seoul National University, Seoul, September 2–3, 2016.

Broadberry, S., B. Campbell, A. Klein, M. Overton and B. Van Leeuwen. 2015. *British Economic Growth, 1270–1870*. Cambridge.

Broadberry, S. and L. Gardner. 2015. 'Economic Development in Africa and Europe: Reciprocal Comparisons', *Revista de Historia Economica/Journal of Iberian and Latin American Economic History*, 34: 1, pp. 11–37.

Broadberry, S., H. Guan and D. D. Li. 2018. 'China, Europe, and the Great Divergence: A Study in Historical National Accounting, 980–1850', *Journal of Economic History*, 78: 4, pp. 955–1000.

Broadberry, S. and B. Gupta. 2006. 'The Early Modern Great Divergence: Wages, Prices and Economic Development in Europe and Asia, 1500–1800', *Economic History Review*, 59: 1, pp. 2–31.

Brunner, O. 1968. 'Das Ganze Haus und die Alteuropäische Ökonomik' in *Neue Wege der Sozialgeschichte*, ed. O. Brunner. Göttingen.

Campbell, B. M. S. 1984. 'Population Pressure, Inheritance and the Land Market in a Fourteenth-Century Peasant Community' in *Land, Kinship and Life-Cycle*, ed. R. M. Smith. Cambridge.

   2005. 'The Agrarian Problem in the Early Fourteenth Century', *Past & Present*, 188, pp. 3–70.

Carus, A. W. and S. Ogilvie. 2009. 'Turning Qualitative into Quantitative Evidence: A Well-Used Method Made Explicit', *Economic History Review*, 62: 4, pp. 893–925.

Cerman, M. 1996. 'Proto-industrialisierung und Grundherrschaft: ländliche Sozialstruktur, Feudalismus und proto-industrielles Heimgewerbe in Nordböhmen vom 14. bis zum 18. Jahrhundert (1381–1790)'. PhD thesis, University of Vienna.

   1999. 'Gutsherrschaft und untertäniges Gewerbe: die Herrschaften Frýdlant und Liberec in Nordböhmen', *Jahrbücher für Geschichte Osteuropas*, 47: 1, pp. 2–19.

   2008. 'Social Structure and Land Markets in Late Medieval Central and East-Central Europe', *Continuity and Change*, 23: 1, pp. 55–100.

   2012. *Villagers and Lords in Eastern Europe, 1300–1800*. Basingstoke and New York.

Chayanov, A. V., D. Thorner, B. Kerblay and R. E. F. Smith. 1966 [1925]. *The Theory of Peasant Economy*. Homewood, IL.

Cook, P. J., S. Machin, O. Marie and G. Mastrobuon, eds. 2013. *Lessons from the Economics of Crime: What Reduces Offending?* Cambridge, MA.

Coppola, M. 2010. 'The Biological Standard of Living in Germany before the Kaiserreich, 1815–1840: Insights from English Army Data', *European Review of Economic History*, 14: 1, pp. 71–109.

Czap, P. 1978. 'Marriage and the Peasant Joint Family in Russia', in *The Family in Imperial Russia: New Lines of Historical Research*, ed. D. L. Ransel. Urbana.

Dennison, T. 2006. 'Did Serfdom Matter? Russian Rural Society, 1750–1860', *Historical Research*, 79: 203, pp. 74–89.

2011. *The Institutional Framework of Russian Serfdom*. Cambridge.

Dennison, T. and S. Ogilvie. 2007. 'Serfdom and Social Capital in Bohemia and Russia', *Economic History Review*, 60: 3, pp. 513–44.

Dyer, C. 1980. *Lords and Peasants in a Changing Society: The Estates of the Bishopric of Worcester, 680–1540*. Cambridge.

2007. 'The Ineffectiveness of Lordship in England, 1200–1400', *Past & Present*, 195, pp. 69–86.

Enders, L. 1995. 'Individuum und Gesellschaft: bäuerliche Aktionsräume in der frühneuzeitlichen Mark Brandenburg' in *Gutsherrschaft als soziales Modell: vergleichende Betrachtungen zur Funktionsweise frühneuzeitlicher Agrargesellschaften*, ed. J. Peters. Munich.

Figes, O. 1989. *Peasant Russia, Civil War: The Volga Countryside in Revolution (1917–1921)*. Oxford.

Fogel, R. W. and G. R. Elton. 1983. *Which Road to the Past? Two Views of History*. New Haven.

Freeze, G. L. 1976. 'The Disintegration of Traditional Communities: The Parish in Eighteenth-Century Russia', *Journal of Modern History*, 48: 1, pp. 32–50.

Hagen, W. W. 2002. *Ordinary Prussians: Brandenburg Junkers and Villagers 1500–1840*. Cambridge.

Hatcher, J. 1981. 'English Serfdom and Villeinage: Towards a Reassessment', *Past & Present*, 90, pp. 3–39.

Hatekar, N. 2003. 'Farmers and Markets in the Pre-Colonial Deccan: The Plausibility of Economic Growth in Traditional Society', *Past & Present*, 178: 1, pp. 116–47.

Hilton, R. H. 1975. *The English Peasantry in the Later Middle Ages*. Oxford.

Himl, P. 2003. *Die 'armben Leüte' und die Macht: die Untertanen der südböhmischen Herrschaft Český Krumlov/Krumau im Spannungsfeld zwischen Gemeinde, Obrigkeit und Kirche (1680–1781)*. Stuttgart.

Hoch, S. 1996. 'The Serf Economy and the Social Order in Russia' in *Serfdom and Slavery: Studies in Legal Bondage*, ed. M. L. Bush. Harlow.

Hodgskin, T. 1820. *Travels in the North of Germany: Describing the Present State of the Social and Political Institutions, the Agriculture, Manufactures, Commerce, Education, Arts and Manners in that Country Particularly in the Kingdom of Hannover*. Edinburgh.

Homans, G. C. 1941. *English Villagers of the Thirteenth Century*. New York.

Jensen, P. S., C. V. Radu, B. Severgnini and P. Sharp. 2018. 'The Introduction of Serfdom and Labor Markets', CEPR Discussion Paper DP13303.

Klein, A. 2014. 'The Institutions of the "Second Serfdom" and Economic Efficiency: Review of the Existing Evidence for Bohemia' in *Schiavitu e servaggio nell'economia europea. Secc. XI–XVIII/Slavery and Serfdom in the European Economy from the 11th to the 18th Centuries*, ed. S. Cavaciocchi. Florence.

Kula, W. 1972. 'La seigneurie et la famille paysanne dans la Pologne du XVIIIe siècle', *Annales. Histoire, Sciences Sociales*, 27: 4–5, pp. 949–58.

Levett, A. E. 1938. *Studies in Manorial History*. Oxford.

Little, I. M. D. 1982. *Economic Development: Theory, Policy, and International Relations*. New York.

Markevich, A. and E. Zhuravskaya. 2018. 'The Economic Effects of the Abolition of Serfdom: Evidence from the Russian Empire', *American Economic Review*, 108: 4–5, pp. 1074–1117.

Melton, E. 1988. 'Gutsherrschaft in East Elbian Germany and Livonia, 1500–1800: A Critique of the Model', *Central European History*, 21: 4, pp. 315–49.

Mironov, B. N. 1990. 'The Russian Peasant Commune after the Reforms of the 1860s' in *The World of the Russian Peasant: Post-Emancipation Culture and Society*, ed. B. Eklof and S. Frank. Boston and London.

Moon, D. 1996. 'Reassessing Russian Serfdom', *European History Quarterly*, 26: 4, pp. 483–526.

North, M. 2014. 'Serfdom and Corvee Labour in the Baltic Area 16th–18th Centuries' in *Schiavitu e servaggio nell'economia europea. Secc. XI–XVIII/ Slavery and Serfdom in the European Economy from the 11th to the 18th Centuries*, ed. S. Cavaciocchi. Florence.

Ogilvie, S. 2001. 'The Economic World of the Bohemian Serf: Economic Concepts, Preferences and Constraints on the Estate of Friedland, 1583–1692', *Economic History Review*, 54: 3, pp. 430–53.

  2005. 'Communities and the "Second Serfdom" in Early Modern Bohemia', *Past & Present*, 187, pp. 69–119.

  2014a. 'Choices and Constraints in the Pre-Industrial Countryside' in *Population, Welfare and Economic Change in Britain, 1290–1834*, ed. C. Briggs, P. Kitson and S. J. Thompson. Woodbridge.

  2014b. 'Serfdom and the Institutional System in Early Modern Germany' in *Schiavitu e servaggio nell'economia europea. Secc. XI–XVIII/Slavery and Serfdom in the European Economy from the 11th to the 18th Centuries*, ed. S. Cavaciocchi. Florence.

  2014c. 'Slavery and Serfdom in the European Economy: Contribution to Tavola Rotunda' in *Schiavitu e servaggio nell'economia europea. Secc. XI– XVIII/Slavery and Serfdom in the European Economy from the 11th to the 18th Centuries*, ed. S. Cavaciocchi. Florence.

Ogilvie, S. and A. W. Carus. 2014. 'Institutions and Economic Growth in Historical Perspective' in *Handbook of Economic Growth*, ed. S. Durlauf and P. Aghion, vol. IIA. Amsterdam.

Ogilvie, S. and J. Edwards. 2000. 'Women and the "Second Serfdom": Evidence from Early Modern Bohemia', *Journal of Economic History*, 60: 4, pp. 961–94.

Pallot, J. 1999. *Land Reform in Russia, 1906–1917: Peasant Responses to Stolypin's Project of Rural Transformation*. Oxford.

Plakans, A. 1973. 'Peasant Families East and West: A Comment on Lutz K. Berkner's "Rural Family Organization in Europe: A Problem in Comparative History"', *Peasant Studies Newsletter*, 2: 3, pp. 11–16.

  1975. 'Seigneurial Authority and Peasant Life: The Baltic Area in the Eighteenth Century', *Journal of Interdisciplinary History*, 5: 4, pp. 629–54.

Polanyi, K. 1957. *The Great Transformation*. Boston.

Popkin, S. 1979. *The Rational Peasant: The Political Economy of Rural Society in Vietnam*. Berkeley.

Raftis, J. A. 1996. *Peasant Economic Development within the English Manorial System*. Stroud.

Rasmussen, C. P. 2014. 'Forms of Serfdom and Bondage in the Danish Monarchy' in *Schiavitu e servaggio nell'economia europea. Secc. XI–XVIII/ Slavery and Serfdom in the European Economy from the 11th to the 18th Centuries*, ed. S. Cavaciocchi. Florence.

Razi, Z. 1980. *Life, Marriage and Death in a Medieval Parish: Economy, Society and Demography in Halesowen 1270–1400*. Cambridge.

　　1993. 'The Myth of the Immutable English Family', *Past & Present*, 140, pp. 3–44.

Redfield, R. 1956. *Peasant Society and Culture: An Anthropological Approach to Civilization*. Chicago.

Scott, J. C. 1976. *The Moral Economy of the Peasant: Rebellion and Subsistence in Southeast Asia*. New Haven.

Seppel, M. 2020. 'The Semiotics of Serfdom: How Serfdom was Perceived in the Swedish Conglomerate State, 1561–1806', *Scandinavian Journal of History*, 45: 1, pp. 48–70.

Shanin, T. 1971. 'Introduction: Peasantry as a Concept' in *Peasants and Peasant Societies*, ed. T. Shanin. London.

Smith, R. M. 1974. 'English Peasant Life-Cycles and Socio-Economic Networks: A Quantitative Geographical Case Study'. PhD thesis, University of Cambridge.

Stanziani, A. 2014a. *Bondage: Labor and Rights in Eurasia from the Sixteenth to the Early Twentieth Centuries*. New York.

　　2014b. 'Russian Serfdom: A Reappraisal', *Ab Imperio*, 2, pp. 71–99.

Štefanová, D. 1997. 'Herrschaft und Untertanen: ein Beitrag zur Existenz der rechtlichen Dorfautonomie in der Herrschaft Frýdlant in Nordböhmen (1650–1700)' in *Gutsherrschaftsgesellschaften im europäischen Vergleich*, ed. J. Peters. Berlin.

　　1999. *Erbschaftspraxis und Handlungsspielräume der Untertanen in einer gutsherrschaftlichen Gesellschaft: die Herrschaft Frýdlant in Nordböhmen, 1558–1750*. Munich.

Stone, D. 1997. 'The Productivity of Hired and Customary Labour: Evidence from Wisbech Barton in the Fourteenth Century', *Economic History Review*, 50: 4, pp. 640–56.

Van Bavel, B. J. P. 2008. 'The Organization and Rise of Land and Lease Markets in Northwestern Europe and Italy, c. 1000–1800', *Continuity and Change*, 23: 1, pp. 13–53.

Whittle, J. 1998. 'Individualism and the Family–Land Bond: A Reassessment of Land Transfer Patterns among the English Peasantry', *Past & Present*, 160, pp. 25–63.

Wolf, E. R. 1969. *Peasant Wars of the Twentieth Century*. New York.

Wunder, H. 1985. 'Der dumme und der schlaue Bauer' in *Mentalitat und Alltag im Spatmittelalter*, ed. C. Meckseper and E. Schraut. Göttingen.

15 The Return of Depression Economics: Paul Krugman and the Twenty-First-Century Crisis of American Democracy

Adam Tooze

In the first decades of the twenty-first century there was no more influential analyst of the crises of liberal America than Paul Krugman. As an author and columnist for the *New York Times* he has a huge following. He is one of the first generation of commentators whose career was born on the internet. As of the summer of 2022 he had 4.6 million Twitter followers.

Krugman is an economist, a Nobel Prize winner no less. As such it is tempting to say that what he has chronicled over the last three decades are the crises of neo-liberalism. Krugman does not shy away from using that loaded term.[1] However, what is actually at stake is something more general, what in economics is referred to as the neo-classical synthesis, the framework within which economics emerged as a policy discipline in the mid-twentieth century. Whereas neo-liberalism and the market revolution are indelibly associated with the University of Chicago in the 1970s, the neo-classical synthesis of economic policy advising in the USA was forged above all at Krugman's Alma Mater, MIT.[2] It made MIT's Economics department into by far the most practically influential centre of economic analysis in the United States, and thus in the world. It remains so. For Krugman, MIT's neo-classical synthesis subsumed Milton Friedman's monetarism as one of its variants. What Krugman is diagnosing is, therefore, something more far reaching than the crisis of neo-liberalism. What has come apart in the early twenty-first century is the basic structure for coordinating power and expert knowledge in America's democracy. What is more, Krugman did not merely declare the crisis of the neo-classical synthesis, he historicised it. If it is Krugman's economic expertise that gives him his platform of authority, what earns him his audience is his ability to articulate the crisis of liberal America as dramatic political and

---

[1] Krugman 2018.
[2] On some of the background see Applebaum 2019.

economic narrative. His writings and commentary are self-consciously historicising interventions. In fact, history is everywhere in Krugman's thought.

All too often neo-liberalism and the market revolution are associated with the end of history.[3] In the classic formulation of Francis Fukuyama this depended on aligning history with questions of political and constitutional order, thus putting revolutionary upheavals centre stage: 1789–1917–1989.[4] But, if one views technology and the spatial expansion of economic development as rising to the status of history, this was always unconvincing. The era of 'hyperglobalisation' from the 1990s onwards was a world historic drama.[5] Explaining the global division of labour, first to his fellow economists and then to a wider public, was how Krugman originally conceived his role. The economics for which he won the Nobel Prize is an irreducibly historical theory of the division of labour and of economic geography. Up to 2000 Krugman was a fierce defender of the status quo. It was the upheaval in American politics in the early twenty-first century that forced him to historicise his role in more critical terms. If he has moved from being an admittedly self-absorbed professional economist to being a political actor he insists that this is not just a matter of his personal development but impelled by broader historical forces. Krugman diagnosed three trends – in American economy and society, in American politics and in the intellectual dynamics of the field of economics – which converged between 2008 and 2013 to produce a profound break in the once-confident neo-classical synthesis. Beyond the inherent interest of this or that intellectual and political intervention and the enjoyment to be gained from his robust prose, it is this broader crisis that gives larger meaning to Krugman's trajectory.

Perhaps the drama of Krugman's development was prefigured by its beginning. As he tells his story, he did not set out to be a pundit, nor did he set out to be an economist. His 'first love was history'.[6] In fact, not history but psychohistory.

In autobiographical reflections after winning the Nobel Prize, Krugman described his domestic and high school existence in the suburbs of New York in the 1960s as entirely mundane except for 'those science fiction novels. Indeed, they may have been what made me go into

[3] Hartog 2016.
[4] Fukuyama 1993.
[5] Kessler and Subramanian 2013.
[6] Krugman 2020, p. 396.

economics.' His particular favourite was Isaac Asimov's classic *Foundation* trilogy. 'It is one of the few science fiction series that deals with social scientists – the "psychohistorians", who use their understanding of the mathematics of society to save civilization as the Galactic Empire collapses.'[7] Psychohistory, as Asimov imagined it, was a projection into the future of nineteenth-century positivist sociology, a science not of man but of 'man-masses', the science of mobs, 'mobs in their billions'.[8] 'I loved *Foundation*', Krugman confessed to a journalist of the *New Yorker* in 2010, 'and in my early teens my secret fantasy was to become a psychohistorian.'[9]

Like a young person of Koselleck's 'Sattelzeit', Krugman imagined his future in terms of a character in a historical novel, in this case an omniscient Comtean social scientist in a Cold War age. Like any good *Bildungsroman*, this egohistoire has a twist. Unfortunately for Krugman, when he arrived at Yale in 1970 he discovered that 'no such thing' as psychohistory actually existed '(yet)'. The actual academic history that he encountered was 'too much about what and when and not enough about why'. It was this disappointment that led him to economics. Economics examined the same infinitely complicated social reality, but sought to explain it with simple basic forces. Moving to MIT as a graduate student he encountered the Polish–Russian emigré Evsey Domar, one of the legendary figures of early growth economics. Domar addressed history in terms that Krugman could appreciate. He posed questions such as 'Why did some societies have serfs or slaves while others did not? You could talk about culture and national character and climate and changing mores and heroes and revolts.' Or 'You could argue that if peasants are barely surviving there's no point in enslaving them. But if good new land becomes available it makes sense to enslave them, because you can skim off the difference between their output and what it takes to keep them alive. Suddenly, a simple story made sense of a huge and baffling swath of reality.'[10] For Krugman, economics was the struggle to bring intellectual clarity to the complexity of history.

Krugman went on to discover that this divergence between history and economics has its own history. It was 'a development that Keynes had helped to bring about'. In American Economics departments prior to the late 1930s 'economics had been more like history: institutional economics was dominant, and, in opposition to neoclassical economics,

[7] Krugman n.d.a.
[8] Asimov 2010, pp. 205, 411.
[9] MacFarquhar 2010.
[10] MacFarquhar 2010. For Domar's argument see Domar 1970.

emphasized the complicated interactions between political, social, and economic institutions and the complicated motives that drove human economic behavior'. 'Then', Krugman said, 'came the Depression, and the one question that people wanted economists to answer was "What should we do?"' 'The institutionalists said, "Well, it's very deep, it's complex ... ". Keynes by contrast, "coming out of the model-based tradition ... basically said, 'Push this button.'"'[11] That was both intellectually clarifying and, as Krugman was to realise, politically enabling. 'Thinking about economic situations as infinitely complex, with any number of causes going back into the distant past tended to induce a kind of fatalism.'[12] It was the ability of economics to identify simple mechanisms that created the precondition both for thought and for agency. The freedom for clear-sighted analysis and for action depended on refusing the fullest historical determination of reality.

This desire for simplification defines Krugman's relationship not just to history but to economics as well. Krugman was never a highly technical mathematical economist. He is known not as a technician but as a poet. His preferred tools are small and elegant models, also known as 'toy' models. This differentiates him also from the more orthodox Keynesians. Many true-believing Keynesians are driven by the need to rescue the deepest insights of 'the master' lost by subsequent academic and technocratic appropriation.[13] The model most commonly blamed for Keynes's bowdlerisation is IS-LM. Proposed by John R. Hicks in 1937 it reduced Keynes's *General Theory of Employment, Interest and Money* to two equations that can be mapped in a single graph.[14] Joan Robinson denounced IS-LM as the progenitor of 'bastard Keynesianism'.[15] IS-LM is Krugman's favourite analytical device. He likes it so much that he has gone to the trouble of providing a simplified explanation to the millions of readers of his blog.[16]

Krugman's primary intellectual and professional attachment is not to the Keynes of inter-war Britain, but to the home-grown American tradition of which the founding text is Paul Samuelson's 1948 textbook, *Economics*.[17] As Krugman put it: 'It's an approach that combines the grand tradition of microeconomics, with its emphasis on how the invisible hand leads to generally desirable outcomes, with Keynesian macroeconomics,

---

[11] MacFarquhar 2010.
[12] MacFarquhar 2010.
[13] For a pop version see Akerlof 2009.
[14] Hicks 1937.
[15] Blackhouse and Laidler 2004.
[16] Krugman 2011a.
[17] Samuelson 1955.

which emphasizes the way the economy can develop magneto trouble, requiring policy intervention.'[18] The neo-classical synthesis is thus based on an intellectual dualism, a dualism with practical policy implications. As Samuelson put it in a famous line: 'Solving the vital problems of monetary and fiscal policy by the tools of income analysis will validate and bring back into relevance the classical verities.'[19] Politics was confined to the realm of macroeconomics so that microeconomics could follow its own rules. Or, in Krugman's words: 'The basic idea is that if you can get macro right then micro will follow. In Samuelson's synthesis, one must count on the government to ensure more or less full employment; only once that can be taken as given do the usual virtues of free markets come to the fore.'[20]

In the post-war period, with Samuelson as its anchor, MIT became the leading Economics department worldwide. Though Chicago tends to hog the limelight, and has attracted an inordinate amount of attention from intellectual historians, it was in fact MIT that framed the model of technical but practically relevant economics.[21] From Nobel Prize winners to central bank governors and prime ministers such as Stanley Fischer and Mario Draghi, its influence is all-pervasive.

Given this backdrop, Krugman explains the emergence of the intellectual project that would define his academic career at MIT, and earn him the Nobel Prize, in environmental terms.[22] The main preoccupation of the MIT department was to work on the dualism laid down by Samuelson. An urgent question was how loosening restrictive assumptions about the microeconomic realm might have macroscopic effects. For Krugman, treading in the footsteps of the young Joseph Stiglitz, this meant focusing on problems of increasing returns, externalities and imperfect competition. Why these issues were so disturbing to conventional equilibrium economics is that if a production process realises lower costs per unit as production increases, this may trigger a runaway process. Greater production leads to lower prices, leads to more demand, leads to greater production and lower cost and so on. One might think that this was, in fact, a good description of economic growth, but from an equilibrium-modelling point of view it is not very tractable. It was not by accident that these difficult calculations became more feasible in the 1970s. As Krugman put it, 'the availability of easy computation'

---

[18] Krugman 2020, pp. 407–8.
[19] Samuelson 1955, p. vii.
[20] Krugman 2020, pp. 407–8.
[21] Weintraub 2014.
[22] Krugman 1999a.

encouraged the exploration of 'nonlinear dynamics' that had previously been prohibitively expensive.[23]

In this creative milieu, with new tools at his disposal, Krugman built manageable models incorporating increasing returns to scale and externalities, which, under the influence of Rudiger Dornbusch, he applied to international trade. The payoff was to explain how centres of industrial production and competitive advantage emerged, between which trade could then take place. The effect of this analytical move was to explain international trade not by reference to natural conditions or initial factor endowments but as the result of path-dependent processes and, thus, history. As Krugman remarked:

I think Henry Ford once said that history is just one damn thing after another. Maybe not, but explanations of economic location are almost always historical, and the history does tend to have a 'one damn thing after another' character. ... If you try to explain why a particular region is home to a particular industry, you usually end up explaining it largely by describing the sequence of events that caused the industry to be there.[24]

This was a major analytical achievement, but it also had immediate significance in explaining the world. For trade theorists, one of the puzzles of the post-war growth boom was that the majority of trade was no longer between commodity producers on the one hand and manufacturing workshop economies on the other. That older 'colonial model' of trade was well explained by basic Ricardian trade theory. After 1945, increasingly, trade was between high-income countries exchanging different brands of automobile or washing machine. Krugman's model explained why. It also posed the question of whether one could change such patterns. That too was an urgent practical question. Krugman presented his foundational paper to the National Bureau of Economic Research in the summer of 1979, just as the worst of Western de-industrialisation was beginning.[25] The subsequent decade was one of traumatic adjustment and increasing global competition. Many readers saw in Krugman's work a licence for government intervention and so-called strategic trade policy.[26] If you knew that a particular industrial concentration was the result of a history of cumulative causation, why not intervene to change the pattern?

Krugman was certainly an advocate of the need for change. He wrote his first popular book, *The Age of Diminished Expectations*, to puncture

[23] Krugman 1999b.
[24] Krugman n.d.a.
[25] Krugman 1979.
[26] Krugman 1986.

the complacency of the Reagan era. Compared to the 1960s the American economy was not doing well, and what growth was happening was generating benefits only for those at the top of the income distribution.[27] For all his dissatisfaction with the status quo, however, Krugman had no truck with the protectionism of much of the Democratic Party under Bill Clinton. In the 1990s Krugman entered the ring of public debate above all as a scourge of left-leaning critics of globalisation.[28] Specifically, it was at a seminar at Little Rock, Arkansas, in December 1992, as the Clinton transition team prepared for power, that Krugman realised the gulf that separated policy from the state of the art in economics.[29] Over the following years he engaged in violent polemics with Clinton's labour secretary, Robert Reich, and industrial-policy advocate Lester Thurow. Krugman attacked their pessimistic accounts of the threat posed by Japan and China. The contemporary obsession with 'competitiveness' was a piece of business-school nonsense that conflated the perspective of corporations with that of national economies.[30] The proper focus of policy was on broad-based technological change, education and domestic tax and welfare policies.

Krugman was finally reconciled to the Clinton administration in 1995 when Robert Rubin, formerly CEO of Goldman Sachs, and Larry Summers, Krugman's contemporary at MIT, took over the reins at the US Treasury. These finally were the 'mature, skillful economic leaders' that America and the world needed, who 'in a pinch would do what had to be done. They would insist on responsible fiscal policies; they would act quickly and effectively to prevent a repeat of the jobless recovery of the early 90s, let alone a slide into Japanese-style stagnation.'[31] They fully understood the new classical synthesis position. The thing for macro-economic policy to do was not to pick winners, but to stabilise the overall economic parameters and let markets take care of the rest.

Krugman's emphasis on the need for macroeconomic leadership was heightened by the emerging-market financial crises that began in Mexico in 1995 and ended in Argentina and Turkey in 2001. For Krugman, the worrying thing about globalisation was not the long-run structural change it produced, but the challenge it posed for macroeconomic management.

This was the argument that Krugman made in *The Return of Depression Economics*, which he rushed into print in 1999. The echoes of the 1930s

---

[27] Krugman 1997.
[28] Hirsch 2019.
[29] Krugman 1996.
[30] Krugman 2009c.
[31] Krugman 2003, p. 19.

in his title were deliberate. The emerging-market crises of the late 1990s were a throwback in a double sense. The crises in Mexico, Thailand, Indonesia and South Korea resulted from a once-familiar combination of collapsing confidence, financial panic and real economic recession. This was made worse by the failure of policy to respond with sufficient force and speed. That was the doubled meaning of 'return'. It was not just that Keynesian economics had a new relevance as an explanation of crises. The case needed to be made, once again, for prompt and effective policy action.

What Krugman argued was that the market revolution of the 1980s and 1990s had created a kind of time warp.[32] It had turned the clock back, re-creating both the advantages and risks of the Edwardian and inter-war eras. It was large-scale global capital mobility, financial innovation, low inflation and a commitment to balanced budgets that set the world up for a repeat of a 1930s-style recession. The remedy was to go back to the future, to the era of Bretton Woods, out of which Samuelson's neo-classical synthesis had emerged: 'Sooner or later we will have to turn the clock at least part of the way back: to limit capital flows for countries that are unsuitable for either currency unions or free floating; to reregulate financial markets to some extent; and to seek low but not too low inflation rather than price stability. We must heed the lessons of Depression economics, lest we be forced to relearn them the hard way.'[33]

The one thing that reassured Krugman at the time was that the problem was not (yet) American. So far, the risks were concentrated in the emerging markets. To make sense of this temporal and geographical displacement, Krugman used the language of emerging infectious diseases and biohazards that was very much en vogue in the late 1990s. As Krugman put it in 2009, looking back to the first edition of 1999: 'At the time, I thought of it this way: it was as if bacteria that used to cause deadly plagues, but had long been considered conquered by modern medicine, had reemerged in a form resistant to all the standard antibiotics.'[34]

Krugman continued to trust in the quality of American leadership. Indeed, the assumption of a competent American hegemony was the premise on which he made the transformational career decision in 1999 to join the *New York Times* as a regular columnist. As he later described it, his hiring was due to the view of the 'paper's editorial page editor' that

---

[32] Intriguingly, a hostile neo-Austrian review of Krugman's book chose to label him as a 'post-modern' palaeo-Keynesian. See Ritenour 2000.
[33] Krugman 1999c, p. 74.
[34] Krugman 2009a, p. 5.

in an age when, more than ever, the business of America was business, *The Times* needed to broaden its Op-Ed commentary beyond the traditional focus on foreign affairs and domestic politics. I was brought on in the expectation that I would write about the vagaries of the new economy, the impacts of globalization, and bad policies in other countries. I didn't expect to spend a lot of time on domestic politics, since everyone assumed that American policy would remain sensible and responsible.[35]

That was not how things worked out.

Rather than Gore succeeding Clinton and the likes of Rubin and Summers continuing to anchor the global order, the disputed election of 2000 yielded the Bush presidency. The 9/11 attacks triggered the war on terror and the Bush administration flanked its campaign with a tax cut that chiefly benefited the most affluent Americans. It was, as far as Krugman was concerned, a triple shift: in politics, geopolitics and economic policy that fundamentally destabilised his understanding of America and its place in the world. He wasn't just confronting a bad government. His historical sense told him he was dealing with something far more momentous.

In the early 2000s Krugman stumbled on Henry Kissinger's famous study of the Congress of Vienna, *A World Restored*, published in 1957.[36] 'One wouldn't think that a book about the diplomatic efforts of Metternich and Castlereagh is relevant to US politics in the twenty-first century,' Krugman told his readers. 'But the first three pages of Kissinger's book sent chills down my spine.'[37] What Krugman took from Kissinger was his warning about the failure of established political systems to take seriously the challenge posed by 'revolutionary powers', forces that do not accept the system's legitimacy. The immediate historical reference was to Revolutionary France, but, as Krugman pointed out, Kissinger clearly also had in mind the disastrous appeasement policy pursued towards the 'totalitarian regimes' of the 1930s. Transposing the same model to the early 2000s, Krugman came to see the Republican Party 'as a revolutionary power in Kissinger's sense. That is, it is a movement whose leaders do not accept the legitimacy of our current political system.'[38] The threat was compounded by the fact that it was not recognised as such. Liberals found it well nigh impossible to take the GOP seriously. They tended to dismiss Krugman himself as alarmist. They fundamentally underestimated the threat to American democracy.

---

[35] Krugman 2003, pp. 21–2.
[36] Kissinger 2017 [1957].
[37] Krugman 2003, pp. 28–9.
[38] Krugman 2003, p. 29.

Whereas Krugman's argument about the reappearance of the histori-cal threat of Keynesian recessions was addressed to a more technical audience, his political call to arms appealed to the public at large. It was in this phase that Krugman's bond with the internet audience was forged.[39] In reaction to the right-wing shock jocks of the 1990s, an alter-native public sphere of the left was emerging, more outspoken, based on its own sense of American identity. Krugman's rallying cry was that of Democrat Howard Dean: 'I want my country back.'[40] It was Krugman's willingness to name the scale of the political threat that quite suddenly made him into a spokesman for the left.

As Krugman himself admitted in *The Great Unraveling*, published in August 2003, the ultimate driving force behind movement conservatism was at first a puzzle to him. 'I am not entirely sure why ... we are now faced with such a radical challenge to our political and social system.'[41] After all, rich people and American corporations were doing well. Why the sudden push to attack all forms of regulation and redistribution? By 2007 Krugman had an answer, and again it came from history. *The Conscience of a Liberal* married his long-standing interest in inequality to a sweeping seventy-year political history of the United States.[42] What he now came to appreciate was that movement conservatism was not a product of the recent past. It was the latest incarnation of the reaction-ary bloc in American society that since the era of the New Deal had resisted the levelling of social and economic inequality in the United States. In the era known amongst economists as the 'great compression', between the 1930s and the 1970s, it had been on the back foot.[43] Since the Reagan era it had gone on the offensive. To do so, movement con-servatism recruited mass support, especially in the South, through dog-whistle racial appeals. If there was a single variable that explained why the United States had no comprehensive welfare state, it was the scar of racism, going back to the age of slavery.[44] Welfare in the United States was code for race, and for black dependency in particular.[45]

The Bush era was a shock to Krugman's understanding of American democracy, but it did not shake his economics. Indeed, his commitment to the Clinton-era agenda of budget balance and globalisation provided him with another stick with which to beat the Bush administration.

[39] Wallace-Wells 2011.
[40] Burkeman 2003.
[41] Krugman 2003, p. 35.
[42] Krugman 2009b.
[43] Goldin and Margo 1992.
[44] Krugman 2015.
[45] Fraser and Gordon 1994.

Irresponsible and socially inequitable tax cuts were running up large deficits and making China and Japan into America's largest creditors.

The crisis that Krugman foresaw before 2008 was a dollar shock.[46] At some point foreign investors would lose patience with America's debt and a collapse in the dollar would ensue. Krugman was not, however, an alarmist. He favoured devaluation. It might be painful in the short run but it would rebalance the American economy away from imports towards exports and help to create new jobs. It confirmed that the Bush administration was on an unsustainable course that would need to be unwound by a future Democratic administration as Clinton had done with the legacy of Reagan and Bush senior.

As it turned out, Krugman and many others of his cohort were focused on the wrong crisis.[47] Whilst they were worrying about America's balance of payments and its government budget deficits, a far more dangerous threat was developing in its financial system, centred on securitised mortgage debt and the structures of what became known as 'shadow banking'. By November 2008 even Queen Elizabeth would be asking: why had none of the economists seen this coming?

Krugman was defensive of the profession. He rejected as 'absurd' the idea that economists should have predicted that 'Lehman Brothers would go down on September 15, 2008, and take much of the world economy with it. In fact, it's not reasonable to criticize economists for failing to get the year of the crisis right, or any of the specifics of how it played out, all of which probably depended on detailed contingencies and just plain accident.'[48]

This was making excuses, of course, but Krugman's stance was fully consistent with his understanding of the relationship between economics and history back to Isaac Asimov, Samuelson and the neo-classical synthesis. The role of the economists was not to predict individual bank failures but to get the basic parameters right. If spotting the trouble at Lehman was anyone's job it was that of bank regulators and market analysts.

What Krugman conceded, 'indeed, what I sometimes berate myself for', is that mainstream economists had failed to warn that a crisis of the 2008 type was a 'fairly likely event'. The rise of shadow banking and unstable funding such as repo should have set off alarm bells.

Economists, of all people, should have been on guard for the fallacy of misplaced concreteness, should have realized that not everything that functions like a bank and creates bank-type systemic risks looks like a traditional bank,

---

[46] Krugman 2007. More broadly on this expectation see Tooze 2018.
[47] DeLong 2008.
[48] Krugman 2012a.

a big marble building with rows of tellers. ... I plead guilty to falling into that fallacy. I was vaguely aware of the existence of a growing sector of financial institutions that didn't look like conventional banks, and weren't regulated like conventional banks, but engaged in bank-like activities. Yet I gave no thought to the systemic risks.[49]

More broadly, economists should have recognised the risks of high indebtedness. As Krugman pointed out, already in 1933 Irving Fisher, the grandfather of monetarism, had published a well-known paper about the risk of debt deflation and the way that 'high levels of debt create the possibility of a self-reinforcing downward spiral'.[50]

'I plead guilty to negligence,' Krugman conceded. 'I had especially little excuse for being oblivious to these dangers given that I had actually laid great stress on balance-sheet factors in causing financial crises in emerging markets.'[51] Of course the crises of the 1990s in the emerging markets had a lot to do with currency mismatch, but in general terms the risks were similar. Indeed, so similar that the effect of hindsight was dizzying. Krugman had failed to see 2008 coming, but, once it was under way, 'I had a more or less ready-made intellectual framework to accommodate these revelations: at a meta level, this was very much the same kind of crisis as Indonesia 1998 or Argentina 2002.'[52]

Once the problem was recognised, the effect on Krugman was electrifying. The immediate need was for massive stimulus. The risk was of slumping into a Japanese-style state of prolonged deflation, a so-called liquidity trap. Central bank policy could only do so much. If interest rates could not go below zero there was a limit to how far you could stimulate investment. It was fiscal policy that would have to do the work. In a rush, Krugman prepared a new edition of *The Return of Depression Economics*, updated to take into account the disaster of 2008.[53]

If the economic policy imperative was clear, so too, in Krugman's view, was the political opportunity. The shambolic end of the Bush administration opened the door to the Obama presidency with a majority in both houses of Congress. The Obama administration was stocked with veterans of Rubin and Summers' period at the Treasury, all true-believing adherents to the MIT tradition. And yet the upshot was bitterly disappointing.

The Obama administration embarked on a stimulus response, but it was spectacularly inadequate. By the best estimates it was half what

---

[49] Krugman 2012a.
[50] Krugman 2012a.
[51] Krugman 2012a.
[52] Krugman 2009d.
[53] Krugman 2009a.

was needed.[54] The economy stopped collapsing but the recovery was painfully slow. 'The overall narrative', in Krugman's terms, was 'tragic. A policy initiative that was good but not good enough ended up being seen as a failure, and set the stage for an immensely destructive wrong turn.'[55] The political failure was even worse. The Obama administration had fallen straight into the trap of which Krugman had been warning. Rather than waging war on movement conservatism, the Obama administration tried to bargain with it. The result was that the Tea Party was running rampant. In November 2010 the Republicans retook control of Congress.

The effort to make sense of what had gone wrong forced Krugman to bring his understanding of the role of economics and economic policy into line with his jaundiced appreciation of the forces driving American politics.[56]

Krugman was never an enthusiastic supporter of Barack Obama. He preferred left wingers such as Howard Dean in 2004 and John Edwards in 2008. Hillary Clinton at least would have no illusions about bipartisanship. Obama's efforts at bipartisanship were a predictable failure. Of course, the Congressional politics of reform in 2009 were intensely difficult. The administration was juggling health care and other priorities. It was precisely for that reason that Krugman favoured a more aggressive approach. What dismayed him even more deeply was the failure of the economics profession to solidly back the giant stimulus that the US economy so badly needed.[57] The opposition of conservative colleagues was perhaps predictable, but it was Larry Summers, working inside the administration, who cut off the push for a more adequate stimulus.[58]

The failure to react adequately to the emerging-market crises of the late 1990s had been a warning. Now the historical narrative that had organised Krugman's professional life was up-ended: 'We used to pity our grandfathers, who lacked both the knowledge and the compassion to fight the Great Depression effectively; now we see ourselves repeating all the old mistakes.'[59] Nor could this be dismissed as an accident. In a remarkable short piece in November 2010 entitled 'The Instability of Moderation' Krugman re-framed the entire history of policy advice in the United States.[60] 'Watching the failure of policy over the past three

---

[54] Tooze 2018.
[55] Krugman 2020, p. 120.
[56] Wallace-Wells 2011.
[57] Krugman 2012a.
[58] Krugman 2009f.
[59] Krugman 2020, p. 407.
[60] Krugman 2010e. Also in Krugman 2020, p. 407.

years, I find myself believing, more and more, that ... we were in some sense doomed to go through this.'[61] He now suspected that the neo-classical synthesis, 'a regime that by and large lets markets work, but in which the government is ready both to rein in excesses and fight slumps – is inherently unstable. It's something that can last for a generation or so, but not much longer.'[62]

The Samuelson synthesis was unstable at three levels: intellectual, political and economic. It was unstable intellectually because it was based on a dualism, what Krugman dubbed a 'strategic inconsistency'. When doing microeconomics, MIT economists assumed rational individuals and rapidly clearing markets. To animate their macro-models they built in frictions and ad hoc behavioural assumptions to generate market failure. As Krugman insisted: 'Inconsistency in the pursuit of useful guidance is no vice. The map is not the territory, and it's OK to use different kinds of maps depending on what you're trying to accomplish.' The risk was the intellectual restlessness induced by the inconsistency on the dividing line between micro and macro. That tension demanded to be resolved, 'which in practice has meant trying to make macro more like micro, basing more and more of it on optimization and market-clearing'.[63] The result was what Krugman called the 'Dark Age of macroeconomics', in which 'large numbers of economists literally knew nothing of the hard-won insights of the thirties and forties'.[64] As Krugman cruelly quipped, the so-called Freshwater school of economics redefined the Great Depression as the Great Vacation – a voluntary downward adjustment in labour supply perversely supported by unemployment benefits and exaggerated union wages.[65] This was absurd but, understood in terms of the foundational inconsistency of the neo-classical synthesis, it was an accident waiting to happen.

The Samuelson synthesis was also politically labile. Conservatives had never really been friends of Keynesianism, but in practical terms they could not deny the need for macroeconomic stabilisation. Friedman was the answer. The monetarist fashion of the 1970s and early 1980s was, for Krugman, 'an attempt to assuage conservative political prejudices without denying macroeconomic realities'. Even more than Keynesianism, it was a button-pushing approach to policy. It made policy 'technical and largely mechanical'. It was the job of the central bank to stabilise

---

[61] Krugman 2020, p. 407.
[62] Krugman 2020, p. 407.
[63] Krugman 2020, p. 408.
[64] Krugman 2020, p. 408.
[65] Krugman 2009e.

the money supply 'and aside from that, let freedom ring!' By the 1980s monetarism as a policy formula was a busted flush but what persisted was the cult of the independent central banker. 'Put a bunch of bankerly men in charge ... insulate them from political pressure, and let them deal with the business cycle; meanwhile, everything else can be conducted on free-market principles.' That worked well up to 2007, in part because central banks were insulated not just against politics but against prevailing fashions in university Economics departments too. Once more Krugman let his historical imagination run wild:

> If we're living in a Dark Age of macroeconomics, central banks have been its monasteries, hoarding and studying the ancient texts lost to the rest of the world. Even as the real business cycle people [the ultimate anti-Keynesians, AT] took over the professional journals, to the point where it became very hard to publish models in which monetary policy, let alone fiscal policy, matters, the research departments of the Fed system continued to study counter-cyclical policy in a relatively realistic way.[66]

This compromise worked, so long as there was no shock that exceeded the capacity of the central banks to handle it. Once a real crisis broke out, they had to call on fiscal policy and then the entire fragile edifice collapsed. The conservative backlash would run riot and not even the central bankers would be safe.[67] And such a crisis, Krugman now finally conceded, was more likely than not to arrive.

The basic premise of the Samuelson synthesis had been that macroeconomic stabilisation would permit market mechanisms to operate as efficiently as neo-classical economics promised. But what if the reverse were true? What if successful macroeconomic stabilisation actually encouraged financial innovation, leverage and destabilising speculation? Here, Krugman paid at least nodding respects to the maverick post-Keynesian Hyman Minsky, long ignored by the economics establishment.[68] Periods of relative stability, Krugmam now acknowledged, tended to lead to 'greater risk-taking, greater leverage, and, finally, a huge deleveraging shock'. When that occurred it demanded a huge and immediate policy response for which there was no longer a political basis. 'In the end, then, the era of the Samuelsonian synthesis was, I fear, doomed to come to a nasty end. And the result is the wreckage we see all around us.'[69]

The blockage that Krugman had first identified in the emerging markets in 1999 was now paralysing policy in the very heart of the global

---

[66] Krugman 2020, p. 409.
[67] Krugman 2020, p. 409.
[68] Eggertsson and Krugman 2012.
[69] Krugman 2020, pp. 409–10.

economy, in the United States. The aftermath of 2008 looked like a rerun of the 1930s. A systemic financial shock opened the door to a prolonged recession. The failure by liberals to mount an effective policy response opened the door to a dangerous wave of right-wing extremism. In the United States movement conservatism morphed into the Tea Party, whilst in Europe there was an upsurge of nationalist populism. What was the way out?

The New Deal was the obvious answer. For Krugman it was a model above all in a political sense. In the 1930s there was 'a genuine attempt to say who the evildoers were', he argued.[70] By contrast, despite the moral and financial bankruptcy of Wall Street, the Obama administration had shrunk from a decisive confrontation with money power. The consequences, Krugman believed, were serious: 'My sense is that in the face of this catastrophe, people needed some sign, a kind of symbolic sense of who was to blame.'[71] By failing to define an enemy, Obama helped create a political monster, the Tea Party, 'that's now come and bitten him. If you're not going to point fingers at the people who actually caused the problem, then those fingers may end up pointed at you.'[72]

That was the politics. As far as economic policy was concerned, Krugman was too good a student of American economic history to imagine that the New Deal could serve as a role model. Despite the propagandistic noise around organisations such as the Works Progress Administration, its fiscal effort had been modest. There had been a fiscal experiment in the 1930s; but it was not in the democracies, it was in the dictatorships. Whereas FDR had hesitated, Krugman believed that 'Hitler managed to override the usual objections to stimulus'.[73] American democracy in the 1930s was not capable of matching that performance, until it was galvanised into action by the war. 'It would have been much better if the Depression had been ended' by the New Deal 'with massive spending on useful things, on roads and railroads and schools and parks. But the political consensus for spending on a sufficient scale never materialized; we needed Hitler and Hirohito instead.'[74] 'The fact is', Krugman opined, 'the Great Depression ended largely thanks to a guy named Adolf Hitler. He created a human catastrophe, which also led to a lot of government spending.'

As Krugman insists: '*economics is not a morality play*. It's not a happy story in which virtue is rewarded and vice punished.'[75] Nevertheless,

---

[70] Tasini and Krugman n.d.
[71] Tasini and Krugman n.d.
[72] Tasini and Krugman n.d.
[73] Krugman 2012b.
[74] Krugman 2010d.
[75] Krugman 2010d.

invoking Hitler as a role model of economic policy did not make Krugman comfortable. In the blogosphere he had to introduce rules to control comments on the subject.[76] Nor could he resist drawing gloomy conclusions about modern America. 'Everybody in the world except us is doing a lot of investment in infrastructure and education. This is the country of the Erie Canal and the Interstate Highway System. ... Can you imagine doing that in 21st century America? We really have slid backward for the past 200 years.' On the other hand, Krugman the sci-fi addict mused, 'if it were announced that we faced a threat from space aliens and needed to build up to defend ourselves, we'd have full employment in a year and a half'.[77]

If finding a suitable enemy was the problem, there was one obvious option. In 2010 Krugman focused repeatedly on China.[78] In the desperate winter of 2010–11, following the Tea Party's triumphant march into Congress, Krugman and Robin Wells, his wife, economist and co-author, argued that the Democrats should rally support by challenging China over its currency manipulation.

Democrats could ... demand that the administration ... act on the problem of China's currency manipulation, which keeps the renminbi artificially cheap compared to the dollar. While China's actions are not the main factor in our economic woes, they are a factor. China's unprecedented level of currency manipulation siphons off demand for US products that is much needed in our depressed economy. ... The obvious American response is to threaten, and if necessary actually impose, countervailing duties on Chinese exports. ... Such a move would have overwhelming Democratic support in Congress, and would put Republicans on the spot if they tried to block it.[79]

In February 2012 Krugman doubled down: 'Under current circumstances, with mass unemployment and a complete absence of policy levers to do anything about it, China is hurting us, period ... Chinese policy right now is our enemy.'[80]

Of course, a trade war with China to rally the Democratic troops was not the same thing as an anti-fascist crusade against imperial Japan and Hitler's Germany. The historical precedent that Krugman cited was Richard Nixon's surcharge on undervalued German and Japanese imports.[81] Hardly the stuff of global conflagration. But even that was too much for the Obama administration. Why?

[76] Kampeas 2011.
[77] Tasini and Krugman n.d.
[78] Krugman 2010b.
[79] Krugman and Wells 2011.
[80] Tasini and Krugman n.d.
[81] Economist 2010.

There were no doubt broader diplomatic considerations. Some Americans continued to worry about Beijing no longer buying American Treasuries. As Krugman explained, that was completely misguided. A fall in the dollar should be welcome. But, 'aside from unjustified financial fears, there's a more sinister cause of US passivity: business fear of Chinese retaliation'.[82] As Krugman noted, American business was 'wary of filing trade cases, fearing Chinese officials' reputation for retaliating against joint ventures in their country and potentially denying market access to any company that takes sides against China'.[83] Similar intimidation had no doubt helped discourage action on the currency front. 'This', Krugman remarked, 'is a good time to remember that what's good for multinational companies is often bad for America, especially its workers.'[84]

Krugman had been concerned with inequality as early as the 1980s. What had come ever more sharply into focus in his commentary since the early 2000s was not just inequality but class warfare, the active struggle by the rich to secure their interests by all means necessary, what Krugman called 'top-down class war'.[85] Whereas inequality generated by technological change had a history that ran over decades, top-down class war was a day-to-day affair, directly tied to politics. It mattered who controlled Washington.[86]

Despite his disillusionment with the Obama administration, Obama's second victory in November 2012 was thus for Krugman a decisive moment. 'This was very much an election pitting the interests of the very rich against those of the middle class and the poor,' he declared. What pleased and impressed Krugman was that 'the Obama campaign won largely by disregarding the warnings of squeamish "centrists" and … stressing the class-war aspect of the confrontation. This ensured not only that President Obama won by huge margins among lower-income voters, but that those voters turned out in large numbers, sealing his victory.' Whilst the election was won, the class war wasn't. What Krugman now warned about was the effort by the monied interests that had backed Romney to 'win by stealth – in the name of fiscal responsibility – the ground they failed to gain in an open election … to smuggle in plutocrat-friendly policies under the pretence that they're just sensible responses to the budget deficit'.[87] Given America's continuing levels of unemployment, any talk of budget consolidation, once the Clinton-era common sense, was now suspect.

[82] Krugman 2010c.
[83] Krugman 2010c.
[84] Krugman 2010c.
[85] Krugman 2010a.
[86] Krugman 2006.
[87] Krugman 2012c.

Krugman's embrace of the analytic of class war completed his dismantling of the neo-classical synthesis. If the entire realm of what he had once confidently described as 'sensible' economic policy was shot through with class interest, cloaked in terms such as 'confidence' and 'responsibility', that provided a key to the failure of Keynesian policy. If Samuelson in 1948 had laid out how a macro stabilisation policy would ideally enable private enterprise to operate efficiently, Krugman was now forced to recognise that the Polish Marxist Keynesian Michall Kalecki had spelled out five years beforehand, in 1943, why delivering stabilisation policy in a sustained way might not actually be possible.[88] At the depths of the crisis, Keynesians would be summoned to do the minimum that was necessary, but as soon as the worst of the crisis was passed, well before the economy reached full employment, the same policies would be anathematised as undermining 'confidence'. The balance of what was 'sensible' would be set by the interests of the wealthiest and most secure. As Krugman remarked:

When I first read [Kalecki's] essay, I thought it was over the top. Kalecki was, after all, a declared Marxist. ... But, if you haven't been radicalized by recent events, you haven't been paying attention; and policy discourse since 2008 has run exactly along the lines Kalecki predicted. First came the 'pivot' – the sudden switch to the view that budget deficits, not mass unemployment, were the crucial policy issue. Then came the Great Whine – the declaration by one leading business figure after another that President Obama was undermining confidence by saying mean things about businesspeople and doing outrageous things like helping the uninsured. Finally, just as happened with the claims that slashing spending is actually expansionary and terrible things happen if government debt rises, the usual suspects found an academic research paper to adopt as mascot ... showing that rising levels of 'economic policy uncertainty' were holding the economy back.[89]

Taken together, the elements of Krugman's new narrative delivered a deeply pessimistic verdict on the neo-classical synthesis. The development of the financial system generated the risk of major systemic shocks. They had the potential to tip the economy into a loss of confidence so severe that conventional monetary policy was powerless. That, according to the Samuelson formula, was the moment for classical Keynesian fiscal remedies to be applied, but the economics profession was divided against itself, the Republican Party was a destructive force bent on sabotaging any Democratic administration and powerful social interests were systematically unreliable, calling for stimulus only when it suited their

---

[88] Kalecki 1943.
[89] Krugman 2013a.

selfish and short-sighted interests, bitterly denouncing it when it actually might deliver truly full employment and thus shift the balance of power in the labour market in favour of working people.

The conclusion, in Krugman's view, was that policy could no longer confine itself to the boundaries as defined by the neo-classical synthesis.

At the very least ... we need 'macroprudential' policies – regulations and taxes designed to limit the risk of crisis – even during good years, because we now know that we can't count on an effective cleanup when crisis strikes. And I don't just mean banking regulation ... the logic of this argument calls for policies that discourage leverage in general, capital controls to limit foreign borrowing, and more. What's more, you have to ask why, if markets are imperfect enough to generate the massive waste we've seen since 2008, we should believe that they get everything else right. I've always considered myself a free-market Keynesian – basically, a believer in Samuelson's synthesis. But I'm far less sure of that position than I used to be.[90]

Nor was it just the specific balance of fiscal and monetary policy that was in question; it was the role of the expert in general.

In 2011 Krugman still saw himself as a defender of the technocrats: 'Am I against technocrats? Not at all. I like technocrats ... we need technical expertise to deal with our economic woes. But our discourse is being badly distorted by ideologues and wishful thinkers ... pretending to be technocrats. And it's time to puncture their pretensions.'[91]

By 2013 he had shifted to a more sceptical view: 'the desire of some pundits to depoliticize our economic discourse, to make it technocratic and nonpartisan' limited the conversation, particularly when it touched on the most sensitive issues such as inequality and class. It was 'a pipe dream. Even on what may look like purely technocratic issues, class and inequality end up shaping – and distorting – the debate.'[92]

By 2020 Krugman's message was even more stark: 'In 21st-century America, everything is political. In many cases, accepting what the evidence says about an economic question will be seen as a partisan act. Indeed, in some cases even asking certain questions is seen as a partisan act.'[93] 'This means that the technocratic dream – the idea of being a politically neutral analyst helping policymakers govern more effectively – is, for now at least, dead.'[94]

[90] Krugman 2013b.
[91] Krugman 2011b.
[92] Isquith 2013.
[93] Krugman 2020, pp. 1–2.
[94] Krugman 2020, p. 5.

In the neo-classical synthesis, expertise was directed towards stabilising the broad context of the economy so that markets could operate. The structure of the economy and of politics were taken as givens, as was the freedom of economic expertise in relation to both. By 2013 for Krugman that model had disintegrated. Successive financial crises demonstrated the need to intervene in the development of markets themselves to avoid shocks that affect the entire economy. Expertise had divided against itself along lines of class interest. So too had American democratic politics, in which the right wing had become radically anti-systemic. The Trump presidency merely confirmed Krugman's earlier diagnosis.

In this embattled situation, progressive expertise, which now had no option but to own that label, had not only to diagnose the immediate situation but to struggle to secure the conditions of its own existence and to win the argument even within its own camp. That was the bitter lesson of the Obama administration. It was the lesson that Krugman and others hammered home relentlessly over the following decade. In that respect at least they have succeeded not just in interpreting history but in making it. If there is one idea that motivated the policy team of the Biden administration in early 2021 it was the determination to avoid a repeat of 2009, to resist the blandishments of bipartisanship, to 'go big'.[95] With the enthusiastic backing of Krugman, in the face of objections from the likes of Larry Summers, Biden launched a giant stimulus bill followed by an infrastructure package.[96] The hope was that this would stave off a social crisis, restore full employment, solidify the Democrats' wafer-thin Congressional majority and in so doing uphold the political conditions for the efficacy of economic expertise. It is a test of the Krugmanian diagnosis on the largest scale.

It is not an application of technocratic fine-tuning in the manner once imagined by the neo-classical synthesis. Nor is it the radical programme of structural transformation proposed by the Green New Deal.[97] It is, however, a programme of fiscal and monetary policy of unprecedented scale that reflects the historic stakes. It is a desperate effort – perhaps a last-ditch effort – to steer American democracy away from the abyss towards which, as Krugman has warned us as loudly as anyone, it has been steering for a quarter of a century.

---

[95] Dorning, Taylor and Epstein 2020; Grim 2021.
[96] Coy 2021.
[97] 116th Congress 2019.

References

116th Congress 1st Session. H. Res. 109. 2019. 'Recognizing the Duty of the Federal Government to Create a Green New Deal', www.congress .gov/116/bills/hres109/BILLS-116hres109ih.pdf.

Akerlof, G. A. 2009. *Animal Spirits: How Human Psychology Drives the Economy, and why it Matters for Global Capitalism*. Princeton.

Applebaum, B. 2019. *The Economists' Hour: False Prophets, Free Markets, and the Fracture of Society*. New York.

Asimov, I. 2010. *The Foundation Trilogy: Foundation and Empire*. New York.

Blackhouse, R. E. and D. Laidler. 2004. 'What was Lost with IS-LM', *History of Political Economy*, 36: 1, pp. 25–56, https://doi.org/10.1215/00182702-36-Suppl_1-25.

Burkeman, O. 2003. '"I Do Get Rattled"', *The Guardian*, 19 September, www .theguardian.com/world/2003/sep/19/usa.internationaleducationnews.

Coy, P. 2021. 'Summers and Krugman Debate Stimulus: Here's a Blow-by-Blow Account', *Bloomberg*, 12 February, www.bloomberg.com/news/ articles/2021-02-12/summers-and-krugman-debate-stimulus-here-s-a-blow-by-blow-account?sref=wOrDP8KX.

DeLong, B. 2008. 'The Wrong Financial Crisis', *VoxEU*, 10 October, https:// voxeu.org/article/wrong-financial-crisis; https://voxeu.org/article/new-insight-role-imbalances-global-crisis.

Domar, E. D. 1970. 'The Causes of Slavery or Serfdom: A Hypothesis', *Journal of Economic History*, 30, pp. 18–32.

Dorning, M., J. Taylor and J. Epstein. 2020. 'Biden's 2009 Lessons for Now: Spend Big, No Coddling Wall Street', *Bloomberg*, 17 August, www.bloomberg.com/news/articles/2020-08-17/biden-s-2009-lessons-for-now-spend-big-no-coddling-wall-street.

Economist. 2010. 'Tricky Dick and the Dollar', 20 March, www.economist .com/node/15770808/print?story_id=15770808.

Eggertsson, G. B. and P. Krugman. 2012. 'Debt, Deleveraging, and the Liquidity Trap: A Fisher–Minsky–Koo Approach', *Quarterly Journal of Economics*, 127: 3, pp. 1469–1513, https://doi.org/10.1093/qje/qjs023.

Fraser, N. and L. Gordon. 1994. '"Dependency" Demystified: Inscriptions of Power in a Keyword of the Welfare State', *Social Politics: International Studies in Gender, State and Society*, 1: 1, pp. 4–31, https://doi.org/10.1093/ sp/1.1.4.

Fukuyama, F. 1993. *The End of History and the Last Man*. New York.

Goldin, C. and R. A. Margo. 1992. 'The Great Compression: The Wage Structure in the United States at Mid-Century', *Quarterly Journal of Economics*, 107: 1, pp. 1–34, www.jstor.org/stable/2118322.

Grim, R. 2021. 'Democrats Actually Learned from the Failures of 2009', *The Intercept*, 3 February, https://theintercept.com/2021/02/03/democrats-covid-stimulus-obama-lessons/.

Hartog, F. 2016. *Regimes of Historicity*. New York.

Hicks, J. R. 1937. 'Mr. Keynes and the "Classics": A Suggested Interpretation', *Econometrica* 5: 2, pp. 147–59, doi:10.2307/1907242.

Hirsch, M. 2019. 'Economists on the Run', *Foreign Policy*, 22 October, https://foreignpolicy.com/2019/10/22/economists-globalization-trade-paul-krugman-china/.

Isquith, E. 2013. 'Paul Krugman: Inequality is "the Defining Challenge of our Time"', *Salon*, 16 December, www.salon.com/2013/12/16/paul_krugman_inequality_is_the_defining_challenge_of_our_time/.

Kalecki, M. 1943. 'Political Aspects of Full Employment', *Political Quarterly*, 14: 4, pp. 322–31, https://doi.org/10.1111/j.1467-923X.1943.tb01016.x.

Kampeas, R. 2011. 'Paul Krugman's No Nazi Rule', *Jewish Telegraphic Agency*, 12 January, www.jta.org/2011/01/12/culture/paul-krugmans-no-nazi-rule.

Kessler, M. and A. Subramanian. 2013. 'The Hyperglobalization of Trade and its Future', Peterson Institute for International Economics, Working Paper Series WP13-6, http://dx.doi.org/10.2139/ssrn.2297994.

Kissinger, H. 2017 [1957]. *A World Restored: Metternich, Castlereagh, and the Problems of Peace, 1812–22*. n.p.

Krugman, P. n.d.a. 'Incidents from my Career', www.princeton.edu/~pkrugman/incidents.html.

n.d.b. 'Some Chaotic Thoughts on Regional Dynamics', http://web.mit.edu/krugman/www/temin.html.

1979. 'Increasing Returns, Monopolistic Competition, and International Trade', *Journal of International Economics*, 9: 4, pp. 469–79, https://doi.org/10.1016/0022-1996(79)90017-5.

1996. *Pop Internationalism*. Cambridge, MA.

1997. *The Age of Diminished Expectations*. Cambridge, MA.

1999a. 'Talking about a Revolution', *Slate*, 19 August, https://slate.com/business/1999/08/talking-about-a-revolution.html.

1999b. 'Was it all in Ohlin?', http://web.mit.edu/krugman/www/ohlin.html.

1999c. 'The Return of Depression Economics', *Foreign Affairs*, 78: 1, pp. 56–74, doi:10.2307/20020239.

2003. *The Great Unraveling: Losing our Way in the New Century*. New York.

2006. 'Wages, Wealth, and Politics', *New York Times*, 18 August, www.nytimes.com/2006/08/18/opinion/18krugman.html?hp.

2007. 'Will there be a Dollar Crisis?', *Economic Policy*, 22: 51, pp. 436–67, https://doi.org/10.1111/j.1468-0327.2007.00183.x.

2009a. *The Return of Depression Economics and the Crisis of 2008*. New York.

2009b. *The Conscience of a Liberal*. New York.

2009c. *A Country is not a Company*. Cambridge, MA.

2009d. 'Views Differ on Shape of Macroeconomics', *New York Times*, 17 July, https://krugman.blogs.nytimes.com/2009/07/17/views-differ-on-shape-of-macroeconomics/.

2009e. 'How Did Economists Get it So Wrong?', *New York Times Magazine*, 2 September, www.nytimes.com/2009/09/06/magazine/06Economic-t.html.

2009f. 'The Story of the Stimulus', *New York Times*, 5 October, https://krugman.blogs.nytimes.com/2009/10/05/the-story-of-the-stimulus/.

2010a. 'A Depressing Budget', *New York Times*, 1 February, https://krugman.blogs.nytimes.com/2010/02/01/a-depressing-budget/.

2010b. 'Taking on China', *New York Times*, 14 March, www.nytimes
.com/2010/03/15/opinion/15krugman.html.

2010c. 'China, Japan, America and the Renminbi', *New York Times*, 12
September, www.nytimes.com/2010/09/13/opinion/13krugman.html.

2010d. 'Economics is not a Morality Play', *New York Times*, 28 September,
https://krugman.blogs.nytimes.com/2010/09/28/economics-is-not-a-
morality-play/.

2010e. 'The Instability of Moderation', *New York Times*, 26 November,
https://krugman.blogs.nytimes.com/2010/11/26/the-instability-
of-moderation/.

2011a. 'IS-LMentary', *New York Times*, 9 October, https://krugman.blogs
.nytimes.com/2011/10/09/is-lmentary/.

2011b. 'Boring Cruel Romantics', *New York Times*, 20 November, www
.nytimes.com/2011/11/21/opinion/boring-cruel-euro-romantics.html.

2012a. 'Economics in the Crisis', *New York Times*, 5 March, https://
krugman.blogs.nytimes.com/2012/03/05/economics-in-the-crisis/.

2012b. 'Bubble, Bubble, Conceptual Trouble', *New York Times*, 20
October, https://krugman.blogs.nytimes.com/2012/10/20/bubble-bubble-
conceptual-trouble/.

2012c. 'Class Wars of 2012', *New York Times*, 29 November, www.nytimes
.com/2012/11/30/opinion/krugman-class-wars-of-2012.html.

2013a. 'Phony Fear Factor', *New York Times*, 8 August, www.nytimes
.com/2013/08/09/opinion/krugman-phony-fear-factor.html.

2013b. 'Synthesis Lost', *New York Times*, 12 August, https://krugman.blogs
.nytimes.com/2013/08/12/synthesis-lost/.

2015. 'Slavery's Long Shadow', *New York Times*, 22 June, www.nytimes
.com/2015/06/22/opinion/paul-krugman-slaverys-long-shadow.html.

2018. 'Capitalism, Socialism, and Unfreedom', *New York Times*, 26 August,
www.nytimes.com/2018/08/26/opinion/capitalism-socialism-and-
unfreedom.html.

2020. *Arguing with Zombies: Economics, Politics, and the Fight for a Better
Future*. New York.

Krugman, P., ed. 1986. *Strategic Trade Policy and the New International
Economics*. Cambridge, MA.

Krugman, P. and R. Wells. 2011. 'Where Do we Go from Here?', *New York
Review of Books*, 13 January, www.nybooks.com/articles/2011/01/13/
where-do-we-go-here/.

MacFarquhar, L. 2010. 'The Deflationist: How Paul Krugman
Found Politics', *New Yorker*, 1 March, www.newyorker.com/
reporting/2010/03/01/100301fa_fact_macfarquhar#ixzz2HupVHWPE.

Ritenour, S. 2000. 'Post-Modern Economics: The Return of Depression
Economics. By Paul Krugman. New York: WW Norton and Company,
1999', *Quarterly Journal of Austrian Economics*, 3: 1, pp. 79–83.

Samuelson, P. A. 1955. *Economics*, 3rd ed. New York.

Tasini, J. and P. Krugman. n.d. 'Playboy Interview: Paul Krugman',
Working Life, www.workinglife.org/jonathan-tasinis-columns/playboy-
interview-with-paul-krugman/.

Tooze, A. 2018. *Crashed: How a Decade of Financial Crises Changed the World.* New York.

Wallace-Wells, B. 2011. 'What's Left of the Left', *New Yorker*, 22 April, https://nymag.com/news/politics/paul-krugman-2011-5.

Weintraub, E. Roy, ed. 2014. 'MIT and the Transformation of American Economics', *History of Political Economy*, 46: 1, https://read.dukeupress.edu/hope/issue/46/suppl_1.

16   Anthropology and the Turn to History

Joel Isaac

Among the social sciences, the discipline of anthropology displays perhaps the greatest affinity for the methods and assumptions of historical enquiry. Anthropology's turn to history began as early as the 1950s,
with the influential writings of E. E. Evans-Pritchard. The relationship
between the two fields was cemented a generation later. During the
1970s the Young Turks of social history began to turn to anthropological
notions of culture and ideology, while many anthropologists, especially
in the United States, embraced a more historical conception of culture
than they had hitherto been willing to countenance. These developments
have entered the lore of both disciplines. Anthropologists speak of their
discipline's 'journey into history', while historians look back on the 'marriage' between history and anthropology that marked the rise of cultural
history.[1]

Since it is now disciplinary folklore, the precise character of anthropology's turn to history is less well understood than it should be. It is
one thing to observe that anthropologists have become more concerned
than they once were to account for change over time in the societies they
study, or that they seek to explain social change in terms of causal mechanisms embedded within social structures. These commitments have
certainly drawn anthropologists towards distinctively historical forms of
explanation. Yet it is critical to stress that we cannot assume that this
apparent enthusiasm for historical argument is an act of epistemological
deference. In this chapter I seek to explain why the methods of historical
enquiry became so attractive to a generation of anthropologists. What
did they think it could do for them that other modes of explanation –
most notably, the functionalism or structuralism of an earlier generation – could not? There is no general explanation for why and to what
extent the social sciences or humanities have embraced history; we need

My thanks to Richard Bourke and Quentin Skinner for their comments on an earlier
draft of this paper.
[1] See Geertz 2004; Agnew 1990.

to understand what, in each case, made the problem of change over time and its explanation so central to practitioners of a given discipline. In the case of anthropology, I shall argue, it was the problem of the origins and persistence of *institutions* that drew social and cultural anthropologists towards history. It is this singular and characteristic concern that has marked anthropology's historical turn.

The history of anthropological theory, as it is conventionally written, is not organised around the challenge of explaining institutions. In the standard history, methodological and epistemological debates are treated as the main drivers of theoretical innovation. This is in part a product of the fact that the historiography of anthropology has been deeply shaped by the history of science.[2] By contrast, in this chapter I will stress the political character of these theoretical shifts, which are visible, as we shall see, in the seminal writings of Durkheim, and which remain prominent in the works of the leaders of the profession throughout the twentieth century. The politics implicit in such works are clearest when our focus is on the explanation of institutions in anthropology.

For now, however, let us return to the standard history. The lineaments of this story have long been clear. It begins with the British evolutionists. Victorian anthropology was a notoriously eclectic affair, which combined broad speculation on human origins with positivist reflections on the progress of human rationality and comparative studies of 'primitive' law and institutions.[3] The central idea of the evolutionist school was that all societies were composed of a set of basic elements, whose development into more complex forms was governed by universal principles. The study of primitive society was to provide a kind of 'deep history' of the human race, whose purpose was to discern the building blocks that formed modern society.[4] The Victorians believed that the empirical disciplines of comparative philology, evolutionary science and ethnological research would yield a less 'conjectural', more realistic account of the primitive conditions of mankind. This positivist streak left ample room for both the Enlightenment belief in a progressive and universal human history and Darwinist musings about a hierarchy of the races.

At the start of the twentieth century, evolutionism was challenged by an anti-universalist and anti-racialist ethnology from Germany. Instead of arguing for the unity and inexorable progress of human culture,

---

[2] The dean of the history of anthropology is, of course, the anthropologist-turned-historian of science George C. Stocking, Jr.

[3] The classic texts are still Burrow 1966 and Stocking 1987. For general guides to the historiography of anthropology see Stocking 1968 and Kuper 2003.

[4] Kuper 2005; Stocking 1995, pp. 1–14.

pioneer figures such as Rudolf Virchow and Adolf Bastian argued that all races and cultures were hybrids – the product of long-term and contingent processes of imitation and borrowing among societies.[5] Bronislaw Malinowski was not wrong to describe the method of the so-called diffusionists as consisting in 'a careful mapping out of cultural similarities over large portions of the globe and in speculative reconstructions as to how the similar units of culture have wandered from one place to another'.[6] The diffusionist approach would find its most influential exponent in Franz Boas, a student of both Virchow and Bastian, who established one of the first Anthropology departments in the United States.

By the First World War evolutionism was in crisis. Its ideological character had become clear to many ethnologists, and this offended the pride of the would-be science of anthropology. A new school sought the prize of a scientific theory of human behaviour. These developments are usually associated with the commanding figures of Malinowski and A. R. Radcliffe-Brown. But the professionalisation of anthropology and, especially, its embrace of scholar-led fieldwork, was the work of a generation.[7] At any rate, by the 1920s the message was clear: anthropology was to join the mainstream of the social sciences. It was to do so in the form of either (largely British) 'social' or (largely American) 'cultural' anthropology. In inter-war France – another hotbed of ethnological research – anthropology was not sharply separated from sociology, thanks to the early efflorescence of the latter in the hands of the Saint-Simonians, Auguste Comte and, most importantly, Émile Durkheim.[8]

The turn away from purely synchronic forms of analysis – functionalism and structuralism being alike in this respect, if not others – began after the Second World War. The social convulsions triggered by the collapse of European empires in Africa and Asia set the scene for this reassessment. As early as 1950, Evans-Pritchard scandalised his colleagues by claiming that 'social anthropology is a kind of historiography, and therefore ultimately of philosophy or art'.[9] His remarks were primarily intended as a repudiation of what he had come to see as the fruitless search for scientific laws of society by adherents of the functionalist school; but his recommendation that anthropology be assimilated to the historical sciences was in earnest, and soon found support from his colleagues across the Atlantic. In the United States, Clifford

---

[5] Stocking 1996; Kuper 2003, pp. 360–2.
[6] Malinowski 1937, p. 624.
[7] See esp. Stocking 1995 and Kuper 2015.
[8] Lévi-Strauss 1945, pp. 503–4.
[9] Evans-Pritchard 1950, p. 123.

Geertz spoke of 'anthropology's journey into history' during this time, by which he meant its shift of focus from 'out-of-the-way peoples in out-of-the-way places' to 'differentiated societies enclosed in multiplex civilizations'.[10] There was no chance of treating these societies as examples of the 'primitive'. Anthropologists were coming to recognise that the 'field' was already deeply marked by the forces of global trade, economic development, cultural innovation, population growth and interaction with Europe. The only solution to the ubiquity of 'modernity' in the field was to find a method capable of interpreting the meanings of the highly changeable and fragile institutions, customs and narratives that had some kind of grip in these worlds. This method was typically 'historical', or at any rate attentive to the ways in which social structures and cultural meanings absorbed the relentless change they faced. Examples of this new, refined 'historical' approach abound: Geertz issued a call for ethnography as 'thick description'; Marshall Sahlins for the attention to the phenomenon of 'mytho-praxis'; James Scott for the adaptable 'infrapolitics' of the global peasantry; Louis Dumont for what he called a 'radical' comparative analysis between modern and non-modern societies; Eric Wolf and Sidney Mintz for a history of European capitalism as a global economic system.[11]

In so far as there is a politics in this standard history of the discipline, it is a Whiggish one. The Victorians sought exotic specimens from the empire for the purposes of explaining the unique character of their own society; the functionalists went into the field to hunt for specimens of primitive societies that they could place under glass for scientific analysis; finally, the new historically aware generation of cultural anthropologists recognised the putative modernity of the decolonising societies they studied, and folded the 'developing' world into the history of the birth of the modern world. This politics is in reality an ethics of the discipline, according to which the profession has shifted, or ought to shift, from being a tool of empire to a critical resource against structures of domination. In the rest of this chapter I shall try to move the discussion about anthropology's politics away from professional ethics and towards the categories of political theory, since it is these categories that allow us to better understand the meaning of the discipline's turn to history. And the central category, as I have noted, is that of the institution.

Why institutions? To answer this question, we need to begin at the beginning, which means with Durkheim. The professionalisation of

---

[10] Geertz 2004, p. 577.
[11] Geertz 1973; Sahlins 1985; Scott 1990; Dumont 1986; Wolf 1982; Mintz 1985.

anthropology is owed in large part to Durkheim's teachings.[12] The Frenchman wrote extensively on anthropology, both on his own (including his famous essay on the incest taboo in the first volume of the journal he founded, the *Année Sociologique*, as well as swathes of *The Division of Labour in Society* (1893) and all of *The Elementary Forms of Religious Life* (1912)), and with Marcel Mauss. It was Mauss who blazed the trail for Durkheim's approach in anthropology, first in collaboration with archaeologist and sociologist Henri Hubert, and then, after the First World War and the death of Durkheim, in his epoch-making essay on the gift.[13] The great scholar of early Roman law Paul Huvelin was drawn into the circle of Durkheim and Mauss, and wrote on magic under the influence of the Durkheimian school.[14] The legal sociologist and seminal theorist of social rights Georges Gurvitch was also part of this circle, as was the philosopher and ethnologist Lucien Lévy-Bruhl. French anthropology lived under the shadow of Durkheim's sociology far into the twentieth century. English-speaking anthropologists quickly took notice of this powerful French group of writers on anthropology. Malinowski was converted to Durkheim's account of sociology before he landed on the Trobriand Islands during the war.[15] Radcliffe-Brown was an even more careful reader of the Durkheimians, and took care to cite Henri Hubert as well as Durkheim in his own methodological writings.[16] He described his own version of social anthropology as, simply, an exercise in 'comparative sociology'. In the 1930s Radcliffe-Brown brought the good word to the United States, where Robert Redfield – already a serious student of sociology in the mould of Robert Park – soon genuflected towards Durkheim, as did the influential follower of Franz Boas, Robert Lowie.[17] Durkheim's view of social science set the terms in which most professional anthropologists (of whom there were still very few in the 1930s and 1940s) thought about the aims and scientific purport of their fledgling discipline.

In the preface to the second edition of *The Rules of Sociological Method* Durkheim remarks that sociology may be 'defined as the science of institutions, their genesis and their functioning'. Following the lead of Mauss and his collaborator Paul Fauconnet, Durkheim invoked the concept of the institution because, he wrote, it 'expresses moderately well the

---

[12] Kuper 2015, pp. 29–31; Stocking 1995, pp. 321–3.
[13] Mauss 2016.
[14] Lévi-Strauss 1945, pp. 511–12; Frank 2016.
[15] Stocking 1995, pp. 249–50.
[16] See Radcliffe-Brown 1922, p. 325 n 1; Radcliffe-Brown 1935, p. 394.
[17] Redfield 1941, pp. x, 343; Lowie 1937.

special kind of existence' enjoyed by what he called *faits sociaux*, social facts. It was a key tenet of Durkheim's methodology that institutions were irreducible to the individual psychological states of the persons who participated in them. To explain institutions in terms of individual psychology was to make unintelligible the defining mark of the institution, which was that it was felt by the individual as an external 'social constraint'. Durkheim therefore insisted that 'collective ways of acting and thinking possess a reality existing outside of individuals, who, at every moment, conform to them'. These *représentations collectives*, were, for Durkheim,

things that have their own existence. The individual encounters them when they are already completely fashioned and he cannot cause them to cease to be or to be different from what they are. Willy-nilly he is therefore obliged to take them into account; it is all the more difficult (although we do not say it is impossible) for him to modify them because in varying degrees they partake of the material and moral supremacy that society exerts over its members. No doubt the individual plays a part in their creation. But in order for a social fact to exist, several individuals at the very least must have interacted together and the resulting combination must have given rise to some new production. As this synthesis occurs outside each one of us (since a plurality of consciousnesses are involved) it has necessarily the effect of crystallizing, of instituting outside ourselves, certain modes of action and certain ways of judging which are independent of the particular individual will considered separately.[18]

As a specifically social fact, however, this collective 'reality' was not identical to that of natural phenomena such as molecules or biological processes – although, like the latter, social facts were forces that impinged on persons. It was the key feature of social facts, which was embodied most vividly in institutions, that they had to be explained only with reference to other social facts. Durkheim was insistent that social facts could not otherwise be understood – for example, with reference to the laws governing individual psychology.

I shall pass over most of the well-documented difficulties encountered by Durkheim's master concepts. I wish to focus instead on a tension in Durkheim's account of the proper explanation of institutions. For it is a tension that has set the terms in which anthropologists generally have grappled with the importance of 'historical' versus some form of 'functional' or 'structural' explanation. Malinowski famously described Durkheim as the father of functionalism, but the truth is more complicated. We may recall that, after defining sociology as the 'science of institutions', Durkheim goes on to stipulate that this science would

---

[18] Durkheim 2013, pp. 14–15.

be concerned with the 'genesis and ... functioning' of institutions. But which is it? Functional explanations are teleological: they account for the existence of an institution by citing its beneficial effects. In contrast, genetic or historical explanations explain the existence of an institution in terms of its efficient causes. To cite an institution's causal antecedents is to say nothing about its function or purpose. Indeed, genetic explanations allow for the possibility that an institution may not have any beneficial effects; or that it had such effects and then lost them, or now has different favourable effects. In his *Rules*, Durkheim was perfectly clear on the difference between these two kinds of explanation, and did not favour functionalism as a matter of principle, as is clear from his remark that 'it is a proposition true in sociology as in biology, that the organ is independent of its function, i.e. while staying the same it can serve different ends. Thus the causes that give rise to its existence are independent of the ends it serves.'[19] In Durkheim's view this variability of ends was matched by the plasticity of human needs and the infinite range of means by which those needs, including the most basic, could be met. For a serious sociology of the kind Durkheim sought to establish, this thought precluded getting functional explanation off the ground by citing a fixed range of basic human needs, and then explaining any and all institutions on that basis (a temptation that, as we shall see, later functionalists such as Malinowski would find irresistible). Instead, Durkheim recommended a dual approach, in which the sociologist would seek a genetic account of an institution – marriage customs, property rules, taboos and so on – and separately asked what function such an institution might serve.[20]

Durkheim's methodology was, at least in this respect, broad-minded, but, in practice, the two modes of explanation were contradictory. This was what Claude Lévi-Strauss claimed as early as 1945 in an article (published in English) on 'French Sociology'. The clash between the functional and the historical – that is, the teleological and the causal – showed up vividly, Lévi-Strauss wrote, in the grand opening passages of *The Elementary Forms of Religious Life*, in which Durkheim pronounced that, while 'simple', the totemic religion of the Australian aborigines contained – and thus, properly understood, explained – all of the main ideas and rituals found in more complex modern religions. According to Lévi-Strauss, Durkheim's thesis blended the genetic and the functional in precisely the way that the *Rules* had warned against:

---

[19] Durkheim 2013, p. 79.
[20] This was one of Durkheim's rules: 'Therefore when one undertakes to explain a social phenomenon the efficient cause which produces it and the function it fulfills must be investigated separately' (Durkheim 2013, p. 81).

If, as Durkheim himself says ... every religion, while being 'a kind of delirium', cannot be 'a pure illusion'; if, although the objects of religious thought are 'imaginary', 'no human institution can be established upon a ground made of errors and lies', then the direct study of any religion should suffice to bring out its explanation, i.e., the function it fulfills in the society where it is found. If on the other hand, the study of 'anterior' forms is requested, it can only be because the considered phenomenon cannot be explained anymore on a functional basis. ... If this were true, the historical method should be predominant in sociology ... however it is an entirely different principle of explanation that Durkheim finally accepts: 'the primary origin of every social process of importance must be looked for in the internal structure of the social group'.[21]

Determined to vouchsafe a realm of social facts with their own unique explanatory laws, Durkheim bounced back and forth between functionalism and genetic explanation, undermining the independence of both while vindicating neither. According to Lévi-Strauss, this kind of 'oscillation between what would today be called the functional and the historical approaches' was typical of the social sciences of the first half of the twentieth century. As he put it in his doctoral thesis, published as *The Elementary Structures of Kinship* (1949), social theorists during this period tended to assume that a 'human institution has only two possible origins, either historical and irrational, or as in the case of the legislator, by design'. That is to say, where no 'rational motive' could be found for an institution – Lévi-Strauss's case at hand was cross-cousin marriage – it was concluded that it must be 'the result of a series of historical accidents which in themselves are insignificant'.[22] The reference here to functional explanations implying a 'legislator' or conscious designer is revealing, as we shall see below.

What was at stake in this debate over the extent to which human institutions exhibited purpose or order? Anthropology has always been concerned with the fundamental question of whether the human mind is one or many: is thought a universal process (which may be expressed in different ways by different cultures) or does each culture have its own mind, which is incomparable with the values and beliefs of other groups?[23] In the moral sciences or *Geisteswissenschaften*, as these took shape as distinct disciplines during the nineteenth century, it was reasonable to expect answers to these questions from the investigation of institutions: to what extent were the singular customs, mores and institutions of particular peoples rationally ordered wholes? And if they could be so understood, was that rational order universal or perhaps even transcendental in

---

[21] Lévi-Strauss 1945, pp. 516–17.
[22] Lévi-Strauss 1969 [1949], p. 100.
[23] Descombes 2001, pp. 47–8.

character? These issues were explored in Durkheim and Mauss's reflections on the social origins of the categorisation of experience, which were directly inspired (especially in Durkheim's case) by Kant's critical philosophy.[24] Lévi-Strauss's famous symbolic account of the mental foundations of human institutions was an attempt to defend the universality of the human mind on a-priori but non-transcendental grounds – a move very much in keeping with the neo-Kantian theory of symbolism that swept across the human sciences during this period.[25]

The controversy about the purportedly universal structures of the human mind was not only a problem in the philosophy of mind, however. In fact, the debate about the role of institutions as expressions of the human mind has its roots in politics. The concern about the relationship between the human mind and the explanation of institutions is, at root, a concern about human sociability. For each position implies a view about sociability: to claim, as do cognitivists like Lévi-Strauss, that the human mind is one, but also that it 'unconsciously' structures customs and mores, is to defend a strong view of human natural sociability, since it leads to the conclusion that human beings will tend, if given autonomy, to live in rationally ordered, purposive institutions.[26] To suppose, on the other hand, that institutions are either created whole cloth by a legislator, in a founding political act, or are otherwise the product of random historical chance with no underlying rational principle, is to imply that humans are in fact very weakly sociable. They are forced into order by a determining will, or otherwise left to the vagaries of chance.

For Durkheim and his associates, the immediate source of these political questions about sociability was the intellectual heritage of Montesquieu and Rousseau, whom Durkheim himself read as 'proto-sociologists'.[27] Rousseau was an especially important figure for Durkheim and those who sought to go beyond him. Like Montesquieu, Rousseau stressed the need to go beyond the formal mechanics of political sovereignty. His contractual theory of sovereignty was not intended to close the discussion on the proper means of securing the constitution, but to open it. The alienation of one's person and one's goods to the community was the precondition for the formation of the general will, but the return of all those powers to the citizen required the transposition of the love of self in the natural state into the love of oneself as a citizen,

---

[24] Durkheim and Mauss 1963; Schmaus 2004.
[25] For a compendium of symbolist thinking written at this time see Langer 1942.
[26] This may explain Noam Chomsky's attraction to anarchism, and his argument that it is not unsociable human beings, but the corruptible modern state, and the private interests that seize control of it, that is the main source of social conflict.
[27] Durkheim 1960.

as a member of a 'common unity' governed by the general will.[28] This process whereby the 'I' was made to coincide with the communal 'We' of the general will was the work of education, in particular, and of what Rousseau called (in *Considerations on the Government of Poland*) 'national institutions' in general.[29] In his discussion of the legislative system established by the social contract, Rousseau was emphatic that 'the most important' category of law in the state 'graven not in marble or in bronze, but in the hearts of the Citizens; which is the State's genuine constitution; which daily gathers force; which when the other laws age or die out, revives and replaces them, and imperceptibly the force of habit for that of authority. I speak of morals, customs, and above all of opinion.'[30] What Rousseau's careful attention to national institutions implied was that the general will is a historical entity, which is meant to exist through time, and which encompasses future citizens as well as present ones. As Vincent Descombes notes, Rousseau's politics demands that we

> introduce the temporal dimension and the succession of generations. What makes possible the expression of a general will would then be that the elders look after the education of the young, concerning themselves with their entry into adult life and with inculcating good manners within them. Rousseau can then write that it is within such education that the real constitution of the city should be sought.[31]

But this power to ground a political community over time is also the power to create community – that is to say, to make the 'I' coincide with the 'We'. Rousseau described this process metaphorically as the founding of the polity by the heroic figure of the legislator. Yet this instituting power, which literally invents or establishes a custom or tradition, cannot in fact be given to one person, since institutions exist only in so far as their members recognise and act upon the self-understandings implicit in the institution. This re-institution is never simply given, and indeed it is reasonable to expect either radical innovation from time to time, or else a kind of 'drift' in the character of institutions as they are re-enacted over and over again.[32] In this light, Rousseau's positing of the figure of the heroic legislator may be understood as an attempt to soothe any worries about the open-ended character of this process of institutional reproduction, since the intentions of the founder could always be consulted.[33]

---

[28] Rousseau 1979, pp. 39–40.
[29] Rousseau 1997, pp. 179–89.
[30] Rousseau 1997, p. 81.
[31] Descombes 2016, p. 178.
[32] On rapid conceptual shifts and their place in the study of intellectual history see Skinner 2002, p. 180.
[33] Descombes 2016, pp. 177–80.

This was just the point that Durkheim seized on in his reading of Rousseau: it was wrong to suppose that a conjectural account of the founding of society by a far-sighted legislator could explain the formation of the institutions that made society possible. Durkheim's mistake, in Lévi-Strauss's view, was to have still held this act of self-conscious founding by a legislator as the gold standard of a 'functional' or purposive institution. Where conscious design could not be found, Durkheim concluded, the only explanation for its existence was sheer historical contingency – an argument that robbed institutions of the rational orderliness necessary for them to hold society together. In tacit recognition of this gap in his theory, Durkheim therefore kept a space for functional, rather than genetic, explanation. Lévi-Strauss's theory of the formally structured symbolic origins of society was a response to this impasse in Durkheimian social science – and a return to an ahistorical view of strong natural sociability.

As an attempt at a solution to what I have been suggesting is a pre-eminently political problem, Lévi-Strauss's structural anthropology had one major drawback. Because it relied on symbolic relations as unconscious mechanisms of understanding, it completely neglected the issue of the temporality of 'structures' and the open-endedness of institutional reproduction – open-ended because, as I have said, it is up to participants in an institution to interpret the norms or constitutive rules that underpin it. Lévi-Strauss left no room for this historical view of constructed sociability through institutions. For him, the institutional stability we are able to secure as social creatures is a function of the unconscious psychological structures that govern individual action within institutions.

Yet to reject the claim that a-priori structures of the human mind, or some other kind of universal mechanism, provided the basis of social order was to cast in one's lot with history. It was this response to the politics of the explanation of institutions, and not mere epistemological disagreement, that drove the historical turn in anthropology. Or so, at least, I shall now try to show. In the remainder of this chapter I depart from the French tradition and focus on British social anthropology and American cultural anthropology. My case studies are the writings of the functionalist Bronislaw Malinowski and the historically oriented anthropology of Clifford Geertz. Geertz, in particular, has become associated with anthropology's turn to history. My claim is that this turn is the result of his attempt to address the problem of institutional reproduction without political sovereignty, but while avoiding the functionalist (and structuralist) temptation towards positing universal or a-priori structures to explain the durability of social order.

The charge typically laid against the functionalism of early British social anthropology is that it is very boring or very wrong, and probably both. After Malinowski's death in 1942 his reputation suffered a precipitous decline. In 1957 one of his students, Raymond Firth, attempted to revive interest in his mentor's work, but the resulting book, which featured a star-studded list of contributors, 'did rather more', as Clifford Geertz wryly noted, 'to justify the neglect than to end it'.[34] Almost every aspect of Malinowski's oeuvre was found to be dated or misleading. His insistence upon the functionalist explanation of institutions was said to be rooted in a crude biological determinism, but also to be too unsystematic to merit the title of a serious social theory. The publication of Malinowski's field diaries, replete with racial epithets and often sneering appraisals of the natives (although the most frequent target of his ire was himself), set the seal: he was neither a pioneer theorist nor even, as was widely thought, a savant in the field.[35]

Radcliffe-Brown was more careful, but also much less interesting. He thought of himself as a 'comparative sociologist' who looked for patterns of kinship across different societies with the aim of discovering structures that could be studied as universal social forms.[36] Evidence that a given set of kinship relations was found in radically different cultures was a prima facie case for its efficacy; the next task was to discover the 'function' the structure had in sustaining social order. Radcliffe-Brown's careful comparison of the various structures of kinship systems threw new light on the role of lineage organisation in underpinning large-scale 'pre-modern' societies, especially in Africa, where most social anthropologists did their work. This was grist to the mill of a certain kind of political anthropology, especially in the 1950s when Radcliffe-Brown was the undisputed leader of his discipline, with his Oxford colleagues Evans-Pritchard and Meyer Fortes as his allies.[37] In the final analysis, however, Radcliffe-Brown was a fossil-hunter rather than a student of human behaviour. When, after the war, anthropologists became more interested in flesh-and-blood actors living in complex, often jumbled modernising societies, Radcliffe-Brown's analytics of kinship fell out of favour.[38]

The case of Malinowski is more complicated. His reputation sank during an age in which theoretical consistency and rigour, modelled on the natural sciences, became watchwords for social scientists. And it is true

---

[34] Geertz 2010, p. 15; Firth 1957.
[35] Malinowksi 1967.
[36] See, esp., Radcliffe-Brown 1957.
[37] Fortes and Evans-Pritchard 1940.
[38] Kuper 2015, p. 40.

that he did ground the development of institutions – and thus the whole of 'culture' – in biological human needs. But it is wrong to conclude that Malinowski was simply an undisciplined thinker, seduced by organic analogies to such an extent that he believed 'culture was a gigantic metaphorical extension of the physiological processes of digestion'.[39] On the contrary, Malinowski was a vigorous political theorist who engaged questions similar to those that had animated the French tradition: could institutions – or, in aggregate, 'culture' – socialise human beings without the intercession of the state? Could these institutions provide all of the elements of law and order later ascribed to the modern state? If so, what could explain their reproduction across the generations, and thereby the existence of a durable and (relatively) well-ordered society without a constitution? Malinowski's answers to the first two questions – and here he was in line with the Durkheimians – was affirmative. His reply to the last question, the question of reproduction, was that biological needs drove the whole system of culture, even if the means by which those needs were satisfied varied across cultures. Malinowski was indeed guilty of biologism, but it emerged within his thought as a solution to the problem (as it was posed to critics of the modern state) of institutional reproduction. What the more historically sensitive writers who followed Malinowski did was to drop his biologism while maintaining the thesis of the stable institutional reproduction of society without the requirement of a constitution or sovereign state. It is in the shift from the one regulative principle of institutional reproduction to the other that we can see the transition from 'functionalism' to 'historicism'. So I shall now argue through a reading of Malinowski's texts and then those of Clifford Geertz.

Malinowski did not hide his interest in political questions as they emerged from the Durkheimian tradition. In one of his fullest statements of his theory of culture, published in the *Encyclopedia of the Social Sciences* in 1930, Malinowski signalled his fealty to Durkheim's institutionalism while also distinguishing his account of institutional socialisation from Durkheim's ambiguous treatment of that topic. He declared that the 'primary concern of functional anthropology is with the function of institutions, customs, implements, and ideas'; and that, of those four elements, the 'real component units of cultures which have a considerable degree of permanence, universality and independence are the organized systems of human activities called institutions'. 'Every institution centers around a fundamental need, permanently unites a group of people in a

---

[39] Sahlins 1976, p. 4.

cooperative task and has its particular body of doctrine and its technique of craft.' Yet Malinowski rejected Durkheim's claim that institutions had any kind of autonomous existence or independent power over those who participated in them. Therefore, while he admitted that the central issue in the 'understanding of culture is to be found in the process of its production by succeeding generations and in the way in which it produces in each new generation the appropriately molded organism', he scorned the 'metaphysical concepts of a group mind, collective sensorium or consciousness', especially 'Durkheim's theory of moral constraint by the direct influence of the social being'. According to Malinowski, sociologists of this persuasion had simply misinterpreted the significance of Durkheim's distinction between social facts and the facts of individual psychology: this did not, for Malinowski, rise to the level of an antinomy, since all it did was record the fact that, in a more or less behaviourist fashion, individuals within the same society or small group were conditioned by the same elements – technologies, habits, customs – and so had the same reactions to these features of their environment: 'Thus the reality of the superindividual consists in the body of material culture, which remains outside any individual, and yet influences him in the ordinary physiological manner. There is nothing mystical therefore in the fact that culture is at the same time psychological and collective.'[40]

This breezy physiological account of the basis of institutions no doubt encouraged Malinowski to argue that the fundamental human biological needs – for food, shelter, clothing and entertainment – set the pace of cultural development, no matter how complex the 'derived imperatives' governing economic life, matters of justice, and education. But it is equally clear that Malinowski came to see culture – the complex institutional life of society – as something like a functioning modern society without the need of sovereign power to solve coordination problems. Malinowski agreed with the traditional claim that culture was for man (here I follow his gendered language) a 'second nature', which developed his capacities far beyond those he possessed in his natural state. Indeed, it took him into the civil state without need of a constitution:

Culture thus transforms individuals into organized groups and gives these an almost definite continuity. Man is certainly not a gregarious animal in the sense that his concerned actions are due to physiological and innate endowment and carried on it patterns common to the whole species. Organization and all concerted behavior, the results of traditional continuity, assume a different form for every culture. Culture deeply modifies human innate endowment,

---

[40]   Malinowski 1937, pp. 625–6, 623.

and in doing this it not only bestows blessings but also imposes obligations and demands the surrender of a great many personal liberties to the common welfare. The individual has to submit to order and law; he has to learn to obey tradition; he has to twist his tongue and to adjust his larynx to a variety of sounds and to adapt his nervous system to a variety of habits. He works and produces objects which others will consume, while in turn he is always dependent upon alien toil.

Although it remained true that 'culture is primarily born out of biological needs', that claim licensed a strikingly modern picture of how those needs were conceived and met: 'Man has his wants as ... a toiling unit within a cooperative body of men, as one who is haunted by the past or in love with it, as one whom the events to come fill with hopes and with anxieties and finally as one to whom the division of labor and the provisions for the future have given leisure and opportunities to enjoy color, form, and music.'[41]

If this sounded like a description of a modern, commercial society, composed of deeply interdependent but also rivalrous, ambitious and self-involved people, that is because this obverse of Malinowski's biologism – his inscription of bourgeois attitudes in non-modern societies – had marked his work from the very beginning. In Malinowski's view, tribal society was, for good and ill, as 'civilised' as modern society. It, too, had its own quasi-commercial sociability, and was not to be viewed as backward or primitive in its institutions. In *Crime and Custom in Savage Society* (1926) Malinowski attacked the 'dogma of the absence of individual rights and liabilities among the savages'. He noted that this 'dogma' was at the core of the famous thesis of primitive communism, which become an obsession for students of comparative jurisprudence in both Germany and Britain during the last third of the nineteenth century. The basis of the idea of primitive communism, wrote Malinowski, was 'the assumption that in primitive societies the individual is completely dominated by the group – the horde, the clan, or the tribe – that he obeys the commands of his community, its traditions, its public opinion, its decrees, with a slavish, passive obedience'. Malinowski insisted that even in his own time 'the dogma of automatic submission to custom dominates the whole inquiry into primitive law'. Ethnologists were working with a model of legal obligation which tacitly assumed that the modern state was a necessary condition for the existence of law: 'Accustomed as we are to look for a definite machinery of enactment, administration, and enforcement of law, we cast round for something in a savage community

---

[41] Malinowski 1937, pp. 628, 645.

and, failing to find there any similar arrangements, we conclude that all law is obeyed by this mysterious propensity of the savage to obey it.' In the absence of anything that could be understood as law by modern standards, commentators concluded that the apparent deference of 'savages' to the forces of custom and tradition could only be explained by 'automatic acquiescence, [the] instinctive submission of every member of the tribe to its law'. On the contrary, it was Malinowski's purpose to show that the savage's 'observance of the rules of law under the normal conditions ... is at best partial, conditional, and subject to evasions' and, most importantly of all, that this observance 'is not enforced by any wholesale motive like fear of punishment, or a general submission to all tradition, but by very complex psychological and social inducements'. More concretely, Malinowski insisted that there existed among the people he knew best, the Trobriand Islanders of New Guinea, a form of what could be called 'primitive civil law', composed of 'rules with a definite binding obligation', which '[stood] out from the mere rules of custom'.[42]

But what sense could be made of Malinowski's claim that premodern societies such as those of the Melanesians contained a system of 'individual rights and liabilities'? Such a claim was a direct challenge to the most famous thesis of the Victorian anthropologists, which was that human history was marked by a fundamental shift from 'status' to 'contract': from societies in which status was tied to wholly ascriptive kinship relations to societies in which statuses were based on voluntary agreements between individuals enforced by positive law. In order to defend his claim about primitive civil law, Malinowski returned to the complexities of economic exchange among the Melanesians, which he had described in the book that made his reputation, *Argonauts of the Western Pacific* (1922). In *Argonauts* Malinowski had focused his attention on the *kula*, the elaborate system of ceremonial exchange that linked tribes across the Trobriand archipelago. The *kula* was highly ritualised, since it was regulated by a dense collection of rules and conventions, including various magical rites and public ceremonies. Yet these apparently purely symbolic rituals, which centred on the circulation of shell necklaces and bracelets, provided the infrastructure for a vast range of economic production and exchange, from the trade of fish and vegetables to the building of the canoes necessary to carry on hunting, trade and the *kula* itself. What the *kula* did brilliantly, as Malinowski saw it, was to create a set of obligations and reciprocal exchanges among the Trobrianders that solved the basic economic problem of life, but which,

[42] Malinowski 1926, pp. 3–5, 14, 11, 15, 30.

as a carefully constructed system of rights and obligations, could not be reduced to the pure exchange of utilities posited by the marginal theory of value of the neo-classical economists. The *kula* 'presents to us a new type of phenomenon, lying on the borderland between the commercial and the ceremonial and expressing a complex and interesting attitude of mind'.[43] In *Crime and Custom* Malinowski extended this argument to cover almost every aspect of the life of the primitive community: not just the *kula*, but canoe building, the organisation of tribes into moieties, the tears of the widow in mortuary rituals, and the rules of marriage. All of these institutions had a crucial 'legal side', in so far as their performance created a dense network of mutual obligations among those who participated in them. This was why one could speak of individual rights and liabilities: in giving a gift, or helping with the construction of a canoe, one became entitled to expect an equivalent service or action in return; while, in receiving a gift or aid, one acquired the duty to reciprocate. To witness these exchanges was to understand their 'social function in safeguarding the continuity and adequacy of mutual services'.[44] Malinowski's basic point was that it was wrong to think of societies in binary terms as being either pre-modern or modern. Not from status to contract, but always status and contract: this was the lesson of Malinowski's anthropology of law.

Malinowski therefore had no compunction about describing primitive societies as defined by the division of labour, and as bound together by a delicate tissue of civil rights organised around property, the labour process and exchange. But he went even further towards merging the pre-modern and the modern. Contrary to other anthropological depictions of tribal societies, Malinowski's Trobrianders were not mindlessly attempting to satisfy basic needs; nor were they mere puppets of the rules and structures that guided their lives. They were mentally and emotionally complex: in Rousseau's terms, they had already shown their capacity for 'perfectibility' – the development of mental faculties and the refinement of appetites and desires. They thought about the 'laws' that governed their transactions with one another: about how to evade them, and the costs of getting caught. 'Whenever the native can evade his obligations without the loss of prestige, or without the prospective loss of gain, he does so, exactly as a civilized business man would do.' Two considerations kept the Trobrianders more or less in line. First, 'enlightened self-interest', according to which the keeping of an obligation was clearly better than the alternative. Obeying the dictates of the

[43] Malinowski 2014 [1922], p. 530.
[44] Malinowski 1926, pp. 33, 24.

kula or marriage rites meant that one would be obliging others to provide one with needed 'services'; more negatively, a consistent refusal to reciprocate would consign the individual in question to social opprobrium and perhaps even banishment. They would be cast out of the 'civil' order and left to the state of nature – a prospect few in Melanesia, or anywhere else, could contemplate with equanimity. Besides self-interest, the other factor keeping the Trobriander's sense of legal obligation in place was 'obedience to his social ambitions and sentiments'. The Melanesians linked power with wealth, and wealth with the ability to give gifts and feasts of great extravagance.

> Nothing has greater sway over the Melanesian's mind than ambition and vanity associated with a display of food and wealth. ... Generosity is the highest virtue to him, and wealth the essential element of influence and rank. The association of a semi-commercial transaction with definite public ceremonies supplies another binding force of fulfilment through a special psychological mechanism: the desire for display, the ambition to appear munificent, the extreme esteem for wealth and for the accumulation of food.[45]

Malinowski was here clearly undermining the very idea of a careful development sequence of stages leading from the primitive order to the modern commercial state. Yet this erasure of the difference between the primitive and the modern, between 'natural' man and political society, also foreclosed on the possibility of novelty or historical change. For Malinowski, the fundamental elements of culture – religion, magic, myth, law, language, kinship – were not governed by their own unique, internal logic. These were 'derived' or 'secondary' imperatives, dictated by the primary imperatives of food, sex and shelter – in short, the basic human desire for safety and ease. The necessities of life were the source of the reproduction of society, with institutions thus rendered the vehicle of those basic needs. From this perspective, the quasi-commercial or selfish social sentiments that Malinowski attributed to his Trobrianders could never serve as the basis of further psychological and historical development, governed by its own, open-ended principles of change. This was a radical departure from earlier theorists of ambition and status seeking among the members of commercial states. No modern state, no history: Malinowski would not have minded that conclusion.

Anthropology has come a long way from Malinowski's Trobriand Islanders. After the war the discipline rejected the functionalist treatment of 'primitive' peoples existing outside history, fated to recapitulate their social forms without end. Instead, anthropologists began to stress

---

[45] Malinowski 1926, pp. 31, 29.

the obvious fact that the cultures they study are not trapped in amber, but rather have histories which are marked by the forces of global trade, capitalist production, imperialism and state formation. Indeed, theorists of the 'world system' insist that all modern states, whether in the global north or the global south, share the same history, since they have historically been linked by mutual dependencies rooted in labour, trade and economic exploitation. Likewise, writers in the Marxist tradition such as Eric Wolf suggest that capitalist development is in fact best understood from the perspective of the 'people without history' whose labour and dispossession underpinned the system.[46] Even liberal writers such as Clifford Geertz made the transitional character of the societies they studied the central focus of their research.[47] In short, these anthropologists came to understand the field in which they worked as the product of history: specifically, the history of the impact of modernising economic and social forces on the places they investigated. Just as significantly, they also began to write and think historically, whether by outright producing works of history or by developing theories of culture and ethnographic method that could account for the transformation or revaluation of 'traditional' customs and institutions, as seemed to be happening across the partially developed, partially urbanised countries in which they did their fieldwork.

Yet we would be wrong to conclude that these changes entailed a revolution in anthropological theory. To be sure, these writers had spotted a real weakness in Malinowski and Radcliffe-Brown's anti-historical approach to institutions, with its crude reliance upon biological foundations. But they shared with Malinowski two characteristic beliefs: that their subjects had a very keen sense of their rights and liabilities within a carefully structured social order; and that the sovereign state was neither a necessary nor a sufficient condition for the stable existence of such a system of justice, rights and obligations.[48] Where they differed was on the historical formation and reproduction of these non-state civil institutions. In this final section of the chapter I examine one important example of this shift towards historicism: the work of Clifford Geertz, whose contributions to political theory are perhaps less well understood than they deserve to be.

Geertz began his career writing about religion and economic development, not politics. His doctoral research on the religious traditions of

---

[46] Wolf 1982.
[47] Isaac 2018.
[48] This is the basic idea behind the notion of 'moral economy', which swept anthropology after the publication of Scott 1976.

Java fitted perfectly with his training in Harvard's department of Social Relations. Devoted to the study of the 'modernisation' process, Social Relations sent its graduate students into the field to look for the equivalents of the social changes that led to the rise of capitalism in the West. In search of an Indonesian analogue of Weber's Protestant ethic, Geertz found an approximation in the worldview of the reformist Muslims, the *santri*, of east-central Java.[49] In later work he compared incipient trends towards capitalist enterprise in Java with the 'aristocratic' society of Bali, with an eye to explaining the possibilities and limits of economic development in Indonesia.[50] Geertz's signature theory of culture was already visible in his earliest methodological writings on the sociology of religion. Based on the principles of the symbolic theory of Susanne Langer, Kenneth Burke and Walker Percy, this semiotic conception of culture would provide the basis for Geertz's later, historian-friendly plea for 'thick description' in the study of alien beliefs and rituals.[51] Yet the most interesting feature of Geertz's thought is not the revelation that his hermeneutic approach to social science pre-dated his break with the modernisation theory of his Harvard mentors. Rather, it is the way in which his theory of culture was formed in dialectic with his theory of economic and social change. His long-running effort to conceptualise the 'intermediate' or semi-commercialised economic forms of the post-colonial nations offers one vivid example of this dialectic.[52] But his reflection on politics in the new nations provides another, one that has hitherto not received the attention it deserves.

The prompt for Geertz's engagement with political anthropology was his work at the University of Chicago in the Committee for the Comparative Study of the New Nations. A boondoggle of sorts for the social theorist and institutional power broker Edward Shils, the Committee gave Geertz (who was recruited to Chicago by Shils in 1959 and stayed for a decade) an opportunity to extend his analysis of the cultural aspects of social change into the study of politics. Such was the aim of the essays collected in the fourth (and largest) part of Geertz's classic book – the *locus classicus* of interpretive social science: *The Interpretation of Cultures* (1973). In the most important political essay in that volume, 'The Integrative Revolution: Primordial Sentiments and Civil Politics in the New States' (1963/1973), Geertz took his cue from Shils. Shils sought to replace Tönnies's classic distinction between *Gemeinschaft* and

---

[49] Geertz 1956; Geertz 1960, esp. pp. 131–47.
[50] Geertz 1963, p. 49.
[51] Geertz 1957. On Geertz's debts to Langer see Isaac 2020.
[52] See Isaac 2018.

Gesellschaft (which itself derived, at least in part, from Tönnies's scholarship on Hobbes[53]) with a fourfold distinction that split *Gemeinschaft* – or what Shils called the 'primary group' – into three distinct categories: groups based on 'primordial' attachments of kinship, place or language; groups based on personal attachments, as among soldiers thrown into battle who fight more for each other than for the larger cause; and groups based on ideological affinity or charisma, as in the case of a religious sect or revolutionary vanguard.[54] Within Shils's schema, *Gesellschaft* remained the realm of citizenship, which promised formal legal status, but lacked the strength of the ties of the primary group. For Shils the challenge for modern, state-centred politics was to stabilise civic attachments by at once harnessing and neutralising the three forms of primary group.[55] When he turned his attention to the post-colonial nations, Shils noted that civil sentiments there were weak, if only because they were so new, while primordial attachments were unusually strong.[56]

Geertz ran with this idea but added his own twist. The tension between primordial forms of sociability – blood, language, territory – and the paler attractions of civic politics was greatly aggravated by the twin imperatives of the post-colonial polities. 'The peoples of the new states are simultaneously animated by two powerful, thoroughly interdependent yet distinct and often actually opposed motives – the desire to be recognized as responsible agents whose wishes, acts, hopes, and opinions "matter", and the desire to build an efficient, dynamic modern state.' Although in the ideal type of a nationalist movement those two desires would be realised together in the form of the ethnically homogeneous nation-state, in the new states these motives pulled apart from one another. The desire for recognition of one's identity pointed towards 'the gross actualities of blood, race, language, locality, religion or tradition' while the desire for statehood implied the need to 'subordinate these specific and familiar identifications in favor of a generalized commitment to an overarching and somewhat alien civil order'. The state threatened primordial identities while also increasing competition among ethnic and kinship groups as they vied for control of the state – a new and powerful prize within

---

[53] Hont 2015, p. 5.
[54] Shils 1957. Shils intended to publish his *magnum opus* on this topic, but the volume he envisaged, *Love, Belief, and Civility*, was never finished.
[55] Following Weber, Shils argued that ideological groups or sects – what Weber had called the *Bund* – could undermine civic sentiments and so had to be carefully contained within the civil order. Personal attachments were often thought to connect the local to the national, but Shils had his doubts about that. I take up the issue of primordial attachments in the main text.
[56] Shils 1960.

these societies. Hence the main political challenge of the new states was to find a way of transforming the primordial and the civic so that the two imperatives of the politics of the post-colonial states, rather than heightening parochialism, could somehow be integrated in the name of a project of national unity. This was the 'integrative revolution' that these states would have to undergo, and (ominously) at the same time that they faced the social revolutions of industrialisation, urbanisation and 'restratification'. This basic problem of reconciling *Gesellschaft* with the post-colonial states' peculiar forms of *Gemeinschaft* was at the heart of Geertz's political thought throughout his career.[57]

But how exactly would this integrative revolution come about, if the state was such an alien graft onto primordial social sentiments? It is on this question that the political dimension of Geertz's semiotic conception of culture becomes clear. In 'The Integrative Revolution' Geertz did not fully draw out the implications of his cultural theory, but he hinted at them in his suggestion that the route to the integration of the civic and primordial lay in what he described as the 'domestication' of primordial sentiments, or elsewhere as the 'modernization' of 'ethnocentrism'. Primordial ties had to be reconciled to 'the unfolding civil order by divesting them of their legitimizing force with respect to governmental authority, [and] by neutralizing the apparatus of the state in relationship to them'. This was to be done by transforming brute essentialist identities into 'ethnic blocs', on the model (although Geertz did not say this outright) of the post-war United States. Will Herberg's famous study of the ethnicisation of American society, *Protestant, Catholic, Jew*, hovered in the background of Geertz's remarks. Ethnic blocs would not remove conflict from the political system, but rather channel it into a less corrosive form – a team politics, as it were.[58]

The question remained exactly how the modernisation of primordial loyalties was to be achieved. Geertz's essay 'Ideology as a Cultural System' (1964) gave the answer. It was based on Geertz's attempt to make the 'science of symbolic action' the key method in social research. He characterised rituals and institutions as 'symbol systems' through which individual agents interpreted and acted upon the world. Quite simply, these were vehicles for cognising experience and organising one's moods and emotions, just as Geertz's great inspiration, the symbolic theorist Susanne Langer, had argued. It was helpful to think of

---

[57] Geertz 1973, pp. 258, 277.
[58] Geertz 1973, pp. 307–8; Herberg 1955.

symbolic systems – religion or ideology or art – as '"programs": they provide a template or blueprint for the organization of social and psychological processes, much as genetic systems provide such a template for the organization of organic processes'. Geertz asserted that the 'central rituals of religion – a mass, a pilgrimage, a corroboree' are 'symbolic models ... of a particular sense of the divine, a certain sort of devotional mood, which their continual re-enactment tends to produce in their participants'. But these cultural systems were not fixed: the world in which these symbolic networks operated could change, thereby rendering the existing 'program' in some way limited or obsolete; or new symbolic connections could be made through the use of such rhetorical tropes as metaphor, metonymy and irony. Ideology, in particular, was in the business of manufacturing new meanings and thereby providing new models in terms of which to interpret and act upon reality (never, of course, with any guarantee that such attempts would not misfire, or have bad consequences): 'it is through the construction of ideologies, schematic images of the social order, that man makes himself for better or worse a political animal'. In short, if primordial sentiments were to be made safe for politics in the new states, they had to be ideologised: they had to be converted from obstacles to civic politics into the very means of such politics. 'Whatever else ideologies may be – projections of unacknowledged fears, disguises for ulterior motives, phatic expressions of group solidarity – they are, most distinctively, maps of problematic social reality and matrices for the creation of collective conscience.'[59]

Geertz's symbolic theory of culture described a power that lay deeper than, and provided the conditions of possibility for, political institutions. The idea of the ethnic bloc, or other basic primordial identity, had to be rendered into a model for political action, most likely through the metaphoric connection of traditional models of social life with modern conditions. In fact, this was just what Geertz glimpsed in Indonesia in the early 1960s, before the purges of 1965–6. To be sure, Geertz already recognised that this process was to some extent being reversed as tribal political affiliations began to overwhelm Indonesian society. Still, Geertz noted how the classical Hindu conception of government, based on the principle of the exemplary centre, had survived through the period of Islamification and was now the subject of several attempts to 'construct ... an essentially metaphoric reworking of it, a new symbolic framework within which to give form and meaning to the emerging republican

[59] Geertz 1973, pp. 214, 216, 218, 220.

polity'. If there was to be a viable politics in post-revolutionary Indonesia, it was to come through such 'ideological' modes of politics.[60]

It is worth emphasising what Geertz was doing here in contradistinction to Malinowski. Broadly speaking, he accepted Malinowski's claim that culture was the source of social order, since it was what bound persons together and socialised them, even as they often strained against the limits of their institutions. But Geertz took two important steps beyond Malinowski. First, he cut culture loose from biological needs – or perhaps one should say he snapped a few more cords connecting the two than Malinowski could allow. The latter had a sequential view of this relationship: first, the physiological development of the human animal, with its basic needs; then institutions develop to meet those needs, in forms that, where varying in their outward aspects, serve the same basic function – hence his specification, late in life, of a list of 'universal institutional types'. Geertz stressed instead how little of human behaviour was programmed by genetics or universal needs, and how cultural systems had been involved in the development of *Homo sapiens* alongside physiological factors. Given the hypertrophy of the human nervous system, the only way humans could act intelligibly at all was to 'rely more and more heavily on cultural sources – the accumulated fund of significant symbols. ... We are, in sum, incomplete or unfinished animals who complete ourselves through culture – and not culture in general but through highly particular forms of it: Dobuan and Javanese, Hopi and Italian, upper-class and lower-class, academic and commercial.'[61] It followed that there were no cultural universals of the kind that Malinowski (and, it should be said, most of his contemporaries) envisaged.

The second step followed from the first. If there were no cultural universals; and if symbolic systems were always particular, and also subject to reworking and obsolescence thanks to the self-conscious 'instituting' actions of individuals; if this were true then there could be nothing so general as Malinowski's 'primitive civil law', or state-like culture, with its accompanying form of quasi-bourgeois sociability. Where Malinowski saw status and contract, pre-modern and modern, mixed together everywhere, Geertz's vision was more localised and fragmentary. Yet, as we have seen, the starting point of his writings on

---

[60] Geertz 1973, p. 224. Geertz returned to the pre-colonial Balinese state in Geertz 1980. Notably, when he did so, he had given up on the idea that this model of a state-without-sovereignty could be 'metaphorically reworked' in a productive way for modern Indonesian politics – hence his focus on the nineteenth century. At best, the Balinese theatre state was an interesting counter-case in political theory, not a 'program' that could be leveraged into a stable form of national politics.

[61] Geertz 1973, p. 49.

political anthropology was the brute fact of the existence of the post-colonial state, and the challenge of giving persons civic motivations when they had only primordial sentiments to draw upon in attempting to relate themselves to the state. In that respect, Geertz took the modern state more seriously than his functionalist predecessors had done. His view of the adaptation of cultural systems, and especially the possibilities inherent in the process of the metaphor-driven 'ideologisation' of primordial identities, suggested the possibility of a healthy, institution-led development of sociability. Therefore, by embracing a particularist and historicist view of culture and institutions, Geertz replaced Malinowski's vision of a natural but still fractious sociability with a more plastic view of human social propensities, which would depend on the context and scope for symbolic action. This opened the door to genuinely historical explanations in anthropology, since there were no universal principles to appeal to in understanding cultural formations; only local, empirical, causal explanations of changing cultural systems would do.

In the end, however, Geertz chafed – as did so many anthropologists – against the nation-state as the standard against which the politics of the modern world should be judged. During the latter part of his career Geertz devoted a number of studies to showing how provincial the post-Hobbesian view of politics was when the polities of the global south were taken into account. The entire logic of nation-state-centred political theory, he argued, had to be replaced with a more neutral language that allowed for cultural difference and radical ideological change: a language of 'country' and 'town' instead of 'nation' and 'city'. In a word, Geertz had given up on the state as the proper vehicle for politics – a gesture that had been constitutive of anthropological theory since Malinowski. The goal of a new, truly postmodern political theory was to embrace the universalisation of particularity and difference – the logic of a 'world in pieces'.[62]

We can return, in conclusion, to where we began. After the First World War anthropology set itself a very specific problem: to show that a stable society was possible without the state. Contra Hobbes, there *was* a difference between society and political society. This argument led the anthropologists to place enormous stress on the socialising role of institutions or (to take a society's set of institutions in aggregate) 'culture'. Anthropology was to be the 'science' of institutions (Durkheim) or the 'science' of culture (Malinowski). But this argument, in turn,

---

[62] Geertz 1995; Geertz 2000, pp. 159–88.

raised the question of social reproduction: what made a society stable over time – indeed, conceivable as a community – if not a constitution? In what sense were institutions binding on their participants if they did not avail themselves of sovereign power? Durkheim concluded that 'collective representations' had a direct coercive power over their subjects, much like the external and coercive power of the state, but this assumption led to a split in his theory into which Lévi-Strauss drove a further wedge. Ultimately, while seeking to evade the modern state, anthropologists kept in play a set of ideas about sociability that had underpinned debates about the origins and necessity of the state. I have suggested that structuralists adopted a version of the thesis of strong natural sociability, now rooted in the natural propensity of human beings to establish rationally ordered social institutions. In contrast, the functionalists and the historicists refused to ground the stable reproduction of society in universal structures of the human mind. Instead, they were impressed by the idea that human mental faculties and social propensities were constructed by institutions. They shared a developmental model of human sociability, which implied that human societies could have something analogous to a 'civil society', replete with possibilities for 'autonomy', ambition and specialisation, but without the need for either the modern representative state or modern industry. Where figures such as Malinowski and Geertz diverged was on the developmental possibilities of this quasi-political society. For Malinowski, comparative analysis suggested that institutional possibilities were fixed within a narrow realm, and his biological essentialism became the necessary premise of his social theory. But Geertz came to believe that closer attention to the agent's view of the possibilities for social action showed that the scope for institutional innovation was open-ended and allowed for radical change. Human modes of sociability were both historically constructed and remarkably variegated.

If this view of the discipline has merit, its history is much less segmented than the standard contrasts between evolutionism, functionalism and historicism have supposed. Indeed, we can think of anthropology's anti-political institutionalism as representing a single position on the compulsory character of modern, post-Hobbesian politics. Whether, in the end, it succeeds in evading the 'constitutional delusion' it so vehemently rejects is a separate topic. The fact that it has reinvented so many of its problems – the sources of legal obligation, the corrosiveness of self-interest and its potential redirection into socially beneficial ends, the dangers of national enmity in global politics – perhaps suggests that it has not. But that is a question for another time.

References

Agnew, Jean Christophe. 1990. 'History and Anthropology: Scenes from a Marriage', *Yale Journal of Criticism*, 3: 2, pp. 29–50.

Burrow, John. 1966. *Evolution and Society: A Study in Victorian Social Theory*. Cambridge.

Descombes, Vincent. 2001. *The Mind's Provisions: A Critique of Cognitivism*, trans. Stephen Adam Schwartz. Cambridge, MA.

2016. *Puzzling Identities*, trans. Stephen Adam Schwartz. Cambridge, MA.

Dumont, Louis. 1986. *Essays on Individualism: Modern Ideology in Anthropological Perspective*. Chicago.

Durkheim, Émile. 1960. *Montesquieu and Rousseau: Forerunners of Sociology*, trans. Ralph Manheim. Ann Arbor.

2013. *The Rules of Sociological Method, and Selected Texts on Sociology and its Method*, ed. Steven Lukes, trans. W. D. Halls. New York.

Durkheim, Émile and Marcel Mauss. 1963. *Primitive Classification*, trans. Rodney Needham. Chicago.

Evans-Pritchard, E. E. 1950. 'Social Anthropology: Past and Present', *Man*, 198, pp. 118–24.

Firth, Raymond, ed. 1957. *Man and Culture: An Evaluation of the Work of Bronislaw Malinowski*. London.

Fortes, Meyer and E. E. Evans-Pritchard. 1940. *African Political Systems*. London.

Frank, Stephanie. 2016. 'The "Force in the Thing": Nonauthoritarian Sociality in The Gift', *Hau: Journal of Ethnographic Theory*, 6: 2, pp. 255–77.

Geertz, Clifford. 1956. 'Religious Belief and Economic Behavior in a Central Javanese Town: Some Preliminary Considerations', *Economic Development and Cultural Change*, 4: 2, pp. 134–58.

1957. 'Ethos, World View, and the Analysis of Sacred Symbols', *Antioch Review*, 17: 4, pp. 421–37.

1960. *The Religion of Java*. New York.

1963. *Peddlers and Princes: Social Change and Economic Modernization in Two Indonesian Towns*. Chicago.

1973. *The Interpretation of Cultures: Selected Essays*. New York.

1980. *Negara: The Theatre State in Nineteenth-Century Bali*. Princeton.

1995. *After the Fact: Two Countries, Four Decades, One Anthropologist*. Cambridge, MA.

2000. *Available Light: Anthropological Perspectives on Philosophical Topics*. Princeton.

2004. 'What is a State if not a Sovereign? Reflections on Politics in Complicated Places', *Current Anthropology*, 45: 5, pp. 577–93.

2010. *Life among the Anthros*, ed. Fred Inglis. Princeton.

Herberg, Will. 1955. *Protestant, Catholic, Jew: An Essay in American Religious Sociology*. New York.

Hont, Istvan. 2015. *Politics in a Commercial Society: Jean-Jacques Rousseau and Adam Smith*. Cambridge, MA.

Isaac, Joel. 2018. 'The Intensification of Social Forms: Economy and Culture in the Thought of Clifford Geertz', *Critical Historical Studies*, pp. 237–66.

2020. 'Susanne K. Langer, Philosophy in a New Key (1942)', *Public Culture*, 32: 2, pp. 355–61.

Kuper, Adam. 2003. 'Anthropology' in *The Cambridge History of Science*, vol. VII: *The Modern Social Sciences*, ed. Theodore Porter and Dorothy Ross. Cambridge.

2005. *The Reinvention of Primitive Society: Transformations of a Myth*, 2nd ed. London and New York.

2015. *Anthropology and Anthropologists: The British School in the Twentieth Century*, 4th ed. New York and London.

Langer, Susanne K. 1942. *Philosophy in a New Key: A Study in the Symbolism of Reason, Rite, and Art*. Cambridge, MA.

Lévi-Strauss, Claude. 1945. 'French Sociology' in *Twentieth Century Sociology*, ed. Georges Gurvitch and Wilbert E. Moore. New York.

1969 [1949]. *The Elementary Structures of Kinship*, rev. ed., ed. Rodney Needham, trans. James Harle Bell and John Richard von Sturmer. Boston.

Lowie, Robert. 1937. *The History of Ethnological Theory*. New York.

Malinowski, Bronislaw. 1926. *Crime and Custom in Savage Society*. London.

1937. 'Culture' in *Encyclopedia of the Social Sciences*, vol. IV, ed. Edwin R. A. Seligman and Alvin Johnson. New York.

1967. *A Diary in the Strict Sense of the Term*, trans. Norbert Guterman. New York.

2014 [1922]. *Argonauts of the Western Pacific: An Account of Native Enterprise and Adventure in the Archipelagoes of Melanesian New Guinea*. London and New York.

Mauss, Marcel. 2016. *The Gift*, expanded ed., ed. and trans. Jane Guyer. Chicago.

Mintz, Sidney. 1985. *Sweetness and Power: The Place of Sugar in Modern History*. New York.

Radcliffe-Brown, A. R. 1922. *The Andaman Islanders: A Study in Social Anthropology*. Cambridge.

1935. 'On the Concept of Function in Social Science', *American Anthropologist*, 37: 3, pp. 394–402.

1957. *A Natural Science of Society*. Glencoe, IL.

Redfield, Robert. 1941. *The Folk Culture of the Yucatan*. Chicago.

Rousseau, Jean-Jacques. 1979. *Emile; or Education*, ed. and trans. Allan Bloom. New York.

1997. *The Social Contract and Other Later Political Writings*, ed. Victor Gourevitch. Cambridge.

Sahlins, Marshall. 1976. *The Use and Abuse of Biology: An Anthropological Critique of Sociobiology*. Ann Arbor.

1985. *Islands of History*. Chicago.

Schmaus, Warren. 2004. *Rethinking Durkheim and his Tradition*. Cambridge.

Scott, James C. 1976. *The Moral Economy of the Peasant: Rebellion and Subsistence in Southeast Asia*. New Haven.

1990. *Domination and the Arts of Resistance*. New Haven.

Shils, Edward. 1957. 'Primordial, Personal, Sacred and Civil Ties: Some Particular Observations on the Relationship of Sociological Research and Theory', *British Journal of Sociology*, 8: 2, pp. 130–45.

1960. 'Political Development in the New States', *Comparative Studies in Society and History*, 2: 3, pp. 265–92.

Skinner, Quentin. 2002. *Visions of Politics*, vol. I: *Regarding Method*. Cambridge.

Stocking, George W., Jr. 1968. *Race, Culture, and Evolution: Essays in the History of Anthropology*. New York.

1987. *Victorian Anthropology*. New York.

1995. *After Tylor: British Social Anthropology, 1888–1951*. Madison.

Stocking, George W., Jr., ed. 1996. *Volksgeist as Method and Ethic: Essays on Boasian Ethnography and the German Anthropological Tradition*. Madison.

Wolf, Eric. 1982. *Europe and the People without History*. Berkeley.

Index

408

www.ingramcontent.com/pod-product-compliance
Ingram Content Group UK Ltd.
Pitfield, Milton Keynes, MK11 3LW, UK
UKHW020453010325
455719UK00016B/558